Lecture Notes in Computer Science 14603

Founding Editors

Gerhard Goos
Juris Hartmanis

Editorial Board Members

The series Lecture Notes in Computer Science (LNCS), including its subseries Lecture Notes in Artificial Intelligence (LNAI) and Lecture Notes in Bioinformatics (LNBI), has established itself as a medium for the publication of new developments in computer science and information technology research, teaching, and education.

LNCS enjoys close cooperation with the computer science R & D community, the series counts many renowned academics among its volume editors and paper authors, and collaborates with prestigious societies. Its mission is to serve this international community by providing an invaluable service, mainly focused on the publication of conference and workshop proceedings and postproceedings. LNCS commenced publication in 1973.

Qiang Tang · Vanessa Teague
Editors

Public-Key Cryptography – PKC 2024

27th IACR International Conference
on Practice and Theory of Public-Key Cryptography
Sydney, NSW, Australia, April 15–17, 2024
Proceedings, Part III

Springer

Editors
Qiang Tang
The University of Sydney
Sydney, NSW, Australia

Vanessa Teague
The Australian National University
Acton, ACT, Australia

ISSN 0302-9743   ISSN 1611-3349 (electronic)
Lecture Notes in Computer Science
ISBN 978-3-031-57724-6   ISBN 978-3-031-57725-3 (eBook)
https://doi.org/10.1007/978-3-031-57725-3

This Springer imprint is published by the registered company Springer Nature Switzerland AG
The registered company address is: Gewerbestrasse 11, 6330 Cham, Switzerland

Paper in this product is recyclable.

Preface

The 27th International Conference on Practice and Theory of Public-Key Cryptography (PKC 2024) was held in Sydney, Australia, on April 15–17, 2024. It was sponsored by the International Association for Cryptologic Research (IACR) and is the main IACR-sponsored conference with an explicit focus on public-key cryptography. PKC 2024 authors represented 24 different countries, bringing a vibrant international community of cryptography researchers to Australia.

The conference received 176 submissions, reviewed by the Program Committee of 68 cryptography experts (including four area chairs) working with 183 external reviewers. The reviewing process took two months and selected 54 papers to appear in PKC 2024. Papers were reviewed in the usual double-blind fashion with an average of just over three reviews per paper. Program committee members and general chairs were limited to 3 submissions (4 if all with students), and their submissions were scrutinized more closely. The two program chairs were not allowed to submit papers. PKC 2024 was the first major cryptography conferences to accept SoK papers.

PKC 2024 welcomed Nadia Heninger (University of California, San Diego) and Aggelos Kiayias (University of Edinburgh) as the invited speakers. The Program Committee also selected two best papers: *An algorithm for efficient detection of (N, N)-splittings and its application to the isogeny problem in dimension 2* by Maria Corte-Real Santos, Craig Costello and Sam Frengley, and *Quantum CCA-Secure PKE, Revisited* by Navid Alamati and Varun Maram.

The award committee (Masayuki Abe, Alexandra Boldyreva, Qiang Tang, Vanessa Teague, Moti Yung) also chose the PKC Test of Time Award for 2024.

PKC is a remarkable undertaking, possible only through the hard work and significant contributions of many people. We would like to express our sincere gratitude to all the authors, as well as to the Program Committee and external reviewers, session chairs and presenters. Special thanks to the area chairs: Steven Galbraith, Giuseppe Persiano, Kazue Sako and Vassilis Zikas. Their specialist knowledge and good judgement were critical for making good decisions.

Additionally, we would like to thank Willy Susilo, Fuchun Guo and the team at the University of Wollongong for making the general arrangements such a success. Also, as always, Kay McKelly and Kevin McCurley provided invaluable support for all things technical behind the scenes.

All of this happens against a backdrop in which even some democratic governments are working to undermine encrypted communications in the name of "safety." In Australia, exporting a new encryption algorithm without a permit can be punished with years in jail. Open, scientific, internationally collaborative research in cryptography is more important than ever.

We hope you enjoyed the conference and the warm welcome of Sydney.

April 2024

Qiang Tang
Vanessa Teague

Organization

General Chairs

Fuchun Guo   University of Wollongong, Australia
Willy Susilo   University of Wollongong, Australia

Program Committee Chairs

Qiang Tang   The University of Sydney, Australia
Vanessa Teague   Democracy Developers Ltd., The Australian
                                 National University and Thinking
                                 Cybersecurity Pty. Ltd., Australia

Steering Committee

Masayuki Abe   NTT, Japan
Alexandra Boldyreva   Georgia Tech, USA
Jung Hee Cheon   Seoul National University, South Korea
Yvo Desmedt   University of Texas at Dallas, USA
Goichiro Hanaoka   National Institute of Advanced Industrial Science
                                 and Technology, Japan
Tibor Jager   University of Wuppertal, Germany
Aggelos Kiayias   University of Edinburgh, UK
Vladimir Kolesnikov   Georgia Tech, USA
Tanja Lange   Eindhoven University of Technology,
                                 The Netherlands
Jiaxin Pan   NTNU, Norway & University of Kassel, Germany
David Pointcheval   École Normale Supérieure Paris, France
Qiang Tang   The University of Sydney, Australia
Vanessa Teague   Democracy Developers Ltd., The Australian
                                 National University and Thinking
                                 Cybersecurity Pty. Ltd., Australia
Moti Yung (Secretary)   Google Inc. & Columbia University, USA
Yuliang Zheng (Chair)   University of Alabama at Birmingham, USA

Area Chairs

Steven Galbraith

The University of Auckland,
Aotearoa-New Zealand
*Post-quantum cryptography, quantum
cryptography, Math & Attacks*

Giuseppe Persiano

University of Salerno, Italy and Google, USA
*Theoretical Foundations & Advanced
Primitives*

Kazue Sako

Waseda University, Japan
*Applied Cryptography, SNARKs & Verifiable
Computation*

Vassilis Zikas

Purdue University, USA
Multiparty computation & consensus

Program Committee

Divesh Aggarwal	National University of Singapore, Singapore
Christian Badertscher	Input Output Global, Switzerland
Foteini Baldimtsi	George Mason University, USA
Sofia Celi	Brave, Portugal
Suvradip Chakraborty	Visa Research, USA
Long Chen	Chinese Academy of Sciences, China
Yilei Chen	Tsinghua University, China
Rongmao Chen	National University of Defense Technology, China
Jung Hee Cheon	Seoul National University, Republic of Korea
Amy Corman	RMIT University, Australia
Luca De Feo	IBM Research Europe, Switzerland
Yi Deng	Chinese Academy of Sciences, China
Xiong Fan	Rutgers University, USA
Hanwen Feng	The University of Sydney, Australia
Rishab Goyal	University of Wisconsin-Madison, USA
Debayan Gupta	Ashoka University, India
Thomas Haines	The Australian National University, Australia
Goichiro Hanaoka	AIST, Japan
Cheng Hong	Ant Research, China
Tibor Jager	University of Wuppertal, Germany
Zhengzhong Jin	MIT, USA
Dmitry Khovratovich	Ethereum Foundation, Luxembourg
Fuyuki Kitagawa	NTT Social Informatics Laboratories, Japan

Jiaheng Zhang   National University of Singapore, Singapore
Dominique Schroeder   Friedrich-Alexander University of
                             Erlangen-Nürnberg, Germany
Wessel van Woerden   University of Bordeaux, France

Additional Reviewers

Aydin Abadi
Behzad Abdolmaleki
Masayuki Abe
Miguel Ambrona
Arathi Arakala
Sven Argo
Benedikt Auerbach
Renas Bacho
Weihao Bai
Shi Bai
Fabio Banfi
Andrea Basso
Fabrice Benhamouda
Olivier Bernard
Daniel J. Bernstein
Siddhartha Bhoi
Alex Bienstock
Katharina Boudgoust
Charles Bouillaguet
Pedro Branco
Fabian Buschkowski
Rohit Chatterjee
Binyi Chen
Hyeongmin Choe
Arka Rai Choudhuri
Hao Chung
Michele Ciampi
Valerio Cini
Alexandru Cojocaru
Pierrick Dartois
Poulami Das
Koen de Boer
Paola de Perthuis
Benne de Weger
Giovanni Deligios
Lalita Devadas
Jesus Diaz

Jelle Don
Léo Ducas
Pranjal Dutta
Keita Emura
Daniel Escudero
Muhammed F. Esgin
Thomas Espitau
Prastudy Fauzi
Danilo Francati
Daniele Friolo
Yao Jiang Galteland
Gayathri Garimella
Riddhi Ghosal
Aarushi Goel
Lenaick Gouriou
Anna Guinet
Hui Guo
Kyoohyung Han
Lucjan Hanzlik
Charlotte Hoffmann
Alex Hoover
Yao-Ching Hsieh
David Hu
Zhicong Huang
Andreas Hülsing
Nikai Jagganath
Aayush Jain
Xiaoyu Ji
Haodong Jiang
Haohao Jiang
Ioanna Karantaidou
Sabyasachi Karati
Handan Kilinc Alper
Suhri Kim
Dongwoo Kim
Seongkwang Kim
Sungwook Kim

Miran Kim
Kamil Kluczniak
Anders Konrig
Swastik Kopparty
Alexis Korb
Abhiram Kothapalli
Elisabeth Krahmer
Sabrina Kunzweiler
Kaoru Kurosawa
Qiqi Lai
Georg Land
Changmin Lee
Yun Li
Yanan Li
Xiao Liang
Yao-Ting Lin
Qipeng Liu
Zeyu Liu
Weiran Liu
Fengrun Liu
Wen-jie Lu
Varun Madathil
Lorenzo Magliocco
Monosij Maitra
Easwar Mangipudi
Elisaweta Masserova
Takahiro Matsuda
Daniel McVicker
Simon-Philipp Merz
Ruiqi Mi
Peihan Miao
Arash Mirzaei
Anuja Modi
Johannes Mono
Ethan Mook
Kirill Morozov
Marta Mularczyk
Ky Nguyen
Ryo Nishimaki
Alice Pellet-Mary
Nikhil Pappu
Jeongeun Park
Guillermo Pascual Perez
Alain Passelegue
Rutvik Patel

Sihang Pu
Ludo Pulles
Octavio Pérez Kempner
Wei Qi
Tian Qiu
Wenjie Qu
Willy Quach
Ahmadreza Rahimi
Omar Renawi
Mahshid Riahinia
Jan Richter-Brockmann
Guilherme Rito
Damien Robert
Maxime Roméas
Lawrence Roy
Luigi Russo
Sagnik Saha
Yusuke Sakai
Robert Schaedlich
Sven Schäge
Jacob Schuldt
Mahdi Sedaghat
Sruthi Sekar
Joon Young Seo
Jun Jie Sim
Yongha Son
Bruno Sterner
Atsushi Takayasu
Gang Tang
Guofeng Tang
Yuhao Tang
Khai Hanh Tang
Stefano Tessaro
Junichi Tomida
Monika Trimoska
Yiannis Tselekounis
Akhil Vanukuri
Benedikt Wagner
Hendrik Waldner
Han Wang
Yuchen Wang
Li-Ping Wang
Zhedong Wang
Yi Wang
Jiabo Wang

Charlotte Weitkämper
Chenkai Weng
Jie Xu
Anshu Yadav
Aayush Yadav
Shota Yamada
Takashi Yamakawa
Dan Yamamoto
Zhaomin Yang

Yusuke Yoshida
Zuoxia Yu
Shang Zehua
Xinyu Zhang
Liangfeng Zhang
Raymond K. Zhao
Hong-Sheng Zhou
Tanping Zhou
Zidi Zhuang

Contents – Part III

Theoretical Foundations

A Refined Hardness Estimation of LWE in Two-Step Mode

Wenwen Xia[1,2,5], Leizhang Wang[3], Geng Wang[4,5(✉)], Dawu Gu[1,4(✉)], and Baocang Wang[3]

[1] School of Cyber Engineering, Xidian University, Xi'an 710071, China
xiawenwen@stu.xidian.edu.cn
[2] Lab of Cryptology and Computer Security, Shanghai Jiao Tong University, Shanghai 200240, China
[3] State Key Laboratory of Integrated Service Networks, Xidian University, Xi'an 710071, China
lzwang_2@stu.xidian.edu.cn, bcwang@xidian.edu.cn
[4] School of Electronic, Information and Electrical Engineering, Shanghai Jiao Tong University, Shanghai 200240, China
{wanggxx,dwgu}@sjtu.edu.cn
[5] State Key Laboratory of Cryptology, P.O.Box 5159, Beijing 100878, China

Abstract. Recently, researchers have proposed many LWE estimators, such as lattice-estimator (Albrecht et al, Asiacrypt 2017) and leaky-LWE-Estimator (Dachman-Soled et al, Crypto 2020), while the latter has already been used in estimating the security level of Kyber and Dilithium using only BKZ. However, we prove in this paper that solving LWE by combining a lattice reduction step (by LLL or BKZ) and a target vector searching step (by enumeration or sieving), which we call a Two-step mode, is more efficient than using only BKZ.

Moreover, we give a refined LWE estimator in Two-step mode by analyzing the relationship between the probability distribution of the target vector and the solving success rate in a Two-step mode LWE solving algorithm. While the latest Two-step estimator for LWE, which is the "primal-bdd" mode in lattice-estimator (https://github.com/malb/lattice-estimator), does not take into account some up-to-date results and lacks a thorough theoretical analysis. Under the same gate-count model, our estimation for NIST PQC standards drops by 2.1–3.4 bits (2.2–4.6 bits while considering more flexible block-size and jump strategy) compared with leaky-LWE-Estimator.

Furthermore, we also give a conservative estimation for LWE from the Two-step solving algorithm. Compared with the Core-SVP model, which is used in previous conservative estimations, our estimation relies on weaker assumptions and outputs higher evaluation results than the Core-SVP model. For NIST PQC standards, our conservative estimation is 4.17–8.11 bits higher than the Core-SVP estimation. Hence our estimator can give a closer estimation for both upper bound and lower bound of LWE hardness.

Keywords: Lattice-based Cryptanalysis · Security Strength · LWE estimator · Two-step mode

© International Association for Cryptologic Research 2024
Q. Tang and V. Teague (Eds.): PKC 2024, LNCS 14603, pp. 3–35, 2024.
https://doi.org/10.1007/978-3-031-57725-3_1

1   Introduction

As an important branch in post-quantum cryptography, lattice-based cryptography has shown its potential in several cryptographic primitives, such as key establishment [1], digital signature [2,3], hash function [4] and other more advanced cryptography constructions like identity-based encryption [5], attribute-based encryption [6], functional encryption [7], and homomorphic encryption [8].

One of the advantages of lattice-based cryptography is that the security of lattice-based cryptography schemes is guaranteed by the hardness of lattice problems with worst-case to average-case reduction, such as the Learning with Errors problem (LWE). It has been proved that solving the LWE problem is at least as hard as some worst-case lattice problem like the Shortest Independent Vector problem (SIVP) or the Bound Distance Decoding (BDD) problem. In the post-quantum standardization process held by the National Institute of Standards and technique (NIST), many lattice-based cryptographic schemes (e.g. [1–3]) are selected as standards to resist the threat of quantum computer. One of the most important problems in standardization is the parameter selection. To select more compact but still safe security parameters for lattice-based schemes, it is necessary to give a concrete hardness estimation for lattice-based problems. In this paper, we focus on LWE, which is the most widely used lattice-based problem.

There are various methods for solving LWE, such as BDD attack [9], Arora-Ge attack [10], BKW attack [11], primal attack [12,13], dual attack [14] and hybrid attacks [15] based on lattice reduction algorithm. Among them, the primal attack [12,13] is most practical in breaking actual LWE-based schemes, and the concrete hardness of LWE is often estimated by calculating the cost of the primal attack. A primal attack translates LWE to a unique Shortest Vector Problem (uSVP) by constructing a special lattice basis with Kannan's embedding technique [16].

In particular, a long series of works, e.g. [12,13,17–19] have proposed the evaluation of the hardness of LWE under the primal attack. In 2015, the work of Albrecht et al. [17] gives concrete estimations for various families of LWE instances. Later, a simple yet conservative estimation method was given by [12] named the Core-SVP model. It proposed a success condition in solving LWE by BKZ with fixed blocksize β and estimated its cost as a single call to the SVP oracle, which is a lattice sieve with dimension β. Since the Core-SVP model ignores both the number of calls to the SVP oracle in one BKZ tour and the number of BKZ tours, the evaluation result by the Core-SVP model is often considered to be conservative enough. In 2017, Albrecht et al. [13] verified the attack success condition proposed in [12] by experiments.

However, the experiment results shown in [13,20] both illustrate that when the blocksize of BKZ is smaller than the estimation given in [12], it still has a non-negligible probability in solving the LWE instance. This phenomenon is mainly caused by the randomness of the target vector which actually follows the discrete Gaussian distribution rather than a fixed expected value. To solve this problem, Dachman-Soled et al. [19] proposed the first estimator which describes the relationship between the probability of successfully solving LWE and the blocksize β of BKZ used in solving LWE, which is called "leaky-LWE-Estimator". According to the experiment results of [21], the estimator proposed in [19] and their simplified version [21] can well predict the behavior of BKZ solving LWE with smaller blocksize β. In fact, the leaky-LWE-Estimator has been used for estimating the concrete security strength of the lattice-based post-quantum cryptography (PQC) standardization [1,2] selected by NIST [22] in 2022.

Specifically, the leaky-LWE-Estimator first uses the technique in [19] to calculate the expected value of BKZ blocksize of solving LWE and calculate the total number of logic circuit gates needed to solve LWE by calling the gate-count algorithm proposed in [23]. It is noticeable that the leaky-LWE-Estimator also considers the influence of dimension-for-free (d4f) technique [24], which leads to a decrease in the estimation result. Moreover, it is worth pointing out that the Core-SVP model did not consider the influence brought by d4f, which threatens the conservativeness of the Core-SVP model.

However, the main problem in the leaky-LWE-Estimator and Core-SVP model is that they only use the BKZ algorithm as the underlying LWE solver, instead of combining BKZ reduction with a final search step (we call it a Two-step mode for solving LWE). In this work, we prove that the Two-step LWE-solving strategy is more efficient than the underlying LWE solver in earlier LWE estimators (such as leaky-LWE-Estimator [19]) which only uses BKZ, thus the BKZ-only estimators may output an over-optimistic estimation.

A Two-step LWE-solving strategy is divided into a lattice reduction step (by LLL or BKZ) and a target vector searching step (by enumeration or sieving). Although the Two-step mode is often considered a folklore approach to solving LWE, only few works bring it into practice. The first Two-step LWE-solving attack was proposed in [9], where they reduce LWE into a BDD problem, and call an enumeration for finding the closest vector in the last searching step. In [25], the authors show that an additional post-processing step using enumeration can increase the success rate in solving γ-SVP with $\gamma = 1.05$, but it is not known whether the post-processing step has same acceleration when applied to LWE. For solving LWE with sieving instead of enumeration, the G6K framework [26] presented a solving algorithm that is also a combination of BKZ and conditional sieving. However, it is different from the Two-step strategy in previous works, and its efficiency has not been theoretically analyzed.

In the context of LWE estimation, Albrecht et al use the "`primal_bdd`" function in lattice-estimator [27] to estimate the hardness of LWE through a primal attack using one BKZ reduction and a sieve in the searching step. However, in estimating the dimension of the last sieving, "`primal_bdd`" estimation only considers the expected norm of the target vector rather than analyzing the relationship between the probability distribution of the target vector and the solving success rate of Two-step mode. So it is necessary to give a more refined Two-step LWE estimator that considers the success probability of the last sieve algorithm and provides extensive experimental evidence of its accuracy. Besides, the Two-step attack proposed in [28] can also improve the efficiency of the Two-step attack in "`primal_bdd`" by applying the improved progressive BKZ reduction and allowing PnjBKZ with jump value ¿ 1.

Furthermore, there is an open question proposed in Sect. 5.3 (Q7) of Kyber's document that a security estimation error interval exists in NIST lattice-based standardization. This security estimation error interval is caused by using different reduction strategies to evaluate the security. Particularly, the reduction strategy considered by leaky-LWE-Estimator [19] is a trivial progressive BKZ, and in [12,13,17,18] they consider a fixed blocksize BKZ algorithm to solve LWE. The paper [29] mentioned that a large dimension of sieve in the final process costs less than a BKZ. The trivial reduction strategies above can be further improved by a more efficient reduction strategy like the optimized blocksize and jump selection strategy proposed in [28] which has already shown its efficiency in solving LWE instances[1]. To ensure the security and narrow the security estimation error interval of lattice-based NIST standard schemes, it is necessary to evaluate the impact of the combination of the Two-step solving strategy and the optimized blocksize and jump selection strategy on the security of NIST selected lattice-based schemes.

Contributions. In this paper, we improve the estimation of LWE hardness from the following aspects:

- We formally prove that the Two-step mode is more efficient in solving uSVP than the BKZ-only mode under Geometric Series Assumption, and extend the result to solving LWE which considers the distribution of LWE error term.
- We construct an LWE hardness estimator which underlying LWE solver is the Two-step LWE solving algorithm, and we calculate the success probability for solving LWE at each step. In the reduction phase, we give a heuristic assumption that each BKZ tour totally randomizes the lattice basis, which is also implicitly implied by the leaky-LWE-estimator [19], so that the success probability of different BKZ tours can be considered independent. In the searching phase, however, the success probability is accumulated after each step. By calculation of the success rate, we show that the expected cost for solving LWE by Two-step mode is much lower than by BKZ-only mode as in [19].
- To verify the accuracy of our estimation, we did extensive experiments of solving LWE by different sieving dimensions in the searching phase. The results of these experiments are consistent with our estimation, which means the expected time cost of solving LWE by our estimator is accurate. Moreover, we re-evaluate the security bit of NIST PQC schemes by our Two-step LWE hardness estimator. When using the same trivial reduction strategy in leaky-LWE-Estimator [19], the security bit drops by 2.1–3.4 bits. Besides, when

---

[1] See latest TU Darmstadt LWE challenge records $(n, \alpha) \in \{(40, 0.035), (90, 0.005), (50, 0.025), (55, 0.020), (40, 0.040)\}$ in https://www.latticechallenge.org/lwe_ challenge.php.

using the optimized blocksize and jump selection strategy proposed in paper [28], the security bit drops by 2.2–4.6 bits.
- We also give a more accurate lower bound estimation which is a conservative Two-step solving mode estimation for LWE. Compared with the commonly used Core-SVP model, our conservative estimation relies on weaker assumptions. Meantime, our conservative estimation has higher estimation results than the Core-SVP model (while d4f not considered). For NIST PQC standards, our conservative estimation is 4.17–8.11 bits higher than the Core-SVP estimation. Therefore, we give more accurate estimations on both the upper bound and lower bound of the hardness of LWE.

All detailed codes of our Two-step LWE Estimator with different reduction strategies are already open-sourced[2].

Organization. In Sect. 2 we give the preliminaries, notations, and the basic knowledge of lattice problems. In Sect. 3 we prove that the Two-step solving mode is more efficient in solving uSVP than the BKZ-only mode. In Sect. 4 we construct a refined Two-step security estimator for solving LWE. The experiments results in Sect. 5 verify the accuracy of our Two-step security estimator and the efficiency of the Two-step solving mode. In Sect. 6 we give a conservative estimation for LWE from a Two-step solving algorithm. Based on our Two-step security estimator and lower bound estimation estimator we give more accurate both upper bound and lower bound estimation of LWE in NIST PQC schemes in Sect. 7.

2 Preliminaries

2.1 Notations and Basic Definitions

In this paper, all vectors are denoted by bold lowercase letters and are to be read as column vectors. We write a matrix $\mathbf{B}$ as $\mathbf{B} = (\mathbf{b}_0, \cdots, \mathbf{b}_{d-1})$ where $\mathbf{b}_i$ is the $(i+1)$-th column vector of $\mathbf{B}$. The Euclidean norm of a vector $\mathbf{v}$ is denoted by $\|\mathbf{v}\|$. A lattice $\mathcal{L}$ generated by the basis $\mathbf{B}$ is denoted by $\mathcal{L}(\mathbf{B}) = \{\mathbf{Bx} | \mathbf{x} \in \mathbb{Z}^d\}$. Here lattice basis matrix $\mathbf{B} \in \mathbb{R}^{d \times d}$ needs to be full rank d. We denote $\mathbf{B}^* = (\mathbf{b}_0^*, \cdots, \mathbf{b}_{d-1}^*)$ as the Gram-Schmidt orthogonalization of $\mathbf{B}$, in which $\mathbf{b}_i^* = \mathbf{b}_i - \sum_{j=0}^{i-1} \mu_{i,j} \mathbf{b}_j^*$, $\mu_{i,j} = \langle \mathbf{b}_i, \mathbf{b}_j^* \rangle / \|\mathbf{b}_j^*\|^2$. We denote the orthogonal projection to the span of $(\mathbf{b}_0, \cdots, \mathbf{b}_{i-1})$ by π_i, for $i \in \{0, \cdots, d-1\}$, i.e. $\forall \mathbf{v}, \pi_i(\mathbf{v}) = \mathbf{v} - \sum_{j=0}^{i-1} \omega_j \mathbf{b}_j^*$, in which $\omega_j = \langle \mathbf{v}, \mathbf{b}_j^* \rangle / \|\mathbf{b}_j^*\|^2$. For $i, j \in \mathbb{Z}_d$ and $0 \le i < j \le d-1$, given an arbitrary d-dimensional vector $\mathbf{v} = (v_0, \cdots, v_{d-1})$, define $\mathbf{v}_{[i:j]}$ as $(v_i, \cdots, v_{j-1})$ with size $j-i$. For a lattice basis $\mathbf{B}$, let $\mathbf{B}_{[i:j]} \leftarrow (\mathbf{b}_i, \cdots, \mathbf{b}_{j-1})$. Moreover, we denote $\mathbf{B}_{\pi[i:j]}$ as the local projected block $(\pi_i(\mathbf{b}_i), \cdots, \pi_i(\mathbf{b}_{j-1}))$, and call $\mathcal{L}_{\pi[i:j]}$ the lattice generated by $\mathbf{B}_{\pi[i:j]}$. We use $\mathbf{B}_{\pi[i]}$ and $\mathcal{L}_{\pi[i]}$ as shorthands for $\mathbf{B}_{\pi[i:d]}$ and $\mathcal{L}_{\pi[i:d]}$. An important invariant

---

[2] Batch "refined-lwe-estimator" in https://github.com/Summwer/lwe-estimator-with-pnjbkz.git.

value of the lattice $\mathcal{L}(\mathbf{B})$ is its volume $\mathrm{Vol}(\mathcal{L}(\mathbf{B})) = \prod_{i=0}^{d-1} \|\mathbf{b}_i^*\|$. The length of the shortest non-zero vector of a lattice $\mathcal{L}(\mathbf{B})$ can be denoted by $\lambda_1(\mathcal{L}(\mathbf{B}))$. We use the abbreviations $\mathrm{Vol}(\mathbf{B}) = \mathrm{Vol}(\mathcal{L}(\mathbf{B}))$ and $\lambda_1(\mathbf{B}) = \lambda_1(\mathcal{L}(\mathbf{B}))$.

Notations for Algorithms Description. Let BKZ-β/PnjBKZ-(β, J) be an abbreviation of a one-tour BKZ/PnjBKZ with blocksize β and jump value J, and J is omitted when $J = 1$. Assume $\mathbf{B} = (\mathbf{b}_0, \cdots, \mathbf{b}_{d-1})$, its Gram-Schmidt basis is $\mathbf{B}^* = (\mathbf{b}_0^*, \cdots, \mathbf{b}_{d-1}^*)$. Let $\mathrm{rr}(\mathbf{B}) = (\|\mathbf{b}_0^*\|, \cdots, \|\mathbf{b}_{d-1}^*\|)$, abbreviate to rr. $\mathrm{rr}_{[i:j]} = (\|\mathbf{b}_{i-1}^*\|, \cdots, \|\mathbf{b}_{j-1}^*\|)$. Let $\mathrm{rr}[i]$ be the $(i+1)$-th element of rr.

Denote BKZSim as the BKZ simulator proposed in [30]. The simulation for PnjBKZ is denoted as $\mathrm{PnjBKZSim}(\mathrm{rr}(\mathbf{B}), \beta, J, t)$ which simulates a PnjBKZ-(β, J) with t tours on lattice $\mathcal{L}(\mathbf{B})$ and return the new lengths, where the PnjBKZ simulator was proposed in [28]. Moreover, if we have a blocksize and jump strategy S that stores a series of (β_i, J_i), then $\mathrm{PnjBKZSim}(\mathrm{rr}, \mathsf{S})$ means iteratively calling a tour of PnjBKZ-(β_i, J_i) simulator on rr, where $(\beta_i, J_i) \in \mathsf{S}$. Let BKZ-$\beta$ reduced basis be the lattice basis after calling sufficient tours of BKZ-β. For simplification, we use β to imply the quality of a BKZ-β reduced basis. Let $\sharp\mathrm{tours}(\text{BKZ-}\beta)/\sharp\mathrm{tours}(\text{PnjBKZ-}(\beta, J))$ be the minimum tours for BKZ-β/PnjBKZ-(β, J) to reach a BKZ-β/PnjBKZ-(β, J) reduced basis, abbreviated as $\sharp\mathrm{tours}$. Denote t as the number of tours for implementing BKZ/PnjBKZ with a fixed blocksize (and jump) $\beta/(\beta, J)$.

Let $T_{\mathrm{BKZ}}(\beta)/T_{\mathrm{pnjBKZ}}(\beta, J)$ be the time cost of one BKZ/PnjBKZ tour with blocksize β and jump value J. For a specific blocksize and jump strategy $\mathsf{S} = [(\beta_0, J_0), \cdots, (\beta_{n-1}, J_{n-1})]$, we let $T_{\mathrm{BKZs}}(\mathsf{S})/T_{\mathrm{pnjBKZs}}(\mathsf{S})$ be total time cost for a series of BKZ/PnjBKZ reduction with strategy S, abbreviate it as $T_{\mathrm{BKZs}}/T_{\mathrm{pnjBKZs}}$.

In the searching step, we will consider a high dimension sieve and we denote $T_{\mathrm{sieve}}(d_{\mathrm{svp}})$ as the time cost of sieve dimension d_{svp}, abbreviate it as T_{sieve}. Let PSC be the expected sieve cost to find the target vector.

Definition 1. *(The Gaussian Distribution [21]) Let $\sigma, u \in \mathbb{R}$ be the standard deviation and the mean value respectively, a continuous Gaussian Distribution denoted as $N(u, \sigma^2)$. Its probabilistic density function $\rho_{N(u,\sigma^2)} = e^{-\frac{(x-u)^2}{2\sigma^2}}/\sigma\sqrt{2\pi}$.*

Definition 2. *(Chi-Squared Distribution [21]) Given n random variables $X_i \sim N(0, 1)$, the random variables $X_0^2 + \cdots + X_{n-1}^2$ follows a chi-squared distribution χ_n^2 over $\mathbb{R}^*$ of mean n and variance $2n$ with probabilistic density function $\rho_{\chi_n^2}(x) = x^{\frac{n}{2}-1}e^{-\frac{x}{2}}/2^{\frac{n}{2}}\Gamma(n/2)$. Given n random variables $Y_i \sim N(0, \sigma^2)$, the random variables $Y_0^2 + \cdots + Y_{n-1}^2$ follows a scaled chi-squared distribution $\sigma^2 \cdot \chi_n^2$ over $\mathbb{R}^*$ of mean $n\sigma^2$ and variance $2n\sigma^2$.*

Heuristic 1. *(Gaussian Heuristic [24]) The expected first minimum of a lattice $\mathcal{L}$ (denoted as $\lambda_1(\mathcal{L}(\mathbf{B}))$) according to the Gaussian Heuristic denoted by $\mathrm{GH}(\mathcal{L})$ is given by $\lambda_1(\mathcal{L}(\mathbf{B})) \approx \mathrm{GH}(\mathcal{L}) = \left(\Gamma(\frac{d}{2}+1) \cdot \mathrm{Vol}(\mathcal{L})\right)^{\frac{1}{d}}/\sqrt{\pi} \approx \sqrt{d/(2\pi e)} \cdot \mathrm{Vol}(\mathcal{L})^{\frac{1}{d}}$ We also write $\mathrm{GH}(\mathbf{B}) = \mathrm{GH}(\mathcal{L}(\mathbf{B}))$ and $\mathrm{GH}(\mathrm{rr}_{[i:j]}) = \mathrm{GH}(\mathbf{B}_{\pi[i:j]})$.*

Definition 3. *(HKZ reduction and BKZ reduction [24]) The basis* **B** *of a lattice* $\mathcal{L}$ *is HKZ reduced if* $\mathbf{b}_i^* = \lambda_1(\mathcal{L}(\mathbf{B}_{\pi[i:d]}))$, *for all* $i < d$. $\mathcal{L}$ *is BKZ-β reduced if* $\mathbf{b}_i^* = \lambda_1(\mathcal{L}(\mathbf{B}_{\pi[i:\min\{i+\beta,d\}]}))$, *for all* $i < d$.

Definition 4. *(Root Hermite Factor [31]) For a basis* **B** *of d-dimensional lattice, the root Hermite factor is defined as* $\delta = \left(\|\mathbf{b}_0\|/\mathrm{Vol}(\mathbf{B})^{1/d}\right)^{1/d}$, *for estimating the equality of the output vector of BKZ. For larger blocksize, it follows the asymptotic formula* $\delta(\beta)^{2(\beta-1)} = \frac{\beta}{2\pi e}(\beta\pi)^{1/\beta}$.

Heuristic 2. *(Geometric Series Assumption (GSA) [26]) Let* **B** *be a lattice basis after lattice reduction, then Geometric Series Assumption states that* $\|\mathbf{b}_i^*\| \approx \alpha \cdot \|\mathbf{b}_{i-1}^*\|$, $0 < \alpha < 1$. *Combine the GSA with root-Hermite factor (Definition 4) and* $Vol(\mathcal{L}(\mathbf{B})) = \prod_{i=0}^{d-1}\|\mathbf{b}_i^*\|$, *it infers that* $\alpha = \delta^{-\frac{2d}{d-1}} \approx \delta^{-2}$.

2.2 Lattice Hard Problems

Definition 5. *(unique Shortest Vector Problem($uSVP_\gamma$) [32]) Given an arbitrary basis* **B** *on lattice* $\mathcal{L} = \mathcal{L}(\mathbf{B})$, $\mathcal{L}$ *satisfies the condition* $\gamma\lambda_1(\mathbf{B}) < \lambda_2(\mathbf{B})$ $(\gamma > 1, \lambda_2(\mathbf{B})$ *is norm of the second shortest vector which is linearly independent to the shortest vector), find the shortest non-zero vector* **v** *s.t.* $\|\mathbf{v}\| = \lambda_1(\mathbf{B})$.

Definition 6. *(LWE_{m,n,q,D_σ} Distribution [33–35]) Given some samples $m \in \mathbb{Z}$, a secret vector length $n \in \mathbb{Z}$, a modulo $q \in \mathbb{Z}$, a probability distribution D_σ. Uniformly sample a matrix $\mathbf{A} \in \mathbb{Z}_q^{m \times n}$ and sample a secret vector $\mathbf{s} \in \mathbb{Z}_q^n$ from a specific distribution, randomly sample a relatively small noise vector $\mathbf{e} \in \mathbb{Z}_q^m$ from Gaussian distribution D_σ whose standard deviation is σ. The LWE distribution Ψ is constructed by the pair $(\mathbf{A}, \mathbf{b} = \mathbf{As} + \mathbf{e}) \in (\mathbb{Z}_q^{m \times n}, \mathbb{Z}_q^m)$ sampled as above.*

Definition 7. *(Search LWE_{m,n,q,D_σ} problem [33–35]) Given a pair $(\mathbf{A}, \mathbf{b})$ sampled from LWE distribution Ψ compute the pair $(\mathbf{s}, \mathbf{e})$.*

2.3 Primal Attack

Albrecht *et al.* [36] firstly presented the primal attack for the LWE problem, which reduced Standard Form LWE problem to an $uSVP_\gamma$ by Kannan's embedding technique [16]. $(\mathbf{A}, \mathbf{b})$ are LWE instances and the form of the embedding lattice basis is as $\mathbf{B}_{\mathbf{A}',\mathbf{b}} = \begin{pmatrix} \mathbf{A}' & \mathbf{b} \\ \mathbf{0}^T & 1 \end{pmatrix}$, $\mathbf{A}' = \mathbf{P}^{-1}\begin{pmatrix} q\mathbf{I}_{m-n} & \bar{\mathbf{A}} \\ \mathbf{O} & \mathbf{I}_n \end{pmatrix}$, here $\mathbf{P} \in \mathbb{Z}^{m \times m}$ is a permutation matrix such that $\mathbf{P} \cdot \mathbf{A} = \left(\bar{\mathbf{A}}^T, \mathbf{I}_n\right)^T$. Then there is a unusually short lattice vector $\mathbf{v} = (\mathbf{e}, 1)$ in this embedding lattice $\mathbf{B}_{\mathbf{A}',\mathbf{b}}$ whose norm $\|\mathbf{v}\| \approx \sigma\sqrt{m}$ is shorter than $\lambda_2(\mathcal{L})$. Thus LWE is reduced to a uSVP on the embedding lattice.

2.4 Core-SVP Model [12]

Core-SVP model [12] only considers using the BKZ algorithm with a fixed blocksize β to perform Primal Attack and evaluate the time cost. [12,13] give a success condition of such attack: For the minimal blocksize β in the BKZ algorithm (or its variant) to ensure that the following inequality is satisfied $\|\mathbf{v}\|\sqrt{\beta/d} \leq \delta^{2\beta-d}\mathrm{Vol}(\mathcal{L}(\mathbf{B}))^{1/d}$, the unique shortest vector $\mathbf{v}$ will be found by BKZ in time $T(\beta)$ which is an exponential function of β. This success condition based on GSA (Heuristic 2) is a brief justification for the estimation given in [12]. Here δ is the root of the Hermit factor of lattice basis. [37] gives the following relation between the blocksize and the root Hermite factor $\delta(\beta) \approx \left(((\pi\beta)^{1/\beta}\beta)/(2\pi e)\right)^{1/(2(\beta-1))}$.

Core-SVP model considers neither the number of calls to β-dimension SVP Oracle during one tour of the BKZ algorithm with blocksize β, nor the number of BKZ tours needed to satisfy the success condition. Therefore, the Core-SVP model [12] is considered a conservative LWE security evaluation model. The accurate upper bound number of BKZ tours needed to reach BKZ-β reduced basis is still unknown [38], but [30] suggests that a polynomial number of BKZ-β tours seems sufficient to obtain a lattice basis with Hermite factor near $\delta(\beta)$. When the SVP Oracle used by the BKZ algorithm is BDGL sieving [39], the time cost of solving LWE under Core-SVP model is $T(\beta) \approx O(2^{0.292\beta})$.

2.5 PnjBKZ

PnjBKZ is a BKZ-type reduction algorithm that uses `Pump` as its SVP oracle. Unlike classical BKZ, PnjBKZ performs the SVP oracle with an adjustable jump no less than 1. Specifically, running a PnjBKZ with blocksize β and jump=J, after executing the SVP oracle on a certain block $\mathbf{B}_{[i:i+\beta]}$, the next SVP oracle will be executed on the $\mathbf{B}_{[i+J:i+\beta+J]}$ block with a jump count J rather than $\mathbf{B}_{[i+1:i+\beta+1]}$.

2.6 Dimension for Free (d4f) Technique

D4f technique [24] can bring sub-exponential time speedup and memory decrease for sieve algorithms. In this paper, we consider the theoretical d4f estimation given in [24] as d4f$(\beta) = \beta\ln(4/3)/\ln(\beta/2\pi e)$, which means that solving β-dimension SVP needs only $\beta - $ d4f(β) dimensional sieving.

2.7 Leaky-LWE-Estimator

The leaky-LWE-Estimator [19] proposed a probabilistic method in LWE estimation as opposed to the GSA-intersect, which relates the solving probability of LWE instance to BKZ blocksizes. The estimator was later applied to the NIST PQC standards such as Kyber and Dilithium along with the estimation in [39], which gives an accurate estimation for LWE rather than a conservative lower bound like Core-SVP model [12]. The leaky-LWE-Estimator [19] computes an expected value $\bar{\beta}$ of the blocksize needed to solve an LWE instance by simulating how the quality of the lattice basis changes during lattice reduction, and estimating the success probability in finding the target vector at each block of the progressive BKZ. Then it substitutes $\bar{\beta}$ into the gate count and memory cost by the list decoding estimation in [23] and obtains a cost estimation for LWE with specific input parameters. Besides, to simplify the calculation process in Leaky-LWE-Estimator, [21] presented a simpler version that has the same estimation results as [19].

One main difference between leaky-LWE-Estimator and Core-SVP model is that leaky-LWE-Estimator uses the BKZ 2.0 simulator [30] denoted as BKZSim to simulate how the lattice basis changed during the reduction of progressive BKZ, which can be used to estimate the number of calls to SVP Oracle with different dimensions and the quality of the lattice basis reduced by a series of BKZ. Another difference is that the leaky-LWE-Estimator considers the length of the target vector as a random variable that follows the chi-square distribution rather than some fixed value. In addition, the leaky-LWE-Estimator uses the gate count method proposed in [23] instead of computational complexity to estimate the hardness of LWE. The detail of the leaky-LWE-Estimator is given in Algorithm 1. Here χ_β^2 in Algorithm 1 is the chi-squared distribution with degree β of freedom.

---

input: d, **t**;
output: $\bar{\beta}$;

1 **Function** LeakyLWEEstimator$(d, \mathbf{t})$:
2     $p_{\text{tot}} \leftarrow 0$, $\bar{\beta} \leftarrow 0$
3   rr $\leftarrow$ GSA profile of an LLL reduced, rank d, LWE instance
4   **for** $\beta \leftarrow 3$ **to** d **do**
5   rr $\leftarrow$ BKZSim(rr, β);
6        $p_{\text{lift}} \leftarrow$ Pr[**t** recovered in $\lfloor d/\beta \rfloor$ rounds $\mid \pi_{d-\beta+1}(\mathbf{t})$ recovered this round]
7        $p_{\text{rec}} \leftarrow$ Pr[$x \leftarrow \chi_\beta^2 : x \le (\text{rr}[d-\beta])^2$]
8        $p_{\text{new}} \leftarrow (1 - p_{\text{tot}}) \cdot p_{\text{rec}} \cdot p_{\text{lift}}$
9        $\bar{\beta} \leftarrow \bar{\beta} + p_{\text{new}} \cdot \beta$
10   **if** $p \ge 0.999$ **then**
11   break

12   **return** $\bar{\beta}$

Algorithm 1: leaky LWE Estimator proposed in [19]. [21] shows that p_{lift} is always close to 1 and could be deleted in the computation.

After calling Algorithm 1 to obtain the expected value of BKZ blocksize $\bar{\beta}$ for solving LWE, leaky-LWE-Estimator will call the Gate-count algorithm in [23] to calculate the number of gates (time cost): ppgate$(\bar{\beta}) = C^2 \cdot$ agps20gates$(\bar{\beta} -$ d4f$(\bar{\beta}))$ and memory cost: bit$(\bar{\beta}) = 8(\bar{\beta} - $d4f$(\bar{\beta})) \cdot$ agps20vectors$(\bar{\beta} - $d4f$(\bar{\beta}))$ for solving the LWE respectively. Here the Gate-count algorithm [23] can analyze the cost of sieving with a classical and quantum circuit and $C = \frac{1}{1-2^{-0.292}}$ is a constant used to simulate the time cost of progressive sieving when BDGL16 sieving [39] is used and progressive BKZ blocksize. More detail about functions agps20gates$(\cdot)$ can be seen in [40].

2.8   PnjBKZ Simulator

The first step in the two-step solving mode is using a series of well-chosen BKZ tours to reduce the lattice basis. Compared with classical BKZ algorithm, the PnjBKZ algorithm (see Sect. 2.5 and Algorithm 3 for more detail) is a more efficient lattice reduction algorithm which allows more flexible choice of blocks to be processed in BKZ which uses a sieving algorithm Pump as its SVP oracle.

The PnjBKZ simulator is a polynomial time algorithm to simulate how the quality of the lattice basis changes during the reduction by using the optimized reduction strategy of PnjBKZ-(β, J) with $J > 1$ in [28] without actually running the time-consuming (exponential time cost according to blocksize) PnjBKZ algorithm. The PnjBKZ simulator uses the Gaussian Heuristic and the property of HKZ reduction to estimate how the logarithms of the Gram-Schmidt norms of lattice basis changed after one tour of PnjBKZ-(β, J). For convenience, we declare the notation of PnjBKZ simulation in Sect. 2.

3   Efficiency of Two-Step Solving Mode

In this section, we will show that the Two-step solving mode is more efficient in solving uSVP$_\gamma$ compared with the BKZ-only mode. We use Theorem 1 to illustrate this claim and give the corresponding proof under GSA.

Theorem 1. *Assume Gaussian Heuristic (Heuristic 1), GSA (Heuristic 2) and Heuristic 4 in [28] hold. Let d be the dimension of lattice, $d \geq 100$, we assume that the uSVP$_\gamma$ instance can be solved by BKZ-only mode through a BKZ-β reduced basis with $\frac{d+16}{9} \leq \beta \leq \frac{d}{2}$, and let the time cost for sieving on d-dimensional lattice be $2^{c \cdot d + c_0}$ where $c \leq 0.35$. Then there exists a parameter choice for the Two-step mode which solves the uSVP$_\gamma$ instance in less time than the BKZ-only mode.*

Proof. Let $\mathcal{L}$ be the lattice, $\mathbf{B}$ be its basis and d be the dimension of $\mathcal{L}$, suppose the unique shortest vector is $\mathbf{v}$. Without loss of generality, we set $\text{Vol}(\mathcal{L}) = 1$, let $M = \|\mathbf{v}\|$ be the length of its unique shortest vector. Assume all the orthogonal projections of $\mathbf{v}$ onto the k-dimensional projection sub-lattice $\mathcal{L}_{\pi[d-k]}$ have expected norm $\sqrt{\frac{k}{d}} \cdot M$. Let $\delta(\beta)$ be the root Hermite factor of a BKZ-β reduced basis. Assuming GSA holds, the length of the basis can be estimated by $(\delta(\beta)^d, \delta(\beta)^{d \cdot \frac{d-3}{d-1}}, ..., \delta(\beta)^{-d})$.

Since the projection $\pi_{d-\beta}(\mathbf{v})$ is expected to be the shortest non-zero vector of $\mathcal{L}_{\pi[d-\beta]}$, i.e. $\|\pi_{d-\beta}(\mathbf{v})\| \leq \lambda_1(\mathcal{L}_{\pi[d-\beta]}) \approx \text{GH}(\mathcal{L}_{\pi[d-\beta]})$, then

$$\sqrt{\frac{\beta}{2\pi e}} \cdot \delta(\beta)^{-\frac{d(d-\beta)}{d-1}} \geq \sqrt{\frac{\beta}{d}} \cdot M$$

Next, suppose that the same instance is solved by a Two-step mode on a BKZ-β' reduced basis with a d_{svp} dimensional sieving, where $\beta' < \beta < d_{\text{svp}}$.

Then:

$$\sqrt{\frac{d_{\text{svp}}}{2\pi e}} \cdot \delta(\beta')^{-\frac{d(d-d_{\text{svp}})}{d-1}} \geq \sqrt{\frac{d_{\text{svp}}}{2\pi e}} \cdot \delta(\beta)^{-\frac{d(d-\beta)}{d-1}} \geq \sqrt{\frac{d_{\text{svp}}}{d}} \cdot M$$

We find a condition such that the inequality above holds. Since $d_{\text{svp}} > \beta$, we only need to ensure that $\delta(\beta')^{-\frac{d(d-d_{\text{svp}})}{d-1}} \geq \delta(\beta)^{-\frac{d(d-\beta)}{d-1}}$. Take logarithm on both sides, and consider that $\delta(\beta) = (\frac{\beta}{2\pi e} \cdot (\beta\pi)^{\frac{1}{\beta}})^{\frac{1}{2(\beta-1)}}$, we need to ensure that:

$$\frac{d-\beta}{d-d_{\text{svp}}} \geq \frac{\frac{1}{2(\beta'-1)} \cdot (\log\frac{\beta'}{2\pi e} + \frac{1}{\beta'}\log(\beta'\pi))}{\frac{1}{2(\beta-1)} \cdot (\log\frac{\beta}{2\pi e} + \frac{1}{\beta}\log(\beta\pi))}$$

Since $0 < \beta' < \beta$, it infers that $\beta'\log\frac{\beta'}{2\pi e} + \log(\beta'\pi) < \beta\log\frac{\beta}{2\pi e} + \log(\beta\pi)$ always holds. We only need to ensure that:

$$\frac{d-\beta}{d-d_{\text{svp}}} \geq \frac{\beta(\beta-1)}{\beta'(\beta'-1)}$$

Here we consider a special case where $\beta' = \beta - 1$, since if the condition is satisfied under this case, then it is surely satisfied for the optimal choice of β', d_{svp}. We write $d_{\text{gap}} = d_{\text{svp}} - \beta$. We choose d_{gap} to satisfy the condition above, which means that:

$$1 + \frac{d_{\text{gap}}}{d-\beta-d_{\text{gap}}} \geq 1 + \frac{2}{\beta-2}$$

Let T be the time to generate a BKZ-$(\beta-1)$ reduced basis, under the heuristic assumption that generating a BKZ-β reduced basis requires at least one BKZ-β tour, the time of BKZ-only mode $T_{\text{BKZ-only}} \geq T + T_{\text{BKZ}}(\beta)$, and the time of Two-step mode $T_{\text{Two-step}} = T + T_{\text{sieve}}(\beta + d_{\text{gap}})$, so we only need to show that for a choice of d_{gap} satisfies the condition above, $T_{\text{sieve}}(\beta+d_{\text{gap}}) \leq (d-\beta+1)T_{\text{sieve}}(\beta) \leq T_{\text{BKZ}}(\beta)$. Let $T_{\text{sieve}}(d) = 2^{c \cdot d + c_0}$ be the sieve cost model, then we only need to show that $2^{c \cdot d_{\text{gap}}} \leq d - \beta + 1$.

Now we choose $d_{\text{gap}} = \frac{2(d-\beta+1)}{\beta-2}$ which satisfies the condition. By our assumption, $d \leq 9\beta - 16$, so we have that $d_{\text{gap}} \leq 16$. For $c \leq 0.35$, $2^{c \cdot d_{\text{gap}}} \leq 49$, since we assume that $d \geq 100$ and $d \geq 2\beta$, $d - \beta \geq 50$, thus the condition is satisfied. $\square$

All current LWE estimators only consider the security strength of LWE under the BKZ-only solving mode. However, according to Theorem 1, we know that a Two-step mode is more efficient in solving uSVP$_\gamma$ and we should analyze the impact of Two-step mode on the hardness of LWE which can be reduced to uSVP$_\gamma$ under primal attack. So in the following section, we propose a refined Two-step LWE Estimator to evaluate the concrete hardness of LWE by considering Two-step solving mode.

4   A Refined Two-Step Security Estimator for Solving LWE

In this section, we give the details of our refined Two-step security estimator for solving LWE. The detail of our Two-step LWE Estimator is shown in Sect. 4.1. Then the verification experiments of our Two-step LWE Estimator are shown in Sect. 5. In addition, we re-estimate the hardness of LWE instances in NIST PQC schemes by our Two-step LWE Estimator under a trivial reduction strategy and an optimized reduction strategy [28] respectively in Sect. 7.1.

In this section, we build our estimator mainly based on leaky-LWE estimator [19]. In fact, constructing our Two-step LWE Estimator based on other security evaluators (such as the LWE-estimator by Albrecht et al. [17]) can also obtain similar conclusions that the Two-step mode of solving LWE will result in a decrease of the estimated security bit. More analysis and estimation results can be seen in Appendix A.

4.1   Two-Step LWE Estimator with Trivial Strategy

In this part, we give the detail about our Two-step LWE Estimator (Algorithm 2) (See footnote 2).

> **input** : $n, m, q, \chi, \mathsf{S}$;
> **output**: $\mathsf{GB}_{\min}$;
> 1 **Function** TwoStepLWEEstimator($n, m, q, \chi, \mathsf{S}$):
> 2 $\quad$ $\mathsf{GB}_{\min} \leftarrow (+\infty, +\infty)$; $\mathsf{GB} \leftarrow (0,0)$; $\mathsf{GB}_{\mathrm{pre}} \leftarrow (0,0)$; $p_{\mathrm{tot}} \leftarrow 0$;
> 3 $\quad$ $\mathrm{rr} \leftarrow$ expected length of GS-basis of an LLL reduced $\mathrm{LWE}_{n,m,q,\chi}$ instance;
> 4 $\quad$ **for** $\beta \in \mathsf{S}$ *or* $(\beta, J) \in \mathsf{S}$ **do**
> 5 $\quad\quad$ $\mathrm{rr} \leftarrow$ BKZSim(rr, β); // PnjBKZSim(rr, β, J) if $J > 1$;
> 6 $\quad\quad$ $P(\beta) \leftarrow \Pr\left[x \leftarrow \chi_\beta^2 \middle| x \le (\mathrm{rr}[d - \beta])^2\right]$;
> 7 $\quad\quad$ $\mathsf{GB}_{\mathrm{cum}} \leftarrow (\sum_{b=\beta_0}^{\beta} \mathtt{pbgate}(b - \mathtt{d4f}(b)), \mathtt{bit}(\beta - \mathtt{d4f}(\beta)))$;
> 8 $\quad\quad$ $\mathsf{GB}_{\mathrm{pre}} \leftarrow \mathsf{GB}_{\mathrm{pre}} + \mathsf{GB}_{\mathrm{cum}} \cdot (1 - p_{\mathrm{tot}}) \cdot P(\beta)$;
> 9 $\quad\quad$ $p_{\mathrm{tot}} \leftarrow p_{\mathrm{tot}} + (1 - p_{\mathrm{tot}}) \cdot P(\beta)$; $\mathsf{GB}_{\mathrm{csieve}} \leftarrow (0,0)$; $P(d_{\mathrm{start}} - 1) \leftarrow 0$;
> 10 $\quad\quad$ **for** $d_{\mathrm{svp}} \leftarrow d_{\mathrm{start}}$ **to** d **do**
> 11 $\quad\quad\quad$ $P(d_{\mathrm{svp}}) \leftarrow \Pr\left[x \leftarrow \chi_{d_{\mathrm{svp}}}^2 \middle| x \le (\mathrm{GH}(\mathrm{rr}_{[d - d_{\mathrm{svp}}:d]}))^2\right]$;
> 12 $\quad\quad\quad$ $\mathsf{GB}_{\mathrm{cum}}[0] \leftarrow \mathsf{GB}_{\mathrm{cum}}[0] + \mathtt{pgate}(d_{\mathrm{svp}} - \mathtt{d4f}(d_{\mathrm{svp}}))$;
> 13 $\quad\quad\quad$ $\mathsf{GB}_{\mathrm{cum}}[1] \leftarrow \max\{\mathsf{GB}_{\mathrm{cum}}[1], \mathtt{bit}(d_{\mathrm{svp}} - \mathtt{d4f}(d_{\mathrm{svp}}))\}$;
> 14 $\quad\quad\quad$ $\mathsf{GB}_{\mathrm{csieve}} \leftarrow \mathsf{GB}_{\mathrm{csieve}} + \mathsf{GB}_{\mathrm{cum}} \cdot (1 - p_{\mathrm{tot}}) \cdot (P(d_{\mathrm{svp}}) - P(d_{\mathrm{svp}} - 1))$;
> 15 $\quad\quad\quad$ **if** $p_{\mathrm{tot}} + (1 - p_{\mathrm{tot}}) \cdot P(d_{\mathrm{svp}}) \ge 0.999$ **then**
> 16 $\quad\quad\quad\quad$ break;
> 17 $\quad\quad$ $\mathsf{GB} \leftarrow \mathsf{GB}_{\mathrm{pre}} + \mathsf{GB}_{\mathrm{csieve}}$;
> 18 $\quad\quad$ **if** $\mathsf{GB}[0] < \mathsf{GB}_{\min}[0]$ **then**
> 19 $\quad\quad\quad$ $\mathsf{GB}_{\min} \leftarrow \mathsf{GB}$;
> 20 $\quad$ **return** $\mathsf{GB}_{\min}$;

Algorithm 2: Two-step LWE Estimator

Before we give details of our Two-step LWE Estimator, let us briefly review the leaky-LWE-Estimator which we mainly focus on. Leaky-LWE-Estimator is used by NIST selected PQC schemes [1,2] to evaluate the security strength of LWE, and is more refined than previous LWE estimators as it considers the randomness of target vector rather than fixed expected value and uses BKZ simulator rather than an estimation from GSA. For BKZ reduction, it used the trivial progressive strategy where the blocksize β is increased by 1 each tour.

We use similar notations in [21]: W be the event of solving LWE during running Progressive PnjBKZ or the final high-dimension Pump of Two-step mode, $W_\beta^{(1)}$ be the event of solving LWE by using BKZ-β, $F_\beta^{(1)} = \neg W_\beta^{(1)}$ and $W_{(d_{\mathrm{svp}})}^{(2)}$ as the event that a d_{svp}-dimension Pump solved LWE. Here $\Pr[W_\beta^{(1)}] = \Pr\left[x \leftarrow \chi_\beta^2 \mid x \leq (\mathrm{rr}[d - \beta])^2\right]$, and $\mathrm{rr}[d - \beta]$ is the length of the first Gram-Schmidt vector of projective sub-lattice $\mathcal{L}_{\pi[d-\beta:d]}$ of current lattice basis which has been reduced by Progressive BKZ with reduction strategy $S = \{\beta_i = i + 2 \mid i = 1, ..., \mathrm{end}\}$. In Two-step mode we partition W as:

$$\Pr[W] = \Pr[W_{\beta_1}^{(1)}] + \Pr[W_{\beta_2}^{(1)} \wedge F_{\beta_1}^{(1)}] + \Pr[W_{\beta_3}^{(1)} \wedge F_{\beta_2}^{(1)} \wedge F_{\beta_1}^{(1)}]$$

$$+ \cdots + \Pr\left[W_{\beta_{\mathrm{end}}}^{(1)} \wedge \bigwedge_{j=1}^{\mathrm{end}-1} F_{\beta_j}^{(1)}\right] + \Pr\left[W_{d_{\mathrm{svp}}}^{(2)} \wedge \bigwedge_{j=1}^{\mathrm{end}} F_{\beta_j}^{(1)}\right] \quad (1)$$

$$= \sum_{i=1}^{\mathrm{end}} \Pr\left[W_{\beta_i}^{(1)} \wedge \bigwedge_{i>1,j=1}^{i-1} F_{\beta_j}^{(1)}\right] + \Pr\left[W_{d_{\mathrm{svp}}}^{(2)}\right] \cdot \Pr\left[\bigwedge_{j=1}^{\mathrm{end}} F_{\beta_j}^{(1)}\right]$$

Here $W_{d_{\mathrm{svp}}}^{(2)}$ means during the process of the final sieve, d_{svp}-dimension progressive sieving finds the projection vector of the target vector and $F_{d_{\mathrm{svp}}}^{(2)} = \neg W_{d_{\mathrm{svp}}}^{(2)}$. Event $W_{d_{\mathrm{svp}}}^{(2)}$ happened means all BKZ-β in the reduction step fail to find the target vector, other else it will not call the final high-dimension sieve. So event $W_{d_{\mathrm{svp}}}^{(2)}$ is independent with all events $F_{\beta_j}^{(1)}$. When evaluating the concrete hardness of a LWE instance, the value of d_{svp} will be set to solve this LWE with a probability above 0.999. Set end as the index of the last block in the BKZ reduced sequence and d_{start} is the dimension of the initial projection sub-lattice in the final sieve.

It is worth noticing that leaky-LWE-Estimator is based on a Heuristic assumption that events $W_{\beta_i}^{(1)}$ and $F_{\beta_j}^{(1)}$ for $i \neq j$ are independent. See the discussion in Sect. 4.1 of [21] or the implementation of leaky-LWE-Estimator: Algorithm 1 for more details. The Heuristic assumption that events $W_{\beta_i}^{(1)}$ and $F_{\beta_j}^{(1)}$ for $i \neq j$ are independent which leaky-LWE-Estimator based on, is reasonable to some extent if we assume that the lattice basis will be re-randomized each time it is reduced by a stronger BKZ reduction. Below we reformulate this assumption formally:

Heuristic 3. *The lattice basis is randomized each time by a reduction of BKZ-β with larger β. Then events $W_{\beta_i}^{(1)}$ and $F_{\beta_j}^{(1)}$ for $i \neq j$ are independent.*

Besides, set event $E^{(1)}_{\beta_i}$ for $i \in \{1, 2, ...\}$ as the event that solving LWE during the process of running Progressive BKZ: BKZ-β_1, $\cdots$, BKZ-β_i. Based on Heuristic 3, we have $\Pr\left[W^{(1)}_{\beta_i} \wedge \bigwedge^{i-1}_{i>1,j=1} F^{(1)}_{\beta_j}\right] = \Pr\left[W^{(1)}_{\beta_i}\right] \cdot \Pr\left[\bigwedge^{i-1}_{i>1,j=1} F^{(1)}_{\beta_j}\right]$ and

$$\Pr[E^{(1)}_{\beta_i}] = \Pr[E^{(1)}_{\beta_{i-1}}] + \Pr[W^{(1)}_{\beta_i}] \cdot \left(1 - \Pr[E^{(1)}_{\beta_{i-1}}]\right). \tag{2}$$

We will use Eq. (2) to calculate the cumulative probability of solving LWE during reduction step, see line 8 of Algorithm 2.

However, the same method cannot be used to calculate the probability of solving LWE during the final sieve. Specifically, we use a progressive sieve algorithm as the final sieve, thus we also need to calculate the probability of solving LWE during each step of the progressive sieve. Specifically, we use $W^{(2)}_i, F^{(2)}_i$ as the success rate and failing rate that LWE can be solved using a i-dimensional progressive sieve (which performs sieving on projected sub-lattices with dimensions from 2 to i). Unlike in a progressive BKZ, the lattice basis will not change during sieving. Therefore, the similar Heuristic assumption that events $W^{(2)}_i$ and $F^{(2)}_j$ for $i \neq j$ are independent cannot be established.

On the contrary, instead of considering that events $W^{(2)}_{(i)}$ and $F^{(2)}_{(j)}$ for $i \neq j$ are independent, we consider that there is an inclusive relationship between $W^{(2)}_{(i)}$ and $W^{(2)}_{(j)}$ for $j \leq i$, i.e. $W^{(2)}_{(i)} \supseteq W^{(2)}_{(j)}$. Since the lattice basis will not change during the progressive sieving of Pump and running an i-dimension progressive sieving, it will run a j-dimension progressive sieving at first, for $j \leq i$.

Setting event $E^{(2)}_\beta$ as the progressive sieving finds the projection of the target vector exactly after a β-dimensional sieve. More specifically, during one progressive sieving, all the sieving dimensions smaller than β failed to find the target vector but succeeded when the sieving dimension equals β. We give the following Heuristic assumption.

Heuristic 4. For $i \in \{2, ..., d_{\text{svp}}\}$, $W^{(2)}_i \supseteq W^{(2)}_{i-1} \supseteq W^{(2)}_{i-2} \cdots \supseteq W^{(2)}_2$. Then $E^{(2)}_i = W^{(2)}_i - W^{(2)}_{i-1}$.

Set $\Pr\left[W^{(2)}_{d_{\text{start}}-1}\right]=0$, based on Heuristic 4 we calculate $\Pr\left[E^{(2)}_{d_{\text{svp}}}\right]$ by

$$\Pr\left[E^{(2)}_{d_{\text{svp}}}\right] = \Pr\left[W^{(2)}_{d_{\text{svp}}}\right] - \Pr\left[W^{(2)}_{d_{\text{svp}}-1}\right], \tag{3}$$

which is the key equality to calculate the number of gate in searching step. Then, the cumulative probability of solving LWE in Two-step LWE estimator can be expressed by

$$\begin{aligned} \Pr[W] &= \Pr[E^{(1)}_{\beta_{\text{end}}}] + \left(1 - \Pr[E^{(1)}_{\beta_{\text{end}}}]\right) \sum_{i=d_{\text{start}}}^{d_{\text{svp}}} \Pr\left[E^{(2)}_i\right] \\ &= \Pr[E^{(1)}_{\beta_{\text{end}}}] + \left(1 - \Pr[E^{(1)}_{\beta_{\text{end}}}]\right) \Pr\left[W^{(2)}_{d_{\text{svp}}}\right], \end{aligned} \tag{4}$$

see the line 15 of Algorithm 2 for more details.

Gates Count of Reduction Step. In this part, we introduce how to count the number of Gates when we solved LWE in the reduction step. After we calculate each $\Pr[E_{\beta_i}^{(1)}]$ value for $i \in \{1, 2, ...\}$ by using Eq. (2) in the reduction step, we can calculate the expected value of gate count G_1 of reduction step. We evaluate the expected value of gates counts G_1 of reduction step by Eq. (5), see line 7 of Algorithm 2 for more details. Let $\mathtt{gate}(\beta)$ be the gate count of a sieve algorithm with dimension β, $\mathtt{pgate}(\beta) = C \cdot \mathtt{gate}(\beta)$ be the gate count of a progressive sieve algorithm with dimension β and let $\mathtt{pbgate}(\beta) = \mathtt{pgate}(\beta) \cdot (d - \beta + 1)$ be the gate count of a BKZ-β, then G_1 can be expressed as

$$G_1 = \sum_{i=1}^{\text{end}} \Pr[W_{\beta_i}^{(1)}] \cdot \left(1 - \Pr[E_{\beta_{i-1}}^{(1)}]\right) \cdot \left[\sum_{l=0}^{i} \mathtt{pbgate}(\beta_l - \mathtt{d4f}(\beta_l))\right]. \tag{5}$$

Gates Count of Searching Step. In this part, we introduce how to calculate the numbers of Gates when we solved LWE in the searching step. When we solved uSVP in the searching step, it meant that all the BKZ tours in the reduction step failed to find the target vector. Thus, based on Eq. (3) to calculate $\Pr\left[E_i^{(2)}\right]$, $i \in \{d_{\text{start}}, \ldots, d_{\text{svp}}\}$, we use Eq. (6) to calculate the expected value of gates of the searching step, see line 14 of Algorithm 2 for more details.

$$G_2 = \sum_{i=d_{\text{start}}}^{d_{\text{svp}}} \Pr\left[E_i^{(2)}\right] \cdot \left(1 - \Pr[E_{\beta_{\text{end}}}^{(1)}]\right) \cdot \\ \left[\left(\sum_{l=0}^{\text{end}} \mathtt{pbgate}\left(\beta_l - \mathtt{d4f}(\beta_l)\right)\right) + \mathtt{pgate}\left(i - \mathtt{d4f}(i)\right)\right] \tag{6}$$

When considering the cost of solving LWE during the searching step, it means that all BKZ tours in the reduction step failed to find the target vector. We calculate the $\Pr\left[\bigwedge_{j=1}^{\text{end}} F_{\beta_j}^{(1)}\right]$ in Eq. (6) to represent the probability of all BKZ tours in the reduction step failed to find the target vector. Besides, before starting the large dimensional sieve in the searching step, the total time cost of solving the uSVP in the searching step already contains the full-time cost of all BKZ tours in the reduction step. Therefore, the total gate count of the reduction step is $\sum_{l=0}^{\text{end}} \mathtt{pbgate}(\beta_l - \mathtt{d4f}(\beta_l))$ and when the dimension of SVP Oracle we considered equals to d_{svp}, the gate count of searching step is $\mathtt{pgate}(d_{\text{svp}} - \mathtt{d4f}(d_{\text{svp}}))$. Here, the $\mathtt{d4f}(j)$ is calculated by Sect. 2.6.

Finally, the total gate count for the Two-step mode of solving LWE $G :=$ $G_1 + G_2$.

Memory Count of Two-Step LWE Concrete Estimator. The memory count of the Two-step LWE concrete estimator is similar to gate count, just replace the function $\mathtt{gate}(\beta)$ with the memory cost function $\mathtt{bit}(\beta)$ which declares the memory cost of one sieve algorithm with dimension β. Since the memory cost of the final sieve and (progressive) BKZ with the same dimension is equal to the memory cost of one sieve algorithm with the same dimension, the memory count of the reduction process in our Two-step LWE Estimator is

$$B_1 = \sum_{i=1}^{end} \left[\Pr[W_{\beta_i}^{(1)}] \cdot \left(1 - \Pr[E_{\beta_{i-1}}^{(1)}] \right) \right] \cdot \mathtt{bit}(\beta_l - \mathtt{d4f}(\beta_l)), \tag{7}$$

and the memory count of searching step is

$$B_2 = \sum_{i=d_{start}}^{d_{svp}} \Pr\left[E_i^{(2)}\right] \cdot \left(1 - \Pr[E_{(\beta_{end})}^{(1)}] \right) \cdot \max\{\mathtt{bit}\,(\beta_{end} - \mathtt{d4f}(\beta_{end})), \mathtt{bit}\,(i - \mathtt{d4f}(i))\}. \tag{8}$$

The total memory count for Two-step mode of solving LWE $B := B_1 + B_2$.

4.2 Two-Step LWE Estimator with Refined Strategy

In this section, we adapt the Two-step LWE-estimator to Improved Progressive PnjBKZ [28], which calls a series of PnjBKZ to reduce the basis first and finds a good timing to use a Pump algorithm to search the unique shortest vector. The concrete process is as Algorithm 3.

---

input : $\mathbf{B}$, $F(\star, \mathcal{D})$;
output: The approximate shortest vector $\mathbf{v}$;
1 **Function** ProPnjBKZ($\mathbf{B}$, $F(\star, \mathcal{D})$):
2     $\mathbf{B} = \mathtt{LLL}(\mathbf{B})$;
3   Generate Strategy S using EnumBS or BSSA [28];
4   **for** $(\beta, J, \sharp tours) \in S$ **do**
5   **for** t **from** 1 **to** $\sharp tours$ **do**
6           $\mathbf{B} \leftarrow \mathtt{PnjBKZ}(\mathbf{B}, \beta, J, \sharp tours)$;
7     $d_{svp}, \_ \leftarrow \mathtt{ProSieveDimEst}(\mathtt{rr}(\mathbf{B}), F(\star, \mathcal{D}))$; $f \leftarrow \mathtt{d4f}(d_{svp})$;
8     $\mathbf{B} \leftarrow \mathtt{Pump}(\mathbf{B}, d - d_{svp}, d_{svp}, f)$;
9   **return** $\mathbf{v} \leftarrow \mathbf{b}_0$;

Algorithm 3: Improved Progressive PnjBKZ

We point out the main differences between the estimator with improved progressive PnjBKZ and the estimator in Sect. 4.1. First, the use of PnjBKZ allows us to adjust the reduction strategy more freely. Instead of the trivial reduction strategy $S = \{(\beta_i = i + 2, J_i = 1) \mid i = 1, \cdots\}$ used in leaky-LWE-Estimator and Sect. 4.1, we can choose a more efficient reduction strategy given by the blocksize and jump strategy enumeration algorithm (EnumBS) in [28].

Secondly, we use the PnjBKZ simulator [28] instead of the original BKZ simulator to simulate how the quality of lattice basis changes during the reduction by a series of PnjBKZ with $J > 1$. The simulator is purely based on the Gaussian Heuristic, which avoids the problem that GSA (Heuristic 2) is not strictly held during the reduction of PnjBKZ. Also, the gate count of a PnjBKZ-(β, J) tour is calculated as $\mathtt{pbgate}(\beta, J) = \mathtt{pgate}(\beta) \cdot (d - \beta + 1)/J$.

The gate count and memory count can be calculated similarly, we only need to replace the events $W_{\beta_i}^{(1)}, F_{\beta_i}^{(1)}$ by $W_{(\beta_i, J_i)}^{(1)}, F_{(\beta_i, J_i)}^{(1)}$ which allow $J > 1$ when calculating the probability. We omit further details here.

5 Experiments on Verifying the Accuracy of Two-Step LWE Estimator

In Sect. 5.1, we mainly focus on the success probabilities of solving LWE by Two-step mode, especially the success probabilities of the last sieve with different sieving dimensions. We give the detail of our verification experiments to verify Heuristic 4 and the accuracy of Eq. (3) and Eq. (4) which are the key equations to calculate the gate number of the searching step. Then we give an experiment to verify the efficiency of the Two-step mode compared with the BKZ-only mode in Sect. 5.2. Finally in Sect. 5.3 we compare the Two-step LWE Estimator using different reduction strategies with the leaky-LWE-Estimator.

5.1 Verification Experiments for Success Probability

In particular, we use different parameters of the LWE instances[3] to test the success probabilities of the final sieve when using different progressive sieving dimensions shown in Fig. 1.[4] We choose four different LWE parameters ($n = 40$, $\alpha = 0.005$, $q = 1601$, $m = 1600$), ($n = 40$, $\alpha = 0.015$, $q = 1601$, $m = 1600$), ($n = 60, \alpha = 0.005, q = 3607$), ($n = 45, \alpha = 0.010, q = 2027, m = 2025$) for our experiments. For each LWE parameter, we initialize 100 random LWE instances to construct 100 different lattice bases. Each lattice basis corresponds to an uSVP instance with a different target vector. Then we use BKZ/PnjBKZ to do pre-processing by some trivial reduction strategy S. Using LWE parameter ($n = 40$, $\alpha = 0.005, q = 1601, m = 1600$) for example, we set $S = \{\beta_1 = 10, ..., \beta_{\mathrm{end}} = 17\}$. Here, 100 different LWE instances under the same parameter are used to fit the distribution of the error vector.

After pre-processing, we set the key parameter $\kappa \in \{0, ..., d-1\}$ to determine the size of the final sieve in the searching phase. In [12], it is assumed that one can solve an LWE by solving a $d - \kappa$ dimension SVP on $\mathcal{L}_{\pi[\kappa:d]}$ as long as $\sigma\sqrt{d - \kappa} <$ $\mathrm{GH}(\mathcal{L}_{\pi[\kappa,d]})$. Here $\sigma\sqrt{d - \kappa}$ is the expected norm of the projected target vector. However, since we consider the square sum of the length of the projected target vector as a chi-squared distribution with $d - \kappa$ degrees of freedom, we calculate the cumulative probability of solving LWE when using a high-dimension Pump in Sect. 4 by Eq. (4), and the line 15 of Algorithm 2. To verify the Heuristic 4 and

---

[3] https://www.latticechallenge.org/lwe_challenge/challenge.php.
[4] We've uploaded our verification experiment in the file "lwe_prob_test.py" in the website https://github.com/Summwer/test-for-refined-lwe-estimator.

the accuracy of Eq. (4), we test the actual success rate of solving LWE under different lattice sieving with different κ value.

More precisely, we set $d_{svp} = d - \kappa$ in lattice sieving from 30 to d by adjusting the value of κ and use each sieve with different d_{svp} value to try to find the solution of LWE on 100 different lattice basis after pre-processing. Meantime, we record the actual success rate of each sieve with different d_{svp} values on 100 different lattice bases. Finally, we compare the actual success rate of each sieve with different d_{svp} with our estimation success rate of solving LWE by the final sieve in Eq. (4), and the line 15 of Algorithm 2. See Fig. 1 for more detail.

From Fig. 1 we can see that the predication of the success rate of solving LWE given by Eq. (4) is consistent with the experimental results, which means our analysis and estimation in Sect. 4.1 is accurate.

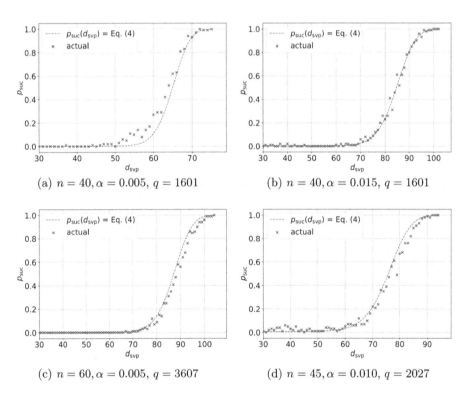

(a) $n = 40, \alpha = 0.005, q = 1601$

(b) $n = 40, \alpha = 0.015, q = 1601$

(c) $n = 60, \alpha = 0.005, q = 3607$

(d) $n = 45, \alpha = 0.010, q = 2027$

Fig. 1. Verification experiments of the fitness of the theoretical total success probability $P(d_{svp}) = $ Eq. (4) (the dashed line) to the actual success probability. Test 100 trials and count the success rate for each d_{svp}.

5.2   Verification Experiments for Efficiency of Two-Step Mode

In this part, we give an experiment to verify the efficiency of the Two-step mode. In the experiment, we test the public keys of Kyber512, Kyber1024, Dilithium-II, and Dilithium-V as the input LWE instances, then call a Two-step Estimator with $\mathsf{S}[\beta] = \{\beta_i | 3 \leq \beta_i \leq \beta\}$. The estimator stops at $\beta = \beta_{\mathrm{end}}$ such that the accumulated probability of $\mathsf{S}[\beta_{\mathrm{end}}]$ is no less than 0.999, i.e. $\sum_{i=1}^{\mathrm{end}} \left[\Pr[W_{\beta_i}^{(1)}] \cdot \left(1 - \Pr[E_{i-1}^{(1)}] \right) \right] \geq 0.999$, which is also the condition in leaky-LWE-Estimator.

The Fig. 2 shows the gate count [23] of Two-step mode under different reduction strategy $\mathsf{S}[\beta]$, where $\beta \in \{3, \ldots, \beta_{\mathrm{end}}\}$ and estimated the number of gates given by the leaky-LWE-Estimator. The x-axis of Fig. 2 is the final blocksize β in reduction strategy $\mathsf{S}[\beta]$. Figure 2 reflects that in solving LWE, the Two-step mode is more efficient than that of using BKZ reduction only and the security estimation given by the leaky-LWE-Estimator [19] is indeed an over-optimistic estimation. Besides, there is optimal timing β_{op} for ending the reduction and entering the searching step as the quality of the lattice basis improved gradually by progressive BKZ.

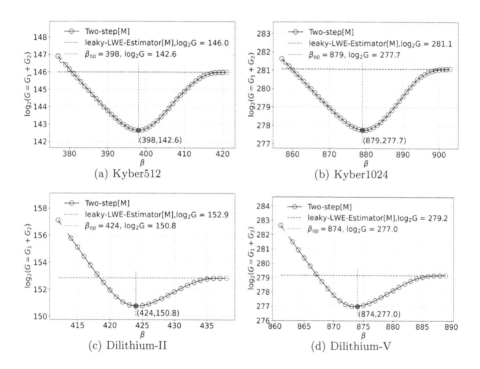

Fig. 2. Two-step efficiency verification Experiment.

5.3   The Comparison of Different Estimation Modes

In this part, we compare our Two-step mode estimator using different reduction strategies and different gate count models with the leaky-LWE-Estimator.

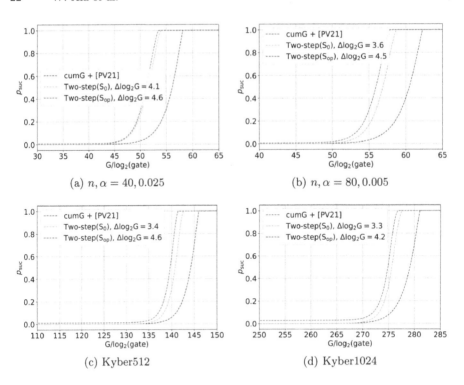

Fig. 3. The relation among the growth of cumulated cost and the success probability. Comparison between the output of cumulated Cost Version of [21](Algorithm 1) and Two-step mode(Algorithm 2, this work) for lwe challenge $(n, \alpha) \in \{(40, 0.025), (80, 0.005)\}$ and on Kyber 512 and Kyber 1024 [1]. "Two-step(S_0)" uses a trial progressive BKZ+Pump in Two-step mode to estimate security. "Two-step(S_{op})" uses a progressive BKZ+Pump with the optimized strategy selected by EnumBS [28] in Two-step mode to estimate security. We set $\Delta \log_2 G$ as the gate count difference between our estimator and the leaky-LWE-estimator both using the same gate count (See footnote 5).

We draw Fig. 3 to describe the relationship between the success rate of solving LWE estimated by different estimators and the corresponding number of gates. The blue line in Fig. 3 is the relationship between the expected gates count and the accumulation success probability of solving LWE by pure progressive BKZ with trivial reduction strategy S_0. These Two-step lines in Fig. 3 are the relationship between the expected gates count and the accumulation success probability of solving LWE by Two-step mode whose reduction step also used a trivial reduction strategy $S_1 : S_1 \subsetneq S_0$ (In Two-step mode the reduction step will end earlier than in BKZ-only mode). These Enumbs lines in Fig. 3 are also the relationship between the expected gates count and the accumulation success probability of solving LWE by Two-step mode while the reduction strategy is the optimized blocksize and jump selection strategy.[5]

From Fig. 3 we can see that in both the LWE challenge instances and the LWE instances in NIST standard algorithms, the accumulation success probability of solving LWE by Two-step mode approaches 1 is much faster than that of the leaky-LWE-Estimator. In addition, the expected number of gates in the Two-step solving mode is smaller than that of the leaky-LWE-Estimator when the accumulation success probability of solving LWE approaches 1. Therefore, the evaluation result shows that the leaky-LWE-Estimator gives an optimistic estimation. Besides, both the optimized blocksize and jump selection strategy and the improved list-decoding technique proposed in [41], which fixed the estimate done in [23] of the list decoding technique proposed in [39], can further decrease the estimated security strength by replacing the trivial reduction strategy or gate-count model in Two-step mode. See Fig. 3 for more details about the difference between different estimation models.

6 Improved Conservative Estimation for LWE

Above we consider the LWE estimation by practical solving algorithms. However, since lattice solving algorithms have been developing fast in recent years, such estimation can hardly be considered stable. Many researchers in the field prefer using a theoretical and conservative estimation to estimate the security level of a lattice-based algorithm. In literature, the most used theoretical estimation for LWE-based cryptosystems is the Core-SVP model, first given in NewHope [12]. Many lattice-based algorithms including Kyber and Dilithium use the estimation result of the Core-SVP model to match the security level requirements proposed by NIST.

However, the Core-SVP model can hardly be called accurate. First, the Core-SVP model ignores many coefficients in the estimation, which lowers the estimation result from one aspect. Second, the dimension for free technique has not been taken into account, which causes the estimation result to be higher than expected from another aspect. Despite these two weaknesses of Core-SVP model, there is another main problem in the Core-SVP model, as the underlying solving algorithm in the Core-SVP model is of BKZ-only mode. So for the Core-SVP estimation to hold, it must implicitly assume that a BKZ-only mode lattice solving algorithm is optimal, while such assumption is overthrown by our discussion in Sect. 3 that a Two-step mode is more efficient than a BKZ-only mode.

In this section, we give a new theoretical lower-bound security estimation for LWE hardness, based on the Two-step solving mode, which relies on weaker assumption than the Core-SVP model. By our estimation result (see Sect. 7.2), our estimation is higher than the Core-SVP model without considering d4f.

---

[5] We use the gate-count model which adopts the improved list-decoding technique proposed in [41]. It fixed the estimate done in [23] of the list-decoding technique proposed in [39].

While taking d4f into consideration, our estimation turns out to be lower than the Core-SVP estimation, which shows that the original Core-SVP model is in fact not conservative enough without d4f.

6.1   Theoretical Lower-Bound Security Estimation of LWE Hardness

The idea is simple: we use the time cost of the last lattice sieving in a Two-step mode to estimate the hardness of solving uSVP$_\gamma$ or LWE. Considering that Two-step mode is currently the most efficient way in solving uSVP$_\gamma$ and we omit the time cost of the BKZ reduction step, our estimation is conservative enough.

The main problem in constructing such a lower-bound estimation is to determine the lattice basis quality as the input of lattice sieving step, since we are impossible to give the optimal strategy for BKZ reduction step. So we take an alternative approach: we find the exact basis length rr, such that the best strategy for solving uSVP$_\gamma$ from a basis with length rr is by performing sieving algorithm on a d_{svp} dimensional sublattice rather than performing more BKZ tours before the final lattice sieving.

For simplicity reason, we also assume geometric series assumption (GSA, see Heuristic 2) as in Core-SVP model, so rr can be uniquely determined by the lattice volume V and the root Hermite factor (RHF) δ of the basis. Let $\mathrm{rhf}(\delta, \beta)$ be the new RHF of the basis after current basis with RHF δ reduced by a BKZ-β tour, and $d_{\mathrm{svp}} = \mathrm{md}(\delta, M)$ be the minimum dimension such that a d_{svp} dimension sieving on $\mathcal{L}_{\pi[d-d_{\mathrm{svp}}:d]}$ can recover the unique shortest vector of length M from a lattice basis with RHF δ.

Moreover, we can take dimension for free into account, and let the time cost of sieving on a d_{svp} dimensional lattice be $T_{\mathrm{sieve}}(d_{\mathrm{svp}}) = 2^{c(d_{\mathrm{svp}} - \mathtt{d4f}(d_{\mathrm{svp}}))}$, and $T_{\mathrm{BKZ}}(\beta) = (d - \beta + 1) \cdot 2^{c(\beta - \mathtt{d4f}(\beta))}$. Then the condition above can be expressed as the following inequality: $\forall \beta, T_{\mathrm{sieve}}(\mathrm{md}(\delta, M)) \leq T_{\mathrm{BKZ}}(\beta) + T_{\mathrm{sieve}}(\mathrm{md}(\mathrm{rhf}(\delta, \beta), M))$.

It is not hard to show that if δ satisfies this condition, then any $\delta' < \delta$ also satisfies this condition. We only need to find the maximum δ satisfying this condition, and we use $T_{\mathrm{sieve}}(\mathrm{md}(\delta, M))$ for the estimation. Next, we explain how to calculate the value $\mathrm{rhf}(\delta, \beta)$ and $\mathrm{md}(\delta, M)$.

Let $\delta(\beta)$ be the RHF of a BKZ-β reduced basis. Then if $\delta > \delta(\beta)$, using Gaussian Heuristic, the length of $\mathbf{b}_1$ in the lattice basis after a BKZ-β tour can be estimated as: $\mathrm{GH}(\mathrm{rr}_{[0:\beta]} = (\delta^d V^{1/d}, \alpha \delta^d V^{1/d}, ..., \alpha^{\beta-1} \delta^d V^{1/d}))$, where $\alpha = \delta^{-\frac{d-1}{2d}}$ and d is the dimension of lattice basis. Then the RHF of the basis after a BKZ-β tour can be calculated by: $\mathrm{rhf}(\delta, \beta) \approx (\sqrt{\frac{\beta}{2\pi e}} \cdot \delta^{\frac{d \cdot (d-\beta)}{d-1}})^{\frac{1}{d}} = \delta^{\frac{d-\beta}{d-1}} \cdot (\sqrt{\frac{\beta}{2\pi e}})^{\frac{1}{d}}$ and for $\delta \leq \delta(\beta)$, we simply let $\mathrm{rhf}(\delta, \beta) = \delta$.

Next, we estimate the expected dimension of the last lattice sieving. Let M be the expected length of the unique shortest vector, and $M_{d_{\mathrm{svp}}} = M \cdot \sqrt{d_{\mathrm{svp}}/d}$ be the expected length of the projection of M on a d_{svp} dimensional sublattice. We should have that $M_{d_{\mathrm{svp}}} < \mathrm{GH}(\mathrm{rr}_{[d-d_{\mathrm{svp}}:d]} = (\delta^{-d} \cdot V^{1/d} \cdot \alpha^{-d_{\mathrm{svp}}+1}, ..., \delta^{-d} \cdot V^{1/d} \cdot \alpha^{-1}, \delta^{-d} \cdot V^{1/d}))$. Thus we have:

$$M \cdot \sqrt{d_{\mathrm{svp}}/d} < V^{1/d} \cdot \sqrt{\frac{d_{\mathrm{svp}}}{2\pi e}} \cdot \delta^{\frac{d \cdot (d_{\mathrm{svp}} - d)}{d-1}}$$

and the minimum d_{svp} can be recovered by solving the inequation above.

Combining all the things above, we get a lower bound estimation for solving LWE using the Two-step mode. We also explicitly write out the algorithm for lower bound estimation by Algorithm 4.

---

input : M, $V \leftarrow \mathrm{Vol}(\mathcal{L})$;
output: T;
1 **Function** LowerBoundEst$(M, V \leftarrow \mathrm{Vol}(\mathcal{L}))$:
2   **for** $\beta \leftarrow \beta_0$ **to** d **do**
3   con $\leftarrow$ true;
4      $d_{\mathrm{svp}} \leftarrow \mathsf{md}(\delta(\beta), M)$;
5   **for** $\beta' \leftarrow \beta + 1$ **to** d **do**
6        $\delta' \leftarrow \mathsf{rhf}(\delta(\beta), \beta')$;
7   **if** $T_{\mathrm{sieve}}(d_{\mathrm{svp}}) > T_{\mathrm{BKZ}}(\beta') + T_{\mathrm{sieve}}(\mathsf{md}(\delta', M))$ **then**
8   con $\leftarrow$ false; break;

9   **if** con **then**
10      $\beta_{\mathrm{optimal}} \leftarrow \beta$;
11   **return** β_{optimal}, d_{svp}, $T_{\mathrm{sieve}}(d_{\mathrm{svp}})$;

Algorithm 4: Lower Bound Estimation

Note that in Algorithm 4, we only perform searching on all BKZ-β reduced basis to ensure that the estimation can be done in a reasonable time. This may decrease the estimated time by a small amount, so the estimation only becomes more conservative.

We prove that the new estimation is conservative enough under GSA and two simple heuristic assumptions. We show that our assumptions are strictly weaker than the implicit assumptions in the Core-SVP model, so our estimation is in fact more solid than the Core-SVP estimation.

Heuristic 5. *BKZ is the optimal algorithm for lattice reduction, i.e. generating a lattice basis satisfying GSA.*

Since the Core-SVP model only uses BKZ to estimate the hardness of LWE and also assumes GSA on BKZ-β reduce basis, our assumption is obviously weaker than the implicit assumption in the Core-SVP model.

Heuristic 6. *The best way of solving uSVP$_\gamma$ or LWE is by performing lattice sieving on a projected sublattice on a reduced lattice basis satisfying GSA.*

We note that in the underlying solving algorithm of the Core-SVP model, the unique shortest vector is recovered by sieving on the last β-size block in the lattice, which is only a special case of our assumption. So our assumption is also strictly weaker than the implicit assumption in Core-SVP model.

Theorem 2. *Assume that Gaussian Heuristic (Heuristic 1), GSA (Heuristic 2), Heuristic 5, 6, and Heuristic 4 in [28] hold, then the estimated cost of our lower bound estimation is strictly lower than the actual cost for solving uSVP$_\gamma$ in almost all lattices.*

Proof. Let δ, d_{svp} be the intermediate result in our lower bound estimation, i.e. the unique shortest vector is found by performing d_{svp}-dimensional lattice sieving on a lattice basis satisfying GSA which RHF is δ.

Let $\mathcal{A}$ be the optimal algorithm in solving uSVP$_\gamma$. By Heuristic 6, we assume that $\mathcal{A}$ solves uSVP$_\gamma$ by performing d'_{svp}-dimensional lattice sieving on a lattice basis satisfying GSA which RHF is δ'. Furthermore, since in Heuristic 5, we assume that a lattice basis satisfying GSA should be found by BKZ, let β' be the blocksize of the last BKZ tour before the final sieving, and δ'' be the RHF of lattice basis before this BKZ-β' tour. We consider the following cases.

(1) $\delta' \geq \delta$, so $d'_{\text{svp}} \geq d_{\text{svp}}$, thus the running time of $\mathcal{A}$ is larger than $T_{\text{sieve}}(d_{\text{svp}})$.
(2) $\delta'' \leq \delta$, by the definition of δ, we can see that $T_{\text{BKZ}}(\beta') + T_{\text{sieve}}(d'_{\text{svp}}) > T_{\text{sieve}}(\text{md}(\delta'', M))$, so by replacing the final BKZ-β' tour and lattice sieving with a single lattice sieving, the running time of $\mathcal{A}$ decreases, which contradicts with the optimality of $\mathcal{A}$.
(3) $\delta' < \delta < \delta''$. Then $\text{rhf}(\delta, \beta') < \delta'$, so $T_{\text{BKZ}}(\beta') + T_{\text{sieve}}(d'_{\text{svp}}) > T_{\text{BKZ}}(\beta') + T_{\text{sieve}}(\text{md}(\text{rhf}(\delta, \beta'), M)) \geq T_{\text{sieve}}(d_{\text{svp}})$.

Thus we have the result.   □

7   Two-Step Security Estimation of LWE in NIST Schemes

In this section based on our refined Two-step security estimator, we give a more accurate upper bound estimation of LWE in NIST PQC schemes in Sect. 7.1. Next, based on our conservative estimation for LWE in Sect. 6, we give the lower bound estimation of LWE in NIST PQC schemes in Sect. 7.2.

7.1   Security Upper Bound Estimation of LWE in NIST PQC Schemes

Two-Step Security Estimation of LWE of NIST PQC Schemes. In this part, we will estimate the security strength of LWE instances of NIST PQC schemes by our Two-step LWE hardness estimator in Sect. 4.1. Besides we use the same blocksize and jump selection strategy: trivial $S_0 = [\beta_0 = 3, \beta_1 = 4, ..., \beta_{\text{end}}]$ strategy in the reduction step of Two-step mode and the only difference between with leaky-LWE-Estimator is that we consider a Two-step LWE solving mode.

The evaluation results show that even without further optimizing the blocksize and jump selection, the Two-step mode strategy can effectively reduce the estimated security bit of LWE instances in NIST PQC schemes. In particular, under the RAM model, i.e., it assumes that access into even exponentially large

Table 1. Security Upper bound Estimation results of different estimators for NIST schemes with different blocksize and jump solving strategies.[♮]

	$\log_2 G/\log_2$ (gates)			$\log_2 B/\log_2$ (bit)			$\Delta\log_2 G$	
	Previous	Two-step		Previous	Two-step			
		S_0	S_{op}		S_0	S_{op}	S_0	S_{op}
Kyber512	146	142.6	141.4	93.97	99.1	98.1	3.4	4.6
Kyber768	208.9	205.5	204.4	138.73	144.0	143.2	3.4	4.5
Kyber1024	281.07	277.7	276.9	189.78	195.4	194.6	3.3	4.2
Dilithium-II	152.85	150.8	150.6	97.95	104.3	104.4	2.1	2.3
Dilithium-III	210.23	207.9	207.9	138.8	145.3	145.3	2.3	2.3
Dilithium-V	279.17	277.0	277.0	187.52	194.1	194.1	2.2	2.2

♮ The column "Previous" is the security estimation in the statement of Kyber and Dilithium. Strategy "S_0" uses a trial progressive BKZ+Pump in Two-step mode to estimate security. Strategy "S_{op}" uses a progressive BKZ+Pump with the optimized strategy selected by EnumBS [28] in Two-step mode to estimate security. $\Delta\log_2 G$ is the difference between "Previous" and "Two-step" under the RAM model in strategy S_0 and S_{op} in the logarithm of gate count with base 2. The gate count of all estimations in this Table uses the same improved list-decoding technique proposed by MATZOV [41]. (See footnote 5)

memory is free, the estimated security bit of LWE in NIST schemes [22] can be reduced by 2.1–3.4 bits. See Table 1 for details. Here G and B in Table 1 respectively represent the total log number of logic circuits for event W happened and the maximum memory needed for event W happened, that both are calculated by Gate-count algorithm [23].

Optimized Blocksize and Jump Selection Strategy and Two-Step Mode. In this part, we quantitatively analyze the impact of the combination of the Two-step LWE solving mode and optimized blocksize and jump selection strategy proposed in [28] on NIST PQC schemes. We change the reduction strategy in the reduction step of Two-step mode from trivial S_0 to the optimized blocksize and jump selection strategy S_{op} proposed in [28]. In other words, we still use Eq. (1), but the reduction strategy used in Eq. (1) is replaced by the optimized blocksize and jump selection strategy proposed in [28].

The evaluation results show that the combination of the optimized blocksize and jump selection and the Two-step mode strategy can indeed effectively reduce the estimated security bit of LWE. Specifically, under the RAM model, the estimated security bit of LWE in NIST schemes [22] can be reduced by 2.2–4.6 bits. See Table 1 for details. Here G and B in Table 1 respectively represent the total log number of logic circuits for event W happened and the maximum memory needed for event W happened, that both are calculated by Gate-count algorithm [23] under the optimized blocksize and jump selection.

Table 2. The security lower bound estimation of NIST lattice-based standardization[†].

	Kyber512	Kyber768	Kyber1024	DilithiumII	DilithiumIII	DilithiumV
Lattice Dim d	1003	1424	1885	2049	2561	3582
BKZ β	406	625	877	423	624	863
CoreSVP	118	182	256	123	182	252
Lattice Dim d	1025	1477	1954	2039	2672	3461
$\beta_{optimal}$	392	608	857	415	614	853
d_{svp}	423	641	891	449	649	889
LBE	123.52	187.17	260.17	131.11	189.51	259.59
LBE (d4f)	112.44	172.32	241.24	119.57	174.52	240.69
ΔHardness	5.52	5.17	4.17	8.11	7.51	7.59
ΔHardness (d4f)	−5.56	−9.68	−14.76	−3.43	−7.48	−11.31

[†] Here the row of "LBE" is the lower bound estimation evaluated by Algorithm 5, the row of "LBE (d4f)" is the lower bound estimation by considering d4f technique, and the row of "CoreSVP" represents the security strength evaluated by the CoreSVP model. "Lattice Dim d" is the dimension for constructing the embedding lattice in primal attack.

In practice, without considering the RAM model, a large `Pump` dimension in Two-step mode will indeed lead to an extra cost while accessing exponentially large memory, which will somewhat partially offset the above-claimed decrease of security hardness. However, it is unclear what the practical influence of increasing memory cost is on the total time cost. In fact, it is still an open question, see Q5 in Sect. 5.3 of [1]. Besides, although [42] gave an experimental analysis of an idealized model for the sieve algorithm, its theoretical analysis of hidden probabilistic overhead in near-neighbors search still remains an open problem. So our analysis in this section does not address these two parts.

7.2 Lower Bound Estimation of LWE in NIST PQC Schemes

In this part, we will calculate the lower-bound security estimation of NIST lattice-based standardization. As the dimension of the embedding lattice basis $d = m + n + 1$ can be further optimized by appropriately choosing the number of LWE samples $m \in \{1, ..., m_{max}\}$. We numerically optimize the number of LWE samples m to minimize the lower-bound security estimation by Algorithm 5. See Table 2 for more detail. Table 2 illustrates that by optimizing the number of LWE samples m, compared with the conservative estimation given by the Core-SVP model, the lower-bound security estimation of NIST lattice-based standardization calculated by Algorithm 5 increased by $4.17 \sim 8.11$ bits. However, when considering d4f technique, compared with the conservative estimation given by the Core-SVP model, the security bit of NIST lattice-based standardization will decrease by 3.42–14.76 bits under our new lower-bound security estimation. It indicates that the Core-SVP model is not conservative enough to offset the influence of the d4f technique.

Furthermore, Table 2 also shows that there indeed exist a β_{optimal} s.t $d_{\text{svp}} = \text{md}(\delta(\beta_{\text{optimal}}), M)$, for any $\beta' \in \{\beta_{\text{optimal}} + 1, ..., d\}, \delta' = \text{rhf}(\delta(\beta), \beta')$ satisfied $T_{\text{sieve}}(d_{\text{svp}}) < T_{\text{BKZ}}(\beta') + T_{\text{sieve}}(\text{md}(\delta', M))$ under the parameter of NIST lattice-based standardization [1, 2]. See Table 2 for more detail.

---

input : $m_{\max}, n, \sigma, q$;
output: $\beta_{\text{optimal}}, d_{\text{svp}}, T_{\text{sieve}}(d_{\text{svp}})$;

1 **Function** LowerBoundEstWithOptimalM($m_{\max}, n, \sigma, q$):
2 $\quad d_{\text{svp}}^* \leftarrow m_{\max} + n + 1; m_{\text{optimal}} \leftarrow m_{\max}; \beta_{\text{optimal}} \leftarrow m_{\max} + n + 1;$
3 $\quad$ **for** $m \leftarrow m_{\max}$ **to** 1 **do**
4 $\quad\quad d \leftarrow n + m + 1; M \leftarrow \sigma \cdot \sqrt{d}; V \leftarrow q^m;$
5 $\quad\quad \beta_{\text{current}}, d_{\text{svp}}, T_{\text{sieve}}(d_{\text{svp}}) \leftarrow$ LowerBoundEst(M, V);
6 $\quad\quad$ **if** $d_{\text{svp}}^* > d_{\text{svp}}$ **then**
7 $\quad\quad\quad d_{\text{svp}}^* \leftarrow d_{\text{svp}}; m_{\text{optimal}} \leftarrow m; \beta_{\text{optimal}} \leftarrow \beta_{\text{current}};$

8 $\quad d_{\text{optimal}} \leftarrow m_{\text{optimal}} + n + 1;$
9 $\quad$ **return** $d_{\text{optimal}}, \beta_{\text{optimal}}, d_{\text{svp}}^*, T_{\text{sieve}}(d_{\text{svp}}^*)$;

Algorithm 5: Lower Bound Estimation with Optimal m

8   Conclusion

In this paper, we construct a Two-step LWE hardness estimator which estimates the hardness of LWE under primal attack using a combination of BKZ and sieving. To verify the accuracy of our Two-step LWE hardness estimator, we did extensive experiments, and the experiment results are consistent with our estimation. Besides, we also propose a conservative estimation for LWE considering the attack in Two-step mode. Compared with the most conservative Core-SVP model, our conservative estimation relies on weaker assumptions.

To figure out the influence of the Two-step mode on security estimation of NIST PQC schemes, We re-evaluate the concrete hardness of schemes by our Two-step LWE hardness estimator with a trivial reduction strategy and optimized blocksize and jump selection strategy. Evaluation results show that the upper bound security estimation given by the leaky-LWE-Estimator [19] is an over-optimistic estimation and the security bit drops by 2.1–3.4 bits under trivial reduction strategy and drops by $2.2 - -4.6$ bits under optimized blocksize and jump selection strategy. For the lower bound security bit of NIST PQC schemes, our conservative estimation is $4.17 - -8.11$ bits higher than the Core-SVP estimation. Therefore, we give more accurate estimations on both the upper bound and lower bound of the hardness of LWE.

Acknowledgments. This work was supported in part by the National Key R&D Program of China under Grant No. 2023YFB4403500, the National Natural Science Foundation of China (Nos. U2336210, 62272362), and Shanghai Science and Technology Innovation Action Plan (No. 23511100300). L. Wang is funded by the China Scholarship Council (No. 202006960055).

A   Appendix. Two-Step LWE Estimator Based on Classical LWE Estimator

In this Appendix A, we will show that based on other lwe estimators for instance the lwe estimator proposed by Albrecht *et al* in [33], to construct Two-step LWE estimator. The evaluation results show that Two-step mode also is more efficient in solving LWE than using BKZ algorithm only.

In particular, same as the LWE estimation proposed in [33], we also based on GSA to give a time cost model of the Two-step solving mode. Then we show that there is an optimal timing for ending the reduction and entering the searching step as the quality of lattice basis improved gradually by progressive BKZ.

Two-Step LWE Solving Mode. The Two-step mode we considered here will call progressive BKZ first for lattice reduction and call a Pump algorithm to find the target vector on the well-reduced lattice basis at the searching step. We set $T_1(\beta)$ as the time cost of obtaining a BKZ-β reduced basis in the reduction step. Then we set $T_2(\beta)$ as the time cost of calling Pump to find the target vector on BKZ-β reduced basis in the searching step. Then the total cost of such a special Two-step LWE solving mode control by reduction parameter β is $T_1(\beta) + T_2(\beta)$.

In the following parts, we will consider that Two-step mode is more efficient than bkz-only mode in the evaluation model of lattice-estimator [17].

Simple Time Cost Model of Reduction Step. Let ♯tours be the minimum number of tours that each BKZ-β during progressive BKZ reduction needed to obtain the BKZ-β reduced basis. First of all, we set $T_1(\beta) = $ ♯tours $\cdot \sum_{i=2}^{\beta}(d - i + 1) \cdot 2^{c \cdot i} \leq$ ♯tours $\cdot C(d - \beta + 1) \cdot 2^{c\beta}$ be the time cost of progressive BKZ from BKZ-2 to BKZ-β. Here c is the coefficients related to the sieving algorithm. For example, when using BDGL sieving $c = 0.292$ by using the classical computer and $c = 0.265$ by using the quantum computer. And $C = 1/(1 - 2^{-c}) \approx 5.46$ as the limit of ratio between $\sum_{i \leq \beta} 2^{ci + o(i)}$ and $2^{c\beta + o(\beta)}$ when β grows. When using the heuristic used in lattice-estimator [17] ♯tours=1, which assumed that after reduction of the progressive BKZ-β for each blocksize running once only, one can obtain the BKZ-β reduced basis. Thus, we get the time cost $T_1(\beta)$ of the reduction step which can obtain a BKZ-β reduced basis.

Simple Time Cost Model of Search Step. Secondly, to evaluate the time cost of the search step, we need to describe the relationship between the quality of the lattice basis and the time cost of a final pump in the search step of the Two-step mode. We choose the estimation in [43] which is based on GSA and uses the information of the current lattice basis to give a more refined upper bound of d4f value when solving LWE compared to the asymptotically upper bound of the d4f value proposed in [24]. The asymptotically upper bound of d4f value given in [24] holds if and only if that lattice $\mathcal{L}$ needs to be BKZ-$d/2$ reduced. Here d is the dimension of the lattice basis. Since we use a progressive reduction to gradually improve the quality of the lattice basis, at the beginning of reduction, the quality of the initial lattice basis is far away from BKZ-$d/2$ reduced. Therefore the asymptotically upper bound of d4f value given in [24] is inaccurate until proper reduction is done to achieve that lattice $\mathcal{L}$ is BKZ-$d/2$ reduced.

Here we directly use the result of [43] that for the embedding lattice, $\mathcal{L}$ in prime attack with dimension d and the root hermit factor of this lattice basis is $\delta(\beta)$, to find the target vector $\mathbf{t} = (\mathbf{e}, 1)$ in this lattice $\mathcal{L}$ by final sieve. Here $\mathbf{e}$ is the error vector of the LWE instance. Based on GSA, $\lambda_1\left(\mathcal{L}_{[f:d]}\right) = \sqrt{\frac{d-f}{2\pi e} \frac{|\det(L)|^{\frac{1}{d}}}{\delta(\beta)^f}}$ and Substituting it into the optimistic condition GH $\left(\mathcal{L}_{[f:d]}\right) \sqrt{4/3} \geq \pi_f(\lambda_1(\mathcal{L})) \approx \sqrt{\frac{d-f}{d}}\sigma\sqrt{d}$ from [24], we get the sieving dimension of the last sieve in searching step $d_{\text{sieving}}(\delta(\beta))$:

$$d_{\text{sieving}}(\delta(\beta)) \geq d - \log_{\delta(\beta)} \frac{|\det(\mathcal{L})|^{\frac{1}{d}} \sqrt{2}}{\sigma\sqrt{3\pi e}} \tag{9}$$

where the optimistic condition GH $\left(\mathcal{L}_{[f:d]}\right) \cdot \sqrt{4/3} \geq \pi_f(\lambda_1(\mathcal{L}))$ given in [24] by accounting the fact that the $d - f$ dimensional sieving algorithm on $\mathcal{L}_{[f:d]}$ heuristically finds all vectors up to norm GH $\left(\mathcal{L}_{[f:d]}\right) \cdot \sqrt{4/3}$ and σ is the standard deviation of LWE instances. In standard form LWE the expected length of the target vector in the embedding lattice is $\sigma\sqrt{d}$[6]. Here $\delta(\beta)$ is the root Hermit factor of the current lattice basis which is one of the lattice basis quality measurement values controlled by β.

Then we set $T_2(\beta) = 2^{c \cdot d_{\text{sieving}}(\delta(\beta))}$ as the simple time cost evaluation of the searching step which calls a pump on a BKZ-β reduced lattice basis with sieving dimension $d_{\text{sieving}}(\delta(\beta))$. Here minimum $d_{\text{sieving}}(\delta(\beta))$ is calculated by Eq. (9) which describes the relationship between the current quality of lattice basis and the sieving dimension of the last pump in searching step. It shows that a better BKZ-β reduced basis (smaller δ value) can decrease the time cost of $T_2(\beta)$ since a more reduced lattice basis can obtain a bigger dimension for free value when we use the high dimension pump to search the projected of target vector.

Simple Time Cost Model of Two-Step Mode. Finally, we give a simple time cost model $T(\beta)$ of a special Two-step mode that ends BKZ reduction when the lattice basis is BKZ-β reduced and use the Pump to find the target vector by considering the length of the target vector as fixed expected value. We calculate $T(\beta)$ by Eq. (10):

$$T(\beta) = T_1(\beta) + T_2(\beta) = \sharp\text{tours} \cdot C(d - \beta + 1) \cdot 2^{c\beta} + 2^{c \cdot d_{\text{sieving}}(\delta(\beta))} \tag{10}$$

---

[6] Note that we consider the length of the target vector by its expected value the same as what lattice-estimator did.

Comparison Between Two-Step Mode and BKZ-Only Mode. We set $T_{\text{bkz-only}} = \sharp\text{tours} \cdot C(d - \beta_{\text{adps16}} + 1) \cdot 2^{c\beta_{\text{adps16}}}$. Here β_{adps16} is the blocksize estimated from [12] which is minimal β_{adps16} s.t $\sigma\sqrt{\beta_{\text{adps16}}} \approx \|\pi_{d-\beta_{\text{adps16}}}(\mathbf{t})\| \leq \text{GH}(\mathbf{B}_{\pi[d-\beta_{\text{adps16}}]})$ holds. This β_{adps16} is minimal blocksize to make BKZ-only mode successful. In the calculation of both $T_1(\beta)$ and $T_{\text{bkz-only}}$, we use the same heuristic that after one tour reduction of the progressive BKZ-β that blocksize β gradually increased from 2 to β, one can obtain the BKZ-β reduced basis. Finally, we choose the parameters of Kyber-1024 and Dilithum-V as an example, we set $c = 0.292$ and respectively calculate $T(\beta)$ under different lattice reduction qualities and $T_{\text{bkz-only}}$. See Fig. 4 for more detail.

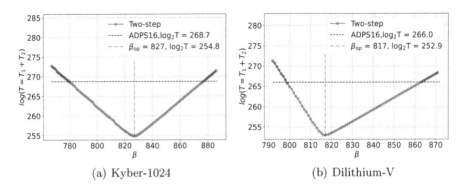

(a) Kyber-1024   (b) Dilithium-V

Fig. 4. $T(\beta)$ by Eq. (10) with different reduction quality.

From Fig. 4 we can see that as the quality of the lattice basis increased (the x-axis reflects that the current lattice basis is BKZ-β reduced), the total time cost $T(\beta)$ of solving LWE by using Two-step mode under our simple time cost model will decrease first then increase. So there is an optimal timing of entry in the searching step to make the $T(\beta)$ minimum, which we use the red line to indicate this location. Besides the minimum total cost of solving LWE by using Two-step mode $T(\beta)$ is smaller than that of $T_{\text{bkz-only}}$ which only uses progressive BKZ to solve LWE. In fact all blue points in Fig. 4 have a smaller time cost compared with $T_{\text{bkz-only}}$. Therefore, we observed that in solving LWE, the Two-step mode is more efficient than that of using BKZ reduction only based on the model of Albrecht et al. to construct the Two-step estimator.

References

1. Avanzi, R., et al.: Kyber (Round 3), p. 42 (2020)
2. Ducas, L., Eike Kiltz, T.L., Lyubashevsky, V., Schwabe, P., Seiler, G., Stehlé, D.: Dilithium (Round 3). NIST PQC project (2020)
3. Pornin, T., Prest, T.: More efficient algorithms for the NTRU key generation using the field norm. In: Lin, D., Sako, K. (eds.) PKC 2019. LNCS, vol. 11443, pp. 504–533. Springer, Cham (2019). https://doi.org/10.1007/978-3-030-17259-6_17

4. Steinfeld, R., et al.: Cryptanalysis of LASH. In: Nyberg, K. (ed.) FSE 2008. LNCS, vol. 5086, pp. 207–223. Springer, Heidelberg (2008). https://doi.org/10.1007/978-3-540-71039-4_13

5. Ducas, L., Lyubashevsky, V., Prest, T.: Efficient identity-based encryption over NTRU lattices. In: Sarkar, P., Iwata, T. (eds.) ASIACRYPT 2014. LNCS, vol. 8874, pp. 22–41. Springer, Heidelberg (2014). https://doi.org/10.1007/978-3-662-45608-8_2

6. Boyen, X.: Attribute-based functional encryption on lattices. In: Sahai, A. (ed.) TCC 2013. LNCS, vol. 7785, pp. 122–142. Springer, Heidelberg (2013). https://doi.org/10.1007/978-3-642-36594-2_8

7. Mera, J.M.B., Karmakar, A., Marc, T., Soleimanian, A.: Efficient lattice-based inner-product functional encryption. In: Hanaoka, G., Shikata, J., Watanabe, Y. (eds.) PKC 2022. LNCS, vol. 13178, pp. 163–193. Springer, Cham (2022). https://doi.org/10.1007/978-3-030-97131-1_6

8. Cheon, J.H., Kim, A., Kim, M., Song, Y.: Homomorphic encryption for arithmetic of approximate numbers. In: Takagi, T., Peyrin, T. (eds.) ASIACRYPT 2017. LNCS, vol. 10624, pp. 409–437. Springer, Cham (2017). https://doi.org/10.1007/978-3-319-70694-8_15

9. Liu, M., Nguyen, P.Q.: Solving BDD by enumeration: an update. In: Dawson, E. (ed.) CT-RSA 2013. LNCS, vol. 7779, pp. 293–309. Springer, Heidelberg (2013). https://doi.org/10.1007/978-3-642-36095-4_19

10. Arora, S., Ge, R.: New algorithms for learning in presence of errors. In: Aceto, L., Henzinger, M., Sgall, J. (eds.) ICALP 2011. LNCS, vol. 6755, pp. 403–415. Springer, Heidelberg (2011). https://doi.org/10.1007/978-3-642-22006-7_34

11. Kirchner, P., Fouque, P.-A.: An improved BKW algorithm for LWE with applications to cryptography and lattices. In: Gennaro, R., Robshaw, M. (eds.) CRYPTO 2015. LNCS, vol. 9215, pp. 43–62. Springer, Heidelberg (2015). https://doi.org/10.1007/978-3-662-47989-6_3

12. Alkim, E., Ducas, L., Pöppelmann, T., Schwabe, P.: Post-quantum Key Exchange - a new hope, pp. 327–343 (2016)

13. Albrecht, M.R., Göpfert, F., Virdia, F., Wunderer, T.: Revisiting the expected cost of solving uSVP and applications to LWE. In: Takagi, T., Peyrin, T. (eds.) ASIACRYPT 2017. LNCS, vol. 10624, pp. 297–322. Springer, Cham (2017). https://doi.org/10.1007/978-3-319-70694-8_11

14. Albrecht, M.R.: On dual lattice attacks against small-secret LWE and parameter choices in HElib and SEAL. In: Coron, J.-S., Nielsen, J.B. (eds.) EUROCRYPT 2017. LNCS, vol. 10211, pp. 103–129. Springer, Cham (2017). https://doi.org/10.1007/978-3-319-56614-6_4

15. Espitau, T., Joux, A., Kharchenko, N.: On a dual/hybrid approach to small secret LWE: a dual/enumeration technique for learning with errors and application to security estimates of FHE schemes. In: Bhargavan, K., Oswald, E., Prabhakaran, M. (eds.) INDOCRYPT 2020. LNCS, vol. 12578, pp. 440–462. Springer, Cham (2020). https://doi.org/10.1007/978-3-030-65277-7_20

16. Kannan, R.: Improved algorithms for integer programming and related lattice problems. In: Proceedings of the Fifteenth Annual ACM Symposium on Theory of Computing. STOC '83, pp. 193–206. Association for Computing Machinery, New York, NY, USA, December 1983

17. Albrecht, M.R., Player, R., Scott, S.: On the concrete hardness of learning with errors. J. Math. Cryptol. **9**(3), 169–203 (2015)

18. Albrecht, M.R., et al.: Estimate all the LWE, NTRU schemes! In: Catalano, D., De Prisco, R. (eds.) SCN 2018. LNCS, vol. 11035, pp. 351–367. Springer, Cham (2018). https://doi.org/10.1007/978-3-319-98113-0_19

19. Dachman-Soled, D., Ducas, L., Gong, H., Rossi, M.: LWE with side information: attacks and concrete security estimation. In: Micciancio, D., Ristenpart, T. (eds.) CRYPTO 2020. LNCS, vol. 12171, pp. 329–358. Springer, Cham (2020). https://doi.org/10.1007/978-3-030-56880-1_12

20. Bai, S., Miller, S., Wen, W.: A refined analysis of the cost for solving LWE via uSVP. In: Buchmann, J., Nitaj, A., Rachidi, T. (eds.) AFRICACRYPT 2019. LNCS, vol. 11627, pp. 181–205. Springer, Cham (2019). https://doi.org/10.1007/978-3-030-23696-0_10

21. Postlethwaite, E.W., Virdia, F.: On the success probability of solving unique SVP via BKZ. In: Garay, J.A. (ed.) PKC 2021. LNCS, vol. 12710, pp. 68–98. Springer, Cham (2021). https://doi.org/10.1007/978-3-030-75245-3_4

22. Information Technology Laboratory, Computer Security Resource Center: Post-quantum cryptography PQC selected algorithms 2022. https://csrc.nist.gov/Projects/post-quantum-cryptography/selected-algorithms-2022

23. Albrecht, M.R., Gheorghiu, V., Postlethwaite, E.W., Schanck, J.M.: Estimating quantum speedups for lattice sieves. In: Moriai, S., Wang, H. (eds.) ASIACRYPT 2020. LNCS, vol. 12492, pp. 583–613. Springer, Cham (2020). https://doi.org/10.1007/978-3-030-64834-3_20

24. Ducas, L.: Shortest vector from lattice sieving: a few dimensions for free. In: Nielsen, J.B., Rijmen, V. (eds.) EUROCRYPT 2018. LNCS, vol. 10820, pp. 125–145. Springer, Cham (2018). https://doi.org/10.1007/978-3-319-78381-9_5

25. Aono, Y., Wang, Y., Hayashi, T., Takagi, T.: Improved progressive BKZ algorithms and their precise cost estimation by sharp simulator. In: Fischlin, M., Coron, J.-S. (eds.) EUROCRYPT 2016. LNCS, vol. 9665, pp. 789–819. Springer, Heidelberg (2016). https://doi.org/10.1007/978-3-662-49890-3_30

26. Albrecht, M.R., Ducas, L., Herold, G., Kirshanova, E., Postlethwaite, E.W., Stevens, M.: The general sieve kernel and new records in lattice reduction. In: Ishai, Y., Rijmen, V. (eds.) EUROCRYPT 2019. LNCS, vol. 11477, pp. 717–746. Springer, Cham (2019). https://doi.org/10.1007/978-3-030-17656-3_25

27. Albrecht, M.R., Yun, C., Hunt, H.: lattice-estimator. https://github.com/malb/lattice-estimator

28. Xia, W., Wang, L., Wang, G., Gu, D., Wang, B.: Improved progressive BKZ with lattice sieving. Cryptology ePrint Archive, Paper 2022/1343 (2022). https://eprint.iacr.org/archive/2022/1343/1697360937.pdf

29. Zhao, Z., Ding, J.: Practical improvements on BKZ algorithm. In: Dolev, S., Gudes, E., Paillier, P. (eds.) CSCML 2023. LNCS, vol. 13914, pp. 273–284. Springer, Cham (2023). https://doi.org/10.1007/978-3-031-34671-2_19

30. Chen, Y., Nguyen, P.Q.: BKZ 2.0: better lattice security estimates. In: Lee, D.H., Wang, X. (eds.) ASIACRYPT 2011. LNCS, vol. 7073, pp. 1–20. Springer, Heidelberg (2011). https://doi.org/10.1007/978-3-642-25385-0_1

31. Chen, P.-Q., Nguyen, Y.: Réduction de réseau et sécurité concrète du chiffrement complètement homomorphe. Ph.D. thesis (2013)

32. Lyubashevsky, V., Micciancio, D.: On bounded distance decoding, unique shortest vectors, and the minimum distance problem. In: Halevi, S. (ed.) CRYPTO 2009. LNCS, vol. 5677, pp. 577–594. Springer, Heidelberg (2009). https://doi.org/10.1007/978-3-642-03356-8_34

33. Albrecht, M.R., Player, R., Scott, S.: On the concrete hardness of learning with errors. J. Math. Cryptol. **9** (2015)

34. Peikert, C.: A decade of lattice cryptography. Found. Trends Theor. Comput. Sci. **10**, 283–424 (2016). Place: Hanover, MA, USA Publisher: Now Publishers Inc
35. Xagawa, K.: Cryptography with Lattices, p. 244 (2010)
36. Albrecht, M.R., Fitzpatrick, R., Göpfert, F.: On the efficacy of solving LWE by reduction to unique-SVP. In: Lee, H.-S., Han, D.-G. (eds.) ICISC 2013. LNCS, vol. 8565, pp. 293–310. Springer, Cham (2014). https://doi.org/10.1007/978-3-319-12160-4_18
37. Chen, Y.: Réduction de réseau et sécurité concrète du chiffrement complètement homomorphe (2013)
38. Hanrot, G., Pujol, X., Stehlé, D.: Analyzing blockwise lattice algorithms using dynamical systems. In: Rogaway, P. (ed.) CRYPTO 2011. LNCS, vol. 6841, pp. 447–464. Springer, Heidelberg (2011). https://doi.org/10.1007/978-3-642-22792-9_25
39. Becker, A., Ducas, L., Gama, N., Laarhoven, T.: New directions in nearest neighbor searching with applications to lattice sieving. In: Proceedings of the Twenty-Seventh Annual ACM-SIAM Symposium on Discrete Algorithms. SODA '16, USA, pp. 10–24. Society for Industrial and Applied Mathematics, January 2016
40. Ducas, L., Rossi, M.: leaky-lwe-estimator. https://github.com/lducas/leaky-LWE-Estimator/tree/NIST-round3
41. MATZOV: Report on the Security of LWE: Improved Dual Lattice Attack, April 2022
42. Ducas, L.: Estimating the hidden overheads in the BDGL lattice sieving algorithm. In: Cheon, J.H., Johansson, T. (eds.) PQCrypto 2022. LNCS, vol. 13512, pp. 480–497. Springer, Cham (2022). https://doi.org/10.1007/978-3-031-17234-2_22
43. Wang, L., Wang, Y., Wang, B.: A trade-off SVP-solving strategy based on a sharper PNJ-BKZ simulator. In: Proceedings of the 2023 ACM Asia Conference on Computer and Communications Security. ASIA CCS '23, pp. 664-677. Association for Computing Machinery, , New York, NY, USA (2023)

A Simpler and More Efficient Reduction of DLog to CDH for Abelian Group Actions

Steven Galbraith[1], Yi-Fu Lai[1,2(✉)], and Hart Montgomery[3]

[1] University of Auckland, Auckland, New Zealand
s.galbraith@auckland.ac.nz
[2] Ruhr-University Bochum, Bochum, Germany
Yi-Fu.Lai@ruhr-uni-bochum.de
[3] Linux Foundation, San Francisco, USA

Abstract. Abelian group actions appear in several areas of cryptography, especially isogeny-based post-quantum cryptography. A natural problem is to relate the analogues of the computational Diffie-Hellman (CDH) and discrete logarithm (DLog) problems for abelian group actions. Galbraith, Panny, Smith and Vercauteren (Mathematical Cryptology '21) gave a quantum reduction of DLog to CDH, assuming a CDH oracle with perfect correctness. Montgomery and Zhandry (Asiacrypt '22, best paper award) showed how to convert an unreliable CDH oracle into one that is correct with overwhelming probability. However, while a theoretical breakthrough, their reduction is quite inefficient: if the CDH oracle is correct with probability ϵ then their algorithm to amplify the success requires on the order of $1/\epsilon^{21}$ calls to the CDH oracle.

We revisit this line of work and give a much simpler and tighter algorithm. Our method only takes on the order of $1/\epsilon^4$ CDH oracle calls and is conceptually simpler than the Montgomery-Zhandry reduction. Our algorithm is also fully black-box, whereas the Montgomery-Zhandry algorithm is slightly non-black-box. Our main tool is a thresholding technique that replaces the comparison of distributions in Montgomery-Zhandry with testing equality of thresholded sets.

1 Introduction

Abelian group actions appear in several areas of cryptography. In isogeny-based post-quantum cryptography there have been several new instantiations of group actions, such as CSIDH [CLM+18], CSI-FiSh [BKV19, EKP20], and SCALLOP [FFK+23]. Isogeny-based group actions have been proven to be versatile in many applications, including but not limited to signature schemes [BKV19, EKP20, DG19], UC-secure oblivious transfer protocols [LGD21, BMM+23], threshold signatures [DM20], (linkable/accountable) ring and group signatures [BKP20, BDK+22], blind signatures [KLLQ23], and PAKE [AEK+22].

A natural problem is to relate the analogues of the computational Diffie-Hellman (CDH) and discrete logarithm (DLog) problems for abelian group actions, which we abbreviate GA-CDH and GA-DLog, respectively, since key

© International Association for Cryptologic Research 2024
Q. Tang and V. Teague (Eds.): PKC 2024, LNCS 14603, pp. 36–60, 2024.
https://doi.org/10.1007/978-3-031-57725-3_2

exchange protocols based on these instantiations are build upon the group action CDH assumption (GA-CDH) but the underlying group action DLog assumptions (GA-DLog) are much better studied and understood from a hardness perspective. Galbraith, Panny, Smith and Vercauteren [GPSV21] gave a quantum reduction of GA-DLog to GA-CDH, assuming a GA-CDH oracle with *perfect correctness*. Subsequently, Montgomery and Zhandry [MZ22] devised a novel approach and a series of sophisticated procedures to transform an unreliable GA-CDH oracle into one that is correct with an overwhelming probability and showed how to use this in the [GPSV21] framework to build a full quantum reduction of GA-DLog to GA-CDH.

However, [MZ22] is quite inefficient: more precisely, if a GA-CDH oracle is correct with probability ϵ, then the Montgomery-Zhandry algorithm to amplify the success probability to an exponentially low amount, which is necessary for their reduction from GA-CDH to GA-DLog to work, takes on the order of $1/\epsilon^{21}$ calls to the original GA-CDH oracle. To put this into perspective, given a GA-CDH oracle with success rate $1/8$, it requires at least 2^{63} oracle calls in [MZ22] to obtain a GA-CDH a GA-DLog solver with an overwhelming advantage. While [MZ22] was a theoretical breakthrough, its inefficiency means it can only have an extremely limited effect on practical parameter setting for group actions or isogenies.

This brings us to the primary objective of this work:

Can we have tighter and simpler approaches for the reduction between CDH *and DLog and to amplify a* CDH *circuit for abelian group actions?*

We answer this question in the affirmative. We show a GA-CDH to GA-DLog reduction that only requires on the order of $1/\epsilon^4$ calls to a GA-CDH oracle that succeeds with probability ϵ. Moreover, our techniques are considerably simpler than the heavy mathematical machinery used in [MZ22], providing a much more understandable reduction as well.

1.1   Group Actions and Computational Problems

Let G be an abelian group acting transitively on set $\mathcal{X}$ via the operation $\star$. We denote group actions as tuples $(G, \mathcal{X}, \star)$. In this paper we assume this is an effective group action (EGA), meaning that there is an efficient algorithm to compute $g \star x$ for any $g \in G$ and $x \in \mathcal{X}$. The isogeny-based primitive CSIDH [CLM+18], which is one of the main motivations for this work, was originally not known to be an effective group action, but recent work by Page and Robert [PR23] gives a solution to this problem, and in the context of our work this issue can be bypassed using a technique of Wesolowski [Wes22]. We note there are seemingly hard barriers to making a GA-DLog to GA-CDH reduction work for non-EGAs (*restricted* effective group actions), and we refer interested readers to [MZ22] for this, where there is an extensive discussion on the topic.

We now introduce the two main computational problems that arise in (abelian) group action cryptography. The discrete logarithm problem is also known as *vectorization*, and the computational Diffie-Hellman problem as *parallelization*.

GA-DLog: Given $(x, g \star x) \in \mathcal{X}^2$, compute g.

GA-CDH: Given $(x, a \star x, b \star x) \in \mathcal{X}^3$, compute $(ab) \star x$.

Galbraith, Panny, Smith and Vercauteren [GPSV21] showed a quantum reduction of GA-DLog to GA-CDH (vectorization to parallelization) for *perfect* adversaries. At a high level the idea is the following: let $\mathcal{A}$ be a (quantum) oracle such that $\mathcal{A}(a \star x, b \star x) = (ab) \star x$ with overwhelming correctness. Given a GA-DLog instance $(x, a \star x)$ one can use the oracle as $\mathcal{A}(a^m \star x, a^n \star x) = (a^{m+n}) \star x$ to compute $(a^t) \star x$ for any desired $t \in \mathsf{Z}$. Suppose for simplicity that G is cyclic and let g be a generator of G. Define $f : \mathsf{Z}^2 \to \mathcal{X}$ by $f(s, t) = (g^s) \star (a^t) \star x$. One can compute f using the oracle $\mathcal{A}$. Applying Shor's algorithm [Sho94] for the hidden subgroup problem returns an element in the lattice $L = \{(s, t) \in \mathsf{Z}^2 : g^s a^t = 1\}$. If $\gcd(t, |G|) = 1$ then we can solve the discrete logarithm of a to the base g, and hence can compute a.

The intuition of [GPSV21] is that the ability to compute GA-CDH allows us to turn a group action into a group, since we can "multiply" elements using the GA-CDH oracle. This means we can directly apply Shor's algorithm for solving discrete log on groups.

1.2   The Montgomery-Zhandry Approach

Montgomery and Zhandry [MZ22] showed how to handle an oracle that is only correct with probability ϵ. Since the decisional Diffie-Hellman problem for group actions is hard, and since we lack the algebraic tools used in to resolve this problem in the case of CDH in groups, there seems to be no easy way to determine whether or not an output of the oracle is correct or not. We sketch some of the main ideas of their work.

For $y, z \in \mathcal{X}$ define $\mathcal{A}_0(y, z)$ to be the algorithm that samples uniformly at random group elements $a', b' \in G$, and returns $(a'b')^{-1} \star \mathcal{A}(a' \star y, b' \star z)$. Let $\mathcal{D}$ be the output distribution of $\mathcal{A}_0(x, x)$. Montgomery and Zhandry show that $\Pr[x \leftarrow \mathcal{D}] = \epsilon$ and that the output distribution of $\mathcal{A}_0(a \star x, b \star x)$ is the same as the shift of the distribution $\mathcal{D}$, which we denote as $(ab) \star \mathcal{D}$ (meaning $\Pr[w \leftarrow (ab) \star \mathcal{D}] := \Pr[((ab)^{-1} \star w) \leftarrow \mathcal{D}]$). We also use $\mathcal{A}_0$ in this work, as it is a very basic self-reduction. We explain $\mathcal{A}_0$ in more detail in the body of the paper.

The next core component of [MZ22] is an algorithm $\mathcal{A}_1(y, z)$ that runs $\mathcal{A}_0(y, z)$ for a number T (to be determined later) of times to get a list L of outputs (some may be repeated multiple times), which provides an empirical distribution $\tilde{\mathcal{D}}$ of the distribution $\mathcal{D}$. When $T \gg 1/\epsilon$, the correct answer $(ab) \star x$ will be on the list with an overwhelming probability. Then for each $w \in L$, they run $\mathcal{A}_0(x, w)$ for T times. When $w = (ab) \star x$ then the resulting distribution will be the same as $\mathcal{D}$. The idea is that if $w \neq (ab) \star x$ then we would like to eliminate it from the list, but this does not always work. We will use a similar "shifting" approach here, but our algorithm is somewhat different and our analysis is considerably different from [MZ22].

One of the main insights of [MZ22] is that the only obstruction is due to small subgroups. We briefly explain this now.

Define $\mathcal{D}_w$ to be the output distribution of $\mathcal{A}_0(x, w)$, and let $\tilde{\mathcal{D}}_w$ be an empirical distribution of $\mathcal{D}_w$ obtained by taking T samples from $\mathcal{D}_w$. Let $\Delta(\cdot, \cdot)$ be the statistical distance function. [MZ22] considers the distance function $\|\mathcal{D} - \mathcal{D}'\|_\infty = \max_{u \in \mathcal{X}} |\Pr[u \leftarrow \mathcal{D}] - \Pr[u \leftarrow \mathcal{D}']|$. Let $L'' \subseteq G$ be the set of $g \in G$ such that $\Delta(\mathcal{D}_{g \star x}, \mathcal{D}) \leq \delta/2$. Let H be the subgroup of G generated by L''. Montgomery and Zhandry show (Lemma 15 of [MZ22]) that if $\delta \leq \epsilon^4/8$ then $|H| < 1/\epsilon + 1$.

The full specification of algorithm $\mathcal{A}_1(y, z)$ is as follows:

1. Run $\mathcal{A}_0(y, z)$ for T times to get a list L of outputs and an estimate $\tilde{\mathcal{D}}$ of the distribution $\mathcal{D}$.
2. Set $L' = \{\}$.
3. For each $w \in L$, run $\mathcal{A}_0(x, w)$ for T times and calculate estimate $\tilde{\mathcal{D}}_w$ of distribution $\mathcal{D}_w$.
4. If $\Delta(\tilde{\mathcal{D}}_w, \tilde{\mathcal{D}}) \leq \delta/2$ then add w to L'.
5. Return L'.

Montgomery and Zhandry then define an algorithm $\mathcal{A}_2(y, z)$ that "fills out" the subgroup so that it outputs the set $\{(gab) \star x : g \in H\}$, where H is the subgroup above mentioned. This algorithm now has overwhelming success. The analysis of $\mathcal{A}_2$ is intricate, and we have intentionally omitted it from our own work. We refer an interested reader to [MZ22].

The full [MZ22] reduction on input a GA-DLog instance $(x, a \star x)$ and with quantum access to circuit $\mathcal{A}$ is as follows:

1. Choose the parameters δ, T.
2. Determine H.
3. Run the algorithm of [GPSV21] with respect to action of G/H on $(G/H) \star x$, using the $\mathcal{A}_2(\cdot, \cdot)$ as the parallelization circuit. Here G/H and $(G/H) \star x$ are represented in $O(1/\epsilon + 1)$ space as cosets/orbits. The algorithm returns the coset aH with noticeable probability.
4. Perform a brute-force search over all elements g within the coset aH, where $a \in aH$, to deduce the group element a using the known set element of $a \star x$.

Our overall approach in this work is similar, although our parameterizations and algortms are quite different.

Finally, we note that in their published work, Montgomery and Zhandry claim the number of queries to $\mathcal{A}$ is $O(1/\epsilon^{13})$. However, there is a miscalculation in the complexity of the algorithm $\mathcal{A}_1$ as presented in [MZ22]. According to their analysis, the algorithm $\mathcal{A}_1$ requires $T^2 + T$ queries of the circuit $\mathcal{A}$, where T is taken to be $T = \tilde{O}(\epsilon^{-8})$. It is crucial to note that the condition $T = \tilde{O}(\epsilon^{-8})$ is necessary to ensure that the subgroup generated by the error terms of $\mathcal{A}_1$ approximates ϵ^{-1}. However, due to this requirement, it actually implies that $\mathcal{A}_1$ performs $\tilde{O}(\epsilon^{-16})$ queries to $\mathcal{A}$ instead of the originally stated $\tilde{O}(\epsilon^{-8})$. Consequently, when provided with a GA-CDH oracle with a success rate of ϵ, solving a GA-DLog problem using $\mathcal{A}_1$ would actually require $\tilde{O}(\epsilon^{-21})$ queries to the CDH oracle, as opposed to the claim of $\tilde{O}(\epsilon^{-13})$ made in the paper.

1.3 Technical Overview

We show a new approach to the problem based on thresholding. For a GA-CDH challenge $(a \star x, b \star x)$, we essentially show that there is a set of "heavy" elements that contains the required value $(ab) \star x$ that can be accurately computed using a sufficient number of queries to the oracle. Unlike in [MZ22], we can show that, across different queries the same set of elements, up to shifting by some value, always shows up in an output set. This makes our statistical analysis much easier and more lightweight– [MZ22] has to use a number of complicated theorems from algebra, while the most complicated math we use is a simple Chernoff bound–as well as dramatically more efficient. We outline the steps in our reduction in the remainder of this subsection.

We also assume in this overview we are working with a regular group action $(G, \mathcal{X}, \star)$ with origin element x. Consider a GA-CDH oracle $\mathcal{A}$ that outputs the correct set element with probability ϵ. We show how to use $\mathcal{A}$ to build an algorithm that outputs either the correct set element or all elements in a coset of a subgroup containing the correct set element with extremely high probability; from there, we can apply the work of [GPSV21] and [MZ22] to complete the GA-CDH to GA-DLog reduction.

The simple randomized self-reduction. As we outlined earlier, one of the core algorithms in [MZ22] and in our work is the simple random self-reduction $\mathcal{A}_0$ for GA-CDH instances on a group action. Suppose we are given GA-CDH challenge set elements $(y = a \star x, z = b \star x)$ and want to query $\mathcal{A}$ to output $(ab) \star x$. $\mathcal{A}$ could just refuse to work on certain inputs; its success probability is over all combinations of set elements. However, we can have an efficient self-reduction: by randomly selecting g and h from the group G and calculating $(gh)^{-1} \star \mathcal{A}(g \star x, h \star y)$, we obtain the correct result if and only if $\mathcal{A}$ correctly evaluates the query. Furthermore, since $g \star x$ and $h \star y$ constitute uniformly random and independent set elements (we assume here that the group action is regular), we obtain the distribution that represents the "average" output of the adversary.

Following [MZ22] we refer to this algorithm as $\mathcal{A}_0$. The distribution resulting from $\mathcal{A}_0(x, x)$ is denoted as $\mathcal{D}$, and can be viewed as the "reference" distribution. We adopt straightforward proofs from [MZ22] to establish that, for any $g \in G$, $g \star \mathcal{D} = A_0(x, g \star x)$, which we denote as $\mathcal{D}_g$.

In essence, we are asserting that if we modify the input to $\mathcal{A}_0$, the distribution of the adversary's output will shift accordingly. This is because the inputs to $\mathcal{A}$ from $\mathcal{A}_0$ are entirely randomized, preventing $\mathcal{A}$ from engaging in any strategic maneuvers or attempts to deceive.

Approximating the oracle's success probability ϵ. In contrast to [MZ22], our reduction commences with a concrete approximation of the given GA-CDH oracle's success probability, denoted as ϵ. Establishing a tight lower bound on ϵ, denoted by $\epsilon_{\min}$, is a crucial step in our reduction process. This lower bound serves a vital role in enabling a *fully black-box reduction*, a distinction from [MZ22].

To determine $\epsilon_{\min}$, we execute $\mathcal{A}_0(x, x)$ a sufficient number of times and count the instances where x is the output. Given that we are aware of the value of x and its correctness as a solution to a CDH query on (x, x), this procedure is straightforward and efficient. For the sake of simplicity in this overview, we assume that $\epsilon = \epsilon_{\min}$ and that we know the value of ϵ. However, it's important to note that our results do not hinge on this assumption being the case.

Building a threshhold list. As per our assumption above, we know the adversary $\mathcal{A}$ succeeds with probability ϵ, and we can leverage $\mathcal{A}_0$ to ensure this success rate on any query. Our next goal is to show we can, requiring roughly (asymptotically) $1/\epsilon^3$ queries to $\mathcal{A}_0$, "threshhold" the output such that, in response to any CDH challenge query (y, z), we generate a list of precisely I elements. Here, I is a fixed integer where $I = O\left(\frac{1}{\epsilon}\right)$, and this list consists of the top I elements from the distribution $\mathcal{A}_0(y, z)$.[1]

By assumption, we have that the adversary must output the correct answer to the CDH challenge with probability ϵ. Suppose we rank the elements output by $\mathcal{D}$–the output distribution of $\mathcal{A}_0$ by likelihood of appearing. The most likely element x_1 occurs with probability p_1, the second most likely element x_2 occurs with probability p_2, and so forth. If x_c is the correct element, we claim that there must be some elements x_i, x_{i+1} where $i \geq c$ and $p_i - p_j \geq k\epsilon^2$ for some constant k and some $i \leq \frac{2}{\epsilon}$. This follows from summing the p_is using the Gaussian summation formula (see, we told you, simple math!): if there is no gap of the appropriate size, the probabilities will sum to something larger than 1.

It turns out that if we sample $\mathcal{A}_0(x, x)$ enough times, we can find I and this gap by just seeing where a large gap lies. We use Chernoff bounds to show that asymptotically $1/\epsilon^3$ samples are enough to do this, and this turns out to be the bulk of the writing in our proof. If we provided the Chernoff bounds out of thin air, then our already short proof would be extremely short. We call this algorithm for gap-finding $\mathcal{A}_I$, and we note that it works, for any input values (x, y). We do, however, write down and keep track of I for our future algorithms, because it could be possible that there are two gaps of similar size, and we want to make sure that we use the same set of elements (of the same size) every time we attempt to threshold.

A "shifting" algorithm. At this point, we borrow conceptually from [MZ22], but our algorithms will be different. We define a new algorithm which we refer to as $\mathcal{A}_1$, which is conceptually similar to the algorithm of the same name from [MZ22]. $\mathcal{A}_1$ does almost the exact same thing as $\mathcal{A}_I$, except it uses the knowledge of I to always output I elements. So, $\mathcal{A}_1(y, z)$ outputs a set of I elements $z_1, ..., z_I$, one of which must be the correct GA-CDH answer. Suppose, for each z_i, we compute $\mathcal{A}_1(x, z_i)$. For the correct z_i, we know that $\mathcal{D}_{y,z} = \mathcal{D}_{x,z_i}$, where we are overloading the notation of $\mathcal{D}$ in the natural way, because $\mathcal{A}_0$ is "shift invariant." Hence, it is very straightforward to see that, with an overwhelming chance, we have $\mathcal{A}_1(y, z) = \mathcal{A}_1(x, z_i)$, if z_i is the correct answer. As a result, after the

---

[1] Note this is very different from the algorithm of the same name in [MZ22].

execution of $\mathcal{A}_1(x, z_i)$ for each i, we can eliminate all z_i for which $\mathcal{A}_1(y, z) \neq \mathcal{A}_1(x, z_i)$ from our candidate list of correct solutions. We will call this algorithm $\mathcal{A}_2$ and denote the resulting list L.

The authors of [MZ22] opt for a more intricate shifting and pruning algorithm. Without thresholding, they cannot ensure that each "run" of their $\mathcal{A}_1$ will consistently produce the same list of elements (although they may be shifted). This crucial distinction is the primary reason why our algorithm stands out as simpler and significantly more efficient than theirs.

Why we have a full subgroup. The primary challenge, which is also a key source of inefficiency in [MZ22], revolves around the necessity of finding a "complete" coset (i.e. the set elements generated by $H \star x$ for some subgroup H). In the reduction, this step is indispensable, as it paves the way for the application of Shor's algorithm in the final step. However, in our case here, it is straightforward to show that the list L constitutes a complete coset already. To see this, every element in L needs to be "shift invariant" onto the set L with respect to $\mathcal{A}_1$: in other words, we have $\mathcal{A}_1(x, L) = L$, or else $\mathcal{A}_2$ would have pruned these elements. It is straightforward to derive a contradiction if L is not a complete coset: we either break the "shift invariance" of $\mathcal{A}_0$ and $\mathcal{A}_1$, or the fact that $\mathcal{A}_2$ should have eliminated certain elements.

Cleaning up. Now that we have outlined how our improved reduction outputs a set L that is a complete coset containing the correct solution to a GA-CDH instance, all that remains is to show that we can clean up correctly. We do this exactly as in [MZ22] and [GPSV21]. We can use L and Shor's algorithm to find a subgroup H that generates L from the correct solution, run the core algorithm from [GPSV21] on the induced group action $(G/H, G/H \star x, \star)$, and then "brute force" over all elements of H to get a final answer.

Our total running time is proportional to $1/\epsilon^4$ and some polynomial in $\log(|G|)$, which is a substantial improvement over $\tilde{O}(\epsilon^{-21})$ from the previous work.

2   Preliminaries

We begin by defining basic background material. A reader knowledgeable in group actions and cryptography may safely skip this section.

2.1   Cryptographic Group Actions

We define cryptographic group actions following Alamati *et al.* [ADMP20], which are based on those of Brassard and Yung [BY91] and Couveignes [Cou06]. Our presentation here is based on that of [MZ22].

Definition 1. *(Group Action) A group G is said to act on a set $\mathcal{X}$ if there is a map $\star : G \times \mathcal{X} \to \mathcal{X}$ that satisfies the following two properties:*

1. *Identity: If e is the identity of G, then $\forall x \in \mathcal{X}$, we have $e \star x = x$.*
2. *Compatibility: For any $g, h \in G$ and any $x \in \mathcal{X}$, we have $(gh) \star x = g \star (h \star x)$.*

We may use the abbreviated notation $(G, \mathcal{X}, \star)$ to denote a group action. We extensively consider group actions that are *regular*:

Definition 2. *A group action $(G, \mathcal{X}, \star)$ is said to be* regular *if, for every $x_1, x_2 \in \mathcal{X}$, there exists a* unique *$g \in G$ such that $x_2 = g \star x_1$.*

We emphasize that most results in group action-based cryptography have focused on regular actions. As emphasized by [ADMP20], if a group action is regular, then for any $x \in \mathcal{X}$, the map $f_x : g \mapsto g \star x$ defines a bijection between G and $\mathcal{X}$; in particular, if G (or $\mathcal{X}$) is finite, then we must have $|G| = |\mathcal{X}|$.

In this paper, unless we specify otherwise, we will work with *effective* group actions (EGAs). An effective group action $(G, \mathcal{X}, \star)$ is, informally speaking, a group action where all of the (well-defined) group operations and group action operations are efficiently computable, there are efficient ways to sample random group elements, and set elements have unique representation. Since the focus of this paper is on abelian group actions in a quantum world, we note that we can efficiently map any abelian group to $\mathbf{Z}_p$ for some integer p , and all of the less obvious properties needed for EGAs follow automatically. Formally speaking, we define an *effective group action* (EGA) as follows:

Definition 3. (Effective Group Action) *A group action $(G, \mathcal{X}, \star)$ is effective if the following properties are satisfied:*

1. *The group G is finite and there exist efficient (PPT) algorithms for:*
   (a) *Membership testing, i.e., to decide if a given bit string represents a valid group element in G.*
   (b) *Equality testing, i.e., to decide if two bit strings represent the same group element in G.*
   (c) *Sampling, i.e., to sample an element g from a distribution $\mathcal{D}_G$ on G. In this paper, We consider distributions that are statistically close to uniform.*
   (d) *Operation, i.e., to compute gh for any $g, h \in G$.*
   (e) *Inversion, i.e., to compute g^{-1} for any $g \in G$.*
2. *The set $\mathcal{X}$ is finite and there exist efficient algorithms for:*
   (a) *Membership testing, i.e., to decide if a bit string represents a valid set element.*
   (b) *Unique representation, i.e., given any arbitrary set element $x \in \mathcal{X}$, compute a string $\hat{x}$ that canonically represents x.*
3. *There exists a distinguished element $x_0 \in \mathcal{X}$, called the* origin, *such that its bit-string representation is known.*
4. *There exists an efficient algorithm that given (some bit-string representations of) any $g \in G$ and any $x \in \mathcal{X}$, outputs $g \star x$.*

2.2   Computational Problems

We next define problems related to group action security. We emphasize that we are defining *problems* here and not *assumptions* because these are easier to use in reductions. Again our presentation is based on that of [MZ22].

Definition 4. (Group Action Discrete Logarithm (DLog))   *Given a group action $(G, \mathcal{X}, \star)$ and distributions $(\mathcal{D}_\mathcal{X}, \mathcal{D}_G)$, the group action discrete logarithm problem is defined as follows: sample $g \leftarrow \mathcal{D}_G$ and $x \leftarrow \mathcal{D}_\mathcal{X}$, compute $y = g \star x$, and create the tuple $T = (x, y)$. We say that an adversary solves the group action discrete log problem if, given T and a description of the group action and sampling algorithms, the adversary outputs g.*

Definition 5. (Group Action Computational Diffie-Hellman (CDH))   *Given a group action $(G, \mathcal{X}, \star)$ and distributions $(\mathcal{D}_\mathcal{X}, \mathcal{D}_G)$, the group action CDH problem is defined as follows: sample $g \leftarrow \mathcal{D}_G$ and $x, x' \leftarrow \mathcal{D}_\mathcal{X}$, compute $y = g \star x$, and create the tuple $T = (x, y, x')$. We say that an adversary solves the group action CDH problem if, given T and a description of the group action and sampling algorithms, the adversary outputs $y' = g \star x'$.*

Remark 1. The above definitions allow for different distributions $\mathcal{D}_\mathcal{X}$ on $\mathcal{X}$. In particular, $\mathcal{D}_\mathcal{X}$ could be uniform over $\mathcal{X}$, or it could be a singleton distribution that places all its weight on a single fixed x. Whether x is fixed or uniform potentially changes the the nature of these problems (see [BMZ19] for an exploration in the group-based setting). Looking ahead, as in [MZ22], our reduction between DLog and CDH will preserve x, and therefore it works no matter how x is modeled.

2.3   Chernoff Bounds

In our forthcoming argument, we will rely on Chernoff bounds. To this end, we present a specific formulation of a Chernoff bound below.

Theorem 1.   *Let $X = \sum_{i=1}^{T} X_i$, where X_i are independent random variables with a Bernoulli distribution with $\Pr[X_i = 1] = p_i$ and $\Pr[X_i = 0] = 1 - p_i$. Let $\mu = \mathbb{E}[X] = \sum_{i=1}^{T} p_i$. Then, we have*

$$\Pr\left[X - \mu \geq \eta\mu\right] \leq e^{-\mu\eta^2/(2+\eta)}$$

for any $\eta \geq 0$, and

$$\Pr\left[X - \mu \leq -\eta\mu\right] \leq e^{-\mu\eta^2/2}$$

for any $\eta \in (0, 1)$.

If $p_i = p$ for all $i \in [T]$ for some $p \in [0, 1]$, then we can restate the inequalities as follows:

$$\Pr\left[X - Tp \geq \eta Tp\right] \leq e^{-Tp\eta^2/(2+\eta)}$$

for any $\eta \geq 0$, and

$$\Pr\left[X - Tp \leq -\eta Tp\right] \leq e^{-Tp\eta^2/2}$$

for any $\eta \in (0,1)$. Moreover, for any $\eta \in (0,1)$ we have

$$\Pr\left[|X - Tp| \geq \eta Tp\right] \leq 2e^{-Tp\eta^2/3}.$$

3   The Main Reduction

We state our main result.

Theorem 2. *Let* $(G, \mathcal{X}, \star)$ *be an effective group action. If DLog is post-quantum hard in* $(G, \mathcal{X}, \star)$, *then so is CDH. More precisely, given a CDH adversary* $\mathcal{A}$ *there exists an oracle algorithm* $\mathcal{R}^{\mathcal{A},(G,\mathcal{X},\star)}(y)$ *that runs in time* $O\left(\mathsf{poly}(\log|G|)/\epsilon^4\right)$ *with* $\mathsf{poly}(\log|G|)/\epsilon^4$ *queries to* $\mathcal{A}$ *and the group action* $(G, \mathcal{X}, \star)$ *such that*

$$\mathsf{Adv}_{\mathsf{DLog}}^{(G,\mathcal{X},\star)}\left(\mathcal{R}^{\mathcal{A},(G,\mathcal{X},\star)}\right) \geq 0.99,$$

where $\epsilon := \mathsf{Adv}_{\mathsf{CDH}}^{(G,\mathcal{X},\star)}(\mathcal{A})$.

The running time and number of calls to $\mathcal{A}$ of the black-box reduction $\mathcal{R}$ depend on the success probability ϵ of $\mathcal{A}$. Nonetheless, we are not required to know ϵ in advance and the estimation is also a part of our reduction. The remainder of this section is devoted to proving Theorem 2.

3.1   Preparation

Our basic setup very closely mirrors that of [MZ22], so we borrow their presentation for much of the beginning of this section. Let $x \in \mathcal{X}$ be a fixed set element. Define CDH to be the function which correctly solves CDH relative to x: $\mathsf{CDH}(a \star x, b \star x) = (ab) \star x$. We extend the oracle CDH to accept a vector of elements as input, operating as follows: $\mathsf{CDH}(a_1 \star x, \cdots, a_n \star x) = (a_1 \cdots a_n) \star x$. Moreover, we permit CDH to process distribution(s) over the set $\mathcal{X}$ as input. In such cases, CDH will naturally yield a corresponding distribution as its output. We will later use a very similar argument as in [MZ22] in Sect. 3.9 and explain how to extend our reduction to non-regular abelian actions.

Let $a, b \in G$ be group elements, and let $y = a \star x$ and $z = b \star x$. Suppose $\mathcal{A}$ is an efficient (quantum) algorithm such that

$$\epsilon := \mathsf{Adv}_{\mathsf{CDH}}^{(G,\mathcal{X},\star)}(\mathcal{A}) = \Pr_{a,b\in G}[\mathcal{A}(x, a \star x, b \star x) = (ab) \star x]$$

is a non-negligible function in the security parameter, where a and b are random elements in G, and the probability is over the randomness of a and b and $\mathcal{A}$.

Our goal is to turn $\mathcal{A}$ into a quantum algorithm for discrete logarithms. As a first step, we will introduce the basic random self-reduction for CDH from [MZ22].

Algorithm $\mathcal{A}_0$.

- On input $y = a \star x$, $z = b \star x$, choose elements $a', b' \in G$ uniformly at random.
- Assign $(y', z') \leftarrow (a' \star y, b' \star z)$.
- Run $w' \leftarrow \mathcal{A}(x, y', z')$.
- Output $w \leftarrow (a'b')^{-1} \star w'$.

Note that each run of $\mathcal{A}_0$ runs $\mathcal{A}$ exactly once, and uses a constant number of group action operations. This reduction preserves the correctness of $\mathcal{A}$, since, if $\mathcal{A}$ is correct, then we output

$$w = (a'b')^{-1} \star \mathsf{CDH}\left((a'a) \star x, (b'b) \star x\right) = (a'b')^{-1} (aa'bb') \star x = (ab) \star x$$

which is the correct output for CDH on input (y, z). Furthermore, as the set elements y' and z' are uniformly distributed over $\mathcal{X}$, the success rate of $\mathcal{A}_0$ will be independent of the input.

Let $\mathcal{D}$ represent the output distribution of $\mathcal{A}_0(x, x)$. While the answer to $x = \mathsf{CDH}(x, x)$ is trivial, the distribution $\mathcal{D}$ provides crucial clues for our analysis.

Lemma 1. *(Lemma 10, [MZ22])* $\Pr[x \leftarrow \mathcal{D}] = \epsilon$.

Proof. Recall that $\mathcal{D}$ is the distribution $\mathcal{A}_0(x, x)$. $\mathcal{A}_0$ on input (x, x) calls $\mathcal{A}(a' \star x, b' \star x)$ for random $a', b' \in G$. With probability ϵ, $\mathcal{A}(a' \star x, b' \star x)$ returns $(a'b') \star x$, and in this case we have $w = x$ as desired.   □

We next generalize our notation. For any $y, z \in X$ where $y = a \star x$ and $z = b \star x$ for some $a, b \in G$, let $\mathcal{D}_{y,z}$ be the distribution of outputs of $\mathcal{A}_0(y, z)$.

Lemma 2. *(Lemma 11, [MZ22])* *For every $y, z \in \mathcal{X}$ such that there exist $a, b \in G$ where $y = a \star x$ and $z = b \star x$, $\mathcal{D}_{y,z} = \mathsf{CDH}(y, z, \mathcal{D})$, where $\mathsf{CDH}(\cdot, \cdot, \cdot)$ is the 3-way CDH function. In other words, $\mathcal{A}_0(a \star x, b \star x)$ is identically distributed to $(ab) \star \mathcal{A}_0(x, x)$.*

Proof. Fix $a, b \in G$. Consider the probability that $\mathcal{A}_0(a \star x, b \star x)$ outputs w:

$$\Pr[\mathcal{A}_0(a \star x, b \star x) = w] = \Pr_{a', b' \in G}[(a'b')^{-1} \star \mathcal{A}((aa') \star x, (bb') \star x) = w]$$

$$= \Pr_{a', b' \in G}[\mathcal{A}((aa') \star x, (bb') \star x) = (a'b') \star w]$$

$$= \Pr_{a'', b'' \in G}[\mathcal{A}(a'' \star x, b'' \star x) = (a''b'' (ab)^{-1}) \star w]$$

$$= \Pr[\mathcal{A}_0(x, x) = (ab)^{-1} \star w]$$

Thus, $\mathcal{A}_0(a \star x, b \star x)$ is just the distribution $\mathcal{A}_0(x, x)$, but shifted by ab.   □

For some intuition on this lemma, we emphasize that $\mathcal{A}_0$ completely re-randomizes the output that the adversary sees. In other words, on an input $(a \star x, b \star x)$ to $\mathcal{A}_0$, the adversary sees a CDH tuple $(x, (ga) \star x, (hb) \star x)$ for uniformly random group elements g and h. Then, $\mathcal{A}_0$ takes whatever set element

x' that the adversary returns and outputs $(gh)^{-1} \star x'$. Note that, even if the adversary could solve GA-DLog, it couldn't output a constant element: even if it can solve for (ga) and (hb), it information-theoretically doesn't know what a is (or g for that matter). For instance, if the adversary got $(x, c \star x, d \star x)$ and always tried to output $(cd)^{-1} \star z$ for some fixed set element z, A_0 wouldn't actually output a constant element: if $c = g$ and $d = h$, then A_0 would just output z (i.e. the case where $a = b = 1$), but if $c = ga$ and $d = hb$, then A_0 would output $(ab) \star z$, as the lemma states.

Using this "shift invariance" we can define $\mathcal{D}_w := \mathcal{D}_{w,x} = \mathcal{D}_{x,w} = \mathcal{D}_{y,z}$, if $\mathsf{CDH}(y, z) = w$. Lemma 2 shows that $\mathcal{D}_{y,z}$ outputs $\mathsf{CDH}(y, z)$ with probability ϵ. Thus, by running $\mathcal{A}_0$ many times, the right answer is almost certainly amongst the list of outputs. However, to amplify the success probability, we would need to know which element of the list of outputs is the correct answer; we cannot determine this yet.

3.2   Estimating ϵ

At this point, we deviate from the approach taken in [MZ22]. We will need to have a precise estimation of a lower bound for ϵ in our later algorithms; luckily, this is easy enough for us to compute. Although we need to use some statistical tests, our approach is straightforward: we just run $\mathcal{A}_0(x, x)$ "enough" times and keep track of how many times we get x as an output. We generate a (w.h.p.) lower bound for ϵ which we call $\epsilon_{\min}$.

Algorithm $\mathcal{A}_\epsilon(\lambda, \lambda')$ (Estimating ϵ).

- On input (security) parameters λ, λ' where λ' can be chosen linearly in the security parameter λ, do the following:
- Set $c = \lambda^2 \lambda'$.
- Set $T = 0, i = 0$.
- While $i < c$:
  - Run $x' \leftarrow \mathcal{A}_0(x, x)$.
  - If $x' == x$ then $i + +$.
  - $T + +$.
- Output $\epsilon_{\min} = \left(1 - \frac{1}{\lambda}\right) \frac{c}{T}$.

We next prove some bounds on our estimation of $\epsilon_{\min}$. We use a simple Chernoff bound.

Lemma 3.   *Let all parameters be defined as above. When $\lambda > 2$, except with probability that decays exponentially in λ', we have $\epsilon_{\min} < \epsilon$.*

Proof. We assume that $\epsilon T < c$, or otherwise our bound holds trivially. Note that

$$\Pr\left[\epsilon_{\min} \geq \epsilon\right] = \Pr\left[\left(1 - \frac{1}{\lambda}\right) \cdot \frac{c}{T} \geq \epsilon\right] = \Pr\left[c - \epsilon T \geq \frac{c}{\lambda}\right]$$

Using a Chernoff bound, we have

$$\Pr\left[c - \epsilon T \geq \eta \epsilon T\right] \leq e^{-\epsilon T \eta^2/2 + \eta}.$$

for any $\eta > 0$. Suppose we set $\eta \epsilon T = \frac{c}{\lambda}$ for our parameter λ. If we continue to assume that $\epsilon T < c$, we have $\eta \geq \frac{1}{\lambda}$. This gives us

$$\Pr\left[c - \epsilon T \geq \eta \epsilon T\right] \leq e^{-\epsilon T \eta^2/2 + \eta} \leq e^{-\frac{c}{\lambda} \cdot \frac{\eta}{\eta+2}} \leq e^{-\frac{c}{3\lambda^2}}.$$

Setting $c = \lambda^2 \lambda'$ makes this equation decay exponentially in λ', as desired. □

We can think of λ and λ' as essentially security parameters. We leave these undefined for now because we will need to make the error probability in our final algorithm dependent on the group size. We now prove an upper bound on ϵ.

Lemma 4. *Let all parameters be defined as above, and let $\lambda \geq 5$. Except with probability that decays exponentially in λ', we have $\epsilon < \left(1 + \frac{3}{\lambda}\right) \epsilon_{\min}$.*

Proof. When $\epsilon T \leq c$, the statement holds trivially if $\lambda \geq 2$. This is because $(1 + \frac{3}{\lambda})(1 - \frac{1}{\lambda}) > 1$ when $\lambda \geq 2$. Hence, we assume $\epsilon T > c$.

At this point, the result follows from another Chernoff bound. Note that

$$\Pr\left[\epsilon T - c \geq \eta \epsilon T\right] \leq e^{-\epsilon T \eta^2/2}.$$

for any $\eta \in (0,1)$. Recall that $\epsilon_{\min} = \left(1 - \frac{1}{\lambda}\right)\frac{c}{T}$, and therefore we have that $c = \frac{\epsilon_{\min} T}{1 - \frac{1}{\lambda}}$. If we take $\eta = \frac{2\lambda - 3}{\lambda^2 + 2\lambda - 3}$, then we have

$$\Pr\left[\epsilon T - c \geq \eta \epsilon T\right] = \Pr\left[\epsilon T - \frac{\epsilon_{\min} T}{1 - \frac{1}{\lambda}} \geq \frac{2\lambda - 3}{\lambda^2 + 2\lambda - 3} \epsilon T\right].$$

Some basic algebra gives us that

$$\Pr\left[\epsilon T - \frac{\epsilon_{\min} T}{1 - \frac{1}{\lambda}} \geq \frac{2\lambda - 3}{\lambda^2 + 2\lambda - 3} \epsilon T\right] = \Pr\left[\epsilon \geq \left(1 + \frac{3}{\lambda}\right)\epsilon_{\min}\right]$$

as desired. Thus, by taking $\eta = \frac{2\lambda-3}{\lambda^2+2\lambda-3}$, with the Chernoff bound, we have

$$\Pr\left[\epsilon \geq \left(1 + \frac{3}{\lambda}\right)\epsilon_{\min}\right] \leq e^{-\frac{T\epsilon\eta^2}{2}} \leq e^{-\frac{T\epsilon}{2\lambda^2}} \leq e^{-\frac{c}{2\lambda^2}},$$

where $\eta \in (0,1)$ and $\eta > 1/\lambda$ when $\lambda \geq 5$. Since $c = \lambda^2 \lambda'$, the statement holds except with probability $e^{-\frac{\lambda'}{2}}$. □

We can now easily determine the running time of $\mathcal{A}_\epsilon$.

Lemma 5. *Let all parameters be defined above, and let $\lambda \geq 5$. Algorithm $\mathcal{A}_\epsilon$ terminates in time $O\left(\frac{1}{\epsilon}\lambda^2\lambda'\right)$ with probability one minus a function exponentially decaying in λ'.*

Proof. This follows as an immediate corollary of Lemma 4. □

We now know that we can closely estimate ϵ, and we can find such an estimate ϵ_{min} efficiently.

3.3   Thresholding

We know from earlier that $A_0(x, x)$ outputs elements according to some "true" distribution $\mathcal{D}$, and that using different set elements instead of x only shifts this distribution. We know that, by assumption $A_0(x, x)$ outputs x with probability $\epsilon > \epsilon_{\min}$, which is a fact we will use extensively. Below, we formally define some properties of this distribution that will be useful to us for building an algorithm.

Let the distribution $\mathcal{D}$ be supported on $x_1, x_2, x_3, \ldots$ in $\mathcal{X}$ such that, writing $p_i = \Pr(x_i \leftarrow \mathcal{D})$ we have $p_1 \geq p_2 \geq p_3 \geq \cdots$. Then $p_1 \geq \epsilon$. The following result shows that fairly quickly there is a noticeable "gap" $p_i - p_{i+1}$ that we can use for thresholding. Since we don't exactly know ϵ (and thus, can't use it), we will write the lemmas below for $\epsilon_{\min}$, which we know is relatively close to ϵ.

Lemma 6.   *Let $p_i = \Pr(x_i \leftarrow \mathcal{D})$ be defined as above, so that $p_1 \geq \epsilon$ and $p_1 \geq p_2 \geq p_3 \geq \cdots$. Let $0 < \epsilon_{\min} \leq \epsilon$ be any real number. Let i_0 be the smallest integer such that $p_{i_0} > \epsilon_{\min}$ and $p_{i_0+1} \leq \epsilon_{\min}$. Let $\ell > 0$ be an integer such that ℓ is divisible by 2, and let $\delta \in (0, 1)$ be a real number. If $\ell\left(\epsilon_{\min} - \frac{\ell\delta}{2}\right) > 1$, then there is some integer $i < i_0 + \ell$ such that $p_i \leq \epsilon$ and $p_i - p_{i+1} \geq \delta$.*

Proof. Because the p_i are probabilies, we know that $\sum_{i=1}^{|G|} p_i = 1$. Let i_0 be the smallest integer such that $p_{i_0} > \epsilon_{\min}$ and $p_{i_0+1} \leq \epsilon_{\min}$. Hence $p_{i_0+1} \leq \epsilon$.

If $p_{i_0+1} < \epsilon_{\min} - \delta$ then, since there is some i such that $p_i = \epsilon$, it follows that $p_{i_0} \leq \epsilon$. The result holds in this case by taking $i = i_0$. Hence it suffices to consider the case $p_{i_0+1} \geq \epsilon_{\min} - \delta$. Suppose, for the purposes of contradiction, that for all i such that $i_0 < i < i_0 + \ell$ we have $p_i - p_{i+1} < \delta$.

We have

$$\sum_{i=1}^{i_0+\ell} p_i \leq 1.$$

Since we know that $p_{i_0} > \epsilon_{\min}$, as well as for all $i_0 < i < i_0 + \ell$, $p_i - p_{i+1} < \delta$, we have

$$\sum_{i=1}^{i_0+\ell} p_i > \sum_{i=1}^{i_0} \epsilon_{\min} + \sum_{k=1}^{\ell} p_{i_0+k} > i_0\epsilon_{\min} + \sum_{k=1}^{\ell} (\epsilon_{\min} - k\delta).$$

By the Gauss summation formula, this implies that

$$\sum_{i=1}^{i_0+\ell} p_i > i_0\epsilon_{\min} + \ell\left(\epsilon_{\min} - \frac{(\ell+1)\delta}{2}\right) = (\ell + i_0)\epsilon_{\min} - \ell(\ell+1)\delta/2.$$

However, we have assumed that $\ell\left(\epsilon_{\min} - \frac{\ell\delta}{2}\right) > 1$, which implies that $\sum_{i=1}^{\ell} p_i > 1$. This gives us the desired contradiction and completes the proof.   □

Concretely, one can verify that $\delta = \epsilon_{\min}^2/4$ and $\ell = 2\lceil 1/\epsilon_{\min}\rceil$ satisfy the equation $\ell\left(\epsilon_{\min} - \frac{\ell\delta}{2}\right) > 1$. Note also that for $\ell < 2/\epsilon_{\min}$ we have

$$\epsilon_{\min} - \ell\delta > \epsilon_{\min} - \frac{2}{\epsilon_{\min}}\frac{\epsilon_{\min}^2}{4} = \frac{\epsilon_{\min}}{2}.$$

Hence the hard case of thresholding is when there are p_i such that $\epsilon > p_i > \epsilon_{min}/2$. Since $i_0 \leq 1/\epsilon_{min}$, we have $i_0 + \ell \leq 3/\epsilon_{min} + 2$. Since $\epsilon < \epsilon_{min}(1 + 3/\lambda)$ we have

$$i_0 + \ell \leq 2 + 3/\epsilon_{min} < 2 + 3(1 + 3/\lambda)/\epsilon = O(1/\epsilon). \tag{1}$$

Remark 2. Note that the above result also applies if p_i are (good) estimations of the true probabilities from some empirical distribution based on a fixed number of samples, up to some (small) margin of error, of course. In practice, the bounds will largely be interchangeable with ϵ rather than ϵ_{min} (up to constant factors, assuming we picked λ and λ' large enough when finding ϵ_{min}). But in our algorithm below we will actually be working with the empirical estimate ϵ_{min} and estimates of the p_i.

3.4   Finding a Gap

Our intuition for how we find a gap is fairly simple: choose some security parameter λ, which will impact the failure probability of our simulation. Then, compute an estimated lower bound ϵ_{min} as we described in the previous subsection and set $\delta = \epsilon_{min}^2/4$. Then, we will query $\mathcal{A}_0(x, x)$ enough times so that, if there is a gap of size at least $\delta = \frac{\epsilon_{min}^2}{4}$ between two (estimated) probabilities p_i, p_{i+1}, there will be a noticeable difference in the number of x_i's and x_{i+1}'s that we see over all of the outputs. Then, by standard sampling theorems, if λ'' is large enough, the gap in sampled elements will be at least $k\lambda''$ for some constant k. We can use a similar analysis to show that, with high probability, we don't incorrectly find a small gap either (although we might not find the largest gap). The full algorithm and proof are below.

Algorithm $\mathcal{A}_I (\epsilon_{min}, \lambda'', \delta, T)$ (Gap-finding algorithm) On input a positive number λ'', which can be chosen linearly to the security parameter λ, and all previous parameters as previously stated. The algorithm $\mathcal{A}_I$ proceeds as follows:

- Initialize an empty database $\mathcal{D}$ consisting of tuples $(x \in \mathcal{X}, t \in \mathbb{Z})$ where $\mathcal{X}$ is the set and t is a nonnegative integer.
- For $(i = 0; i \leq T; i++)$:
  • Set $z_i = \mathcal{A}_0(x, x)$, where each z_i is a "fresh" call of $\mathcal{A}_0(x, x)$.
  • If z_i is the first entry in some tuple $(z_i, t) \in \mathcal{D}$, increment t by 1 in the tuple and update $\mathcal{D}$.
  • If z_i has not yet been added to $\mathcal{D}$, add the tuple $(z_i, 1)$ to $\mathcal{D}$.
- Sort (and relabel) the tuples in $\mathcal{D}$ in *decreasing order of t*, getting a database of tuples $(z_1, t_1), (z_2, t_2), \ldots$, such that, for all i, $t_i \geq t_{i+1}$.
- Find the smallest integer i such that $t_{i+1} \leq (\epsilon_{min} - \delta/2)T$ and $t_i - t_{i+1} \geq T\delta/2$ and output that i. If no such i exists then output $\perp$.

Proving that we find a gap. We next claim that the above algorithm outputs some i with high probability if λ'' is large enough. More precisely, we show that it outputs a gap close to the "best" with high probability, which is good enough for us.

First we need a basic lemma about how well our estimates t_i/T approximate the true values p_i, for values p_i in the worst case zone $\epsilon_{\min} \geq p_i > \epsilon_{\min}/2$ handled by Lemma 6.

Lemma 7. *Let $\epsilon_{\min} \leq \epsilon$ and $\delta = \epsilon_{\min}^2/4$. Let $T = \lambda'' \left(\frac{3072}{\epsilon_{\min}^3} \right)$ for some λ''. Let i be an integer, t_i be the number of times element x is sampled in an experiment where x is sampled T times independently with probability p_i. We have*

1. *If $\epsilon_{\min} \geq p_i$, then $t_i/T - p_i < \delta/8$ holds except for the probability that decays exponentially in λ''.*
2. *Moreover, if $\epsilon_{\min} \geq p_i \geq \epsilon_{\min}/2$, then $|t_i/T - p_i| \leq \delta/8$ with probability that decays exponentially in λ''.*

Proof. Firstly, since

$$\Pr\left[t_i/T - p_i \geq \frac{\delta}{8} \right] = \Pr\left[t_i - p_iT \geq \frac{\delta}{8}T \right] = \Pr\left[t_i - p_iT \geq \left(\frac{\epsilon_{\min}^2}{32p_i} \right) p_iT \right],$$

by taking $\eta = \frac{\epsilon_{\min}^2}{32p_i} \geq 0$ for the Chernoff bound, we have

$$\Pr\left[t_i/T - p_i \geq \frac{\delta}{8} \right] \leq e^{-p_iT\eta^2 \frac{1}{2+\eta}}$$

$$= e^{-T \cdot \frac{p_i \cdot \epsilon_{\min}^4}{1024 \cdot p_i^2} \cdot \frac{1}{2+\eta}}$$

$$= e^{-\frac{T \cdot \epsilon_{\min}^3}{1024} \cdot \frac{\epsilon_{\min}}{p_i} \cdot \frac{1}{2+\eta}}$$

$$= e^{-3\lambda'' \cdot \frac{\epsilon_{\min}}{p_i} \cdot \frac{1}{2+\eta}}$$

$$= e^{-3\lambda'' \cdot \frac{\epsilon_{\min}}{p_i} \cdot \frac{32p_i}{64p_i + \epsilon_{\min}^2}}$$

$$\leq e^{-3\lambda'' \cdot \frac{32\epsilon_{\min}}{64\epsilon_{\min} + \epsilon_{\min}^2}}$$

$$\leq e^{-3\lambda'' \cdot \frac{32}{65}}$$

$$\leq e^{-\lambda''}.$$

Similarly, we have

$$\Pr\left[|t_i/T - p_i| \geq \frac{\delta}{8} \right] = \Pr\left[|t_i - p_iT| \geq \frac{\delta}{8}T \right] = \Pr\left[|t_i - p_iT| \geq \left(\frac{\delta}{8p_i} \right) p_iT \right].$$

Since $\epsilon_{\min} \geq p_i \geq \epsilon_{\min}/2$ we have $1 \leq \epsilon_{\min}/p_i \leq 2$, so

$$\Pr\left[|t_i - p_iT| \geq \left(\frac{\delta}{8p_i} \right) p_iT \right] \leq \Pr\left[|t_i - p_iT| \geq \left(\frac{\epsilon_{\min}}{32} \right) p_iT \right]$$

By the Chernoff bound, with $\eta = \epsilon_{min}/32 \in (0,1)$, this is bounded by

$$2e^{-p_i T\eta^2/3} \leq 2e^{-(\epsilon_{min}/2)T(\epsilon_{min}/32)^2/3} = 2e^{-\lambda''/2}$$

which proves the result. $\square$

Lemma 8. *Consider all parameters as previously stated. Consider the smallest choice of i such that $p_i - p_{i+1} \geq \delta = \frac{\epsilon_{min}^2}{4}$ and $p_i \leq \epsilon_{min}$. It is the case that algorithm $\mathcal{A}_I$ outputs some integer less than or equal to i with probability that decays exponentially in λ''.*

Proof. Let i be the index from Lemma 6, so that $p_i \leq \epsilon$ and $p_i - p_{i+1} \geq \delta$. It follows that $p_i \geq \epsilon_{min}/2$ and $\epsilon - \delta \geq p_{i+1} \geq \epsilon_{min}/2 - \delta$. By Lemma 7 (Item 2) we have $|t_i/T - p_i| < \delta/8$.

Since $\epsilon_{min} \geq p_i > p_{i+1}$, by Lemma 7 (Item 1) we have $t_{i+1}/T - p_{i+1} < \delta/8$. (Recall that p_{i+1} might not less than $\epsilon_{min}/2$.) It follows that

$$t_i/T - t_{i+1}/T > (p_i - \delta/8) - (p_{i+1} + \delta/8) = (p_i - p_{i+1}) - \delta/4 > \delta/2.$$

This proves the result. $\square$

Lemma 9. *Consider all parameters as previously stated. Let I be the output of algorithm $\mathcal{A}_I$. The probability that $p_I - p_{I+1} \leq \delta/4 = \frac{\epsilon_{min}^2}{16}$ is a function that decays exponentially in λ''.*

Proof. Suppose $p_I - p_{I+1} \leq \delta/4$ for the purpose of contradiction. Then we claim that $t_I - t_{I+1} \geq T\delta/2$ holds with a negligible chance.

Since $\epsilon_{min} \geq p_I \geq \epsilon_{min}/2$, we have $p_{I+1} \geq p_I - \delta/4$ where $\delta = \epsilon_{min}^2/4$. Since $\epsilon_{min}/4 \geq \epsilon_{min}^2/16$ always holds, we have $p_{I+1} \geq \epsilon_{min}/4$.

Similar to the proof of Lemma 7, write

$$\Pr\left[|t_{I+1}/T - p_{I+1}| \geq \frac{\delta}{8}\right] = \Pr\left[|t_{I+1} - p_{I+1}T| \geq \frac{\delta}{8}T\right]$$

$$= \Pr\left[|t_{I+1} - p_{I+1}T| \geq \left(\frac{\delta}{8p_{I+1}}\right)p_{I+1}T\right].$$

Since $\epsilon_{min} \geq p_{I+1} \geq \epsilon_{min}/4$ we have $1 \leq \epsilon_{min}/p_{I+1} \leq 4$, so

$$\Pr\left[|t_{I+1} - p_{I+1}T| \geq \left(\frac{\delta}{8p_{I+1}}\right)p_{I+1}T\right] \leq \Pr\left[|t_{I+1} - p_{I+1}T| \geq \left(\frac{\epsilon_{min}}{32}\right)p_{I+1}T\right]$$

By the Chernoff bound, with $\eta = \epsilon_{min}/32 \in (0,1)$, this is bounded by

$$2e^{-p_{I+1}T\eta^2/3} \leq 2e^{-(\epsilon_{min}/4)T(\epsilon_{min}/32)^2/3} = 2e^{-\lambda''/4}.$$

Hence, $|t_{I+1}/T - p_{I+1}| < \frac{\delta}{8}$ with an overwhelming chance. By applying Lemma 7 (Item 2) to the term of index I, we have $|t_I/T - p_I| < \frac{\delta}{8}$ with an overwhelming chance. By combining together, we have $t_I/T - t_{I+1}/T < \delta/4 + p_I - p_{I+1} < \delta/2$ except for a probability that decays exponentially in λ''. That is, $t_I - t_{I+1} \geq T\delta/2$ holds only with a negligible chance, which proves the result. $\square$

To conclude, algorithm $\mathcal{A}_I$ runs in time proportional to $1/\epsilon^3$ and outputs an index $I = O(1/\epsilon)$ such that $p_I \leq \epsilon$ and $p_I - p_{I+1} > \delta/4$.

3.5   Using the Fixed Set of Elements

From the previous section, we know that there will be some index $I \leq \frac{2}{\epsilon_{min}}$ such that we can efficiently find (in time proportional to $\frac{\lambda}{\epsilon_{min}^3}$), for some λ'' independent[2] of ϵ_{min}, the set of elements $x_1, \ldots, x_I$ that appear with highest probability. Note that this set is invariant across calls to different inputs to $\mathcal{A}_0$, and we will exploit this in our algorithms.

Algorithm $\mathcal{A}_1 (y, z, I, T)$ (Algorithm to find heavy elements)

- Initialize an empty database $\mathcal{D}$ consisting of tuples $(x, t) \in \mathcal{X} \times \mathbb{Z}$ where $\mathcal{X}$ is the set and t is a nonnegative integer.
- For $(i = 0; i \leq T; i++)$:
  - Set $z_i = \mathcal{A}_0 (y, z)$, where each z_i is a "fresh" call of $\mathcal{A}_0 (y, z)$.
  - If z_i is the first entry in some tuple $(z_i, t) \in \mathcal{D}$, increment t by 1 in the tuple and update $\mathcal{D}$.
  - If z_i has not yet been added to $\mathcal{D}$, add the tuple $(z_i, 1)$ to $\mathcal{D}$.
- Sort (and relabel) the tuples in $\mathcal{D}$ in *decreasing order of t*, getting a database of tuples $(z_1, t_1), (z_2, t_2), \ldots$, such that, for all i, $t_i \geq t_{i+1}$.
- Return the set $\{z_1, ..., z_I\}$.

The following lemma shows that if $T = \lambda'' \left(\frac{3072}{\epsilon_{min}^3} \right)$ then with overwhelming probability Algorithm $\mathcal{A}_1$ does output the I elements that are heaviest, in the sense that the corresponding probabilities p_i are the highest.

Lemma 10.   *Consider all parameters as previously stated. Let $T = \lambda'' \left(\frac{3072}{\epsilon_{min}^3} \right)$ for some λ''. Then algorithm $\mathcal{A}_1$ outputs the I heaviest elements in the distribution except with probability that decays exponentially in λ''.*

Proof. From Lemma 9 we have $p_I - p_{I+1} > \delta/4$. Algorithm $\mathcal{A}_I$ ensures $t_{I+1} \leq (\epsilon_{min} - \delta/2)T$. Hence, $p_{I+1} < \epsilon_{min} - \delta/4$. It suffices to show that the heaviest I elements all appear with frequency strictly larger than $(p_{I+1} + \delta/8)T$ and that the remaining elements all appear with frequency strictly smaller than $(p_{I+1} + \delta/8)T$. Note that $p_{I+1} + \delta/4 < \epsilon_{min}$.

If $p_i \geq \epsilon \geq \epsilon_{min} > p_{I+1} + \delta/4$ then

$$\Pr\left[t_i > (p_{I+1} + \delta/8)T\right] = \Pr\left[t_i > (p_i - (p_i - (p_{I+1} + \delta/8)))T\right]$$
$$= \Pr\left[t_i - p_iT > -(1 - (p_{I+1} + \delta/8)/p_i)p_iT\right].$$

The Chernoff bound with $\eta = 1 - (p_{I+1} + \delta/8)/p_i \in (0, 1)$ shows this holds with an overwhelming chance. That is,

$$\Pr\left[t_i - p_iT \leq -(1 - (p_{I+1} + \delta/8)/p_i)p_iT\right] \leq e^{-\frac{\eta^2 p_i T}{2}}.$$

The next case is $i \leq I$ where $p_I < \epsilon_{min}$. We apply the union bound to the $O(1/\epsilon_{min})$ values of i in this case. Note that $\epsilon > p_i > \epsilon_{min}/2$ in this case, so we

---

[2] λ'' may be dependent on $\log |G|$.

can apply Lemma 7. Hence, $|t_i/T - p_i| \le \delta/8$ with overwhelming probability. $t_i/T \le p_i + \delta/8$. It follows that for $i \le I$ we have $t_i/T \ge p_i - \delta/8$, and then $t_i \ge Tp_{i+1} + T\delta/8$ with an overwhelming chance.

Finally, we need to handle the case when $i > I$ (so $p_i \le p_{I+1}$). For any specific i then the Chernoff bound shows that t_i does not exceed $(p_{I+1} + \delta/8)T$ except with probability that decays exponentially in λ''. But since there are exponentially many such i we need to argue that, for all $j \le I$ and all $k > I$, the probability that $\mathcal{A}_1$ outputs any z_j fewer times than any z_k decays exponentially in λ''.

To handle this, suppose we group each of the z_k's (recall $k > I$) into sets $\tilde{z}_1, \tilde{z}_2, \ldots$ in the following way: starting with z_{I+1}, add set elements in increasing order to the set $\tilde{z}_1$ as long as the total sum of probabilities of elements in the set is less than p_I. Once $\tilde{z}_1$ is "full", continue this process with the "unused" set elements in increasing order until $\tilde{z}_2$ is "full", and then continue this process until all of the set elements z_k have been placed in a set $\tilde{z}_{k'}$. We note that such a process may not be efficient, but we do not need it to be.

Since the p_i are decreasing, it follows that the probability mass of each set $\tilde{z}_{k'}$ (except perhaps the last one) is at least $p_I/2$. Hence there are a maximum of $\frac{2}{p_I}$ sets $\tilde{z}_{k'}$, or otherwise the sum $\sum_{k=i}^{\infty} p_k > 1$, which is a contradiction. Moreover, note that the probability that some z_k is output more than some z_j is less than the probability that elements in the set $\tilde{z}_{k'}$ containing z_k are output more than the z_j.

Therefore, the probability that $\mathcal{A}_1$ does not output the I heaviest elements is at most $I\frac{2}{p_I}$ multiplied by the probability that $\mathcal{A}_1$ outputs z_{I+1} more than z_I. Since I and p_I are independent of λ'', the statement claimed in the lemma holds.   □

Consider the following algorithm, where all parameters are as previously stated. We assume as inputs a CDH challenge $(y, z) = (a \star x, b \star x)$ and all relevant parameters.

Algorithm $\mathcal{A}_2(y, z, I, T)$ (Pruning)

_____

– Run the algorithm $\mathcal{A}_1(y, z, I, T)$ from the previous section with oracle calls $\mathcal{A}_0(y, z)$ to get a set of elements $\mathcal{S} = \{z_1, \ldots, z_I\}$. Record all of these.
– Create a list L of set elements intialized to be empty.
– For each $j \in [1, I]$:
  • Run the algorithm $\mathcal{A}_1(x, z_j, I, T)$ getting a set of elements $\mathcal{S}_j$.
  • If $\mathcal{S}_j = \mathcal{S}$ then add z_j to L.
  Output L.

We next prove a lemma about the running time of this algorithm.

Lemma 11.   *Algorithm $\mathcal{A}_2$ runs in time $O\left(\frac{1}{\epsilon_{\min}^4}\right)$ in $\epsilon_{\min}$ and in time polynomial in all other factors.*

Proof. Since $I \leq \frac{c}{\epsilon_{min}}$ for some constant c, and this algorithm makes I calls to our previous algorithm, it has running time $O\left(\frac{1}{\epsilon_{min}^4}\right)$, ignorning the λ'' factors, which are technically independent of ϵ_{min} (i.e. λ must be proportional to something in $\log|G|$). $\qquad\square$

In the next section we show that L consists of either a single element $(ab) \star x$ or else there is a subgroup H such that $L = \{(hab) \star x : h \in H\}$.

3.6 Proof of Finding the Subgroup

Let $S = \mathcal{A}_1(x,x)$ be the set of heavy elements output by the gap-finding algorithm on instance x. We have $x \in S$ with overwhelming probability. For $w \in \mathcal{X}$ let $S_w = \mathcal{A}_1(x,w)$. Let $L = \mathcal{A}_2(x,x)$ be the list (a subset of S) output by the pruning algorithm. We know that if $x \in L$ then $x \in S$. For $w \in \mathcal{X}$ let $L_w = \mathcal{A}_2(x,w)$.

For any set $S = \{x_1, \ldots, x_I\}$ and $g \in G$ define $g \star S = \{g \star x_1, \ldots, g \star x_I\}$. Ditto for $g \star L$. From lemma 2, we know that $\mathcal{A}_0(x, g \star x) = g \star \mathcal{A}_0(x,x)$.

Lemma 12. *Let notation be as above. The following properties hold:*

1. $S_{g \star x} = g \star S$.
2. $\mathcal{A}_1(x, g \star x) = g \star \mathcal{A}_1(x,x)$.
3. $L_{g \star x} = g \star L$.
4. $\mathcal{A}_2(x, g \star x) = g \star \mathcal{A}_2(x,x)$.

Proof. To prove the first item, note that $S_{g \star x}$ is the set of thresholded outputs of $\mathcal{A}_0(x, g \star x)$. But $\mathcal{A}_0(x, g \star x) = g \star \mathcal{A}_0(x,x)$. So $S_{g \star x} = g \star S$.

The second part is immediate, since $\mathcal{A}_1(x, g \star x) = S_{g \star x} = g \star S = g \star \mathcal{A}_1(x,x)$.

Finally,

$$
\begin{aligned}
L_{g \star x} &= \{w \in S_{g \star x} : \mathcal{A}_1(x,w) = \mathcal{A}_1(x, g \star x)\} \\
&= \{w \in S_{g \star x} : \mathcal{A}_1(x,w) = g \star \mathcal{A}_1(x,x)\} \\
&= \{w \in S_{g \star x} : g \star \mathcal{A}_1(x, g^{-1} \star w) = g \star \mathcal{A}_1(x,x)\} \\
&= \{w \in g \star S : \mathcal{A}_1(x, g^{-1} \star w) = S\}.
\end{aligned}
$$

Hence $L_{g \star x} = g \star L$. The fourth part, in a similar argument to the second part, is immediate since $\mathcal{A}_2(x, g \star x) = L_{g \star x} = g \star L = g \star \mathcal{A}_2(x,x)$. $\qquad\square$

Now we let $H = \{g \in G : g \star x \in L\}$ and we show H is a subgroup. For a set S we define $H \star S = \{h \star w : h \in H, w \in S\}$.

Corollary 1. *Let notation be as above and assume $x \in L$. Let $H = \{g \in G : g \star x \in L\}$. Then H is a subgroup of G and $H \star L = L$. Finally $|H| = |L| \leq |S| = O(1/\epsilon_{min})$.*

Proof. Since our group action is regular, we can define $H = \{g \in G : g \star x \in L\}$. Since $x \in L$ we have $1 \in H$ and H is non-empty.

Let $w \in L$ and let $g \in H$ be such that $w = g\star x$. Recall that $L = \mathcal{A}_2(x, x)$ and $\mathcal{A}_2$ takes as input the set $\mathcal{S}$. It then computes all $w \in \mathcal{S}$ such that $\mathcal{A}_1(x, w) = \mathcal{S}$.

By definition of L, we have $L = \mathcal{A}_2(x, x)$. Note that, for any $w \in L$, we have $\mathcal{A}_1(x, w) = \mathcal{A}_1(x, x)$ by definition, and thus we immediately see that $\mathcal{A}_2(x, w) = \mathcal{A}_2(x, x)$, since we will prune identically in both cases. Finally, we have

$$\mathcal{A}_2(x, w) = \mathcal{A}_2(x, g \star x) = g \star \mathcal{A}_2(x, x) = g \star L$$

Hence $g \star L = L$. It follows that $H * L = L$.

(As an aside, going back to $g \star L = L$, by induction we have $g^n \star L = L$ for all integers n. Hence the order of g is at most $|L|$.)

Finally, let $g_1, g_2 \in H$. By definition of $\mathcal{A}_2$, this means $\mathcal{A}_2(x, g_1 \star x) = \mathcal{A}_2(x, g_2 \star x)$. But this implies $g_1 \star L = \mathfrak{g}_2 \star L =:$. Then $\mathcal{A}_2(x, (g_1 g_2)x) = g_1 \star \mathcal{A}_2(x, g_2 \star x) = g_1 \star L = L$. Hence, $g_1 g_2 \in H$. □

The outcome of all this is that L is a coset of a subgroup H of G. Just like in [MZ22], we can output a complete subgroup H in which our solution is guaranteed to lie.

3.7 Putting It All Together

We are now in a position to state an overall algorithm. We are given a group action $(G, \mathcal{X}, \star)$, a fixed x, and an oracle $\mathcal{A}$. First, we do several precomputations: We run Algorithm $\mathcal{A}_\epsilon$ to compute $\epsilon_{\min}$, and then Algorithm $\mathcal{A}_I$ to compute I, and finally we use Algorithm $\mathcal{A}_2$ to compute the list L and hence the subgroup H. The cost of the precomputation is $O\left(\frac{\lambda^2 \lambda'}{\epsilon} + \frac{\lambda''}{\epsilon^4}\right)$, assuming $\lambda > 5$.

When provided with a GA-CDH challenge (x, y, z) we run $\mathcal{A}_2(y, z, I, T)$, which does the pruning to $\mathcal{S}$ and outputs L, which is a coset with respect to a subgroup H.

Lemma 13. *The probability that $\mathcal{A}_2$ does not output a correct L (meaning that L is a complete coset of a subgroup G/H for some subgroup H) decays exponentially in λ, λ', and λ'' assuming $\lambda > 5$.*

Proof. This follows from Lemmas 3, 4 8, 9, 10, and Corollary 1. □

This essentially allows us to minimize our error exponentially by only growing λ' and λ'' linearly.

3.8 Using the Subgroup

At this point, we can go back to the template of [MZ22]. Once we have the appropriate set L, we just need to follow their approach for finishing the overall algorithm. We mirror both their techniques and presentation in this subsection. While we could just cite their results, we present them here for the sake of completeness and point out the text here is only slightly modified from their work.

Removing Superfluous Information. We will next want to run quantum period-finding algorithms which make queries to $\mathcal{A}_2$ on superpositions of inputs. These algorithms, however, assume $\mathcal{A}_2$ is a function. Unfortunately, our algorithm generates significant side information, namely all the intermediate computations used to arrive at the final answer. Fortunately, since our algorithm outputs a single answer with overwhelming probability, we can use the standard trick of purifying the execution of $\mathcal{A}_2$ and then un-computing all the intermediate values. The result is that $\mathcal{A}_2$ is negligibly close to behaving as the function mapping $(y, z) \mapsto H \star \mathsf{CDH}(y, z)$. From now on, we will therefore assume that $\mathcal{A}_2$ is such a function.

Computing H. Given algorithm $\mathcal{A}_2$, we can compute the subgroup H using quantum period-finding [BL95]. Concretely, the function $a \mapsto \mathcal{A}_2(a \star x, x)$ will output $(aH) \star x$, which is periodic with set of periods H. Therefore, applying quantum period finding to the procedure $a \mapsto \mathcal{A}_2(a \star x, x)$ will recover H. This will make $O(\log |G|)$ calls to $\mathcal{A}_2(a \star x, x)$.

Solving DLog in G/H. Notice that $\mathcal{A}_2$ is a (near) perfect CDH-solver, just in the group action corresponding to G/H. Concretely, the group G/H acts on the set $X/H := \{H \star y : y \in X\}$ in the obvious way; the distinguished element of X/H is $H \star x$. Our algorithm $\mathcal{A}_2$ gives a perfect CDH algorithm for this group action: we compute $\mathsf{CDH}(H \star y, H \star z)$ as $\mathcal{A}_2(y', z')$ for an arbitrary $y' \in H \star y, z' \in H \star z$.

We apply Galbraith et al. [GPSV21] to our CDH adversary for $(G/H, X/H)$ to obtain a DLog adversary $\mathcal{B}(gH \star x)$ which computes gH. For completeness, we sketch the idea: Let $\mathbf{a}$ be a set of generators for G/H. Since G is abelian, we can write any g as $\mathbf{a}^{\mathbf{v}}$ for some vector $\mathbf{v} \in \mathbb{Z}_{n_1} \times \cdots \times \mathbb{Z}_{n_k}$ where n_i is the period of a_i. We assume the n_i are fully reduced, so that the choice of $\mathbf{v}$ is unique. Shor's algorithm is used in this step, and we note that Shor's algorithm will not necessarily work if G is not abelian and our group action is not regular, which is why we need this restriction.

The CDH oracle allows, given $h \star (H \star x)$, to compute $h^y \star (H \star x)$ in $O(\log y)$ steps using repeated squaring. Given a DLog instance $g \star (H \star x) = \mathbf{a}^{\mathbf{v}} \star (H \star x)$, we define the function $(\mathbf{x}, y) \mapsto \mathbf{a}^{\mathbf{x}+y\mathbf{v}} \star (H \star x)$, which can be computed using the CDH oracle[3]. Then this function is periodic with period $(\mathbf{v}, -1)$. Running quantum period-finding therefore gives $\mathbf{v}$, which can be used to compute h.

Solving DLog in G We now have an algorithm which solves, with overwhelming probability, DLog in G/H. We now turn this into a full DLog adversary, which works as follows:

- Given $y = c \star x$, first apply the DLog adversary for G/H, which outputs cH.
- For each $a \in cH$ (which is polynomial sized), test if $y = a \star x$. We output the unique such a.

Overall, assuming ϵ is small relative to $\log |G|$, the running time of the algorithm is dominated by the cost of running $\mathcal{A}_2$.

---

[3] The original paper [GPSV21] needed to solve close vector problems in the relation lattice, but Wesolowski [Wes22] (proof of Theorem 3) has shown that one can bypass this by using the CDH oracle.

3.9 Extending to Non-regular Group Actions

We also borrow the text in this section almost verbatim from [MZ22] for the sake of completeness. The above assumed a regular group action, which captures all the cryptographic abelian group actions currently known. Here, we briefly sketch how to extend to an arbitrary abelian group action. The idea is that, within any ablelian group action, we can pull out a regular group action, and then apply the reduction above.

Concretely, we first consider restricting $(G, X, \star)$ to the orbit of x under G, namely $G \star x$. Let $S \subseteq G$ the the set of a that "stabilizes" x, namely $a \star x = x$. Then S is a subgroup. Moreover, for any $y \in G \star x$, the set of a that stabilize y is also exactly S.

The first step is to compute the (representation of the) subgroup S. Let $f : G \to X$ be defined as $f(a) = a \star x$. Then f is an instance of the abelian hidden subgroup problem with hidden subgroup exactly S. Therefore, we can find S using Shor's quantum algorithm.

Then we can define the new group action $(G/S, G \star x, \star)$, which is a regular abelian group action. CDH in this group action is identical to CDH in the original group action, in that a CDH adversary for one is also a CDH adversary for the other. We can also solve DLog in $(G, X, \star)$ by solving DLog in $(G/S, G \star x, \star)$, and then lifting $a \in G/S$ to $a' = (a, g) \in G$ for an arbitrary $g \in S$.

The main challenge is that our CDH adversary $\mathcal{A}$ may not always output elements in $G \star x$, and it may be infeasible to tell when it outputs an element in $G \star x$ versus a different orbit. Nevertheless, the same reduction as used above applies, and the analysis can be extended straightforwardly but tediously to handle the fact that $\mathcal{A}$ may output elements in different orbits. The rough idea is that S outputted by $\mathcal{A}_1$ may have pieces from elements from different orbits. But $S \cap G \star x$ is still going to contain a solution, and elements in different cosets will be pruned since they are inherently unreachable. This is enough to ensure that we obtain a near-perfect CDH algorithm on $(G/S)/H$.

Acknowledgements. We thank the anonymous reviewers and Benjamin Wesolowski for comments and suggestions. Galbraith and Lai thank the New Zealand Ministry for Business and Employment for financial support. Yi-Fu Lai is also supported by the European Union (ERC AdG REWORC - 101054911).

References

ADMP20. Alamati, N., De Feo, L., Montgomery, H., Patranabis, S.: Cryptographic group actions and applications. In: Moriai, S., Wang, H. (eds.) ASIACRYPT 2020. LNCS, vol. 12492, pp. 411–439. Springer, Cham (2020). https://doi.org/10.1007/978-3-030-64834-3_14

AEK+22. Abdalla, M., Eisenhofer, T., Kiltz, E., Kunzweiler, S., Riepel, D.: Password-authenticated key exchange from group actions. In: Lecture Notes in Computer Science, pp. 699–728, Santa Barbara, CA, USA. Springer, Heidelberg, Germany (2022). https://doi.org/10.1007/978-3-031-15979-4_24

BDK+22. Beullens, W., Dobson, S., Katsumata, S., Lai, Y.F., Pintore, F.: Group signatures and more from isogenies and lattices: generic, simple, and efficient. In: Lecture Notes in Computer Science, pp. 95–126. Springer, Heidelberg, Germany (2022). https://doi.org/10.1007/978-3-031-07085-3_4

BKP20. Beullens, W., Katsumata, S., Pintore, F.: Calamari and Falafl: logarithmic (linkable) ring signatures from Isogenies and Lattices. In: Moriai, S., Wang, H. (eds.) ASIACRYPT 2020. LNCS, vol. 12492, pp. 464–492. Springer, Cham (2020). https://doi.org/10.1007/978-3-030-64834-3_16

BKV19. Beullens, W., Kleinjung, T., Vercauteren, F.: CSI-FiSh: efficient isogeny based signatures through class group computations. In: Galbraith, S.D., Moriai, S. (eds.) ASIACRYPT 2019. LNCS, vol. 11921, pp. 227–247. Springer, Cham (2019). https://doi.org/10.1007/978-3-030-34578-5_9

BL95. Boneh, D., Lipton, R.J.: Quantum cryptanalysis of hidden linear functions. In: Coppersmith, D. (ed.) CRYPTO 1995. LNCS, vol. 963, pp. 424–437. Springer, Heidelberg (1995). https://doi.org/10.1007/3-540-44750-4_34

BMM+23. Badrinarayanan, S., Masny, D., Mukherjee, P., Patranabis, S., Raghuraman, S., Sarkar, P.: Round-optimal oblivious transfer and MPC from computational CSIDH. In: Lecture Notes in Computer Science, pp. 376–405. Springer, Heidelberg, Germany (2023). https://doi.org/10.1007/978-3-031-31368-4_14

BMZ19. Bartusek, J., Ma, F., Zhandry, M.: The distinction between fixed and random generators in group-based assumptions. In: Boldyreva, A., Micciancio, D. (eds.) CRYPTO 2019. LNCS, vol. 11693, pp. 801–830. Springer, Cham (2019). https://doi.org/10.1007/978-3-030-26951-7_27

BY91. Brassard, G., Yung, M.: One-Way group actions. In: Menezes, A.J., Vanstone, S.A. (eds.) CRYPTO 1990. LNCS, vol. 537, pp. 94–107. Springer, Heidelberg (1991). https://doi.org/10.1007/3-540-38424-3_7

CLM+18. Castryck, W., Lange, T., Martindale, C., Panny, L., Renes, J.: CSIDH: an efficient post-quantum commutative group action. In: Peyrin, T., Galbraith, S. (eds.) ASIACRYPT 2018. LNCS, vol. 11274, pp. 395–427. Springer, Cham (2018). https://doi.org/10.1007/978-3-030-03332-3_15

Cou06. Couveignes, J.M.: Hard homogeneous spaces. Cryptology ePrint Archive, Report 2006/291 (2006). https://eprint.iacr.org/2006/291

DG19. De Feo, L., Galbraith, S.D.: SeaSign: compact Isogeny signatures from class group actions. In: Ishai, Y., Rijmen, V. (eds.) EUROCRYPT 2019. LNCS, vol. 11478, pp. 759–789. Springer, Cham (2019). https://doi.org/10.1007/978-3-030-17659-4_26

DM20. De Feo, L., Meyer, M.: Threshold schemes from Isogeny assumptions. In: Kiayias, A., Kohlweiss, M., Wallden, P., Zikas, V. (eds.) PKC 2020. LNCS, vol. 12111, pp. 187–212. Springer, Cham (2020). https://doi.org/10.1007/978-3-030-45388-6_7

EKP20. El Kaafarani, A., Katsumata, S., Pintore, F.: Lossy CSI-FiSh: efficient signature scheme with tight reduction to decisional CSIDH-512. In: Kiayias, A., Kohlweiss, M., Wallden, P., Zikas, V. (eds.) PKC 2020. LNCS, vol. 12111, pp. 157–186. Springer, Cham (2020). https://doi.org/10.1007/978-3-030-45388-6_6

FFK+23. De Feo, L., et al.: SCALLOP: scaling the CSI-FiSh. In: Boldyreva, A., Kolesnikov, V., editors, PKC 2023, vol. 13940 of Lecture Notes in Computer Science, pp. 345–375. Springer (2023). https://doi.org/10.1007/978-3-031-31368-4_13

GPSV21. Galbraith, S., Panny, L., Smith, B., Vercauteren, F.: Quantum equivalence of the DLP and CDHP for group actions. Math. Cryptol. **1**(1), 40–44 (2021)

KLLQ23. Katsumata, S., Lai, Y.F., LeGrow, J.T., Qin, L.: CSI -otter: isogeny-based (partially) blind signatures from the class group action with a twist. In: Lecture Notes in Computer Science, pp. 729–761, Santa Barbara, CA, USA. Springer, Heidelberg, Germany (2023). https://doi.org/10.1007/978-3-031-38548-3_24

LGD21. Lai, Y.-F., Galbraith, S.D., Delpech de Saint Guilhem, C.: Compact, efficient and UC-secure isogeny-based oblivious transfer. In: Lecture Notes in Computer Science, pp. 213–241. Springer, Heidelberg, Germany (2021). https://doi.org/10.1007/978-3-030-77870-5_8

MZ22. Montgomery, H., Zhandry, M.: Full quantum equivalence of group action DLog and CDH, and more. In: Lecture Notes in Computer Science, pp. 3–32. Springer, Heidelberg, Germany (2022). https://doi.org/10.1007/978-3-031-22963-3_1

PR23. Page, A., Robert, D.: Introducing Clapoti(s): evaluating the isogeny class group action in polynomial time. IACR Cryptol. ePrint Arch. 2023/1766 (2023)

Sho94. Shor, P.W.: Algorithms for quantum computation: discrete logarithms and factoring. In: 35th Annual Symposium on Foundations of Computer Science, pp. 124–134, Santa Fe, NM, USA, November 20–22 (1994). IEEE Computer Society Press

Wes22. Wesolowski, B.: Orientations and the supersingular endomorphism ring problem. In: Lecture Notes in Computer Science, pp. 345–371. Springer, Heidelberg, Germany (2022). https://doi.org/10.1007/978-3-031-07082-2_13

R3PO: Reach-Restricted Reactive Program Obfuscation and Its Applications

Kaartik Bhushan[1]([⊠]), Sai Lakshmi Bhavana Obbattu[2], Manoj Prabhakaran[1], and Rajeev Raghunath[1]

[1] IIT Bombay, Mumbai, Mumbai, India
{kbhushan,mp,mrrajeev}@cse.iitb.ac.in
[2] IIT (BHU) Varanasi, Varanasi, India

Abstract. In recent breakthrough results, novel use of grabled circuits yielded constructions for several primitives like Identity-Based Encryption (IBE) and 2-round secure multi-party computation, based on standard assumptions in public-key cryptography. While the techniques in these different results have many common elements, these works did not offer a modular abstraction that could be used across them.

Our main contribution is to introduce a novel notion of obfuscation, called Reach-Restricted Reactive-Program Obfuscation (R3PO) that captures the essence of these constructions, and exposes additional capabilities. We provide a powerful composition theorem whose proof fully encapsulates the use of garbled circuits in these works.

As an illustration of the potential of R3PO, and as an important contribution of independent interest, we present a variant of Multi-Authority Attribute-Based Encryption (MA-ABE) that can be based on (single-authority) CP-ABE in a blackbox manner, using only standard cryptographic assumptions (e.g., DDH) in addition. This is in stark contrast to the existing constructions for MA-ABE, which rely on the random oracle model and supports only limited policy classes.

1 Introduction

Consider the following approach to Identity-Based Encryption (IBE):

- The master key pair is a verification/signing key pair for a signature scheme.
- The decryption key for an identity is simply a signature on the identity.
- The ciphertext is an *obfuscation* of the following program: it checks if its input is a valid signature on a target identity, and if so, it outputs the message.

With the right notion of obfuscation, as we shall see, *this construction indeed translates to a secure IBE scheme!* Further, such an obfuscation can be instantiated using standard cryptographic assumptions like DDH, based on the tools in [19, 20].

The motivation of this work comes from the breakthrough results of [6, 16, 20, 27]. These results were surprising not only because of the end results, but

© International Association for Cryptologic Research 2024
Q. Tang and V. Teague (Eds.): PKC 2024, LNCS 14603, pp. 61–91, 2024.
https://doi.org/10.1007/978-3-031-57725-3_3

also because the central tools involved – garbled circuits, oblivious transfer, smooth projective hash functions, etc. – were all well known for a long time. The power behind these results lay in a *machinery* that carefully meshed these tools together.

However, this line of works has lacked reusable high-level abstractions, even as the low-level techniques were clearly similar across multiple works. Even the few abstractions of this machinery that appeared subsequently, e.g., in the form of hash-garbling [23], were not comprehensive enough to capture the multifarious applications of the machinery itself.

The main contribution of this work is to develop a versatile abstraction of the common machinery underlying the above works, and take it beyond the current set of applications. Our abstraction involves a strong form of obfuscation, which can be realized for *programs that are appropriately sampled*. The obfuscation formulation gives an intuitive description of potential solutions, and facilitates realizing it via a *novel composition theorem*. This not only aids in understanding the current constructions better, but also shows the way to new applications. As an illustration, *and as an important contribution of independent interest*, we present a variant of Multi-Authority Attribute-Based Encryption (MA-ABE) that can be based on (single-authority) ABE in a blackbox manner, using only standard cryptographic assumptions (e.g., DDH) in addition. This is in stark contrast to the constructions available for the original formulation of MA-ABE, which rely on specific assumptions, are for special restricted policy classes and/or are in the random oracle model [15,17,40,46].

1.1   Our Contributions

Our contributions are in two parts – (1) developing a powerful new framework to capture several important results from the recent literature, and (2) using it to construct a multi-authority version of ABE.

The R3PO Framework. Our primary contribution is to develop the notion of *Reach-Restricted Reactive Program Obfuscation* (R3PO) that modularly encapsulates and extends the powerful techniques behind the surprising results of [6,16,20,24,27]. Our definition of R3PO allows an intuitive description of prior constructions like IBE [20] (with an easy extension to Identity-Based Functional Encryption [54]), 2-Round MPC [6,27], and RBE [24], all of them using obfuscation of natural reactive programs.

- We present a **library** of useful R3PO schemes. The library includes obfuscations for non-reactive programs that check a commitment opening, verify a signature, and verify the (partial) opening of a hashed value.
- We present a **composition theorem** that can be used to obtain an R3PO scheme for a reactive program from R3PO schemes for smaller (non-reactive) programs (like those in the library above) into which it *decomposes*.
- For each of the applications we consider (as well as some of the programs in the library), we define an appropriate reactive program, construct an R3PO for it and use it to complete our construction. The requisite R3PO maybe

directly available from the library, or is constructed using the composition theorem.

The grabled circuit technique is entirely encapsulated within the proof of the composition theorem above. This is in contrast with prior work that used these techniques, where the proof would use a sequence of indistinguishability arguments interleaving garbled circuit simulation with other arguments specific to the construction. Indeed, one of the main technical challenges we overcome is to allow disentangling the garbled circuits from the other cryptographic elements, in these security proofs, using a strong simulation based definition of R3PO and our novel notion of *decomposition*.

Private Multi-Authority ABE. Another important contribution of this work is a new version of *Multi-Authority Attribute-Based Encryption* (called Private Multi-Authority ABE or p-MA-ABE), and a construction for it, conceived in terms of an R3PO.

The motivation for p-MA-ABE stems from the natural use-case for MA-ABE (or even ABE) where a user has privacy requirements against an attribute authority (e.g., they may want to obtain attributes corresponding to a city and a state that they consider their primary home, but without revealing the name of those locations to the authority). Correspondingly, the authority would be willing to issue attributes that satisfy a (possibly private) *attribute-granting policy* (e.g., issue the attributes for any one state and any one city within that state). The privacy requirement is that the authority (or authorities) shall not learn *anything* about the attributes of a user, and the user shall not learn anything about the attribute-granting policy, beyond whether the policy is met by the attribute set.

Now, a non-private MA-ABE (or ABE) scheme can be easily converted into a private version, via secure 2-party computation of a function to which the user's input is their attribute request, and the authority's input is its master secret key and its attribute-granting policy. Since such a 2PC protocol can be implemented in two rounds (e.g., a simple protocol based on Yao's Garbled Circuit works, as we consider the authorities to be honest-but-curious), this only requires the user to send a single message to the server – which we call an *attribute request* – before the server responds.

p-MA-ABE captures this trade-off: allow the user to initiate the contact with the authority,[1] and in return obtain a strong privacy guarantee. Though the above transformation shows that standard MA-ABE can be easily turned into p-MA-ABE, the former is known to be realizable only for very limited functions and in the random oracle model. In contrast, our results show that p-MA-ABE is as widely realizable as ABE itself!

We give a construction for p-MA-ABE from any (single-authority, ciphertext-policy) ABE scheme in a blackbox manner, using R3PO for (non-reactive) programs for signature checking and commitment opening, that is provably secure

---

[1] We remark that in a practical situation, this extra round comes at virtually no cost, since anyway a user would first need to establish a secure channel and authenticate itself with the authority before receiving its credentials.

in the standard model. The scheme supports general access policies as supported by the underlying ABE scheme, and is policy-hiding if the ABE is policy-hiding.

1.2   Related Work

We mention a few related works below, and discuss how R3PO relate to other notions in Sect. 2.7.

Obfuscation. A large variety of notions of obfuscation have been studied in the literature leading to several important breakthroughs along the way (e.g., [2,4,5,7,22,31,35–37,41,49,51]). Like R3PO, many of these require security only when the program being obfuscated is generated appropriately [4,7,33,51].

Composition. Composition has been considered in the context of cryptographic protocols, leading up to UC security and its variants [3,11–13,18,21,32,45,47, 52], as well as alternate approaches like Constructive Cryptography [44]. Composition for obfuscation has received far less attention, although it was explicitly considered in an early work [43].

Garbled Circuits. Garbled circuits were conceived by Yao [53]. The techniques of chaining multiple garbled circuits appeared in garbled RAM schemes [25,26, 28,42], and later several results like Laconic OT [16], IBE from DDH [19,20], 2-round MPC [6,27], and several extensions of these works have all relied on these techniques.

Multi-Authority Attribute Based Encryption (MA-ABE). The notion of Ciphertext Policy-Attribute Based Encryption (CP-ABE) was introduced in [48] and formally defined in [30]. There is a rich sequence of works realizing ABE, based on lattice based (LWE) [9,29] and pairing based assumptions [30,34,39]. But for MA-ABE, first proposed in [15], realizations so far have been limited. In the standard GID model, [40] formalized the notion of decentralized MA-ABE (where in, no trusted setup algorithm other than a common reference string is allowed), and gave a scheme for it under appropriate bilinear maps assumptions in the random oracle model (supporting general policy structures). A sequence of works culminated in [17], where they gave a scheme under the Learning With Errors (LWE) assumption in the random oracle model for policies corresponding to DNF formulae. Concurrently, [46] modified the definition to consider sender security (policy hiding) as well as receiver security (attribute hiding), and gave a construction for it under the k-linear assumption in the random oracle model for a special subset of policies. More recently, [50] gave a (current state-of-the-art) construction for MA-ABE in the plain model for subset policies (including DNF formulae) from the new evasive LWE assumption. Their construction however requires a global setup.

[38] proposed a variant of MA-ABE called the OT model. It is a relaxed model where there is no global identity fixed for the users. However, as pointed out in [17], this allows multiple users to pool their attributes, defeating one of the main goals of ABE. Our model has a global identity that an authority would incorporate into the key issued for a party, and as captured in the security definition, the user can combine only attributes that are issued for the same

global id. Another drawback of [38] was that it used a global setup; we do not. Our setup is local to each authority (as in the global id model). Our model much more closely resembles the standard global id model, but with an additional key request step in the syntax. On the other hand, our results are much stronger than those available in the standard model (which are in the random oracle model and/or for limited function classes). We also offer further flexibility by not requiring each attribute to be attached to a unique authority.

We also note that MA-ABE can be modeled as an appropriate functionality in the framework of public-key Multi-Party Functional Encryption (MPFE) [1]. Their work gives a construction for public-key MPFE for general functionalities. However, this does not yield the result in our work due to the following limitations. Their construction uses an interactive setup, forcing the authorities to be aware of and interact with each other, while we require the MA-ABE authorities to only use "local" setup. Further, their construction is based on Multi-Input Functional Encryption for general functionalities (which is a strong assumption that implies iO). In contrast, we rely only on ABE and standard assumptions. Indeed, the main motivation behind R3PO and the entire line of work leading to it, is to be able to base various cryptographic schemes on simpler assumptions, and to avoid the need for assumptions like iO.

2 Technical Overview

2.1 Motivating Examples

We start with a few motivating constructions, along the lines of the IBE construction mentioned at the beginning of this paper, which we seek to base on our new notion of obfuscation. In the general case, we would be obfuscating a *reactive* program (or more specifically, a *Moore machine*), which at each step, accepts an input, updates its state, and produces an output based on the new state.

Identity-Based Functional Encryption. IBFE is an extension of IBE where each identity id is associated with a unique function f_{id} (not known to the encryptor), so that when an encryption of a message m addressed to id is decrypted using the key for f_{id}, one receives $f_{id}(m)$. An IBFE scheme can be obtained by simply modifying the IBE scheme above so that the obfuscated program takes a signature on (id, f) (where id is already fixed in the program, but f is not), and transitions to a state encoding f, where it outputs $f(m)$.

IBFE has been explored in a prior work [54], but their definition is incomparable to our notion above. On the one hand, their definition does not allow the adversary to obtain any function keys – under any IDs – for a function f such that $f(m_0)$ and $f(m_1)$ are not equal; on the other hand, it is not made very clear if the adversary is restricted to obtaining a single function key for the challenge id, as is the case in our definition. Finally, they offer a construction for the primitive only for a very restricted class of functions, while our construction supports general functionalities.

2-Round MPC. Following the constructions in [6,27], an underlying (multi-round) MPC protocol can be reinterpreted as evaluating a blinded circuit, in which each boolean gate is owned by a party, and the protocol amounts to evaluating the wires of this circuit publicly. The wire values are public, but each gate is private to its owner.

The 2-round MPC constructed from the blinded circuit is as follows. In the first round, each party broadcasts a commitment to the 4 bits (separately) of the truth table of each of its gates. In the second round, each party broadcasts the obfuscation of the following reactive program:

- The program maintains a public state consisting of all the wire values of the circuit, evaluated thus far.
- If the next gate is owned by another party, the program accepts as input the output wire value of the gate, along with an opening of the corresponding commitment in the gate. If the opening verifies, it updates its state to correspond to having evaluated this wire. It produces no output for this transition.
- If the next gate is owned by this party, then it takes no input, transitions to a state that includes the output wire value of this gate, and outputs the opening of the corresponding commitment.

Finally, given these obfuscated reactive programs, the parties evaluate the blinded circuit gate by gate, at each step first running the program from the owner of the gate, and then feeding its inputs to all the other programs.

Laconic OT. This is a version of OT in which the receiver has a vector D of choice-bits, which it commits to by sending a short string y to the sender. Later, on input (i, x_0, x_1), the sender should send a string to the receiver from which the latter should learn only x_{D_i}.

We consider the following implementation of Laconic OT: Using a hash that supports "selective opening" of a bit in the hashed string, with a collision resistance guarantee that prevents opening any bit in two different ways, the receiver hashes D to obtain y. On input (i, x_0, x_1), the sender obfuscates the following (small) program and sends it over to the receiver: The program accepts as input an opening of y at position i to a bit b, and if the opening is valid, then it outputs x_b.

Each of the above simplistic constructions relied on an intuitive notion of "obfuscation." In the sequel, we develop a formal notion of obfuscation which will let us make the above descriptions precise, while retaining their simplicity. Importantly, our new obfuscation notion is indeed realizable in all the above cases, using the same standard cryptographic assumptions as in the prior works which introduced these constructions.

2.2   Defining R3PO

At a high-level, we consider obfuscation of *reactive programs*. A reactive program (a finite-state machine, or more precisely, a Moore machine) takes inputs over multiple rounds, updating its state and producing an output based on the state at each round. It is specified by a start state, a transition function π and a message function μ, so that, on reaching a state σ, the program outputs $\mu(\sigma)$.

Before discussing the definitions, it will be useful to have a couple of running examples in mind. In these examples, μ is arbitrary (and secret), and a public π is as specified below.

- **Commitment.** π_c incorporates a commitment string c. On input d at the start state, if d decommits c to m, then π_c transitions to a state σ_m encoding m.
- **Signature.** A signature verification key vk is encoded in the start state σ_{vk} of π (denoted as $\pi[\sigma_{\mathsf{vk}}]$), from where, given a valid signature on a message m as input, it transitions to a state σ_m encoding m.

These are both instances of "one-step programs" which have transitions only out of the start state. (We shall later explain the slightly different choices for how the values c and vk are incorporated into π in the two cases.) In these examples, π is not hidden, and the goal of obfuscating such a program would be to hide μ. More generally, π and μ can both have secrets in them (when defining reactive programs formally, we will denote them as $\pi^{(\alpha)}$ and $\mu^{(\beta)}$, where α and β are the secrets).

Reach Extraction and Simulation. Our simulation-based notion of obfuscation requires that a "reach-extractor" should exist for the program being obfuscated. A reach extractor would predict all the states of a reactive program that are reachable using inputs that can be efficiently computed by any adversary. Then, the obfuscation of the program should be simulated using only the outputs produced by the program at those states. We elaborate on reach-exaction and the rest of the simulation below.

Reach Extractability. Which states in a program π are efficiently reachable is a consequence of *the process that generates the program* (analogous to how an "evasive program" being evasive is a consequence of sampling it from a distribution). This process involves a *generator* G and an *adversary* Q. A *reach extractor* for an adversary Q is a program that passively (possibly in a non-blackbox manner) observes Q as it interacts with G, and then predicts (a superset of) the set of states that the adversary will be able to reach in the program output by G. This prediction is made explicitly in the form of inputs to a (possibly different) reactive program Π that will reach all the states reachable by the adversary, and perhaps more. Here we allow the extractor to specify Π, which belongs to a transition function family $\mathring{\mathcal{P}}$ that may be different from the transition program family $\mathcal{P}$ that is obfuscated. We refer to this as the "reach bounding" guarantee of the reach extractor.

We illustrate a reach extractor for the two running examples.

- **Commitment:** G accepts a commitment string c from Q, and then outputs π_c. A reach extractor can extract a value m from the commitment, either when Q is semi-honest, or when a setup is used that the extractor can control. Now, m is not a decommitment as expected by π_c. Instead, we allow the extractor to specify a different program Π_m which accepts m itself as the input and transitions to σ_m.

This extractor is reach bounding, because, due to the binding property of the commitment scheme, the only state Q could reach in π_c is also σ_m.

- **Signature:** In this case, G internally samples a pair $(\mathsf{sk}, \mathsf{vk})$ of signing and verification keys. It sends vk to Q, and further may answer signature requests by Q. An extractor can collect all the signatures Q receives from G and output them as a reach-bounding set of inputs for $\Pi \overset{\circ}{=} \pi[\sigma_{\mathsf{vk}}]$. Note that here the program family to be used by the extractor $\overset{\circ}{\mathcal{P}}$ is the same as the one being obfuscated $\mathcal{P}$ (and it has only one program in it but with various start states). The reach bounding property follows from unforgeability of the signature scheme.

Simulation. An obfuscator for a generator R3PO security definition requires that a 2-stage simulation exists for any adversary Q, as follows:

- Stage 1: After Q finishes interacting with G, a reach extractor observing Q specifies a set of reachable states (in the form of a program Π and inputs to it).
- Stage 2: Given the output of the original message function μ on those states, a simulated obfuscation is produced. This should be indistinguishable from the obfuscation of the reactive program produced by G, even given auxiliary information output by both G and Q.

Note that this is a *stronger notion of simulation than even VBB obfuscation*, which only requires the simulation of one predicate at a time, rather than a simulation of the entire obfuscated program. Indeed, requiring such a simulator would typically entail that the program is learnable and hence trivial to obfuscate. What keeps our definition from becoming trivial is the fact that *the extracted inputs are a function of the program generation process*, and are not available to the obfuscator.

Reach Restriction. The final component in our definition of R3PO is in the form of an additional requirement on the reach extractor in Stage 1 above. This requirement stems from the "one-time" nature of Yao's Garbled Circuits, a key ingredient in the constructions that we wish to capture. Intuitively, these constructions require that an adversary can evaluate any garbled circuit on only one set of inputs. We incorporate a corresponding *reach restriction* requirement into our definition of reach extractability of a reactive program (Definition 3), which leads to the name *reach-restricted reactive programs* (R3P).[2]

To define reach restriction, we require the state space of the reactive programs to be *a priori* partitioned into a polynomial number of parts, $\Sigma = \Sigma_1 \cup \cdots \cup \Sigma_N$. Then, informally, the reach restriction property of a reactive program is that no efficient adversary would be able to find inputs that take π to *two different states that belong to the same part*. Formally, the reach restriction property is imposed on the reachable states produced by the reach-extractor.

We return to our running examples.

---

[2] Formally, we do not define R3P, but only an R3P Generator, as a program generator (Definition 2) that has a reach extractor.

- **Commitment:** We let Σ_1 consist only of the start state and Σ_2 consist of all states of the form σ_m. Since the extractor outputs only one message m, the reach restriction property already holds.
- **Signature:** We let Σ_1 consist of all the potential start states σ_{vk} and Σ_2 consist of all states of the form σ_m (the two kind of states are encoded so that $\Sigma_1 \cap \Sigma_2 = \emptyset$). To be reach restricting, we will require that the generator G gives out at most one signature. Further, we would want to enforce that breaking reach restriction in Π must correspond to forging signatures with respect to the key sampled by G. This is enforced by keeping vk in the start state of $\pi[\mathsf{vk}]$ (rather than in the transition function itself), which in turn forces Π to use the same start state and hence the same verification key.

2.3   R3PO Composition Theorem

As noted earlier, a major motivation of this work is to encapsulate a range of powerful techniques using garbled circuits in a reusable form. This result takes the form of a composition theorem, which allows obfuscating a reactive program via an obfuscation of its various components.

The high-level idea is to view a reactive program $\pi \in \mathcal{P}$, over a state space $\Sigma = \Sigma_1 \cup \cdots \cup \Sigma_N$ as consisting of separate programs $\widehat{\pi}_1, \ldots, \widehat{\pi}_N$, such that $\widehat{\pi}_i$ is identical to π on states $\sigma \in \Sigma_i$, and in other states it ignores all inputs (i.e., remains at the same state). Let $\mathcal{P}_i$ denote the class of such programs $\widehat{\pi}_i$. W.l.o.g. (due to reach-restriction), we require π to not have any transitions between states in the same part, and hence each $\widehat{\pi}_i$ is a "one-step" (or non-reactive) program that halts after its first transition out of the start state. However, attempting to formalize this leads to a couple of conundrums.

Conundrum 1: Dynamically Determined Programs. As a naïve starting point, one could try building an obfuscator for $\mathcal{P}$ from obfuscators for $\mathcal{P}_i$. However, this runs into an immediate problem: When executing a program in $\mathcal{P}$, the state reached in Σ_i is dynamically determined by the inputs used, whereas when obfuscating a program in $\mathcal{P}_i$, its start state needs to be fixed. The resolution of this conundrum, which goes back to [16,19,20,25,26,28,42], is to provide a **garbled circuit** that can dynamically compute the obfuscation of $\widehat{\pi}_i[\sigma_i]$ with the correct start state σ_i; the input to this garbled circuit would be the labels encoding σ_i, which in turn would be released by the obfuscation of a previous program $\pi_j[\sigma_j]$ on an input x such that $\pi_j(\sigma_j, x) = \sigma_i$.

However, the price we pay for using garbled circuits is that only one set of labels can be made available to the adversary for each garbled circuit, in turn resulting in the reach-restriction requirement.

Conundrum 2: Intertwined Generators. Recall that to formalize reach restriction, our definition needed to take into account the generators. Now, when we try to map the different parts of a single reactive program as being generated by multiple generators, *the generators can become deeply intertwined*, sharing secret keys and state variables. Further, the program generated by one generator needs to have a start state that is determined by the outputs produced by programs in other parts. So it may not always be possible to view a (reach-restricted) reactive program produced by a generator as the composition of single-step reactive programs produced by separate generators.

The resolution to this conundrum is to require some additional relation between the generator for the reactive program and the generators for the one-step programs. This leads us to the notion of *decomposition*.

Decomposition. Unlike in the case of MPC protocols, wherein the subprotocols are explicitly executed by a composite protocols, a reactive program generator need not have "sub-generators" running within it. Indeed, this presents a challenge to composition that is *fundamentally different from composition in MPC*.

Our novel solution is to define decomposition in terms of a *bisimulation* requirement. Roughly, for G to decompose into a smaller generator H (and additional computation), we require that G *can be viewed* as H via a simulator, and *vice versa*. More precisely, we require that there be two simulators J and Z such that $\boxed{\genfrac{}{}{0pt}{}{G}{J}}$ (denoting that J internally runs G as a black box) and $\boxed{\genfrac{}{}{0pt}{}{Z}{H}}$ are indistinguishable from each other from the point of view of any adversary Q (or more precisely, for $\boxed{\genfrac{}{}{0pt}{}{Q}{W}}$, where the wrapper W is also part of the simulation). This by itself can be trivially arranged by letting $J = H$ and $Z = G$. We need to further capture the requirement that the program $\widehat{\pi}$ produced by H corresponds to a single step in the program π produced by G. More precisely, the state space of the generator H corresponds to a *part* Σ_i of the state space of G, and we require that the start state of $\widehat{\pi}$ is the same as the only state in Σ_i that is reachable in π.

Now, by requiring this, we require J to know the reachable state in π produced by G. While this is possible in some cases (e.g., when the reachable state is determined by a signed message sent by G), in certain other cases it is not possible (e.g., when it is determined by a message hidden in a commitment). To accommodate these different situations, we allow J to obtain this information from the wrapper W, which is in turn allowed to obtain this from a reach-extractor for G (or more precisely, from a "partial" reach extractor which only extracts the reach within Σ_i).

Finally, for use in our composition theorem, we shall require a uniformly sampled message function to be associated with the reactive program produced by J. (While the definition of decomposition allows arbitrary message function class here, the composition theorem is for decomposition that uses a particular message function class.)

We refer the reader to Sect. 4.1 for a more detailed discussion and a precise definition of decomposition.

Composition. Having defined decomposition, we turn to stating and proving the composition theorem. Informally, it states that if a generator G decomposes into generators $(H_1, \ldots, H_N)$ (for a partition of its state space $(\Sigma_1, \ldots, \Sigma_N)$), and if each H_i has an R3PO scheme $\mathcal{O}_i$, then there is one for G as well. The construction uses garbled circuits, following the outline at the beginning of this section. The final obfuscation consists of one garbled circuit GC_i for each part

Σ_i, such that on reaching $\sigma \in \Sigma_i$, an evaluator would have the labels that encode σ as input for GC_i, and GC_i would then output $\mu(\sigma)$ as well as an obfuscation $\mathcal{O}_i(\widehat{\pi}_i[\sigma], \widehat{\mu}_i)$ (using a hard-coded random tape). Feeding an input x to this obfuscated program will release the labels for the state $\widehat{\pi}_i(\sigma, x) = \pi(\sigma, x)$.

To prove that this construction yields an R3PO for G, we use a sequence of hybrids that would replace one garbled circuit at a time with a simulated one, which in turn outputs not the actual obfuscation $\mathcal{O}_i(\widehat{\pi}_i[\sigma], \widehat{\mu}_i)$, but a simulated one. At each step, we will be able to apply the decomposition guarantee (using an inductively maintained partial reach extractor) to go from G to $\boxed{\frac{\boxed{G}}{J_i}}$ to $\boxed{\frac{Z_i}{\boxed{H_i}}}$, wherein we use the R3PO guarantee to replace the actual obfuscation used to simulate GC_i with a simulated one (while also extending the partial extractor); then we move back from $\boxed{\frac{Z_i}{\boxed{H_i}}}$ to $\boxed{\frac{\boxed{G}}{J_i}}$ and then G.

2.4   R3PO Library

We present R3PO schemes for a few basic program classes which can be combined together in a variety of constructions.

- *Commitment-Opening.* This is similar to the running example presented above. In the full version, we realize the R3PO for a couple of flavors of this (UC secure commitment, and "weakly secure" commitment that is suitable for semi-honest committers), based on the standard assumption of 2-round OT.
- *Signature-Checking.* We provide an R3PO for signature-checking programs as in the running example. To facilitate full security in applications like IBE and IBFE, we support *puncturable* signature schemes.[3] We instantiate a puncturable signature scheme and give an R3PO scheme for this program family assuming an OTSE scheme in the full version.
- *Hash-Opening.* This is similar to the commitment opening reactive program, but with a compressing hash instead of a binding commitment. The R3PO for this program class can be constructed from Laconic OT [16]. Alternately, we can use our composition theorem to bootstrap from an R3PO for the same class instantiated with a factor-2 compressing laconic OT (see Sect. 2.5 below).
- *ϵ-Transition* While specifying reactive programs using the above building blocks, often it is useful to transition from state reached via one building block to a state that is suitable as the start state of another building block. ϵ-transitions provide the essential syntactic sugar to enable this. R3PO for an ϵ-transition is implemented using a garbled circuit.

---

[3] In our constructions of IBE and IBFE, the ciphertext corresponds to an obfuscated program. For full security, the adversary must be allowed to make key queries even after receiving the ciphertext. But, no interaction is allowed between the program generator and the adversary after the program has been generated. Hence, we consider a generator which gives out an appropriately punctured signing key before the interaction finishes.

2.5   Applications: The Different Ways of Using R3PO

Our R3PO library and our composition theorem form a versatile toolkit for instantiating new and old constructions. There are a few different ways in which they can be put to use.

Off-the-Shelf Without Composition. In certain cases, the components in our library are already powerful enough off-the-shelf to yield a construction for a desired application. An illustrative example is that an R3PO for (puncturable) signature-checking can be used to construct an IBFE scheme (and, as a special case, IBE), as sketched in Sect. 2.1 and elaborated in the full version. The security proof is fairly direct, by using a generator for the R3PO that models the security experiment of IBFE.

Using Composition. We illustrate a typical "workflow" for using the R3PO composition theorem in a higher-level application. We use the example of Laconic OT [16], which is one of the early constructions that form the inspiration for this work. For the sake of readability we use slightly imprecise terminology.

- We start by identifying a reactive program family, such that an R3PO for it directly yields our application.In the case of laconic OT, this reactive program traverses a pre-determined path along a Merkle tree, with states holding the hash value at each node, and making a transition if the input "explains" the hash at that node. The Merkle tree uses an underlying hash scheme which compresses by a factor of 2.
- We consider the one-step restrictions of this reactive program as another reactive program family, and carry out the following two steps:
  • We show that the original reactive programs can be decomposed into its one-step restrictions. This involves matching the definition of decomposition with straightforward constructions.
  • We give an R3PO scheme for these one-step restrictions. This can be directly based on the construction in [16] for factor-2-compression laconic OT (not involving garbled circuit chaining).
- Then we *simply invoke our composition theorem* to obtain an R3PO for the original program family.
- We package the original reactive program as another one-step program, so that it can be included in our R3PO library for various applications (see the full version). Laconic OT is a direct consequence of an R3PO for this one-step program.

Another example of this workflow is in the construction of the R3PO for signature-checking that was mentioned above as part of our library (where the smaller non-reactive programs used correspond to one-time signature checking).

R3PO as a Component. In the above examples, once an R3PO is constructed, the final application is fairly immediately realized. However, it is also possible to use R3PO as a component in a larger construction, wherein the step from R3PO to the final security proof may be non-trivial. The proof may involve multiple hybrids, with R3PO security used to replace a real obfuscation in one hybrid with the simulated obfuscation in the next. One such example is the 2-round MPC protocol of [6, 27], which we rederive in the full version using R3PO for commitment opening. In this construction, as sketched in Sect. 2.1, several programs obfuscated using R3PO are involved. The security of R3PO can be used to move to an "ideal" execution of the MPC protocol (or more precisely, build a simulator for the 2-round MPC using the simulators of R3PO and the simulator for the underlying MPC protocol).

Our main application of p-MA-ABE (discussed below) also falls into this category, where the security of the final construction depends on several components, one of which is an R3PO scheme. This construction also illustrates the possibility of combining multiple library components (commitment-opening and signature-checking) in the same reactive program.

2.6   Private Multi-Authority ABE

In this section, we give a brief overview of the new variant of MA-ABE that we introduce, called *Private Multi-Authority ABE* (p-MA-ABE), and the main ideas behind our construction for it. Our construction is intuitive in terms of an obfuscation of a reactive program, and can indeed be realized using R3PO. The flexibility of the new framework allows a relatively easy construction, using existing ABE schemes, and with a robust security definition. The full description can be found in Sect. 5.

Defining p-MA-ABE: The setting of p-MA-ABE (as well as MA-ABE) involves a set of mutually distrusting authorities (say $A_1, \ldots, A_N$), a sender and a receiver. The algorithms in an p-MA-ABE scheme are as follows:

- Setup: At the start of the execution, each authority A_i does a local (decentralized) setup to generate its public and secret keys $(\mathsf{mpk}_i, \mathsf{msk}_i)$ and shares the public key mpk_i with the other users in the system.
- Key-Request: a receiver can construct a set of key-requests $\mathsf{req} = (\mathsf{req}_1, \ldots, \mathsf{req}_N)$ for a global identifier gid and attribute set $\bar{x}$ from the public keys. It can then submit a key-request query (of the form $(\mathsf{gid}, \mathsf{req}_i)$) to an authority A_i and get back a key-component $\mathsf{sk}_{\mathsf{gid},\mathsf{req}_i}$ from A_i (req will hide $\bar{x}$).
- Key-Gen: an authority A_i receives as input a key-request req_i for a global identifier gid, and outputs a key-component $\mathsf{sk}_{\mathsf{gid},\mathsf{req}_i}$ that incorporates an attribute-granting policy Θ_i^{gid} (which, for simplicity, we do not consider a secret).
- Encryption: a sender can encrypt a message m with a ciphertext policy ϕ, using the public keys of the authorities to produce a ciphertext $\mathsf{ct}_{m,\phi}$.
- Decryption: a receiver can decrypt a ciphertext $\mathsf{ct}_{m,\phi}$ using key components of the form $(\mathsf{sk}_{\mathsf{gid},\mathsf{req}_1}, \cdots, \mathsf{sk}_{\mathsf{gid},\mathsf{req}_N})$ where all the requests req_i were generated using gid and $\bar{x}$ such that $\Theta_i^{\mathsf{gid}}(\bar{x}) = 1$ for all i, and $\phi(\bar{x}) = 1$.

Compared to the original definition of MA-ABE, there are two main differences in p-MA-ABE: Firstly, since the attributes are to be kept private even from the authorities, there is a key-request step, wherein the user generates the key-request messages to all the authorities based on its desired set of attributes. Secondly, we allow each authority to use an arbitrary attribute-granting policy, which depends on the entire attribute vector.[4]

We define security w.r.t. a corruption model where the adversary is allowed to maliciously corrupt the receivers and semi-honestly corrupt any subset of authorities. If a receiver is honest, we require that the key-request req reveals nothing about $\bar{x}$ to the authorities, even if all of them collude. When the receiver is corrupt, we guarantee that, for any choice of (ϕ, m_0, m_1), the adversary cannot distinguish between the encryptions of m_0 and m_1 w.r.t. a policy ϕ, unless for a pair $(\mathsf{gid}, \bar{x})$ such that $\Theta_i^{\mathsf{gid}}(\bar{x}) = 1$ for *all* honest authorities A_i, $\phi(\bar{x}) = 1$ and the adversary sent a valid key request for $(\mathsf{gid}, \bar{x})$ (i.e., a request that can be produced by the Key-Request algorithm on those inputs) to at least one honest authority (and it could have sent it to the others as well).

A p-MA-ABE Scheme: Our scheme is easily described in terms of obfuscating a reactive program. The key-request req_i is a commitment to $\bar{x}$ (using a common random string in the public-key of A_i). The key issued by each authority is the obfuscation of a reactive program; the reactive programs by the different authorities "talk" to each other and confirm that they all agree on granting the same attribute $\bar{x}$ to gid, and if so, issue standard CP-ABE keys for $\bar{x}$. More precisely, the reactive program $(\pi^{(\alpha)}, \mu^{(\beta)})$ works as follows (with A_i's CP-ABE master secret-key constituting the secret β; α can be empty, or alternately, can be used to store Θ_i^{gid} privately):

- at the start state accepts a decommitment for req_i and transitions to a state with $\bar{x}$. There, if $\Theta_i^{\mathsf{gid}}(\bar{x}) = 1$, then it outputs a signature on $(\mathsf{gid}, \bar{x})$, using A_i's signature key.
- Then, it moves through $\mathsf{N} - 1$ states accepting signatures on $(\mathsf{gid}, \bar{x})$ from all the other servers.
- On reaching the last of these states, it outputs a CP-ABE key for the attribute $\bar{x}$, under a (standard) CP-ABE scheme for which A_i is the authority.

If $\Theta_i^{\mathsf{gid}}(\bar{x}) = 1$ for all i, then the receiver can obtain the CP-ABE keys for $\bar{x}$ under all the authorities. Now, to encrypt a message under a policy ϕ, one simply secret-shares m into N shares, and encrypts each share under the CP-ABE public key of the corresponding authority.

Note that if even one (honest) authority's key component is missing, no honest authority's CP-ABE key can be obtained. This is crucial because the CP-ABE keys do not involve gid and cannot prevent the use of keys obtained using multiple gids.

Using the composition theorem, we show that there is an R3PO for a suitably defined generator that models the p-MA-ABE security game. (As it turns out, we need to do this for two different generators to handle two different hybrids;

---

[4] In particular, it captures the standard formulation of MA-ABE, where each authority A_i "owns" a set of attributes and its key-issuing decision is based on the values of the attributes it owns.

the first hybrid does not rely on the unforgeability of the signatures, and lets the adversary specify all the signing keys. We show that the same obfuscator $\mathcal{O}$ is an R3PO scheme for both the generators.)

2.7   Comparison of R3PO with Existing Primitives

It is instructive to compare R3PO with various existing primitives and techniques.

Hash Garbling. This abstraction from [23] gives a similar interface to R3PO *for a specific class of program generators*, namely, "Hash Opening." More precisely, hash garbling involves a hash-opening check as well as a circuit evaluation, which corresponds to a reactive program that carries out a hash-opening transition followed by an epsilon transition (that evaluates the circuit).

{Batch, Hash, Chameleon, OneTime Signature}-Encryption. These flavors of encryption that were introduced in prior work [8,19,20] correspond to R3PO schemes for one-step programs that are included in our library (Hash Opening and Signature Checking). While these original definitions differ in their details, R3PO provides a simulation-based definition that can be uniformly used in all their applications.

Witness Encryption over Commitments (cWE). cWE, recently defined in [10], is quite similar to an R3PO for "Commitment Opening" followed by an epsilon transition. It was instantiated from Oblivious Transfer (OT) and garbled circuits, just as the R3PO scheme obtained directly from our library and the composition theorem is.

Garbled Circuit Chaining. The *technique* of garbled circuit chaining has appeared in a long line of works [6,20,24,27,42]. We note that R3PO allows different one-step programs (for example combining commitment and signature in p-MA-ABE), while all prior works used garbled circuit chaining with links that correspond to a single cryptographic element. Also, as already mentioned, the prior works do not separate out the chaining from the cryptographic elements that are chained together.

Obfuscation Notions. Our notion of R3PO is different in many ways from the other notions of obfuscation. Many notions of obfuscation are either unrealizable in general or inhabit "obfustopia," requiring a combination of relatively strong assumptions, and are not practical in terms of efficiency [2,4,5,7,7,14,35]. But there are a few exceptions for specialized applications, like obfuscation of reencryption based on bilinear pairings [33] or compute-and-compare obfuscation based on LWE [51]. R3PO could be considered to be in the latter group, but with a much richer class of applications compared to the others.

The original notions of obfuscation require worst-case security, but there are several others, including obfuscation of evasive circuit families [4], strong iO [7], reencryption obfuscation [33], compute-and-compare obfuscation [51], etc. which require only *distributional security*, when the program being obfuscated is sampled from distributions with particular properties. Again, R3PO falls into the latter class here, with the sampling process being interactive.

3   The R3PO Framework

3.1   Reactive Programs and Generators

Below we define a reactive program as a stateful machine that takes inputs, transitions its state and produces outputs as a function of its state. Formally, such a program consists of a deterministic transition function π and a deterministic message function μ, both of which can be parameterized by (secret) values α, β (hardwired into circuits $\pi^{(\cdot)}$, $\mu^{(\cdot)}$ respectively).

Definition 1 (Reactive Program over ($\mathcal{X}$, Σ, $\mathcal{A}$, $\mathcal{B}$, M). A *reactive program* $(\pi^{(\alpha)}, \mu^{(\beta)})$, with input alphabet $\mathcal{X}$, a state-space Σ, a start-state $\mathsf{start} \in \Sigma$ and secret spaces $\mathcal{A}$, $\mathcal{B}$ is specified by a deterministic *transition* program $\pi^{(\alpha)} : \Sigma \times \mathcal{X} \to \Sigma$ parameterized by a secret $\alpha \in \mathcal{A}$ and a deterministic[5] message function $\mu^{(\beta)} : \Sigma \to \mathsf{M}$ parameterized by a secret $\beta \in \mathcal{B}$, that on input sequence $(x_1, \ldots, x_\ell) \in \mathcal{X}$, *reaches* a state σ_ℓ, where $\sigma_i = \pi^{(\alpha)}(\sigma_{i-1}, x_i)$ for $i = 1, \ldots, \ell$ and $\sigma_0 = \mathsf{start}$, and *outputs* a message $\mu^{(\beta)}(\sigma_\ell)$. We also define $\mathrm{REACH}_{\pi^{(\alpha)}}(x_1, \ldots, x_\ell) = \{\sigma_0, \cdots, \sigma_\ell\}$ and $\overline{\pi}^{(\alpha)}(x_1, \ldots, x_\ell) = \sigma_\ell$.   ◁

Reactive programs have an associated implicit security parameter κ; specifically, we require that the states in Σ and secrets in $\mathcal{A}$, $\mathcal{B}$ are represented as binary strings of length polynomial in the security parameter κ, and the functions $\pi^{(\alpha)}$ and $\mu^{(\beta)}$ are polynomial in κ. Throughout the rest of the paper, we shall omit κ and implicitly refer to "polynomial in κ" as simply being polynomial. Partition Function and Program Class. A transition function class $\mathcal{P}$ refers to a set of transition functions along with an associated partition function $\mathcal{I}$ that maps states to integers, i.e., $\mathcal{I} : \Sigma \to [N]$ for some positive integer N. We say that $\mathcal{I}$ partitions the state space Σ into $\Sigma_1, \cdots, \Sigma_N$ where,

$$\Sigma_i = \mathcal{I}^{-1}(i) := \{\sigma \mid \sigma \in \Sigma, \mathcal{I}(\sigma) = i\}$$

Unless otherwise stated, the start state of a reactive program is assumed to be in Σ_1. We say that a transition function $\pi^{(\alpha)}$ is **tree-ordered** with respect to $\mathcal{I}$, if the directed graph over $[N]$ (each partition as a vertex) with an edge-set

$$\{(i,j) \mid \exists \text{ distinct } \sigma \in \Sigma_i, \sigma' \in \Sigma_j, \exists x \in \mathcal{X} \text{ s.t } \pi^{(\alpha)}(\sigma, x) = \sigma'\}$$

is a tree, and all its edges (i,j) satisfy $i < j$. That is, for any partition j, there is at most a single partition $i < j$ from which states in partition j can be transitioned to. Further, we say that a transition function class $\mathcal{P}$ is tree-ordered if every $\pi^{(\alpha)} \in \mathcal{P}$ is tree-ordered w.r.t. the partition associated with $\mathcal{P}$.

A program class $(\mathcal{P}, \mathcal{M})$ is a set of reactive programs $(\pi^{(\alpha)}, \mu^{(\beta)})$ with $\pi^{(\alpha)} \in \mathcal{P}$ and $\mu^{(\beta)} \in \mathcal{M}$.

---

[5] As described in the full version, restricting our obfuscations to deterministic message functions is without loss of generality, even if we are interested in randomized message functions.

Reactive Program Generator. We now describe the process which generates a reactive program to be obfuscated. A PPT program G (which we call the generator) interacts with a PPT program Q (which we call the adversary) over many rounds; at the end G outputs a reactive program $(\pi^{(\alpha)}, \mu^{(\beta)})$. Both G and Q are also allowed to produce auxiliary outputs.

Definition 2 (($\mathcal{P},\mathcal{M}$)-Generator G). A $(\mathcal{P}, \mathcal{M})$-generator G for a transition function class $\mathcal{P}$ and message function class $\mathcal{M}$ is a PPT interactive program that interacts with an arbitrary PPT program Q. We write

$$\left((\pi^{(\alpha)}, \mu^{(\beta)}), a_G;\ a_Q \right) \leftarrow \langle G : Q \rangle$$

to indicate that at the end of the interaction, G outputs $\left((\pi^{(\alpha)}, \mu^{(\beta)}), a_G \right)$ and Q outputs a_Q (where $\pi^{(\alpha)} \in \mathcal{P}$, $\mu^{(\beta)} \in \mathcal{M}$). A *generator class* is simply a set of generators.   ◁

An adversary class $\mathcal{Q}$ is simply a set of adversaries Q. Some useful adversary classes depending on the application are: set of all PPT machines (for active corruption) and set of "semi-honest" PPT machines which follow a given protocol. We also consider adversary classes with *setup*. For any T that is a program in a setup class $\mathcal{T}$, we use Q^T to denote an adversary Q that gets oracle access to an honest execution of T.

3.2   Reach Extractor

To define a reach extractor, we introduce some notation. We write $Q\hat{|}\mathcal{E}$ to denote a composite machine in which $\mathcal{E}$ semi-honestly runs Q internally in a straight-line manner (where $\mathcal{E}$ can read the internal state of Q), letting Q directly communicate externally (with a generator). $\mathcal{E}$ produces the final auxiliary output. For an adversary class with a setup, given an adversary Q^T in the composite machine $Q^T\hat{|}\mathcal{E}$, $\mathcal{E}$ is allowed to replace T with any program from $\mathcal{T}$. For example, to capture common reference strings as a setup, $\mathcal{T}$ would correspond to {Setup, Setup$_{\mathrm{Sim}}$}, where Setup is the standard setup algorithm and Setup$_{\mathrm{Sim}}$ produces a simulated CRS.

$\mathcal{E}$ is a valid reach-extractor if the following hold: in the IDEAL interaction, $\mathcal{E}$ observes the adversary Q and produces an extra output (Π, X^*) such that the states reached in Π using X^* (that is, REACH$_\Pi(X^*)$) is an upper bound on what D can reach in $\pi^{(\alpha)}$; further the output is such that it reaches at-most a single state in each partition.[6]

Definition 3 (Reach-Extractor for Q w.r.t. $(\mathcal{G}, \overset{\circ}{\mathcal{P}})$). A *reach-extractor* for an adversary $Q \in \mathcal{Q}$ w.r.t. a $(\mathcal{P},\mathcal{M})$-generator class $\mathcal{G}$ and a transition function class $\overset{\circ}{\mathcal{P}}$, is a PPT program $\mathcal{E}$ such that, for all $G \in \mathcal{G}$ and PPT D, the

---

[6] As discussed just before Sect. 2.3, the reach-restriction condition is to enable our composition theorem (which depends on the use of garbled circuits).

output X produced by the following two experiments are indistinguishable:

REAL(G, Q, D):
$$\left((\pi^{(\alpha)}, \mu^{(\beta)}), a_G; a_Q\right) \leftarrow \langle G : Q \rangle$$
$$\text{output } X \leftarrow D(\pi^{(\alpha)}, \mu^{(\beta)}, a_G, a_Q)$$

IDEAL$(G, Q|\hat{\mathcal{E}}, D)$:
$$\left((\pi^{(\alpha)}, \mu^{(\beta)}), a_G; a_Q, \Pi, X^*\right) \leftarrow \langle G : Q|\hat{\mathcal{E}} \rangle$$
$$\text{output } X \leftarrow D(\pi^{(\alpha)}, \mu^{(\beta)}, a_G, a_Q)$$

and further the following hold:

– In IDEAL$(G, Q|\hat{\mathcal{E}}, D)$, $\Pi \in \overset{\circ}{\mathcal{P}}$.
– Suppose $\mathcal{I}$ partitions Σ into N parts $\Sigma_1, \cdots, \Sigma_N$. Then
  • **Reach-Bound:** For all $i \in [N]$, $\Pr[(\text{REACH}_{\pi^{(\alpha)}}(X) \cap \Sigma_i) \not\subseteq (\text{REACH}_\Pi(X^*) \cap \Sigma_i)]$ is negligible.
  • **Reach-Restriction:** For all $i \in [N]$, $|\text{REACH}_\Pi(X^*) \cap \Sigma_i| \leq 1$.   ◁

Real and Ideal Program Classes. Note that, in the above definition, $\mathcal{E}$ in the ideal world is allowed to extract an idealized reactive program $\Pi \in \overset{\circ}{\mathcal{P}}$ to describe the set of states reachable by the adversary Q. While in many of our examples, $\overset{\circ}{\mathcal{P}}$ is the same as $\mathcal{P}$, the class of "real world" reactive programs being obfuscated, this is not mandatory. This flexibility in the ideal world can help with enabling reach extraction while remaining useful in a higher level application. Please refer to the full version for more details.

3.3   Reach-Restricted Reactive Program Obfuscation

Recall that, our goal in obfuscating a reactive program is to hide the parameters α, β, except for the states an adversary can reach. Let $\mathcal{E}$ be a reach-extractor for Q w.r.t. $\mathcal{G}$ s.t. $\mathcal{E}$ outputs Π, X^* and REACH$_\Pi(X^*)$ bounds the reach of the adversary in $\pi^{(\alpha)}$. Then, we define a secure obfuscation as requiring a simulator Sim which, given only the circuits $\pi^{(\cdot)}$, $\mu^{(\cdot)}$ and the reachable states $(\overline{x}, \mu^{(\beta)}(\Pi(\overline{x})))$ for input sequences $\overline{x} \in X^*$, can output an obfuscation indistinguishable from a real obfuscation.

Definition 4 (R3PO scheme $\mathcal{O}$ for $(\mathcal{G}, \mathcal{Q}, \overset{\circ}{\mathcal{P}})$). A PPT program $\mathcal{O}$ is an *Reach-Restricted Reactive Program Obfuscation (R3PO) scheme* for a $(\mathcal{P}, \mathcal{M})$-Generator class $\mathcal{G}$ and transition function class $\overset{\circ}{\mathcal{P}}$, if the following hold: [7]

– **Correctness:** For all $\pi^{(\alpha)} \in \mathcal{P}$, $\mu^{(\beta)} \in \mathcal{M}$, $\rho \leftarrow \mathcal{O}(\pi^{(\alpha)}, \mu^{(\beta)})$, and $\overline{x} \in \mathcal{X}^*$, it holds that $\rho(\overline{x}) = \mu^{(\beta)}(\pi^{(\alpha)}(\overline{x}))$.
– **Security:** There exists a PPT program Sim s.t. $\forall Q \in \mathcal{Q}$, there exists a reach-extractor $\mathcal{E}$ w.r.t. $(\mathcal{G}, \overset{\circ}{\mathcal{P}})$, so that $\forall \, G \in \mathcal{G}$, the outputs of the following two experiments are indistinguishable:

---

[7] We assume that the programs $\pi^{(\alpha)}, \mu^{(\beta)}, \mathcal{I}, \mathcal{O}$ are all specified as circuits. Further, $\pi^{(\alpha)}$ and $\mu^{(\beta)}$ are given as circuits for $\pi^{(\cdot)}$ and $\mu^{(\cdot)}$ (resp.), which take α and β (resp.) as an input.

$$\left((\pi^{(\alpha)}, \mu^{(\beta)}), a_G; a_Q\right) \leftarrow \langle G : Q \rangle$$

REAL(G, Q): $\rho \leftarrow \mathcal{O}(\pi^{(\alpha)}, \mu^{(\beta)})$

output (ρ, a_G, a_Q)

$$\left((\pi^{(\alpha)}, \mu^{(\beta)}), a_G; a_Q, \Pi, X^*\right) \leftarrow \langle G : Q | \mathcal{E} \rangle$$

IDEAL(G, Q): $\rho \leftarrow \mathsf{Sim}\left(\pi^{(\cdot)}, \mu^{(\cdot)}, \Pi, \{\overline{x}, \mu^{(\beta)}(\Pi(\overline{x}))\}_{\overline{x} \in X^*}\right)$

output (ρ, a_G, a_Q)

◁

4   A Composition Theorem for R3PO

We now describe our composition theorem that enables building an R3PO for a generator class from R3POs for generator classes that produces smaller "one-step" (or non-reactive) programs. First we formalize the notion of decomposition.

4.1   Decomposition

The goal of decomposition is to view the transition function π of a reactive program produced by a generator G, as consisting of several one-step transitions π_i of reactive programs produced by generators H_i. Below, we define the notion of a σ-restriction of π at a state σ.

One-Step Restriction of a Transition Function. Given a reactive program's transition function $\pi^{(\alpha)}$ and one of its states σ, we define a *one-step σ -restriction of $\pi^{(\alpha)}$* as a transition function $\widehat{\pi}_\sigma^{(\alpha)}$ with start state σ, where

$$\widehat{\pi}_\sigma^{(\alpha)}(\sigma', x) = \begin{cases} \pi^{(\alpha)}(\sigma, x) & \text{if } \sigma' = \sigma \\ \sigma & \text{otherwise.} \end{cases}$$

(i.e., in $\widehat{\pi}_\sigma^{(\alpha)}$, the only transitions allowed are from its start state σ).

Note that the state space Σ of π can be exponentially large in κ, and correspondingly π consists of that many one-step transition functions. When decomposing π, we will group them into polynomially many classes of transition functions, using the partition $\mathcal{I}$ of the state space, $\Sigma = \Sigma_1 \cup \cdots \cup \Sigma_N$ associated with π. This imposes the following structure on the class of transition functions $\mathcal{P}$ to which π belongs.

The transition function class $\mathcal{P}_1 \times \cdots \times \mathcal{P}_N$. For any set of N classes $\mathcal{P}_1, \cdots, \mathcal{P}_N$ over the (same) state space Σ and partition function $\mathcal{I} : \Sigma \to [N]$, we define $\mathcal{P}_1 \times \cdots \times \mathcal{P}_N$ to consist of transition functions $\pi^{(\alpha)}$ such that for each state $\sigma \in \Sigma_i$, the one-step σ-restriction of $\pi^{(\alpha)}$ is in $\mathcal{P}_i$. That is, for all $\sigma \in \Sigma$ and inputs x, $\pi^{(\alpha)}(\sigma, x) = \widehat{\pi}_\sigma^{(\alpha)}(\sigma, x)$ where $\widehat{\pi}_\sigma^{(\alpha)} \in \mathcal{P}_{\mathcal{I}(\sigma)}$.

Though π can have exponentially many states, we would like to view it as composed of N transition functions, $\widehat{\pi}_{\sigma_i} \in \mathcal{P}_i$, where $\sigma_i \in \Sigma_i$. Thanks to the reach-restriction requirement on the reactive programs that we are interested in, for each i, there would indeed be only one state $\sigma_i \in \Sigma_i$ that we need to consider. However, recall that π is dynamically generated by a generator G interacting with an adversary Q, and the reachable states in π are determined by this interaction. So the decomposition should be framed at the level of the interactive generators, rather than individual transition functions.

This leads us to a bi-simulation based definition of decomposition that views the generator G as incorporating another generator H (which produces one-step programs), and gives a two-way equivalence between them. To formalize this notion of bi-simulation, we introduce the following notation of composite machines.

Composite Machines. It will be convenient to define a few different ways in which a program (a generator or an adversary) can be wrapped by another program. As described below, a generator will be wrapped by a blackbox simulator, J or Z.[8] We also introduce a non-blackbox wrapper W which will be used to adapt an adversary Q (that expects to interact with G) so that it can interact with both G and H.

- For a generator H, we write $\boxed{\frac{Z}{\boxed{H}}}$ to denote a composite machine in which Z runs H internally in a blackbox straight-line manner. The reactive program output by the composite generator is produced H, and the auxiliary output produced by it contains outputs from both H and Z. H may communicate with Z, and further the composite machine can communicate externally as described shortly. The running time of $\boxed{\frac{Z}{\boxed{H}}}$ is bounded by that of H plus an *additive* $\mathsf{poly}(\kappa)$ overhead that depends on Z.

- For a generator G, we write $\boxed{\frac{\boxed{G}}{J}}$ to denote a slightly different composite machine, which is similar to $\boxed{\frac{J}{\boxed{G}}}$ (G is run internally by J in a blackbox straight-line manner, and the auxiliary information is produced by both) but the reactive program it produces is output by J. The external communication pattern is also different as described below.

- For an adversary Q, we write $\boxed{\frac{\boxed{Q}}{W}}$ to denote a composite machine in which W internally runs Q in a straight-line manner with additive overhead, *but W can read the internal state of Q*. The auxiliary output of this composite machine is the entire view of W (which includes the auxiliary information a_Q produced by Q). The communication pattern is described below.

- Each of $\boxed{\frac{\boxed{G}}{J}}$, $\boxed{\frac{Z}{\boxed{H}}}$ and $\boxed{\frac{\boxed{Q}}{W}}$ has three external communication channels – one used by the internal machine (shown boxed) and the other two by the wrapper machine. In all machines the "middle" channel is used by the wrapper (J, Z and W, respectively); the "top" channel is used by G, Z and Q (resp.); the "bottom" channel is used by J, H and W (resp.). Note that when $\boxed{\frac{\boxed{G}}{J}}$ is

---

[8] Looking ahead, the role of J below is to simulate the presence of a one-step generator H when the actual execution involves the generator G, and the role of Z is to simulate the presence of G when the actual execution involves H.

connected to $\boxed{\overset{[\bar{Q}]}{W}}$, Q directly interacts with G, whereas when $\boxed{\frac{Z}{H}}$ is connected to $\boxed{\overset{[\bar{Q}]}{W}}$, Q interacts with Z.

For the ease of writing expressions, we shall denote $\boxed{\frac{G}{J}}$ by $G\|J$, and $\boxed{\frac{Z}{H}}$ by $H\|Z$. We will denote $\boxed{\overset{[\bar{Q}]}{W}}$ by $Q\lfloor W$; in fact, we will be interested in $\boxed{\overset{[\bar{Q}\hat{\varepsilon}]}{W}}$ (where $Q\hat{\varepsilon}$ itself is a composite machine involving a reach-extractor which interacts with Q as defined in Definition 3); we shall denote it by $Q\hat{\varepsilon}\lfloor W$.

Partial Reach-Extractor: For a valid decomposition, it will be important to have a bi-simulation that maps π to a one-step restriction π_σ such that σ is the unique reachable state in a subset of states Σ_i. To enforce this, we shall rely on an extractor for the adversary Q w.r.t. the generator G that produces π. However, the purpose of decomposition and composition is to be able to obtain an extractor for Q w.r.t. G along with a simulator, as in the definition of R3PO (Definition 4). To break this apparent circularity, we use the notion of a partial reach extractor: An $(i-1)$-partial reach extractor will be sufficient for defining decomposition "at part Σ_i," and it can be extended to an i-partial reach extractor, using the R3PO guarantee for the one-step generator.

Formally, a t-*partial reach-extractor* is defined identically to Definition 3, but with the relaxation that the reach-bound condition needs to hold only for $i \leq t$, instead of $i \leq N$. (The reach-restriction condition is still required to hold for all $i \in N$.) Thus, an N-partial reach extractor is a "full" reach-extractor.

Now we are ready to state the definition of decomposition. While informally we shall refer to decomposing a reactive program (or even a transition function) to one-step programs, formally, the decomposition is of a generator class to a sequence of generator classes, specified along with corresponding adversary classes and relaxed program classes.

Definition 5 (Decomposition of $(\mathcal{G}, \mathcal{Q})$ to $\mathcal{L}$). Let $\mathcal{G}$ be a $(\mathcal{P}, \mathcal{M})$-generator class where $\mathcal{P} = \mathcal{P}_1 \times \cdots \times \mathcal{P}_N$ is tree-ordered. Let $\mathcal{L} = (\mathcal{H}, \mathcal{Q}, \mathring{\mathcal{P}})$, where $\mathcal{H} = \{H\|Z \mid \text{PPT } Z\}$ for a fixed $(\mathcal{P}_i, \mathcal{M}_i)$-generator H, $\mathcal{Q}$ is an adversary class, and $\mathring{\mathcal{P}}$ is a transition function class.

Then, a generator $G \in \mathcal{G}$ is said to be *decomposable at part i to $\mathcal{L}$* if, there exist PPT J, Z, W so that $\forall Q \in \mathcal{Q}$, and all $(i-1)$-partial reach-extractors $\mathcal{E}$ for Q w.r.t. $(\mathcal{G}, \mathring{\mathcal{P}})$, it holds that $Q\hat{\varepsilon}\lfloor W \in \mathcal{Q}$ and:

- **Indistinguishability:** $\langle G\|J : Q\hat{\varepsilon}\lfloor W \rangle \approx \langle H\|Z : Q\hat{\varepsilon}\lfloor W \rangle$.
- In $\langle G\|J : Q\hat{\varepsilon}\lfloor W \rangle$, let the output of G be $((\pi^{(\alpha)}, \mu^{(\beta)}), a_G)$, and of $\mathcal{E}$ be (a_Q, Π, X^*); then J outputs $((\hat{\pi}_\sigma^{(\alpha)}, \hat{\mu}_\sigma^{(\beta)}), a_J)$ s.t.
  - **Correct One-Step Restriction:** $\text{REACH}_\Pi(X^*) \cap \Sigma_i \subseteq \{\sigma\}$.
  - **Correct Message Function:** $\hat{\mu}_\sigma^{(\beta)} \leftarrow \mathcal{M}_i$ is uniformly sampled at the end of the execution.

$(\mathcal{G}, \mathcal{Q})$ is said to be *decomposable into* $\mathcal{L} = (\mathcal{L}_1, \ldots, \mathcal{L}_N)$ if $\forall G \in \mathcal{G}$, $i \in [N]$, it holds that $\mathcal{L}_i = (\mathcal{H}_i, \mathcal{Q}_i, \mathring{\mathcal{P}}_i)$ where $\mathcal{Q}_i \supseteq \mathcal{Q}$, and G is decomposable at part i to $\mathcal{L}_i$. ◁

Above, we require two simulations to produce indistinguishable outputs (which includes their communication, as $Q|\mathcal{E}\lfloor W$ outputs its entire view as part of output), with J mimicking H, and Z mimicking G. The "correct one-step restriction" condition forces J (and hence H) to output a one-step restriction whose start state is the state that is reachable, as reported by a (partial) reach-extractor for G.

4.2 Composition Theorem

Above, decomposition related the transition functions in $\mathcal{P} = \mathcal{P}_1 \times \cdots \times \mathcal{P}_N$ to those in each $\mathcal{P}_i$. Before stating our composition theorem, we need to specify the message function space $\widehat{\mu}_i$ of these one-step programs as well.

As described in Sect. 2.3, $\widehat{\mu}_i$ should release garbled circuit labels for the state at which it is evaluated. For our purposes, it will be helpful to consider a labeling function (denoted below as $\widehat{\beta}$) which takes the part index i as an input, along with a bit position j and bit value b. Then $\widehat{\mu}_i$ will be of the form $\mathsf{encode}_{\widehat{\beta}}^{\mathcal{I},t}$ defined below, which only retains the part of $\widehat{\beta}$ for parts $i > t$.

Parameters: Program classes $\mathcal{P} = \mathcal{P}_1 \times \cdots \times \mathcal{P}_N$ with state-space $\Sigma = \{0,1\}^n$, and partition function $\mathcal{I} : \Sigma \to [N]$. A message function class $\mathcal{M}$.

Given One-Step Obfuscators: For each $i \in [N]$, $\mathcal{O}_i$ (taking inputs in $\mathcal{P}_i \times \widehat{\mathcal{M}}_{\mathcal{I},i}$)

Garbling Scheme: Let $(\mathsf{GCGarble}, \mathsf{GCEval})$ be a garbling scheme.

Obfuscator $\mathcal{O}$:
- **Input:** $(\pi^{(\alpha)}, \mu^{(\beta)})$, where $\pi^{(\alpha)} \in \mathcal{P}$, $\mu^{(\beta)} \in \mathcal{M}$.
- Uniformly randomly sample $\widehat{\beta} : [N] \times [n] \times \{0,1\} \to \{0,1\}^\kappa$
- For each $i \in [N]$,
  * Define $\widehat{\mu}_i$ to be $\mathsf{encode}_{\widehat{\beta}}^{\mathcal{I},i}$.
  * Define the function f_i as follows (with a fresh random tape hard-coded for $\mathcal{O}_i$ and, if needed, $\mu^{(\beta)}$):

$$f_i(\sigma) = \left(\mathcal{O}_i(\widehat{\pi}_\sigma^{(\alpha)}, \widehat{\mu}_i), \ \mu^{(\beta)}(\sigma) \right)$$

  * Let $\mathsf{GC}_i \leftarrow \mathsf{GCGarble}(f_i, \widehat{\beta}_i)$, where $\widehat{\beta}_i(\ell, b) = \widehat{\beta}(i, \ell, b)$ for $\ell \in [n], b \in \{0,1\}$.
- Let $i_0 = \mathcal{I}(\mathsf{start})$, where start is the start-state of $\pi^{(\alpha)}$.
  Output $\left(f_{i_0}(\mathsf{start}), \{\mathsf{GC}_i\}_{i \in [N] \setminus \{i_0\}} \right)$, along with a "driver program."

Fig. 1. Obfuscator $\mathcal{O}$ used to prove Theorem 1.

Definition 6 (Message function space $\widehat{\mathcal{M}}$). Let $\Sigma = \{0,1\}^n$, with a partition function $\mathcal{I} : \Sigma \to [N]$, and $\widehat{\beta} : [N] \times [n] \times \{0,1\} \to \{0,1\}^\kappa$. A *state labeling function* $\mathsf{encode}_{\widehat{\beta}}^{\mathcal{I},t} : \Sigma \to \{0,1\}^{n\kappa}$ is defined as

$$\mathsf{encode}_{\widehat{\beta}}^{\mathcal{I},t}(\sigma) = \begin{cases} \left(\widehat{\beta}(\mathcal{I}(\sigma),1,a_1),\ldots,\widehat{\beta}(\mathcal{I}(\sigma),n,a_n)\right) & \text{if } \mathcal{I}(\sigma) > t, \\ \bot & \text{otherwise,} \end{cases}$$

where $\sigma = (a_1,\ldots,a_n)$. Then, we define $\widehat{\mathcal{M}} = \bigcup_{\mathcal{I}:\Sigma\to[N],t\in[N]} \widehat{\mathcal{M}}_{\mathcal{I},t}$, where

$$\widehat{\mathcal{M}}_{\mathcal{I},t} = \left\{ \left(\mathsf{encode}_{\widehat{\beta}}^{\mathcal{I},t}\right) \mid \widehat{\beta} : [N] \times [n] \times \{0,1\} \to \{0,1\}^\kappa \right\}$$

$\triangleleft$

We are now ready to state our composition theorem.

Theorem 1. *Suppose $\mathcal{G}$ is a $(\mathcal{P},\mathcal{M})$-generator class that is decomposable into $\mathcal{L} = \{\mathcal{H}_i, \mathcal{Q}_i, \mathring{\mathcal{P}}_i\}_{i\in[N]}$, such that, for each $i \in [N]$, $\mathcal{H}_i$ is a $(\mathcal{P}_i, \widehat{\mathcal{M}}_{\mathcal{I},i})$-generator class and there exists an R3PO scheme $\mathcal{O}_i$ for $(\mathcal{H}_i, \mathcal{Q}_i, \mathring{\mathcal{P}}_i)$. Then there exists an R3PO scheme $\mathcal{O}$ for $(\mathcal{G}, \mathcal{Q}, \mathring{\mathcal{P}})$ where $\mathring{\mathcal{P}} = \mathring{\mathcal{P}}_1 \times \cdots \times \mathring{\mathcal{P}}_N$.*

The obfuscator $\mathcal{O}$ used to prove Theorem 1 is shown in Fig. 1. Please refer to the full version for the proof that it is an R3PO scheme.

5   Private Multi-Authority ABE

In this section, we define Private Multi-Authority ABE and show how to instantiate it from any CP-ABE scheme, using R3PO schemes for commitment-opening and signatures together. Section 2.6 gives an overview of the notion and the construction described below.

5.1   Definition for Private Multi-Authority ABE

Let the authorities in the system be $\mathbb{A}_1, \ldots, \mathbb{A}_N$, s.t. each authority $\mathbb{A}_i$ publishes its public key mpk_i after a local non-interactive setup. Each authority $\mathbb{A}_i$ also has an attribute-granting policy Θ_i^{gid} w.r.t. each gid. A sender encrypts a message m with a ciphertext-policy ϕ under the public keys of all the authorities, s.t. a receiver with global identifier gid and attribute vector $\bar{x}$ can decrypt it only if it has attribute key for $\bar{x}$ and each authorities' attribute-granting policies accepts (that is, $\forall i \in [N], \Theta_i^{\mathsf{gid}}(\bar{x}) = 1$) and the ciphertext-policy accepts (that is, $\phi(\bar{x}) = 1$). To get the attribute key for attribute vector $\bar{x}$, the receiver sends a key-request req_i to each authority $\mathbb{A}_i$, gets back a key-component $\mathsf{sk}_{\mathsf{req}_i}$, and combines all the key-components to construct the key $\mathsf{sk}_{\bar{x}}$.

We define security w.r.t. a corruption model where the adversary is allowed to maliciously corrupt the receiver and semi-honestly corrupt any subset of the authorities. If the receiver is honest, we require that any key-request req reveals nothing about $\bar{x}$ to the adversary (even if it semi-honestly corrupts all the authorities). If the receiver is corrupt, we require that the adversary is unable to distinguish between encryptions of any m_0 and m_1 w.r.t. a policy ϕ, if it did not send a key-request for any $\bar{x}$ that satisfies ϕ to the honest authorities.

Definition 7 (Private Multi-Authority ABE (p-MA-ABE)). A p-MA-ABE scheme for N authorities, message space M, class $\mathcal{C}$ of ciphertext-policies and class Θ of attribute-granting policies, both over n-bit attributes, and global identifiers space GID consists of PPT algorithms as follows:

- SetupAuth$(1^\kappa) \to (\mathsf{mpk}, \mathsf{msk})$: On input the security parameter κ, outputs the master keys for an individual authority.
- Encrypt $\left(\{\mathsf{mpk}_i\}_{i\in[N]}, \phi, m\right) \to \mathsf{ct}$: On input the master public keys of all authorities, a policy $\phi : \{0,1\}^n \to \{0,1\}$ in $\mathcal{C}$ and a message $m \in \mathsf{M}$, outputs a ciphertext ct.
- KeyRequest $\left(\{\mathsf{mpk}_i\}_{i\in[N]}, \mathsf{gid}, \bar{x}\right) \to (\mathsf{st}, \{\mathsf{req}_i\}_{i\in[N]})$: On input the master public keys of all authorities, a global identity $\mathsf{gid} \in \mathsf{GID}$ and an attribute vector $\bar{x} \in \{0,1\}^n$, outputs a recipient state st and requests $\{\mathsf{req}_1, \dots, \mathsf{req}_N\}$.
- KeyGen $\left(i, \mathsf{msk}_i, \Theta_i^{\mathsf{gid}}, \mathsf{req}_i, \{\mathsf{mpk}_j\}_{j\in[N]}\right) \to \mathsf{sk}_{\mathsf{req}_i}$: On input an authority index $i \in [N]$, master secret key msk_i, an attribute-granting policy Θ_i^{gid}, a request req_i and the master public keys of all authorities, outputs a key component $\mathsf{sk}_{\mathsf{req}_i}$ or $\bot$.
- KeyCombine $\left(\mathsf{st}, \{\mathsf{sk}_{\mathsf{req}_i}\}_{i\in[N]}\right) \to \mathsf{sk}_{\bar{x}}$: On input a recipient state st and a set of key components $\{\mathsf{sk}_{\mathsf{req}_i}\}_{i\in[N]}$, outputs a secret key $\mathsf{sk}_{\bar{x}}$.
- Decrypt $(\mathsf{sk}_{\bar{x}}, \mathsf{ct}) \to m$: On input a secret key $\mathsf{sk}_{\bar{x}}$ and a ciphertext ct, outputs a message m or $\bot$.

The following correctness and security properties are required:

1. **Correctness**: $\forall$ security parameter κ, number of authorities $N \in \mathbb{N}$, identities $\mathsf{gid} \in \mathsf{GID}$, messages $m \in \mathsf{M}$, ciphertext policies $\phi \in \mathcal{C}$, attribute granting policies $\{\Theta_i^{\mathsf{gid}} \in \Theta\}_{i\in[N]}$, and attribute vectors $\bar{x}$ s.t $\phi(\bar{x}) = 1$ and $\Theta_i^{\mathsf{gid}}(\bar{x}) = 1$ for all $i \in [N]$, it holds that if:

$$\forall i \in [N], \qquad (\mathsf{mpk}_i, \mathsf{msk}_i) \leftarrow \mathsf{SetupAuth}(1^\kappa)$$
$$(\mathsf{st}, \{\mathsf{req}_i\}_{i\in[N]}) \leftarrow \mathsf{KeyRequest}(\{\mathsf{mpk}_i\}_{i\in[N]}, \mathsf{gid}, \bar{x})$$
$$\forall i \in [N], \qquad \mathsf{sk}_{\mathsf{req}_i} \leftarrow \mathsf{KeyGen}\left(i, \mathsf{msk}_i, \Theta_i^{\mathsf{gid}}, \mathsf{req}_i, \{\mathsf{mpk}_i\}_{i\in[N]}\right)$$
$$\mathsf{sk}_{\bar{x}} \leftarrow \mathsf{KeyCombine}\left(\mathsf{st}, \{\mathsf{sk}_{\mathsf{req}_i}\}_{i\in[N]}\right)$$

then $\Pr\left[\mathsf{Decrypt}\left(\mathsf{sk}_{\bar{x}}, \mathsf{Encrypt}(\{\mathsf{mpk}_i\}_{i\in[N]}, \phi, m)\right) = m\right] = 1$.

2. **Security of encryption**: For any PPT adversary $\mathcal{A} = (\mathcal{A}_0, \mathcal{A}_1, \mathcal{A}_2, \mathcal{A}_3)$ with semi-honest corruption of any subset of authorities and malicious corruption of the receiver, there exists a negligible function $\mathsf{negl}(.)$ such that the following holds in the experiment $\mathrm{IND}_{\mathrm{mesg}}^{\mathrm{p\text{-}MA\text{-}ABE}}$ shown in Fig. 2:

$$\Pr[\mathrm{IND}_{\mathrm{mesg}}^{\mathrm{p\text{-}MA\text{-}ABE}}(\mathcal{A}) = 0] \leq \frac{1}{2} + \mathsf{negl}(\lambda).$$

3. **Receiver Privacy against Semi-honest Adversary**: For any PPT adversary $\mathcal{A} = (\mathcal{A}_0, \mathcal{A}_1)$ that corrupts each authority in a semi-honest way, there exists a negligible function $\mathsf{negl}(.)$ such that the following holds in the experiment $\mathrm{IND}_{\mathrm{attr}}^{\mathrm{p\text{-}MA\text{-}ABE}}$ shown in Fig. 2:

$$\Pr[\mathrm{IND}_{\mathrm{attr}}^{\mathrm{p\text{-}MA\text{-}ABE}}(\mathcal{A}) = 0] \leq \frac{1}{2} + \mathsf{negl}(\lambda).$$

$\triangleleft$

5.2   Construction for Private Multi-Authority ABE

In this section, we give a scheme for p-MA-ABE from the following primitives:

- a CP-ABE scheme
- a non-interactive UC secure commitment scheme
- a puncturable signature scheme
- an R3PO scheme $\mathcal{O}_{\mathrm{p\text{-}MA\text{-}ABE}}$ w.r.t. $(\mathcal{G}_{\mathrm{p\text{-}MA\text{-}ABE}}^1, \mathcal{Q}_{\mathrm{p\text{-}MA\text{-}ABE}})$ and $(\mathcal{G}_{\mathrm{p\text{-}MA\text{-}ABE}}^2, \mathcal{Q}_{\mathrm{p\text{-}MA\text{-}ABE}})$, which we describe in the full version.

Let the number of authorities be N, space of access policies $\mathcal{C}$ correspond exactly to the policies supported by the underlying single-authority CP-ABE scheme.

Completeness Requirement of Commitment Scheme: We will additionally require that, given a commitment setup $\mathsf{Com.crs}$, for any c, d s.t. $\mathsf{Com.Open}$ $(\mathsf{Com.crs}, c, d) = m$, it holds that (m, c, d) lies in the support of the commit algorithm, that is: there exists r s.t. $(c, d) \leftarrow \mathsf{Com.Commit}(\mathsf{Com.crs}, m; r)$. Any commitment scheme can be enhanced to have this property, by modifying it as follows.

Parameter: Let κ be the security parameter, N be the number of authorities.

Experiment $\mathbf{IND}_{\mathbf{mesg}}^{\mathbf{p\text{-}MA\text{-}ABE}}$

- $(\mathsf{st}_0, H) \leftarrow \mathcal{A}_0(1^\kappa)$.
- $\{(\mathsf{mpk}_i, \mathsf{msk}_i) \leftarrow \mathsf{SetupAuth}(1^\kappa)\}_{i \in H}$.
- $(\mathsf{st}_1, \{\mathsf{mpk}_i\}_{i \in [\mathsf{N}] \setminus H}) \leftarrow \mathcal{A}_1(\mathsf{st}_0, \{\mathsf{mpk}_i\}_{i \in H})$.
- Let $O_k(y, \{\Theta_i^{\mathsf{gid}}\}_{i \in H}) := \mathsf{KeyGen}\left(k, \mathsf{msk}_k, \Theta_k^{\mathsf{gid}}, y, \{\mathsf{mpk}_i\}_{i \in [\mathsf{N}]}\right)$, where $y = (\mathsf{gid}, c)$.
- $(\mathsf{st}_2, \phi, m_0, m_1) \leftarrow \mathcal{A}_2^{\{O_k(\cdot, \cdot)\}_{k \in H}}(\mathsf{st}_1)$
- $b \leftarrow \{0, 1\}$.
- $\mathsf{ct} \leftarrow \mathsf{Encrypt}\left(\{\mathsf{mpk}_i\}_{i \in [\mathsf{N}]}, \phi, m_b\right)$.
- $b' \leftarrow \mathcal{A}_3^{\{O_k(\cdot)\}_{k \in H}}(\mathsf{st}_2, \mathsf{ct})$.
- If $\mathcal{A}_2$ or $\mathcal{A}_3$ queried any oracle with different key-policies $\{\Theta_i^{\mathsf{gid}}\}_{i \in H}$ for the same globalid gid, output $a \leftarrow \{0, 1\}$.
  If $\exists \mathsf{gid}, \bar{\mathsf{x}}$ s.t. $\phi(\bar{\mathsf{x}}) = 1$ and, $\forall k \in H$, $\Theta_k^{\mathsf{gid}}(\bar{\mathsf{x}}) = 1$, and $\exists r, k^* \in H$ s.t. $\mathcal{A}_2$ or $\mathcal{A}_3$ queried the oracle O_{k^*} with req_{k^*}, where $(\mathsf{st}, \{\mathsf{req}_k\}_{k \in [\mathsf{N}]}) \leftarrow \mathsf{KeyRequest}(\{\mathsf{mpk}_k\}_{k \in [\mathsf{N}]}, \mathsf{gid}, \bar{\mathsf{x}}; r)$, then output $a \leftarrow \{0, 1\}$.
  Else, output $a = b \oplus b'$.

Experiment $\mathbf{IND}_{\mathbf{attr}}^{\mathbf{p\text{-}MA\text{-}ABE}}$

- $(\mathsf{st}_0, \{\mathsf{mpk}_i\}_{i \in [\mathsf{N}]}, \bar{\mathsf{x}}_0, \bar{\mathsf{x}}_1, \mathsf{gid}) \leftarrow \mathcal{A}_0(1^\kappa)$.
- $b \leftarrow \{0, 1\}$.
- $b' \leftarrow \mathcal{A}_1(\mathsf{st}_0, \mathsf{KeyRequest}(\{\mathsf{mpk}_i\}_{i \in [\mathsf{N}]}, \mathsf{gid}, \bar{\mathsf{x}}_b))$.
- Output $b \oplus b'$.

Fig. 2. p-MA-ABE security experiments.

$$\mathsf{Commit}'(\mathsf{Com.crs}, m; r) = \begin{cases} (c, d) & \text{if } r = 0^k \|c\| d \text{ and } \mathsf{Com.Open}(\mathsf{Com.crs}, c, d) = m \\ \mathsf{Com.Commit}(\mathsf{Com.crs}, m; r) & \text{otherwise.} \end{cases}$$

We now prove that the protocol in Fig. 3 is in fact a secure p-MA-ABE scheme.

Lemma 1. *If there exists a CP-ABE scheme, a non-interactive UC secure commitment scheme, a puncturable signature scheme, and an R3PO scheme* $\mathcal{O}_{p\text{-}MA\text{-}ABE}$ *w.r.t.* $(\mathcal{G}_{p\text{-}MA\text{-}ABE}^1, \mathcal{Q}_{p\text{-}MA\text{-}ABE})^9$, *then there exists a secure p-MA-ABE scheme.*

Please refer to the full version for the full details of the proof.

---

[9] Which is also an R3PO w.r.t. $(\mathcal{G}_{p\text{-}MA\text{-}ABE}^2, \mathcal{Q}_{p\text{-}MA\text{-}ABE})$.

Protocol for Private Multi-Authority ABE

Parameter: Let κ be the security parameter, N be the number of authorities.
Primitives:
   A CP-ABE scheme ABE = (ABE.Setup, ABE.KeyGen, ABE.Encrypt, ABE.Decrypt)
   A Commitment scheme Com = (Com.Setup, Com.Commit, Com.Open)
   A puncturable signature scheme Sig = (Sig.gen, Sig.sign, Sig.verify)
   An obfuscation scheme $\mathcal{O}_{\text{p-MA-ABE}}$

– p-MA-ABE.SetupAuth(1^κ):
   • Sample the common random string Com.crs $\leftarrow$ Com.Setup(1^κ).
   • Sample the signature keys (Sig.vk, Sig.sk) $\leftarrow$ Sig.gen(1^κ).
   • Sample the ABE keys (ABE.mpk, ABE.msk) $\leftarrow$ ABE.Setup(1^κ).
   • Set mpk := (Com.crs, Sig.vk, ABE.mpk) and msk := (Sig.sk, ABE.msk).
   • Output (mpk, msk).

– p-MA-ABE.Encrypt (pk, ϕ, m):
   • For all $i \in [N]$, parse mpk_i as (Com.crs$_i$, Sig.vk$_i$, ABE.mpk$_i$).
   • Sample $s_1, \ldots, s_N$ s.t. $s_1 + \ldots + s_N = m$.
   • For all $i \in [N]$, compute ABE.ct$_i$ $\leftarrow$ ABE.Encrypt(ABE.mpk$_i$, ϕ, s_i).
   • Output ct := {ABE.ct$_1$, ..., ABE.ct$_N$}.

– p-MA-ABE.Decrypt (sk$_{\bar{x}}$, ct):
   • Parse sk$_{\bar{x}}$ as {sk$^{\text{ABE}}_{\bar{x},1}$, ..., sk$^{\text{ABE}}_{\bar{x},N}$}.
   • Parse ct as {ABE.ct$_1$, ..., ABE.ct$_N$}.
   • For all $i \in [N]$, set $s_i = $ ABE.Decrypt(ABE.mpk$_i$, sk$^{\text{ABE}}_{\bar{x},i}$, ABE.ct$_i$).
   • Set $m := s_1 + \ldots + s_N$.
   • Output m.

– p-MA-ABE.KeyRequest(pk, gid, $\bar{x}$):
   • For all $i \in [N]$, parse mpk_i as (Com.crs$_i$, Sig.vk$_i$, ABE.mpk$_i$),
     compute $(c_i, d_i) \leftarrow$ Com.Commit(Com.crs$_i$, gid$\|\bar{x}$)
     and set req$_i$:= (gid, c_i).
   • Set st := (gid, $\bar{x}$, $\{d_i\}_{i \in [N]}$).
   • Output (st, $\{\text{req}_i\}_{i \in [N]}$).

– p-MA-ABE.KeyGen(t, msk$_t$, Θ^{gid}_t, req$_t$, pk): Computes
   • Parse msk as (Sig.sk$_t$, ABE.msk$_t$).
   • For all $i \in [N]$, parse mpk_i as (Com.crs$_i$, Sig.vk$_i$, ABE.mpk$_i$).
   • Parse req$_t$ as (gid, c_t).
   • Fix $\pi^{(\alpha)}_{\text{pp}} \in \mathcal{P}_{\text{p-MA-ABE}}$ where pp $= (t, \text{Com.crs}_t, c_t)$, $\alpha = \Theta^{\text{gid}}_t$, and start $= \sigma^1_{\text{pk,gid}}$.
   • Fix $\mu^{(\beta)} \in \mathcal{M}_{\text{p-MA-ABE}}$ where $\beta = (0, \text{Sig.sk}_t, \text{ABE.msk}_t)$.
   • Compute sk$_{\text{req}_t}$ $\leftarrow$ $\mathcal{O}_{\text{p-MA-ABE}}(\pi^{(\alpha)}_{\text{pp}}, \mu^{(\beta)})$.
   • Output sk$_{\text{req}_t}$.

– p-MA-ABE.KeyCombine (st, $\{\text{sk}_{\text{req}_i}\}_{i \in [N]}$):
   • Parse st as (gid, $\bar{x}$, $\{d_i\}_{i \in [N]}$).
   • For all $t \in [N]$, parse sk$_{\text{req}_t}$ as ρ_t and evaluate as $\tau_t \leftarrow \rho_t(d_t)$[11]
   • Finally, for all $t \in [N]$, compute sk$^{\text{ABE}}_{\bar{x},t}$ $\leftarrow \rho_t(\tau_1, \ldots, \tau_N)$.
   • Output $\{\text{sk}^{\text{ABE}}_{\bar{x},t}\}_{t \in [N]}$.

Fig. 3. A secure p-MA-ABE Protocol. (formally, ρ_t also takes as input a state σ_1 and also outputs a state σ_2. for brevity, we ignore mentioning it here.)

References

1. Agrawal, S., Goyal, R., Tomida, J.: Multi-party functional encryption. In: Nissim, K., Waters, B. (eds.) TCC 2021. LNCS, vol. 13043, pp. 224–255. Springer, Cham (2021). https://doi.org/10.1007/978-3-030-90453-1_8
2. Ananth, P., Boneh, D., Garg, S., Sahai, A., Zhandry, M.: Differing-inputs obfuscation and applications. Cryptology ePrint Archive, Report 2013/689 (2013)
3. Backes, M., Pfitzmann, B., Waidner, M.: A general composition theorem for secure reactive systems. In: Naor, M. (ed.) TCC 2004. LNCS, vol. 2951, pp. 336–354. Springer, Heidelberg (2004). https://doi.org/10.1007/978-3-540-24638-1_19
4. Barak, B., Bitansky, N., Canetti, R., Kalai, Y.T., Paneth, O., Sahai, A.: Obfuscation for evasive functions. In: Lindell, Y. (ed.) TCC 2014. LNCS, vol. 8349, pp. 26–51. Springer, Heidelberg (2014). https://doi.org/10.1007/978-3-642-54242-8_2
5. Barak, B., et al.: On the (Im)possibility of obfuscating programs. J. ACM $59(2)$ (2012). ISSN: 0004-5411
6. Benhamouda, F., Lin, H.: k-round multiparty computation from k-round oblivious transfer via garbled interactive circuits. In: Nielsen, J.B., Rijmen, V. (eds.) EUROCRYPT 2018. LNCS, vol. 10821, pp. 500–532. Springer, Cham (2018). https://doi.org/10.1007/978-3-319-78375-8_17
7. Bitansky, N., Canetti, R., Kalai, Y.T., Paneth, O.: On virtual grey box obfuscation for general circuits. In: Garay, J.A., Gennaro, R. (eds.) CRYPTO 2014. LNCS, vol. 8617, pp. 108–125. Springer, Heidelberg (2014). https://doi.org/10.1007/978-3-662-44381-1_7
8. Brakerski, Z., Lombardi, A., Segev, G., Vaikuntanathan, V.: Anonymous IBE, leakage resilience and circular security from new assumptions. In: Nielsen, J.B., Rijmen, V. (eds.) EUROCRYPT 2018. LNCS, vol. 10820, pp. 535–564. Springer, Cham (2018). https://doi.org/10.1007/978-3-319-78381-9_20
9. Brakerski, Z., Vaikuntanathan, V.: Lattice-based FHE as secure as PKE. In: ITCS 2014, pp. 1–12 (2014)
10. Campanelli, M., David, B., Khoshakhlagh, H., Konring, A., Nielsen, J.B.: Encryption to the future: a paradigm for sending secret messages to future (anonymous) committees. Cryptology ePrint Archive, Paper 2021/1423 (2021)
11. Canetti, R.: Universally composable security: a new paradigm for cryptographic protocols. In: Proceedings 42nd IEEE Symposium on Foundations of Computer Science, pp. 136–145 (2001)
12. Canetti, R.: Security and composition of multiparty cryptographic protocols. J. Cryptol. $13(1)$, 143–202 (2000)
13. Canetti, R., Cohen, A., Lindell, Y.: A simpler variant of universally composable security for standard multiparty computation. In: Gennaro, R., Robshaw, M. (eds.) CRYPTO 2015. LNCS, vol. 9216, pp. 3–22. Springer, Heidelberg (2015). https://doi.org/10.1007/978-3-662-48000-7_1
14. Canetti, R., Lin, H., Tessaro, S., Vaikuntanathan, V.: Obfuscation of probabilistic circuits and applications. In: Dodis, Y., Nielsen, J.B. (eds.) TCC 2015. LNCS, vol. 9015, pp. 468–497. Springer, Heidelberg (2015). https://doi.org/10.1007/978-3-662-46497-7_19
15. Chase, M.: Multi-authority attribute based encryption. In: Theory of Cryptography, pp. 515–534 (2007)
16. Cho, C., Döttling, N., Garg, S., Gupta, D., Miao, P., Polychroniadou, A.: Laconic oblivious transfer and its applications. In: Katz, J., Shacham, H. (eds.) CRYPTO 2017. LNCS, vol. 10402, pp. 33–65. Springer, Cham (2017). https://doi.org/10.1007/978-3-319-63715-0_2

17. Datta, P., Komargodski, I., Waters, B.: Decentralized multi-authority ABE for DNFs from LWE. In: Canteaut, A., Standaert, F.-X. (eds.) EUROCRYPT 2021. LNCS, vol. 12696, pp. 177–209. Springer, Cham (2021). https://doi.org/10.1007/978-3-030-77870-5_7

18. Dolev, D., Dwork, C., Naor, M.: Non-malleable cryptography. SIAM J. Comput. **30**, 391–437 (2001)

19. Döttling, N., Garg, S.: From selective IBE to Full IBE and selective HIBE. In: Kalai, Y., Reyzin, L. (eds.) TCC 2017. LNCS, vol. 10677, pp. 372–408. Springer, Cham (2017). https://doi.org/10.1007/978-3-319-70500-2_13

20. Döttling, N., Garg, S.: Identity-based encryption from the Diffie-Hellman assumption. In: Katz, J., Shacham, H. (eds.) CRYPTO 2017. LNCS, vol. 10401, pp. 537–569. Springer, Cham (2017). https://doi.org/10.1007/978-3-319-63688-7_18

21. Dwork, C., Naor, M., Sahai, A.: Concurrent zero-knowledge. J. ACM **51**(6), 851–898 (2004)

22. Galbraith, S.D., Zobernig, L.: Obfuscating finite automata. In: Dunkelman, O., Jacobson, Jr., M.J., O'Flynn, C. (eds.) SAC 2020. LNCS, vol. 12804, pp. 90–114. Springer, Cham (2021). https://doi.org/10.1007/978-3-030-81652-0_4

23. Garg, S., Hajiabadi, M., Mahmoody, M., Rahimi, A.: Registration-based encryption: removing private-key generator from IBE. In: Beimel, A., Dziembowski, S. (eds.) TCC 2018. LNCS, vol. 11239, pp. 689–718. Springer, Cham (2018). https://doi.org/10.1007/978-3-030-03807-6_25

24. Garg, S., Hajiabadi, M., Mahmoody, M., Rahimi, A., Sekar, S.: Registration-based encryption from standard assumptions. In: Lin, D., Sako, K. (eds.) PKC 2019. LNCS, vol. 11443, pp. 63–93. Springer, Cham (2019). https://doi.org/10.1007/978-3-030-17259-6_3

25. Garg, S., Lu, S., Ostrovsky, R.: Black-Box Garbled RAM. Cryptology ePrint Archive, Report 2015/307 (2015)

26. Garg, S., Lu, S., Ostrovsky, R., Scafuro, A.: Garbled RAM from one-way functions. In: STOC 2015, pp. 449–458 (2015)

27. Garg, S., Srinivasan, A.: Two-round multiparty secure computation from minimal assumptions. In: Nielsen, J.B., Rijmen, V. (eds.) EUROCRYPT 2018. LNCS, vol. 10821, pp. 468–499. Springer, Cham (2018). https://doi.org/10.1007/978-3-319-78375-8_16

28. Gentry, C., Halevi, S., Lu, S., Ostrovsky, R., Raykova, M., Wichs, D.: Garbled RAM revisited. In: Nguyen, P.Q., Oswald, E. (eds.) EUROCRYPT 2014. LNCS, vol. 8441, pp. 405–422. Springer, Heidelberg (2014). https://doi.org/10.1007/978-3-642-55220-5_23

29. Gorbunov, S., Vaikuntanathan, V., Wee, H.: Attribute-based encryption for circuits. J. ACM **62**(6), 1–33 (2015)

30. Goyal, V., Pandey, O., Sahai, A., Waters, B.: Attribute-based encryption for fine-grained access control of encrypted data. In: Proceedings of the 13th ACM Conference on Computer and Communications Security, CCS 2006, pp. 89–98 (2006)

31. Hada, S., Tanaka, T.: On the existence of 3-round zero-knowledge protocols. In: Krawczyk, H. (ed.) CRYPTO 1998. LNCS, vol. 1462, pp. 408–423. Springer, Heidelberg (1998). https://doi.org/10.1007/BFb0055744

32. Dennis Hofheinz and Victor Shoup: GNUC: a new universal composability framework. J. Cryptol. **28**(3), 423–508 (2015)

33. Hohenberger, S., Rothblum, G.N., Shelat, A., Vaikuntanathan, V.: Securely obfuscating re-encryption. In: Vadhan, S.P. (ed.) TCC 2007. LNCS, vol. 4392, pp. 233–252. Springer, Heidelberg (2007). https://doi.org/10.1007/978-3-540-70936-7_13

34. Hohenberger, S., Waters, B.: Attribute-based encryption with fast decryption. In: Kurosawa, K., Hanaoka, G. (eds.) PKC 2013. LNCS, vol. 7778, pp. 162–179. Springer, Heidelberg (2013). https://doi.org/10.1007/978-3-642-36362-7_11

35. Ishai, Y., Pandey, O., Sahai, A.: Public-Coin Differing-Inputs Obfuscation and Its Applications. In: Dodis, Y., Nielsen, J.B. (eds.) TCC 2015. LNCS, vol. 9015, pp. 668–697. Springer, Heidelberg (2015). https://doi.org/10.1007/978-3-662-46497-7_26

36. Jain, A., Lin, H., Sahai, A.: Indistinguishability obfuscation from well-founded assumptions. In: STOC 2021, pp. 60–73 (2021)

37. Jutla, C.S., Roy, A.: Shorter Quasi-adaptive NIZK proofs for linear subspaces. In: Sako, K., Sarkar, P. (eds.) ASIACRYPT 2013. LNCS, vol. 8269, pp. 1–20. Springer, Heidelberg (2013). https://doi.org/10.1007/978-3-642-42033-7_1

38. Kim, S.: Multi-authority attribute-based encryption from LWE in the OT model. Cryptology ePrint Archive, Report 2019/280 (2019)

39. Lewko, A., Okamoto, T., Sahai, A., Takashima, K., Waters, B.: Fully secure functional encryption: attribute-based encryption and (hierarchical) inner product encryption. In: Gilbert, H. (ed.) EUROCRYPT 2010. LNCS, vol. 6110, pp. 62–91. Springer, Heidelberg (2010). https://doi.org/10.1007/978-3-642-13190-5_4

40. Lewko, A., Waters, B.: Decentralizing attribute-based encryption. In: Paterson, K.G. (ed.) EUROCRYPT 2011. LNCS, vol. 6632, pp. 568–588. Springer, Heidelberg (2011). https://doi.org/10.1007/978-3-642-20465-4_31

41. Lin, H., Pass, R., Seth, K., Telang, S.: Indistinguishability obfuscation with non-trivial efficiency. In: Cheng, C.-M., Chung, K.-M., Persiano, G., Yang, B.-Y. (eds.) PKC 2016. LNCS, vol. 9615, pp. 447–462. Springer, Heidelberg (2016). https://doi.org/10.1007/978-3-662-49387-8_17

42. Lu, S., Ostrovsky, R.: How to garble RAM programs? In: Johansson, T., Nguyen, P.Q. (eds.) EUROCRYPT 2013. LNCS, vol. 7881, pp. 719–734. Springer, Heidelberg (2013). https://doi.org/10.1007/978-3-642-38348-9_42

43. Lynn, B., Prabhakaran, M., Sahai, A.: Positive results and techniques for obfuscation. In: Cachin, C., Camenisch, J.L. (eds.) EUROCRYPT 2004. LNCS, vol. 3027, pp. 20–39. Springer, Heidelberg (2004). https://doi.org/10.1007/978-3-540-24676-3_2

44. Maurer, U.: Constructive cryptography – a new paradigm for security definitions and proofs. In: Mödersheim, S., Palamidessi, C. (eds.) TOSCA 2011. LNCS, vol. 6993, pp. 33–56. Springer, Heidelberg (2012). https://doi.org/10.1007/978-3-642-27375-9_3

45. Micciancio, D., Tessaro, S.: An equational approach to secure multi-party computation. In: ITCS 2013, pp. 355–372 (2013)

46. Michalevsky, Y., Joye, M.: Decentralized policy-hiding ABE with receiver privacy. In: Lopez, J., Zhou, J., Soriano, M. (eds.) ESORICS 2018, Part II. LNCS, vol. 11099, pp. 548–567. Springer, Cham (2018). https://doi.org/10.1007/978-3-319-98989-1_27

47. Prabhakaran, M., Sahai, A.: New notions of security: achieving universal composability without trusted setup. In: STOC 2004, pp. 242–251 (2004)

48. Sahai, A., Waters, B.: Fuzzy identity-based encryption. In: Cramer, R. (ed.) EURO-CRYPT 2005. LNCS, vol. 3494, pp. 457–473. Springer, Heidelberg (2005). https://doi.org/10.1007/11426639_27

49. Sahai, A., Waters, B.: How to use indistinguishability obfuscation: deniable encryption, and more. In: STOC 2014, pp. 475–484 (2014)

50. Waters, B., Wee, H., Wu, D.J.: Multi-authority ABE from lattices without random oracles. Cryptology ePrint Archive, Paper 2022/1194 (2022). https://eprint.iacr.org/2022/1194

51. Wichs, D., Zirdelis, G.: Obfuscating compute-and-compare programs under LWE. In: FOCS, pp. 600–611 (2017)

52. Wikström, D.: Simplified universal composability framework. In: Kushilevitz, E., Malkin, T. (eds.) TCC 2016. LNCS, vol. 9562, pp. 566–595. Springer, Heidelberg (2016). https://doi.org/10.1007/978-3-662-49096-9_24

53. Yao, A.C.-C.: How to generate and exchange secrets. In: 27th Annual Symposium on Foundations of Computer Science (SFCS 1986), pp. 162–167 (1986)

54. Yun, K., Wang, X., Xue, R.: Identity-based functional encryption for quadratic functions from lattices. In: Naccache, D., et al. (eds.) ICICS 2018. LNCS, vol. 11149, pp. 409–425. Springer, Cham (2018). https://doi.org/10.1007/978-3-030-01950-1_24

Selective Opening Security
in the Quantum Random Oracle Model,
Revisited

Jiaxin Pan[1,2(✉)] and Runzhi Zeng[2]

[1] University of Kassel, Kassel, Germany
jiaxin.pan@uni-kassel.de
[2] Department of Mathematical Sciences, NTNU – Norwegian University of Science
and Technology, Trondheim, Norway
runzhi.zeng@ntnu.no

Abstract. We prove that two variants of the Fujisaki-Okamoto transformations are selective opening (SO) secure against chosen-ciphertext
attacks in the quantum random oracle model (QROM), assuming that
the underlying public-key encryption scheme is one-wayness against
chosen-plaintext attacks (OW-CPA). The two variants we consider are
$\mathsf{FO}^{\not\perp}$ (Hofheinz, Hövelmanns, and Kiltz, TCC 2017) and $\mathsf{U}_m^{\not\perp}$ (Jiang et
al., CRYPTO 2018). This is the *first* correct proof in the QROM.

The previous work of Sato and Shikata (IMACC 2019) showed the SO
security of $\mathsf{FO}^{\not\perp}$ in the QROM. However, we identify a subtle gap in their
work. To close this gap, we propose a new framework that allows us to
adaptively reprogram a QRO with respect to multiple queries that are
computationally hard to predict. This is a property that can be easily
achieved by the classical ROM, but is very hard to achieve in the QROM.
Hence, our framework brings the QROM closer to the classical ROM.

Under our new framework, we construct the *first tightly* SO secure
PKE in the QROM using lossy encryption. Our final application is prov-
ing $\mathsf{FO}^{\not\perp}$ and $\mathsf{U}_m^{\not\perp}$ are bi-selective opening (Bi-SO) secure in the QROM.
This is a stronger SO security notion, where an adversary can addition-
ally corrupt some users' secret keys.

Keywords: Selective opening security · quantum random oracle
model · Fujisaki-Okamoto transformation · tight security

1 Introduction

Public-key encryption (PKE) schemes are a central topic in cryptography. Their
widely accepted security notion is indstinguishability against chosen-ciphertext
attacks (IND-CCA), which states that confidentiality holds even if an adversary $\mathcal{A}$ can adaptively decrypt ciphertexts of its choice, except the challenge
ciphertext. This is a security notion in the single-user, single-challenge setting,

Partially supported by the Research Council of Norway under Project No. 324235.

Q. Tang and V. Teague (Eds.): PKC 2024, LNCS 14603, pp. 92–122, 2024.
https://doi.org/10.1007/978-3-031-57725-3_4

namely, only one user's public key and one challenge ciphertext are exposed to an adversary.

Its multi-user, multi-challenge counterpart is an arguably more realistic setting. Selective opening (SO) security [3,6] is a notion in a multi-challenge setting, where an adversary is given multiple challenge ciphertexts under a single public key and aims at learning some information about the encrypted messages. On top of that, the adversary can open a subset of the challenge ciphertexts and reveal the corresponding messages and randomness used to generate those ciphertexts. SO security guarantees the confidentiality of the remaining unopened challenge ciphertexts. The recent notion, Bi-SO security [28], can be viewed as a stronger variant of the SO security in a multi-user setting, where the adversary is additionally given multiple users' public keys and it can corrupt some of their secret keys.

The aforementioned opening capability is motivated by the fact that cryptographic information is technically hard and expensive to erase in practice and an adversary may break into an encrypter's computer and learn the used randomness. In some applications, such as secure multi-party computation, it is even required to reveal the messages and randomness to make a user's computation publicly verifiable.

Technically speaking, it is challenging to construct a SO secure PKE. At a first glance, one may think that IND-CCA security implies SO security, since each ciphertext is generated using independent randomness. However, this is not true in general. We refer [23] for an overview and useful further reading. We highlight that, from a provable-security point of view, to answer an opening query, a security reduction should be able to 'explain' how it generates a challenge ciphertext by returning the randomness, but in many cases the reduction does not even know the randomness itself. Hybrid arguments are one of the examples, namely, the reduction cannot explain a ciphertext where a challenge is embedded. This is also the inherent reason why the recent updated proof of Sato and Shikata [36] is incorrect. In the recent years, a great amount of effort has been put into defining the right notion of SO security [3,6,23] and construct efficient SO-secure public-key encryption schemes [11,17–20,28].

NOTIONS OF SELECTIVE OPENING SECURITY. Currently, there are two types of notions have been studied in the literature, the indistinguishability-based (IND-based) ones (weak-IND-SO and full-IND-SO) [3,6] and the simulation-based (SIM-based) one (SIM-SO) [3]. They are not polynomial-time equivalent to each other. In this paper we only consider the SIM-based one. Informally, SIM-SO security states that for every SO adversary its output can be efficiently simulated by a simulator that sees only the opened messages. Unlike its IND-based counterpart, SIM-SO does not require the message distribution chosen by the adversary to be efficiently resamplable, conditioned on the opened messages (cf. [3]). Previous work showed that SIM-SO-CCA and full-IND-SO-CCA notions are the strongest SO security [2,6,23]. However, only SIM-SO-CCA has been realized so far [11,17–20]. It is similar for Bi-SO security, and only SIM-based notion is considered so far [28]. For simplicity, we will not write 'SIM' in the following.

OUR GOAL: SELECTIVE OPENING SECURITY IN THE QROM. SO secure PKE schemes are constructed in idealized models [18,19] and in the standard model [3,11,17,20]. Constructions in idealized models are more efficient and hence more relevant to practice. In particular, this paper considers schemes in the random oracle model (ROM).

The increasing threat that quantum computers can break most widely deployed public-key cryptosystems has driven research in the direction of building post-quantum secure public-key primitives, including PKE schemes and key encapsulation mechanisms (KEMs). Currently, the National Institute of Standards and Technology (NIST) in the US has come to a conclusion for the post-quantum standards. Kyber [37], NTRU [8], and Saber [9] were three finalists in the last round for the KEM/PKE category. They all use variants of the Fujisaki-Okamoto (FO) transformation [12–14,21]. It is interesting to consider whether these FO transformations are secure in the SO setting.

The FO transformation turns a relatively weak PKE (e.g. a One-Way CPA secure one) into an IND-CCA secure one. Recently, the FO transformation and its variants have been widely analyzed in both the classical ROM and the quantum (accessible) ROM (QROM) [21,24,27,34,38], but mostly with a focus on establishing IND-CCA security. An exception is the work of Heuer et al. [18] which studied the SO security of the FO transformation in the ROM.

For post-quantum security, proofs in the QROM are more desirable than those in the (classical) ROM, since it models quantum adversaries in a more realistic manner. In this setting, a quantum adversary interacts with a classical network, where "online" primitives (such as encryption) are classical, and computes "offline" primitives (such as hashing) on its own in superposition.

The work of Sato and Shikata [35] proved the SO security of the FO transformation in the QROM. To the best of our knowledge, this is the only work considers SO security in the QROM. However, we identified a subtle gap in their security proof[1]. Even worse, this gap cannot be closed, even if we relax the notion to the weaker, non-adaptive SO security as in [29], where an adversary is not allowed to adaptively open a challenge ciphertext, but commits all its opening indices after seeing the challenge ciphertexts. From a technical point of view, closing the gap in [35] requires new proof techniques in the QROM that allow a security reduction to adaptively reprogram multiple RO-queries in one security game without changing the view of an adversary, where the reprogrammed points are computationally hidden. This is a property not achievable by existing well-known techniques, such as [16,27,39,40]. We provide more discussion about it in Sect. 1.2.

1.1 Our Contributions

We revise the selective opening security in the QROM and prove that two "implicit rejection" variants of the FO transformation (namely, $FO^{\not\perp}$ [24] and $U_m^{\not\perp}$ [21]) are SO-CCA secure if the underlying PKE is one-way CPA (OW-CPA)

---

[1] The authors confirmed this to us.

secure in the QROM. Here we consider PKE schemes, namely, combining KEM $\mathsf{FO}^{\not\perp}$ (or $\mathsf{U}_m^{\not\perp}$) with one-time pad and a message authentication code (MAC). The one with $\mathsf{FO}^{\not\perp}$ is the same scheme considered in [35], but ours is the first correct proof in the QROM. Since the proofs for $\mathsf{FO}^{\not\perp}$ and $\mathsf{U}_m^{\not\perp}$ are similar, we leave the one for $\mathsf{U}_m^{\not\perp}$ in our full version [33], and there we only prove the Bi-SO-CCA for $\mathsf{U}_m^{\not\perp}$, since it implies SO-CCA security.

Our core technical contribution is a computational adaptive reprogramming framework in the QROM that enables a security reduction to *adaptively* and *simultaneously* reprogram polynomially many RO-queries which are computationally hidden from a quantum adversary. This is a property that cannot be provided by previous techniques in the QROM, such as the (adaptive) one-way to hiding (O2H) lemma [39,40], the semi-classical O2H lemma [1], and the measure-rewind-measure O2H lemma [27]. Our framework brings the QROM closer to the classical ROM, and it generalizes and improves the adaptive reprogramming framework by Grilo et al. [16].

Tight SO Security from Lossy Encryption in the QROM. Our second contribution is a tightly SO-CCA secure PKE from lossy encryption [3,22]. This is the *first* tight scheme in the QROM. A recent work of Pan, Wagner, and Zeng has constructed the first tightly multi-user (without corruptions), multi-challenge IND-CCA in the QROM [31], but it did not get extended to the (stronger) SO setting. Another related work is also due to Pan and Zeng [32], where a compact and tightly SO-CCA secure PKE is proposed in the classical random oracle model. However, it is unclear if it can be transformed to the QROM. Our result on tight SO security is established in the QROM, and it improves both aforementioned work.

Bi-SO Security of FO Transformations. As another application of our framework, we prove that the aforementioned variants of FO transformation, namely, $\mathsf{FO}^{\not\perp}$ and $\mathsf{U}_m^{\not\perp}$, are furthermore Bi-SO-CCA secure [28] in the QROM, assuming OW-CPA security of the underlying PKE scheme. This notion is stronger than the SO-CCA security, since it additionally allows secret key corruption for the adversaries. The only known Bi-SO-CCA secure construction is in the classical ROM. Our work is the first one in the QROM.

Impacts on the NIST Finalists. The NIST finalists Kyber and Saber use tweaked verions of transformation $\mathsf{FO}^{\not\perp}$, and NTRU uses $\mathsf{U}_m^{\not\perp}$. Hence, analysis of these FO transformations is more fundamental than directly analyzing these concrete schemes. Although our results strongly indicate that the NIST finalists are SO-CCA secure and Bi-SO-CCA in the QROM, we leave the formal proof of it as a future direction, and we are optimistic that our approaches can be extended naturally in achieving it.

1.2   Technical Details

We provide some details about our technical contribution, computational adaptive reprogramming framework.

OUR STARTING POINT. The work of Heuer et al. [18] is the first one proving that practical PKEs via the OAEP and FO transformation are SO-CCA secure in the (classical) ROM. Their work considered the original FO transformation [14]. Motivated by Heuer et al.'s work, we can show that the combination of $\mathsf{FO}^{\not\perp}$ and one-time pad is SO-CPA secure in the classical ROM by adaptively reprogramming the ROs. Here we describe some key idea. Note that our final goal is SO-CCA, but for the simplicity of our discussion here, we only consider SO-CPA.

A ciphertext of message m in the $\mathsf{FO}^{\not\perp}$ transformation, (e, d), is defined as follow:

$$e := \mathsf{Enc}_0(\mathsf{pk}, r; G(r)) \quad \text{for} \quad r \xleftarrow{\$} \mathcal{M}'$$
$$d := H(r, e) \oplus m \tag{1}$$

where Enc_0 is the randomized encryption algorithm of a OW-CPA secure PKE with message space $\mathcal{M}'$, $G(r)$ is the explicit randomness used in Enc_0, and G, H are two hash functions with suitable domains and ranges. Public and secret keys of $\mathsf{FO}^{\not\perp}$ is the same as those of the OW-CPA secure PKE, and the decryption is defined in the straightforward way. We refer Fig. 6 for the full description.

EFFICIENT OPENABILITY IN THE ROM. To show the SO-CPA security, we require "efficient openability" of ciphertexts [3,11]. This property states that one can generate some ciphertexts and later they can be efficiently opened to arbitrary messages by using some trapdoor (in the standard model) or reprogramming ROs (in the ROM) in a suitable way. In the classical ROM, our ciphertexts (defined by Eq. (1)) have efficient openability. More precisely, a security reduction $\mathcal{R}$ can choose random r_i^*, R_i^*, and d_i^* and return the challenge ciphertexts $(\mathsf{Enc}_0(\mathsf{pk}, r_i^*; R_i^*), d_i^*)_{1 \le i \le \mu}$ to the SO-CPA adversary $\mathcal{A}$. For these challenge ciphertexts, the reduction $\mathcal{R}$ can open a ciphertext $(\mathsf{Enc}_0(\mathsf{pk}, r_i^*; R_i^*), d_i^*)$ to arbitrary message m_i by reprogramming $G(r_i^*) := R_i^*$ and $H(r_i^*, e_i^*) := d_i^* \oplus m_i$. Moreover, $\mathcal{R}$ will embed the OW-CPA challenge to one of the unopened ciphertexts. Here, r_i^* are only computationally hidden from the adversary.

For the SO-CPA security, the aforementioned reprogramming is required to be *adaptive*, since an adversary can submit an opening query adaptively. Moreover, a SO-CPA adversary can submit multiple opening queries in one security game or hybrid. Therefore, our reprogramming strategy should be able to reprogram multiple RO-queries in one security game. We call this last requirement as multipoint reprogramming. We stress that hybrid arguments are already not useful for SO security. This is because a standard hybrid argument will embed a OW-CPA challenge into the SO-CPA ciphertexts one-by-one. After it is embedded to the i-th ciphertext, $G(r_i^*)$ cannot be reprogrammed to R_i^*, since R_i^* is unknown to the reduction $\mathcal{R}$. Thus, the opening query cannot be correctly answered.

EXISTING APPROACHES IN THE QROM. Reprogramming a quantum (accessible) RO is highly non-trivial, since a query in superposition can be viewed as a query that might contain all possible input values at once. To correctly reprogram a value to a particular QRO query, it needs to measure and extract classical preimages of a quantum query, which will cause a change in the adversary's view. Although many works have been done to provide reprogrammability in the QROM [1,16,27,39,40], reprogramming in the QROM is still much more challenging than in the ROM.

For the SO security, the situation is more complicated. Essentially, existing approaches (such as [1,16,27,39,40]) cannot easily achieve the requirements for SO security in the QROM. We use the semi-classical O2H lemma [1] as an example to elaborate on this. Fix a random set $S \subseteq \mathcal{X}$. Let $H, H' : \mathcal{X} \to \mathcal{Y}$ be two different ROs such that, for all $x \in \mathcal{X} \setminus S$, $H(x) = H'(x)$ (denoted by $H \setminus S = H' \setminus S$). The semi-classical O2H lemma states that a quantum adversary $\mathcal{A}$ cannot tell the difference between H and H' by giving only quantum access to them, unless $\mathcal{A}$ finds an element from S. Here set S needs to be defined before defining H and H'.

In the work of Sato and Shikata [35], their security proofs viewed S as the set containing all the randomness used in the opened ciphertexts (cf. the step between Game$_1$ and Game$_2$ in [35, Section 3.1] and the one between Game$_5$ and Game$_6$ in [35, Section 3.2]). Essentially, S is equivalent to the set of opening indices which are adaptively decided by the adversary $\mathcal{A}$. However, to use the semi-classical O2H lemma, S must be fixed at the beginning of the security game, even before generating the public key. Therefore, this technical gap in their proofs cannot be closed, and it will be the case, even if we consider the weaker, non-adaptive variant of SO security as in [29], namely, an adversary cannot adaptively open challenge ciphertexts, but commits to opening indices after receiving the challenge ciphertexts.

The recent measure-rewind-measure O2H lemma [27] has a similar flavor as the semi-classical O2H lemma, and it does not allow to define S adaptively. The adaptive O2H lemma [39] allow us to reprogram a single query adaptively. However, we require adaptive reprogramming multiple queries for SO security, since if we only reprogram wrt one opening query, an adversary can distinguish the simulation by opening multiple ciphertexts.

OUR APPROACH. To solve the technical difficulties, we propose the computational adaptive reprogramming framework. It is more general than the algorithmic O2H lemma [39] and the adaptive reprogramming framework [16] in the sense that our framework allows a reduction to reprogram polynomial many RO queries in the QROM. Different to the work of Grilo et al., our reprogrammed points can be only computationally hidden from the adversary.

In a nutshell, our framework considers two security games, NONADA and ADA. The RO H' in NONADA will never be reprogrammed, but the RO H in ADA will be adaptively reprogrammed for multiple times according to the adversary's behavior. We require $H' \setminus S = H \setminus S$, but S can be modified adaptively by a security reduction. Intuitively, an adversary $\mathcal{A}$ can distinguish NONADA and ADA if it queries $x \in S$. This event can be detected easily in the classical setting, but is problematic in the quantum setting. Our high-level approach is to bound the probability of this event by randomly measuring $\mathcal{A}$. Details are given in Sect. 3. We stress that our approach is not a "hybrid argument" extension of the existing techniques. In fact, as pointed out by Bellare, Hofheinz, and Yilek [3], it is unknown if a simple hybrid argument is useful in proving SO security.

Very unfortunately, the latest revision[2] of [35] is a concrete example for why it does not work. The proof of their Lemma 1 is essentially a hybrid argument. A counterexample is simply: Imagine an adversary that always opens the first ciphertext, then their first hybrid always fails since the OPEN oracle will abort when the adversary opens the first ciphertext, and thus their hybrid argument cannot prove the SO security.

MORE COMPARISON WITH RELATED WORK. Recently, Grilo et al. proposed the adaptive reprogramming framework [16] and used it to give a QROM proof for Fiat-Shamir's signatures. The main difference between our work and Grilo et al.'s work is that their framework requires the reprogramming points to have high statistical entropy, while our framework requires the reprogramming points are computationally hard to find (which cover the case of statistical entropy). When proving the SO security of the FO transformation, their framework cannot be used since the reprogramming points are computationally hidden by OW-CPA security of some underlying PKEs.

We also compare our framework to the measure-and-reprogram framework of Don, Fehr, and Majenz [10] and the lifting theorem in [41] that are used to prove security of the Fiat-Shamir (FS) signature in the QROM. In a nutshell, the difference between our frameworks is similar to that between the security proofs of the FO encryption and FS signature in the classical setting. More precisely, in the proof of FO encryption, we argue that it is infeasible for an adversary to learn the reprogramming points and thus we can reprogram the random oracle without changing the adversary's view. However, in the proof of FS signature, an adversary can learn the reprogramming points, since they are the hash values of signing messages and some (public) commitments of the Σ protocol. Hence, the measure-and-reprogram framework is conceptually different to us and cannot be used in proving SO or Bi-SO security in the QROM. The lifting theorem (cf. [41, Theorem 4.2]) has a similar flavor as the measure-and-reprogram framework.

FUTURE WORK. We leave exploring more applications of our computational adaptive reprogramming framework as a future direction, since reprogramming a (quantum) random oracle on multiple computationally hidden points is an interesting technique and we are optimistic that it may yield new applications. Moreover, we are optimistic that our approach can work for the simulatable DEM framework of SO secure PKEs. We leave a formal treatment of it as another future direction.

2   Preliminaries

Let n be an integer. $[n]$ denotes the set $\{1, ..., n\}$. Let $\mathcal{X}$ and $\mathcal{Y}$ be two finite sets and $f : \mathcal{X} \to \mathcal{Y}$ be a function. $f(\mathcal{X}) := \{f(x) | x \in \mathcal{X}\}$. $x \xleftarrow{\$} \mathcal{X}$ denotes sampling a uniform element x from $\mathcal{X}$ at random. If S is a subset of $\mathcal{X}$, then $\mathcal{X} \backslash S$ denotes the set $\{x \in \mathcal{X} | x \notin S\}$. Let $\mathcal{A}$ be an algorithm. If $\mathcal{A}$ is probabilistic, then $y \leftarrow \mathcal{A}(x)$ means that the variable y is assigned to the output of $\mathcal{A}$ on input

---

[2] https://eprint.iacr.org/archive/2022/617/20230108:160413.

x. If $\mathcal{A}$ is deterministic, then we write $y := \mathcal{A}(x)$. We write $\mathcal{A}^{\mathcal{O}}$ to indicate that $\mathcal{A}$ has classical access to oracle $\mathcal{O}$. We write $\mathbf{T}(\mathcal{A}_0) \approx \mathbf{T}(\mathcal{A}_1)$ if the running times of $\mathcal{A}_0$ and $\mathcal{A}_1$ are polynomially close to each other. All (quantum) algorithms are (quantum) probabilistic polynomial time, unless we state it.

GAMES. We use code-based games [4] to define and prove security. We implicitly assume that Boolean flags are initialized to false, numerical types are initialized to 0, sets are initialized to $\emptyset$, while strings are initialized to the empty string ϵ. $\Pr[\mathbf{G}^{\mathcal{A}} \Rightarrow 1]$ denotes the probability that the final output $\mathbf{G}^{\mathcal{A}}$ of game $\mathbf{G}$ running an adversary $\mathcal{A}$ is 1. Let $\mathtt{Ev}$ be an (classical and well-defined) event. We write $\Pr[\mathtt{Ev} : \mathbf{G}]$ to denote the probability that $\mathtt{Ev}$ occurs during the game $\mathbf{G}$.

ONE-TIME MESSAGE AUTHENTICATION CODE (MAC). We use MAC schemes that have one-time strong existential unforgeability under chosen message attack (otSUF-CMA) as building block. Let $\mathsf{MAC} := (\mathsf{Tag}, \mathsf{Vrfy})$ be an one-time MAC scheme with key space $\mathcal{K}^{\mathrm{mac}}$. The otSUF-CMA security game is given in Fig. 1.

Definition 1 (otSUF-CMA). *For a forger $\mathcal{F}$, its advantage against otSUF-CMA security of* MAC *is defined as*

$$\mathsf{Adv}_{\mathsf{PKE}}^{\mathsf{otSUF\text{-}CMA}}(\mathcal{F}) := \Pr[\mathsf{otSUF\text{-}CMA}_{\mathsf{MAC}}^{\mathcal{F}} \Rightarrow 1]$$

MAC *is otSUF-CMA secure if for all $\mathcal{F}$*, $\mathsf{Adv}_{\mathsf{PKE}}^{\mathsf{otSUF\text{-}CMA}}(\mathcal{F}) = \mathsf{negl}(\lambda)$.

One-time MAC schemes can be constructed by using pair-wise independent hash function family, and they are otSUF-CMA secure against *unbounded* adversaries. Here TAG cannot be queried with quantum superposition.

GAME otSUF-CMA$_{\mathsf{MAC}}^{\mathcal{F}}$	TAG(m) // Only one query
01 $b := 0, K^{\mathrm{mac}} \xleftarrow{\$} \mathcal{K}^{\mathrm{mac}}$	07 $\tau \leftarrow \mathsf{Tag}(K^{\mathrm{mac}}, m)$
02 $(m^*, \tau^*) \leftarrow \mathcal{F}^{\mathrm{TAG, VRFY}}()$	08 $(m_0, \tau_0) := (m, \tau)$
03 **if** $(m^*, \tau^*) \neq (m_0, \tau_0)$	09 **return** τ
04 $\quad$ **and** $\mathsf{Vrfy}(K^{\mathrm{mac}}, m^*, \tau^*) = 1$	
05 $\quad b := 1$	VRFY(m, τ)
06 **return** b	10 **return** $\mathsf{Vrfy}(K^{\mathrm{mac}}, m, \tau)$

Fig. 1. Security games one-time MAC schemes

2.1 Public-Key Encryption

A Public Key Encryption (PKE) scheme PKE consists of three algorithms (KG, Enc, Dec) and a message space $\mathcal{M}$ that is assumed to be efficiently recognizable. The three algorithms work as follows:

– The key generation algorithm KG, on input the security parameter λ, outputs a public and secret key pair $(\mathsf{pk}, \mathsf{sk})$. pk also defines a finite randomness space $\mathcal{R} := \mathcal{R}(\mathsf{pk})$ and a ciphertext space $\mathcal{C} := \mathcal{C}(\mathsf{pk})$. For sake of simplicity, in this paper, we ignore the input λ and simply write the process as $(\mathsf{pk}, \mathsf{sk}) \leftarrow \mathsf{KG}$.

- The encryption algorithm Enc, on input pk and a message $m \in \mathcal{M}$, outputs a ciphertext $c \in \mathcal{C}$. We also write $c := \mathsf{Enc}(\mathsf{pk}, m; r)$ to indicate the randomness $r \in \mathcal{R}$ explicitly.
- The (deterministic) decryption algorithm Dec, on input sk and a ciphertext c, outputs a message $m' \in \mathcal{M}$ or a rejection symbol $\bot \notin \mathcal{M}$.

Definition 2 (PKE Correctness). *A PKE scheme* $\mathsf{PKE} := (\mathsf{KG}, \mathsf{Enc}, \mathsf{Dec})$ *with message space* $\mathcal{M}$ *is* $(1 - \delta)$-*correct if*

$$\mathbb{E}\left[\max_{m \in \mathcal{M}} \Pr\left[\mathsf{Dec}(\mathsf{sk}, c) \neq m : c \leftarrow \mathsf{Enc}(\mathsf{pk}, m)\right]\right] \leq \delta,$$

where the expectation is taken over $(\mathsf{pk}, \mathsf{sk}) \leftarrow \mathsf{KG}$ *and randomness of* Enc. *PKE has perfect correctness if* $\delta = 0$.

Definition 3 (Collision Probability of Key Generation). *Let*

$$\eta_{\mathsf{PKE}} := \max\left[\Pr\left[\mathsf{pk}_0 = \mathsf{pk}_1 : (\mathsf{pk}_0, \mathsf{sk}_0) \leftarrow \mathsf{KG}, (\mathsf{pk}_1, \mathsf{sk}_1) \leftarrow \mathsf{KG}\right]\right]$$

be the collision probability of KG *of* PKE. *The maximum is taken over all* $\mathsf{pk}_0, \mathsf{pk}_1$. *In this paper, we assume that for any OW-CPA-secure* PKE, $\eta_{\mathsf{PKE}} = \mathsf{negl}(\lambda)$

Let $\mathsf{PKE} := (\mathsf{KG}, \mathsf{Enc}, \mathsf{Dec})$ be a PKE scheme with message space $\mathcal{M}$ and ciphertext space $\mathcal{C}$. We focus on two security notions for PKE: onewayness under chosen-plaintext attacks (OW-CPA) and selective-opening security under chosen-ciphertext-attacks (SO-CCA).

Definition 4 (OW-CPA). *For an adversary* $\mathcal{A}$, *its advantage against* OW-CPA *security of* PKE *is defined as*

$$\mathsf{Adv}_{\mathsf{PKE}}^{\mathsf{OW\text{-}CPA}}(\mathcal{A}) := \Pr\left[m' = m^* : (\mathsf{pk}, \mathsf{sk}) \leftarrow \mathsf{KG}, m^* \xleftarrow{\$} \mathcal{M},\right.$$
$$\left. c^* \leftarrow \mathsf{Enc}(\mathsf{pk}, m^*), m' \leftarrow \mathcal{A}(\mathsf{pk}, c^*)\right].$$

PKE *is* OW-CPA *secure if for all PPT adversaries* $\mathcal{A}$, $\mathsf{Adv}_{\mathsf{PKE}}^{\mathsf{OW\text{-}CPA}}(\mathcal{A}) = \mathsf{negl}(\lambda)$.

(ADAPTIVE) SELECTIVE OPENING SECURITY. Selective Opening (SO) security preserves confidentiality even if an adversary opens the randomnesses of some ciphertexts. We use simulation-based approach to define SO security as in [18]. We consider the SO security against Chosen-Plaintext Attacks (SO-CPA) and Chosen-Ciphertext Attacks (SO-CCA), respectively.

We note that a non-adaptive variant of SO security has been used in [29], where an adversary must declare the opening index set I after receiving the challenge ciphertexts, while our SO security is *adaptive* in the sense that OPEN can be asked adaptively. Intuitively, our adaptive security is harder to achieve, since an adversary can change its opening queries after seeing the answers of previous ones.

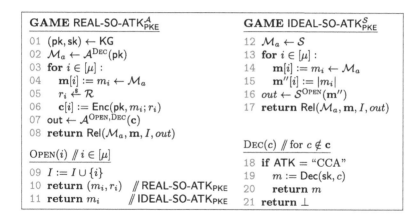

Fig. 2. The SO security games for PKE schemes.

Definition 5 (SO security). *Let* PKE *be a PKE scheme with message space* $\mathcal{M}$ *and randomness space* $\mathcal{R}$ *and* $\mathcal{A}$ *be an adversary against* PKE. *For security parameter* λ, $\mu := \mu(\lambda) > 0$ *is a polynomially bounded function. Let* Rel *be a relation. We consider two games defined in Fig. 2, where* $\mathcal{A}$ *is run in* REAL-SO-ATK$_{\mathsf{PKE}}$ *and a SO simulator* $\mathcal{S}$ *in* IDEAL-SO-ATK$_{\mathsf{PKE}}$. $\mathcal{M}_a$ *is a distribution over* $\mathcal{M}$ *chosen by* $\mathcal{A}$, *and* $\mathcal{A}$ *is not allowed to issue* OPEN *queries before it outputs* $\mathcal{M}_a$ *and receives challenge ciphertexts* **c**. *Messages sampled from* $\mathcal{M}_a$ *may be dependent on each other.* DEC *is not available in SO-CPA security.*

We define the SO-ATK (ATK = 'CPA' or 'CCA') advantage function

$$\mathsf{Adv}_{\mathsf{PKE}}^{\mathsf{SO-ATK}}(\mathcal{A}, \mathcal{S}, \mu, \mathsf{Rel})$$

$$:= \left| \Pr \left[\mathsf{REAL\text{-}SO\text{-}ATK}_{\mathsf{PKE}}^{\mathcal{A}} \Rightarrow 1 \right] - \Pr \left[\mathsf{IDEAL\text{-}SO\text{-}ATK}_{\mathsf{PKE}}^{\mathcal{S}} \Rightarrow 1 \right] \right|,$$

PKE *is SO-ATK secure if, for every adversary* $\mathcal{A}$ *and every PPT relation* Rel, *there exists a simulator* $\mathcal{S}$ *such that* $\mathsf{Adv}_{\mathsf{PKE}}^{\mathsf{SO-ATK}}(\mathcal{A}, \mathcal{S}, \mu, \mathsf{Rel}) \le \mathsf{negl}(\lambda)$.

(ADAPTIVE) BI-SELECTIVE-OPENING SECURITY. In this paper, we also consider a stronger SO security definition: Bi-SO-ATK [28]. This security definition considers a multi-user setting and allows the adversary to corrupt some users (namely, obtains their secret keys) adaptively. The Bi-SO-ATK definition in [28] is non-adaptive, that is, the SO adversary is required to tell the game simulator which users it wants to corrupted and which challenge ciphertexts it wants to open at once. In this paper, we enhance the security definition to be adaptive. The adversary can adaptively issues OPEN queries and CORRUPT queries in any order. The enhanced definition is also simulation-based. If $\mathcal{A}$ corrupts a user j, then the messages of challenge ciphertexts that encrypted by j are also revealed (see Items 15 and 16).

Definition 6 (Bi-SO security). *Let* PKE *be a PKE scheme and* $\mathcal{A}$ *be a Bi-SO adversary against* PKE. *For security parameter* λ, *let* $\mu := \mu(\lambda)$ *and* $p := p(\lambda)$

GAME REAL-Bi-SO-ATK$_{\mathsf{PKE}}$	**GAME** IDEAL-Bi-SO-ATK$_{\mathsf{PKE}}$
01 **for** $j \in [p]$: $(\mathsf{pk}_j, \mathsf{sk}_j) \leftarrow \mathsf{KG}$	17 $\mathcal{M}_a \leftarrow \mathcal{S}$
02 $\mathcal{M}_a \leftarrow \mathcal{A}^{\mathrm{DEC}}(\mathsf{pk}_1, \dots \mathsf{pk}_p)$	18 **for** $j \in [p]$:
03 **for** $j \in [p]$:	19 **for** $i \in [\mu]$:
04 **for** $i \in [\mu]$	20 $\mathbf{m}[j,i] := m_{j,i} \leftarrow \mathcal{M}_a$
05 $\mathbf{m}[j,i] := m_{j,i} \leftarrow \mathcal{M}_a$	21 $\mathbf{m}''[j,i] := |m_{j,i}|$
06 $r_{j,i} \xleftarrow{\$} \mathcal{R}'$	22 $out \leftarrow \mathcal{S}^{\mathrm{OPEN,CORRUPT}}(st, \mathbf{m}'')$
07 $\mathbf{c}[j,i] := \mathsf{Enc}(\mathsf{pk}, m_{j,i}; r_{j,i})$	23 **return** $\mathsf{Rel}(\mathcal{M}_a, \mathbf{m}, J, I, out)$
08 $out \leftarrow \mathcal{A}^{\mathrm{OPEN,CORRUPT,DEC}}(\mathbf{c})$	
09 **return** $\mathsf{Rel}(\mathcal{M}_a, \mathbf{m}, J, I, out)$	$\underline{\mathrm{DEC}(j,c)}$
	24 **if** ATK = "CCA"
$\mathrm{OPEN}(j,i)$ // for $j \in [p], i \in [\mu]$	25 **if** $\exists i \in [\mu]$ s.t. $c = \mathbf{c}[j,i]$
10 $I := I \cup \{(j,i)\}$	26 $m := \bot$
11 **return** $(m_{j,i}, r_{j,i})$ // REAL-Bi-SO-CPA$_{\mathsf{PKE}}$	27 **else** $m := \mathsf{Dec}(\mathsf{sk}_j, c)$
12 **return** $m_{j,i}$ // IDEAL-Bi-SO-CPA$_{\mathsf{PKE}}$	28 **return** m
	29 **return** $\bot$
$\mathrm{CORRUPT}(j)$ // for $j \in [p]$	
13 $J := J \cup \{j\}$, $\mathbf{m}_j := \emptyset$	
14 **for** $i \in [\mu]$: $\mathbf{m}_j[i] := \mathbf{m}[j,i]$	
15 **return** $(\mathsf{sk}_j, \mathbf{m}_j)$ // REAL-Bi-SO-CPA$_{\mathsf{PKE}}$	
16 **return** $\mathbf{m}_j$ // IDEAL-Bi-SO-CPA$_{\mathsf{PKE}}$	

Fig. 3. The Bi-SO-ATK security game for PKE schemes

that are both polynomially bounded. Let Rel *be a relation. We consider two games defined in Fig. 3, where* $\mathcal{A}$ *is run in* REAL-Bi-SO-ATK$_{\mathsf{PKE}}$ *and a Bi-SO simulator* $\mathcal{S}$ *in* IDEAL-Bi-SO-ATK$_{\mathsf{PKE}}$*.* $\mathcal{M}_a$ *is a distribution over* $\mathcal{M}$ *chosen by* $\mathcal{A}$*, and* $\mathcal{A}$ *is not allowed to issue* OPEN *or* CORRUPT *queries before it outputs* $\mathcal{M}_a$ *and receives challenge ciphertexts* $\mathbf{c}$*. Messages sampled from* $\mathcal{M}_a$ *may be dependent on each other.* DEC *is not available in Bi-SO-CPA security.*

We define the Bi-SO-ATK (ATK = 'CPA' or 'CCA') advantage function

$$\mathsf{Adv}_{\mathsf{PKE}}^{\mathsf{Bi\text{-}SO\text{-}ATK}}(\mathcal{A}, \mathcal{S}, p, \mu, \mathsf{Rel})$$
$$:= \left| \Pr\left[\text{REAL-Bi-SO-ATK}_{\mathsf{PKE}}^{\mathcal{A}} \Rightarrow 1 \right] - \Pr\left[\text{IDEAL-Bi-SO-ATK}_{\mathsf{PKE}}^{\mathcal{S}} \Rightarrow 1 \right] \right|.$$

PKE *is adaptive Bi-SO-ATK secure if, for any adversary* $\mathcal{A}$ *and PPT relation* Rel*, there exists a simulator* $\mathcal{S}$ *such that* $\mathsf{Adv}_{\mathsf{PKE}}^{\mathsf{Bi\text{-}SO\text{-}ATK}}(\mathcal{A}, \mathcal{S}, p, \mu, \lambda) = \mathsf{negl}(\lambda)$*.*

SECURITY IN THE QUANTUM RANDOM ORACLE MODEL. The (Bi-)SO security of PKE schemes containing hash functions can be analyzed in the quantum random oracle model (cf. Sect. 2.2). If we model a hash function H as quantum random oracle, then the adversary $\mathcal{A}$ has quantum access to H during the SO security games (e.g., Fig. 7).

2.2 Quantum Computation

We refer to [30] for detailed background about quantum mechanism. Here we only recall some necessary notations and lemmas.

Pure quantum states can be described by qubits. For a λ-bit-string x, $|x\rangle \in \mathbb{C}^{2^\lambda}$ denotes the (pure) quantum state of x encoded in the standard computational basis. Quantum register is used to store multiple qubits. In this paper, we assume that any polynomially long object x can be encoded as a (unique) bit string, and if we "store" x in a quantum register X, $|x\rangle$ is the quantum state of this register. A λ-qubits quantum superposition state $|\phi\rangle$ can be written as $\sum_{x\in\{0,1\}^\lambda} \alpha_x|x\rangle$ where $\sum_{x\in\{0,1\}^\lambda} |\alpha_x|^2 = 1$.

By performing measurement on a quantum state, we obtain classical information about the state, and the state collapses after measurement. Let $|x\rangle$ be an quantum state, $x' \leftarrow \mathsf{Measure}(|x\rangle)$ denote the process that $|x\rangle$ is measured and the measurement outcome is x'. We assume that all measurement are performed with respect to the standard computational basis.

Let $\mathcal{O} : \mathcal{X} \to \mathcal{Y}$ be an random oracle with sets $\mathcal{X}, \mathcal{Y}$. We implicitly assume that the elements in $\mathcal{X}$ and $\mathcal{Y}$ are expressed as bit strings. In quantum random oracle model (QROM) [7], the oracle $\mathcal{O}$ are described as the unitary transformation $U_\mathcal{O} : |x\rangle|y\rangle \to |x, y \oplus \mathcal{O}(x)\rangle$, and the adversary can query random oracles on quantum states. For an quantum adversary $\mathcal{A}$, the notation $\mathcal{A}^{|\mathcal{O}\rangle}$ indicates that $\mathcal{A}$ has quantum access to the $U_\mathcal{O}$. Without loss of generality, we directly write $\mathcal{O}$ to denote the unitary $U_\mathcal{O}$.

In this paper, we say an event is classical if it can be determined by only using classical algorithm (namely, without using any quantum mechanism).

Lemma 1 gives a probabilistic bound for adversary (has a quantum access to oracles) to distinguish $h(s, \cdot)$ and h', where s is secret, h and h' are QRO and have the same image set. When the image is large enough, the adversary cannot distinguish these two oracles.

Lemma 1 (Lemma 2.2 in [34]). *Let k be an integer. Let $h : \mathcal{X}' \times \mathcal{X} \to \mathcal{Y}$ and $h' : \mathcal{X} \to \mathcal{Y}$ be two independent random oracles. If an unbounded time quantum adversary $\mathcal{A}$ that queries h at most q_h times, then we have*

$$\left| \Pr\left[1 \leftarrow \mathcal{A}^{|h\rangle, |h(s,\cdot)\rangle}() \middle| s \xleftarrow{\$} \mathcal{X}' \right] - \Pr\left[1 \leftarrow \mathcal{A}^{|h\rangle, |h'\rangle}() \right] \right| \leq 2q_h/\sqrt{|\mathcal{X}'|}$$

3   Computational Adaptive Reprogramming in the QROM

We propose a computational adaptive reprogramming framework in the QROM. In our full version [33], we review Unruh's adaptive O2H lemma [39] and discuss why our lemma (namely, Lemma 2) cannot be proved by using hybrid arguments of Unruh's adaptive O2H lemma.

Let $\mathcal{A}$ be an adversary that has quantum access to $\mathcal{H} : \mathcal{X} \to \mathcal{Y}$ and takes in_0 as input and terminates by outputting out_n. During its execution, $\mathcal{A}$ outputs some out_i and then takes in_{i+1} as input ($0 \leq i \leq n - 1$). We view $\mathcal{A}$ as a $(n+1)$-stage adversary, $(\mathcal{A}_0, ..., \mathcal{A}_n)$, where $\mathcal{A}_i$ takes in_i as input and outputs out_i. Here $\mathsf{in}_0, \mathsf{out}_0, \mathsf{in}_1, ..., \mathsf{in}_n$, and out_n can be arbitrary classical information. In this paper, we consider post-quantum setting where adversaries have quantum access to hash functions. The classical information $\mathsf{in}_0, \mathsf{out}_0, \mathsf{in}_1, ..., \mathsf{in}_n, \mathsf{out}_n$ capture the interaction between $\mathcal{A}$ and the security game simulator, and they will be specified in a concrete use of our framework.

We write $\mathcal{A} = (\mathcal{A}_0, ..., \mathcal{A}_n)$ to divide $\mathcal{A}$ into $n + 1$ stages for better analysis. By writing $\text{out}_i \leftarrow \mathcal{A}_i(\text{in}_i)$ we mean that at stage i $\mathcal{A}$ receives input in_i and outputs out_i at the end of the stage. The index indicates the stage number of $\mathcal{A}$. So, all $\mathcal{A}_i$ are the same adversary $\mathcal{A}$ in different stages, and they share the quantum registers of $\mathcal{A}$. The same notation (of dividing $\mathcal{A}$ into different stages) is also used in Unruh's adaptive O2H lemma [39].

Games NONADA and ADA (as in Fig. 4) are used to define our framework. $\mathcal{A}$ has quantum access to $\mathcal{H}$ which is either H or H_i. In NONADA, H will never get reprogrammed, while in ADA different stages of $\mathcal{A}$ will have access to different ROs H_i. That is, $\mathcal{A}_i$ queries H_i, and according to $\mathcal{A}_i$'s output out_i H_i will be reprogrammed and become H_{i+1} (cf. Items 07, 17 and 18). To formalize this, we define three algorithms INIT, $\mathsf{F_s}$, and $\mathsf{Repro_s}$ in Fig. 4 as:

- INIT outputs $((\mathbf{s}, \text{in}_0), \mathsf{H}, \mathsf{H}_0)$ (cf. Items 01 and 11), where $\mathbf{s}$ is some parameter that used in a security reduction, in_0 is the initial input to $\mathcal{A}$, and H and H_0 are two random oracles. Here the tuple $((\mathbf{s}, \text{in}_0), \mathsf{H}, \mathsf{H}_0)$ may have an arbitrary joint distribution.
- $\mathsf{F_s}$ takes out_i as input and computes $(\text{in}_{i+1}, \text{in}'_{i+1})$, where in_{i+1} is the input to $\mathcal{A}_{i+1}$ and in'_{i+1} is the information for reprogramming H_i. Here in'_{i+1} is used to capture the fact that $\mathcal{H}$ can be reprogrammed according to $\mathcal{A}_i$'s behavior, and the algorithm $\mathsf{Repro_s}$ (described below) will take it as input. To make our lemma general and useful for a wider class of applications, we only require that $\mathsf{F_s}$ does not have access to random oracles.
- $\mathsf{Repro_s}$ is defined to reprogram $\mathcal{H}$ in ADA (cf. Item 17). $\mathsf{Repro_s}$ takes in'_i and H_{i-1} as input. It returns a random oracle H_i which is from reprogramming H_{i-1}. The concrete reprogramming operation of $\mathsf{Repro_s}$ depends on the concrete use of our framework. Here we only require $\mathsf{Repro_s}$ to be deterministic.

Let S_i be a set such that $\mathsf{H} \backslash S_i = \mathsf{H}_i \backslash S_i$ (namely, for all $x \in \mathcal{X}$, if $x \in S_i$, then $\mathsf{H}(x) \neq \mathsf{H}_i(x)$). $\mathcal{A}$ can only distinguish ADA and NONADA, if it queries a $x \in S_i$ (where $i \in \{0, ..., n\}$). Since $\mathcal{A}$'s QRO queries are superposition states, we need to define extractor $\mathcal{B}_i$ as in Fig. 5 to bound the difference between NONADA and ADA. This follows the works in [27,34,39]. Lemma 2 formalizes our framework. Its proof is postponed to our full version [33].

Lemma 2. *Let $\mathcal{A}$ be an adversary that can be divided into $(n + 1)$ stages as in Fig. 4 and has quantum access to random oracle $\mathcal{H}$ $(= \mathsf{H}$ in NONADA or H_i in ADA). Let Ev be a classical event that may be raised by $\mathcal{A}$ in NONADA or ADA. Suppose that $\mathcal{A}$ queries $\mathcal{H}$ at most q_i times in its i-th stage and at most $q := q_0 + \cdots q_n$ times in total during the game. Then for all algorithms INIT, $\mathsf{F_s}$, and $\mathsf{Repro_s}$ (as described earlier), there exists adversaries $\mathcal{B}_i$ for $i \in \{0, ..., n\}$ (shown in Fig. 5) such that*

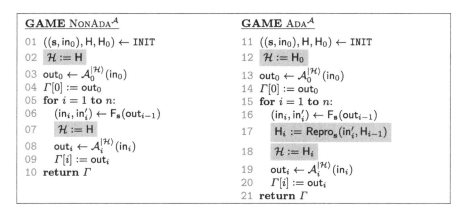

Fig. 4. Games NONADA and ADA used in Lemma 2. The main difference between two games is highlighted with gray box. In both games, $\mathcal{A}$ is divided into $n + 1$ stages, namely, $(\mathcal{A}_0, ..., \mathcal{A}_n)$. The input and output of $\mathcal{A}$ in each stage are classical information because we consider post-quantum settings. The list Γ stores $\mathcal{A}$'s outputs in each stage. $\mathsf{F_s}$ is a deterministic algorithm that provides inputs for each stage of $\mathcal{A}$. $\mathsf{Repro_s}$ is a deterministic algorithm that reprograms QROs. For a concise presentation, we assume that $\mathcal{A}_i$ takes $\mathcal{A}_{i-1}$'s final state as its initial state. In our framework, $\mathsf{H_0}$ can be different to H.

$$\left| \Pr\left[\mathsf{Ev} : \mathrm{NONADA}^{\mathcal{A}}\right] - \Pr\left[\mathsf{Ev} : \mathrm{ADA}^{\mathcal{A}}\right] \right|$$

$$\leq \sum_{k=0}^{n}\sum_{i=0}^{k} 2q_i\sqrt{\Pr\left[x' \leftarrow \mathcal{B}_i^{\mathcal{H}} \ s.t. \ x' \in S_i : \mathrm{ADA}^{\mathcal{B}_i}\right]}, \quad (2)$$

where S_i is a set such that $\mathsf{H} \backslash S_i = \mathsf{H}_i \backslash S_i$. Such an S_i is defined by the operations in $\mathsf{Repro_s}$. $\Pr\left[\mathsf{Ev} : \mathrm{NONADA}^{\mathcal{A}}\right]$ and $\Pr\left[\mathsf{Ev} : \mathrm{ADA}^{\mathcal{A}}\right]$ are the probabilities that $\mathcal{A}$ triggers Ev in NONADA and in ADA, respectively.

DISCUSSIONS ON LEMMA 2. In ADA, reprogramming the RO is captured by algorithm $\mathsf{Repro_s}$. How the reprogramming is done will be specified in a concrete use of Lemma 2. This is to make our framework general. The difference between NONADA and ADA is that between H and H_i caused by $\mathsf{Repro_s}$.

Concretely, in i-th stage, $\mathsf{Repro_s}$ will define a set S_i such that $\mathsf{H} \backslash S_i = \mathsf{H}_i \backslash S_i$. For any $k \in \{0, ..., n\}$, if $\mathcal{A}$ queries $\mathcal{H}$ with an $x \in \cup_{0 \leq i \leq k} S_k$ before the end of its k-th stage, then $\mathcal{A}$ can distinguish NONADA and ADA. To bound this in the quantum setting, our approach is to randomly measure $\mathcal{A}$'s queries to $\mathcal{H}$, which is captured by $\mathcal{B}_i$ (in Fig. 5). The advantage of $\mathcal{A}$ distinguishing NONADA and ADA is bounded by the probability that $\mathcal{B}_i$'s output falls into S_i.

MORE DISCUSSIONS ON F AND Repro IN FIG. 4. When defining our framework, we do not make any requirement on the efficiencies of $\mathsf{F_s}$ and $\mathsf{Repro_s}$. However, when we use this framework to construct (efficient) reduction, $\mathsf{F_s}$ and $\mathsf{Repro_s}$ are required to be efficient (namely, running in quantum probabilistic polynomial time) and the description of QRO is polynomially bounded [7,25,42]. For

$$
\begin{array}{|l|}
\hline
\mathcal{B}_i^{|\mathcal{H}\rangle}(\mathsf{in}_0)\text{:} \quad /\!/ \; \mathcal{H} \text{ is defined as in ADA} \\
\hline
01 \quad t^* \xleftarrow{\$} [q_i] \\
02 \quad \textbf{for } j = 0 \textbf{ to } i-1\text{:} \\
03 \qquad \mathsf{out}_j \leftarrow \mathcal{A}_j^{|\mathcal{H}\rangle}(\mathsf{in}_j) \\
04 \qquad \text{Output } \mathsf{out}_j \text{ to ADA} \\
05 \qquad \text{Receive } \mathsf{in}_{j+1} \text{ from ADA} \\
06 \quad \text{Run } \mathcal{A}_i^{|\mathcal{H}\rangle}(\mathsf{in}_i) \text{ until it issues } t^*\text{-th quantum query to } \mathcal{H} \\
07 \quad \text{Let } |\varphi\rangle \text{ be the } t^*\text{-th quantum query to } \mathcal{H} \\
08 \quad x' \leftarrow \mathsf{Measure}(|\varphi\rangle) \\
09 \quad \textbf{return } x' \\
\hline
\end{array}
$$

Fig. 5. Algorithm $\mathcal{B}_i$ (used in Lemma 2) plays Game ADA (where $i \in [n]$). $\mathcal{B}_i$ proceeds identically with $(\mathcal{A}_1, ..., \mathcal{A}_i)$, except that $\mathcal{B}_i$ measures the t^*-th QRO query issued by $\mathcal{A}_i$ and then outputs the measurement outcome.

instance, we can use a $2q$-independent hash function [42] and the list of reprogramming points (which are inputs to the hash and polynomial-bounded) to describe this QRO.

WHY OUR FRAMEWORK COVERS THE WORK OF GRILO ET AL. By specifying $\mathsf{F_s}$ and $\mathsf{Repro_s}$, we can describe Grilo et al.'s framework using our framework (though the bound of our framework is less tight than Grilo et al.'s one). In Grilo et al.'s framework [16], the i-th output of $\mathcal{A}$ is a distribution $\mathsf{out}_i := p_i$. $\mathsf{F_s}$ can be defined as, on input p_i, it samples a reprogramming point (x_i, x'_i) from p_i and an independently random y_i and outputs $(\mathsf{in}_{i+1} := (x_i, x'_i), \mathsf{in}'_{i+1} := (x_i, x'_i, y_i))$[3]. $\mathsf{Repro_s}$ can be defined as, on input $\mathsf{in}'_{i+1} := (x_i, x'_i, y_i)$, it reprograms the QRO $\mathcal{H} := \mathcal{H}[(x_i, x'_i) \rightarrow y_i]$ and returns the reprogrammed QRO. Their framework implicitly requires that the probability bound for $\mathcal{A}$ to learn x_i, x'_i (before seeing them) is information-theoretic. Namely, p_i should have enough entropy. Some important advantage of our framework, compared with Grilo et al.'s [16], are as follows:

- Grilo et al.'s framework requires the reprogramming points have high entropy and it is hard to find them even for unbounded adversary, while our framework does not have such restrictions. If $\mathcal{A}$ is a QPPT adversary, our framework provides efficient extractors $\mathcal{B}_i$'s to bound the difference of $\mathcal{A}$ in NONADA and ADA. In our proofs, we need to instantiate INIT, $\mathsf{F_s}$, and $\mathsf{Repro_s}$ efficiently. This $\mathcal{B}_i$ can be used to do a reduction in breaking some computational hard problem, for instance, the OW-CPA security. However, the Grilo et al. framework cannot be used to do any efficient reduction.
- Our framework allows NONADA and ADA to start from different QROs, while the Grilo et al. framework starts from the same QRO. Starting from different QROs allows us to consider more complicated cases of adaptive reprogramming. All security proofs in this paper are examples for this, and for SO and Bi-SO security we require this.

---

[3] The randomness for sampling can be included in s, since it is captured by the game simulator.

- Our framework also supports delayed analysis. In some complicated proofs, the difference between non-reprogramming and reprogramming games cannot be immediately bounded, and we may need extra game sequences to postpone such a bound. Our framework supports delayed analysis, since we can use extra game sequences to bound the winning probability of $\mathcal{B}_i$ (i.e. $\mathcal{B}_i$ outputs $x \in S_i$). In particular, our tightly-secure SO-CCA PKE scheme in Sect. 5 requires delayed analysis.

4 Selective Opening Security of Fujisaki-Okamoto's PKE in the QROM

We prove the selective-opening (SO) security of two Fujisaki-Okamoto(FO)-style PKE schemes in the QROM. As a warm-up, our first scheme is SO secure against chosen-plaintext attacks (SO-CPA), and the scheme follows the idea of hybrid encryption. It offers a simple example about how to use our framework. Our second scheme is SO secure against chosen-ciphertext attacks (SO-CCA). It is the same scheme as in [35, Section 3.2], but our proof is showing adaptive SO-CCA security, while the original proof in [35] has a subtle gap and the gap still exists even if we consider the non-adaptive security notion (cf. discussion in Introduction).

In both schemes, let $\mathsf{PKE} := (\mathsf{KG}_0, \mathsf{Enc}_0, \mathsf{Dec}_0)$ be a $(1 - \delta)$-correct PKE scheme with message space $\mathcal{M}'$, ciphertext space $\mathcal{C}'$, and randomness space $\mathcal{R}'$. Let $G : \mathcal{M}' \to \mathcal{R}'$ be a hash function.

4.1 Selective Opening Security Against Chosen-Plaintext Attacks

Let $H : \mathcal{M}' \times \mathcal{C}' \to \mathcal{M}$ be a hash function. Our first PKE scheme $\mathsf{wPKE} = (\mathsf{wKG}, \mathsf{wEnc}, \mathsf{wDec})$ (where 'w' stands for weak) with message space $\mathcal{M}$ and is defined as in Fig. 6. Theorem 1 states that wPKE is adaptive SO-CPA secure when modeling G and H as QROs.

wKG	wEnc($\mathsf{pk}, m \in \mathcal{M}$)	wDec($\mathsf{sk}, (e, d)$)
01 $(\mathsf{pk}, \mathsf{sk}) \leftarrow \mathsf{KG}_0$	03 $r \xleftarrow{\$} \mathcal{M}'$	08 $r' := \mathsf{Dec}_0(\mathsf{sk}, e)$
02 **return** $(\mathsf{pk}, \mathsf{sk})$	04 $e := \mathsf{Enc}_0(\mathsf{pk}, r; G(r))$	09 $K := H(r', e)$
	05 $K := H(r, e)$	10 $m := K \oplus d$
	06 $d := K \oplus m$	11 **return** m
	07 **return** (e, d)	

Fig. 6. A SO-CPA secure PKE scheme $\mathsf{wPKE} = (\mathsf{wKG}, \mathsf{wEnc}, \mathsf{wDec})$

Theorem 1. *If* PKE *is OW-CPA secure, then* wPKE *in Fig. 6 is adaptive SO-CPA secure (Definition 5). Concretely, for security parameter* λ *and*

Game $\mathbf{G}_0$-$\mathbf{G}_3$		Open(i)
01 $(\mathsf{pk}, \mathsf{sk}) \leftarrow \mathsf{KG}_0$		17 $I := I \cup \{i\}$
02 $\mathcal{M}_a \leftarrow \mathcal{A}^{\lvert G \times H \rangle}(\mathsf{pk})$		18 **return** (m_i, r_i)
03 **for** $i \in [\mu]$		
04 $\mathbf{m}[i] := m_i \leftarrow \mathcal{M}_a, r_i \xleftarrow{\$} \mathcal{R}'$		$H(r, e)$
05 $R_i := G(r_i)$		19 **if** $\exists i \in I$ s.t. $(r, e) = (r_i, e_i)$ // $\mathbf{G}_2$-$\mathbf{G}_3$
06 $R_i \xleftarrow{\$} \mathcal{R}'$	// $\mathbf{G}_2$-$\mathbf{G}_3$	20 **return** K_i // $\mathbf{G}_2$
07 $e_i := \mathsf{Enc}_0(\mathsf{pk}, r_i; R_i)$		21 **return** $d_i \oplus m_i$ // $\mathbf{G}_3$
08 $K_i := H(r_i, e_i)$	// $\mathbf{G}_0$-$\mathbf{G}_1$	22 **return** $h(r, e)$
09 $K_i \xleftarrow{\$} \mathcal{M}$	// $\mathbf{G}_2$	
10 $d_i := K_i \oplus m_i$	// $\mathbf{G}_0$-$\mathbf{G}_2$	$G(r)$
11 $d_i \xleftarrow{\$} \mathcal{M} \setminus \{d_1, ..., d_{i-1}\}$	// $\mathbf{G}_3$	23 **if** $\exists i \in I$ s.t. $r = r_i$ // $\mathbf{G}_2$-$\mathbf{G}_3$
12 $\mathbf{c}[i] := (e_i, d_i)$		24 **return** R_i // $\mathbf{G}_2$-$\mathbf{G}_3$
13 **if** $\exists i \neq j$ s.t. $K_i = K_j$	// $\mathbf{G}_1$-$\mathbf{G}_2$	25 **return** $g(r)$
14 **abort**	// $\mathbf{G}_1$-$\mathbf{G}_2$	
15 $out \leftarrow \mathcal{A}^{\text{Open}, \lvert G \times H \rangle}(\mathbf{c})$		
16 **return** $\mathsf{Rel}(\mathcal{M}_a, \mathbf{m}, I, out)$		

Fig. 7. Games $\mathbf{G}_0$-$\mathbf{G}_3$ for proving Theorem 1.

$\mu := \mu(\lambda)$ *(polynomially bounded), for any SO-CPA adversary $\mathcal{A}$ and relation* Rel, *there exist a simulator $\mathcal{S}$ and an adversary $\mathcal{B}'$ such that* $\mathbf{T}(\mathcal{S}) \approx \mathbf{T}(\mathcal{A}) \approx \mathbf{T}(\mathcal{B}')$ *and*

$$\mathsf{Adv}^{\mathsf{SO\text{-}CPA}}_{\mathsf{wPKE}}(\mathcal{A}, \mathcal{S}, \mu, \mathsf{Rel}) \leq 2(n_O + 1)^2 q \sqrt{2\mu \mathsf{Adv}^{\mathsf{OW\text{-}CPA}}_{\mathsf{PKE}}(\mathcal{B}')} + \frac{\mu^2}{|\mathcal{M}|} + \frac{\mu^2}{|\mathcal{M}'|} + \frac{2\mu q}{\sqrt{|\mathcal{M}'|}},$$

where μ, q_G, q_H, and n_O are the maximum numbers of $\mathcal{A}$'s challenge ciphertexts, $\mathcal{A}$'s queries to G, H, and Open, *respectively. $q = q_G + q_H$.*

Proof. Let $h : \mathcal{M}' \times \mathcal{C}' \to \mathcal{M}$ and $g : \mathcal{M}' \to \mathcal{R}'$ be two internal quantum-accessible random oracles that are used to respond queries to H and G, respectively. Following the convention in [25,34], in our proof we simulate H and G using two internal quantum-accessible random oracles $h : \mathcal{M}' \times \mathcal{C}' \to \mathcal{M}$ and $g : \mathcal{M}' \to \mathcal{R}'$, respectively.

Our proof consists a sequence of games defined in Fig. 7. We will use our framework in Sect. 3 to finish the proof. To fit into the syntax of our framework, we combine G and H as one random oracle $G \times H$ such that $G \times H(r', r, e) := (G(r'), H(r, e))$. If $\mathcal{A}$ only queries $G(r')$, we view it as querying $G \times H(r', r, e)$ for some dummy (r, e) and ignoring $H(r, e)$ in the response. $\mathcal{A}$ can query $G \times H$ at most $q = q_H + q_G$ times. This was also used in [24]. $\mathbf{G}_0$ is equivalent to REAL-SO-CPA$_{\mathsf{wPKE}}$, thus

$$\Pr\left[\mathsf{REAL\text{-}SO\text{-}CPA}^{\mathcal{A}}_{\mathsf{wPKE}} \Rightarrow 1\right] = \Pr\left[\mathbf{G}_0^{\mathcal{A}} \Rightarrow 1\right]$$

Game $\mathbf{G}_1$: If in the challenge ciphertexts there exist K_i and K_j for $i \neq j$ such that $K_i = K_j$, then we abort the game. Such K_i and K_j collide only if r_i and r_j collide or $H(r_i, e_i)$ and $H(r_j, e_j)$ collide with different r_i and r_j. By birthday bounds, and we have

$$\left| \Pr\left[\mathbf{G}_0^{\mathcal{A}} \Rightarrow 1\right] - \Pr\left[\mathbf{G}_1^{\mathcal{A}} \Rightarrow 1\right] \right| \leq \frac{\mu^2}{|\mathcal{M}|} + \frac{\mu^2}{|\mathcal{M}'|}$$

Game $\mathbf{G}_2$: R_i and K_i in the challenge ciphertexts are chosen randomly, instead of using G and H. If $\mathcal{A}$ queries $\text{OPEN}(i)$, then we reprogram G and H such that $G(r_i) := R_i$ and $H(r_i, e_i) := K_i$.

In the following, we use Lemma 2 to bound the difference between $\mathbf{G}_1$ and $\mathbf{G}_2$. In $\mathbf{G}_2$, $\mathcal{A}$'s OPEN queries will make QRO $G \times H$ reprogrammed, while in $\mathbf{G}_1$, QRO $G \times H$ does not get reprogrammed. So, we can view $\mathbf{G}_1$ and $\mathbf{G}_2$ as concrete cases of NONADA and ADA, respectively. For simplicity, we denote $\mathcal{A} := (\mathcal{A}_0, (\mathcal{A}_{1,0}, ..., \mathcal{A}_{1,n_O}))$, where $\mathcal{A}_0$ is the initial stage of $\mathcal{A}$ and cannot query OPEN, and $(\mathcal{A}_{1,0}, ..., \mathcal{A}_{1,n_O})$ is the stage that $\mathcal{A}$ receives the challenge ciphertexts $\mathbf{c}$ and can query OPEN. Let $\mathcal{A}_1 := (\mathcal{A}_{1,0}, ..., \mathcal{A}_{1,n_O})$. $\mathcal{A}_1$'s initial state is the final state of $\mathcal{A}_0$. $\mathcal{A}_{1,k}$ is defined with respect to OPEN queries:

- Before any OPEN query (i.e., at the 0-th stage), $\mathcal{A}_{1,0}$ takes $in_0 := \mathbf{c}$ as input and outputs the first opening index $out_0 := (i_1)$.
- At k-th stage ($1 \leq k \leq n_O - 1$), $\mathcal{A}_{1,k}$ receives $in_k = (m_{i_k}, r_{i_k})$ As the result of the $(k-1)$-th OPEN query and finishes the stage by outputting the $(k+1)$-th opening index $out_k := (i_{k+1})$
- Finally, at the n_O stage, $\mathcal{A}_{1,n_O}$ receives $in_{n_O} = (m_{i_{n_O}}, r_{i_{n_O}})$ and terminates by outputting $out_{n_O} = out$ (the final output of SO adversary).

To formally show why $\mathbf{G}_1$ and $\mathbf{G}_2$ are concrete cases of NONADA and ADA, respectively, in Fig. 8, we define INIT, $\mathsf{F_s}$, $\mathsf{Repro_s}$, $\mathbf{G}_1'$ and $\mathbf{G}_2'$. Games $\mathbf{G}_1'$ and $\mathbf{G}_2'$ are only defined to show how our proof follows the syntax of our framework. They have the same forms as NONADA and ADA.

Now we argue that $\mathbf{G}_1$ and $\mathbf{G}_2$ are concrete cases of NONADA and ADA, respectively. Namely, $\mathbf{G}_1$ and $\mathbf{G}_2$ in Fig. 7 are equivalent to $\mathbf{G}_1'$ and $\mathbf{G}_2'$ in Fig. 8, respectively. Firstly, algorithm INIT in Fig. 8 run the codes from Item 01 to Item 12 in Fig. 7. Since in $\mathcal{A}_0$'s view, $\mathbf{G}_1$ is the same as $\mathbf{G}_2$ (it does not see any challenge ciphertexts), the distribution of $\mathcal{M}_a$ and $\mathbf{m}$ in $\mathbf{G}_1$ is the same as the one in $\mathbf{G}_2$, and thus the output of INIT and the final state of $\mathcal{A}_0$ in INIT in $\mathbf{G}_1'$ are the same as those in $\mathbf{G}_2'$. Secondly, $\mathsf{F_s}$ simulates the OPEN oracle and $\mathsf{Repro_s}$ simulates the reprogramming operations on G and H. In $\mathbf{G}_1'$, G and H will not be reprogrammed, but in $\mathbf{G}_2'$, G and H will be reprogrammed, according to $\mathcal{A}$'s output. This is the same as in $\mathbf{G}_2$.

Moreover, when running $\mathcal{A}_{1,k}$, our $\mathsf{Repro_s}$ defines a set

$$S_k := \{(r, (r', e')) \mid \exists i \in [\mu] \backslash I_k \text{ s.t. } r = r_i \text{ or } (r', e') = (r_i, e_i)\} \qquad (3)$$

where $I_k := \{i_1, ..., i_k\}$ is the opening index set I in $\mathcal{A}_1$'s k-th stage. Answers of $G \times H$ on S_k are only different in $\mathbf{G}_1$ (i.e., NONADA) and $\mathbf{G}_2$ (i.e., ADA). For $k = 0$, S_0 is defined at line 35 and $I_0 = \emptyset$.

Now we consider the probability that $\mathsf{Rel}(\mathcal{M}_a, \mathbf{m}, I, out) = 1$. I and out are determined by $\mathcal{A}_1$. $\mathcal{M}_a$ is output by $\mathcal{A}_0$, and $\mathbf{m}$ is determined by $\mathcal{M}_a$. Since in $\mathcal{A}_0$'s view, $\mathbf{G}_1$ is the same as $\mathbf{G}_2$ (since it does not see challenge ciphertexts),

Game $\mathbf{G'_1}$-$\mathbf{G'_2}$	$\mathsf{F_s}(\text{out})$
01 $((\mathbf{s}, \text{in}_0), \mathsf{H}, \mathsf{H}_0) \leftarrow \text{INIT}$	14 **parse** $i := \text{out}$
02 Initialize $\mathcal{A}_{1,0}$ with	15 **parse** $(\mathcal{M}_a, \mathbf{m}, \mathbf{r}, \mathbf{R}, \mathbf{c}) := \mathbf{s}$
the final state of $\mathcal{A}_0$ in INIT	16 $I := I \cup \{i\}$
03 $\mathcal{H} := \mathsf{H}$ // $\mathbf{G'_1}$	17 $r_i := \mathbf{r}[i], m_i := \mathbf{m}[i], (e_i, d_i) := \mathbf{c}[i]$
04 $\mathcal{H} := \mathsf{H}_0$ // $\mathbf{G'_2}$	18 $\text{in} := (m_i, r_i), \text{in}' := (m_i, r_i, e_i, d_i)$
05 $\text{out}_0 \leftarrow \mathcal{A}_{1,0}^{|\mathcal{H}\rangle}(\text{in}_0)$	19 **return** (in, in')
06 $\Gamma[0] := \text{out}_0$	
07 **for** $i = 1$ **to** n_O:	$\mathsf{Repro_s}(\text{in}', (G \times H))$
08 $(\text{in}_i, \text{in}'_i) := \mathsf{F_s}(\text{out}_{i-1})$	20 **parse** $(m, r, e, d) := \text{in}'$
09 $\mathsf{H}_i := \mathsf{Repro_s}(\text{in}'_i, \mathsf{H}_{i-1})$ // $\mathbf{G'_2}$	21 $G' := G[r \to R]$
10 $\mathcal{H} := \mathsf{H}_i$ // $\mathbf{G'_2}$	22 $H' := H[(r, e) \to d \oplus m]$
11 $\text{out}_i \leftarrow \mathcal{A}_{1,i}^{|\mathcal{H}\rangle}(\text{in}_i)$	// Namely, we set $H(r_i, e_i) := K_i$
12 $\Gamma[i] := \text{out}_i$	// and denote the new oracle as H'
13 **return** $\mathsf{Rel}(\mathcal{M}_a, \mathbf{m}, I, \Gamma[n_O])$	23 **return** $G' \times H'$
INIT	
24 $I := \emptyset$	
25 $(\text{pk}, \text{sk}) \leftarrow \mathsf{KG}_0$	
26 $\mathcal{M}_a \leftarrow \mathcal{A}_0^{|g \times h\rangle}(\text{pk})$	
27 Let g' and h' be internal QROs.	
28 **for** $i \in [\mu]$:	
29 $\mathbf{m}[i] := m_i \leftarrow \mathcal{M}_a, \mathbf{r}[i] := r_i \xleftarrow{\$} \mathcal{M}'$	
30 $R_i := g(r_i), \mathbf{R}[i] := R_i$	
31 $e_i := \mathsf{Enc}_0(\text{pk}, r_i; R_i)$	
32 $K_i := h(r_i, e_i), d_i := K_i \oplus m_i$ // By $\mathbf{G_1}$, all K_i's are different.	
33 $\mathbf{c}[i] := (e_i, d_i)$	
34 $\mathbf{s} := (\mathcal{M}_a, \mathbf{m}, \mathbf{r}, \mathbf{R}, \mathbf{c}), \text{in}_0 := \mathbf{c}$	
35 $S_0 := \{r_i\}_{i \in [\mu]} \times \{(r_i, e_i)\}_{i \in [\mu]}$	
36 $G := g, H := h$	
37 Let $G_0 \times H_0$ be a QRO such that $G_0 \times H_0(x) := \begin{cases} g \times h(x), & (x \notin S_0) \\ g' \times h'(x), & (\text{else}) \end{cases}$	
// Namely, $(G_0 \times H_0) \backslash S_0 = (G \times H) \backslash S_0$	
38 **return** $((\mathbf{s}, \text{in}_0), (G \times H), (G_0 \times H_0))$	

Fig. 8. Constructions of INIT, $\mathsf{F_s}$, and $\mathsf{Repro_s}$ and games $\mathbf{G'_1}$ and $\mathbf{G'_2}$. $G' := G[r_i \to R_i]$ (similarly, $H' := H[(r_i, e_i) \to K_i]$) means that we set $G'(r_i) := R_i$ and $G'(r) := G(r)$ for $r \neq r_i$. Oracles $g, g' : \mathcal{M}' \to \mathcal{R}'$, and $h, h' : \mathcal{M}' \times \mathcal{C}' \to \mathcal{M}$ are four independent internal quantum-accessible random oracles.

thus the distribution of $\mathcal{M}_a$ and $\mathbf{m}$ in $\mathbf{G_1}$ is the same as the one in $\mathbf{G_2}$. Therefore, the probability difference between the classical event that $\mathsf{Rel}(\mathcal{M}_a, \mathbf{m}, I, \text{out}) = 1$ in $\mathbf{G_1}$ and the similar event in $\mathbf{G_2}$, is determined by the probability difference between the event that $\mathcal{A}_1$ outputs a particular (I, out) (i.e., Γ in Fig. 8) in $\mathbf{G_1}$ and the similar event in $\mathbf{G_2}$. Therefore, we have

$$\left| \Pr\left[\mathbf{G}_1^{\mathcal{A}} \Rightarrow 1 \right] - \Pr\left[\mathbf{G}_2^{\mathcal{A}} \Rightarrow 1 \right] \right| \leq \left| \Pr\left[\mathbf{G'}_1^{\mathcal{A}_1} \Rightarrow 1 \right] - \Pr\left[\mathbf{G'}_2^{\mathcal{A}_1} \Rightarrow 1 \right] \right| + \frac{2\mu q}{\sqrt{|\mathcal{M}'|}}$$

$$(4)$$

$\mathcal{B}'_i(\mathsf{pk}^*, e^*)$ // (pk^*, e^*) is a OW-CPA challenge of PKE

01 $I := \emptyset$
02 $((\mathbf{s}, \mathsf{in}_0), (G \times H), (G_0 \times H_0)) \leftarrow \mathsf{INIT}$ // INIT is defined in Figure 8 and
                                                  // it uses pk^* instead of KG_0
03 **parse** $(\mathcal{M}_a, \mathbf{m}, \mathbf{r}, \mathbf{R}, \mathbf{c}) := \mathbf{s}$
04 **parse** $\mathbf{c} := \mathsf{in}_0$
05 $t^* \overset{\$}{\leftarrow} [\mu]$, $(e_{t^*}, d_{t^*}) := \mathbf{c}[t^*]$
06 $\mathbf{c}[t^*] := (\boxed{e^*}, d_{t^*})$, $\mathsf{in}_0 := \mathbf{c}$ // embed the challenge
07 Initialize $\mathcal{B}_i$ with $\mathcal{A}_0$'s final state in INIT.
08 **if** $i = 0$: **goto** line 18
09 $\mathsf{out}_0 \leftarrow \mathcal{B}_i^{|G_0 \times H_0\rangle}(\mathsf{in}_0)$
10 **if** $\mathsf{out}_0 = t^*$: **abort**
11 $(\mathsf{in}_1, \mathsf{in}'_1) := \mathsf{F_s}(\mathsf{out}_0)$ // $\mathsf{F_s}$ is defined in Figure 8
12 $(G_1 \times H_1) := \mathsf{Repro_s}(\mathsf{in}'_1, (G_0 \times H_0))$ // $\mathsf{Repro_s}$ is defined in Figure 8
13 **for** $j = 1$ **to** $i - 1$:
14      $\mathsf{out}_j \leftarrow \mathcal{B}_i^{|G_j \times H_j\rangle}(\mathsf{in}_j)$
15   **if** $\mathsf{out}_j = t^*$: **abort**
16      $(\mathsf{in}_{j+1}, \mathsf{in}'_{j+1}) := \mathsf{F_s}(\mathsf{out}_j)$
17      $(G_{j+1} \times H_{j+1}) := \mathsf{Repro_s}(\mathsf{in}'_{j+1}, (G_j \times H_j))$
18 $(r'_0, (r'_1, e')) \leftarrow \mathcal{B}_i^{|G_i \times H_i\rangle}(\mathsf{in}_i)$ // perform measurement
19 $b \overset{\$}{\leftarrow} \{0, 1\}$, $r^* := r'_b$ // randomly choose a solution
20 **return** r^*

Fig. 9. The constructions of OW-CPA adversaries $\mathcal{B}'_i$ for $i \in \{0, ..., n_O\}$. $\mathcal{B}'_i$ simulates $\mathbf{G}'_2$ (which is a concrete case of ADA in Fig. 4) for $\mathcal{B}_i$ to break PKE. F and Repro are defined as in Fig. 8.

This bound includes a term $\frac{2\mu q}{\sqrt{|\mathcal{M}'|}}$, since $\mathcal{A}_0$ also has quantum access to $|G \times H\rangle$, and this term is the probability that the first stage (i.e., $\mathcal{A}_{1,0}$) of $\mathcal{A}_1$ learns r_i before seeing challenge ciphertexts. Such probability is only information-theoretic.

We now use Lemma 2 to bound Eq. (4). Since $\mathbf{G}'_1$ is a NONADA game and $\mathbf{G}'_2$ is an ADA game, by Lemma 2, there exist adversaries $\mathcal{B}_i$ ($0 \le i \le n_O$), which take $\mathsf{in}_0 = \mathbf{c}$ as its input and output $x \in S_k$ where the set S_i is defined in (3), such that

$$\left| \Pr\left[\mathbf{G}'^{\mathcal{A}_1}_1 \Rightarrow 1 \right] - \Pr\left[\mathbf{G}'^{\mathcal{A}_1}_2 \Rightarrow 1 \right] \right| \le \sum_{k=0}^{n_O} \sum_{i=0}^{k} 2 q_i \sqrt{\Pr\left[x \leftarrow \mathcal{B}_i \text{ s.t. } x \in S_i : \mathbf{G}'^{\mathcal{B}_i}_2 \right]} \tag{5}$$

Here $\mathcal{B}_i$ proceeds the same as $(\mathcal{A}_{1,0}, ..., \mathcal{A}_{1,i})$ except that it randomly measures a QRO query issued by $\mathcal{A}_{1,i}$. Moreover, since $\mathcal{A}_{1,0}$'s initial state is the final state of $\mathcal{A}_0$, $\mathcal{B}_i$ starts with state of $\mathcal{A}_0$ (cf. Item 07).

Based on $\mathcal{B}_i$, we construct an adversary $\mathcal{B}'_i$ (in Fig. 9) to break OW-CPA security of PKE. By the construction of $\mathcal{B}'_i$, if $\mathcal{A}_1$ does not open t^*, and r or r' equals the solution of e^*, then $\mathcal{B}'_i$ wins. So the winning probability for $\mathcal{B}'_i$ to break the OW-CPA challenge is:

$$\mathsf{Adv}^{\mathsf{OW\text{-}CPA}}_{\mathsf{PKE}}(\mathcal{B}'_i) = \frac{1}{2} \frac{\mu - n_O}{\mu} \frac{1}{\mu - n_O} \Pr\left[x \leftarrow \mathcal{B}_i \text{ s.t. } x \in S_i \right],$$

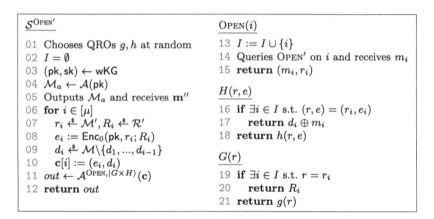

Fig. 10. The simulator $\mathcal{S}$ of the proof of Theorem 1.

and thus we have

$$\Pr\left[x \leftarrow \mathcal{B}_i \text{ s.t. } x \in S_i : \mathbf{G}_2'^{\mathcal{B}_i}\right] \leq 2\mu \mathsf{Adv}_{\mathsf{PKE}}^{\mathsf{OW\text{-}CPA}}(\mathcal{B}_i') \tag{6}$$

Let $\mathcal{B}'$ be the adversary that has highest advantage against PKE among $\{\mathcal{B}_i'\}_{i \in \{0,\dots,n\}}$. Then Eq. (6) can be written as:

$$\Pr\left[x \leftarrow \mathcal{B}_i \text{ s.t. } x \in S_i : \mathbf{G}_2'^{\mathcal{B}_i}\right] \leq 2\mu \mathsf{Adv}_{\mathsf{PKE}}^{\mathsf{OW\text{-}CPA}}(\mathcal{B}'), \text{ for } \forall i \in [\mu] \tag{7}$$

By combining Eqs. (4) to (7), we have

$$\left|\Pr\left[\mathbf{G}_1^{\mathcal{A}} \Rightarrow 1\right] - \Pr\left[\mathbf{G}_2^{\mathcal{A}} \Rightarrow 1\right]\right| \leq 2(n_O+1)^2 q \sqrt{2\mu \mathsf{Adv}_{\mathsf{PKE}}^{\mathsf{OW\text{-}CPA}}(\mathcal{B}')} + \frac{2\mu q}{\sqrt{|\mathcal{M}'|}}$$

Game $\mathbf{G}_3$: We change the generation of K_i and d_i. Now we firstly sample d_i uniformly at random, and replace all K_i as $d_i \oplus m_i$. This change is conceptual since in $\mathbf{G}_2$, all K_i are independently and uniformly random. In $\mathbf{G}_1$, we excluded any collision of K_i, so, in $\mathbf{G}_3$, it is equivalent to sample d_i in a collision-free way. Therefore, we have

$$\Pr\left[\mathbf{G}_2^{\mathcal{A}} \Rightarrow 1\right] = \Pr\left[\mathbf{G}_3^{\mathcal{A}} \Rightarrow 1\right]$$

CONSTRUCTION OF SO SIMULATOR. We construct a SO simulator $\mathcal{S}$ that is simulating $\mathbf{G}_3$ for $\mathcal{A}$ and interacts with the IDEAL-SO-CPA$_{\mathsf{wPKE}}^{\mathcal{S}}$ game. The simulation process is shown in Fig. 10. Obviously, $\mathcal{S}$ can perfectly simulates $\mathbf{G}_3$. So, we have

$$\Pr[\mathbf{G}_3^{\mathcal{A}} \Rightarrow 1] = \Pr[\mathsf{IDEAL\text{-}SO\text{-}CPA}_{\mathsf{wPKE}}^{\mathcal{S}} \Rightarrow 1]$$

In conclusion, for any SO-CPA adversary $\mathcal{A}$, there exists efficient simulator $\mathcal{S}$ such that

$$\left|\Pr[\mathsf{REAL\text{-}SO\text{-}CPA}_{\mathsf{wPKE}}^{\mathcal{A}} \Rightarrow 1] - \Pr[\mathsf{IDEAL\text{-}SO\text{-}CPA}_{\mathsf{wPKE}}^{\mathcal{S}} \Rightarrow 1]\right|$$
$$\leq 2(n_O+1)^2 q \sqrt{2\mu \mathsf{Adv}_{\mathsf{PKE}}^{\mathsf{OW\text{-}CPA}}(\mathcal{B}')} + \frac{\mu^2}{|\mathcal{M}|} + \frac{\mu^2}{|\mathcal{M}'|} + \frac{2\mu q}{\sqrt{|\mathcal{M}'|}}.$$

4.2 Selective Opening Security Against Chosen-Ciphertext Attacks

Let $\mathsf{MAC} = (\mathsf{Tag}, \mathsf{Vrfy})$ be a MAC scheme with key space $\mathcal{K}^{\mathtt{mac}}$, and let $H : \mathcal{R}' \times \mathcal{C}' \to \mathcal{M} \times \mathcal{K}^{\mathtt{mac}}$ be a hash function, where $\mathcal{C}$ is the ciphertext space of PKE. The second PKE scheme $\mathsf{sPKE} = (\mathsf{sKG}, \mathsf{sEnc}, \mathsf{sDec})$ (Fig. 11) is a combination of a modular Fujisaki-Okamoto's transformation $\mathsf{FO}^{\not\perp}$ [PKE, G, H] [21,24], one-time pad, and the one-time MAC scheme MAC. It has similar structure with the scheme in [18,35].

sKG	sEnc(pk, $m \in \mathcal{M}$)	sDec((sk, k), (e, d, τ))
01 (pk, sk) $\leftarrow$ KG$_0$	06 $r \xleftarrow{\$} \mathcal{M}'$	12 $r' := \mathsf{Dec}_0(\mathsf{sk}, e)$
02 $k \xleftarrow{\$} \mathcal{R}'$	07 $e := \mathsf{Enc}_0(\mathsf{pk}, r; G(r))$	13 if $r' = \perp$
03 pk$'$:= pk	08 $(K, K^{\mathtt{mac}}) := H(r, e)$	14 or $e \neq \mathsf{Enc}_0(\mathsf{pk}, r'; G(r'))$
04 sk$'$:= (sk, k)	09 $d := K \oplus m$	15 $(K, K^{\mathtt{mac}}) := H(k, e)$
05 return (pk$'$, sk$'$)	10 $\tau := \mathsf{Tag}(K^{\mathtt{mac}}, d)$	16 else $(K, K^{\mathtt{mac}}) := H(r', e)$
	11 return (e, d, τ)	17 if $\mathsf{Vrfy}(K^{\mathtt{mac}}, \tau) = 1$
		18 $m := K \oplus d$
		19 else $m := \perp$
		20 return m

Fig. 11. A SO-CCA secure PKE scheme $\mathsf{sPKE} = (\mathsf{sKG}, \mathsf{sEnc}, \mathsf{sDec})$

This scheme is adaptive SO-CCA secure when modeling G and H as QROs, as stated in Theorem 2. The main difference between the proof of Theorem 2 and the one of Theorem 1 is that the simulator needs to simulate the decryption oracle for the adversary. We use the encrypt-then-hash technique (widely used in CCA proof of PKE [24,27,34]) to simulate the decryption oracle without using the secret key and add a MAC verification in the decryption so that the adversary cannot forge valid MAC codes for any unopened cipheretext. We postpone the proof of Theorem 2 to our full version [33].

Theorem 2. *If PKE is OW-CPA secure and δ-correct, and MAC is otSUF-CMA secure, then the PKE scheme sPKE in Fig. 11 is adaptive SO-CCA secure (Definition 5). Concretely, for security parameter λ and integer $\mu := \mu(\lambda)$ (polynomially bounded) for any SO-CCA adversary $\mathcal{A}$ and relation Rel, there exist a simulator $\mathcal{S}$ and adversaries $\mathcal{B}'$ and $\mathcal{F}$ such that $\mathbf{T}(\mathcal{S}) \approx \mathbf{T}(\mathcal{A}) \approx \mathbf{T}(\mathcal{B}') \approx \mathbf{T}(\mathcal{F})$ and*

$$\mathsf{Adv}^{\mathsf{SO\text{-}CCA}}_{\mathsf{sPKE}}(\mathcal{A}, \mathcal{S}, \mu, \mathsf{Rel}) \leq 6(n_O + 1)^2 q \sqrt{2\mu \mathsf{Adv}^{\mathsf{OW\text{-}CPA}}_{\mathsf{PKE}}(\mathcal{B}') + \mu \mathsf{Adv}^{\mathsf{otSUF\text{-}CMA}}_{\mathsf{MAC}}(\mathcal{F})}$$

$$+ 3\mu \mathsf{Adv}^{\mathsf{otSUF\text{-}CMA}}_{\mathsf{MAC}}(\mathcal{F}) + \frac{2q_H}{\sqrt{2^k}} + 16(\mu + n_{\mathrm{D}} + q + 1)^2 \delta$$

$$+ \frac{\mu^2}{|\mathcal{M}|} + \frac{\mu^2}{|\mathcal{K}^{\mathtt{mac}}|} + \frac{6\mu q}{\sqrt{|\mathcal{M}'|}} + \frac{\mu n_{\mathrm{D}}}{|\mathcal{C}'| - n_{\mathrm{D}}} + \frac{(2 + \mu)q}{\sqrt{|\mathcal{M}'|}}$$

where $\mu, q_G, q_H, n_O,$ and n_{D} are the maximum numbers of $\mathcal{A}$'s challenge ciphertexts, $\mathcal{A}$'s queries to $G, H, \mathrm{OPEN},$ and DEC, respectively. $q = q_G + q_H$.

5   Tight SO-CCA Security from Lossy Encryption

In this section, we show that if the underlying PKE is a lossy encryption [3,22], then the construction in Fig. 11 is tightly SO-CCA secure. We recall the notion of lossy encryption from [22].

Definition 7 (Lossy Encryption [22]). *Let* $\mathsf{PKE}_1 := (\mathsf{KG}_1, \mathsf{Enc}_1, \mathsf{Dec}_1)$ *be a PKE scheme with message space* $\mathcal{M}'$ *and randomness space* $\mathcal{R}'$. PKE_1 *is lossy if it has the following properties:*

- PKE_1 *is correct according to Definition 2.*
- *Key indistinguishability: We say* PKE_1 *has key indistinguishability if there is an algorithm* LKG_1 *such that, for any adversary* $\mathcal{B}$, *the advantage function*

$$\mathsf{Adv}_{\mathsf{PKE}_1}^{\mathsf{ind\text{-}key}}(\mathcal{B}) := |\Pr[\mathcal{B}(\mathsf{pk}_1) \Rightarrow 1] - \Pr[\mathcal{B}(\mathsf{lpk}_1) \Rightarrow 1]|$$

  is negligible, where $(\mathsf{pk}_1, \mathsf{sk}_1) \leftarrow \mathsf{KG}_1$ *and* $(\mathsf{lpk}_1, \mathsf{lsk}_1) \leftarrow \mathsf{LKG}_1$.
- *Lossiness: Let* $(\mathsf{lpk}_1, \mathsf{lsk}_1) \leftarrow \mathsf{LKG}_1$ *and* m, m' *be arbitrary messages in* $\mathcal{M}'$, *the statistical distance between* $\mathsf{Enc}_1(\mathsf{lpk}_1, m)$ *and* $\mathsf{Enc}_1(\mathsf{lpk}_1, m')$ *is negligible.*
- *Weak Openability: Let* $(\mathsf{lpk}_1, \mathsf{lsk}_1) \leftarrow \mathsf{KG}_1$, *m and* m' *be arbitrary messages, and r be arbitrary randomness. For ciphertext* $c := \mathsf{Enc}_1(\mathsf{lpk}_1, m; r)$, *there exists an algorithm* open_1 *such that* $\mathsf{open}_1(\mathsf{lsk}_1, \mathsf{lpk}_1, c, r, m')$ *outputs* r' *where* $c = \mathsf{Enc}_1(\mathsf{lpk}_1, m'; r')$ *and* r' *is distributed uniformly.* open_1 *can be inefficient.*

The lossiness definition can be extended to a multi-challenge version using a hybrid argument. Since it is only a statistical property, the hybrid argument will not affect tightness of the computational advantage.

Definition 8 (Multi-challenge Lossiness). *For any arbitrary messages* m_1, $m'_1, ..., m_\mu, m'_\mu \in \mathcal{M}'$, *the statistical distance between the following distributions* D *and* D' *is at most* $\epsilon_{\mathsf{PKE}_1}^{\mathsf{m\text{-}ind\text{-}enc}}$, *where* $\epsilon_{\mathsf{PKE}_1}^{\mathsf{m\text{-}ind\text{-}enc}}$ *is negligible:*

$$D := \left\{ (\mathsf{lpk}_1, c_1, ..., c_\mu) \,\middle|\, \begin{array}{l} (\mathsf{lpk}_1, \mathsf{lsk}_1) \leftarrow \mathsf{LKG}_1 \\ c_1 \leftarrow \mathsf{Enc}_1(\mathsf{lpk}_1, m_1), ..., c_\mu \leftarrow \mathsf{Enc}_1(\mathsf{lpk}_1, m_\mu) \end{array} \right\},$$

$$D' := \left\{ (\mathsf{lpk}_1, c'_1, ..., c'_\mu) \,\middle|\, \begin{array}{l} (\mathsf{lpk}_1, \mathsf{lsk}_1) \leftarrow \mathsf{LKG}_1 \\ c'_1 \leftarrow \mathsf{Enc}_1(\mathsf{lpk}_1, m'_1), ..., c'_\mu \leftarrow \mathsf{Enc}_1(\mathsf{lpk}_1, m'_\mu) \end{array} \right\}.$$

5.1   Construction

Let $\mathsf{PKE}_1 = (\mathsf{KG}_1, \mathsf{Enc}_1, \mathsf{Dec}_1)$ be a lossy encryption with message space $\mathcal{M}'$, randomness space $\mathcal{R}'$, ciphertext space $\mathcal{C}'$, and an opening algorithm open_1. Let $\mathsf{MAC} = (\mathsf{Tag}, \mathsf{Vrfy})$ be a MAC scheme with key space $\mathcal{K}^{\mathsf{mac}}$, and $G : \mathcal{M}' \rightarrow \mathcal{R}', H : \mathcal{M}' \times \mathcal{C}' \rightarrow \mathcal{M} \times \mathcal{K}^{\mathsf{mac}}$ be two hash functions. Our PKE scheme $\mathsf{sPKE} = (\mathsf{sKG}, \mathsf{sEnc}, \mathsf{sDec})$ is defined in Fig. 12, which has the same structure with the scheme in Fig. 11.

Theorem 3 shows that sPKE is tightly SO-CCA secure when modeling G and H as QROs. Although there is a loss μ to the otSUF-CMA security of the underlying MAC, if one can use a perfectly otSUF-CMA secure MAC (e.g., the efficient one implicitly in [26]), it will not affect the security loss of sPKE and thus sPKE is tight.

sKG	sEnc(pk = $pk_1, m \in \mathcal{M}$)	sDec((sk_1, k), (e, d, τ))
01 (pk_1, sk_1) ← KG_1	06 $r \xleftarrow{\$} \mathcal{M}'$	12 $r' := Dec_1(sk_1, e)$
02 $k \xleftarrow{\$} \mathcal{M}'$	07 $e := Enc_1(pk_1, r; G(r))$	13 **if** $r' = \bot$
03 pk := pk_1	08 (K, K^{mac}) := $H(r, e)$	**or** $e \neq Enc_1(pk_1, r'; G(r'))$
04 sk := (sk_1, k)	09 $d := K \oplus m$	14 (K, K^{mac}) := $H(k, e)$
05 **return** (pk, sk)	10 $\tau \leftarrow Tag(K^{mac}, (e, d))$	15 **else** (K, K^{mac}) := $H(r', e)$
	11 **return** (e, d, τ)	16 **if** $Vrfy(K^{mac}, (e, d), \tau) = 1$
		17 $m := K \oplus d$
		18 **else** $m := \bot$
		19 **return** m

Fig. 12. A PKE scheme sPKE = (sKG, sEnc, sDec) based on lossy encryption PKE_1.

Theorem 3. *If* PKE_1 *is a lossy encryption scheme and* $(1 - \delta)$-*correct, and* MAC *is otSUF-CMA secure, then the PKE scheme* sPKE *in Fig. 12 is adaptive SO-CCA secure (Definition 5). Concretely, for security parameter* λ *and integer* $\mu := \mu(\lambda)$ *(which is polynomially bounded) for any SO-CCA adversary* $\mathcal{A}$ *and relation* Rel, *there exist a simulator* $\mathcal{S}$ *and an adversary* $\mathcal{F}$ *with* $\mathbf{T}(\mathcal{S}) \approx \mathbf{T}(\mathcal{A})$, $\mathbf{T}(\mathcal{F}) \approx \mathbf{T}(\mathcal{A})$, *and*

$$
\begin{aligned}
Adv_{sPKE}^{SO\text{-}CCA}(\mathcal{A}, \mathcal{S}, \mu, Rel) \\
\leq Adv_{PKE_1}^{ind\text{-}key}(\mathcal{A}) + 3\mu Adv_{MAC}^{otSUF\text{-}CMA}(\mathcal{F}) \\
+ 6(n_O + 1)^2 q \sqrt{\epsilon_{PKE_1}^{m\text{-}ind\text{-}enc} + \frac{\mu q}{|\mathcal{M}'|}} + 16(\mu + n_D + q + 1)^2 \delta \\
+ \frac{(2 + \mu)q}{\sqrt{|\mathcal{M}'|}} + \frac{6\mu q}{\sqrt{|\mathcal{M}'|}} + \frac{\mu^2}{|\mathcal{M}'|} + \frac{\mu^2}{|\mathcal{R}'|} + \frac{\mu^2}{|\mathcal{K}^{mac}|} + \frac{\mu n_D}{|\mathcal{C}' - n_D|} + \frac{\mu^2}{|\mathcal{M}|}
\end{aligned}
$$

where μ, q_G, q_H, n_O, *and* n_D *are the maximum numbers of* $\mathcal{A}$*'s challenge ciphertexts,* $\mathcal{A}$*'s queries to* G, H, OPEN, *and* DEC, *respectively.* $q = q_G + q_H$.

For simplicity, here we only sketch the proof idea and the formal proof of Theorem 3 is postponed to our full version [33]. Roughly, we firstly use the encrypt-then-hash technique [24,27,34] to change security games so that the simulator can simulate decryption oracle without using secret key. Then, we switch the public key of PKE_1 to the lossy mode. By the key indistinguishability of PKE_1, the adversary cannot detect such modification, and the simulation of decryption oracle still works. However, although the public key is switched to lossy mode, we cannot use the lossiness of PKE_1 directly, since there are several correlations between challenge ciphertexts and the QROs. Therefore, at the end of the proof, we use our adaptive reprogramming framework in Sect. 3 and delayed analysis to derelate QROs and challenge ciphertexts, and argue that the adversary cannot learn any information of unopened challenge ciphertexts.

INSTANTIATION FROM LWE. The Regev encryption scheme as defined in [15] is essentially a lossy encryption, and we can use it to instantiate our generic

sKG$_{bi}$	sEnc$_{bi}$(pk, $m \in \mathcal{M}$)	sDec$_{bi}$((pk, sk, k), (e, d, τ))
01 (pk, sk) $\leftarrow$ KG$_0$	06 $r \xleftarrow{\$} \mathcal{M}'$	12 $r' :=$ Dec$_0$(sk, e)
02 $k \xleftarrow{\$} \mathcal{M}'$	07 $e :=$ Enc$_0$(pk, $r; G$(pk, r))	13 if $r' = \perp$
03 pk' := pk	08 $(K, K^{mac}) := H$(pk, r, e)	14 or $e \neq$ Enc$_0$(pk, $r'; G$(pk, r'))
04 sk' := (pk, sk, k)	09 $d := K \oplus m$	15 $(K, K^{mac}) := H'$(pk, k, e)
05 return (pk', sk')	10 $\tau \leftarrow$ Tag(K^{mac}, d)	16 else $(K, K^{mac}) := H$(pk, r', e)
	11 return (e, d, τ)	17 if Vrfy(K^{mac}, τ) = 1
		18 $m := K \oplus d$
		19 else $m := \perp$
		20 return m

Fig. 13. A Bi-SO-CCA secure PKE scheme sPKE$_{bi}$ = (sKG, sEnc, sDec)

construction in Fig. 12. For completeness, we describe the lossy encryption in our full version [33]. Our resulting LWE-based SO-CCA secure PKE is unfortunately only almost tight, since the LWE-based lossy encryption loses a factor depending on the security parameter.

6   Bi-sO Security in the QROM

In this section, we show that two PKE schemes are Bi-sO-CCA secure in the QROM. The first scheme is based on a modular FO transformation FO$^{\not\perp}$ [21,24] (Sect. 6.1). The second scheme is based on another modular FO transformation U$_m^{\not\perp}$ [21] (Sect. 6.2).

6.1   Bi-sO Security of FO$^{\not\perp}$

We show that a multi-user version of sPKE (Fig. 11) is Bi-SO-CCA-secure in the QROM. Using the same building blocks PKE = (KG$_0$, Enc$_0$, Dec$_0$) and MAC as sPKE, we propose sPKE$_{bi}$ (in Fig. 13). This scheme can be viewed as a combination of a modular FO transformation FO$^{\not\perp}$ [PKE, G, H] in [21,24], one-time pad, and the a MAC scheme MAC. Moreover, in sPKE$_{bi}$, each user includes its public key as an input to the hash functions G, H, H'.

Theorem 4 shows that sPKE$_{bi}$ is Bi-SO-CCA secure when modeling G and H as QROs. The proof of Theorem 4 is more complicated than the proofs of Theorem 2, since we also need to simulate CORRUPT oracle. But the proof idea is similar: we change the games so that the game simulator can use the encrypt-then-hash technique to simulate DEC (as we did in the proof of Theorem 2). To use our framework, we divide $\mathcal{A}_1$ with respect to CORRUPT and DEC, since the operations of CORRUPT also reprograms $G \times H$. The proof of Theorem 4 is postponed to our full version [33].

Theorem 4. *If* PKE *is OW-CPA secure, then the PKE scheme* sPKE$_{bi}$ *in Fig. 13 is adaptive Bi-SO-CCA secure (Definition 6). Concretely, for any adversary* $\mathcal{A}$ *and relation* Rel*, there exist a simulator* $\mathcal{S}$ *and adversaries* $\mathcal{B}'$ *and* $\mathcal{F}$ *such that* $\mathbf{T}(\mathcal{S}) \approx \mathbf{T}(\mathcal{A}) \approx \mathbf{T}(\mathcal{B}') \approx \mathbf{T}(\mathcal{F})$ *and*

$$\mathsf{Adv}^{\mathsf{Bi\text{-}SO\text{-}CCA}}_{\mathsf{sPKE}_{\mathsf{bi}}}(\mathcal{A}, \mathcal{S}, p, \mu, \mathsf{Rel})$$

$$\leq 6(n_C + n_O + 1)^2 q \sqrt{2p\mu \mathsf{Adv}^{\mathsf{OW\text{-}CPA}}_{\mathsf{PKE}}(\mathcal{B}^{ow}) + p\mu \mathsf{Adv}^{\mathsf{otSUF\text{-}CMA}}_{\mathsf{MAC}}(\mathcal{F})} + p\eta_{\mathsf{KG}_0}$$

$$+ 3p\mu \mathsf{Adv}^{\mathsf{otSUF\text{-}CMA}}_{\mathsf{MAC}}(\mathcal{F}) + \frac{p\mu n_D}{|\mathcal{C}'| - n_D} + \frac{p^2\mu^2 + p^2}{|\mathcal{M}'|} + \frac{p^2\mu^2}{|\mathcal{R}'|} + \frac{p^2\mu^2}{|\mathcal{M}|} + \frac{p^2\mu^2}{|\mathcal{K}^{\mathtt{mac}}|}$$

$$+ \frac{6p\mu q}{\sqrt{|\mathcal{M}'|}} + 16p(\mu + n_D + q + q_{H'} + 1)^2\delta + \frac{2(n_C + 1)^2\sqrt{pq_{H'}} + 2pq_{H'} + p\mu q}{\sqrt{|\mathcal{M}'|}}$$

where $p, \mu,$ $q_G, q_H, q_{H'}, n_O, n_C,$ *and* n_D *are the number of user in the games and the maximal numbers of challenge ciphertexts per users,* $\mathcal{A}$*'s queries to* $G, H, H', \mathrm{OPEN}, \mathrm{CORRUPT},$ *and* $\mathrm{DEC},$ *respectively.* $q = q_G + q_H.$

6.2 Bi-sO Security of $\mathsf{U}^{\not\perp}_{\mathsf{m}}$

Let $\mathsf{PKE} = (\mathsf{KG}_0, \mathsf{Enc}_0, \mathsf{Dec}_0)$ be a deterministic PKE scheme with public space $\mathcal{PK}'$, plaintext space $\mathcal{M}'$, ciphertext space $\mathcal{C}'$, and plaintext distribution $\mathcal{D}_{\mathcal{M}'}$. Lett MAC be a one-time MAC as in $\mathsf{sPKE}_{\mathsf{bi}}$. Let $H : \mathcal{PK}' \times \mathcal{M}' \rightarrow \mathcal{M} \times \mathcal{K}^{\mathtt{mac}}$ and $H' : \mathcal{PK}' \times \mathcal{M}' \times \mathcal{C}' \rightarrow \mathcal{M} \times \mathcal{K}^{\mathtt{mac}}$ be two hash functions. We define $\mathsf{sPKE}^{\mathsf{m}}_{\mathsf{bi}}$ as in Fig. 14. $\mathsf{sPKE}^{\mathsf{m}}_{\mathsf{bi}}$ can be viewed as a combination of $\mathsf{U}^{\not\perp}_{\mathsf{m}}$ [21], one-time pad and one-time MAC. Similar to $\mathsf{sPKE}_{\mathsf{bi}}$, each user includes its public key into the input of hash functions.

$\mathsf{sKG}^{\mathsf{m}}_{\mathsf{bi}}$	$\mathsf{sEnc}^{\mathsf{m}}_{\mathsf{bi}}(\mathsf{pk}, m \in \mathcal{M})$	$\mathsf{sDec}^{\mathsf{m}}_{\mathsf{bi}}((\mathsf{pk}, \mathsf{sk}, k), (e, d, \tau))$
01 $(\mathsf{pk}, \mathsf{sk}) \leftarrow \mathsf{KG}_0$	06 $r \leftarrow \mathcal{D}_{\mathcal{M}'}$	12 $r' = \mathsf{Dec}_0(\mathsf{sk}, e)$
02 $k \xleftarrow{\$} \mathcal{M}'$	07 $e := \mathsf{Enc}_0(\mathsf{pk}, r)$	13 **if** $r' = \bot$
03 $\mathsf{pk}' := \mathsf{pk}$	08 $(K, K^{\mathtt{mac}}) := H(\mathsf{pk}, r)$	14 $\quad (K, K^{\mathtt{mac}}) := H'(\mathsf{pk}, k, e)$
04 $\mathsf{sk}' := (\mathsf{pk}, \mathsf{sk}, k)$	09 $d := K \oplus m$	15 **else** $(K, K^{\mathtt{mac}}) := H(\mathsf{pk}, r')$
05 **return** $(\mathsf{pk}', \mathsf{sk}')$	10 $\tau \leftarrow \mathsf{Tag}(K^{\mathtt{mac}}, d)$	16 **if** $\mathsf{Vrfy}(K^{\mathtt{mac}}, \tau) = 1$
	11 **return** (e, d, τ)	17 $\quad m = K \oplus d$
		18 **else** $m = \bot$
		19 **return** m

Fig. 14. A Bi-SO-CCA secure PKE scheme $\mathsf{sPKE}^{\mathsf{m}}_{\mathsf{bi}} = (\mathsf{sKG}^{\mathsf{m}}_{\mathsf{bi}}, \mathsf{sEnc}^{\mathsf{m}}_{\mathsf{bi}}, \mathsf{sDec}^{\mathsf{m}}_{\mathsf{bi}})$

Here we consider a variant of OW-CPA security: $\mathcal{D}_{\mathcal{M}'}$-OW-CPA security, namely, OW-CPA security with challenge messages chosen following $\mathcal{D}_{\mathcal{M}'}$. For simplicity, the definition of of $\mathcal{D}_{\mathcal{M}'}$-OW-CPA is given in our full version [33]. Moreover, we require that PKE is *rigid* correct [5], namely, for all $(\mathsf{pk}, \mathsf{sk})$ generated from KG_0, ciphertext e, and plaintext r, $(e = \mathsf{Enc}_0(\mathsf{pk}, r))$ if and only if $(\mathsf{Dec}_0(\mathsf{sk}, e) = r)$. Theorem 5 shows that $\mathsf{sPKE}^{\mathsf{m}}_{\mathsf{bi}}$ is Bi-sO-CCA secure when modeling $G, H,$ and H' as QROs. The proof of Theorem 5 is similar to Theorem 4, and is postponed to our full version [33].

Theorem 5. *Let* PKE *be a deterministic PKE with perfect correctness and rigidity. If* PKE *is* $\mathcal{D}_{\mathcal{M}'}$-*OW-CPA secure, then the PKE scheme* $\mathsf{sPKE}^{\mathsf{m}}_{\mathsf{bi}}$ *in Fig. 14* is adaptive Bi-SO-CCA secure (Definition 6). Concretely, for any Bi-SO-CCA adversary $\mathcal{A}$ and relation Rel, there exist a simulator $\mathcal{S}$ and adversaries $\mathcal{B}^{ow}$ and $\mathcal{F}$ such that $\mathbf{T}(\mathcal{S}) \approx \mathbf{T}(\mathcal{A}) \approx \mathbf{T}(\mathcal{B}') \approx \mathbf{T}(\mathcal{F})$ and

$$\mathsf{Adv}_{\mathsf{sPKE_{bi}}}^{\mathsf{Bi\text{-}SO\text{-}CCA}}(\mathcal{A}, \mathcal{S}, p, \mu, \mathsf{Rel})$$

$$\leq 6(n_\mathrm{C} + n_\mathrm{O} + 1)^2 q \sqrt{2p\mu \mathsf{Adv}_{\mathsf{PKE},\mathcal{D}_{\mathcal{M}'}}^{\mathsf{OW\text{-}CPA}}(\mathcal{B}^{ow}) + p\mu\mathsf{Adv}_{\mathsf{MAC}}^{\mathsf{otSUF\text{-}CMA}}(\mathcal{F})}$$

$$+ 3p\mu\mathsf{Adv}_{\mathsf{MAC}}^{\mathsf{otSUF\text{-}CMA}}(\mathcal{F}) + \frac{6p\mu q}{2^{\epsilon_{\mathcal{D}_{\mathcal{M}'}}}} + \frac{p\mu n_\mathrm{D}}{|\mathcal{C}'| - n_\mathrm{D}} + \frac{p^2\mu^2 + p^2}{|\mathcal{M}'|} + \frac{p^2\mu^2}{|\mathcal{M}|}$$

$$+ p\eta_{\mathsf{KG_0}} + \frac{p^2\mu^2}{|\mathcal{K}^{\mathsf{mac}}|} + \frac{2(n_\mathrm{C} + 1)^2\sqrt{pq_{H'}} + 2pq_{H'} + p\mu q}{\sqrt{|\mathcal{M}'|}}$$

where $p, \mu, q_H, q_{H'}, n_\mathrm{O}, n_\mathrm{C}$, and n_D are the maximum numbers of user in the games and $\mathcal{A}$'s challenge ciphertexts per users, $\mathcal{A}$'s queries to H, H', OPEN, CORRUPT, and DEC, respectively. $\epsilon_{\mathcal{D}_{\mathcal{M}'}}$ is the minimum entropy of $\mathcal{D}_{\mathcal{M}'}$.

Supporting Material

A   Review of Adaptive One-Way-to-Hiding

Let $\mathcal{HF} := \{\{0,1\}^* \to \{0,1\}^n\}$ be a set containing all functions that have $\{0,1\}^*$ as domain and $\{0,1\}^n$ as codomain. Let $\mathcal{A} = (\mathcal{A}_0, \mathcal{A}_1)$ be an adversary that has quantum access to a QRO $\mathcal{H}$ and queries it at most $q_0 + q_1$ times. Unruh's adaptive OW2H lemma [39, Lemma 15] can be described as follows: let

$$P_0^{\mathcal{A}} := \Pr\left[b' = 1 : \mathcal{H} \xleftarrow{\$} \mathcal{HF}, m \leftarrow \mathcal{A}_0^{\mathcal{H}}(), x \xleftarrow{\$} \{0,1\}^l, b' \leftarrow \mathcal{A}_1^{\mathcal{H}}(x, \mathcal{H}(x||m))\right]$$

$$P_1^{\mathcal{A}} := \Pr\Big[b' = 1 : \mathcal{H} \xleftarrow{\$} \mathcal{HF}, m \leftarrow \mathcal{A}_0^{\mathcal{H}}(), x \xleftarrow{\$} \{0,1\}^l,$$
$$B \xleftarrow{\$} \{0,1\}^n, b' \leftarrow \mathcal{A}_1^{\mathcal{H}}(x, B)\Big]$$

$$P_C := \Pr\Big[(x'||m') = (x||m) : \mathcal{H} \xleftarrow{\$} \mathcal{HF}, m \leftarrow \mathcal{A}_0^{\mathcal{H}}(), x \xleftarrow{\$} \{0,1\}^l,$$
$$B \xleftarrow{\$} \{0,1\}^n, j \xleftarrow{\$} [q_0], x'||m' \xleftarrow{\$} C^{\mathcal{H}}(j, x, B)\Big]$$

where q_0, q_1 are the numbers of time $\mathcal{A}_0, \mathcal{A}_1$ queries $\mathcal{H}$ respectively. C is an algorithm that has quantum access to $\mathcal{H}$ and on input (j, B, x), runs $\mathcal{A}_1^{\mathcal{H}}(x, B)$ until its j-th query, measures the QRO query in the computational basis, output the measurement outcome. Then

$$|P_0^{\mathcal{A}} - P_1^{\mathcal{A}}| \leq 2q_1\sqrt{P_C} + q_0 2^{-l/2+2}$$

The bound given in this adaptive OW2H lemma includes two parts: the first part is roughly the search bound of quantum adversaries to find a uniformly random x given $\mathcal{H}(x||m)$ (i.e., $q_0 2^{-l/2+2}$), and the second part is the advantage of $\mathcal{A}_1$ to distinguish two QROs: $\mathcal{H}_{(x||m) \to B}$ and $\mathcal{H}$, where $\mathcal{H}_{(x||m) \to B}$ is the same as $\mathcal{H}$ except that $\mathcal{H}_{(x||m) \to B}(x||m) = B$. Note that this advantage is described by the extracting algorithm C.

Unruh's adaptive OW2H lemma cannot be used to prove the bound of our reprogramming framework Fig. 4 via hybrid arguments. This is because:

- The initial oracles of ADA and NONADA in our framework are not necessarily the same. In this case, our framework considers a stronger QROM adaptive reprogramming setting than the adaptive OW2H (and the adaptive reprogramming framework in [16]).
- Even if the initial oracles are the same, in our framework, sets S_i may not independent to each other, and thus each intermediate hybrid games in the hybrid argument may not independent. This makes it hard to modify the adaptive OW2H lemma to fit in our framework and use hybrid argument. More details will be given in our full version [33].

References

1. Ambainis, A., Hamburg, M., Unruh, D.: Quantum security proofs using semi-classical oracles. In: Boldyreva, A., Micciancio, D. (eds.) CRYPTO 2019, Part II. LNCS, vol. 11693, pp. 269–295. Springer, Heidelberg (2019). https://doi.org/10.1007/978-3-030-26951-7_10
2. Bellare, M., Dowsley, R., Waters, B., Yilek, S.: Standard security does not imply security against selective-opening. In: Pointcheval, D., Johansson, T. (eds.) EUROCRYPT 2012. LNCS, vol. 7237, pp. 645–662. Springer, Heidelberg (2012). https://doi.org/10.1007/978-3-642-29011-4_38
3. Bellare, M., Hofheinz, D., Yilek, S.: Possibility and impossibility results for encryption and commitment secure under selective opening. In: Joux, A. (ed.) EUROCRYPT 2009. LNCS, vol. 5479, pp. 1–35. Springer, Heidelberg (2009). https://doi.org/10.1007/978-3-642-01001-9_1
4. Bellare, M., Rogaway, P.: The security of triple encryption and a framework for code-based game-playing proofs. In: Vaudenay, S. (ed.) EUROCRYPT 2006. LNCS, vol. 4004, pp. 409–426. Springer, Heidelberg (2006). https://doi.org/10.1007/11761679_25
5. Bernstein, D.J., Persichetti, E.: Towards KEM unification. Cryptology ePrint Archive, Report 2018/526 (2018). https://ia.cr/2018/526
6. Böhl, F., Hofheinz, D., Kraschewski, D.: On definitions of selective opening security. In: Fischlin, M., Buchmann, J., Manulis, M. (eds.) PKC 2012. LNCS, vol. 7293, pp. 522–539. Springer, Heidelberg (2012). https://doi.org/10.1007/978-3-642-30057-8_31
7. Boneh, D., Dagdelen, Ö., Fischlin, M., Lehmann, A., Schaffner, C., Zhandry, M.: Random oracles in a quantum world. In: Lee, D.H., Wang, X. (eds.) ASIACRYPT 2011. LNCS, vol. 7073, pp. 41–69. Springer, Heidelberg (2011). https://doi.org/10.1007/978-3-642-25385-0_3
8. Chen, C., et al.: NTRU. Technical report, National Institute of Standards and Technology (2020). https://csrc.nist.gov/projects/post-quantum-cryptography/post-quantum-cryptography-standardization/round-3-submissions
9. D'Anvers, J.P., et al.: SABER. Technical report, National Institute of Standards and Technology (2020). https://csrc.nist.gov/projects/post-quantum-cryptography/post-quantum-cryptography-standardization/round-3-submissions

10. Don, J., Fehr, S., Majenz, C.: The measure-and-reprogram technique 2.0: multi-round fiat-shamir and more. In: Micciancio, D., Ristenpart, T. (eds.) CRYPTO 2020, Part III. LNCS, vol. 12172, pp. 602–631. Springer, Heidelberg (2020). https://doi.org/10.1007/978-3-030-56877-1_21

11. Fehr, S., Hofheinz, D., Kiltz, E., Wee, H.: Encryption schemes secure against chosen-ciphertext selective opening attacks. In: Gilbert, H. (ed.) EUROCRYPT 2010. LNCS, vol. 6110, pp. 381–402. Springer, Heidelberg (2010). https://doi.org/10.1007/978-3-642-13190-5_20

12. Fujisaki, E., Okamoto, T.: How to enhance the security of public-key encryption at minimum cost. In: Imai, H., Zheng, Y. (eds.) PKC 1999. LNCS, vol. 1560, pp. 53–68. Springer, Heidelberg (1999). https://doi.org/10.1007/3-540-49162-7_5

13. Fujisaki, E., Okamoto, T.: Secure integration of asymmetric and symmetric encryption schemes. In: Wiener, M.J. (ed.) CRYPTO 1999. LNCS, vol. 1666, pp. 537–554. Springer, Heidelberg (Aug (1999). https://doi.org/10.1007/3-540-48405-1_34

14. Fujisaki, E., Okamoto, T.: Secure integration of asymmetric and symmetric encryption schemes. J. Cryptol. 26(1), 80–101 (2013)

15. Gentry, C., Peikert, C., Vaikuntanathan, V.: Trapdoors for hard lattices and new cryptographic constructions. In: Ladner, R.E., Dwork, C. (eds.) 40th ACM STOC, pp. 197–206. ACM Press (2008)

16. Grilo, A.B., Hövelmanns, K., Hülsing, A., Majenz, C.: Tight adaptive reprogramming in the QROM. In: Tibouchi, M., Wang, H. (eds.) ASIACRYPT 2021, Part I. LNCS, vol. 13090, pp. 637–667. Springer, Heidelberg (2021). https://doi.org/10.1007/978-3-030-92062-3_22

17. Hemenway, B., Libert, B., Ostrovsky, R., Vergnaud, D.: Lossy encryption: constructions from general assumptions and efficient selective opening chosen ciphertext security. In: Lee, D.H., Wang, X. (eds.) ASIACRYPT 2011. LNCS, vol. 7073, pp. 70–88. Springer, Heidelberg (2011). https://doi.org/10.1007/978-3-642-25385-0_4

18. Heuer, F., Jager, T., Kiltz, E., Schäge, S.: On the selective opening security of practical public-key encryption schemes. In: Katz, J. (ed.) PKC 2015. LNCS, vol. 9020, pp. 27–51. Springer, Heidelberg (2015). https://doi.org/10.1007/978-3-662-46447-2_2

19. Heuer, F., Poettering, B.: Selective opening security from simulatable data encapsulation. In: Cheon, J.H., Takagi, T. (eds.) ASIACRYPT 2016, Part II. LNCS, vol. 10032, pp. 248–277. Springer, Heidelberg (2016). https://doi.org/10.1007/978-3-662-53890-6_9

20. Hofheinz, D.: All-but-many lossy trapdoor functions. In: Pointcheval, D., Johansson, T. (eds.) EUROCRYPT 2012. LNCS, vol. 7237, pp. 209–227. Springer, Heidelberg (2012). https://doi.org/10.1007/978-3-642-29011-4_14

21. Hofheinz, D., Hövelmanns, K., Kiltz, E.: A modular analysis of the Fujisaki-Okamoto transformation. In: Kalai, Y., Reyzin, L. (eds.) TCC 2017, Part I. LNCS, vol. 10677, pp. 341–371. Springer, Heidelberg (2017). https://doi.org/10.1007/978-3-319-70500-2_12

22. Hofheinz, D., Jager, T., Rupp, A.: Public-key encryption with simulation-based selective-opening security and compact ciphertexts. In: Hirt, M., Smith, A.D. (eds.) TCC 2016-B, Part II. LNCS, vol. 9986, pp. 146–168. Springer, Heidelberg (2016). https://doi.org/10.1007/978-3-662-53644-5_6

23. Hofheinz, D., Rupp, A.: Standard versus selective opening security: separation and equivalence results. In: Lindell, Y. (ed.) TCC 2014. LNCS, vol. 8349, pp. 591–615. Springer, Heidelberg (2014). https://doi.org/10.1007/978-3-642-54242-8_25

24. Jiang, H., Zhang, Z., Chen, L., Wang, H., Ma, Z.: IND-CCA-secure key encapsulation mechanism in the quantum random oracle model, revisited. In: Shacham, H., Boldyreva, A. (eds.) CRYPTO 2018, Part III. LNCS, vol. 10993, pp. 96–125. Springer, Heidelberg (2018). https://doi.org/10.1007/978-3-319-96878-0_4

25. Kiltz, E., Lyubashevsky, V., Schaffner, C.: A concrete treatment of Fiat-Shamir signatures in the quantum random-oracle model. In: Nielsen, J.B., Rijmen, V. (eds.) EUROCRYPT 2018, Part III. LNCS, vol. 10822, pp. 552–586. Springer, Heidelberg (2018). https://doi.org/10.1007/978-3-319-78372-7_18

26. Kiltz, E., Pan, J., Wee, H.: Structure-preserving signatures from standard assumptions, revisited. In: Gennaro, R., Robshaw, M.J.B. (eds.) CRYPTO 2015, Part II. LNCS, vol. 9216, pp. 275–295. Springer, Heidelberg (2015). https://doi.org/10.1007/978-3-662-48000-7_14

27. Kuchta, V., Sakzad, A., Stehlé, D., Steinfeld, R., Sun, S.: Measure-rewind-measure: tighter quantum random oracle model proofs for one-way to hiding and CCA security. In: Canteaut, A., Ishai, Y. (eds.) EUROCRYPT 2020, Part III. LNCS, vol. 12107, pp. 703–728. Springer, Heidelberg (2020). https://doi.org/10.1007/978-3-030-45727-3_24

28. Lai, J., Yang, R., Huang, Z., Weng, J.: Simulation-based bi-selective opening security for public key encryption. In: Tibouchi, M., Wang, H. (eds.) ASIACRYPT 2021, Part II. LNCS, vol. 13091, pp. 456–482. Springer, Heidelberg (2021). https://doi.org/10.1007/978-3-030-92075-3_16

29. Lyu, L., Liu, S., Han, S., Gu, D.: Tightly SIM-SO-CCA secure public key encryption from standard assumptions. In: Abdalla, M., Dahab, R. (eds.) PKC 2018, Part I. LNCS, vol. 10769, pp. 62–92. Springer, Heidelberg (2018). https://doi.org/10.1007/978-3-319-76578-5_3

30. Nielsen, M.A., Chuang, I.L.: Quantum Computation and Quantum Information (10th Anniversary edition). Cambridge University Press, Cambridge (2016)

31. Pan, J., Wagner, B., Zeng, R.: Tighter security for generic authenticated key exchange in the QROM. In: Guo, J., Steinfeld, R. (eds.) ASIACRYPT 2023. LNCS, vol. 14441, pp. 401–433. Springer, Heidelberg (2023). https://eprint.iacr.org/2023/1380

32. Pan, J., Zeng, R.: Compact and tightly selective-opening secure public-key encryption schemes. In: Agrawal, S., Lin, D. (eds.) ASIACRYPT 2022, Part III. LNCS, vol. 13793, pp. 363–393. Springer, Heidelberg (2022). https://doi.org/10.1007/978-3-031-22969-5_13

33. Pan, J., Zeng, R.: Selective opening security in the quantum random oracle model, revisited. Cryptology ePrint Archive (2023). https://ia.cr/2023/1682

34. Saito, T., Xagawa, K., Yamakawa, T.: Tightly-secure key-encapsulation mechanism in the quantum random oracle model. In: Nielsen, J.B., Rijmen, V. (eds.) EUROCRYPT 2018, Part III. LNCS, vol. 10822, pp. 520–551. Springer, Heidelberg (2018). https://doi.org/10.1007/978-3-319-78372-7_17

35. Sato, S., Shikata, J.: SO-CCA secure PKE in the quantum random oracle model or the quantum ideal cipher model. In: Albrecht, M. (ed.) IMACC 2019. LNCS, vol. 11929, pp. 317–341. Springer, Heidelberg (2019). https://doi.org/10.1007/978-3-030-35199-1_16

36. Sato, S., Shikata, J.: SO-CCA secure PKE in the quantum random oracle model or the quantum ideal cipher model. Cryptology ePrint Archive, Paper 2022/617 (2022). https://eprint.iacr.org/2022/617. Accessed 21 July 2022

37. Schwabe, P., et al.: CRYSTALS-KYBER. Technical report, National Institute of Standards and Technology (2020). https://csrc.nist.gov/projects/post-quantum-cryptography/post-quantum-cryptography-standardization/round-3-submissions

38. Targhi, E.E., Unruh, D.: Post-quantum security of the Fujisaki-Okamoto and OAEP transforms. In: Hirt, M., Smith, A.D. (eds.) TCC 2016-B, Part II. LNCS, vol. 9986, pp. 192–216. Springer, Heidelberg (2016). https://doi.org/10.1007/978-3-662-53644-5_8

39. Unruh, D.: Quantum position verification in the random oracle model. In: Garay, J.A., Gennaro, R. (eds.) CRYPTO 2014, Part II. LNCS, vol. 8617, pp. 1–18. Springer, Heidelberg (2014). https://doi.org/10.1007/978-3-662-44381-1_1

40. Unruh, D.: Revocable quantum timed-release encryption. In: Nguyen, P.Q., Oswald, E. (eds.) EUROCRYPT 2014. LNCS, vol. 8441, pp. 129–146. Springer, Heidelberg (2014). https://doi.org/10.1007/978-3-642-55220-5_8

41. Yamakawa, T., Zhandry, M.: Classical vs quantum random oracles. In: Canteaut, A., Standaert, F.X. (eds.) EUROCRYPT 2021, Part II. LNCS, vol. 12697, pp. 568–597. Springer, Heidelberg (2021). https://doi.org/10.1007/978-3-030-77886-6_20

42. Zhandry, M.: Secure identity-based encryption in the quantum random oracle model. In: Safavi-Naini, R., Canetti, R. (eds.) CRYPTO 2012. LNCS, vol. 7417, pp. 758–775. Springer, Heidelberg (2012). https://doi.org/10.1007/978-3-642-32009-5_44

On Algebraic Embedding
for Unstructured Lattices

Madalina Bolboceanu[1(✉)], Zvika Brakerski[2], and Devika Sharma[2]

[1] Bitdefender, Bucharest, Romania
mbolboceanu@bitdefender.com
[2] Weizmann Institute of Science, Rehovot, Israel

Abstract. Lattice-based cryptography, the study of cryptographic primitives whose security is based on the hardness of so-called lattice problems, has taken center stage in cryptographic research in recent years. It potentially offers favorable security features, even against quantum algorithms. One of the main obstacles for wide adoption of this type of cryptography is its unsatisfactory efficiency. To address this point, efficient lattice-based cryptography usually relies on the intractability of problems on lattices with additional algebraic structure (such as so-called ideal-lattices or module-lattices). It is an important open question to evaluate the hardness of such lattice problems, and their relation to the hardness of problems on unstructured lattices.

It is a known fact that an unstructured lattice, which is simply an additive discrete group in Euclidean space, can be cast as an ideal-lattice in some *order* of a number field (and thus, in a rather trivial sense, that ideals in orders are as general as unstructured lattices). However, it is not known whether this connection can be used to imply useful hardness results for structured lattices, or alternatively new algorithmic techniques for unstructured lattices.

In this work we establish a gradient of hardness for the Order-LWE problem (a generalization of the well known Ring-LWE problem), as it varies over orders in a number field. Furthermore, we show that, in every number field, there are certain orders such that the corresponding Order-LWE problem is at least as hard as the (unstructured) LWE problem. So in general one should not hope to solve (any) Order-LWE more efficiently than LWE. However, we show that this connection holds in orders that are very "skewed" and hence, perhaps, irrelevant for improving efficiency in cryptographic applications. We further improve the hardness result for Order-LWE, to include *all* ideal lattices, closing a gap left in prior work. This establishes a direct connection between problems on unstructured lattices and the structured problem of Order-LWE.

Keywords: LWE · Order-LWE · Lattice Problems · Number fields

The full version of this work which contains additional definitions and deferred proofs is available at https://eprint.iacr.org/2021/053.
Supported by the Israel Science Foundation (Grant No. 3426/21), and by the European Union Horizon 2020 Research and Innovation Program via ERC Project REACT (Grant 756482).

Q. Tang and V. Teague (Eds.): PKC 2024, LNCS 14603, pp. 123–154, 2024.
https://doi.org/10.1007/978-3-031-57725-3_5

1 Introduction

The Learning with Errors (LWE) problem, as defined by Regev [Reg05], is a convenient way to construct numerous cryptographic primitives such that their security is based on the hardness of solving worst-case lattice problems on integer lattices.[1] See [Pei16] for an exposition. However, there is a drawback in basing cryptographic primitives on LWE in practice. It induces relatively high computational complexity and large instance size, at least quadratically in security parameter; an LWE-based encryption scheme, for instance, has long keys and ciphertexts, along with high encryption complexity.

It was known since the introduction of the NTRU cryptosystems [HPS98] and more rigorously by the results in [LM06, PR06] that the efficiency of the lattice-based cryptosystems could be significantly improved by instead using lattices stemming from algebraic number theory. Popularly known as *ideal lattices*, these are additive discrete groups residing in number fields that, owing to the works of Minkowski, can be viewed as lattices in the Euclidean space as well[2]. This (Minkowski) embedding of the number field into the Euclidean space preserves the algebraic structure. Inspired by this view, in [SSTX09], and then in [LPR10, LPR13], the authors defined the first known algebraic number theoretic analogs of LWE: Polynomial-LWE (PLWE) and Ring-LWE (RLWE), respectively. Roughly, they replaced the abelian group $\mathbb{Z}_q^n$ appearing in LWE by abelian groups that have an additional ring structure. For PLWE, it is the ring of polynomials $\mathbb{Z}[x]/(f(x))$, and for RLWE, it is the ring of integers $\mathcal{O}_K$ in a number field K. We will explain the properties of these algebraic objects below when needed. Similar to Regev's original result, the authors showed that each of these problems, PLWE and RLWE, is as hard as solving worst-case lattice problems on (a certain subset[3] of) their respective *ideal* lattices. Moreover, the PLWE and RLWE problems collapse in a single one, in the case of a power-of-two cyclotomic field.

Naturally, fixing a field K, not all lattices can be expressed as ideals of the ring $\mathcal{O}_K$ considered in the RLWE problem defined over K. Therefore (such) ideal lattices constitute a subset of the class of all lattices. Furthermore, the algebraic structure on these lattices makes ideal-lattice problems potentially easier to solve than their counterparts on general lattices. Indeed, recently it has been shown that on some parameter regimes, state of the art quantum algorithms for ideal lattices asymptotically significantly outperform the best known (classical or quantum) algorithms for general lattices [CGS, CDPR16, CDW17, DPW19, PHS19, BRL20, BLNRL22]. A more recent work, [PXWC21], proves that there

---

[1] We prefer to keep the discussion at a high level at this point and not specify the exact lattice problem. In this context, relevant problems include Discrete Gaussian Sampling (DGS), Shortest Independent Vectors Problem (SIVP) and Bounded Distance Decoding (BDD). See the preliminary section for definitions.

[2] See Sect. 2.3 for details.

[3] This subset is the set of invertible ideals of the polynomial ring considered in PLWE. However, this subset forms the full set of ideals for the ring considered in the RLWE problem.

are prime ideals (lattices) in the power-of-two cyclotomic fields that admit efficient classical SVP algorithms and it is further generalized by [BGP22].

On the other hand, it is known that unstructured integer lattices can be endowed with an algebraic structure by embedding them into a (fixed) number field K. See Sect. 1.1. Under this embedding, the image of an integer lattice is an ideal of a subring (order[4]) in K. But there is no efficient way, known to us, to decide if the set of all integer lattices maps to the subset of ideals captured by the existing hardness results of RLWE (and its variant Order-LWE, described below). Therefore, in spite of making unstructured integer lattices into ideal lattices in this way, one may still not be able to compare the hardness of lattice problems on the two sets. We provide a way out of this problem, in this work, by extending the hardness results to include *all* ideals in K, not just a proper subset.

Since the introduction of Ring-LWE, various algebraically structured variants of the LWE problem have been defined, each with their own worst-case to average-case reduction: Module-LWE [LS12], Middle-Product LWE [RSSS17], and Order-LWE [BBPS19]. The Order-LWE problem, which will be of interest in this work, is a generalization of the Ring-LWE problem, and is obtained by replacing the ring of integers in Ring-LWE by one of its full-rank subrings, i.e. an order.[5] Improving and extending the results from [RSW18], the authors in [PP19] proved that all the above mentioned variants are at least as hard as Ring-LWE (with some order-dependent penalty in the parameters). On the other hand, by merely forgetting the ring (or module) structure on these structured LWE problems, one obtains (multiple) LWE samples, thereby proving that all the algebraically structured LWE problems are not harder than the (unstructured) LWE.

In this paper, we prove that every number field has certain orders such that their corresponding Order-LWE problem is equivalent to the unstructured LWE problem. Therefore, in a sense, Order-LWE can be viewed as a generalization of Regev's LWE. The result emphasizes how devious certain algebraic structures can be, and that it would be naïve to assume that algebraic versions of unstructured problems are necessarily simpler. We describe our work in more detail now.

1.1   This Work: General Lattices as Ideals

To compare lattice problems on (unstructured) integer lattices with the algebraic LWE problems, one may make a lattice into an ideal lattice as follows. Given a number field K over $\mathbb{Q}$ of degree n, the elements in K can be considered as formal polynomials of degree at most $(n-1)$ with rational coefficients. This induces a correspondence between (rational) n-dimensional vectors and field elements

---

[4] See the preliminary section for a definition.

[5] The current authors, in their previous work [BBPS19], provided a detailed background and motivation for the Order-LWE problem, and invite the reader to refer to it, if needed.

known as the *coefficient embedding* (from the field K into $\mathbb{Q}^n \subseteq \mathbb{R}^n$). Once a number field K is chosen and fixed, this correspondence allows to present any (rational) lattice as an additive *subgroup* of K, but not necessarily as an ideal in the aforementioned ring-of-integers. However, it is known that any such (discrete) subgroup $\mathcal{L}$ that corresponds to a full-rank lattice L in $\mathbb{Q}^n$ constitutes an ideal in some *full-rank subring* of the ring of integers (See Sect. 2.3). Such subrings are known as orders, and the maximal order in which the group $\mathcal{L}$ is an ideal is called its ring of multipliers[6], denoted as $\mathcal{O}_{\mathcal{L}}$.

Previously, [BBPS19] showed that solving the Order-LWE problem is at least as hard as solving lattice problems on ideals of that order. We could therefore hope that the above embedding would imply that for any lattice (respectively distribution over lattices) there exists an order (respectively distribution over orders) for which solving Order-LWE is at least as hard as solving short vector problems on this lattice (or distribution). Alas, [BBPS19] only relates the hardness of Order-LWE with the hardness of a subset of ideal lattices in the order, namely the set of *invertible* ideals. We recall that an ideal in the ring is invertible if it has an inverse which is also a (possibly fractional) ideal in the ring. While all ideals of the ring of integers are invertible, this is not necessarily the case for ideals of orders. Although a naive sounding restriction, it left the infinite set of non-invertible ideals uncaptured by an important average-case problem. In particular, the lattice $\mathcal{L}$ is not necessarily invertible in its ring of multipliers and we are unaware of an efficient way of deciding that. Therefore, prior to this work, the above derivation could not be made.

In Sect. 3, we improve the existing hardness result for Order-LWE to show that this problem is at least as hard as solving lattice problems on all ideal lattices of the order, under a regularity condition on the Order-LWE modulus. The approximation factor obtained is identical to the one in [BBPS19]. The novelty of this improvement is our generalization of the so-called Cancellation Lemma that is at the heart of ideal lattice hardness results such as [LPR10, PRSD17,BBPS19].[7] We believe that this extended lemma is of interest beyond the LWE setup. Inspired by the techniques used in the proof of the generalized Cancellation Lemma, we also show an equivalence between two variants of Order-LWE that were defined in [BBPS19] (a *primal* and *dual* variant).

Lastly, in Sect. 3, we extend the Ring-LWE hardness result. The strengthened result now includes solving lattice problems (DGS) for lattices that are not necessarily ideals in the ring of integers, but rather ideals in orders whose index is coprime with the Ring-LWE modulus. This comes at a cost on the approximation factor (for DGS) if the lattice is not an $\mathcal{O}_K$-ideal, which is directly related to

---

[6] Some works, for e.g. [PP19], also call such ring as *coefficient ring*.

[7] The Cancellation Lemma provides a way to map a lattice point into its coefficient vector with respect to a basis of another, fixed and perhaps denser, lattice. The coefficient vector will constitute the LWE secret s. In order to preserve the algebraic structure, this needs to be done via multiplication by a field element. Prior results used the invertibility of the ideal to show that this is possible. See more details in Sect. 1.2.

the conductor of the ring of multipliers of the lattice.[8] This result generalizes the Order-LWE to Ring-LWE reduction proved in [BBPS19]. See Sect. 3 for full statements and proofs.

In Sect. 4, we show that every number field has chain(s) of orders beginning from $\mathcal{O}_K$ such that their corresponding Order-LWE problems become (not necessarily strictly) harder. We prove that this gradient of hardness terminates at special 'skewed' orders. That is, we show that Order-LWE corresponding to these orders is equivalent to the unstructured LWE problem. More precisely, we show that for "reasonable" Gaussian noise, from say D_α, the noise in the (skewed) Order-LWE sample drowns the last $n - 1$ coordinates of the Order-LWE instance. Thus only one coefficient survives, which is distributed like a (standard) LWE sample with a related noise parameter. We call such orders α-drowning and describe a recipe to construct them.

The α-drowning property makes the algebraic structure of the order unuseful for building efficient cryptographic schemes based on the hardness of the corresponding Order-LWE problem. However, in our opinion, since the Order-LWE problem covers the whole spectrum of the LWE problem, structured and unstructured, it is a useful problem to consider. Indeed, the chain of reductions described in Sect. 4, that starts with the Ring-LWE problem, and ends in the LWE problem disguised as an Order-LWE avatar, proposes several intermediate orders such that their corresponding Order-LWE problems are potentially harder than the Ring-LWE problem. This interpolation of Order-LWE between structured and unstructured problems, reminiscent of Module-LWE, sheds light on the interplay of the algebraic structure and the hardness of the LWE problem. It may perhaps in the future help yield an order that may be hard enough and algebraic enough for constructing a secure and yet efficient cryptographic scheme.

1.2 Technical Overview

In this section, we provide a somewhat more technical outline of our results in Sects. 3, 4. To keep this overview simple, we present all the algebraic results for the case of a power-of-two cyclotomic field, i.e., $K = \mathbb{Q}[x]/(x^n + 1)$, where n is a power of two. We will specify when the result holds in more generality, and invite the enthusiastic reader to seek details in the relevant section.

We begin with a brief description of the LWE problem: a secret vector $\vec{s}$ is sampled from $\mathbb{Z}_q^n$, for a modulus q, and an adversary gets access to an oracle that outputs pairs of the form $(\vec{a}, b = \frac{1}{q}\langle \vec{a}, \vec{s} \rangle + e \mod \mathbb{Z})$, for a uniform $\vec{a} \in \mathbb{Z}_q^n$ and a small 'noise' $e \in \mathbb{R}/\mathbb{Z}$, that typically follows a Gaussian distribution. The goal of the adversary is to distinguish this oracle from the one that outputs $(\vec{a}, b)$, with b uniform over $\mathbb{R}/\mathbb{Z}$. The Ring-LWE setup is described in a more algebraic environment, where the sample spaces are algebraic objects isomorphic to $\mathbb{Z}_q^n$.

---

[8] The conductor of an order is the maximal ideal which is shared between the order and the ring of integers. Properties of the conductor are often used to relate the order and the ring of integers.

It is well-known that the *ring of integers* of K is the ring of integer polynomials $\mathcal{O}_K := \mathbb{Z}[x]/(x^n + 1)$.[9] Observe that $\mathcal{O}_K$ is a $\mathbb{Z}$-module of rank n, much like an integer lattice. Further, one can also define the dual $\mathcal{O}_K^\vee$ of $\mathcal{O}_K$, exactly like the dual of a lattice.[10] There is a canonical way of embedding the field K into $\mathbb{R}^n$ (more accurately, a copy of $\mathbb{R}^n$ that lies inside $\mathbb{C}^n$), with the so-called Minkowski embedding of K. (See Sect. 2.3.) The $\mathbb{R}$-vector space generated by the image of K is denoted by $K_\mathbb{R}$. Under this embedding one can view ideals in K as lattices in $K_\mathbb{R}$. For a modulus q, the Ring-LWE problem is defined as follows: for a secret polynomial $s \in \frac{\mathcal{O}_K^\vee}{q\mathcal{O}_K^\vee}$, the adversary gets access to an oracle that outputs pairs of the form

$$\left(a, \frac{1}{q} \cdot a \cdot s + e\right) \in \frac{\mathcal{O}_K}{q\mathcal{O}_K} \times \frac{K_\mathbb{R}}{\mathcal{O}_K^\vee},$$

where a is drawn uniformly over $\frac{\mathcal{O}_K}{q\mathcal{O}_K}$, and e is drawn from a small Gaussian over $K_\mathbb{R}$. Intuitively, in this case, e can be thought of as a polynomial with very small coefficients. The goal of the adversary here is to distinguish between the output of this oracle and the output of an oracle that gives uniform pairs over the same domain.

The (*primal* variant of the) Order-LWE problem is a genuine generalization of the Ring-LWE problem. For, once $\mathcal{O}_K$ is replaced by an *order* $\mathcal{O}$, a full rank subring of $\mathcal{O}_K$, the problem is defined exactly as above and denoted as $\mathcal{O}$-LWE. Some simple examples of orders to keep in mind could be the ring $\mathcal{O}_K$ itself, or $\mathbb{Z} + d\mathcal{O}_K$, for any integer d, or the ring of integer polynomials modulo f, i.e., $\mathbb{Z}[x]/(f)$, if the field in discussion is defined as $K = \mathbb{Q}[x]/(f)$. Moreover, in this problem the integer modulus q can be replaced by an $\mathcal{O}$ ideal modulus $\mathcal{Q}$, but for the sake of simplicity, we will present here our results with an integer modulus. A *dual* variant of this problem is defined by swapping the domains of the secret s and of the a.[11]

Extended Hardness Result of Order-LWE (Sect. 3). The authors in [BBPS19] defined the Order-LWE problem and showed that it is at least as hard as solving lattice problems on the 'invertible' ideal (lattices) of the order. When specialized to the order $\mathcal{O}_K$, this is the hardness result as proved in [LPR10,PRSD17], where there is no mention of invertibility of the ideal lattices considered, since all $\mathcal{O}_K$-ideals are invertible. This distinction only arises when working with ideals of a proper order $\mathcal{O}$ $(\neq \mathcal{O}_K)$.[12] As the proof of the Order-LWE hardness result given in [BBPS19] followed the exact same blueprint

---

[9] See [Was83, Theorem 2.6] for a proof.

[10] Formally this is done by replacing the Euclidean inner product by its number-theoretic analog, the bilinear Trace map $Tr : K \times K \to \mathbb{Q}$. The trace coincides with the Hermitian inner product on the Minkowski space $K_\mathbb{R}$, as $\langle \sigma(x), \overline{\sigma(y)} \rangle := Tr(xy)$, where $\sigma(x)$, $\sigma(y)$ are the images of x, y in $K_\mathbb{R}$, respectively, via the Minkowski embedding σ and $\overline{\sigma(y)}$ is the complex conjugate of $\sigma(y)$.

[11] This *primal-dual* terminology, from [BBPS19], differs from the one of [RSW18,PP19], as there, only the domain of s differs: in the primal variant, it is $\mathcal{O}_K/q\mathcal{O}_K$, whereas in the dual variant, it is $\mathcal{O}_K^\vee/q\mathcal{O}_K^\vee$.

[12] There exist ideals in orders that are not invertible. See [Conb, Example 3.5].

described for the hardness of Ring-LWE [PRSD17], it needed, using additionally discrete Gaussian samples (DGS) over an $\mathcal{O}$-ideal $\mathcal{I}$, to convert Bounded Distance Decoding (BDD) samples on its dual to LWE samples. This conversion required compatible isomorphisms, namely $\mathcal{I}/q\mathcal{I} \simeq \mathcal{O}/q\mathcal{O}$, respectively its dual counterpart, that send the discrete Gaussian sample to the first coordinate of an $\mathcal{O}$-LWE sample, respectively the BDD secret to the $\mathcal{O}$-LWE secret (See Sect. 2.5 for more details on the blueprint of the Order-LWE hardness proof.). Prior to this work, these maps were constructed using the so-called Cancellation Lemma, which necessarily required the $\mathcal{O}$-ideal involved in DGS to be invertible. That was the only reason the $\mathcal{O}$-LWE hardness result needed to be restricted to this sub-class of invertible $\mathcal{O}$-ideals. In this work, we show that the conclusion of the Cancellation Lemma holds even if the ideal is not invertible, as long as a regularity condition is satisfied (i.e., the LWE modulus q is coprime to the index $[\mathcal{O}_K : \mathcal{O}]^{13}$). To prove this lemma, we use a generalization of ideal factorization, known as Jordan-Hölder filtration. To the best of our knowledge, the Jordan-Hölder filtration has not been used in this context prior to this work. Using this filtration, we observe that $\mathcal{I}$, a non-invertible $\mathcal{O}$-ideal, can be viewed as a sublattice of an invertible $\mathcal{O}$-ideal $\mathfrak{p}$. Therefore, we can apply the (usual) Cancellation Lemma to $\mathfrak{p}$ and map the elements of $\mathcal{I}$ to the elements of $\mathfrak{p}$ using the inclusion relation. The latter (inclusion) relation is of course not an isomorphism of $\mathcal{O}$-modules, a condition that is necessary to maintain the algebraic structure. However, in the context of Order-LWE reduction, what we need is an $\mathcal{O}$-isomorphism between the modulo q versions of these ideals (where q is the LWE modulus). Indeed, we show that under the aforementioned regularity condition, the inclusion relation between the ideals implies an $\mathcal{O}$-isomorphism modulo q.[14] This suffices to allow the proof to go through.

Additionally, under the coprimality condition, $(q, [\mathcal{O}_K : \mathcal{O}]) = 1,$[15] we show that the dual and the primal $\mathcal{O}$-LWE problems from [BBPS19] are equivalent, thereby further strengthening the hardness result for the dual Order-LWE problem, as well. Previously, [BBPS19] showed the equivalence between these problems, but requiring a more involved condition on the order in use and not on the LWE modulus.

In the same section, we also extend the Ring-LWE hardness result. We described the details of the strengthened results previously. See the introduction above.

---

[13] This holds more generally, for arbitrary ideal moduli $\mathcal{Q}$ coprime with $[\mathcal{O}_K : \mathcal{O}]\mathcal{O}$, but for the simplicity of exposition, we treat the LWE modulus as integer.

[14] A concurrent work, namely an updated version of [PP19], showed that Cancellation Lemma also holds for non-invertible ideals, but requires instead *invertibility modulo an ideal* $\mathcal{Q}$. In our case, the ideal modulus $\mathcal{Q}$ is coprime with $[\mathcal{O}_K : \mathcal{O}]\mathcal{O}$, therefore, in particular, coprime with the conductor as well. This implies, by their remark, that all fractional ideals are invertible modulo $\mathcal{Q}$. Therefore, [PP19, Lemma 2.14] provides an isomorphism $\mathcal{O}/\mathcal{Q}\mathcal{O} \simeq \mathcal{I}/\mathcal{Q}\mathcal{I}$, for all fractional ideals $\mathcal{I}$ and thus, an alternative proof to ours.

[15] This holds more generally, for arbitrary ideal moduli coprime with the conductor of the order.

Equivalence of Order-LWE and (Unstructured) LWE (Sect. 4). Let K be the power-of-two cyclotomic and let p be a prime such that $p\mathcal{O}_K = \mathfrak{p}_1\mathfrak{p}_2\cdot\ldots\cdot\mathfrak{p}_n$, where $\mathfrak{p}_i$'s are prime ideals in $\mathcal{O}_K$. Then, the following chain of orders exists

$$\mathcal{O}_K \supseteq \mathbb{Z} + \mathfrak{p}_1 \supseteq \mathbb{Z} + \mathfrak{p}_1\mathfrak{p}_2 \supseteq \ldots \supseteq \mathbb{Z} + \mathfrak{p}_1\cdot\ldots\cdot\mathfrak{p}_{n-1} \supseteq \mathbb{Z} + p\mathcal{O}_K.$$

As proven in [PP19, Theorem 4.7], for orders $\mathcal{O}' \subseteq \mathcal{O}$, there is an error preserving reduction from $\mathcal{O}$-LWE to $\mathcal{O}'$-LWE, as long as the modulus q is coprime to $[\mathcal{O} : \mathcal{O}']$. Therefore we can derive the following chain of error preserving reductions, as long as $(p, q) = 1$,

$$\mathcal{O}_K\text{-LWE} \to (\mathbb{Z}+\mathfrak{p}_1)\text{-LWE} \to \ldots \to (\mathbb{Z}+\mathfrak{p}_1\cdot\ldots\cdot\mathfrak{p}_{n-1})\text{-LWE} \to (\mathbb{Z}+p\mathcal{O}_K)\text{-LWE}.$$

Observe that the $\mathbb{Z}$-basis of the order $\mathbb{Z} + p\mathcal{O}_K$ is given by the set $\{1, p\zeta, \ldots, p\zeta^{n-1}\}$, as $\mathcal{O}_K = \mathbb{Z}[\zeta]$, for a primitive root of unity ζ. For a large p, one of these basis elements is much shorter than the rest. It is in this sense that we call this order 'skewed'. We show that this skewed order is α-drowning. That is, for $p \geq \frac{1}{\alpha}$, the error sampled from a spherical Gaussian distribution D_α over $K_\mathbb{R}$ drowns the last $n-1$ coordinates of $K_\mathbb{R}/\mathcal{O}^\vee$ and it is only the coefficient corresponding to the basis element 1 that survives in this Order-LWE sample and looks like the second coordinate of an LWE sample. This implies that the Order-LWE problem corresponding to $\mathbb{Z}+p\mathcal{O}_K$ is equivalent to the unstructured LWE problem. To get an intuitive idea of the proof that $\mathbb{Z}+p\mathcal{O}_K$ is α-drowning, observe that the set $(\mathbb{Z} + p\mathcal{O}_K)^\vee$, in this special case, looks like[16]

$$(\mathbb{Z} + p\zeta\mathbb{Z} + \ldots + p\zeta^{n-1}\mathbb{Z})^\vee = \frac{1}{n}\mathbb{Z} + \frac{1}{pn}\zeta\mathbb{Z} + \ldots + \frac{1}{pn}\zeta^{n-1}\mathbb{Z}.$$

Consider a noise term e drawn from a spherical (in $K_\mathbb{R}$) Gaussian D_α.[17] Its coefficients in this basis are Gaussian with a diagonal covariance matrix whose diagonal entries are $(\alpha^2 n, \alpha^2 p^2 n, \ldots, \alpha^2 p^2 n)$. In the specified choice of parameters, $\alpha p\sqrt{n}$ is greater than the smoothing parameter of $\mathbb{Z}$, thereby proving that the last $n-1$ coefficients of e are indistinguishable from uniform elements in $\mathbb{R}/\mathbb{Z}$. Whereas the first coefficient looks like a part of a LWE-sample with error from $D_{\alpha\sqrt{n}}$. In Sect. 4, we describe α-drowning orders in any number field K and show that Order-LWE corresponding to them is equivalent to LWE. The proof, in this general case, requires a more involved analysis since the covariance matrix of the Gaussian over the basis of the order is not in general diagonal which makes it much more difficult to analyze.

Related Work. A concurrent work, [JL22], showed a variant of Cancellation Lemma, by presenting the isomorphisms $\mathcal{I}/q\mathcal{I} \simeq \mathcal{O}/q\mathcal{O}$, for all ideals $\mathcal{I}$ of the order $\mathcal{O}$ and for an integer modulus q satisfying $(q, [\mathcal{O}_K : \mathcal{O}]) = 1$. The map is

---

[16] See [Conc, Theorem 3.7] for a proof.

[17] The Order-LWE problem is often considered with noise sampled from an elliptical Gaussian, or even a family of elliptical Gaussians, but we can simply consider the largest spherical Gaussian that is contained in that distribution.

described as multiplication by some special element t, obtained by a randomized algorithm and is classically efficient, without knowing the factorization of q. Using the [PRSD17] framework as we do, they develop the hardness result of decision Order-LWE for all ideals $\mathcal{I}$ in the given order, under the coprimality condition. We present the hardness result using any $\mathcal{O}$ ideal modulus $\mathcal{Q}$, as long as it is coprime with $[\mathcal{O}_K : \mathcal{O}]\mathcal{O}$, although the maps we describe for its proof are quantum efficient with the knowledge of factorization of the modulus.

2 Preliminaries

We describe the well-known results and some standard notations. Given a distribution D, when writing $x \leftarrow D$, we mean an element x sampled from this distribution. Given a set X, we denote by $U(X)$, the uniform distribution over this set. For a vector $\mathbf{x} \in \mathbb{C}^n$, we let $\|\mathbf{x}\|$ be its Euclidean norm, defined as $\|\mathbf{x}\| = (\sum_i |x_i|^2)^{1/2}$ and its infinity norm, defined as $\|\mathbf{x}\|_\infty = \max_i |x_i|$. We include more preliminary details in the full version of this paper.

2.1 The Space H

To be able to speak about the geometric properties of a number field K of degree $n = s_1 + 2s_2$, (defined below), we embed it into the following space,

$$H = \{\mathbf{x} \in \mathbb{R}^{s_1} \times \mathbb{C}^{2s_2} | x_{s_1+s_2+j} = \overline{x_{s_1+j}}, \text{ for any } 1 \le j \le s_2\} \subseteq \mathbb{C}^n.$$

H is an n-dimensional vector space over $\mathbb{R}$, equipped with the inner product induced on $\mathbb{C}^n$, and hence isomorphic to (a copy of) $\mathbb{R}^n$. This is the space $K_\mathbb{R}$, up to an isomorphism, mentioned in the introduction.

2.2 Lattices

Given a finite dimensional vector space V over $\mathbb{R}$ (e.g. $\mathbb{R}^n$ or $H \subseteq \mathbb{C}^n$) a $\mathbb{Z}$-lattice $\mathcal{L}$ is an (discrete) additive group generated by a set (basis) $B = \{\mathbf{v}_1, \mathbf{v}_2, \ldots, \mathbf{v}_k\} \subseteq V$ of elements that are linearly independent over $\mathbb{R}$. In other words,

$$\mathcal{L} := \{\sum_{i=1}^{k} a_i \mathbf{v}_i : a_i \in \mathbb{Z}, \mathbf{v}_i \in B\}.$$

The integer k is called the rank of the lattice $\mathcal{L}$ and when $k = \dim_\mathbb{R} V$, the lattice $\mathcal{L}$ is said to be of full rank. Under the inner product on V (e.g. the Euclidean product for $\mathbb{R}^n$ or the Hermitian product for H), the dual lattice $\mathcal{L}^*$, is of the same rank as $\mathcal{L}$, and is defined as

$$\mathcal{L}^* := \{\mathbf{v} \in V : \langle \mathbf{v}, \mathbf{x} \rangle \in \mathbb{Z} \ \forall \mathbf{x} \in \mathcal{L}\}.$$

Let $B(0, r)$ denote the closed Euclidean ball of radius r around 0. The successive minimum of the lattice $\mathcal{L}$ is defined, for $1 \le i \le n$, as

$$\lambda_i(\mathcal{L}) := \inf\{r > 0 : \text{rank}_\mathbb{Z}(\text{span}_\mathbb{Z}(\mathcal{L} \cap B(0, r))) \ge i\}.$$

Lemma 2.1 ([Ban93]). $1 \leq \lambda_1(\mathcal{L}) \cdot \lambda_n(\mathcal{L}^*) \leq n$.

Gaussians and Smoothing Parameter. Let V be a real inner product space of dimension n with an orthonormal basis $(\mathbf{v}_i)_{1 \leq i \leq n}$. We identify an element $x \in V$ in a unique way with a vector $\mathbf{x} \in \mathbb{R}^n$, of its coordinates with respect to this basis. Recall that a symmetric matrix $\Sigma \in M_n(\mathbb{R})$ is said to be *positive (semi)definite* if $\mathbf{x}^T \Sigma \mathbf{x} > 0$ (or $\mathbf{x}^T \Sigma \mathbf{x} \geq 0$, resp.), for any non-zero $\mathbf{x} \in \mathbb{R}^n$. This property puts a partial order on the set of symmetric matrices: $\Sigma_1 \geq \Sigma_2$ if $\mathbf{x}^T(\Sigma_1 - \Sigma_2)\mathbf{x} \geq 0$, for any nonzero $\mathbf{x} \in \mathbb{R}^n$.

Definition 2.2. *For a positive definite matrix $\Sigma \in M_n(\mathbb{R})$ and a mean vector $\mathbf{c} \in \mathbb{R}^n$, define the Gaussian function $\rho_{\mathbf{c}, \sqrt{\Sigma}} : V \to (0, 1]$ as $\rho_{\mathbf{c}, \sqrt{\Sigma}}(x) = e^{-\pi(\mathbf{x}-\mathbf{c})^T \Sigma^{-1}(\mathbf{x}-\mathbf{c})}$. We denote by $D_{\mathbf{c}, \sqrt{\Sigma}}$, the normalized continuous Gaussian distribution over V corresponding to $\rho_{\mathbf{c}, \sqrt{\Sigma}}$.*

When $\mathbf{c}$ is the zero vector, it is dropped from the subscript. When $\Sigma = \mathrm{diag}(r_i^2)$, for some $\mathbf{r} = (r_1, \ldots, r_n) \in \mathbb{R}^n$, the distribution is called an elliptical Gaussian and is denoted as $\rho_{\mathbf{r}}$ and $D_{\mathbf{r}}$. If all r_i's equal r, it is called a spherical Gaussians and is written as ρ_r and D_r. We will frequently use the fact that if x follows a Gaussian distribution of covariance matrix Σ, i.e., $x \leftarrow D_{\sqrt{\Sigma}}$, then $Tx \leftarrow D_{\sqrt{T\Sigma T^*}}$, where T is a linear transformation on V, and T^* is the conjugate-transpose operator. When working with elliptical Gaussians over H, we restrict our parameters to belong to the set $G = \{\mathbf{r} \in (\mathbb{R}^+)^n \mid \mathbf{r}_{s_1+s_2+j} = \mathbf{r}_{s_1+j}, 1 \leq j \leq s_2\}$. We say for $\mathbf{r}_1$ and $\mathbf{r}_2$ in G that $\mathbf{r}_1 \geq \mathbf{r}_2$ if $\mathbf{r}_{1i} \geq \mathbf{r}_{2i}$, for all $1 \leq i \leq n$, and by $\mathbf{r} \geq r$ we mean that $\mathbf{r}_i \geq r$, for all $1 \leq i \leq n$.

Given a lattice $\mathcal{L}$ in V and a real positive definite matrix Σ, we define the discrete Gaussian distribution $D_{\mathcal{L}, \sqrt{\Sigma}}$ on $\mathcal{L}$ as $D_{\mathcal{L}, \sqrt{\Sigma}}(x) := \frac{\rho_{\sqrt{\Sigma}}(x)}{\rho_{\sqrt{\Sigma}}(\mathcal{L})}$, for any $x \in \mathcal{L}$.

Definition 2.3 (Smoothing Condition [Pei10, Definition 2.2, 2.3]). *For a lattice $\mathcal{L}$ in V of rank n and a parameter $\varepsilon > 0$, we define the smoothing parameter of $\mathcal{L}$, $\eta_\varepsilon(\mathcal{L})$, as the smallest $r > 0$ such that $\rho_{1/r}(\mathcal{L}^* \setminus \{0\}) \leq \varepsilon$. For a positive definite matrix Σ, we say that $\sqrt{\Sigma} \geq \eta_\varepsilon(\mathcal{L})$ if $\rho_{\sqrt{\Sigma^{-1}}}(\mathcal{L}^* \setminus \{0\}) \leq \varepsilon$.*

We drop ε from the subscript of $\eta_\varepsilon(\mathcal{L})$ when it is an unspecified negligible function in n.

Lattice Problems. Let $\mathcal{L}$ be a full-rank lattice in a n dimensional real space V. We state the following standard lattice problems:

Definition 2.4 (Shortest Independent Vector Problem). *For an approximation factor $\gamma = \gamma(n) \geq 1$ and a family of rank-n lattices $\mathfrak{L}$, the $\mathfrak{L}$-SIVP_γ problem is: given a lattice $\mathcal{L} \in \mathfrak{L}$, output n linearly independent lattice vectors of norm at most $\gamma \cdot \lambda_n(\mathcal{L})$.*

Definition 2.5 (Discrete Gaussian Sampling). *For a family of rank-n lattices, $\mathfrak{L}$, and a function $\gamma : \mathfrak{L} \to G = \{\mathbf{r} \in (\mathbb{R}^+)^n \mid \mathbf{r}_{s_1+s_2+j} = \mathbf{r}_{s_1+j}, 1 \leq$

$j \leq s_2\}$, where $n = s_1 + 2s_2$, the $\mathfrak{L}$-DGS$_\gamma$ problem is: given a lattice $\mathcal{L} \in \mathfrak{L}$ and $r \geq \gamma(\mathcal{L})$, output a sample $x \in \mathcal{L}$ which follows a distribution statistically indistinguishable from $D_{\mathcal{L},r}$.

Definition 2.6 (Bounded Distance Decoding). *For a family of rank-n lattices $\mathfrak{L}$ and a function $\delta : \mathfrak{L} \to \mathbb{R}^+$, the $\mathfrak{L}$-BDD$_\delta$ problem is: given a lattice $\mathcal{L} \in \mathfrak{L}$, a distance bound $d \leq \delta(\mathcal{L})$ and a coset $e + \mathcal{L}$, where $\|e\| \leq d$, find e.*

Definition 2.7 (Gaussian Decoding Problem [PRSD17]). *For a rank-n lattice $\mathcal{L} \subset H$ and a Gaussian parameter $g > 0$, the $\mathcal{L}$-GDP$_\gamma$ problem is: given as input a coset $e + \mathcal{L}$, where $\boldsymbol{e} \in H$ is drawn from D_g, output $\boldsymbol{e}$.*

We recall here the reduction from SIVP to DGS from [Reg09].

Lemma 2.8 ([Reg09, Lemma 3.17]). *For $\varepsilon = \varepsilon(n) \leq \frac{1}{10}$ and $\gamma \geq \sqrt{2}\eta_\varepsilon(\mathcal{L})$, there is a reduction from $\mathcal{L} - $ SIVP$_{2\sqrt{n}/\lambda_n(\mathcal{L})\cdot\gamma}$ to $\mathcal{L} - $ DGS$_\gamma$.*

2.3 Lattices in Number Fields: Orders and Ideals

A *number field* $K := \mathbb{Q}(\theta)$ of degree n is a $\mathbb{Q}$-vector space obtained by attaching a root θ of a monic, irreducible polynomial $f(x)$ of degree n. It is well-known that each such K has exactly n field embeddings $\sigma_i : K \to \mathbb{C}$, that map θ to each complex root of the minimal polynomial f. Embeddings whose image lie in $\mathbb{R}$ are called *real embeddings*, otherwise they are called *complex embeddings*. It is via these (s_1 real and $2s_2$ complex) embeddings that K is embedded into the space H, defined in Sect. 2.1. This is known as the Minkowski embedding, $\sigma : K \hookrightarrow H$. The $\mathbb{R}$-vector space generated by $\sigma(K)$ in H is called the Minkowski space $K_\mathbb{R}$. Given a geometric norm $\| \cdot \|$ on H, such as the Euclidean or infinity norm, we can define a norm on field elements by identifying them with their Minkowski embeddings, i.e. $\|x\| = \|\sigma(x)\|$, for any $x \in K$. By a lattice in K, we mean the image in $K_\mathbb{R}$, of a finitely generated $\mathbb{Z}$-module in K. The most extensively studied lattice in K is its ring of integers

$$\mathcal{O}_K := \{\beta \in K : \exists \text{ (monic) } g(x) \in \mathbb{Z}[x] \text{ such that } g(\beta) = 0\}.$$

This ring is a full-rank lattice in K, i.e., $rank_\mathbb{Z} \ \mathcal{O}_K = n$. If $\mathcal{O}_K$ happens to coincide with $\mathbb{Z}[\theta]$, we say K is monogenic. A subring $\mathcal{O}$ of $\mathcal{O}_K$ satisfying $rank_\mathbb{Z} \ \mathcal{O} = n$ is said to be an *Order*. In other words, an order $\mathcal{O}$ equals $\mathbb{Z}g_1 \oplus \ldots \oplus \mathbb{Z}g_n$, for some basis $\{g_1, g_2, \ldots, g_n\} \subseteq \mathcal{O}$ of $K/\mathbb{Q}$. The set of all orders is a partial ordered set with respect to set containment and has $\mathcal{O}_K$ as the unique maximal element. See full version for a proof of the next result.

Lemma 2.9. *Let $\mathcal{O}$ be an order in K. Then, $\mathcal{O}$ has a $\mathbb{Z}$-basis containing 1.*

An (integral) *ideal* $\mathcal{I}$ in $\mathcal{O}$ is an additive subgroup that is closed under scalar multiplication by $\mathcal{O}$, i.e. $x \cdot a \in \mathcal{I}$ for every $x \in \mathcal{O}$ and $a \in \mathcal{I}$. Every ideal is a $\mathbb{Z}$-module of rank n. Further, ideals in K can be thought of as integers in $\mathbb{Z}$, since they can be added, multiplied and (sometimes) divided. We invite the reader to refer to the full version of the paper for a full exposition on ideals in K. A *fractional ideal* $\mathcal{I} \subset K$ of $\mathcal{O}$ is an ideal such that $d\mathcal{I} \subset \mathcal{O}$ for some $d \in \mathcal{O}$. A fractional ideal $\mathcal{I}$ is *invertible* if there exists a fractional ideal $\mathcal{J}$ such that $\mathcal{I} \cdot \mathcal{J} = \mathcal{O}$. If there exists such a $\mathcal{J}$, then it is unique and equal to $(\mathcal{O} : \mathcal{I}) = \{x \in K | x\mathcal{I} \subseteq \mathcal{O}\}$, and is denoted by $\mathcal{I}^{-1}$. In general, an ideal in an order may not be invertible. See [Conb, Example 3.5]. However, in the special case where $\mathcal{O} = \mathcal{O}_K$ is the maximal order, *every* fractional ideal is invertible. Integral ideals $\mathcal{I}, \mathcal{J}$ of $\mathcal{O}$ are *coprime*, if $\mathcal{I} + \mathcal{J} = \mathcal{O}$ and therefore we also have, $\mathcal{I}\mathcal{J} = \mathcal{I} \cap \mathcal{J}$ and $(\mathcal{I} \cap \mathcal{J})\mathcal{L} = \mathcal{I}\mathcal{L} \cap \mathcal{J}\mathcal{L}$, for any ideal $\mathcal{L}$. For the sake of this work, we assume that orders and ideals in K are described in terms of their $\mathbb{Z}$-bases.

The following lemma, known as the Cancellation Lemma, plays a crucial role in the hardness result for algebraic LWE's. Note that it uses the invertibility of the ideal $\mathcal{I}$.

Lemma 2.10 ([BBPS19, **Theorem 2.35**]). *Let $\mathcal{I}$ and $\mathcal{J}$ be integral ideals of an order $\mathcal{O}$ and $\mathcal{M}$ a fractional ideal. Assume that $\mathcal{I}$ is an invertible ideal. Then, given the associated primes $\mathfrak{p}_1, \ldots, \mathfrak{p}_r$ of $\mathcal{J}$, and an element $t \in \mathcal{I} \setminus \bigcup_{i=1}^{r} \mathcal{I}\mathfrak{p}_i$, the multiplication by t map θ_t, $\theta_t(x) = t \cdot x$, induces the following isomorphism of $\mathcal{O}$-modules*

$$\frac{\mathcal{M}}{\mathcal{J}\mathcal{M}} \xrightarrow{\sim} \frac{\mathcal{I}\mathcal{M}}{\mathcal{I}\mathcal{J}\mathcal{M}}.$$

This map can be efficiently inverted using $\mathcal{I}$, $\mathcal{J}$, $\mathcal{M}$ and t can be found using $\mathcal{I}$ and $\mathfrak{p}_1, \ldots, \mathfrak{p}_r$.

Remark 2.11. The above result is proved in [BBPS19, Theorem 2.35] under a condition weaker than demanding that $\mathcal{I}$ be an invertible $\mathcal{O}$-ideal. The proof only requires the tuple $(t, \mathcal{I}, \mathcal{J}, \mathcal{M})$ to satisfy $t\mathcal{M} + \mathcal{I}\mathcal{J}\mathcal{M} = \mathcal{I}\mathcal{M}$.

In the improved hardness result in Sect. 3.1, we will deal with the scenario of non-invertible ideals. To circumvent this issue in some cases, we use the following result, which shows that under a coprimality condition, the inclusion induces an isomorphism. For general cases, where the coprimality condition does not hold, we give another recipe. See Sect. 3.1 for details.

Lemma 2.12 ([PP19, **Lema 2.15**]). *Let $\mathcal{L}' \subseteq \mathcal{L}$ be two lattices in an order $\mathcal{O}$ in a number field K and $\mathcal{Q}$ an $\mathcal{O}$ ideal modulus such that it is coprime with $(\mathcal{L}' : \mathcal{L}) = \{x \in K : x\mathcal{L} \subseteq \mathcal{L}'\}$. Then the natural inclusion $\mathcal{L}' \subseteq \mathcal{L}$ induces the bijections*

$$f : \frac{\mathcal{L}'}{\mathcal{Q}\mathcal{L}'} \xrightarrow{\sim} \frac{\mathcal{L}}{\mathcal{Q}\mathcal{L}} \quad f(x) = x + \mathcal{Q}\mathcal{L}, \quad f^\vee : \frac{\mathcal{L}^\vee}{\mathcal{Q}\mathcal{L}^\vee} \xrightarrow{\sim} \frac{\mathcal{L}'^\vee}{\mathcal{Q}\mathcal{L}'^\vee} \quad f^\vee(x) = x + \mathcal{Q}\mathcal{L}'^\vee.$$

Moreover, this map is efficiently computable and invertible given a basis of $\mathcal{L}'$ relative to a basis of $\mathcal{L}$.

Notice that the result above holds also for ideal moduli being coprime with the (principal $\mathcal{O}$ ideal generated by the) index $[\mathcal{L} : \mathcal{L}']$, since this condition implies the coprimality with the set $(\mathcal{L}' : \mathcal{L})$, as $[\mathcal{L} : \mathcal{L}']\mathcal{O} \subseteq (\mathcal{L}' : \mathcal{L})$. We denote by $\xrightarrow{\sim}$ the isomorphism induced by the inclusion considered.

Duality. For an element $a \in K$, the trace $Tr(a)$ is the sum $\sum_{i=1}^{n} \sigma_i(a)$, of images of a under all the embeddings of K. In other words, it is the sum of all coordinates of $\sigma(a)$.

Definition 2.13. *The dual of the lattice $\mathcal{L}$ is defined as*

$$\mathcal{L}^{\vee} = \{x \in K | \ Tr(x \cdot \mathcal{L}) \subseteq \mathbb{Z}\}.$$

The space $H \subseteq \mathbb{C}^n$ inherits the usual Hermitian inner product from $\mathbb{C}^n$. Therefore, for x, $y \in K$, the trace $Tr(xy) = \sum_{i=1}^{n} \sigma_i(xy) = \sum_{i=1}^{n} \sigma_i(x)\sigma_i(y) = \langle \sigma(x), \overline{\sigma(y)} \rangle$. This implies that $\sigma(\mathcal{L}^{\vee}) = \overline{\sigma(\mathcal{L})^*}$.

Embedding Lattices into Number Fields. We describe the (inverse of the) well-known coefficient embedding. Let $\vec{\theta} = (1, \theta, \theta^2, \ldots, \theta^{n-1})$. Let

$$L = \mathbb{Z}\vec{a}_1 + \mathbb{Z}\vec{a}_2 + \cdots + \mathbb{Z}\vec{a}_n \subseteq \mathbb{Z}^n,$$

be an integer lattice generated by n linearly independent elements $\vec{a}_1, \ldots, \vec{a}_n \in \mathbb{Z}^n$, with $\vec{a}_i = (a_{1i}, a_{2i}, \ldots a_{ni})^t$. In Sect. 3, we will deal with a special class of integer lattices, known as *p-ary integer lattices*, i.e., integer lattices L that satisfy $p\mathbb{Z}^n \subseteq L \subseteq \mathbb{Z}^n$. Embed $\vec{a}_i$ in K as $a_i = \langle \vec{a}_i, \vec{\theta} \rangle = a_{1i} + a_{2i}\theta + \ldots + a_{ni}\theta^{n-1}$. It follows from the definition of the Trace function on K that a_i's are $\mathbb{Z}$-linearly independent and hence form an n-dimensional lattice in K. Denote by

$$\mathcal{L} = \mathbb{Z}a_1 + \mathbb{Z}a_2 + \cdots \mathbb{Z}a_n \subseteq \mathbb{Z}[\theta],$$

the embedding of L in K via this coefficient embedding. Define the Minkowski embedding; $\sigma : K \longrightarrow \mathbb{C}^n$ as $\sigma(a) = (\sigma_1(a), \sigma_2(a) \ldots \sigma_n(a))$, where σ_i's are the field embeddings defined earlier. Let $V_f = (\sigma_i(\theta^{j-1}))_{1 \leq i,j \leq n}$ denote the Vandermonde matrix corresponding to f. Then, the coefficient and the Minkowski embedding are related as follows: for any $a \in K$, the image $\sigma(a) = V_f \cdot \text{coef}(a)$, where $\text{coef}(a) \in \mathbb{Q}^n$ is made of the coefficients of a with respect to the power basis $\vec{\theta}$. In other words, the image of $\mathcal{L}$, under the Minkowski map, equals the image of L, under the $\mathbb{C}$-linear transformation defined by V_f: $\sigma(\mathcal{L}) = V_f \cdot L$. We would like to clarify that we consider $\sigma(\mathcal{L})$ as a lattice in $K_{\mathbb{R}}$ and hence a lattice in $\mathbb{R}^n$.

Let $s_n(V_f) \leq \ldots \leq s_1(V_f)$ be the singular values of V_f. Recall that the spectral norm of V_f is given by the maximum singular value, $s_1(V_f)$, whereas the spectral norm of V_f^{-1} is given by the inverse of the smallest singular value, $s_n(V_f)$. The following result describes how the embedding distorts the Euclidean norm and volume. A proof is included in the full version of the paper.

Lemma 2.14. *Let $\mathcal{L}$ be the image of L in K, under the coefficient embedding, with respect to $\vec{\theta}$. Then,*

(i) $s_n(V_f) \cdot \lambda_1(L) \leq \lambda_1(\mathcal{L}) \leq s_1(V_f) \cdot \lambda_1(L)$.
(ii) $\mathcal{L}$-DGS$_\alpha$ is equivalent to L-DGS$_{\alpha \cdot \sqrt{(V_f^* V_f)^{-1}}}$.

The Ring of Multipliers. For any lattice $\mathcal{L}$ in a number field K, we define a *multiplier* of $\mathcal{L}$ as an element $x \in K$ such that $x\mathcal{L} \subseteq \mathcal{L}$. It turns out that the set of these multipliers has a ring structure, and moreover, forms an order in the field K. For more details, see [Neu99, Chapter 1, Sect. 12].

Definition 2.15. *For a lattice $\mathcal{L} \subset K$, we define its ring of multipliers as*

$$\mathcal{O}_{\mathcal{L}} = \{x \in K \mid x\mathcal{L} \subseteq \mathcal{L}\}.$$

Both $\mathcal{L}$ and $\mathcal{L}^{\vee}$ are ideals of $\mathcal{O}_{\mathcal{L}}$. In fact, $\mathcal{O}_{\mathcal{L}}$ is the largest such order. In particular, if the lattice $\mathcal{L}$ is an order itself, then it is its own ring of multipliers. An interesting and important characterisation of $\mathcal{O}_{\mathcal{L}}$ is that $\mathcal{O}_{\mathcal{L}}^{\vee} = \mathcal{L}\mathcal{L}^{\vee}$. (See [Conb, Remark 4.2].) The following result describes an order that is contained in $\mathcal{O}_{\mathcal{L}}$. See full version for a proof.

Lemma 2.16. *Let $\mathcal{O}$ be an order in K and let $\mathcal{I}$ be an integral $\mathcal{O}$-ideal. Then, the set $\mathbb{Z} + \mathcal{I}$, contained in $\mathcal{O}$, is an order in K. Further, given an additive subgroup $\mathcal{L} \subseteq \mathcal{O}$, it is an ideal of the order $\mathbb{Z} + m\mathcal{O}$, where m is the exponent of the (additive) quotient group $\mathcal{O}/\mathcal{L}$.*

Remark 2.17. When L is a p-ary integer lattice, i.e., $p\mathbb{Z}^n \subseteq L \subseteq \mathbb{Z}^n$, the embedded lattice $\mathcal{L} \subseteq K$ satisfies $p\mathcal{O}_K \subseteq \mathcal{L} \subseteq \mathcal{O}_K$. It is straightforward to check that $\mathcal{L}$ is closed under scalar multiplication by elements of $\mathbb{Z} + p\mathcal{O}_K$, which is an order, by Lemma 2.16.

The Conductor Ideal. The non-maximality of an order $\mathcal{O}$ is reflected in a special ideal of $\mathcal{O}$ called the conductor ideal. We describe how this ideal is also closely related to the invertibility and unique factorization of $\mathcal{O}$-ideals.

Definition 2.18. *The* conductor *of an order $\mathcal{O}$ is defined to be the ideal*

$$\mathcal{C}_{\mathcal{O}} = (\mathcal{O} : \mathcal{O}_K) := \{x \in K : x\mathcal{O}_K \subseteq \mathcal{O}\}.$$

It is the maximal $\mathcal{O}_K$-ideal contained in $\mathcal{O}$.

There is a distinction between $\mathcal{O}$-ideals, based on invertibility. This distinction did not exist when dealing with $\mathcal{O}_K$-ideals, since all $\mathcal{O}_K$-ideals are invertible. But the picture is not all that bad.

Theorem 2.19. *[Conb, Theorem 3.8, Corollary 3.11] The nonzero $\mathcal{O}$-ideals coprime to $\mathcal{C}_{\mathcal{O}}$ are invertible and also have unique factorization into prime ideals over $\mathcal{O}$. Further, they are in a multiplicative bijection with the set of nonzero $\mathcal{O}_K$-ideals coprime to $\mathcal{C}_{\mathcal{O}}$, via the maps $\mathcal{I} \mapsto \mathcal{I}\mathcal{O}_K$ and $\mathcal{J} \mapsto \mathcal{J} \cap \mathcal{O}$.*

Jordan-Hölder Filtrations. Jordan-Hölder filtrations may be considered as the analog of unique decomposition into prime ideals for $\mathcal{O}$-ideals, when $\mathcal{O}$ is a non-maximal order. Let $m = [\mathcal{O}_K : \mathcal{O}]$ be the index of $\mathcal{O}$ in $\mathcal{O}_K$. As $m\mathcal{O}_K$ is an $\mathcal{O}_K$-ideal contained in $\mathcal{O}$, we have $\mathcal{C}_{\mathcal{O}}|m\mathcal{O}_K$. Recall that, given two $\mathcal{O}$-ideals

$\mathcal{I}$, $\mathcal{J}$, we say that $\mathcal{I}$ divides $\mathcal{J}$, i.e. $\mathcal{I}|\mathcal{J}$, if there exists an $\mathcal{O}$-ideal $\mathcal{L}$ such that $\mathcal{J} = \mathcal{IL}$. Define, for an ideal $\mathcal{I}$ of a ring R, $Spec_R(\mathcal{I})$ to be the set of prime ideals in R that contain $\mathcal{I}$. This set coincides with the set of associated primes of $\mathcal{I}$, defined in full version.

Theorem 2.20 ([Cond, **Theorem 8.9**]). *Let $\mathcal{O}$ be an order. Then for any integral ideal $\mathcal{I}$ there is a descending chain of ideals*

$$\mathcal{O} = \mathcal{I}_0 \supset \mathcal{I}_1 \supset \ldots \supset \mathcal{I}_l = \mathcal{I}, \tag{2.3.1}$$

where each quotient $\mathcal{I}_i/\mathcal{I}_{i+1}$ is a simple $\mathcal{O}$-module, i.e. for any $0 \leq i \leq l - 1$, $\mathcal{I}_i/\mathcal{I}_{i+1} \sim \mathcal{O}/\mathfrak{p}_i$ for some prime ideal $\mathfrak{p}_i$ of $\mathcal{O}$. These primes are the primes of $\mathcal{O}$ that contain $\mathcal{I}$ and their number is independent on the choice of the series. Furthermore, $[\mathcal{O} : \mathcal{I}] = \prod_{i=0}^{l-1}[\mathcal{O} : \mathfrak{p}_i]$.

Definition 2.21. *A finite chain for an $\mathcal{O}$-ideal $\mathcal{I}$ as in Theorem 2.20 is called a Jordan-Hölder filtration of $\mathcal{I}$.*

Lemma 2.22. *Let $\mathcal{I}$ be an integral $\mathcal{O}$-ideal. Then, there exists an invertible ideal $\mathfrak{q}$ such that $\mathcal{I} \subseteq \mathfrak{q} \subseteq \mathcal{O}$ and $Spec_{\mathbb{Z}}([\mathfrak{q} : \mathcal{I}]) \subseteq Spec_{\mathbb{Z}}(m)$, where $[\mathfrak{q} : \mathcal{I}]$ denotes the index of $\mathcal{I}$ in $\mathfrak{q}$. Further, given $\mathbb{Z}$ bases for $\mathcal{I}$, $\mathcal{O}$, $\mathcal{O}_K$, a $\mathbb{Z}$-basis for such a $\mathfrak{q}$ can be computed quantumly efficient.*

See full version for a detailed proof.

2.4   The LWE Problem

Let n and q be positive integers.

Definition 2.23 (LWE distribution). *For $\vec{s} \in (\mathbb{Z}/q\mathbb{Z})^n$ and an error distribution ψ over $\mathbb{R}/\mathbb{Z}$, define a sample of the distribution $A_{\vec{s},\psi}$ by generating $\vec{a} \leftarrow U((\mathbb{Z}/q\mathbb{Z})^n)$, $e \leftarrow \psi$ and outputting the pair $(\vec{a}, \frac{1}{q} \cdot \langle \vec{a}, \vec{s} \rangle + e \mod \mathbb{Z})$.*

Definition 2.24 (LWE, Average-Case Decision problem). *Let $q = q(n)$ be an integer and Υ a family of error distributions over $\mathbb{R}/\mathbb{Z}$. The average case decision LWE problem, denoted as $\mathrm{LWE}_{n,q,\psi}$ requires to distinguish independent samples from the distribution $A_{\vec{s},\psi}$, where $\vec{s} \leftarrow U((\mathbb{Z}/q\mathbb{Z})^n)$ and $\psi \leftarrow \Upsilon$, and the same number of samples from the uniform distribution over $(\mathbb{Z}/q\mathbb{Z})^n \times \mathbb{R}/\mathbb{Z}$.*

Definition 2.25 (LWE, Average-Case Search problem). *Let $q = q(n)$ be an integer and Υ a family of error distributions over $\mathbb{R}/\mathbb{Z}$. The search LWE problem, denoted as search $\mathrm{LWE}_{q,\varphi}$, requires, given samples from the distribution $A_{\vec{s},\varphi}$, where $\vec{s} \leftarrow U((\mathbb{Z}/q\mathbb{Z})^n)$ and $\varphi \leftarrow \Upsilon$, find $\vec{s}$.*

2.5   The Order LWE Problem

There is a line of work in studying algebraic versions of LWE: Ring-LWE [LPR10], Polynomial-LWE [SSTX09], Order-LWE [BBPS19] and $\mathcal{L}$-LWE [PP19]. In this paper we will focus on Order-LWE. To set it up, let K be a number field, $\mathcal{O}$ an order in it, $\mathcal{Q}$ an integral ideal of $\mathcal{O}$ and $u \in (\mathcal{O} : \mathcal{Q}) := \{x \in K \mid x\mathcal{Q} \subseteq \mathcal{O}\}$. For fractional $\mathcal{O}$-ideals $\mathcal{I}$ and $\mathcal{J}$, we denote by $\mathcal{I}_{\mathcal{J}} := \mathcal{I}/\mathcal{J}\mathcal{I}$. We let $\mathbb{T}_{\mathcal{O}^\vee} := K_\mathbb{R}/\mathcal{O}^\vee$. The Order-LWE distribution and problem are stated as follows:

Definition 2.26 ($\mathcal{O}$-LWE distribution). *For $s \in \mathcal{O}_\mathcal{Q}^\vee$ and an error distribution ψ over $\mathbb{T}_{\mathcal{O}^\vee}$, define a sample of the distribution $\mathcal{O}_{s,\psi,u}$ over $\mathcal{O}_\mathcal{Q} \times \mathbb{T}_{\mathcal{O}^\vee}$ by generating $a \leftarrow U(\mathcal{O}_\mathcal{Q})$, $e \leftarrow \psi$ and outputting the pair $(a, b = u{\cdot}a{\cdot}s + e \bmod \mathcal{O}^\vee)$.*

Definition 2.27 ($\mathcal{O}$-LWE, Average-Case Decision problem). *Let Υ a family of error distributions over $K_\mathbb{R}$. The average case decision $\mathcal{O}$-LWE problem, denoted as $\mathcal{O}$-LWE$_{(\mathcal{Q},u),\Upsilon}$, requires to distinguish independent samples from the distribution $\mathcal{O}_{s,\psi,u}$, where $s \leftarrow U(\mathcal{O}_\mathcal{Q}^\vee)$ and $\psi \leftarrow \Upsilon$ and the same number of samples from the uniform distribution over $\mathcal{O}_\mathcal{Q} \times \mathbb{T}_{\mathcal{O}^\vee}$.*

Definition 2.28 ($\mathcal{O}$-LWE, Average-Case Search problem). *Let Υ a family of error distributions over $K_\mathbb{R}$. The average case search $\mathcal{O}$-LWE problem, denoted as search $\mathcal{O}$-LWE$_{(\mathcal{Q},u),\Upsilon}$, requires, given independently many samples from the distribution $\mathcal{O}_{s,\psi,u}$, where $s \leftarrow U(\mathcal{O}_\mathcal{Q}^\vee)$ and $\psi \leftarrow \Upsilon$, find s.*

In Sect. 3 we will also deal with the *dual* variant of the $\mathcal{O}$-LWE problem, denoted as the $\mathcal{O}^\vee$-LWE problem, and defined in [BBPS19, Definition 3.3]. The only difference lies in swapping the domains of the secret s, $\mathcal{O}^\vee/\mathcal{Q}\mathcal{O}^\vee$, and of the a, $\mathcal{O}/\mathcal{Q}\mathcal{O}$, in the definitions above.[18]

We mention that when $\mathcal{O} = \mathcal{O}_K$, $\mathcal{Q} = q\mathcal{O}_K$ and $u = 1/q$, the Order-LWE problem becomes the Ring-LWE problem. We describe the proof of the hardness result for the decision $\mathcal{O}$-LWE problem defined in Definition 2.27. The hardness results of Ring-LWE ([PRSD17]) and Order-LWE ([BBPS19]) involve the following family of error distributions. We denote by s_1 the number of real embeddings and by $2s_2$ the number of complex embeddings of the field. Recall the definition of the set G from Sect. 2.2.

Definition 2.29 ([BBPS19, Definition 3.6]). *Fix an arbitrary $f(n) = \omega(\sqrt{\log n})$. For a positive real α and $u \in K$, a distribution sampled from $\Upsilon_{u,\alpha}$ is an elliptical Gaussian $D_\mathbf{r}$, where $\mathbf{r} \in G$ has the entries sampled as follows: for each $1 \leq i \leq s_1$, sample $x_i \leftarrow D_1$ and set $r_i^2 = \alpha^2(x_i^2 + (f(n){\cdot}|\sigma_i(u)| / \|u\|_\infty)^2)/2$. For each $s_1 + 1 \leq i \leq s_1 + s_2$, sample $x_i, y_i \leftarrow D_{1/\sqrt{2}}$ and set $r_i^2 = r_{i+s_2}^2 = \alpha^2(x_i^2 + y_i^2 + (f(n){\cdot}|\sigma_i(u)| / \|u\|_\infty)^2)/2$. When $u \in K$ is such that $|\sigma_i(u)| = \|u\|_\infty$, for all i, we denote the distribution as Υ_α.*

The proof of the hardness results for algebraic LWE (Ring-LWE [LPR10,PRSD17], Polynomial-LWE [SSTX09], Module-LWE [LS12], Order-LWE [BBPS19]) follow the same blueprint. For a detailed proof, we refer the

---

[18] We stress on the fact that we use the terminology from [BBPS19], which differs from the *primal-dual* terminology from [RSW18,PP19].

reader to [BBPS19]. Briefly, it iterates the following quantum step: given discrete Gaussian samples and an oracle for algebraic LWE, the quantum algorithm outputs narrower discrete Gaussian samples. To do this, it first transforms an $\mathcal{O}$-LWE oracle, using polynomially many discrete Gaussian samples, into a BDD solver, and then uses the BDD solver to output discrete Gaussian samples of narrower parameter. A sufficient condition required to make BDD-samples on a dual lattice $\mathcal{L}^\vee$, along with discrete Gaussian samples over $\mathcal{L}$, into $\mathcal{O}$-LWE samples is that there must exist ($\mathcal{O}$-module) isomorphisms $f : \mathcal{L}/\mathcal{QL} \xrightarrow{\sim} \mathcal{O}/\mathcal{QO}$, and $g : \mathcal{O}^\vee/\mathcal{QO}^\vee \xrightarrow{\sim} \mathcal{L}^\vee/\mathcal{QL}^\vee$, that satisfy the compatibility condition $u \cdot z \cdot x = u \cdot f(z) \cdot g^{-1}(x) \bmod \mathcal{O}^\vee$, for all $z \in \mathcal{L}/\mathcal{QL}$, $x \in \mathcal{L}^\vee/\mathcal{QL}^\vee$ with $u \in (\mathcal{O} : \mathcal{Q})$. For efficiency reasons, we require the isomorphisms f and g to be both efficiently computable and invertible. The compatibility condition yields well-defined LWE samples. Formally,

Theorem 2.30. *Let K be an arbitrary number field of degree n and let $\mathcal{O} \subset K$ an order. Let $\mathcal{Q}$ be an integral $\mathcal{O}$-ideal, $u \in (\mathcal{O} : \mathcal{Q})$ and let $\alpha \in (0,1)$ be such that $\alpha/\|u\|_\infty \geq 2 \cdot \omega(1)$. Let $\mathcal{S}$ be a subset of $\mathcal{O}$-ideal lattices such that, for any $\mathcal{L} \in \mathcal{S}$, there exist ($\mathcal{O}$-module) isomorphisms $f : \mathcal{L}/\mathcal{QL} \xrightarrow{\sim} \mathcal{O}/\mathcal{QO}$ and $g : \mathcal{O}^\vee/\mathcal{QO}^\vee \xrightarrow{\sim} \mathcal{L}^\vee/\mathcal{QL}^\vee$, both efficiently computable and invertible, such that $u \cdot z \cdot x = u \cdot f(z) \cdot g^{-1}(x) \bmod \mathcal{O}^\vee$ for any $x \in \mathcal{L}^\vee/\mathcal{QL}^\vee$ and $z \in \mathcal{L}/\mathcal{QL}$. Then, there is a polynomial-time quantum reduction from $\mathcal{S}$-DGS$_\gamma$ to $\mathcal{O}$-LWE$_{(\mathcal{Q},u),\Upsilon_{u,\alpha}}$, where*

$$\gamma = max\left\{ \eta(\mathcal{QL}) \cdot \sqrt{2}\|u\|_\infty/\alpha \cdot \omega(1), \frac{\sqrt{2n}}{\lambda_1(\mathcal{L}^\vee)} \right\}.$$

Proof. (Overview) We first prove that the compatibility condition yields well-defined Order-LWE samples. Recall that the isomorphism f maps the discrete Gaussian sample z to the a part of the LWE sample, whereas the isomorphism g^{-1} maps the BDD-secret x to the LWE secret s. Then the compatibility condition yields $u \cdot z \cdot x = u \cdot a \cdot s \bmod \mathcal{O}^\vee$. Under well chosen parameters, as in Lemma [BBPS19, Lem 3.16], the discrete Gaussian distribution over $\mathcal{L} \bmod \mathcal{QL}$ is almost the uniform distribution over $\mathcal{L}/\mathcal{QL}$ (see full version) and since f is an isomorphism, a is almost uniform over $\mathcal{O}/\mathcal{QO}$. Let $y = x + e$ be the BDD coset and e', an additional error term. Then the LWE samples are defined as,

$$\begin{aligned} (a,b) &= (f(z), u \cdot z \cdot y + e' \mod \mathcal{O}^\vee) \\ &= (f(z), u \cdot z \cdot x + \tilde{e} \mod \mathcal{O}^\vee) \\ &= (f(z), u \cdot a \cdot s + \tilde{e} \mod \mathcal{O}^\vee). \end{aligned}$$

For a detailed analysis of the error term, we refer the reader to the proof of [BBPS19, Lemma 2.36]. This shows that the compatibility condition implies the well-defined LWE samples and hence the algorithm in Lemma [BBPS19, Lemma 3.16].

As described earlier, the hardness proof relies on applying Lemma [BBPS19, Lemma 3.15] iteratively for transforming discrete Gaussian samples into discrete Gaussian samples of a narrower parameter. This iterative step uses

Lemma [BBPS19, Lemma 3.16] and Lemma [PRSD17, Lemma 6.7]. As a starting point for the iteration, samples from a discrete Gaussian distribution of a large enough parameter are efficiently generated using [Reg05, Lemma 3.2]. □

Hardness results for Ring-LWE [LPR10, PRSD17], Polynomial-LWE [SSTX09] and Order-LWE [BBPS19] use invertibility of the ideal lattices considered, to derive the compatible maps f and g.

Remark 2.31. Although Theorem 2.30 presents the hardness result for Order-LWE, a similar proof also derives the hardness result for the dual setting of Order-LWE, as defined in [BBPS19, Definition 3.3], where $a \in \mathcal{O}^\vee/\mathcal{Q}\mathcal{O}^\vee$ and $s \in \mathcal{O}/\mathcal{Q}\mathcal{O}$. The only difference consists in switching the maps f and g in the BDD-to-$\mathcal{O}^\vee$-LWE reduction.

Gaussian Distributions Over $K_\mathbb{R}$ and $K_\mathbb{R}/\mathcal{O}^\vee$. The proofs of the following results follow from basic properties of the Gaussian vector distributions. See full version for more details. For an order $\mathcal{O} \subseteq K$ with a $\mathbb{Z}$-basis $\{p_i\}_{1 \leq i \leq n}$, let $P_{\mathcal{O}} = (Tr(p_i \cdot \overline{p_j}))_{1 \leq i,j \leq n}$.

Lemma 2.32 ([PP19, Section 5.3.]). *Let e be drawn according to a Gaussian distribution D_α over $K_\mathbb{R}$. Then the coefficients of e with respect to a $\mathbb{Z}$-basis of $\mathcal{O}^\vee$ satisfy a Gaussian distribution over $\mathbb{R}^n$ of covariance matrix $\alpha^2 \cdot P_{\mathcal{O}}$. In particular, $e \mod \mathcal{O}^\vee$ follows a Gaussian distribution over $\mathbb{R}^n \mod \mathbb{Z}^n$ of the same covariance matrix.*

3   New Hardness Results for $\mathcal{O}$-LWE

In this section, we extend and enhance the hardness results for decision Order-LWE from [BBPS19] as follows:

– We prove extended versions of worst-case hardness results for both decision primal and dual variants of Order-LWE that follow for all $\mathcal{O}$-ideals, with same approximation factors as in the previous hardness statements for Order-LWE and Ring-LWE.
– We extend the worst-case hardness result for decision Ring-LWE that follows not only for $\mathcal{O}_K$-ideals, but also for $\mathcal{O}$-ideals, for any order $\mathcal{O}$ of index coprime to the Ring-LWE ideal modulus $\mathcal{Q}$. However, it incurs a penalty in the approximation factor, which depends on the conductor of the order. This result is complementary to [BBPS19, Theorem 3.8 & Corollary 5.2].

We mention that these reductions are non-uniform, as short ring elements and $\mathbb{Z}$-bases of orders and ideals involved are given as advice.

3.1   Worst-Case Hardness for All $\mathcal{O}$-Ideals

We begin this section with a non-maximal order $\mathcal{O}$ in the number field K. Let $m = [\mathcal{O}_K : \mathcal{O}]$ be the index of $\mathcal{O}$ in $\mathcal{O}_K$ and $\mathcal{C}_\mathcal{O}$ its conductor. Recall that for an ideal $\mathcal{I}$ of a ring R, $Spec_R(\mathcal{I})$ is the set of all prime ideals in R that contain $\mathcal{I}$. We denote by $\mathrm{Id}(\mathcal{O})$ the set of all fractional $\mathcal{O}$-ideals and further remark that $\mathrm{Id}(\mathcal{O}_K) \subsetneq \mathrm{Id}(\mathcal{O})$. For an ideal modulus $\mathcal{Q}$ coprime with the principal $\mathcal{O}$ ideal generated by the index $[\mathcal{O}_K : \mathcal{O}]$ and $u \in (\mathcal{O} : \mathcal{Q}) = \{x \in K | x\mathcal{Q} \subseteq \mathcal{O}\}$, we denote the primal Order-LWE problem as $\mathcal{O}$-LWE$_{(\mathcal{Q},u)}$ and the dual Order-LWE problem ([BBPS19, Definition 3.3]) as $\mathcal{O}^\vee$-LWE$_{(\mathcal{Q},u)}$. Our improved hardness results for these decision problems are as follows.

Theorem 3.1. *Let K be an arbitrary number field of degree n. Choose an ideal modulus $\mathcal{Q}$, coprime to $[\mathcal{O}_K : \mathcal{O}]\mathcal{O}$ and $u \in (\mathcal{O} : \mathcal{Q})$. Let $\alpha \in (0,1)$ such that $\alpha/\|u\|_\infty \geq 2 \cdot \omega(1)$. Then there are polynomial time quantum reductions*

$$\mathrm{Id}(\mathcal{O})\text{-DGS}_\gamma \longrightarrow \mathcal{O}\text{-LWE}_{(\mathcal{Q},u),\Upsilon_{u,\alpha}} \tag{3.1.1}$$

$$\mathrm{Id}(\mathcal{O})\text{-DGS}_\gamma \longrightarrow \mathcal{O}^\vee\text{-LWE}_{(\mathcal{Q},u),\Upsilon_{u,\alpha}} \tag{3.1.2}$$

where $\gamma = max\left\{\eta(\mathcal{QL}) \cdot \sqrt{2}\|u\|_\infty/\alpha \cdot \omega(1), \frac{\sqrt{2n}}{\lambda_1(\mathcal{L}^\vee)}\right\}$.

As mentioned in the introduction, the hardness result for Order-LWE, as proved in [BBPS19], showed that $\mathcal{O}$-LWE is at least as hard as lattice problems on lattices that are *invertible* $\mathcal{O}$-ideals. The theorem above extends the result to include non-invertible $\mathcal{O}$-ideals as well, thereby closing the gap. We, however, restrict to the ideal modulus being coprime to $[\mathcal{O}_K : \mathcal{O}]\mathcal{O}$, which also implies being coprime with the conductor ideal $\mathcal{C}_\mathcal{O} = (\mathcal{O} : \mathcal{O}_K)$, as $[\mathcal{O}_K : \mathcal{O}]\mathcal{O} \subseteq \mathcal{C}_\mathcal{O}$. In the case of $\mathcal{Q} = q\mathcal{O}$ and $u = 1/q$, for some integer q, we can choose q as being coprime with the index $[\mathcal{O}_K : \mathcal{O}]$. No such assumption was made on the modulus in [BBPS19, Theorem 3.8].

Note that both the hardness results compare the LWE problems with lattice problems on the same set of number field lattices, the $\mathcal{O}$-ideals. This is because the $\mathcal{O}$-LWE and $\mathcal{O}^\vee$-LWE problems are equivalent as long as the ideal modulus $\mathcal{Q}$ is coprime to $\mathcal{C}_\mathcal{O}$. This equivalence was also studied in [BBPS19, Remark 3.5], but under a stronger assumption of $\mathcal{O}^\vee$ being an invertible $\mathcal{O}$-ideal. Moreover, this equivalence is also a consequence of [PP19, Corollary 4.3], under the assumption of $\mathcal{O}$ and $\mathcal{O}^\vee$ being both *invertible modulo $\mathcal{Q}$* ([PP19, Definition 2.10]), a condition already implied by our choice of $\mathcal{Q}$.

Proposition 3.2. *Let K be an arbitrary number field of degree n and $\mathcal{O}$ be an order. Choose an $\mathcal{O}$ ideal modulus $\mathcal{Q}$, coprime to $\mathcal{C}_\mathcal{O}$, $u \in (\mathcal{O} : \mathcal{Q})$, and Υ a distribution over a family of error distributions over $K_\mathbb{R}$. Then, given bases for $\mathcal{O}$ and $\mathcal{O}_K$, the (search or decision) $\mathcal{O}$-LWE$_{(\mathcal{Q},u),\Upsilon}$ and the (search or decision) $\mathcal{O}^\vee$-LWE$_{(\mathcal{Q},u),\Upsilon}$ problems are equivalent by an efficient reduction, given bases of $\mathcal{O}$, $\mathcal{O}_K$, $\mathcal{O}_K^\vee$, $\mathcal{O}^\vee$, $\mathcal{Q}$ and prime ideals containing $\mathcal{Q}$.*

Proof. Define a map $f : \frac{\mathcal{O}}{\mathcal{Q}\mathcal{O}} \longrightarrow \frac{\mathcal{O}^\vee}{\mathcal{Q}\mathcal{O}^\vee}$ as a composition of the following three isomorphisms

$$\frac{\mathcal{O}}{\mathcal{Q}\mathcal{O}} \overset{\sim}{\hookrightarrow} \frac{\mathcal{O}_K}{\mathcal{Q}\mathcal{O}_K} \overset{\sim}{\longrightarrow} \frac{\mathcal{O}_K^\vee}{\mathcal{Q}\mathcal{O}_K^\vee} \overset{\sim}{\hookrightarrow} \frac{\mathcal{O}^\vee}{\mathcal{Q}\mathcal{O}^\vee}$$

$$a \rightarrow a + \mathcal{Q}\mathcal{O}_K \rightarrow ta + \mathcal{Q}\mathcal{O}_K^\vee \rightarrow ta + \mathcal{Q}\mathcal{O}^\vee := f(a)$$

The first and the last isomorphisms follow from Lemma 2.12, under the coprimality condition on $\mathcal{Q}$. The middle map is an application of the Cancellation Lemma 2.10 and we let $t \in \mathcal{O}_K^\vee$ be the element, multiplication by which, yields the isomorphism. The multiplier can be efficiently computed as in previous works [RSW18, Theorem 3.1], [BBPS19, Proposition 4.7], [PP19, Lemma 2.13].[19] Then, for $a \in \mathcal{O}/\mathcal{Q}\mathcal{O}$ and $s \in \mathcal{O}^\vee/\mathcal{Q}\mathcal{O}^\vee$, the cosets $u \cdot a \cdot s + \mathcal{O}^\vee$ and $u \cdot f(a) \cdot f^{-1}(s) + \mathcal{O}^\vee$ are equal. To see this, let $s' = f^{-1}(s) \in \mathcal{O}/\mathcal{Q}\mathcal{O}$. Notice that, as f is isomorphism, then $f(a)$ and $f^{-1}(s')$ are uniform over their corresponding sets, as a and s are. Then,

$$\begin{aligned}
u \cdot a \cdot s + \mathcal{O}^\vee &= u \cdot a \cdot f(s') + \mathcal{O}^\vee \\
&= u \cdot a \cdot (ts' + \mathcal{Q}\mathcal{O}^\vee) + \mathcal{O}^\vee \\
&= u \cdot ta \cdot s' + \mathcal{O}^\vee &\text{as } u \cdot a \cdot \mathcal{Q}\mathcal{O}^\vee \subseteq \mathcal{O}^\vee \\
&= u \cdot (ta + \mathcal{Q}\mathcal{O}^\vee) \cdot s' + \mathcal{O}^\vee &\text{as } u \cdot s' \cdot \mathcal{Q}\mathcal{O}^\vee \subseteq \mathcal{O}^\vee \\
&= f(a) \cdot f^{-1}(s) + \mathcal{O}^\vee
\end{aligned}$$

Therefore, the $\mathcal{O}$-LWE samples $(a, b := u \cdot a \cdot s + e \mod \mathcal{O}^\vee)$, where $e \leftarrow \varphi$ for some $\varphi \leftarrow \Upsilon$, can be transformed to $\mathcal{O}^\vee$-LWE samples by considering $(f(a), b := u \cdot f(a) \cdot f^{-1}(s) + e \mod \mathcal{O}^\vee)$, where $f(a) \in \mathcal{O}^\vee/\mathcal{Q}\mathcal{O}^\vee$ and $f^{-1}(s) \in \mathcal{O}/\mathcal{Q}\mathcal{O}$. Conversely, the $\mathcal{O}^\vee$-LWE samples $(a', b' := u \cdot a' \cdot s' + e' \mod \mathcal{O}^\vee)$, where $e' \leftarrow \varphi$ for some $\varphi \leftarrow \Upsilon$, can be made into $\mathcal{O}$-LWE samples by taking $(f^{-1}(a'), b := u \cdot f^{-1}(a') \cdot f(s') + e' \mod \mathcal{O}^\vee)$, where $f^{-1}(a') \in \mathcal{O}/\mathcal{Q}\mathcal{O}$ and $f(s') \in \mathcal{O}^\vee/\mathcal{Q}\mathcal{O}^\vee$. It is easy to check that the transformation above sending (a, b) to $(f(a), b)$ maps uniform samples over $\mathcal{O}/\mathcal{Q}\mathcal{O} \times K_\mathbb{R}/\mathcal{O}^\vee$ to uniform samples over $\mathcal{O}^\vee/\mathcal{Q}\mathcal{O}^\vee \times K_\mathbb{R}/\mathcal{O}^\vee$.   □

Taking the particular case of Theorem 3.1 for $\mathcal{Q} = q\mathcal{O}$ and $u = 1/q$, coupled with the reduction from SIVP to DGS (see Lemma 2.8) yields the following generalization of [LPR10, Theorem 3.6], [PRSD17, Corollary 6.3]. See full version for a proof.

Corollary 3.3. *Let K be an arbitrary number field of degree n. Let $\alpha \in (0, 1)$ satisfy $\alpha \cdot q \geq 2\omega(1)$ and q be an integer coprime to $[\mathcal{O}_K : \mathcal{O}]$. Then there is a polynomial time quantum reduction from*

$$Id(\mathcal{O})\text{-}SIVP_{\gamma'} \longrightarrow \mathcal{O}\text{-}LWE_{(q\mathcal{O}, 1/q), \Upsilon_\alpha},$$

where $\gamma' = \omega(\frac{1}{\alpha})$.

---

[19] The size of the multiplier is not relevant here.

In order to prove Theorem 3.1, we need the following lemma.

Lemma 3.4. *Let $\mathcal{Q}$ be an ideal modulus coprime to $m\mathcal{O}$, for $m := [\mathcal{O}_K : \mathcal{O}]$ and $u \in (\mathcal{O} : \mathcal{Q})$. Let $\mathcal{I}$ be an integral $\mathcal{O}$-ideal. Then, there exist (quantumly) efficiently computable and invertible $\mathcal{O}$-module isomorphisms,*

$$f : \frac{\mathcal{I}}{\mathcal{Q}\mathcal{I}} \xrightarrow{\sim} \frac{\mathcal{O}}{\mathcal{Q}\mathcal{O}} \quad and \quad g : \frac{\mathcal{O}^\vee}{\mathcal{Q}\mathcal{O}^\vee} \xrightarrow{\sim} \frac{\mathcal{I}^\vee}{\mathcal{Q}\mathcal{I}^\vee},$$

given bases of $\mathcal{I}$, $\mathcal{I}^\vee$, $\mathcal{O}$, $\mathcal{O}^\vee$, $\mathcal{Q}$ and prime ideals containing $\mathcal{Q}$. Further, if $a \in \mathcal{O}/\mathcal{Q}\mathcal{O}$ is the image of $z \in \mathcal{I}/\mathcal{Q}\mathcal{I}$ and $s \in \mathcal{O}^\vee/\mathcal{Q}\mathcal{O}^\vee$ is the pre-image of $x \in \mathcal{I}^\vee/\mathcal{Q}\mathcal{I}^\vee$, then $u \cdot z \cdot x = u \cdot a \cdot s \mod \mathcal{O}^\vee$.

Proof. Let $\mathfrak{p}$ be the invertible ideal that contains $\mathcal{I}$ as described in Lemma 2.22. Moreover, a basis of this ideal can be found quantumly efficient, thanks to the same lemma. Then, the modulus $\mathcal{Q}$ is coprime with $[\mathfrak{p} : \mathcal{I}]\mathcal{O}$, as $Spec_{\mathbb{Z}}([\mathfrak{p} : \mathcal{I}]) \subseteq Spec_{\mathbb{Z}}(m)$. Indeed, assume by contrary that $\mathcal{Q}$ is not coprime to the index $[\mathfrak{p} : \mathcal{I}]$. Then there exists a maximal ideal $\mathfrak{m}$ for which $\mathcal{Q} + [\mathfrak{p} : \mathcal{I}]\mathcal{O} \subseteq \mathfrak{m}$. In particular, this says $\mathcal{Q} \subseteq \mathfrak{m}$ and $[\mathfrak{p} : \mathcal{I}]\mathcal{O} \subseteq \mathfrak{m}$. Denote by $[\mathfrak{p} : \mathcal{I}] = p_1^{n_1} \cdot \ldots \cdot p_k^{n_k}$, for some prime integers p_i of positive integer exponents n_i. Then since $\prod_i (p_i \mathcal{O})^{n_i} = [\mathfrak{p} : \mathcal{I}]\mathcal{O} \subseteq \mathfrak{m}$ and $\mathfrak{m}$ is in particular a prime ideal, we also have $p_i \mathcal{O} \subseteq \mathfrak{m}$, for some $i \in \{1, \ldots, k\}$. Moreover, as $Spec_{\mathbb{Z}}([\mathfrak{p} : \mathcal{I}]) = \{p_1, \ldots, p_k\} \subseteq Spec_{\mathbb{Z}}(m)$, we get that $m\mathcal{O} \subseteq p_i \mathcal{O} \subseteq \mathfrak{m}$. Together with $\mathcal{Q} \subseteq \mathfrak{m}$, we reach a contradiction with our choice of $\mathcal{Q}$.

As $\mathcal{Q}$ is indeed coprime with $[\mathfrak{p} : \mathcal{I}]\mathcal{O}$, it becomes also coprime with $(\mathcal{I} : \mathfrak{p})$, as needed in Lemma 2.12, since $[\mathfrak{p} : \mathcal{I}]\mathcal{O} \subseteq (\mathcal{I} : \mathfrak{p})$. By Lemma 2.12, this yields the following (classically) efficiently computable and invertible isomorphisms induced by inclusion,

$$f_1 : \frac{\mathcal{I}}{\mathcal{Q}\mathcal{I}} \xhookrightarrow{\sim} \frac{\mathfrak{p}}{\mathcal{Q}\mathfrak{p}} \quad and \quad g_1 : \frac{\mathfrak{p}^\vee}{\mathcal{Q}\mathfrak{p}^\vee} \xhookrightarrow{\sim} \frac{\mathcal{I}^\vee}{\mathcal{Q}\mathcal{I}^\vee}$$

$$z \mapsto f_1(z) = \tilde{z} \qquad \tilde{x} \mapsto g_1(\tilde{x}) = x$$

$$z + \mathcal{Q}\mathfrak{p} = \tilde{z} + \mathcal{Q}\mathfrak{p} \qquad \tilde{x} + \mathcal{Q}\mathcal{I}^\vee = x + \mathcal{Q}\mathcal{I}^\vee$$

Invertibility of $\mathfrak{p}$ and the Cancellation Lemma (Lemma 2.10) yield a $t \in \mathfrak{p}$ such that multiplication by t^{-1} induces the following efficiently computable and invertible isomorphisms:

$$f_2 : \frac{\mathfrak{p}}{\mathcal{Q}\mathfrak{p}} \xrightarrow{\sim} \frac{\mathcal{O}}{\mathcal{Q}\mathcal{O}} \quad and \quad g_2 : \frac{\mathcal{O}^\vee}{\mathcal{Q}\mathcal{O}^\vee} \xrightarrow{\sim} \frac{\mathfrak{p}^\vee}{\mathcal{Q}\mathfrak{p}^\vee}$$

$$\tilde{z} \mapsto f_2(\tilde{z}) = t^{-1}\tilde{z} := a \qquad s \mapsto g_2(s) = t^{-1}s := \tilde{x}$$

$$t^{-1}\tilde{z} + \mathcal{Q}\mathcal{O} = a + \mathcal{Q}\mathcal{O} \qquad t^{-1}s + \mathcal{Q}\mathfrak{p}^\vee = \tilde{x} + \mathcal{Q}\mathfrak{p}^\vee$$

The above map uses the fact that $\mathfrak{p}^\vee = \mathfrak{p}^{-1}\mathcal{O}^\vee$. See full version for details. The multiplier can be efficiently computed as in previous works [RSW18, Theorem 3.1], [BBPS19, Proposition 4.7], [PP19, Lemma 2.13].[20] Define $f = f_2 \circ f_1 :$

---

[20] The size of the multiplier is not relevant here.

$\mathcal{I}/\mathcal{QI} \to \mathcal{O}/\mathcal{QO}$ and $g = g_1 \circ g_2 : \mathcal{O}^{\vee}/\mathcal{QO}^{\vee} \to \mathcal{I}^{\vee}/\mathcal{QI}^{\vee}$. Since all the maps involved are efficiently computable $\mathcal{O}$-module isomorphisms, so are f and g.

Finally, we prove that f and g are compatible, i.e., for all $z \in \mathcal{I}/\mathcal{QI}$ and $x \in \mathcal{I}^{\vee}/\mathcal{QI}^{\vee}$, $u \cdot z \cdot x = u \cdot a \cdot s$ mod $\mathcal{O}^{\vee}$, whenever $f(z) = a$ and $g(s) = x$. Consider the coset,

$$
\begin{aligned}
u \cdot z \cdot x + \mathcal{O}^{\vee} &= u \cdot z \cdot (x + \mathcal{QI}^{\vee}) + \mathcal{O}^{\vee} && \text{as } u \cdot z \cdot \mathcal{QI}^{\vee} \subset u\mathcal{QII}^{\vee} \subseteq \mathcal{O}^{\vee} \\
&= u \cdot z \cdot (\tilde{x} + \mathcal{QI}^{\vee}) + \mathcal{O}^{\vee} \\
&= u \cdot z \cdot \tilde{x} + \mathcal{O}^{\vee} \\
&= u \cdot (z + \mathcal{Qp}) \cdot \tilde{x} + \mathcal{O}^{\vee} && \text{as } u \cdot \mathcal{Qp} \cdot \tilde{x} \subset u \cdot \mathcal{Qpp}^{\vee} \subseteq \mathcal{O}^{\vee} \\
&= u \cdot (\tilde{z} + \mathcal{Qp}) \cdot \tilde{x} + \mathcal{O}^{\vee} \\
&= u \cdot \tilde{z} \cdot \tilde{x} + \mathcal{O}^{\vee}.
\end{aligned}
$$

Therefore, $u \cdot z \cdot x = u \cdot \tilde{z} \cdot \tilde{x}$ mod $\mathcal{O}^{\vee}$. According to the notations, $a = f_2(\tilde{z})$ and $s = g_2^{-1}(\tilde{x})$. Using the definitions of f_2 and g_2,

$$
\begin{aligned}
u \cdot \tilde{z} \cdot \tilde{x} + \mathcal{O}^{\vee} &= u \cdot t^{-1}(\tilde{z} + \mathcal{Qp}) \cdot t(\tilde{x} + \mathcal{Qp}^{\vee}) + \mathcal{O}^{\vee} \\
&= u \cdot (a + \mathcal{QO}) \cdot (s + \mathcal{QO}^{\vee}) + \mathcal{O}^{\vee} \\
&= u \cdot a \cdot s + \mathcal{O}^{\vee},
\end{aligned}
$$

therefore $u \cdot a \cdot s = u \cdot \tilde{z} \cdot \tilde{x}$ mod $\mathcal{O}^{\vee}$. This concludes the proof. $\qquad \square$

Notice that the maps from Lemma 3.4 are constructed as quantumly efficient, because of the quantum construction of the basis of the intermediary ideal $\mathfrak{p}$ from Lemma 2.22.[21]

Proof (of Theorem 3.1). We use Theorem 2.30 to prove the hardness results. We show that in this case the set $\mathcal{S}$, as described in Theorem 2.30, equals the set of all $\mathcal{O}$-ideals for both $\mathcal{O}$-LWE and $\mathcal{O}^{\vee}$-LWE. The novelty of this generalization is in the fact that we convert BDD samples on non-invertible $\mathcal{O}$-ideals into LWE samples. Previously, as in the proof of [BBPS19, Theorem 3.7 & 3.8], this step used the Cancellation Lemma (Lemma 2.10) which unavoidably required the ideal for the BDD problem (or the dual ideal, which ever is relevant), to be invertible. We overcome this by using the improved cancellation Lemma 3.4. Let $\mathcal{I}$ be a non-invertible $\mathcal{O}$-ideal. Recall that without loss of generality, we may assume that $\mathcal{I} \subset \mathcal{O}$. Then, for all ideal moduli $\mathcal{Q}$ coprime to $[\mathcal{O}_K : \mathcal{O}]\mathcal{O}$, we obtain isomorphisms $f : \mathcal{I}/\mathcal{QI} \xrightarrow{\sim} \mathcal{O}/\mathcal{QO}$ and $g : \mathcal{O}^{\vee}/\mathcal{QO}^{\vee} \xrightarrow{\sim} \mathcal{I}^{\vee}/\mathcal{QI}^{\vee}$. Further, Lemma 3.4 shows that these maps are compatible with respect to the condition mentioned in Theorem 2.30.

Now, let $\mathcal{I}$ be an integral $\mathcal{O}$-ideal. Given a BDD sample $y = x + e$ on $\mathcal{I}^{\vee}$ and a discrete Gaussian sample z from $\mathcal{I}$, we define $(a, b) \in \mathcal{O}/\mathcal{QO} \times K_{\mathbb{R}}/\mathcal{O}^{\vee}$ as

---

[21] This is improved in a concurrent work, [JL22, Lemma 5.7], which presents in their *Ideal Clearing Lemma* a classical efficient algorithm to construct the same isomorphisms, for an ideal modulus $\mathcal{Q}$ generated by an integer q coprime to the index of the order.

$a = f(z)$ and $b = u \cdot z \cdot y + e'$ mod $\mathcal{O}^\vee$, for a small error e'. The compatibility of the maps f and g implies that the tuple (a, b) is a well-defined $\mathcal{O}$-LWE sample, i.e. $b = u \cdot f(z) \cdot g^{-1}(x) + \tilde{e}$ mod $\mathcal{O}^\vee$, for an error $\tilde{e}$ depending on e and e'. Equation (3.1.2) then follows from the equivalence of $\mathcal{O}$-LWE and $\mathcal{O}^\vee$-LWE, Proposition 3.2. □

3.2   Ring-LWE Hardness for Some Non $\mathcal{O}_K$-Ideal Lattices

The authors in [LPR10,PRSD17] showed that solving Ring-LWE is at least as hard as solving short vector problems on the set of all ideals of the ring of integers $\mathcal{O}_K$. We extend this result to include lattice problems on lattices that are not necessarily ideals of $\mathcal{O}_K$. Although, in our reduction, we extend the set of lattices to a strict superset of $\mathcal{O}_K$-ideal lattices, a lattice $\mathcal{L}$ that is not an $\mathcal{O}_K$-ideal incurs a cost of an $\mathcal{O}_\mathcal{L}$-dependent factor in the approximation factor γ. We prove our generalized hardness result for Ring-LWE, often denoted as $\mathcal{O}_K$-LWE, by giving a polynomial time reduction from $\mathcal{O}$-LWE to $\mathcal{O}_K$-LWE and pre-composing it with our hardness result, Theorem 3.1, for $\mathcal{O}$-LWE. In our $\mathcal{O}$-LWE to $\mathcal{O}_K$-LWE reduction, the error parameter gets inflated by the conductor $\mathcal{C}_\mathcal{O}$ of $\mathcal{O}$ in $\mathcal{O}_K$.

Fix an order $\mathcal{O}$. Let $\mathcal{Q}$ be an $\mathcal{O}$ ideal modulus coprime to the conductor $\mathcal{C}_\mathcal{O} = (\mathcal{O} : \mathcal{O}_K)$, and therefore by Theorem 2.19 admits a unique factorization into a product of prime ideals over $\mathcal{O}$. Let $Spec_\mathcal{O}(\mathcal{Q}) := \{\mathfrak{q}_1, \ldots, \mathfrak{q}_r\}$. Let $u \in (\mathcal{O} : \mathcal{Q})$. Notice that by definition, it also belongs to $(\mathcal{O}_K : \mathcal{Q}\mathcal{O}_K)$.

Proposition 3.5. *Let K be a number field and $\mathcal{O} \subset \mathcal{O}_K$, an order. Let $\mathcal{Q}$ be an ideal modulus coprime with $\mathcal{C}_\mathcal{O}$, $u \in (\mathcal{O} : \mathcal{Q})$. Let Υ be a distribution over a family of error distributions over $K_\mathbb{R}/\mathcal{Q}\mathcal{O}^\vee$, and let $t \in \mathcal{C}_\mathcal{O} \setminus \bigcup_i \mathfrak{q}_i\mathcal{C}_\mathcal{O}$. Then there is a polynomial time reduction from (search or decision) $\mathcal{O}$-LWE$_{(\mathcal{Q},u),\Upsilon}$ to (search or decision) $\mathcal{O}_K$-LWE$_{(\mathcal{Q}\mathcal{O}_K,u),t\cdot\Upsilon}$, given the bases of $\mathcal{O}$, $\mathcal{O}_K$, $\mathcal{C}_\mathcal{O}$, $\mathcal{Q}$ and the primes $\mathfrak{q}_i$.*

Notice that the reduction increases the noise by a factor of t. We remark that the error parameter of the $\mathcal{O}_K$-LWE problem in Theorem 3.6 would be the least when t is the shortest lattice vector in $\mathcal{C}_\mathcal{O} \setminus \bigcup_i \mathfrak{q}_i\mathcal{C}_\mathcal{O}$. The existence of such a short multiplier can be proven either by using the combinatorial argument from [BBPS19, Lemma 2.36] or by sampling according to a Gaussian distribution over the conductor ideal with a wide parameter, as in [RSW18, Theorem 3.1], [BBPS19, Proposition 4.7].[22] We would like to clarify that the statements in these previous works require that the ideal we sample t from be invertible. Their proofs, however, hold true for the conductor ideal. See full version for a discussion on the size of this multiplier.

---

[22] We would also like to point out that [PP19, Lemma 2.13] shows another efficient way of constructing a multiplier t, via the Chinese Remainder Theorem application, but this does not give any control on its size. Same discussion holds also for [JL22, Lemma 4.1], as the multiplier is constructed via a randomized algorithm that considers a linear combination of basis elements of the involved order.

Proof (of Prop. 3.5). Define the following maps,

$$f : \frac{\mathcal{O}}{\mathcal{Q}\mathcal{O}} \to \frac{\mathcal{O}_K}{\mathcal{Q}\mathcal{O}_K}, \qquad f^\vee : \frac{\mathcal{O}^\vee}{\mathcal{Q}\mathcal{O}^\vee} \xrightarrow{\cdot t} \frac{\mathcal{O}_K^\vee}{\mathcal{Q}\mathcal{O}_K^\vee}.$$

The first map f is induced by the inclusion $\mathcal{O} \subset \mathcal{O}_K$ and is an isomorphism under the assumption that $\mathcal{Q}$ is coprime to the conductor (Lemma 2.12). The second map $f^\vee$ is induced by multiplication by t. It is an isomorphism for $\mathcal{I} = \mathcal{C}_\mathcal{O}$, $\mathcal{J} = \mathcal{Q}$ and $\mathcal{M} = \mathcal{O}^\vee$ as $t\mathcal{M} + \mathcal{I}\mathcal{J}\mathcal{M} = \mathcal{I}\mathcal{M}$. See Remark 2.11 and [BBPS19, Remark 2.33]. Both maps can be efficiently computed. We further extend the second map to $K_\mathbb{R}$, $\overline{f^\vee} : K_\mathbb{R}/\mathcal{O}^\vee \longrightarrow K_\mathbb{R}/\mathcal{O}_K^\vee$ as $\overline{f^\vee}(u \cdot x) = u \cdot t \cdot x$, for any $x \in K_\mathbb{R}/\mathcal{Q}\mathcal{O}^\vee$. With these maps, define the following transformation

$$\frac{\mathcal{O}}{\mathcal{Q}\mathcal{O}} \times \frac{K_\mathbb{R}}{\mathcal{O}^\vee} \longrightarrow \frac{\mathcal{O}_K}{\mathcal{Q}\mathcal{O}_K} \times \frac{K_\mathbb{R}}{\mathcal{O}_K^\vee}$$
$$(a, b) \mapsto (a' = f(a), \; b' = \overline{f^\vee}(b) := t \cdot b \mod \mathcal{O}_K^\vee).$$

Since the maps, f and $\overline{f^\vee}$ are isomorphisms, this transformation maps uniform samples to uniform samples. Further, if $b = u \cdot a \cdot s + e \mod \mathcal{O}^\vee$ is sampled from the $\mathcal{O}$-LWE distribution $\mathcal{O}_{(\mathcal{Q},u),s,\varphi}$, where s is uniform in $\mathcal{O}^\vee/\mathcal{Q}\mathcal{O}^\vee$ and $e \leftarrow \varphi$, for $\varphi \leftarrow \Upsilon$, then,

$$b' = u \cdot f^\vee(a \cdot s) + \overline{f^\vee}(e) \mod \mathcal{O}_K^\vee$$
$$= u \cdot a \cdot f^\vee(s) + \overline{f^\vee}(e) \mod \mathcal{O}_K^\vee$$
$$= u \cdot f(a) \cdot f^\vee(s) + \overline{f^\vee}(e) \mod \mathcal{O}_K^\vee.$$

The second equality follows from the fact that $f^\vee$ is an $\mathcal{O}$-module homomorphism. The third equality follows from the fact that these cosets are equal: $u \cdot a \cdot f^\vee(s) + \mathcal{O}_K^\vee = u \cdot (a + \mathcal{Q}\mathcal{O}_K) \cdot f^\vee(s) + \mathcal{O}_K^\vee = u \cdot f(a) \cdot f^\vee(s) + \mathcal{O}_K^\vee$. Finally, as $e \leftarrow \varphi$, its image $\overline{f^\vee}(e) \leftarrow t \cdot \varphi$. Moreover, the secret s, as is uniform over $\mathcal{O}^\vee/\mathcal{Q}\mathcal{O}^\vee$, is mapped to $f^\vee(s)$, which is also uniform over $\mathcal{O}_K^\vee/\mathcal{Q}\mathcal{O}_K^\vee$, as $f^\vee$ is an isomorphism. This yields an efficient transformation from $\mathcal{O}$-LWE$_{(\mathcal{Q},u),\Upsilon}$ to $\mathcal{O}_K$-LWE$_{(\mathcal{Q}\mathcal{O}_K,u),t\cdot\Upsilon}$. $\square$

Pre-composing this reduction (Proposition 3.5) by the decision $\mathcal{O}$-LWE hardness result, Theorem 3.1 yields the following improved hardness result for decision $\mathcal{O}_K$-LWE.

Theorem 3.6. *Let K be a number field of degree n and $\mathcal{O} \subset \mathcal{O}_K$, an order. Let $\mathcal{Q}$ be an ideal modulus coprime to $[\mathcal{O}_K : \mathcal{O}]\mathcal{O}$ and $u \in (\mathcal{O} : \mathcal{Q})$. Let $Id(\mathcal{O})$ denote the set of $\mathcal{O}$-ideals. Choose $t \in \mathcal{C}_\mathcal{O} \setminus \bigcup_i \mathfrak{q}_i\mathcal{C}_\mathcal{O}$ and choose $\alpha \in (0,1)$ such that $\alpha/\|u\|_\infty \geq 2\omega(1)$. Then there is a polynomial time quantum reduction from*

$$Id(\mathcal{O})\text{-DGS}_\gamma \longrightarrow \mathcal{O}_K\text{-LWE}_{(\mathcal{Q}\mathcal{O}_K,u),t\cdot\Upsilon_{u,\alpha}},$$

where

$$\gamma = max\left\{ \eta(\mathcal{Q}\mathcal{L}) \cdot \sqrt{2} \cdot \|u\|_\infty/\alpha \cdot \omega(1), \frac{\sqrt{2n}}{\lambda_1(\mathcal{L}^\vee)} \right\}.$$

Comparison with Previous Work. We note that [BBPS19, Theorem 3.8, Cor 5.2] also showed a connection between Order-LWE and Ring-LWE. While the error and the approximation factors obtained from the two reductions are comparable, the results are complementary in terms of other parameters. Further, the prior requires a set of field elements that generate $\mathcal{O}^\vee$ over $\mathcal{O}_K^\vee$ to map between the order and the ring of integers, which is similar to the role of our t. Our result poses a significant improvement in the size of the set of lattices and the set of relevant moduli, since it considers solving lattice problems on the set of all $\mathcal{O}$-ideals, whereas the prior result considers solving lattice problems on the set of $\mathcal{O}$-ideals whose duals are invertible. Our theorem also expands the choice of the moduli for the Ring-LWE problem: the previous result only holds under the assumption that the modulus q be a factor of $[\mathcal{O}_K : \mathcal{O}]$, reducing the choice for q to a finite set, whereas, Theorem 3.6 assumes that the ideal modulus $\mathcal{Q}$ (and in particular, the principal ideal $q\mathcal{O}$) is coprime to $[\mathcal{O}_K : \mathcal{O}]\mathcal{O}$, tapping an infinite set of choices and also complementing the previous result by bridging the gap.

Solving DGS on p-ary Lattices. We view Theorem 3.6 in a different light. We first consider its particular case $\mathcal{Q} = q\mathcal{O}$ and $u = 1/q$, for q an integer coprime with the index $[\mathcal{O}_K : \mathcal{O}]$. Instead of solving DGS on $\mathcal{O}$-ideals, where $\mathcal{O}$ varies over the set of orders of indices coprime to a fixed modulus q, we use the $\mathcal{O}_K$-LWE oracle to solve DGS on the set of (embeddings of) all p-ary lattices. Recall that, when K is a monogenic field, the embedding $\mathcal{L}$ of an integer p-ary lattice satisfies $p\mathcal{O}_K \subseteq \mathcal{L} \subseteq \mathcal{O}_K$. This makes $\mathcal{L}$ an ideal of the order $\mathbb{Z} + p\mathcal{O}_K$. See Remark 2.17. However, this order may be strictly contained in the ring of multipliers $\mathcal{O}_\mathcal{L}$ of $\mathcal{L}$. The reduction described below, would, in turn solve DGS on integer p-ary lattices up to an approximation factor related to the field (of embedding) K. See Lemma 2.14. Owing to the results of [Ajt96, Reg05], it is sufficient to solve lattice problems on p-ary lattices, as solving lattice problems on p-ary lattices is at least as hard as solving lattice problems on general integer lattices.

Before going into the next result, we would like to remark that given a $\mathbb{Z}$-basis of an input lattice $\mathcal{L}$, we can derive a basis for its dual, and hence a set of generators for $\mathcal{O}_\mathcal{L}^\vee = \mathcal{L}\mathcal{L}^\vee$ (See [Conb, Rem 4.2]). Thanks to Hermite Normal Form, we therefore get a basis for $\mathcal{O}_\mathcal{L}^\vee$, and further for $\mathcal{O}_\mathcal{L}$. Moreover, as $\mathcal{C}_{\mathcal{O}_\mathcal{L}}^\vee = \mathcal{O}_K \mathcal{O}_\mathcal{L}^\vee$ ([BBPS19, Lemma 2.32]), we can get a basis for $\mathcal{C}_{\mathcal{O}_\mathcal{L}}^\vee$ and then for $\mathcal{C}_{\mathcal{O}_\mathcal{L}}$. Knowing these bases help us derive the efficient maps involved in Theorem 3.6.

Corollary 3.7. *Let K be a monogenic number field. Let $\mathcal{L} \subset K$ be a lattice such that $p\mathcal{O}_K \subseteq \mathcal{L}$, for a fixed prime p, along with its basis. Let an integer q, coprime to p, and an $\alpha \in (0, 1)$ such that $\alpha q / \|t\|_\infty \geq 2\omega(1)$. Given the primes $\mathfrak{q}_i$ containing $q\mathcal{O}_\mathcal{L}$ and $t \in \mathcal{C}_{\mathcal{O}_\mathcal{L}} \setminus \bigcup_i \mathfrak{q}_i \mathcal{C}_{\mathcal{O}_\mathcal{L}}$, there is a polynomial time quantum reduction*

$$\mathcal{L}\text{-DGS}_{\tilde{\gamma}} \longrightarrow \mathcal{O}_K\text{-LWE}_{(q\mathcal{O}_K, 1/q), \Upsilon_\alpha}, \text{ where } \tilde{\gamma} = max\left\{\eta(\mathcal{L}) \cdot \sqrt{2} \cdot \|t\|_\infty / \alpha \cdot \omega(1), \frac{\sqrt{2n}}{\lambda_1(\mathcal{L}^\vee)}\right\}.$$

See full version of this paper for a proof. Observe that for the embedding $\mathcal{L}$ of an integer p-ary lattice, the approximation factor γ obtained above only makes sense as long as $\|t\|_\infty < p$. This may be achievable if $\mathcal{C}_{\mathcal{O}_\mathcal{L}}$ is a proper factor of $p\mathcal{O}_K$. We also provide in the full version of this paper examples of lattices $\mathcal{L}$ and multipliers t whose infinity norm are less than p. However, the DGS problem on $\mathcal{L}$ can also be solved using either an $\mathcal{O}_\mathcal{L}$-LWE oracle or a $(\mathbb{Z} + p\mathcal{O}_K)$-LWE oracle. The approximation factor from both of these reductions is equal to γ, as in the hardness result, Theorem 3.1, which is an improvement by $\|t\|_\infty$ from the approximation factor in the Corollary 3.7.

4   Gradients of Hardness Between Ring-LWE and LWE

In this section, we describe chains of Order-LWE problems that begin with the well-known Ring-LWE problem (often denoted as $\mathcal{O}_K$-LWE) and increase in hardness until they reach an Order-LWE problem that is equivalent to the unstructured LWE problem. The descending chain of orders (with respect to inclusion) creates a gradient of increasing hardness from Ring-LWE to LWE. Its relevance is two-fold; it describes a collection of orders in K such that their corresponding (Order-)LWE problems lie between Ring-LWE and LWE, the former being the most efficient and the latter, hardest and least efficient. Secondly, it instantiates the LWE problem in an algebraic avatar, as an Order-LWE problem. All the results in this section hold for both search and decision versions of the Order-LWE and LWE problems. Note that the equivalence between the LWE problem and the Order-LWE problem, Theorem 4.4, is non-uniform, since it uses as advice a special $\mathbb{Z}$-basis for the order in consideration.

To ease notation, we denote by $\mathcal{O}$-LWE$_{q,\psi}$, the Order-LWE problem for the order $\mathcal{O}$, with modulus ideal $q\mathcal{O}$, the element $u = 1/q$ and an error distribution ψ over $K_\mathbb{R}$. The following result is a building block in creating the chains. It gives an error preserving reduction between the Order-LWE problems, as long as the index of the two orders is coprime to the LWE modulus.

Theorem 4.1 ([PP19, **Theorem 4.7**]). *Given $\mathcal{O} \subseteq \mathcal{O}'$, an $\mathcal{O}$ ideal modulus $\mathcal{Q}$ such that it is coprime with $(\mathcal{O} : \mathcal{O}') = \{x \in K \; x\mathcal{O}' \subseteq \mathcal{O}\}$ and $u \in (\mathcal{O} : \mathcal{Q})$, there is an efficient, deterministic and error preserving reduction from (search or decision) $\mathcal{O}'$-LWE$_{(\mathcal{Q}\mathcal{O}',u),\psi}$ to (search or decision) $\mathcal{O}$-LWE$_{(\mathcal{Q},u),\psi}$. In particular, if $\mathcal{O}'$ is the maximal order, $\mathcal{O}_K$, then we have an efficient, deterministic and error preserving reduction from $\mathcal{O}_K$-LWE$_{(\mathcal{Q}\mathcal{O}_K,u),\psi}$ to $\mathcal{O}$-LWE$_{(\mathcal{Q},u),\psi}$. Moreover, if $\mathcal{Q} = q\mathcal{O}$ and $u = 1/q$, for an integer q coprime with $[\mathcal{O}_K : \mathcal{O}]$, we have an efficient, deterministic and error preserving reduction from $\mathcal{O}_K$-LWE$_{q,\psi}$ to $\mathcal{O}$-LWE$_{q,\psi}$.*

Notice that it suffices for the ideal $\mathcal{Q}$ to be coprime with $[\mathcal{O}' : \mathcal{O}]\mathcal{O}$ in order for Theorem 4.1 to hold, as again $(\mathcal{O} : \mathcal{O}') \subseteq [\mathcal{O}' : \mathcal{O}]\mathcal{O}$. With repetitive application of Theorem 4.1, we get a chain of algebraic LWEs as follows. Let $\mathcal{L} \subset \mathcal{O}_K$ be a lattice in K. Then, $\mathcal{L}$ is an ideal of the order $\mathbb{Z} + m\mathcal{O}_K$, where m is the exponent of the quotient group $\mathcal{O}_K/\mathcal{L}$. See Lemma 2.16. The order $\mathbb{Z} + m\mathcal{O}_K$ may be strictly contained in the ring of multipliers, $\mathcal{O}_\mathcal{L}$. Hence, the inclusion, $\mathbb{Z} + m\mathcal{O}_K \subseteq \mathcal{O}_\mathcal{L} \subseteq \mathcal{O}_K$, by Theorem 4.1, implies the error preserving reduction

$$\mathcal{O}_K\text{-LWE}_{(\mathcal{Q}\mathcal{O}_K,u),\psi} \longrightarrow \mathcal{O}_\mathcal{L}\text{-LWE}_{(\mathcal{Q}\mathcal{O}_\mathcal{L},u),\psi} \longrightarrow (\mathbb{Z} + m\mathcal{O}_K)\text{-LWE}_{(\mathcal{Q},u),\psi},$$

as long as the $\mathbb{Z} + m\mathcal{O}_K$ ideal modulus $\mathcal{Q}$ is coprime to $m\mathcal{O}$. Coprimality of $\mathcal{Q}$ with $m\mathcal{O}$ is sufficient as both the indices, $[\mathcal{O}_{\mathcal{L}} : (\mathbb{Z}+m\mathcal{O}_K)]$ and $[\mathcal{O}_K : \mathcal{O}_{\mathcal{L}}]$ divide $[\mathcal{O}_K : m\mathcal{O}_K] = m^n$, owing to the fact that $m\mathcal{O}_K \subset \mathbb{Z} + m\mathcal{O}_K$ and therefore, $\mathrm{Spec}([\mathcal{O}_{\mathcal{L}} : (\mathbb{Z}+m\mathcal{O}_K)]\mathcal{O}) \subseteq \mathrm{Spec}(m\mathcal{O})$ and $\mathrm{Spec}([\mathcal{O}_K : \mathcal{O}_{\mathcal{L}}]\mathcal{O}_{\mathcal{L}}) \subseteq \mathrm{Spec}(m\mathcal{O}_{\mathcal{L}})$. This chain of LWE problems, increasing in hardness, may be longer depending on the factorization of $m\mathcal{O}_K$ as an $\mathcal{O}_K$-ideal, as we describe in Theorem 4.2.

Let $Spec_{\mathcal{O}_K}(m\mathcal{O}_K) = \{\mathfrak{m}_1, \mathfrak{m}_2, \ldots, \mathfrak{m}_r\}$. Define $\mathcal{O}_i := \mathbb{Z} + \mathfrak{m}_1 \cdot \ldots \cdot \mathfrak{m}_i$. Then, by Lemma 2.16, each $\mathcal{O}_i$ is an order in K. Further, $\mathcal{O}_i \subset \mathcal{O}_j$, for $i \geq j$, and $\mathbb{Z} + m\mathcal{O}_K \subset \mathcal{O}_i$, for all i. By the same argument, for any lattice, $\mathcal{J} \subseteq \mathcal{O}_K$, the order $\mathbb{Z} + m\mathcal{J} \subseteq \mathbb{Z} + m\mathcal{O}_K$. This yields the following chain of orders: $\mathcal{O}_K \supseteq \mathcal{O}_1 \supseteq \cdots \supseteq \mathcal{O}_r \supseteq \mathbb{Z} + m\mathcal{O}_K \supseteq \mathbb{Z} + m\mathcal{J}$.

Theorem 4.2. *Let m be an integer and $\mathcal{J}$ be a lattice in $\mathcal{O}_K$. Let $\mathcal{Q}$ be an ideal modulus in $\mathbb{Z} + m\mathcal{J}$ such that it is coprime with $m(\mathbb{Z}+m\mathcal{J})$ and $[\mathcal{O}_K : \mathcal{J}](\mathbb{Z} + m\mathcal{J})$. Let $u \in (\mathbb{Z}+m\mathcal{J} : \mathcal{Q})$. Then, we have the following efficient, deterministic and error preserving reductions for the (search or decision) problems*

$$\mathcal{O}_K\text{-LWE}_{(\mathcal{Q}\mathcal{O}_K, u), \psi} \to \cdots \to \mathcal{O}_r\text{-LWE}_{(\mathcal{Q}\mathcal{O}_r, u), \psi} \to$$

$$(\mathbb{Z} + m\mathcal{O}_K)\text{-LWE}_{(\mathcal{Q}(\mathbb{Z}+m\mathcal{O}_K), u), \psi} \to (\mathbb{Z} + m\mathcal{J})\text{-LWE}_{(\mathcal{Q}, u), \psi}.$$

In particular, for $\mathcal{Q} = q(\mathbb{Z} + m\mathcal{J})$ and $u = 1/q$, where q is a positive integer coprime with m and $[\mathcal{O}_K : \mathcal{J}]$, we have the following efficient, deterministic and error preserving reductions for the (search or decision) problems

$$\mathcal{O}_K\text{-LWE}_{q, \psi} \to \cdots \to \mathcal{O}_r\text{-LWE}_{q, \psi} \to (\mathbb{Z}+m\mathcal{O}_K)\text{-LWE}_{q, \psi} \to (\mathbb{Z}+m\mathcal{J})\text{-LWE}_{q, \psi}.$$

See full version of the paper for a proof.

From now on, we focus on the Order-LWE problem with ideal modulus $\mathcal{Q}$ generated by a positive integer q and $u = 1/q$.

We now describe (non-maximal) orders such that the corresponding Order-LWE problems, with error sampled from a spherical Gaussian, become equivalent to the unstructured LWE problem. Suppose $\mathcal{O} \subseteq K$ be such an order. In unison with Theorem 4.2, this result yields various chains of algebraic LWEs in the field K that begin with Ring-LWE and terminate at LWE.

The $\mathbb{Z}$-bases of these special orders satisfy a particular property that we describe now. Some notation: let $\mathcal{O}$ be an order of K and a $\mathbb{Z}$-basis of it of the form $\vec{p} = \{p_0 = 1, p_1, \ldots, p_{n-1}\}$. See Lemma 2.9 for the existence of $\vec{p}$. Denote by $\vec{p}^\vee = \{p_i^\vee\}_{i=0}^{n-1}$, the $\mathbb{Z}$-basis of $\mathcal{O}^\vee$ that satisfies $Tr(p_i p_j^\vee) = \delta_{ij}$, where $Tr = Tr_{K_\mathbb{R}/\mathbb{R}}$.

Definition 4.3. *Let K be a number field of degree n and $e \in K_\mathbb{R}$ be sampled from the distribution D_α over $K_\mathbb{R}$, for some $\alpha > 0$. We say that an order $\mathcal{O}$ in K is α-**drowning** if for a $\mathbb{Z}$-basis $\vec{p}$ of $\mathcal{O}$, as described above, such that the coefficients $(e_0, e_1, \ldots, e_{n-1})$ of e with respect to the $\mathbb{Z}$-basis $\vec{p}^\vee$ of $\mathcal{O}^\vee$ satisfy the following: the marginal distribution of $e_0 \bmod \mathbb{Z}$ is*

$$e_0 \bmod \mathbb{Z} \leftarrow D_{\alpha\sqrt{n}} \bmod \mathbb{Z},$$

and, for any $x_0 \in \mathbb{R}$, the conditional distribution,

$$(e_1, e_2, \ldots, e_{n-1}) \, | e_0 = x_0 \quad \mod \mathbb{Z}^{n-1} \approx_{s.i} U((\mathbb{R}/\mathbb{Z})^{n-1}),$$

where $\approx_{s.i}$ means that the two distributions have statistical distance negligible in n.

Theorem 4.4. Let K be a number field of degree n and let $\mathcal{O}$ be an α-drowning order, for $\alpha \cdot q \geq 2 \cdot \omega(1)$ and $\mathbb{Z}$ bases of $\mathcal{O}$ and $\mathcal{O}^\vee$, $\vec{p}$ and $\vec{p}^\vee$, as above. Then, the (search or decision) $\mathcal{O}$-LWE$_{q,D_\alpha}$ problem is equivalent to the (search or decision) LWE$_{n,q,D_{\alpha \cdot \sqrt{n}}}$ problem.

Proof. We first give a reduction from LWE to $\mathcal{O}$-LWE. This is the non-trivial part of the proof. As is standard, for this reduction, we define a transformation that sends uniform samples over $(\mathbb{Z}/q\mathbb{Z})^n \times \mathbb{R}/\mathbb{Z}$ to uniform samples over $\mathcal{O}/q\mathcal{O} \times K_\mathbb{R}/\mathcal{O}^\vee$ and LWE samples to $\mathcal{O}$-LWE samples.

Let $Tr = Tr_{K_\mathbb{R}/\mathbb{R}}$ denote the trace map. For $i \in [n-1]$, sample uniform elements in $\mathbb{R}/\mathbb{Z}$; $u_i \leftarrow U(\mathbb{R}/\mathbb{Z})$. We define the transformation as follows: given a pair $(\vec{a}, b_0) \in (\mathbb{Z}/q\mathbb{Z})^n \times \mathbb{R}/\mathbb{Z}$, output

$$(a := a_1 p_0 + \ldots + a_n p_{n-1}, \ \ b := b_0 \, p_0^\vee + u_1 \, p_1^\vee + \ldots + u_{n-1} \, p_{n-1}^\vee) \in \mathcal{O}/q\mathcal{O} \times K_\mathbb{R}/\mathcal{O}^\vee.$$

It is straightforward to see that this transformation is well-defined and maps uniform samples from the domain to uniform samples in the range. We claim that if $b_0 = \frac{1}{q} \cdot \langle \vec{a}, \vec{s} \rangle + e$, with a secret $\vec{s} \leftarrow U((\mathbb{Z}/q\mathbb{Z})^n)$ and an error $e \leftarrow D_{\alpha \sqrt{n}}$, then $b \in K_\mathbb{R}/\mathcal{O}^\vee$, as defined above, is statistically indistinguishable from $b' := \frac{1}{q} \cdot a \cdot s + e' \in K_\mathbb{R}/\mathcal{O}^\vee$, where $s := \langle \vec{s}, \vec{p}^\vee \rangle = s_1 p_0^\vee + \ldots + s_n p_{n-1}^\vee \in \mathcal{O}^\vee/q\mathcal{O}^\vee$ and $e' \leftarrow D_\alpha$ over $K_\mathbb{R}$. In fact, we show that the coefficients of b are statistically indistinguishable from the coefficients of b' in the basis $\{p_i^\vee\}_i$ of $\mathcal{O}^\vee$. Notice that (a, b') is an $\mathcal{O}$-LWE$_{q,D_\alpha}$ sample with the uniformly sampled secret s, since $\vec{s} \leftarrow U((\mathbb{Z}/q\mathbb{Z})^n)$.

The linearity of the Trace map along with the equality, $Tr(p_i p_j^\vee) = \delta_{ij}$, implies that $a \cdot s = \sum_{i=0}^{n-1} Tr(a \cdot s \cdot p_i) \, p_i^\vee$, and $Tr(a \cdot s) = \sum_{i=1}^n a_i s_i = \langle \vec{a}, \vec{s} \rangle$. Therefore,

$$b = \frac{1}{q} \cdot \langle \vec{a}, \vec{s} \rangle \, p_0^\vee + e \, p_0^\vee + \sum_{i=1}^{n-1} u_i p_i^\vee = \left(\frac{1}{q} \cdot Tr(a \cdot s) + e \right) \cdot p_0^\vee + \sum_{i=1}^{n-1} u_i p_i^\vee \quad \mod \widetilde{\mathcal{O}}^\vee,$$

whereas

$$b' = \left(\frac{1}{q} \cdot Tr(a \cdot s) + e_0' \right) \cdot p_0^\vee + \sum_{i=1}^{n-1} \left(\frac{1}{q} \cdot Tr(a \cdot s \cdot p_i) + e_i' \right) \cdot p_i^\vee \quad \mod \mathcal{O}^\vee.$$

Here, $e' = \sum_{i=0}^{n-1} e_i' p_i^\vee$ is the representation of the error (from the $\mathcal{O}$-LWE sample) in the $\mathbb{Z}$-basis of $\mathcal{O}^\vee$. Since $\mathcal{O}$ is α-drowning, the marginal distribution of e_0 mod $\mathbb{Z}$ is $D_{\alpha \sqrt{n}}$ mod $\mathbb{Z}$, whereas the conditional distribution of $(e_1', \ldots, e_{n-1}') | e_0'$ equals x_0 mod $\mathbb{Z}^{n-1}$ is statistically indistinguishable from $U((\mathbb{R}/\mathbb{Z})^{n-1})$, for any $x_0 \in \mathbb{R}$. This shows that $(e_0', e_1', \ldots, e_{n-1}')$ mod $\mathbb{Z}^n$ is statistically indistinguishable from $(e, u_1, \ldots, u_{n-1})$ mod $\mathbb{Z}^n \leftarrow (D_{\alpha\sqrt{n}}$ mod $\mathbb{Z}) \times U((\mathbb{R}/\mathbb{Z})^{n-1})$. Therefore, the coefficients of b and of b' with respect to the $\mathbb{Z}$-basis of $\mathcal{O}^\vee$ are statistically indistinguishable, as desired.

The converse, from $\mathcal{O}$-LWE to LWE, is a special case of [PP19, Theorem 6.1]. $\square$

Examples of α-Drowning Orders. We describe two orders and prove in Proposition 4.5 below that they are α-drowning, for an $\alpha > 0$ satisfying $\alpha \cdot q > 2 \cdot \omega(1)$ and well chosen positive integer m.

(i) For a number field K, let $\{1, \theta_1, \ldots, \theta_{n-1}\}$ be a fixed $\mathbb{Z}$-basis for $\mathcal{O}_K$. See Lemma 2.9 for its existence. For a $d \times d$ matrix M, let $e_d(M)$ denote the smallest eigenvalue of M. Let $\tau := e_{n-1}(T)$, where $T = (Tr(\theta_i\bar{\theta}_j) - \frac{1}{n} \cdot Tr(\theta_i)Tr(\theta_j))_{1\leq i,j\leq n-1}$. Choose $r \in \mathbb{N}$ such that $\tau \cdot m^{2r-2} \geq n$. Let $\widetilde{\mathcal{O}} := \mathbb{Z} + m^r\mathcal{O}_K$. Then, a $\mathbb{Z}$-basis for $\widetilde{\mathcal{O}}$ is $\vec{p} := (p_i)_{i=0}^{n-1} = \{1, m^r\theta_1, \ldots, m^r\theta_{n-1}\}$. Let $\vec{p}^\vee = (p_0^\vee, p_1^\vee, \ldots, p_{n-1}^\vee)$ be the (dual) $\mathbb{Z}$-basis for $\widetilde{\mathcal{O}}^\vee$. Then, for $\alpha > 0$ satisfying $\alpha \cdot q \geq 2\omega(1)$, the order $\widetilde{\mathcal{O}}$ is α-**drowning**. When $\mathcal{O}_K$ has an orthogonal $\mathbb{Z}$-basis containing 1, then the matrix T is a diagonal matrix with $\tau = e_{n-1}(T) \geq \sqrt{n}$. Therefore, the condition $\tau \cdot m^{2r-2} \geq n$ is achieved with $r = 1$. See full version for details.

(ii) In fields that are closed under complex conjugation, i.e. $\overline{K} \subseteq K$, one may be able to choose a smaller order $\widetilde{\mathcal{O}}'$ **that is α-drowning**. Note that all Galois fields and totally real number fields are closed under complex conjugation. As $\overline{K} \subseteq K$, we get that $Tr_{K/\mathbb{Q}}(x\bar{y}) \in \mathbb{Q}$, for $x, y \in K$. Therefore, by repeated application of [Cona, Lema 4.6], $K = \mathbb{Q}\cdot1\oplus\mathbb{Q}\cdot\theta_1'\oplus\ldots\oplus\mathbb{Q}\cdot\theta_{n-1}'$, decomposes orthogonally into $\mathbb{Q}$ vector subspaces, for $\theta_i' \in K$. Consider the $\mathbb{Z}$-module generated by this orthogonal basis and call it $\mathcal{J}$. It is a full-rank lattice and hence an ideal in its ring of multipliers. We multiply by the integer scalar m to make sure that $\mathcal{J}$ is an integral ideal. Then, by Lemma 2.16, the set $\widetilde{\mathcal{O}}' := \mathbb{Z}+m\mathcal{J}$ is an order, generated by $\vec{p}' = (p_i')_{i=0}^{n-1} := \{1, m\theta_1', \ldots, m\theta_{n-1}'\}$ over $\mathbb{Z}$. Let $\vec{p}'^\vee = \{p_i'^\vee\}_{i=0}^{n-1}$ be the corresponding $\mathbb{Z}$-basis for $\widetilde{\mathcal{O}}'^\vee$.

Recall that, when $e \leftarrow D_\alpha$ over $K_\mathbb{R}$, the coefficients $(e_0, e_1, \ldots e_{n-1})$ of e, with respect to the $\mathbb{Z}$-basis of the dual of the order in consideration, call it $\mathcal{O}$, follow the Gaussian distribution of covariance matrix $\alpha^2 \cdot P_\mathcal{O}$. (See Lemma 2.32.) To prove that this order is α-drowning, we show that the $n - 1 \times n - 1$ covariance matrix of the conditional distribution of the coefficients $(e_1, \ldots e_{n-1})$ satisfies that the smallest singular value of its square root exceeds the smoothing parameter of $\mathbb{Z}^{n-1}$. This implies that given any value for e_0, the tuple $(e_1, \ldots e_{n-1})$ mod $\mathbb{Z}^{n-1}$ is indistinguishable from a uniform element in $(\mathbb{R}/\mathbb{Z})^{n-1}$. We also show that e_0 mod $\mathbb{Z} \leftarrow D_{\alpha\sqrt{n}}$. We invite the reader to full version for more details of the following proposition and its proof.

Proposition 4.5. *Let K be a number field of degree n and m be an integer greater than q. Then, for $\alpha > 0$ satisfying $\alpha \cdot q > 2 \cdot \omega(1)$,*

(i) $\widetilde{\mathcal{O}}$ is an α-drowning order;

(ii) when $\overline{K} \subseteq K$, the order $\widetilde{\mathcal{O}}'$ is α-drowning.

Proof. For both the cases, let $X_a := e_0$ and $X_b := (e_1, e_2, \ldots, e_{n-1})$. The covariance matrix for the appropriate order $\mathcal{O} = \widetilde{\mathcal{O}}$ or $\widetilde{\mathcal{O}}'$ can be expressed as,

$$\alpha^2 P_{\mathcal{O}} = \alpha^2 \left(Tr(p_i \overline{p_j}) \right)_{ij} = \alpha^2 \begin{pmatrix} \Sigma_{aa} & \Sigma_{ab} \\ \Sigma_{ba} & \Sigma_{bb} \end{pmatrix},$$

where $\Sigma_{aa} \in M_{1 \times 1}(\mathbb{R})$, $\Sigma_{bb} \in M_{n-1 \times n-1}(\mathbb{R})$, and the matrices $\Sigma_{ab} = \Sigma_{ba}^t \in M_{1 \times n-1}(\mathbb{R})$. The marginal distribution of X_a is a Gaussian distribution over $\mathbb{R}$ of covariance matrix $\alpha^2 \cdot \Sigma_{aa} = \alpha^2 \cdot Tr(p_0 \overline{p_0}) = \alpha^2 \cdot n$. The conditional distribution of $X_b | X_a = x_0$ is a Gaussian distribution over $\mathbb{R}^{n-1}$ of mean $x_0 \alpha^2 \Sigma_{ba} (\alpha^2 \Sigma_{aa})^{-1} = \frac{x_0}{n} \cdot \Sigma_{ba}$ and of covariance matrix $\alpha^2 \left(\Sigma_{bb} - \Sigma_{ba} \Sigma_{aa}^{-1} \Sigma_{ab} \right)$.

Proof of (i) When $\mathcal{O} = \widetilde{\mathcal{O}}$, the covariance matrix $\alpha^2 \left(\Sigma_{bb} - \Sigma_{ba} \Sigma_{aa}^{-1} \Sigma_{ab} \right) = \alpha^2 \cdot m^{2r} \cdot T$, where T was defined above. As r was chosen such that $\tau \cdot m^{2r-2} \geq n$, for $\tau = e_{n-1}(T)$, the smallest singular value, $s_{n-1}(\sqrt{T})$, of $\sqrt{T}$ equals $\sqrt{\tau}$, and

$$\alpha \cdot m^r \cdot s_{n-1}(\sqrt{T}) \geq \alpha \cdot m^r \cdot \sqrt{\tau} \geq \alpha \cdot m \cdot \sqrt{n} \geq \omega(1) \cdot \sqrt{n} > \eta(\mathbb{Z}^{n-1}).$$

The last inequality follows from the fact that $\eta(\mathbb{Z}^{n-1}) < \sqrt{n}$, for $\varepsilon = (e^{\pi n}/(2n-2) - 1)^{-1}$. Thus, since $\alpha^2 \cdot m^{2r} \cdot T \geq \alpha^2 \cdot m^{2r} \cdot s_{n-1}(\sqrt{T})^2$, the distribution of $X_b | X_a = x_0 \mod \mathbb{Z}^{n-1}$ is ε-close to the uniform distribution $U((\mathbb{R}/\mathbb{Z})^{n-1})$. Recall that, given symmetric matrices A, B, the standard notation $A \geq B$ means that $A - B$ is a positive semi-definite matrix. This proves the result.

Proof of (ii) When $\mathcal{O} = \widetilde{\mathcal{O}}'$, the $\mathbb{Z}$-basis $\vec{p}'$ is orthogonal. Therefore, the covariance matrix

$$\alpha^2 \left(\Sigma_{bb} - \Sigma_{ba} \Sigma_{aa}^{-1} \Sigma_{ab} \right) = \alpha^2 \cdot diag(m^2 \|\theta_1'\|^2, \ldots, m^2 \|\theta_{n-1}'\|^2).$$

Now, for $1 \leq i \leq n-1$, each e_i is an independent variable drawn from $D_{\sqrt{\alpha_i}}$, with $\alpha_i = \alpha^2 \cdot m^2 \|\theta_i'\|^2$. As $\theta_i' \in \mathcal{O}_K$, $\|\theta_i'\| \geq \sqrt{n}$. Hence,

$$e_i \mod \mathbb{Z} \leftarrow D_{\sqrt{\alpha_i}} \mod \mathbb{Z} \quad \text{for } \sqrt{\alpha_i} \geq \alpha \cdot m \cdot \sqrt{n}.$$

Under the assumption on α and the fact that $m \geq q$, for $i > 0$, the parameter $\sqrt{\alpha_i} > \eta(\mathbb{Z})$. The last inequality follows from the fact that $\eta(\mathbb{Z}) < \sqrt{n}$, for $\varepsilon = (e^{\pi n}/2 - 1)^{-1}$. The distribution $D_{\sqrt{\alpha_i}} \mod \mathbb{Z}$, for $i > 0$, is statistically ε-close to the uniform distribution $U(\mathbb{R}/\mathbb{Z})$. This proves the result. $\qquad \square$

Remark 4.6. The parameters $m \geq q$ in Theorem 4.4 cannot satisfy $m \gg q$, as the Order-LWE problem would become trivially impossible to solve. This is because when $m \gg q$, the error parameter $\alpha > \frac{2\omega(1)}{q} \gg \frac{1}{m}$ is greater than the smoothing parameter of $(\mathbb{Z} + m\mathcal{O}_K)^\vee$, thereby making the second coordinate from the $(\mathbb{Z} + m\mathcal{O}_K)$-LWE problem, $b \in K_\mathbb{R}/(\mathbb{Z} + m\mathcal{O}_K)^\vee$, indistinguishable from uniform.

The α-drowning orders from Proposition 4.5 are particularly easy to describe in the case of the power-of-two cyclotomic extensions. See full version for a proof of the next result.

Corollary 4.7. *Let $K = \mathbb{Q}(\zeta_{2n})$ be a power of two cyclotomic extension. Let m and q be distinct integers, with $m \geq q$. Let $\alpha \in (0,1)$ be such that $\alpha \cdot q \geq 2 \cdot \omega(1)$. Then, for $\widetilde{\mathcal{O}} := \mathbb{Z} + m\mathcal{O}_K$, the problems $\widetilde{\mathcal{O}}$-LWE$_{q,D_\alpha}$ and LWE$_{n,q,D_{\alpha \cdot \sqrt{n}}}$ are equivalent.*

Acknowledgements. We thank the anonymous referees for their useful comments and suggestions.

References

[Ajt96] Ajtai, M.: Generating hard instances of lattice problems (extended abstract). In: Proceedings of STOC, pp. 99–108. ACM (1996)

[Ban93] Banaszczyk, W.: New bounds in some transference theorems in the geometry of numbers. Math. Ann. **296**(1), 625–635 (1993)

[BBPS19] Bolboceanu, M., Brakerski, Z., Perlman, R., Sharma, D.: Order-LWE and the hardness of ring-LWE with entropic secrets. In: Proceedings of ASIACRYPT, pp. 91–120 (2019)

[BGP22] Boudgoust, K., Gachon, E., Pellet-Mary, A.: Some easy instances of ideal-SVP and implications on the partial vandermonde knapsack problem. In: Proceedings of Crypto, pp. 480–509 (2022)

[BLNRL22] Bernard, O., Lesavourey, A., Nguyen, T.-H., Roux-Langlois, A.: Log-s-unit lattices using explicit stickelberger generators to solve approx ideal-svp. In: Proceedings of Asiacrypt, pp. 677–708 (2022)

[BRL20] Bernard, O., Roux-Langlois, A.: Twisted-phs: Using the product formula to solve approx-svp in ideal lattices. In: Proceedings of Asiacrypt, pp. 349-380 (2020)

[CDPR16] Cramer, R., Ducas, L., Peikert, C., Regev, O.: Recovering short generators of principal ideals in cyclotomic rings. In: Proceedings of EUROCRYPT, pp. 559–585 (2016)

[CDW17] Cramer, R., Ducas, L., Wesolowski, B.: Short stickelberger class relations and application to ideal-SVP. In: Proceedings of EUROCRYPT, pp. 324–348 (2017)

[CGS] Campbell, P., Groves, M., Sheperd, D.: Soliloquy: a cautionary tale. ETSI 2nd quantum-safe crypto workshop (2014). https://docbox.etsi.org/workshop/2014/201410_CRYPTO/S07_Systems_and_Attacks/S07_Groves_Annex.pdf

[Cona] Conrad, K.: Bilinear forms. https://kconrad.math.uconn.edu/blurbs/linmultialg/bilinearform.pdf

[Conb] Conrad, K.: The conductor ideal. https://kconrad.math.uconn.edu/blurbs/gradnumthy/conductor.pdf

[Conc] Conrad, K.: The different ideal. https://kconrad.math.uconn.edu/blurbs/gradnumthy/different.pdf

[Cond] K. Conrad. Ideal factorization. https://kconrad.math.uconn.edu/blurbs/gradnumthy/idealfactor.pdf

[DPW19] Ducas, L., Plançon, M., Wesolowski, B.: On the shortness of vectors to be found by the ideal-SVP quantum algorithm. In: Proceedings of CRYPTO, pp. 322–351 (2019)

[HPS98] Hoffstein, J., Pipher, J., Silverman, J.H.: NTRU: a ring-based public key cryptosystem. In: ANTS, pp. 267–288 (1998)

[JL22] Jutla, C.S., Lin, C.: Enhancing ring-LWE hardness using dedekind index theorem (2022). https://eprint.iacr.org/2022/1631

[LM06] Lyubashevsky, V., Micciancio, D.: Generalized compact knapsacks are collision resistant. In: Proceedings of ICALP, pp. 144–155 (2006)

[LPR10] Lyubashevsky, V., Peikert, C., Regev, O.: On ideal lattices and learning with errors over rings. In: Proceedings of EUROCRYPT, pp. 1–23 (2010)

[LPR13] Lyubashevsky, V., Peikert, C., Regev, O.: A toolkit for ring-LWE cryptography. In: Proceedings of EUROCRYPT, pp. 35–54 (2013)

[LS12] Langlois, A., Stehlé, D.: Worst-case to average-case reductions for module lattices. IACR Cryptol. ePrint Arch. **2012**, 90 (2012)

[Neu99] Neukirch, J.: Algebraic number theory (1999)

[Pei10] Peikert, C.: An efficient and parallel gaussian sampler for lattices. In: Rabin, T. (ed.) CRYPTO 2010. LNCS, vol. 6223, pp. 80–97. Springer, Heidelberg (2010). https://doi.org/10.1007/978-3-642-14623-7_5

[Pei16] Peikert, C.: A decade of lattice cryptography. Found. Trends Theor. Comput. Sci. **10**(4), 283–424 (2016)

[PHS19] Pellet-Mary, A., Hanrot, G., Stehlé, D.: Approx-SVP in ideal lattices with pre-processing. In: Proceedings of EUROCRYPT, pp. 685–716 (2019)

[PP19] Peikert, C., Pepin, Z.: Algebraically structured LWE, revisited. In: Proceedings of TCC, pp. 1–23 (2019)

[PR06] Peikert, C., Rosen, A.: Efficient collision-resistant hashing from worst-case assumptions on cyclic lattices. In: Proceedings of TCC, pp. 145–166 (2006)

[PRSD17] Peikert, C., Regev, O., Stephens-Davidowitz, N.: Pseudorandomness of ring-LWE for any ring and modulus. IACR Cryptology ePrint Archive **2017**, 258 (2017)

[PXWC21] Pan, Y., Xu, J., Wadleigh, N., Cheng, Q.: On the ideal shortest vector problem over random rational primes. In: Proceedings of EUROCRYPT, pp. 559–583 (2021)

[Reg05] Regev, O.: On lattices, learning with errors, random linear codes, and cryptography. In: STOC, pp. 84–93 (2005). Full version in [Reg09]

[Reg09] Regev, O.: On lattices, learning with errors, random linear codes, and cryptography. J. ACM **56**(6), 1–40 (2009)

[RSSS17] Rosca, M., Sakzad, A., Stehlé, D., Steinfeld, R.: Middle-product learning with errors. In: Proceedings of CRYPTO, pp. 283–297 (2017)

[RSW18] Rosca, M., Stehlé, D., Wallet, A.: On the ring-LWE and polynomial-LWE problems. In: Proceedings of EUROCRYPT, pp. 146–173 (2018)

[SSTX09] Stehlé, D., Steinfeld, R., Tanaka, K., Xagawa, K.: Efficient public key encryption based on ideal lattices. In: Proceedings of ASIACRYPT, pp. 617–635 (2009)

[Was83] Washington, L.C.: Introduction to cyclotomic fields (1983)

Isogenies and Applications

An Algorithm for Efficient Detection of (N, N)-Splittings and Its Application to the Isogeny Problem in Dimension 2

Maria Corte-Real Santos[1]($\boxtimes$)(ID), Craig Costello[2](ID), and Sam Frengley[3](ID)

[1] University College London, London, UK
maria.santos.20@ucl.ac.uk
[2] Microsoft Research, Redmond, USA
craigco@microsoft.com
[3] University of Cambridge, Cambridge, UK
stf32@cam.ac.uk

Abstract. We develop an efficient algorithm to detect whether a superspecial genus 2 Jacobian is optimally (N, N)-split for each integer $N \leq 11$. Incorporating this algorithm into the best-known attack against the superspecial isogeny problem in dimension 2 (due to Costello and Smith) gives rise to significant cryptanalytic improvements. Our implementation shows that when the underlying prime p is 100 bits, the attack is sped up by a factor of 25; when the underlying prime is 200 bits, the attack is sped up by a factor of 42; and, when the underlying prime is 1000 bits, the attack is sped up by a factor of 160.

Keywords: Isogeny-based cryptography · genus 2 · superspecial · cryptanalysis

1 Introduction

Let C and C' be genus 2 curves with superspecial Jacobians. The general dimension 2 *superspecial isogeny problem* asks us to find an isogeny

$$\phi \colon \operatorname{Jac}(C) \to \operatorname{Jac}(C'),$$

of principally polarised (p.p.) abelian surfaces, where $\operatorname{Jac}(C)$ and $\operatorname{Jac}(C')$ are the Jacobians of C and C' respectively.

We say that the Jacobian $\operatorname{Jac}(C)$ of a genus 2 curve C is *split* (over K) if there exists a separable (polarised) K-isogeny of p.p. abelian surfaces $\operatorname{Jac}(C) \to E_1 \times E_2$ where E_1/K and E_2/K are elliptic curves.

The best known algorithm for solving the superspecial isogeny problem is due to Costello and Smith [13]. It consists of two stages. The first stage computes pseudorandom walks away from the two input Jacobians to find paths to

---

Maria Corte-Real Santos: Supported by the UK EPSRC grant EP/S022503/1.
Sam Frengley: Funded by the Woolf Fisher and Cambridge Trusts.

Q. Tang and V. Teague (Eds.): PKC 2024, LNCS 14603, pp. 157–189, 2024.
https://doi.org/10.1007/978-3-031-57725-3_6

products of two supersingular elliptic curves, i.e., $\varphi\colon \mathrm{Jac}(C) \to E_1 \times E_2$ and $\varphi'\colon \mathrm{Jac}(C') \to E_1' \times E_2'$. Assuming the pseudorandom walks quickly converge to the uniform distribution, the first stage runs in $\widetilde{O}(p)$ classical bit operations, since the proportion of superspecial abelian surfaces that are isomorphic to a product of elliptic curves is $O(1/p)$. The second stage calls the $\widetilde{O}(p^{1/2})$ Delfs-Galbraith algorithm [16] to find paths between E_1 and E_1' and between E_2 and E_2'. These are then glued together to obtain the path $\pi\colon E_1 \times E_2 \to E_1' \times E_2'$ connecting φ and φ' in order to output the full solution $\phi := \widehat{\varphi'} \circ \pi \circ \varphi$. It follows that the entire algorithm runs in $\widetilde{O}(p)$ classical bit operations on average, with the cost dominated by the first step: finding paths to products of elliptic curves.

Isogeny-based cryptography in dimension 2. The product-finding algorithm [13] that we accelerate in this work solves the general superspecial isogeny problem, which underlies the security of various isogeny-based protocols in dimension 2. An example of such a scheme is the dimension 2 analogue of the Charles-Goren-Lauter hash function [10], which was proposed by Takashima [52] and later extended by Castryck, Decru and Smith [9].

The 2022 breaks of SIDH and SIKE [8,41,44] revealed that understanding higher dimensional isogenies is essential to navigate the isogeny graphs in dimension 1. More recently, there has been a line of works leveraging the techniques used in the attacks to propose new cryptosystems that exploit isogeny computations in higher dimensions [1,11,15]. Although the hard problems underlying these schemes are not directly impacted by the algorithm that is optimised in this paper, we believe the trend towards instantiating schemes in higher dimensions will only make the dimension 2 supersingular isogeny problem more relevant to practitioners as the field of isogeny-based cryptography continues to mature.

Based on the present knowledge of attacks in dimension 2, we believe it is reasonable to speculate that the complexity of the product-finding algorithm may eventually be used as an upper-bound on the classical hardness of attacking many schemes that are currently conceivable, even when the underlying instances of the isogeny problem are special cases of its general formulation (provided no superior algorithm for the special problem is found, of course). For example, consider the dimension 2 analogue of the Sigma protocol that proves knowledge of an isogeny of a specified degree (see [19] for the latest on this protocol). In dimension 1, the best known classical attack on this protocol is the van Oorschot–Wiener (vOW) meet-in-the-middle algorithm [54]. In dimension 2, however, the $\widetilde{O}(p)$ product-finding algorithm will solve the general problem at least as fast as the van Oorschot–Wiener meet-in-the-middle algorithm [54], and is likely to become the preferred algorithm[1] for large enough p.

---

[1] For a fixed memory bound w and single processor, taking $n = p^{3/4}$ [24, §4.1] in [54, Equation 4] gives an asymptotic runtime of $O(p^{9/8})$ on a single core. Moreover, parallel processors running vOW must read from, and write to, the huge central storage database (which hampers parallel performance in practice), while product-finding is memory-free and parallelises *perfectly*.

Contributions. We begin with an implementation of the algorithm described above for finding paths to products of elliptic curves. This includes a streamlined version of the Takashima–Yoshida algorithm [53, §5.5] for computing chains of Richelot isogenies. With this optimised algorithm, we provide a toolbox for exploring the $(2, 2)$-isogeny graph. The expansion properties of the $(2, 2)$-isogeny graph are not well understood and our implementation is well suited to exploring this. For example, one could hope to provide evidence towards [23, Conj. 4.10]. Understanding the expansion properties of this graph is crucial to gaining a deeper insight into the hardness of the general isogeny problem in dimension 2.

This lays the foundation for the main contribution of this work: a new algorithm that speeds up the search for paths to products of elliptic curves. At the heart of our algorithm is the work of Kumar [36], who gives explicit parametrisations of the moduli space of genus 2 curves whose Jacobians are split by an (N, N)-isogeny. When we step to a new node in the Richelot isogeny graph, these parametrisations allow us to efficiently test whether *any* of the (N, N)-isogenous neighbours are isomorphic to a product of supersingular elliptic curves without computing any expensive (N, N)-isogenies. For example, over a field whose characteristic is a 100-bit prime, an optimised Richelot isogeny (see Sect. 3) requires 1176 $\mathbb{F}_p$-multiplications. This is the cost of taking a single step in the Richelot isogeny graph, which reveals only one neighbour and is thus the per-node cost of running the attack described in [13]. However, using the new algorithm we describe in Sect. 5 with $N = 3$, we are able to test whether any of the $(3, 3)$-isogenous neighbours are split with a total of 767 $\mathbb{F}_p$-multiplications. Since there are 40 such neighbours, the per-node cost of simultaneously searching these neighbours is less than 20 $\mathbb{F}_p$-multiplications each. The upshot is that when attacking an instance of the superspecial isogeny problem, we can sift through a larger proportion of superspecial Jacobians per unit time, thus reaching an elliptic curve product with fewer $\mathbb{F}_p$-multiplications.

In Sect. 7 we report on a number of experiments conducted over both small primes (where instances of the superspecial isogeny problem can be solved) and large primes of cryptographic size. Applying our accelerated algorithm to find paths to elliptic products when $p = 2^{31} - 1$, we solve 10 instances of the problem using an average of $2^{33.0}$ multiplications in $\mathbb{F}_p$ for an average wall time of $2^{16.3}$ seconds. Our optimised version of the original algorithm from [13] requires an average of $2^{36.8}$ multiplications in $\mathbb{F}_p$ for an average runtime of $2^{20.5}$ seconds to solve the same 10 instances. In Table 1 we give a snapshot of the improvements that were observed in our implementation for a number of large primes of varying bitlength. We see that the relative speedup improves as the prime p grows in size (see Sect. 7 for more details).

Indeed, for primes of at least 150 bits, we argue in Sect. 6.3 that (heuristically) Algorithm 4 requires an expected number of

$$\left(\frac{14 \log_2(p) + 34490}{5 \cdot 664} \right) p + O(\log_2(p))$$

Table 1. An abbreviated version of Table 5. See Sect. 7 for further explanation.

	Walks in $\Gamma_2(2;p)$ without additional searching [13] (optimised in §3)	Walks in $\Gamma_2(2;p)$ with split searching in $\Gamma_2(N;p)$ **This work**		
p (bits)	$\mathbb{F}_p$ muls per node	set $N \in \{\dots\}$	$\mathbb{F}_p$ muls per node	**improv. factor**
50	579	$\{2,3\}$	35	**16.5x**
100	1176	$\{2,3\}$	48	**24.5x**
150	1575	$\{3,4\}$	54	**29.2x**
⋮	⋮	⋮	⋮	⋮
950	9772	$\{4,6\}$	69	**141.6x**
1000	11346	$\{4,6\}$	71	**159.8x**

$\mathbb{F}_p$-multiplications before encountering a product of elliptic curves. Under the same heuristics, our optimised version of the algorithm in [13] would require a larger expected $\left(\frac{12\log_2(p)+129}{5}\right) p + O(\log_2(p))$ $\mathbb{F}_p$-multiplications.

All of the source code accompanying this paper is written in Magma [2] and can be found at

$$\text{https://github.com/mariascrs/SplitSearcher.}$$

Finally, we note that our algorithm for detecting (N, N)-splittings may be of interest outside of our target application of the dimension 2 superspecial isogeny problem. For example, it answers a question posed by Castryck and Decru [8, §11] for $N \le 11$.

Related work. At a high level, our improvements to the dimension 2 superspecial isogeny attack can be viewed as an analogue of those recently given by Corte-Real Santos, Costello and Shi [12] to the Delfs–Galbraith attack [16] in dimension 1. Indeed, both attacks use random walks to find special nodes in the graph to reduce the (remainder of the) algorithm to a comparatively easier isogeny problem: the special nodes in the Delfs–Galbraith algorithm are the isomorphism classes of elliptic curves defined over $\mathbb{F}_p$, while the special nodes in the Costello–Smith algorithm are the isomorphism classes of products of elliptic curves. The key to the improvements in [12] was an efficient method for determining whether modular polynomials have subfield roots without computing any such roots explicitly. This allows many nodes to be simultaneously searched over without being visited by means of expensive isogeny computations. The key to the improvements in this paper stem from Kumar's parametrisations of the moduli space of genus 2 curves whose Jacobians are split by an (N, N)-isogeny [36]. In a similar vein to [12], we show that these can be used to simultaneously search over many neighbours without visiting the corresponding nodes in the isogeny walks.

It is worth noting that, relatively speaking, the improvements found in this work are significantly larger than the improvements reported in [12] in the dimension 1 case. At first glance of Sect. 5, it seems our batch (N, N)-split searching requires a lot more computation than the analogous batch N-isogenous subfield curve searching in [12]. However, in dimension 2 we are processing $O(N^3)$ neighbours simultaneously (see Equation (1)), while the subfield search in dimension 1 is batch testing $O(N)$ neighbours each time. For primes of size 50 to 800 bits, [12, Table 6] report speedups ranging from 3.2× to 17.6×, while the speedups we found for primes of these same sizes (see Table 5) range from 16.5× to 116.3×.

Outline. After giving the necessary background in Sect. 2, we detail our optimised version of the original $\Gamma_2(2; p)$ walk from [13] in Sect. 3. In Sect. 4 we recall standard results concerning moduli spaces for genus 2 curves with split Jacobians and Kumar's formulae [36]. In Sect. 5 we present the main contribution of this work: an efficient algorithm to detect (N, N)-splittings. We give the full algorithm and discuss our implementation in Sect. 6. Finally, we present the experimental results in Sect. 7 before we conclude by mentioning some possible avenues for improving the algorithm.

2   Background

We give a brief account of abelian surfaces and fix notation. Readers looking for an in-depth discussion of higher dimensional abelian varieties and their application in isogeny based cryptography are encouraged to consult [9,13], and [24].

Let A be an abelian surface (i.e., an abelian variety of dimension 2) defined over a field K and write $\widehat{A}$ for the dual abelian variety. A pair (A, λ) is said to be a *polarised abelian surface* if $\lambda \colon A \to \widehat{A}$ is an isogeny (i.e., a surjective finite morphism of group varieties). We say that (A, λ) is *principally polarised* (p.p.) if λ is an isomorphism.

If C/K is a smooth projective curve we write $\mathrm{Jac}(C)/K$ for the Jacobian of C, the abelian variety whose points parametrise degree zero divisors on C up to linear equivalence. Throughout the article we will suppress the implicit choice of (principal) polarisation on A. In particular, when $A = \mathrm{Jac}(C)$ is the Jacobian of a (smooth projective) curve then A is equipped with the (canonical) principal polarisation arising from the theta divisor and when $A = E_1 \times E_2$ is a product of elliptic curves then A is equipped with the product polarisation.

Let (A, λ) and (A', λ') be p.p. abelian surfaces. An isogeny $\phi \colon A \to A'$ is said to be an *isogeny* of p.p. abelian surfaces if there exists an integer $m \geq 1$ such that $\widehat{\phi} \circ \lambda' \circ \phi = [m]\lambda$. If $N \geq 2$ is an integer coprime to the characteristic of K, then for any abelian variety A we have the N-Weil pairing $A[N] \times \widehat{A}[N] \to \mu_N$. When A is equipped with a principal polarisation this gives rise to the N-Weil pairing

$$e_N \colon A[N] \times A[N] \to \mu_N.$$

We say that a subgroup $G \subseteq A[N]$ is *isotropic* (with respect to the N-Weil pairing) if $e_N(P, Q) = 1$ for all $P, Q \in G$. We say G is *maximal isotropic* if moreover there is no isotropic subgroup G' with $G \subsetneq G' \subseteq A[N]$.

Given a maximal isotropic subgroup $G \subseteq A[N]$, the abelian surface $A' = A/G$ comes equipped with a principal polarisation λ' such that $\phi: A \to A'$ is an isogeny of p.p. abelian surfaces and $\phi^* \lambda' = [m]\lambda$ for some integer m. We say that a subgroup $G \subseteq A[N]$ is an (N, N)-subgroup if it is maximal isotropic (with respect to e_N) and isomorphic (as an abstract group) to $(\mathbb{Z}/N\mathbb{Z})^2$. In this case we say that ϕ is an (N, N)-isogeny. The number of (N, N)-subgroups of $A[N]$ is equal to

$$D_N := N^3 \prod_{\substack{\text{primes} \\ \ell \mid N}} \frac{1}{\ell^3}(\ell + 1)(\ell^2 + 1). \tag{1}$$

In particular, when N is prime we have $D_N = (N^2 + 1)(N + 1)$. See e.g., [7, Lemma 2] (see also [13, Lemma 2] and [24, Proposition 3(2)] when N is a prime or prime power, respectively).

2.1 Superspecial Abelian Surfaces

As discussed by Castryck, Decru, and Smith [9, §2], for cryptographic applications the most natural generalisation of the set of supersingular elliptic curves to dimension 2 is the set of *superspecial* p.p. abelian surfaces.

Definition 1. *We say a p.p. abelian surface $A/\overline{\mathbb{F}}_p$ is* supersingular *if the Newton polygon of A is a line of slope $\frac{1}{2}$. We say A is* superspecial *if the Hasse-Witt matrix $M \in \mathbb{F}_p^{2 \times 2}$ vanishes identically.*

If A is superspecial, then it is supersingular. The converse is not necessarily true when $\dim(A) \geq 2$. The condition for superspeciality is a natural generalisation of the fact that when $p > 3$ an elliptic curve is supersingular if and only if it has trace of Frobenius congruent to 0 modulo p. An alternative characterisation is that A is isomorphic (as an abstract abelian variety) to a product of supersingular elliptic curves.

It can be shown that every superspecial p.p. abelian surface $A/\overline{\mathbb{F}}_p$ is $\overline{\mathbb{F}}_p$-isomorphic (as a p.p. abelian variety) to a p.p. abelian surface defined over $\mathbb{F}_{p^2}$ (see [29, Theorem 1]) and moreover this abelian surface may be chosen to have full $\mathbb{F}_{p^2}$-rational 2-torsion when p is odd (see [9, §2]).

The dimension 2 superspecial isogeny problem may be stated precisely as:

Problem 1 (Dimension 2 superspecial isogeny problem). Given a pair of superspecial p.p. abelian surfaces A and A' defined over $\mathbb{F}_{p^2}$, find an $\overline{\mathbb{F}}_p$-isogeny $A \to A'$.

2.2 The Superspecial Isogeny Graph

We now describe the superspecial isogeny graph, and re-frame Problem 1 as a path finding problem.

Let $\mathcal{S}_2(p)$ denote the set of $\overline{\mathbb{F}}_p$-isomorphism classes of superspecial p.p. abelian surfaces. Since every superspecial p.p. abelian surface admits a model over $\mathbb{F}_{p^2}$, the set $\mathcal{S}_2(p)$ is finite. In fact, it can be shown that it has size $O(p^3)$ [9, Theorem 1]. For each integer N coprime to p, we define $\Gamma_2(N; p)$ as the directed weighted multigraph on vertex set $\mathcal{S}_2(p)$, whose edges are $\overline{\mathbb{F}}_p$-isomorphism classes of (N, N)-isogenies (weighted by the number of distinct kernels yielding isogenies in the class). The graph $\Gamma_2(N; p)$ is D_N-regular, where D_N is given by Equation (1) (taking into account multiplicities of each edge).

Though primitives constructed using superspecial p.p. abelian surfaces, such as the Castryck–Decru–Smith hash function [9], assume the rapid convergence of random walks in the graphs $\Gamma_2(N; p)$ to the uniform distribution, it is important to note that these expansion properties are not well understood. The superspecial isogeny graph is connected (see e.g., [33,43]), however, as discussed by Florit and Smith [23, §4.3], the graphs $\Gamma_2(N; p)$ do not fit into the definition of an expander graph as they are directed multigraphs. However, one can still obtain upper bounds on the eigenvalues of these graphs to determine whether $\Gamma_2(N; p)$ is Ramanujan, i.e., has optimal expansion. Jordan–Zaytman [33] give the first counterexample: $\Gamma_2(2; 11)$ is not Ramanujan. Florit–Smith provide evidence that the same behaviour occurs for $\Gamma_2(2; p)$ where $11 \leq p \leq 201$, therefore suggesting that the superspecial $(2, 2)$-isogeny graph fails to be Ramanujan [23, Appendix A]. It would also be interesting to study the expansion properties of $\Gamma_2(N; p)$ for $N > 2$. Despite the lack of *optimal* expansion, Florit–Smith conjecture [23, Conjecture 4.10] that $\Gamma_2(N; p)$ still has *good enough* expansion for cryptographic purposes.

Every p.p. abelian surface is isomorphic to either the Jacobian of a curve of genus 2, or to a product of two elliptic curves with the product polarisation. In the latter case, if the abelian surface is superspecial, then the elliptic curves will be supersingular. Therefore, $\mathcal{S}_2(p)$ is equal to the disjoint union of the following two sets:

$$\mathcal{J}_2(p) := \{A \in \mathcal{S}_2(p) \ : \ A \cong \mathrm{Jac}(C) \text{ for some genus 2 curve } C\} \text{ and}$$
$$\mathcal{E}_2(p) := \{A \in \mathcal{S}_2(p) \ : \ A \cong E_1 \times E_2 \text{ for some } E_1, E_2 \in \mathcal{S}_1(p)\},$$

where the isomorphisms are of p.p. abelian varieties over $\overline{\mathbb{F}}_p$. It can be shown that $\#\mathcal{J}_2(p) = \frac{1}{2880}p^3 + O(p^2)$ and $\#\mathcal{E}_2(p) = \frac{1}{288}p^2 + O(p)$ (combine [51, Theorem V.4.1(c)] with [3, Theorem 3.10(b)] or [30, Theorem 3.3], see [9, Theorem 1] for details). In particular $\#\mathcal{E}_2(p)/\#\mathcal{S}_2(p) = 10/p + O(1/p^2)$.

Important to our work will be the ratio of nodes $A \in \mathcal{E}_2(p)$ to nodes visited while performing a random walk on $\Gamma_2(N; p)$. A natural first guess would be that this ratio matches the proportion of such nodes in the entire graph, i.e., $\sim 10/p$. However, Florit–Smith show that all but $O(p)$ of the products of elliptic curves have reduced automorphism group of order 2, and deduce that the expected proportion of products in a random walk is $\sim \frac{1}{2} \cdot \frac{10}{p} = \frac{5}{p}$ [23, §6.2].

As in the dimension 1 case, we can view the dimension 2 isogeny problem as a path finding problem in the superspecial isogeny graph.

Problem 2. Given superspecial p.p. abelian surfaces A and A' defined over $\mathbb{F}_{p^2}$, find a walk in $\Gamma_2(N; p)$ connecting them (when $p \nmid N$).

2.3   Attacking the General Isogeny Problem in Dimension 2

The best known algorithm for solving Problem 2 exploits the properties of the subset $\mathcal{E}_2(p) \subseteq \mathcal{S}_2(p)$ and is depicted in Algorithm 1. Given two ($\bar{\mathbb{F}}_p$-isomorphism classes of) p.p. abelian surfaces A and $A' \in \mathcal{J}_2(p)$, Steps 1 and 2 find paths $\varphi \colon A \to E_1 \times E_2$ and $\varphi' \colon A' \to E_1' \times E_2'$, where both $E_1 \times E_2 \in \mathcal{E}_2(p)$ and $E_1' \times E_2' \in \mathcal{E}_2(p)$. As $\#\mathcal{J}_2(p) = O(p^3)$ and $\#\mathcal{E}_2(p) = O(p^2)$, we expect to complete both of these steps using $\widetilde{O}(p)$ operations in $\mathbb{F}_p$. Steps 3 and 4 then solve the dimension 1 isogeny problem on input of E_1 and E_1' and on input of E_2 and E_2' to output the paths $\psi_1 \colon E_1 \to E_1'$ and $\psi_2 \colon E_2 \to E_2'$ in the supersingular elliptic curve N-isogeny graph. Both of these steps terminate using on average $\widetilde{O}(\sqrt{p})$ operations in $\mathbb{F}_p$ [16]. If $\mathrm{length}(\psi_1) \equiv \mathrm{length}(\psi_2) \bmod 2$, we can use these to construct a product path $\pi \colon E_1 \times E_2 \to E_1' \times E_2'$, as described in [13, Lemma 3]. The desired path between A and A' is then $\phi := \widehat{\varphi'} \circ \pi \circ \varphi$.[2] Overall, the cost of the algorithm is $\widetilde{O}(p)$ bit operations.

For the rest of this paper we focus on improving the concrete complexity of Steps 1 and 2 of this attack, i.e., on finding paths to the product surfaces, since this is the bottleneck step that determines the concrete complexity of Algorithm 1.

Algorithm 1. Computing isogeny paths in $\Gamma_2(N; p)$ [13]

Input: A and A' in $\mathcal{S}_2(p)$
Output: A path $\phi \colon A \to A'$ in $\Gamma_2(N; p)$

 1: Find a path φ from A to some $E_1 \times E_2$ in $\mathcal{E}_2(p)$
 2: Find a path φ' from A' to some $E_1' \times E_2'$ in $\mathcal{E}_2(p)$
 3: Find a path $\psi_1 \colon E_1 \to E_1'$ using (elliptic curve) path finding
 4: Find a path $\psi_2 \colon E_2 \to E_2'$ using (elliptic curve) path finding
 5: **if** $\mathrm{length}(\psi_1) \not\equiv \mathrm{length}(\psi_2) \pmod 2$ **then**
 6:     **return** $\perp$
 7: **else**
 8:     Construct a path $\pi \colon E_1 \times E_2 \to E_1' \times E_2'$ using ψ_1, ψ_2 as in [13, Lemma 3]
 9:     **return** the path $\phi := \widehat{\varphi'} \circ \pi \circ \varphi$ from A to A'

Applications to cryptanalysis. In the security analysis of their hash function [9], Castryck–Decru–Smith correctly argue that, since the steps taken by their hash function correspond entirely to "good extensions" (see Sect. 3.2), the path returned by [13, Algorithm 1] (which does not only consist of good extensions) is therefore not a valid preimage [9, Footnote 11]. However, more recent

---

[2] If $\mathrm{length}(\psi_1) \not\equiv \mathrm{length}(\psi_2) \bmod 2$, we fail and return $\perp$. Note, however, only three runs of Algorithm 1 are required to successfully return path ϕ. Indeed, if we instead run Algorithm 1 to find paths $\psi_1 \colon E_1 \to E_1'$, $\psi_{2,1} \colon E_2 \to E$, and $\psi_{2,2} \colon E \to E_2'$, where $E \colon y^2 = x^3 + x$ has an endomorphism of degree 2, say τ, then we can set $\psi_2 = \psi_{2,2} \circ \psi_{2,1}$ if $\mathrm{length}(\psi_1) \equiv \mathrm{length}(\psi_{2,1} \circ \psi_{2,2}) \bmod 2$ and $\psi_2 = \psi_{2,2} \circ \tau \circ \psi_{2,1}$, otherwise.

work by Florit and Smith [23, §6.2 - 6.4] shows that collisions in the Castryck–Decru–Smith hash function can be constructed once a walk to an elliptic product is known. So long as we assume our walks approximate the random distribution on $\Gamma_2(2; p)$ (more on this in Remark 1), then we consider it prudent to use the complexity of the product-finding algorithms to classify the security of a given instance of the CDS hash function, even if preimage resistance is the governing security property.

As will become apparent in Sect. 6, our acceleration of the Costello–Smith algorithm will return a $(2^n N, 2^n N)$-isogeny (for some n). However, for many cryptographic protocols in isogeny-based cryptography, the secret isogeny will be of a specified degree, usually a prime power ℓ^k. Though an algorithm that transforms a $(2^n N, 2^n N)$-isogeny to a (ℓ^k, ℓ^k)-isogeny has yet to be developed, for example by generalising the KLPT algorithm [34] to dimension 2, we find it prudent to conjecture such an algorithm exists, rather than betting the security of primitives on the converse.

3   Optimised Product Finding in $\Gamma_2(2; p)$

In this section we describe an optimised instantiation of the product finding algorithm from [13] in the case of dimension 2.

Our instantiation uses pseudo-random walks in the superspecial subgraph of the Richelot isogeny graph [22, Definition 1] and exploits a streamlined version of Takashima and Yoshida's Richelot isogeny algorithm [53] to take efficient steps therein.

3.1   Taking a Step in $\Gamma_2(2; p)$

We start by deriving a streamlined version of Takashima and Yoshida's Richelot isogeny algorithm [53, Algorithm 2] that will be used as the basis for pseudo-random walks in the superspecial subgraph of $\Gamma_2(2; p)$. On input of the six-tuple $a = (a_0, \ldots, a_5) \in (\mathbb{F}_{p^2})^6$ defining[3] the genus 2 curve

$$C/\mathbb{F}_{p^2} : y^2 = (x - a_0) \cdots (x - a_5),$$

the algorithm outputs the six-tuple $a' = (a_0', \ldots, a_5') \in (\mathbb{F}_{p^2})^6$ that defines

$$C'/\mathbb{F}_{p^2} : y^2 = (x - a_0') \cdots (x - a_5'),$$

where $\phi\colon \operatorname{Jac}(C) \to \operatorname{Jac}(C')$ is the Richelot isogeny whose non-trivial kernel is precisely the three points $((x - a_i)(x - a_{i+1}), 0)$ in $\operatorname{Jac}(C)$ with $i \in \{0, 2, 4\}$.

The main modifications we have made to their algorithm are:

---

[3] For odd p, superspecial abelian surfaces always have full $\mathbb{F}_{p^2}$-rational 2-torsion (cf. [9, §2]), which in particular implies that the a_i are defined over $\mathbb{F}_{p^2}$.

- We assume that both the equations for C and C' are indeed given by the sextic polynomials whose six roots are rational elements of $\mathbb{F}_{p^2}$. This avoids the case distinctions made by Takashima and Yoshida that allow for quintic inputs and outputs (i.e., one of the a_i and/or a'_j being at infinity), which are unnecessary for our purposes (they occur with negligible probability, and after a change of coordinates we may assume that C and C' are defined by sextics).
- We do not keep track of the leading coefficient of the sextic, since this merely determines which quadratic twist we are on, which is irrelevant for our application because twists correspond to the same node in $\Gamma_2(2;p)$. This means we avoid the final inversion in Line 33 of [53, Algorithm 2].
- Each of the three iterations of their main loop involve separate inversion and square root computations. In each case we merge the inversion and square root into one combined inverse-and-square-root computation (see Line 7 of Algorithm 2) using the trick described in [45].

On top of a small, fixed, number of field multiplications, Algorithm 2 computes a Richelot isogeny using 3 calls to InvSqrt, which is essentially the same cost as a square root in $\mathbb{F}_{p^2}$ (i.e., 2 exponentiations in $\mathbb{F}_p$). This means our streamlined version saves all of the four additional $\mathbb{F}_{p^2}$ inversions reported by Takashima and Yoshida [53, §5.5]. Otherwise, the notation and description of the algorithm is essentially unchanged: the indices in Line 3 of Algorithm 2 are taken modulo 6, and the indices in Line 5 are taken modulo 3.

Algorithm 2. RIsog(): A Richelot isogeny in the general case

Input: $a = (a_0, \ldots, a_5) \in (\mathbb{F}_{p^2})^6$ defining $C/\mathbb{F}_{p^2} : y^2 = (x - a_0) \cdots (x - a_5)$.
Output: $a' = (a'_0, \ldots, a'_5) \in (\mathbb{F}_{p^2})^6$ defining $C'/\mathbb{F}_{p^2} : y^2 = (x - a'_0) \cdots (x - a'_5)$, where $\phi:$ Jac$(C) \rightarrow$ Jac(C') is a Richelot isogeny whose kernel corresponds to the three quadratic splittings $(x - a_i)(x - a_{i+1})$ for $i = 0, 2, 4$; and split, a boolean that is true if the image of ϕ is in $\mathcal{E}_2(p)$.

1: Initialise $\lambda \leftarrow [a[0] \cdot a[1], a[2] \cdot a[3], a[4] \cdot a[5]], \theta \leftarrow [], a' \leftarrow []$
2: **for** $j = 0$ to 2 **do**
3:   $\quad \rho \leftarrow [a[2j+2]-a[2j+4], a[2j+3]-a[2j+5], a[2j+2]-a[2j+5], a[2j+3]-a[2j+4]]$
4:   $\quad \theta[j] \leftarrow \rho[0] + \rho[1]$
5:   $\quad \nu \leftarrow \lambda[j+1] - \lambda[j+2]$
6:   $\quad \delta \leftarrow \rho[0] \cdot \rho[1] \cdot \rho[2] \cdot \rho[3].$
7:   $\quad (\mu, \kappa) \leftarrow$ InvSqrt(θ_j, δ)
8:   $\quad (a'[2j], a'[2j+1]) \leftarrow ((\nu + \kappa) \cdot \mu, (\nu - \kappa) \cdot \mu)$
9: split $\leftarrow (\lambda[0] \cdot \theta[0] + \lambda[1] \cdot \theta[1] + \lambda[2] \cdot \theta[2]) = 0$
10: **return** (a', split)

Alternatives for computing $(2^n, 2^n)$-isogenies. There are numerous ways to compute chains of $(2, 2)$-isogenies that would be fit for our purposes, but we are yet to find one that can appreciably outperform repeated calls to Algorithm 2. Recall that each such call computes a $(2,2)$-isogeny using a fixed number of $\mathbb{F}_p$-multiplications on top of three calls to the merged inversion-and-square root computation (i.e., InvSqrt). Castryck and Decru's multiradical variant of a Richelot isogeny also requires at least three square root computations in $\mathbb{F}_{p^2}$ [7, §4.2], so the most we could expect to gain using their formulae is in the constant number of additional $\mathbb{F}_p$-operations (assuming any field inversions required in their case can also be absorbed into the square root calls). Kunzweiler's efficient $(2^n, 2^n)$-isogeny algorithm [37] could also be used in our scenario, but in testing this algorithm against ours we observed that, on average, ours performs between 3x and 5x faster for the two primes considered by Kunzweiler. Note, Kunzweiler's formulae were derived with a different target application (i.e., G2SIDH) in mind, meaning computing a chain of $(2,2)$-isogenies of fixed length n is most efficient when $2^n \mid p + 1$. In our algorithm, we compute chains of length much larger than any such n and, as a result, this comparison is unfair to [37]. Our comparison is to ensure that we are not sacrificing efficiency in our context.

3.2   Walking in the Superspecial Subgraph of $\Gamma_2(2; p)$

We now turn to describing walks in the superspecial subgraph of $\Gamma_2(2; p)$ that take steps using the RIsog algorithm developed above. To ensure that these walks are non-backtracking and avoid short cycles, the output of RIsog must first be permuted so that the quadratic splitting implicit to its ordering (see §3.1) corresponds to a *good extension* of the previous $(2,2)$-isogeny (i.e., a $(2,2)$-isogeny whose kernel intersects trivially with the kernel of the dual of the previous $(2,2)$-isogeny).

Kernel permutations corresponding to good extensions. Following Castryck, Decru and Smith [9], there are 8 non-equivalent permutations of our a_i which correspond to good extensions of the previous $(2,2)$-isogeny. Our walks are deterministically defined by pseudorandom bitstrings. Each step uses three bits to choose which of the 8 good extensions defines our next $(2,2)$-isogeny. Using [9, Proposition 3], we define the function $\mathbf{a} \leftarrow$ PermuteKernel$(\mathbf{a}, \mathtt{bits})$ by

$$\mathbf{a} \leftarrow \begin{cases} (\mathbf{a}[0], \mathbf{a}[2], \mathbf{a}[1], \mathbf{a}[4], \mathbf{a}[3], \mathbf{a}[5]), & \mathtt{bits} = 0|0|0; \\ (\mathbf{a}[0], \mathbf{a}[2], \mathbf{a}[1], \mathbf{a}[5], \mathbf{a}[3], \mathbf{a}[4]), & \mathtt{bits} = 0|0|1; \\ (\mathbf{a}[0], \mathbf{a}[3], \mathbf{a}[1], \mathbf{a}[4], \mathbf{a}[2], \mathbf{a}[5]), & \mathtt{bits} = 0|1|0; \\ (\mathbf{a}[0], \mathbf{a}[3], \mathbf{a}[1], \mathbf{a}[5], \mathbf{a}[2], \mathbf{a}[4]), & \mathtt{bits} = 0|1|1; \\ (\mathbf{a}[0], \mathbf{a}[4], \mathbf{a}[1], \mathbf{a}[2], \mathbf{a}[3], \mathbf{a}[5]), & \mathtt{bits} = 1|0|0; \\ (\mathbf{a}[0], \mathbf{a}[4], \mathbf{a}[1], \mathbf{a}[3], \mathbf{a}[2], \mathbf{a}[5]), & \mathtt{bits} = 1|0|1; \\ (\mathbf{a}[0], \mathbf{a}[5], \mathbf{a}[1], \mathbf{a}[3], \mathbf{a}[2], \mathbf{a}[4]), & \mathtt{bits} = 1|1|0; \\ (\mathbf{a}[0], \mathbf{a}[5], \mathbf{a}[1], \mathbf{a}[2], \mathbf{a}[3], \mathbf{a}[4]), & \mathtt{bits} = 1|1|1. \end{cases}$$

Remark 1. Under a mild conjecture on the associated eigenvalues, Florit and Smith [23] show that despite Richelot isogeny graphs not having optimal expansion, walks of length $O(\log p)$ still approximate the stationary distribution on $\Gamma_2(2; p)$ [23, Theorem 6.1]. This statement is implicitly assuming that walks are

unrestricted, i.e., that each step can take any one of the 15 outgoing Richelot isogenies. In choosing to restrict each step in $\Gamma_2(2;p)$ to the 8 good edges
with the aim of avoiding fruitless cycles, we are under the implicit assumption
that these walks also rapidly approximate the stationary distribution. All of our
experiments over small primes produced results that support this assumption
(see Sect. 7), and Florit and Smith also comment in its favour [23, §6.4]. Nevertheless, if future research provides evidence to the contrary, modifying our walks
to include the 6 other extensions is straightforward. In this case we could either
aim to prohibit certain sequences of isogenies that cycle back to prior nodes,
or (since we abandon walks after a small number of steps – see below) simply
tolerate the possibility of revisiting prior nodes. Even if a walk did cycle back
and hit a prior node, in general we would have a 14^{-n} chance of continuing along
the same path for n steps thereafter.

Pseudorandom walks in the superspecial subgraph of $\Gamma_2(2;p)$. A given
step of our pseudorandom walk can now be defined as $\mathbf{a} \leftarrow \mathsf{Step}(\mathbf{a},\mathtt{bits})$, where
the function Step is simply given by

$$\mathsf{Step}(\mathbf{a},\mathtt{bits}) = \mathsf{RIsog}(\mathsf{PermuteKernel}(\mathbf{a},\mathtt{bits})).$$

Recall (from Lines 1 and 2 of Algorithm 1) that our goal is to find a path φ from
$A \in \mathcal{S}_2(p)$ to some $E_1 \times E_2 \in \mathcal{E}_2(p)$. In principle, one could continue walking
deterministically from the input node $A \in \mathcal{S}_2(p)$ for as long as it takes to find
the splitting $E_1 \times E_2 \in \mathcal{E}_2(p)$, but the length of this path would be $O(p)$. To
ensure a compact description of the solution, we instead take a relatively small
number of steps from $A \in \mathcal{S}_2(p)$ before abandoning a walk, returning back to
$A \in \mathcal{S}_2(p)$, and starting again.

Our implementation uses Magma's inbuilt function $\mathsf{SHA1}\colon \{0,1\}^* \to \{0,1\}^{160}$
to generate pseudorandom walks consisting of 160 Richelot isogeny steps
as follows. We start by setting $H_0 := \mathsf{StartingSeed}(\mathbf{a})$, where $\mathbf{a} \in (\mathbb{F}_{p^2})^6$
defines the input node $A \in \mathcal{S}_2(p)$, and where $\mathsf{StartingSeed}$ merely concate-
nates and parses the 12 $\mathbb{F}_p$ components of $\mathbf{a}$ in order to be fed as input into
$\mathsf{SHA1}$. We then define the function $\mathsf{Hash}\colon \{0,1\}^* \to \{0,1\}^{480}$ as $\mathsf{Hash}\colon s \mapsto$
$\mathsf{SHA1}(s)\|\mathsf{SHA1}^2(s)\|\mathsf{SHA1}^3(s)$, where $\mathsf{SHA1}^2(s)$ denotes $\mathsf{SHA1}(\mathsf{SHA1}(s))$, etc.
Our first walk in $\Gamma_2(2;p)$ is defined by $H_1 = \mathsf{Hash}(H_0)$; these 480 bits are used
(three bits at a time) to give 160 steps away from $A \in \mathcal{S}_2(p)$, at which point we
return back to $A \in \mathcal{S}_2(p)$ and repeat the process by using $H_{i+1} = \mathsf{Hash}(H_i)$ for
$i = 1, 2, \ldots$, until one of our calls to RIsog returns $\mathtt{split} = \mathtt{true}$, at which point
our walks have hit a node in $\mathcal{E}_2(p)$. To proceed to the elliptic curve path finding
in Steps 3 and 4 of Algorithm 1, the j-invariants of the elliptic curves in the
product of the final $(2,2)$-isogeny are determined using [9, §6.2]. This concludes
the description of our implementation of the generic product finding algorithm
from [13] that works entirely in $\Gamma_2(2;p)$.

Choice of Optimisations. In our search for product curves we use optimised
walks in $\Gamma_2(2;p)$, rather than adopting Castryck and Decru's multiradical isogenies [7] to walk in $\Gamma_2(3;p)$. Indeed, their hash function built from multiradical

$(3,3)$-isogenies between superspecial genus 2 Jacobians outperforms its $(2,2)$-counterpart by a factor ≈ 9. We first note that the bulk of the Castryck–Decru speedup comes from their hash function processing 3 trits of entropy per $(3,3)$-isogeny, rather than 3 bits of entropy processed by a $(2,2)$-isogeny. In our application, however, entropy is irrelevant and we are only interested in the raw cost of taking one step in the graph. Nevertheless, Castryck and Decru still report a $\approx 2.7\times$ speedup for a multiradical $(3,3)$-isogeny (which is dominated by 3 cube roots over $\mathbb{F}_{p^2}$) compared to a multiradical $(2,2)$-isogeny (which is dominated by 3 square roots over $\mathbb{F}_{p^2}$), with this factor coming directly from the relative performance of cube roots and square roots in $\mathbb{F}_{p^2}$ in Magma. In our implementation, we optimised explicit computation of the square roots in $\mathbb{F}_{p^2}$ in terms of $\mathbb{F}_p$ exponentiations and multiplications using the tricks in [45, §5.3], and we are unaware of analogous (or any) tricks in the cube root case that could outperform the square root computation.

Furthermore, we use walks in $\Gamma_2(2;p)$ that do not store or recycle any information from previous steps. Indeed, we could not see an obvious way to (re)use any of the three square roots in Line 7 of Algorithm 2 to compute the other 7 good extensions. We remark that this is a feature of our choice to walk using only good extensions, and we could in fact recycle these square roots to compute some of the *bad* extensions. If it turns out that there *is* a way to compute all 8 of the image tuples **a** in appreciably fewer operations than calling the RIsog algorithm on all 8 kernels individually, then one could define an octonary tree in an analogous fashion to the binary tree from [12].

4   Explicit Moduli Spaces for Genus 2 Curves with Split Jacobians

We give a brief review of some well known facts about genus 2 curves with split Jacobians and their moduli. The reader wishing for a more in-depth discussion is encouraged to consult e.g., [5, §2], [26,35], or [36].

4.1   The Igusa–Clebsch Invariants of a Genus 2 Curve

Let K be a field of characteristic not equal to 2. Let $\mathcal{M}_2$ denote the variety whose points $[C] \in \mathcal{M}_2(\overline{K})$ correspond to the $\overline{K}$-isomorphism classes of genus 2 curves $C/\overline{K}$.

From the invariant theory of the binary sextic, we may associate to any genus 2 curve C/K its Igusa–Clebsch invariants $I_2(C)$, $I_4(C)$, $I_6(C)$, and $I_{10}(C)$ (here the subscript denotes the weight of the invariant). Moreover the isomorphism class of $C/\overline{K}$ is uniquely determined by its Igusa–Clebsch invariants (see e.g., [31,42]).

This induces a birational K-morphism $\mathcal{M}_2 \hookrightarrow \mathbb{P}(2,4,6,10)$ given by associating to a class $[C]$ its Igusa–Clebsch invariants $[I_2(C) : I_4(C) : I_6(C) : I_{10}(C)]$.

Explicitly, if C/K is a genus 2 curve given by a Weierstrass equation

$$C: y^2 = (x - a_0) \cdots (x - a_5)$$

where $a_0, \ldots a_5 \in K$, we define:

$$I_2(C) := \sum_{15} (01)^2 (23)^2 (45)^2, \quad I_4(C) := \sum_{10} (01)^2 (12)^2 (20)^2 (34)^2 (45)^2 (53)^2,$$

$$I_6(C) := \sum_{60} (01)^2 (12)^2 (20)^2 (34)^2 (45)^2 (53)^2 (03)^2 (14)^2 (25)^2, \quad \text{and}$$

$$I_{10}(C) := \prod_{i<j} (a_i - a_j)^2,$$

where, for any permutation $\sigma \in S_6$, we let (ij) denote the difference $(a_{\sigma(i)} - a_{\sigma(j)})$. Here the sums are taken over all distinct expressions in the a_i as σ ranges over S_6; the subscripts denote the number of expressions in each sum.

4.2 Optimal Splittings of Jacobians of a Genus 2 Curves

Let C be a curve of genus 2 defined over a field K. Recall that we say the Jacobian $\mathrm{Jac}(C)$ of C is *split* (over K) if there exists a (polarised) separable K-isogeny $\phi \colon \mathrm{Jac}(C) \to E_1 \times E_2$ where E_1/K and E_2/K are elliptic curves[4].

To work explicitly with subvarieties of $\mathcal{M}_2$ which parametrise genus 2 curves with split Jacobians, we will restrict our focus to Jacobians which are split by an (N, N)-isogeny. However, without imposing further conditions on the isogeny, our subvarieties will not be irreducible. Following Bruin–Doerksen [5, §2], we make the following definition:

Definition 2. *Let K be a field, C/K be a curve of genus 2, and E/K be an elliptic curve. We say that a cover $\psi \colon C \to E$ of degree N is optimal if N is coprime to the characteristic of K and ψ does not factor through a non-trivial unramified covering.*

We say that a polarised separable isogeny $\phi \colon \mathrm{Jac}(C) \to E_1 \times E_2$ is an optimal (polarised) (N, N)-splitting if ϕ is an (N, N)-isogeny and the covering $C \to E_1$ induced by ϕ and the Abel–Jacobi map is optimal. In this case $\mathrm{Jac}(C)$ is said to be optimally (N, N)-split.

In our application N will be an integer ≤ 11 and K will be the finite field $\mathbb{F}_{p^2}$ for some prime number $p \gg 11$, so the assumption that ϕ is separable will be automatically satisfied.

In fact every splitting factors through an optimal (N, N)-splitting, more precisely:

Proposition 1. *If $\mathrm{Jac}(C)$ is split (over K) then there exists an integer $N \geq 2$ such that $\mathrm{Jac}(C)$ is optimally (N, N)-split (over K).*

Proof. We closely follow [5, Proposition 2.8]. Since $\mathrm{Jac}(C)$ is split, there exists a separable K-isogeny $\phi \colon \mathrm{Jac}(C) \to E_1 \times E_2$ where E_1/K and E_2/K are elliptic curves. Since ϕ is separable, there exists an elliptic curve D_1/K such that the

---

[4] The convention that ϕ is separable contrasts with, e.g., [5, Definition 2.1].

morphism $C \to E_1$ induced by the Abel–Jacobi map and ϕ factors through an optimal cover $\psi: C \to D_1$. By [5, Lemma 2.6], ψ gives rise to an optimal (N, N)-splitting $\mathrm{Jac}(C) \to D_1 \times D_2$, where D_2 is an elliptic curve and N is the degree of ψ.   □

4.3   The Surfaces $\widetilde{\mathcal{L}}_N$ and $\mathcal{L}_N$

We write $\widetilde{\mathcal{L}}_N$ for the surface whose K-points parametrise ($\overline{K}$-isomorphism classes of) pairs (C, ϕ) where C is a curve of genus 2 and $\phi: \mathrm{Jac}(C) \to E_1 \times E_2$ is an optimal (N, N)-splitting.

Replacing ϕ with its composition with the natural isomorphism $E_1 \times E_2 \to E_2 \times E_1$ gives an involution on $\widetilde{\mathcal{L}}_N$. We write $\mathcal{L}_N$ for the quotient of $\widetilde{\mathcal{L}}_N$ by this involution. The natural map $\widetilde{\mathcal{L}}_N \longrightarrow \mathcal{M}_2$, given by $(C, \phi) \longmapsto [C]$, factors via $\widetilde{\mathcal{L}}_N \to \mathcal{L}_N$.

Kumar [36] gave explicit models of the surface $\widetilde{\mathcal{L}}_N$ for each integer $N \leq 11$. In this range the surfaces $\mathcal{L}_N$ are rational (i.e., birational to $\mathbb{A}^2$), and they give an explicit model for the surface $\widetilde{\mathcal{L}}_N$ as a double cover of $\mathcal{L}_N$ together with the moduli interpretation of $\mathcal{L}_N$. More specifically, they compute rational functions $\mathcal{I}_2(r, s), \mathcal{I}_4(r, s), \mathcal{I}_6(r, s), \mathcal{I}_{10}(r, s)$ which (after an appropriate projective rescaling) may be taken to lie in $\mathbb{Z}[r, s]$ and for which the following diagram commutes

$$
\begin{array}{ccc}
\mathbb{A}^2 & \xdashrightarrow{\varphi_N} & \mathbb{P}(2, 4, 6, 10) \\
\vert & & \uparrow \\
\downarrow & & \vert \\
\mathcal{L}_N & \longrightarrow & \mathcal{M}_2
\end{array}
$$

Here the maps on the left and right are birational and the rational map φ_N is given by $(r, s) \mapsto [\mathcal{I}_2(r, s) : \mathcal{I}_4(r, s) : \mathcal{I}_6(r, s) : \mathcal{I}_{10}(r, s)]$.

We will employ the following lemma to detect whether a Jacobian $\mathrm{Jac}(C)$ is optimally (N, N)-split over $\overline{K}$.

Lemma 1. *The Jacobian of a genus 2 curve C/K is split over $\overline{K}$ if and only if there exists an integer $N \geq 2$ such that the point $[C] \in \mathcal{M}_2(\overline{K})$ lies in the image of $\mathcal{L}_N \to \mathcal{M}_2$.*

Proof. If $\mathrm{Jac}(C)$ is split, then it is optimally (N, N)-split for some integer $N \geq 2$ by Proposition 1. In this case, the corresponding point on $\mathcal{L}_N$ maps to $[C]$ on $\mathcal{M}_2$. Conversely, suppose $[C]$ lies in the image of $\mathcal{L}_N \to \mathcal{M}_2$. Since the morphism $\widetilde{\mathcal{L}}_N \to \mathcal{L}_N$ is a surjection on $\overline{K}$-points, there exists an optimal degree N cover $\phi: C \to E$ such that the preimage of $[C]$ under this morphism is $(C, \phi) \in \widetilde{\mathcal{L}}_N(\overline{K})$. Hence $\mathrm{Jac}(C)$ is split.   □

Remark 2. Genus 2 curves C/K with split Jacobians have appeared many times elsewhere in the literature. Indeed when $N \leq 4$ generic families were known classically from work of Legendre, Jacobi, Hermite, Grousat, Burkhardt, Brioschi, and Bolza (as discussed in [36]). More recently, Shaska [46] gave a method for general N for computing the surface $\widetilde{\mathcal{L}}_N$ together with a curve $C/K(\widetilde{\mathcal{L}}_N)$ such that $\mathrm{Jac}(C)$ is (N, N)-isogenous to a product $E_1 \times E_2$. Explicit computations have been performed for $2 \leq N \leq 5$ by Shaska, Magaard, Volklein, Wijesiri, Wolf, and Woodland [40,47–50] and by Gaudry–Schost [27], Bröker–Lauter–Howe–Stevenhagen [4], Bruin–Doerksen [5], and Djukanović [17,18]. If $\mathrm{Jac}(C)$ is (N, N)-isogenous over K to a product of elliptic curves $E_1 \times E_2$ there exists an anti-symplectic Galois equivariant isomorphism $E_1[N] \cong E_2[N]$ (see e.g., [5, Proposition 2.8]). For $N > 11$ this has been considered by Fisher when $N = 13, 17$ [20,21] and Frengley when $N = 12$ [25]. However, while they give the generic elliptic curves E_1 and E_2, they do not give the genus 2 curve C.

4.4   The Image of the Morphism $\mathcal{L}_N \to \mathcal{M}_2$

Recall that we have a map $\mathcal{L}_N \to \mathcal{M}_2 \to \mathbb{P}(2, 4, 6, 10)$ given by the Igusa–Clebsch invariants. The (Zariski closure of) the image of this map is a projective surface given by the vanishing of a polynomial $F_N \in \mathbb{Z}[I_2, I_4, I_6, I_{10}]$ which is homogeneous with respect to the weights.

If K is a field of characteristic coprime to $2N$, the Jacobian of a genus 2 curve C/K is optimally (N, N)-split over $\overline{K}$ if and only if

$$F_N(I_2(C), I_4(C), I_6(C), I_{10}(C)) = 0.$$

For $2 \leq N \leq 5$ the polynomial F_N was computed by Bruin–Doerksen [5,6, Theorem 1.2] and Shaska, Magaard, Volklein, Wijesiri, Wolf, and Woodland [40, 48,50].

Such equations may be computed from Kumar's formulae [36]. For each $N \leq 5$ we interpolate the image of φ_N modulo a small number of primes of approximately 128 bits. Lifting these equations to characteristic zero with the LLL algorithm gives a candidate for F_N.

Since F_N is an irreducible polynomial and the image of φ_N is an irreducible variety, we verify the result in **Magma** by checking that F_N vanishes at the equations defining φ_N. These polynomials are available in the code accompanying this article, and their properties are summarised in Table 2.

Table 2. The number of monomials in the defining equation F_N for the image of $\mathcal{L}_N$ in $\mathbb{P}(2, 4, 6, 10)$ and the total number of bytes required to (naively) store the coefficients of each F_N.

N	Weighted degree of F_N	Number of monomials in F_N	Average bitlength of the coefficients of F_N
2	30	34	~ 16.6
3	80	318	~ 64.3
4	180	2699	~ 197
5	480	43410	~ 617

5   Efficient Detection of (N, N)-Splittings

In this section we present an algorithm to efficiently detect whether, at each step, the p.p. abelian surface $\mathrm{Jac}(C)$ is (N, N)-isogenous (over $\overline{\mathbb{F}}_p$) to a product of elliptic curves, without ever computing an (N, N)-isogeny. In this way we are able to use resultants and gcd computations, rather than inefficient computations of (N, N)-isogenies, therefore avoiding all N^{th}-root calculations and the need to work in extension fields when the N-torsion is not fully $\mathbb{F}_{p^2}$-rational.

A natural starting point to perform this detection is to exploit the equations F_N for the image of the morphism $\mathcal{L}_N \to \mathbb{P}(2, 4, 6, 10)$ (see Sect. 4.4). Indeed, if a genus 2 curve $C/\mathbb{F}_{p^2}$ is (N, N)-split, then $F_N(I_2(C), I_4(C), I_6(C), I_{10}(C)) = 0$. However, as demonstrated in Table 2, both the number of monomials in F_N and the bitlength of its coefficients grow rapidly with N. As a result, computing and storing F_N for $N > 5$ is challenging. Instead, we will use techniques in elimination theory to determine whether $[C]$ lies on the (Zariski closure of) the image of φ_N. Indeed, even for $N \le 5$, evaluating the image at the Igusa–Clebsch invariants of C will not outperform this method.

Lemma 2. *Let $N \ge 2$ be an integer and C/K be a genus 2 curve defined over a field K of characteristic not dividing $2N$. Suppose that the Igusa–Clebsch invariants $I_2(C)$, $I_4(C)$, $I_6(C)$, and $I_{10}(C)$ are non-zero. Write $\alpha_1(C) = \frac{I_4(C)}{I_2(C)^2}$, $\alpha_2(C) = \frac{I_2(C)I_4(C)}{I_6(C)}$, and $\alpha_3(C) = \frac{I_4(C)I_6(C)}{I_{10}(C)}$. If there exist $r_0 \in \overline{K} \cup \{\infty\}$ and $s_0 \in \overline{K}$ satisfying*

$$\begin{cases} \alpha_1(C) = \frac{\mathcal{I}_4(r_0, s_0)}{\mathcal{I}_2(r_0, s_0)^2}, \\ \alpha_2(C) = \frac{\mathcal{I}_2(r_0, s_0)\mathcal{I}_4(r_0, s_0)}{\mathcal{I}_6(r_0, s_0)}, \\ \alpha_3(C) = \frac{\mathcal{I}_4(r_0, s_0)\mathcal{I}_6(r_0, s_0)}{\mathcal{I}_{10}(r_0, s_0)}, \end{cases}$$

then $\mathrm{Jac}(C)$ is optimally (N, N)-split over $\overline{K}$. Here $\mathcal{I}_w(r, s)$ are as in Sect. 4.3.

Proof. The rational map $\psi \colon \mathbb{P}(2, 4, 6, 10) \dashrightarrow \mathbb{A}^3$ given by $[I_2 : I_4 : I_6 : I_{10}] \mapsto \left(\frac{I_4}{I_2^2}, \frac{I_2 I_4}{I_6}, \frac{I_4 I_6}{I_{10}} \right)$ is birational with inverse $(\alpha_1, \alpha_2, \alpha_3) \mapsto \left[1 : \alpha_1 : \frac{\alpha_1}{\alpha_2} : \frac{\alpha_1^2}{\alpha_2 \alpha_3} \right]$. Moreover on the open subvariety of $\mathbb{P}(2, 4, 6, 10)$ where I_2, I_4, I_6, and I_{10} are nonzero the map ψ restricts to an isomorphism onto its image. The claim follows from the discussion preceding the lemma. $\square$

Remark 3. It is common in the literature (e.g., [5, 32]) to choose the affine patch with coordinates the *absolute invariants* $\frac{6(I_2^2 - 16 I_4)}{I_2^2}$, $\frac{-12(5 I_2^3 - 176 I_2 I_4 + 384 I_6)}{I_2^3}$, and $\frac{3888 I_{10}}{I_2^5}$. Our choice is *ad hoc* and made to optimise the algorithms in Sect. 5.2. In particular, the choice in Lemma 2 yields polynomials $P_{i,j}$ in Lemma 3 of smaller degree. Choosing an affine patch of $\mathbb{P}(2, 4, 6, 10)$ so that the analogous polynomials to $P_{i,j}$ in Lemma 3 have minimal degree would likely lead to improved performance of our algorithm.

Remark 4. In the code accompanying this article we provide a function Invari-antsFromWeierstrassPoints that, on input of the 6-tuple $\mathbf{a} = (a_0, \ldots, a_5) \in (\mathbb{F}_{p^2})^6$ of Weierstrass points, computes the 3-tuple $\boldsymbol{\alpha}(C) = (\alpha_1(C), \alpha_2(C), \alpha_3(C)) \in (\mathbb{F}_{p^2})^3$ using a total of 291 multiplications and one (merged) inversion in $\mathbb{F}_p$. This is the first step of Algorithm 4.

Define polynomials $f_k(r, s) \in \mathbb{Z}[\alpha_1, \alpha_2, \alpha_3][r, s]$ by

$$f_1(r, s) = \mathcal{I}_4(r, s) - \alpha_1 \mathcal{I}_2(r, s)^2,$$
$$f_2(r, s) = \mathcal{I}_2(r, s)\mathcal{I}_4(r, s) - \alpha_2 \mathcal{I}_6(r, s),$$
$$f_3(r, s) = \mathcal{I}_4(r, s)\mathcal{I}_6(r, s) - \alpha_3 \mathcal{I}_{10}(r, s).$$

The following proposition follows immediately from Lemma 2.

Proposition 2. *Suppose that C/K is a genus 2 curve with non-zero Igusa–Clebsch invariants. If there exist $r_0 \in \overline{K} \cup \{\infty\}$ and $s_0 \in \overline{K}$ such that for each $w \in \{2, 4, 6, 10\}$ we have $\mathcal{I}_w(r_0, s_0) \neq 0$ and $f_k(r_0, s_0) = 0$, then $\mathrm{Jac}(C)$ is optimally (N, N)-split over $\overline{K}$.*

In Sect. 5.2 we describe a method for determining whether, given a genus 2 curve $C/\mathbb{F}_p$ with superspecial Jacobian, there exists a point $P \in \mathbb{A}^2(\overline{\mathbb{F}}_p)$ such that the polynomials $f_k(r, s)$ vanish at P. Moreover, we determine lower bounds on their costs in terms of $\mathbb{F}_p$-multiplications for each $N \in \{2, 3, \ldots, 11\}$.

5.1   The Resultants of f_j and f_k

Fix an integer $2 \leq N \leq 11$. For each distinct pair $i, j \in \{1, 2, 3\}$, define polynomials[5]

$$R_{i,j}(s) := \mathrm{res}_r(f_i(r, s), f_j(r, s)) \in \mathbb{Z}[\alpha_1, \alpha_2, \alpha_3][s].$$

If C/K is a genus 2 curve then, since resultants are invariant under ring homomorphisms, by the elimination property of the resultant (see e.g., [14, §3.6 Lemma 1]) the specialisations $(R_{i,j})_{[C]}(s) \in K[s]$, given by evaluating the coefficients of $R_{i,j}(s)$ at $\alpha_1(C)$, $\alpha_2(C)$, and $\alpha_3(C)$, vanish at the s-coordinate of any common solution to the specialised polynomials $(f_j)_{[C]}(r, s)$.

However, these resultants (generically) have factors which correspond to unwanted solutions (i.e., where one of the polynomials $\mathcal{I}_w$ vanishes). We make this more precise in the following lemma.

Lemma 3. *Let $L = \mathbb{Q}(\alpha_1, \alpha_2, \alpha_3)$. When $i \neq j$, there exist polynomials $Q_{i,j} \in \mathbb{Z}[\alpha_1, \alpha_2, \alpha_3][s]$ dividing $R_{i,j}$ with the following property: for each pair $r_0, s_0 \in \overline{L}$ such that $f_k(r_0, s_0) = 0$ for $k = 1, 2, 3$ and $Q_{i,j}(s_0) = 0$, then $\mathcal{I}_w(r_0, s_0) = 0$ for some $w \in \{2, 4, 6, 10\}$.*

Moreover, the polynomials $P_{i,j} = \frac{R_{i,j}}{Q_{i,j}} \in \mathbb{Z}[\alpha_1, \alpha_2, \alpha_3][s]$ are coprime.

---

[5] If necessary, we swap the roles of Kumar's r and s so that the polynomials $P_{i,j}$ from Lemma 3 are of lowest degree (as noted in the accompanying code). It would be interesting to find a birational transformation of $\mathbb{A}^2$ which minimises $\deg P_{i,j}$.

Proof. This follows from a direct calculation in `Magma`.   □

Applying [14, §3.6 Corollary 7] we have:

Proposition 3. *Let C/K be a genus 2 curve such that $I_w(C) \neq 0$ for each $w \in \{2, 4, 6, 10\}$. If there exist $r_0, s_0 \in \overline{K}$ such that $(f_i)_{[C]}(r_0, s_0) = 0$ for each $i = 1, 2, 3$ then the degree of $\gcd((P_{1,2})_{[C]}, (P_{2,3})_{[C]})$ is at least 1.*

Conversely if $s_0 \in \overline{K}$ is a root of $\gcd((P_{1,2})_{[C]}, (P_{2,3})_{[C]})$ then there exist $r_0, r_0' \in \overline{K} \cup \{\infty\}$ such that $(f_1)_{[C]}(r_0, s_0) = (f_2)_{[C]}(r_0, s_0) = 0$ and $(f_1)_{[C]}(r_0', s_0) = (f_2)_{[C]}(r_0', s_0) = 0$.

5.2   An Algorithm to Detect (N, N)-Split Jacobians

We now present our algorithm to efficiently detect whether the Jacobian of a genus 2 curve $C/\mathbb{F}_{p^2}$ is (N, N)-split for some integer $2 \leq N \leq 11$. In Proposition 4 we then give an upper bound on the number of $\mathbb{F}_p$-multiplications required by the algorithm.

Precomputation step. We reduce the coefficients of the polynomials $P_{1,2}, P_{2,3} \in \mathbb{Z}[\alpha_1, \alpha_2, \alpha_3][s]$ from Lemma 3 modulo p to obtain polynomials $\widetilde{P}_{1,2}, \widetilde{P}_{2,3} \in \mathbb{F}_p[\alpha_1, \alpha_2, \alpha_3][s]$, which are stored.

Evaluation and gcd step. Our approach is summarised in Algorithm 3. To test a given genus 2 curve $C/\mathbb{F}_{p^2}$ with superspecial Jacobian, we specialise the coefficients of $\widetilde{P}_{1,2}, \widetilde{P}_{2,3}$ at $\boldsymbol{\alpha}(C) = (\alpha_1(C), \alpha_2(C), \alpha_3(C))$, by running the algorithm EvalCoeffs, to obtain the polynomials $(\widetilde{P}_{1,2})_{[C]}, (\widetilde{P}_{2,3})_{[C]} \in \mathbb{F}_{p^2}[s]$. The EvalCoeffs algorithm takes as input $\widetilde{P}_{i,j}$ and the invariants $\boldsymbol{\alpha}(C)$, and evaluates the coefficients of the polynomial at these invariants (see the proof of Proposition 4 for more details).

We then compute the gcd of $(\widetilde{P}_{1,2})_{[C]}$ and $(\widetilde{P}_{2,3})_{[C]}$ using the "inversion-free gcd" algorithm InvFreeGCD from [12, Algorithm 1], modified to output the gcd explicitly, rather than a boolean.

If this gcd has degree ≥ 1 then it has a root $s_0 \in \overline{\mathbb{F}}_p$ and (by Proposition 3) there exist $r_0, r_0' \in \overline{\mathbb{F}}_p \cup \{\infty\}$ such that $(f_1)_{[C]}(r_0, s_0) = (f_2)_{[C]}(r_0, s_0) = 0$ and $(f_1)_{[C]}(r_0', s_0) = (f_2)_{[C]}(r_0', s_0) = 0$. By Proposition 2 to verify that $\mathrm{Jac}(C)$ is (N, N)-split it suffices to show that we may take $r_0 = r_0'$ such that $\mathcal{I}_w(r_0, s_0) \neq 0$ for each $w \in \{2, 4, 6, 10\}$. We verify the first condition by computing the gcd of $(f_1)_{[C]}(r, s_0), (f_2)_{[C]}(r, s_0), (f_3)_{[C]}(r, s_0)$, and if it has degree ≥ 1 computing a root $r_0 \in \overline{\mathbb{F}}_p$. We verify the second condition by checking that $\mathcal{I}_w(r_0, s_0) \neq 0$ for each $w \in \{2, 4, 6, 10\}$ – we abbreviate this to the function IsNonzero.

Remark 5. If $\mathrm{Jac}(C)$ is optimally (N, N)-split then Algorithm 3 will return true with high probability. In this case $[C]$ is an $\mathbb{F}_{p^2}$-point on $\mathcal{L}_N$. Since $\varphi_N \colon \mathbb{A}^2 \dashrightarrow \mathcal{L}_N$ is birational (over $\mathbb{F}_p$) it is an isomorphism outside a closed $\mathbb{F}_p$-subvariety $X \subseteq \mathcal{L}_N$ of dimension 1. But from the Weil conjectures $\#\mathcal{L}_N(\mathbb{F}_{p^2}) = O(p^4)$ and $\#X(\mathbb{F}_{p^2}) = O(p^2)$. In particular except in $O(1/p^2)$ of cases there exist $r_0, s_0 \in \overline{\mathbb{F}}_p$ satisfying the conditions of Proposition 3.

Algorithm 3. IsSplit($\alpha(C), \widetilde{P}_{1,2}, \widetilde{P}_{2,3}, N$):

Input: A tuple $\alpha(C) = (\alpha_1(C), \alpha_2(C), \alpha_3(C))$, the polynomials $\widetilde{P}_{1,2}, \widetilde{P}_{2,3} \in \mathbb{F}_p[\alpha_1, \alpha_2, \alpha_3][r]$, and an integer $2 \leq N \leq 11$.
Output: A boolean which is true if Jac(C) is optimally (N, N)-split.

1: $(\widetilde{P}_{1,2})_{[C]} \leftarrow \mathsf{EvalCoeffs}(\widetilde{P}_{1,2}, \alpha(C))$
2: $(\widetilde{P}_{2,3})_{[C]} \leftarrow \mathsf{EvalCoeffs}(\widetilde{P}_{2,3}, \alpha(C))$
3: $g \leftarrow \mathsf{InvFreeGCD}((\widetilde{P}_{1,2})_{[C]}, (\widetilde{P}_{2,3})_{[C]})$
4: **if** deg $g \geq 1$ **then**
5:    $s_0 \leftarrow \mathsf{ComputeRoot}(g)$
6:    $(\widetilde{f}_1)_{[C]} \leftarrow \mathsf{EvalCoeffs}(\widetilde{f}_1, \alpha(C))$
7:    $(\widetilde{f}_2)_{[C]} \leftarrow \mathsf{EvalCoeffs}(\widetilde{f}_2, \alpha(C))$
8:    $(\widetilde{f}_3)_{[C]} \leftarrow \mathsf{EvalCoeffs}(\widetilde{f}_3, \alpha(C))$
9:    $h \leftarrow \mathsf{InvFreeGCD}(\mathsf{InvFreeGCD}((\widetilde{f}_1)_{[C]}(r, s_0), (\widetilde{f}_2)_{[C]}(r, s_0)), (\widetilde{f}_3)_{[C]}(r, s_0))$
10:    **if** deg $h \geq 1$ **then**
11:      $r_0 \leftarrow \mathsf{ComputeRoot}(h)$
12:      bool $\leftarrow \mathsf{IgNonzero}(r_0, s_0)$
13:      **if** bool $==$ **true** **then**
14:         **return true**
15: **return false**

The cost of Algorithm 3. We now determine an upper bound for the number of $\mathbb{F}_p$-multiplications required for the online part of this method (i.e., ignoring the cost of precomputation). In the analysis that follows we assume that Karatsuba multiplication is used in $\mathbb{F}_{p^2}$, hence we cost one $\mathbb{F}_{p^2}$-multiplication as three $\mathbb{F}_p$-multiplications.

Proposition 4. *Let $N \in \{2, \ldots, 11\}$ be an integer, and let mons(N) be the set of monomials in $\alpha_1, \alpha_2, \alpha_3$ appearing in the coefficients of $\widetilde{P}_{1,2}$ and $\widetilde{P}_{2,3}$ (which lie in $\mathbb{F}_p[\alpha_1, \alpha_2, \alpha_3]$). For each $i = 1, 2, 3$, let*

$$d_i(N) = \max(\{\text{degree of } \alpha_i \text{ in } m \mid m \in \mathsf{mons}(N)\}).$$

The cost of steps 1–3 in Algorithm 3 (with input N) is at most

$$3(d_1(N) + d_2(N) + d_3(N)) + 6m(N) + 2M(N) + \frac{3}{2}(d_P(N) + 2)(d_P(N) + 3) - 27$$

$\mathbb{F}_p$-multiplications, where $d_P(N) = \deg \widetilde{P}_{1,2} + \deg \widetilde{P}_{2,3}$, $m(N) = \#\mathsf{mons}(N)$, and $M(N)$ is the number of monomials in $\alpha_1, \alpha_2, \alpha_3$ appearing in the coefficients of $\widetilde{P}_{1,2}$ and $\widetilde{P}_{2,3}$ counting repetitions.

Proof. We first evaluate the coefficients of $\widetilde{P}_{1,2}, \widetilde{P}_{2,3} \in \mathbb{F}_{p^2}[\alpha_1, \alpha_2, \alpha_3][s]$ at the normalised invariants $\alpha_1(C), \alpha_2(C), \alpha_3(C) \in \mathbb{F}_{p^2}$ using our evaluation algorithm $\mathsf{EvalCoeffs}$ on each polynomial. This runs as follows. We first compute powers $\alpha_1(C)^2, \ldots, \alpha_1(C)^{d_1(N)}$ where $d_1(N)$ is the maximum degree of α_1 appearing in mons(N) (as defined in the statement of the proposition). Similarly we compute powers of $\alpha_2(C)$ and $\alpha_3(C)$ up to $d_2(N)$ and $d_3(N)$ respectively. This step is performed using $d_1(N) + d_2(N) + d_3(N) - 3$ multiplications in $\mathbb{F}_{p^2}$.

From these powers, we obtain the monomials appearing in the coefficients of $(\widetilde{P}_{1,2})_{[C]}(s)$ and $(\widetilde{P}_{2,3})_{[C]}(s)$ in at most $2m(N)$ $\mathbb{F}_{p^2}$-multiplications, where $m(N) = \#\text{mons}(N)$. We then require $2M(N)$ $\mathbb{F}_p$-multiplications (and $2M(N)$ additions) to construct the coefficients of $(\widetilde{P}_{1,2})_{[C]}$ and $(\widetilde{P}_{2,3})_{[C]}$.

The final step computes the gcd of $(\widetilde{P}_{1,2})_{[C]}$ and $(\widetilde{P}_{2,3})_{[C]}$ using InvFreeGCD. This requires $\frac{3}{2}(d_P(N) + 2)(d_P(N) + 3) - 18$ $\mathbb{F}_p$-multiplications by [12, Proposition 2]. □

The cost from Proposition 4 depends only on N. Therefore, for each $2 \leq N \leq 11$, we can determine the total number of $\mathbb{F}_p$-multiplications required for the detection per node revealed in $\mathcal{S}_2(p)$ for any prime p. We give these costs in Table 3.

Noting that, when $N \neq N'$ we may have non-empty intersection $\text{mons}(N) \cap \text{mons}(N')$, our implementation of Algorithm 4 stores all evaluated monomials to avoid repeated computations. In particular, the upper bound in Proposition 4 is often not sharp.

Table 3. Values of $d_1(N), d_2(N), d_3(N), m(N), M(N)$, and $d_P(N)$ for $N \in \{2, \ldots, 11\}$. The final columns respectively list the number of $\mathbb{F}_p$-multiplications in Proposition 4 and the ratio of multiplications to the number of (N, N)-isogenous p.p. abelian surfaces.

N	$d_1(N)$	$d_2(N)$	$d_3(N)$	$m(N)$	$M(N)$	$d_P(N)$	Total #$\mathbb{F}_p$ mults.	Total #$\mathbb{F}_p$ mults. per node revealed
2	1	2	1	6	23	6	175	12.5
3	2	3	2	11	97	16	767	19.2
4	6	8	6	78	1136	35	4882	46.9
5	6	10	6	64	2500	92	18818	120.6
6	7	11	7	91	4118	114	29188	52.1
7	10	14	10	190	24779	294	182641	456.6
8	16	24	16	433	73454	340	325606	395.2
9	12	16	12	271	69648	540	582474	539.3
10	24	32	24	1005	260178	606	1082007	495.4
11	28	38	28	1345	669432	1120	3237198	2211.2

Remark 6. We note that, in practice, when our algorithm enters the if loop on Line 4 in Algorithm 3, we have yet to encounter a case where Steps 5–14 fail to return true. In these cases the bound in Proposition 4 yields a bound on the cost of Algorithm 3. It is however possible to construct examples of polynomials for which they would be necessary – e.g., $f_1(r, s) = r - 1$, $f_2(r, s) = s - r(r + 1)(r - 1)$, and $f_3(r, s) = r + 1$. It would be interesting to put this observation on rigorous footing by showing that with overwhelming probability the roots r_0 and r_0' guaranteed by Proposition 3 are equal.

Alternative approach for $N = 10$ **and** 11. When $N = 10, 11$, several megabytes are required to store the coefficients of the polynomials $\tilde{P}_{i,j}$. Rather than computing the resultants $R_{1,2}$ and $R_{2,3}$ and dividing out by the generic factors described in Lemma 3 to obtain $P_{1,2}$, $P_{2,3}$ as a precomputation, the approach we pursued was to instead perform these two steps during the online phase. Even still, our experiments (which were reinforced by the cost analysis above) revealed that performing the detection for $N = 10, 11$ is suboptimal in our application to SplitSearcher (shown in Algorithm 4) and slows the overall search down, even when the characteristic of the field is very large. Thus, we leave the further optimisation of these computations as future work.

6   The Full Algorithm

In Sect. 3 we discussed our optimised implementation of the product-finding attack [13] that works entirely in the Richelot isogeny graph $\Gamma_2(2; p)$. In this section, we present SplitSearcher, which leverages our efficient detection of (N, N)-splittings from Sect. 5.2 to improve on the concrete complexity of product-finding when solving the dimension 2 isogeny problem.

6.1   SplitSearcher

Each time we take a step using a Richelot isogeny, we will use the methods from the previous section to detect whether the current node is (N, N)-isogenous to a product of elliptic curves, for some subset of integers in $2 \leq N \leq 11$. Using the algorithm from Sect. 5.2 makes this check much more efficient than, say, walking in $\Gamma_2(N; p)$; each node we step to would require computing an (N, N)-isogeny which, at minimum, requires three N-th roots in $\mathbb{F}_{p^2}$ [7].

Each time we take a step and arrive at a new abelian surface, A, we are in one of two cases: either A is isomorphic to a product of elliptic curves, in which case the algorithm terminates, or A is isomorphic to the Jacobian of a genus 2 curve $C/\mathbb{F}_{p^2}$. In the latter case, SplitSearcher calls Algorithm 3 to detect whether A is (N, N)-split for certain $2 \leq N \leq 11$. The set of N's for which this detection is performed is chosen to minimise the number of $\mathbb{F}_p$-multiplications per node revealed (either by stepping on them in $\Gamma_2(2; p)$ or inspecting them via our splitting detection) in $\mathcal{S}_2(p)$. Since it only depends on the prime p, determining this optimal list of N's is performed during precomputation.

If Algorithm 3 determines that A is (N, N)-split, the elliptic curves E_1 and E_2 can be recovered by applying [39, Algorithm 4] to compute all (N, N)-isogenies from A (alternatively, E_1 and E_2 may be recovered from Kumar's equations [36] by solving for r_0 and s_0 in Proposition 2). As both of these costs are negligible and do not affect the cost of finding such a splitting, we may view this as a post-computation step and exclude it from our multiplication counts.

A precise formulation of the full algorithm for finding paths to elliptic curve products is given by Algorithm 4. Along with the target abelian surface $A \in \mathcal{S}_2(p)$, the auxiliary inputs into the algorithm are the polynomials

$\widetilde{P}_{1,2}, \widetilde{P}_{2,3} \in \mathbb{F}_p[\alpha_1, \alpha_2, \alpha_3][r]$ (see Lemma 3), and the optimal set $\mathcal{N} \subseteq \{2, \ldots, 11\}$ (see Sect. 6.2). The hash function on Line 4 is assumed to be of the form $\mathsf{Hash} \colon \{0, 1\}^* \to \{0, 1\}^{3\ell}$, where ℓ is a positive integer, since we use three bits of entropy each time we call the Richelot isogeny (i.e., Step algorithm) in Line 13. In practice we choose ℓ to be large enough that we can expect to find an elliptic product in walks of ℓ steps, but not *too* large, since storing walks of up to ℓ steps requires more storage on average. Once the 3ℓ bits of entropy have been consumed, the hash function is called again and the walk is restarted from a_{start} (more on this in Remark 7). The output returned by Algorithm 4 is of the form (path, N), where path is a sequence of $3k$ bits (with $k \leq \ell$) and N is an integer: the $3k$ bits define a sequence of k Richelot isogenies and the integer N specifies the final (N, N)-isogeny whose image is in $\mathcal{E}_2(p)$.

Algorithm 4. SplitSearcher: finding paths to elliptic curve products

Input: $a_{\mathrm{start}} = (a_0, \ldots, a_5) \in (\mathbb{F}_{p^2})^6$ defining a genus 2 curve $C/\mathbb{F}_{p^2}$ with superspecial Jacobian, and a set $\mathcal{N} \subseteq \{2, 3, \ldots, 11\}$.

Output: A pair (path, N) where path is a path $\varphi \colon \mathrm{Jac}(C) \to \mathrm{Jac}(C')$ in $\Gamma_2(2; p)$ and N is an integer such that $\mathrm{Jac}(C')$ is optimally (N, N)-split.

```
 1: split ← false
 2: H ← StartingSeed(a_start)                                              §3.1
 3: while not split do
 4:    (H, i, path, a) ← (Hash(H), 0, {∅}, a_start)
 5:    while i < ℓ and not split do
 6:       if N ≠ ∅ then
 7:          α(C) ← InvariantsFromWeierstrassPoints(a)                  Remark 4
 8:          for N ∈ N do
 9:             split ← IsSplit(α(C), P̃_1,2, P̃_2,3, N)              Algorithm 3
10:             if split then
11:                return (path, N)
12:       bits ← H[3i] ‖ H[3i + 1] ‖ H[3i + 2]
13:       a, split ← Step(a, bits)                                         §3.2
14:       path ← path ‖ bits
15:       i ← i + 1
16: return (path, 2)
```

Remark 7. In a real-world attack, we would expect to return to Line 4 of Algorithm 4 an exponential number of times before the algorithm terminates. Thus, there are a number of ways one could recycle information computed in the early stages of each walk to avoid recomputing them over and over again. One solution that is easy to implement in view of Algorithm 4 would be to store a hash table whose entries each correspond to the (hash of the) Igusa–Clebsch invariants of any node that is visited and checked for (N, N)-splittings. Upon returning to a given node and finding a collision in the hash table, the walk could simply avoid the tests for (N, N)-splittings between Lines 8 and 11. Another approach would be to build a table of the six-tuples $\boldsymbol{a}$ that are computed after the first t Richelot steps have been taken, alongside the label of the $3t$-bit string that took us there. Each time we return back to Line 4 and iterate the hash function, we simply check to see if the first $3t$ bits are already in the table and, if so, we can skip straight to $\boldsymbol{a}$.

Finally, as is mentioned in [13], parallelising the search for product curves is trivial. For P processors, we would simply compute P unique short walks from our target surface $A \in \mathcal{S}_2(p)$ and send each of the corresponding image surfaces $A_1, \ldots, A_P$ to a unique processor as its assigned input surface.

6.2   Determining the Optimal Set $\mathcal{N}$

Recall that, when we step to a new p.p. abelian surface $A \in \mathcal{S}_2(p)$, we want to determine if it is (N, N)-split for a set $\mathcal{N} \subseteq \{2, \ldots, 11\}$ of N. We wish to determine the optimal subset $\mathcal{N} \subseteq \{2, \ldots, 11\}$, i.e., the subset which minimises the number of $\mathbb{F}_p$-multiplications per node revealed in the graph. The first step towards determining this 'multiplications-per-node' ratio is to count the number of nodes in $\mathcal{S}_2(p)$ that are inspected inside the `for` loop of Algorithm 4 with a finite set of integers $\mathcal{N} \subseteq \mathbb{Z}_{\geq 2}$. A first attempt would be to simply count the number of neighbours a node $A \in \mathcal{S}_2(p)$ has in $\Gamma(N; p)$, i.e., D_N given by Equation (1) in Sect. 2. However, this is an overcount as we now detail.

Suppose we take a non-backtracking walk

$$A_0 \xrightarrow{\phi_0} A_1 \xrightarrow{\phi_1} \cdots \xrightarrow{\phi_{n-1}} A_n \xrightarrow{\phi_n} \cdots \tag{2}$$

in $\Gamma_2(2; p)$ and we inspect (N, N)-splittings for $N \in \mathcal{N}$. If $0 \leq m \leq n$ are integers, let $\phi_{m,n}$ denote the $(2^{n-m}, 2^{n-m})$-isogeny $\phi_{m-1} \circ \cdots \circ \phi_n$ and let $\phi_{n,m}$ denote $\widehat{\phi_{m,n}}$.

Firstly, if both N and $2^k N$ are contained in $\mathcal{N}$ (for $k \geq 1$), then any abelian surfaces (N, N)-isogenous to A_n are automatically $(2^k N, 2^k N)$-isogenous to A_{n+k}. Therefore, we restrict to only considering subsets $\mathcal{N}$ which do not contain pairs of integers $M \neq N$ with $N = 2^k M$.

This restriction is not sufficient to stop double-counting nodes. Indeed, suppose $N \in \mathcal{N}$ with $N = 2M$. Then any abelian surface (N, N)-isogenous to A_n will be (M, M)-isogenous to A_{n+1}. In particular such an abelian surface will also be (N, N)-isogenous to A_{n+2}. To rule out such scenarios, we introduce the following restriction on our paths.

Definition 3. *Let $\mathcal{N} \subseteq \mathbb{Z}_{\geq 2}$ be a finite set of integers and let $\mathcal{P}$ be a walk of $(2, 2)$-isogenies in $\Gamma_2(2; p)$ as in (2).*

Let $M, N \in \mathcal{N}$ and suppose that there exist integers $m, n \geq 0$ and (M, M)- and (N, N)-isogenies $\psi_M \colon A_m \to B$ and $\psi_N \colon A_n \to B$. We say that $\mathcal{P}$ resists collisions for M, N if there exists an integer $i \geq 0$ and an isogeny $\Psi \colon A_i \to B$ such that $\psi_M = \Psi \circ \phi_{m,i}$ and $\psi_N = \Psi \circ \phi_{n,i}$.

We say that $\mathcal{P}$ resists collisions for $\mathcal{N}$ if it resists collisions for every pair $M, N \in \mathcal{N}$.

We are now able to state precisely the number of nodes checked between Lines 8–11 of Algorithm 4, assuming our paths resist collisions for the set $\mathcal{N}$.

Lemma 4. *Let $\mathcal{N} \subseteq \mathbb{Z}_{\geq 2}$ be a finite set of integers such that if $\mathcal{N}$ is non-empty, then there do not exist distinct $M, N \in \mathcal{N}$ with $N = 2^k M$ for any $k \geq 1$.*

Let $\mathcal{P}$ be a path in $\Gamma_2(2; p)$ which resists collisions for $\mathcal{N}$. The number of nodes inspected per step by running Algorithm 4 in $\mathcal{P}$ is at least

$$\mathrm{nodes}_{\mathcal{N}} := \begin{cases} \sum_{N \in \mathcal{N}} D'_N & \text{if } \mathcal{N} \text{ contains a power of 2,} \\ \sum_{N \in \mathcal{N}} D'_N + 1 & \text{otherwise} \end{cases}$$

where

$$D'_N = D_N - \sum_{\substack{1 \leq k \\ 2^k \mid N}} D_{N/2^k}$$

and D_N is the number of neighbours of a node in $\Gamma_2(N; p)$, given in Equation (1). Equality holds for steps taken after $\max_{N \in \mathcal{N}} (2 \log_2(N))$ steps.

Remark 8. It is important to note that the assumption that $\mathcal{P}$ resists collisions for $\mathcal{N}$ is mild in practice. Indeed, when $\mathcal{N}$ contains only odd integers the assumption simplifies to requiring that, in a walk in the $(2, 2)$-isogeny graph, any abelian surface (N, N)-isogenous to A_n is not (M, M)-isogenous to A_m for some m. The set $\mathcal{N}$ will consist only of integers ≤ 11 and our walks have length $O(\log(p))$. A collision of this sort therefore implies that A_n has an endomorphism of degree $O(\log(p))$. Heuristically there should be very few such abelian surfaces. Indeed in the dimension 1 case, by Proposition B.3 in the unpublished appendix to [38], the proportion of supersingular elliptic curves with an endomorphism of degree at most $O(\log(p))$ is $O(\log(p)^{3/2}/p)$.

Proof. Suppose we have taken the following walk in $\Gamma_2(2; p)$

$$A_0 \to A_1 \to \cdots \to A_n \to A_{n+1} \to \cdots,$$

applying Algorithm 4.

First note that if $\mathcal{N}$ contains a power of 2, then each successive p.p. abelian surface A_i is known not to be a product of elliptic curves. By hypothesis, there do not exist distinct $M, N \in \mathcal{N}$ with $N = 2^k M$ for any $k \geq 1$. Therefore, since $\mathcal{P}$ resists collisions for $\mathcal{N}$, for each *distinct* $M, N \in \mathcal{N}$ the p.p. abelian surfaces (M, M)-isogenous to A_m are not (N, N)-isogenous to A_n for all $m, n \geq 0$. In particular it suffices to show that the number of p.p. abelian surfaces (N, N)-isogenous to A_i, but not (N, N)-isogenous to A_j for each $j < i$, is equal to D'_N.

The claim follows immediately when N is odd, since the walk takes place in $\Gamma_2(2; p)$. If N is even, write $N = 2^\ell M$ where $\ell \geq 1$ and M is odd. In this case, for each $1 \leq k \leq \ell$, any p.p. abelian surface $(2^{\ell-k} M, 2^{\ell-k} M)$-isogenous to A_{n-k} is (N, N)-isogenous to both A_{n-2k} and A_n. Therefore, $D_{N/2^k}$ surfaces (N, N)-isogenous to A_n are (N, N)-isogenous to A_{n-2k}.

The claim follows by summing over $1 \leq k \leq \ell$. Note that equality holds if $n - 2k \geq 0$ for each $1 \leq k \leq \ell$, i.e., we have taken at least 2ℓ steps. □

We use the lemma above to determine, for each prime p, an *optimal* set $\mathcal{N}$ for which we perform the detection of (N, N)-splittings during Algorithm 4.

Let c_{step} be the number of $\mathbb{F}_p$-multiplications required to take a step in $\Gamma_2(2; p)$ using Algorithm 2, and let c_{ig} be the number of $\mathbb{F}_p$-multiplications required to compute $\alpha(C)$ using InvariantsFromWeierstrassPoints (see Remark 4). Finally, letting $c_{\text{split}}(N)$ be the total number of $\mathbb{F}_p$-multiplications required by Algorithm 3 (see Proposition 4 and Remark 6), we obtain the following lemma.

Lemma 5. *For a subset* $\mathcal{N} \subseteq \{2, 3, \ldots, 11\}$, *the number of* $\mathbb{F}_p$*-multiplications required to run Steps 7–15 of Algorithm 4 is at most*

$$\text{cost}_{\mathcal{N}} := \begin{cases} c_{\text{step}} + c_{\text{ig}} + \sum_{N \in \mathcal{N}} c_{\text{split}}(N) & \text{if } \mathcal{N} \neq \emptyset, \\ c_{\text{step}} & \text{otherwise.} \end{cases}$$

Proof. Given input defining a genus 2 curve $C/\mathbb{F}_{p^2}$ if $\mathcal{N} = \emptyset$ then Steps 7–15 of Algorithm 4 require a single call to $\text{Step}(a, \text{bits})$, taking c_{step} $\mathbb{F}_p$-multiplications.

Otherwise, Step 7 calls InvariantsFromWeierstrassPoints taking c_{ig} multiplications in $\mathbb{F}_p$. For each $N \in \mathcal{N}$, the contents of the for-loop (i.e., Steps 8–11) require $c_{\text{split}}(N)$ multiplications in $\mathbb{F}_p$. Finally Steps 12–15 call $\text{Step}(a, \text{bits})$, again requiring c_{step} $\mathbb{F}_p$-multiplications. $\square$

We consider subsets of $\{2, \ldots, 11\}$ satisfying the hypotheses of Lemma 4. As a precomputation, amongst these subsets we determine the optimal set $\mathcal{N}$ for Algorithm 4 by choosing $\mathcal{N}$ to minimise the number of $\mathbb{F}_p$-multiplications per node revealed (either visited by the Richelot walk or revealed by IsSplit). That is, we choose the $\mathcal{N}$ that minimises the ratio $\frac{\text{cost}_{\mathcal{N}}}{\text{nodes}_{\mathcal{N}}}$.

6.3   A Bound on the Cost of the SplitSearcher Algorithm

We now discuss a heuristic upper bound for the concrete cost of finding a splitting of a genus 2 Jacobian using the SplitSearcher algorithm combined with an optimised walk in $\Gamma_2(2; p)$.

First recall that our function InvariantsFromWeierstrassPoints terminates with 291 $\mathbb{F}_p$-multiplications and 1 $\mathbb{F}_p$ inversion. Bounding this inversion by $2 \log_2(p)$ $\mathbb{F}_p$-multiplications (i.e., by the worst case where the binary expansion of the exponent consists only of 1's), we have $c_{\text{ig}} \leq 291 + 2 \log_2(p)$.

We now assume that the cost of IsSplit is bounded by the cost of its first 3 steps (see Proposition 4 and Table 3 bounds depending only on N, and Remark 6 for a justification). Finally Rlsog requires 63 $\mathbb{F}_p$-multiplications and 3 calls to InvSqrt which costs at most $22 + 4 \log_2(p)$ $\mathbb{F}_p$-multiplications (with the $\log_2(p)$ terms arising from 2 exponentiations). In particular, Rlsog costs at most $129 + 12 \log_2(p)$ $\mathbb{F}_p$-multiplications.

For primes of at least 150 bits, the set $\mathcal{N} = \{4, 6\}$ is the optimal set discussed in Sect. 6.2, and we obtain an upper bound of

$$\frac{14 \log_2(p) + 34490}{664} \tag{3}$$

$\mathbb{F}_p$-multiplications per node revealed (assuming the heuristics from Remarks 5 and 8). If we assume that the proportion of product nodes (among nodes inspected by Algorithm 4) is equal[6] to $5/p$ we would expect that Algorithm 4 requires

$$\left(\frac{14\log_2(p) + 34490}{5 \cdot 664}\right) p + O(\log_2(p)) \tag{4}$$

$\mathbb{F}_p$-multiplications before encountering a product node.

7   Experimental Results

We conducted experiments over both small and large primes, and the results are reported in Tables 4 and 5, respectively.

The small prime experiments were conducted so that we could run multiple instances of the full $\tilde{O}(p)$ search for product curves to completion. The four Mersenne primes of the form $p = 2^m - 1$ with $m \in \{13, 17, 19, 31\}$ were chosen as the field characteristics, and instances of the product-finding problem were generated by taking a chain of 40 randomised Richelot isogenies away from the superspecial abelian surface[7] corresponding to $C/\mathbb{F}_p\colon y^2 = x^5 + x$. For the three smaller primes, 256 instances were generated, while for $p = 2^{31} - 1$, we generated 10 such instances; each instance is specified by a 6-tuple of Weierstrass points (see Sect. 3.1). All of the instances were solved once using the original walk in $\Gamma_2(2; p)$ described in Sect. 3. and again using our improved SplitSearcher algorithm described in Sect. 6. For all four of these primes, the set $\mathcal{N} = \{2, 3\}$ was optimal for use in SplitSearcher. In Table 4 we report the average number of steps taken in $\Gamma_2(2; p)$ for both algorithms, as well as the average number of $\mathbb{F}_p$-multiplications required to solve the problem. In the case of SplitSearcher, we additionally report the average number of nodes searched. This includes both the nodes that were walked on and those that were inspected using our (N, N)-splitting detection[8]. As we might expect, this is always relatively close to the number of steps taken in the Richelot-only walk.

For cryptographically sized primes, we are unable to solve the product-finding problem, which is why Table 5 instead reports the number of nodes that were searched when the number of $\mathbb{F}_p$-multiplications was bounded at 10^8. The main trend to highlight (in both tables) is that the speedup is increasing steadily as

---

[6] This is the expected proportion of product nodes in a random walk in $\Gamma_2(2, p)$, see [23, §6.2]. However, preliminary experiments (see Table 4) indicate that in our walk (taking only *good extensions*) the proportion may be closer to $1/p$.

[7] The shapes of the primes chosen in both tables is of little consequence: we merely made consistent choices of the prime shape so that the same form of superspecial starting surface could be used throughout the experiments.

[8] Throughout this section we assume that the number of nodes revealed by Split-Searcher after s steps is equal to $s \cdot \text{nodes}_\mathcal{N}$. Indeed, as discussed in Remarks 5 and 8 an overcount should occur with very low probability. In particular, after $O(p)$ steps we would expect to overcount at most $o(p)$ nodes. This heuristic is also supported by the experiments reported in Table 4.

Table 4. Solving the product-finding problem using Richelot isogeny walks in $\Gamma_2(2;p)$ only (left) vs. using Richelot isogeny walks in $\Gamma_2(2;p)$ together with SplitSearcher in $\Gamma_2(N;p)$ (right).

		Walks in $\Gamma_2(2;p)$ without additional searching [13] (optimised in §3)		Walks in $\Gamma_2(2;p)$ with SplitSearcher in $\Gamma_2(N;p)$ **This work**			
prime p	no. inst solved	av. steps taken	av. $\mathbb{F}_p$ muls	av. steps taken	av. nodes covered	av. $\mathbb{F}_p$ muls	**imprv. factor**
$2^{13}-1$	256	6531	1839209	122	6536	188015	**9.8x**
$2^{17}-1$	256	101812	33538079	2154	116305	3474579	**9.7x**
$2^{19}-1$	256	475300	168095438	8593	464008	14104408	**11.9x**
$2^{31}-1$	10	238694656	118336348672	4856252	262237639	8787389743	**13.4x**

the prime grows in size: the number of $\mathbb{F}_p$-multiplications required for a single Richelot isogeny is proportional to the bitlength of p (due to the square root computations), while the number of $\mathbb{F}_p$-multiplications required to inspect the (N,N)-isogenous neighbours (after computing the Igusa–Clebsch invariants) remains fixed as p grows. This is also predicted by Eq. 3, where the coefficient of the dominating $\log_2(p)$ term is $14/664$ versus 12.

Interestingly, as shown in Table 5 the set $\mathcal{N} = \{2,3\}$ is optimal for the 50- and 100-bit primes, the set $\mathcal{N} = \{3,4\}$ is optimal for the 150-bit prime, while the set $\mathcal{N} = \{4,6\}$ takes over and reigns supreme for all other reported bitlengths. Our implementation can be used to obtain the same data for any other prime of interest, and the number of $\mathbb{F}_p$-multiplications used per node can be combined with the (average) number of nodes one expects to search through in order to get a very precise estimate on the concrete classical security of the superspecial isogeny problem.

Possible Improvements. There have been a number of choices made throughout this paper which open up possible avenues for improvement. We conclude by giving a non-exhaustive list of such improvements.

1. The parametrisation of $\mathcal{L}_N$ given by Kumar [36] may be altered through composition with a birational transformation of $\mathbb{A}^2$. There may be better choices of parametrisations for our purposes, i.e., ones which minimise the degree of $P_{i,j}$. Furthermore, as detailed in Remark 3, there are many ways to normalise the Igusa–Clebsch invariants, though it is unclear to us which normalisations minimise the degrees that arise in the resultant computations.
2. Since the Weierstrass points of genus 2 curve with superspecial Jacobian are all $\mathbb{F}_{p^2}$-rational, it may be desirable to work with the Rosenhain invariants which may be computed more efficiently. To use our methods one would need to compute a birational model for the surface $\mathcal{L}_N(2)$ whose points parametrise optimally (N,N)-split Jacobians with full level 2 structure. One approach is described in [28].

Table 5. The approximate number of multiplications required to search a single node using Richelot isogeny walks in $\Gamma_2(2; p)$ only (left) vs. using Richelot isogeny walks in $\Gamma_2(2; p)$ together with SplitSearcher in $\Gamma_2(N; p)$ (right). Note that the shape of the primes chosen has little effect on the multiplication counts since we expect to never find a splitting.

prime p	bits p	Walks in $\Gamma_2(2;p)$ without additional searching [13] (optimised in §3) nodes per 10^8 muls	$\mathbb{F}_p$ muls per node	Walks in $\Gamma_2(2;p)$ with SplitSearcher in $\Gamma_2(N;p)$ This work set $N \in \{\dots\}$	nodes per 10^8 muls	$\mathbb{F}_p$ muls per node	imprv. factor
$2^{11} \cdot 3^{24} - 1$	50	172712	579	$\{2,3\}$	2830951	35	**16.5x**
$2^{44} \cdot 3^{35} - 1$	100	85034	1176		2076517	48	**24.5x**
$2^{27} \cdot 3^{77} - 1$	150	63492	1575	$\{3,4\}$	1858912	54	**29.2x**
$2^{144} \cdot 3^{35} - 1$	200	42088	2376	$\{4,6\}$	1802816	55	**43.2x**
$2^{181} \cdot 3^{43} - 1$	250	34083	2934		1771608	56	**52.4x**
$5 \cdot 2^{193} \cdot 3^{66} - 1$	300	29317	3411		1745712	57	**59.8x**
$2^{201} \cdot 3^{94} - 1$	350	25581	3909		1719152	58	**67.4x**
$2^{231} \cdot 3^{106} - 1$	400	22753	4395		1694584	59	**74.5x**
$2^{204} \cdot 3^{155} - 1$	450	20729	4824		1672672	60	**80.4x**
$2^{113} \cdot 3^{244} - 1$	500	20239	4941		1667360	60	**82.4x**
$2^{293} \cdot 3^{162} - 1$	550	16835	5940		1619552	62	**95.8x**
$5 \cdot 2^{299} \cdot 3^{188} - 1$	600	15679	6378		1599632	63	**101.2x**
$2^{404} \cdot 3^{155} - 1$	650	13848	7221		1562448	64	**112.8x**
$2^{83} \cdot 3^{389} - 1$	700	14530	6882		1580376	63	**109.2x**
$2^{477} \cdot 3^{172} - 1$	750	12046	8301		1517960	66	**125.7x**
$2^{107} \cdot 3^{437} - 1$	800	13228	7560		1548504	65	**116.3x**
$2^{166} \cdot 3^{431} - 1$	850	11968	8355		1515304	66	**126.6x**
$2^{172} \cdot 3^{459} - 1$	900	11427	8751		1500032	67	**130.6x**
$2^{536} \cdot 3^{261} - 1$	950	10233	9772		1443592	69	**141.6x**
$2^{721} \cdot 3^{176} - 1$	1000	8814	11346		1403752	71	**159.8x**

3. It may be possible to improve the complexity of the evaluations performed by EvalCoeffs (see Sect. 5.2) by taking longer walks in the $(2,2)$-graph and then batching the evaluations using multi-point evaluation.

4. Knowledge of explicit equations for the surface $\mathcal{L}_N$ for larger N would allow us to perform efficient detection of (N, N)-splittings beyond $N = 11$. It may be possible to derive these from the pre-existing equations for the surfaces $Z(N, -1)$ (which parametrise pairs of elliptic curves (N, N)-isogenous to a genus 2 Jacobian) in [20, Theorem 2.4], [21, Theorem 1.2], and [25, Theorem 1.1], or by extending Kumar's computations.

5. It is possible to detect $(2N, 2N)$-splittings more efficiently by taking *partial* steps in the $(2,2)$-isogeny graph. Let $C/\mathbb{F}_{p^2}$ be a genus 2 curve given by a Weierstrass equation $y^2 = (x - a_0) \cdots (x - a_5)$. While we cannot take a full step in $\Gamma_2(2; p)$ (recovering the factorisation of the Weierstrass sextic for

each of the $(2,2)$-isogenous curves) without computing square roots, we can compute the Igusa–Clebsch invariants of *all* the neighbours of $\mathrm{Jac}(C)$ using only a small number of $\mathbb{F}_p$-multiplications and a single batched inversion. In this case we may detect $(2N, 2N)$-splittings of $\mathrm{Jac}(C)$ by applying IsSplit to each of the $(2,2)$-neighbours of $\mathrm{Jac}(C)$. In the code attached to this article, this optimisation can be enabled by setting `split_after_22_flag = true`. In our implementation of this idea, and for the primes ranging between 50 and 1000 bits reported in Table 5, we observed additional improvement factors ranging between 1.3-1.6.

Acknowledgements. We thank Thomas Decru, Tom Fisher, and Benjamin Smith for helpful comments on earlier versions of this paper. We also thank Thomas Decru for mentioning to us improvement 5 in Sect. 7.

References

1. Basso, A., Maino, L., Pope, G.: FESTA: fast encryption from supersingular torsion attacks. In: Guo, J., Steinfeld, R. (eds.) ASIACRYPT 2023. LNCS, vol. 14444, pp. 98–126. Springer, Singapore (2023). https://doi.org/10.1007/978-981-99-8739-9_4
2. Bosma, W., Cannon, J., Playoust, C.: The magma algebra system I. the user language. J. Symbolic Comput. **24**(3–4), 235–265 (1997). Computational algebra and number theory
3. Brock, B.: Superspecial curves of genera two and three. PhD thesis, Princeton University (1994)
4. Bröker, R., Howe, E.W., Lauter, K.E., Stevenhagen, P.: Genus-2 curves and Jacobians with a given number of points. LMS J. Comput. Math. **18**(1), 170–197 (2015)
5. Bruin, N., Doerksen, K.: The arithmetic of genus two curves with $(4,4)$-split Jacobians. Canad. J. Math. **63**(5), 992–1024 (2011)
6. Bruin, N., Doerksen, K.: Electronic resources (2011). http://www.cecm.sfu.ca/~nbruin/splitigusa/. Accessed Sept 2022
7. Castryck, W., Decru, T.: Multiradical isogenies. Arithmetic Geom. Crypt. Coding Theory **779**(57), 2022 (2021)
8. Castryck, W., Decru, T.: An efficient key recovery attack on SIDH. In: Hazay, C., Stam, M. (eds.) EUROCRYPT 2023. LNCS, vol. 14008, pp. 423–447. Springer, Cham (2023). https://doi.org/10.1007/978-3-031-30589-4_15
9. Castryck, W., Decru, T., Smith, B.: Hash functions from superspecial genus-2 curves using Richelot isogenies. J. Math. Crypt. **14**(1), 268–292 (2020)
10. Charles, D.X., Lauter, K.E., Goren, E.Z.: Cryptographic hash functions from expander graphs. J. Cryptol. **22**(1), 93–113 (2009)
11. Chen, M., Leroux, A.: SCALLOP-HD: group action from 2-dimensional isogenies. IACR Cryptol. ePrint Arch., 1488 (2023)
12. Corte-Real Santos, M., Costello, C., Shi, J.: Accelerating the Delfs-Galbraith algorithm with fast subfield root detection. In: Dodis, Y., Shrimpton, T. (eds.) CRYPTO 2022. LNCS, vol. 13509, pp. 285–314. Springer, Cham (2022). https://doi.org/10.1007/978-3-031-15982-4_10

13. Costello, C., Smith, B.: The supersingular isogeny problem in genus 2 and beyond. In: Ding, J., Tillich, J.-P. (eds.) PQCrypto 2020. LNCS, vol. 12100, pp. 151–168. Springer, Cham (2020). https://doi.org/10.1007/978-3-030-44223-1_9
14. Cox, D.A., Little, J., O'Shea, D.: Ideals, Varieties, and Algorithms. Undergraduate Texts in Mathematics. Springer, New York (2015)
15. Dartois, P., Leroux, A., Robert, D., Wesolowski, B.: SQISignHD: new dimensions in cryptography. IACR Cryptol. ePrint Arch., 436 (2023)
16. Delfs, C., Galbraith, S.D.: Computing isogenies between supersingular elliptic curves over $\mathbb{F}_p$. Des. Codes Crypt. **78**(2), 425–440 (2016)
17. Djukanović, M.: Split Jacobians and Lower Bounds on Heights. PhD thesis, Leiden University and L'Université de Bordeaux (2017). https://hdl.handle.net/1887/54944
18. Djukanović, M.: Families of (3,3)-split Jacobians. arXiv e-prints arXiv:1811.10075 (2018)
19. De Feo, L., Dobson, S., Galbraith, S.D., Zobernig, L.: SIDH proof of knowledge. In: Agrawal, S., Lin, D. (eds.) ASIACRYPT 2022. LNCS, vol. 13792, pp. 310–339. Springer, Cham (2022). https://doi.org/10.1007/978-3-031-22966-4_11
20. Fisher, T.: On families of 13-congruent elliptic curves. arXiv e-prints arXiv:1912.10777 (2019)
21. Fisher, T.: On pairs of 17-congruent elliptic curves. arXiv e-prints arXiv:2106.02033 (2021)
22. Florit, E., Smith, B.: An atlas of the Richelot isogeny graph. Cryptology ePrint Archive, Paper 2021/013 (2021)
23. Florit, E., Smith, B.: Automorphisms and isogeny graphs of abelian varieties, with applications to the superspecial Richelot isogeny graph. Arithmetic Geom. Crypt. Coding Theory **2021** (2021)
24. Flynn, E.V., Ti, Y.B.: Genus two isogeny cryptography. In: Ding, J., Steinwandt, R. (eds.) PQCrypto 2019. LNCS, vol. 11505, pp. 286–306. Springer, Cham (2019). https://doi.org/10.1007/978-3-030-25510-7_16
25. Frengley, S.: On 12-congruences of elliptic curves. arXiv e-prints arXiv:2208.05842 (2022). To appear in Int. J. Number Theory
26. Frey, G., Kani, E.: Curves of genus 2 covering elliptic curves and an arithmetical application. In: Arithmetic Algebraic Geometry (Texel, 1989), Progress in Mathematics, vol. 89, pp. 153–176. Birkhäuser Boston, Boston, MA (1991). https://doi.org/10.1007/978-1-4612-0457-2_7
27. Gaudry, P., Schost, É.: On the invariants of the quotients of the Jacobian of a curve of genus 2. In: Boztaş, S., Shparlinski, I.E. (eds.) AAECC 2001. LNCS, vol. 2227, pp. 373–386. Springer, Heidelberg (2001). https://doi.org/10.1007/3-540-45624-4_39
28. Gruenewald, D.: Computing Humbert surfaces and applications. In: Arithmetic, Geometry, Cryptography and Coding Theory 2009, Volume 521 of Contemporary Mathematics, pp. 59–69. American Mathematical Society, Providence, RI (2010)
29. Ibukiyama, T., Katsura, T.: On the field of definition of superspecial polarized abelian varieties and type numbers. Compositio Math. **91**(1), 37–46 (1994)
30. Ibukiyama, T., Katsura, T., Oort, F.: Supersingular curves of genus two and class numbers. Compos. Math. **57**(2), 127–152 (1986)
31. Igusa, J.: Arithmetic variety of moduli for genus two. Ann. Math. **2**(72), 612–649 (1960)
32. Igusa, J.: On Siegel modular forms of genus two. Amer. J. Math. **84**, 175–200 (1962)

33. Jordan, B.W., Zaytman, Y.: Isogeny graphs of superspecial abelian varieties and generalized Brandt matrices. arXiv preprint arXiv:2005.09031 (2020)
34. Kohel, D., Lauter, K., Petit, C., Tignol, J.: On the quaternion-isogeny path problem. LMS J. Comput. Mathem. **17**(A), 418–432 (2014)
35. Kuhn, R.M.: Curves of genus 2 with split Jacobian. Trans. Amer. Math. Soc. **307**(1), 41–49 (1988)
36. Kumar, A.: Hilbert modular surfaces for square discriminants and elliptic subfields of genus 2 function fields. Res. Math. Sci. **2**(1), 1–46 (2015)
37. Kunzweiler, S.: Efficient computation of $(2^n, 2^n)$-isogenies. Cryptology ePrint Archive, Paper 2022/990 (2022)
38. Love, J., Boneh, D.: Supersingular curves with small noninteger endomorphisms. Open Book Ser. **4**(1), 7–22 (2020). Appendices, https://arxiv.org/pdf/1910.03180.pdf
39. Lubicz, D., Robert, D.: Fast change of level and applications to isogenies. In: ANTS-XV (2022)
40. Magaard, K., Shaska, T., Völklein, H.: Genus 2 curves that admit a degree 5 map to an elliptic curve. Forum Math. **21**(3), 547–566 (2009)
41. Maino, L., Martindale, C., Panny, L., Pope, G., Wesolowski, B.: A direct key recovery attack on SIDH. In: Hazay, C., Stam, M. (eds.) EUROCRYPT 2023. LNCS, vol. 14008, pp. 448–471. Springer, Cham (2023). https://doi.org/10.1007/978-3-031-30589-4_16
42. Mestre, F.: Construction de courbes de genre 2 à partir de leurs modules. In: Mora, T., Traverso, C. (eds.) Effective Methods in Algebraic Geometry. Progress in Mathematics, vol. 94, pp. 313–334. Springer, Boston (1990). https://doi.org/10.1007/978-1-4612-0441-1_21
43. Oort, F.: A stratification of a moduli space of abelian varieties. In: Faber, C., van der Geer, G., Oort, F. (eds.) Moduli of Abelian Varieties. Progress in Mathematics, vol. 195, pp. 345–416. Birkhäuser, Basel (2001). https://doi.org/10.1007/978-3-0348-8303-0_13
44. Robert, D.: Breaking SIDH in Polynomial Time. In: Hazay, C., Stam, M. (eds.) EUROCRYPT 2023. LNCS, vol. 14008, pp. 472–503. Springer, Cham (2023). https://doi.org/10.1007/978-3-031-30589-4_17
45. Scott, M.: A note on the calculation of some functions in finite fields: tricks of the trade. Cryptology ePrint Archive (2020)
46. Shaska, T.: Curves of genus 2 with (n, n) decomposable Jacobians. J. Symb. Comput. **31**(5), 603–617 (2001)
47. Shaska, T.: Curves of Genus Two Covering Elliptic Curves. University of Florida (2001)
48. Shaska, T.: Genus 2 fields with degree 3 elliptic subfields. Forum Math. **16**(2), 263–280 (2004)
49. Shaska, T., Völklein, H.: Elliptic subfields and automorphisms of genus 2 function fields. In: Christensen, C., Sathaye, A., Sundaram, G., Bajaj, C. (eds.) Algebra, Arithmetic and Geometry with Applications, pp. 703–723. Springer, Berlin (2004). https://doi.org/10.1007/978-3-642-18487-1_42
50. Shaska, T., Wijesiri, G.S., Wolf, S., Woodland, L.: Degree 4 coverings of elliptic curves by genus 2 curves. Albanian J. Math. **2**(4), 307–318 (2008)
51. Silverman, J.H.: The Arithmetic of Elliptic Curves, Volume 106 of Graduate Texts in Mathematics, 2nd (edn.). Springer, Dordrecht (2009)

52. Takashima, K.: Efficient algorithms for isogeny sequences and their cryptographic applications. In: Takagi, T., Wakayama, M., Tanaka, K., Kunihiro, N., Kimoto, K., Duong, D.H. (eds.) Mathematical Modelling for Next-Generation Cryptography. MI, vol. 29, pp. 97–114. Springer, Singapore (2018). https://doi.org/10.1007/978-981-10-5065-7_6

53. Takashima, K., Yoshida, R.: An algorithm for computing a sequence of Richelot isogenies. Bull. Korean Math. Soc. **46**(4), 789–802 (2009)

54. van Oorschot, P.C., Wiener, M.J.: Parallel collision search with cryptanalytic applications. J. Cryptol. **12**(1), 1–28 (1999)

SCALLOP-HD: Group Action from 2-Dimensional Isogenies

Mingjie Chen[1,5(✉)] [iD], Antonin Leroux[2,3], and Lorenz Panny[4]

[1] University of Birmingham, Birmingham, UK
m.chen.1@bham.ac.uk, mjchennn555@gmail.com
[2] DGA-MI, Bruz, France
antonin.leroux@polytechnique.org
[3] IRMAR, UMR 6625, Université de Rennes, Rennes, France
[4] Technical University of Munich, Munich, Germany
lorenz@yx7.cc
[5] Université Libre de Bruxelles, Brussels, Belgium

Abstract. We present SCALLOP-HD, a novel group action that builds upon the recent SCALLOP group action introduced by De Feo, Fouotsa, Kutas, Leroux, Merz, Panny and Wesolowski in 2023. While our group action uses the same action of the class group $\mathrm{Cl}(\mathfrak{O})$ on $\mathfrak{O}$-oriented curves where $\mathfrak{O} = \mathbb{Z}[f\sqrt{-d}]$ for a large prime f and small d as SCALLOP, we introduce a different orientation representation: The new representation embeds an endomorphism generating $\mathfrak{O}$ in a 2^e-isogeny between abelian varieties of dimension 2 with Kani's Lemma, and this representation comes with a simple algorithm to compute the class group action. Our new approach considerably simplifies the SCALLOP framework, potentially surpassing it in efficiency—a claim supported by preliminary implementation results in SageMath. Additionally, our approach streamlines parameter selection. The new representation allows us to select efficiently a class group $\mathrm{Cl}(\mathfrak{O})$ of smooth order, enabling polynomial-time generation of the lattice of relation, hence enhancing scalability in contrast to SCALLOP.

To instantiate our SCALLOP-HD group action, we introduce a new technique to apply Kani's Lemma in dimension 2 with an isogeny diamond obtained from commuting endomorphisms. This method allows one to represent arbitrary endomorphisms with isogenies in dimension 2, and may be of independent interest.

1 Introduction

The group action framework is a powerful abstract tool to build cryptographic protocols such as non-interactive key exchange [CLM+18], signatures [BKV19], threshold schemes [CS20, DFM20], ring signatures [BKP20], group signatures [BDK+23], partial-blind signatures [KLLQ23], updatable encryption [LR22], and, among other things, various applications as discussed in [ADFMP20].

Isogenies provide the only known way to instantiate this framework in a manner resistant to quantum computers. There are two achievable flavours of group

© International Association for Cryptologic Research 2024
Q. Tang and V. Teague (Eds.): PKC 2024, LNCS 14603, pp. 190–216, 2024.
https://doi.org/10.1007/978-3-031-57725-3_7

action: the "restricted" group action (REGA) such as the one introduced for the CSIDH key exchange in [CLM+18], and the "full" variant (EGA) introduced for the CSI-FiSh signature scheme in [BKV19]. While the restricted variant is already interesting, the full variant is required by the more elaborate constructions.

Unfortunately, isogeny-based group actions suffer from various problems. First, the underlying hard problem can be solved in subexponential time by a quantum computer [Kup05] which renders their security hard to estimate and reduces their efficiency. Second, current methods for instantiating the full variant require superpolynomial precomputation as demonstrated in [BKV19, DFFK+23] and reaffirmed in a recent blog post by Panny[1]. This makes it computationally infeasible to obtain the full variant for group sizes of several thousands of bits.

The second obstacle is what motivated the introduction of the recent SCALLOP scheme in [DFFK+23] where the precomputation (while still superpolynomial) is much more practical than in the setting of CSI-FiSh [BKV19]. The authors of SCALLOP demonstrated the interest of their constructions by scaling the parameters to sizes known to be computationally unreachable in the setting of CSI-FiSh. However, the efficiency of SCALLOP is much worse than CSIDH, and the amount of precomputation required to reach the higher levels of security (equivalent to the CSIDH-8192 variant of [CSCDJRH22] for instance) promises to be quite extensive.

The improvements in scalability achieved by SCALLOP, when compared to CSI-FiSh, arise from using a distinct group and set in the group action. However, in order to define their group action, the set elements are no longer just j-invariants of supersingular elliptic curves, but curves together with extra data called "orientation". The necessity of carrying the orientation and computing the group action on the orientation is what renders the efficiency of SCALLOP bad in comparison to CSI-FiSh.

Recently, the field of isogeny-based cryptography has seen a major breakthrough with the successful cryptanalysis of the SIDH key exchange scheme by [CD23, MMP+23, Rob23]. This result was obtained by embedding isogenies between elliptic curves (isogenies of dimension 1) inside isogenies of higher dimension (2, 4 and 8) using Kani's Lemma [Kan97]. Since then, these novel ideas have been used several times to build some post-quantum protocols such as encryption [BMP23], signature [DLRW23], or VRF [Ler23]. In short, our new construction SCALLOP-HD uses these ideas to represent orientations more efficiently and this leads to various improvements over SCALLOP that we list in the next section.

1.1   Contribution

In this work, we revisit the SCALLOP group action with the high dimensional isogenies at the heart of the attacks against SIDH. We show that these new

---

[1] https://yx7.cc/blah/2023-04-14.html.

techniques, and in particular, the idea of Robert [Rob22] that an arbitrary degree isogeny can be efficiently represented using high dimension isogenies allows us to simplify the framework of SCALLOP. Concretely, the improvements of SCALLOP-HD compared to the original SCALLOP can be summarized as follows:

1. A new orientation representation that uses the embedding techniques based of higher dimensional isogenies.
2. A simplified algorithm to compute the group action using Kani's Lemma in dimension 2 that we expect will improve the efficiency.
3. The improvement from a merely subexponential to a polynomial complexity of the computation of the class group's lattice of relation: the bottleneck in the precomputation required by SCALLOP. Hence, the reduction of the lattice of relations remains the only superpolynomial-time part in the precomputation of the SCALLOP-HD group action.

In doing so, we introduce a novel way of applying Kani's Lemma in dimension 2 by building isogeny diamonds from two endomorphisms lying in the same quadratic order. This can be used to represent orientations and endomorphisms in dimension 2. We believe this new technique is interesting in its own right, and it was recently used in [Ler23] to provide a new algorithm to perform the Deuring correspondence using isogenies in dimension 2. We also briefly discuss another example where this new technique can be used in a recent endomorphism division algorithm in Remark 14.

Organization of the Paper. The rest of this paper is organized as follows. In Sect. 2, we introduce necessary mathematical background. Then, Sect. 3 explains how to construct group action from isogenies and outlines the progress towards obtaining a scalable EGA. In Sect. 4, we present the new orientation representation alongside the resulting group action formula. Section 5 introduces the SCALLOP-HD group action and provides example parameter choices. Section 6 discusses some remarks on the secrurity of SCALLOP-HD. We conclude in Sect. 7 by summarizing the paper and discussing future work.

2   Preliminaries

2.1   Quaternion Algebras, Supersingular Elliptic Curves, Isogenies and the Deuring Correspondence

Quaternion Algebras. Let p be a prime and let $\mathcal{B}_{p,\infty}$ denote the unique (up to isomorphism) quaternion algebra ramified precisely at p and ∞. We fix a $\mathbb{Q}$-basis $\langle 1, \mathbf{i}, \mathbf{j}, \mathbf{k} \rangle$ of $\mathcal{B}_{p,\infty}$ that satisfies $\mathbf{i}^2 = -q$, $\mathbf{j}^2 = -p$ and $\mathbf{k} = \mathbf{ij} = -\mathbf{ji}$ for some integer q. A *fractional ideal* I in $\mathcal{B}_{p,\infty}$ is a $\mathbb{Z}$-lattice of rank 4. We denote by $n(I)$ the *norm* of I as the largest rational number such that $n(\alpha) \in n(I)\mathbb{Z}$ for any $\alpha \in I$. An order $\mathcal{O}$ is a subring of $\mathcal{B}_{p,\infty}$ that is also a fractional ideal. An order is called *maximal* when it is not contained in any other larger order. A fractional ideal is *integral* if it is contained in its *left order* $\mathcal{O}_L(I) = \{\alpha \in \mathcal{B}_{p,\infty} \mid \alpha I \subset I\}$, or equivalently in its *right order* $\mathcal{O}_R(I) = \{\alpha \in \mathcal{B}_{p,\infty} \mid I\alpha \subset I\}$.

Supersingular Elliptic Curves and Isogenies. Let E, E_1, E_2 be elliptic curves defined over a finite field of characteristic p. An isogeny from E_1 to E_2 is a non-constant rational map that is simultaneously a group homomorphism. An isogeny from a curve E to itself is an *endomorphism*. The set $\mathrm{End}(E)$ of all endomorphisms of E forms a ring under addition and composition. $\mathrm{End}(E)$ is either an order in an imaginary quadratic field and E is called *ordinary*, or a maximal order in $\mathcal{B}_{p,\infty}$, in which case E is called *supersingular*.

The Deuring Correspondence. Fix a supersingular elliptic curve E_0, and an order $\mathcal{O}_0 \simeq \mathrm{End}(E_0)$. The curve/order correspondence allows one to associate to each outgoing isogeny $\varphi : E_0 \to E_1$ an integral left $\mathcal{O}_0$-ideal, and every such ideal arises in this way (see [Koh96] for instance). Through this correspondence, the ring $\mathrm{End}(E_1)$ is isomorphic to the right order of this ideal. This isogeny/ideal correspondence is defined in [Wat69], and in the separable case, it is explicitly given as follows.

Definition 1. *Given I an integral left $\mathcal{O}_0$-ideal coprime to p, we define the I-torsion $E_0[I] = \{P \in E_0(\overline{\mathbb{F}}_{p^2}) : \alpha(P) = 0 \text{ for all } \alpha \in I\}$. To I, we associate the separable isogeny φ_I of kernel $E_0[I]$. Conversely given a separable isogeny φ, the corresponding ideal is defined as $I_\varphi = \{\alpha \in \mathcal{O}_0 : \alpha(P) = 0 \text{ for all } P \in \ker(\varphi)\}$.*

We summarize properties of the Deuring correspondence in Table 1, borrowed from [DFKL+20].

Table 1. The Deuring correspondence, a summary [DFKL+20].

Supersingular j-invariants over $\mathbb{F}_{p^2}$ $j(E)$ (up to Galois conjugacy)	Maximal orders in $\mathcal{B}_{p,\infty}$ $\mathcal{O} \cong \mathrm{End}(E)$ (up to isomorphism)
(E_1, φ) with $\varphi : E \to E_1$	I_φ integral left $\mathcal{O}$-ideal and right $\mathcal{O}_1$-ideal
$\theta \in \mathrm{End}(E_0)$	Principal ideal $\mathcal{O}\theta$
$\deg(\varphi)$	$n(I_\varphi)$

2.2 Quadratic Orders and Orientations on Supersingular Elliptic Curves

Let d be a positive square-free integer and $K = \mathbb{Q}(\sqrt{-d})$ be an imaginary quadratic field with discriminant D_K. Let $\mathfrak{O} \subseteq K$ be an order with discriminant $D_\mathfrak{O}$. Explicitly, $\mathfrak{O} = \mathbb{Z}[\frac{D_\mathfrak{O} + \sqrt{D_\mathfrak{O}}}{2}]$. Any element $\alpha \in \mathfrak{O}$ can be written as $x + y\frac{D_\mathfrak{O} + \sqrt{D_\mathfrak{O}}}{2}$ with $x, y \in \mathbb{Z}$, and $\{1, \alpha\}$ is a $\mathbb{Z}$-basis of $\mathfrak{O}$ if and only if $y = 1$. One can compute the norm of α and thus derive the norm form $f_\mathfrak{O}$ of $\mathfrak{O}$:

$$f_\mathfrak{O}(x, y) = x^2 + D_\mathfrak{O} xy + y^2 \frac{D_\mathfrak{O}(D_\mathfrak{O} - 1)}{4}.$$

For any order $\mathfrak{O}$, the class group $\mathrm{Cl}(\mathfrak{O})$ consists of the invertible fractional ideals of $\mathfrak{O}$ up to principal factors and is of order $D_{\mathfrak{O}}^{o(1)}$. When $\mathfrak{O} = \mathfrak{O}_K$ is the maximal order with discriminant D_K, computing $\mathrm{Cl}(\mathfrak{O}_K)$ takes time $L_{D_K}(1/2)$ classically [HM89] and polynomial time quantumly [BS16]. When $\mathfrak{O} = \mathbb{Z} + f\mathfrak{O}_K$ where f is a prime and $\mathrm{Cl}(\mathfrak{O}_K) = \{1\}$, there is a simple characterization of $\mathrm{Cl}(\mathfrak{O})$ as discussed in [DFK+23, Appx. A]. Specifically, $\mathrm{Cl}(\mathfrak{O})$ satisfies the following short exact sequence

$$1 \to \mathfrak{O}_K^* / \mathfrak{O}^* \to (\mathfrak{O}_K/(f))^* / (\mathfrak{O}/(f))^* \to \mathrm{Cl}(\mathfrak{O}) \to 1,$$

and they showed that

$$(\mathfrak{O}_K/(f))^* / (\mathfrak{O}/(f))^* \cong \begin{cases} \mathbb{F}_f^* & \text{if } f \text{ splits in } K, \\ \mathbb{F}_{f^2}^* / \mathbb{F}_f^* & \text{if } f \text{ is inert in } K. \end{cases}$$

In particular, this suggests that $\mathrm{Cl}(\mathfrak{O})$ is always cyclic for these orders as it is isomorphic to a quotient of a cyclic group, and $\mathrm{Cl}(\mathfrak{O})$ is easy to compute. Furthermore, this implies that $\#\mathrm{Cl}(\mathfrak{O}) = \left(f - \left(\frac{D_K}{f} \right) \right) \frac{1}{|\mathfrak{O}_K^*|/2}$.

Quadratic orders and their class groups are playing an increasingly important role in isogeny-based cryptography, in particular since Colò and Kohel introduced orientations on supersingular elliptic curves in [CK20]. In what follows, we recall the basic definitions and important properties regarding orientations.

Definition 2. *Let E be a supersingular elliptic curve over $\mathbb{F}_{p^2}$, K be an imaginary quadratic field and $\mathfrak{O} \subseteq K$ be a suborder. Then a K-orientation on E is a ring homomorphism $\iota : K \hookrightarrow \mathrm{End}(E) \otimes \mathbb{Q}$. This K-orientation induces an $\mathfrak{O}$-orientation on E if $\iota(\mathfrak{O}) = \mathrm{End}(E) \cap \iota(K)$. In this case, the pair (E, ι) is called a $\mathfrak{O}$-oriented curve and E is a $\mathfrak{O}$-orientable curve.*

Note that here we use $\mathfrak{O}$-orientation to indicate the *primitive* $\mathfrak{O}$-orientation from [CK20].

Let E' be another supersingular curve and $\varphi : E \to E'$ be an isogeny. Let ι be a K-orientation on E, then there is an induced K-orientation $\iota' = \varphi_*(\iota)$ on E' defined to be $\varphi_*(\iota)(\omega) := \frac{1}{\deg(\varphi)} \varphi \circ \iota(\omega) \circ \widehat{\varphi} \in \mathrm{End}(E') \otimes \mathbb{Q}$. An isogeny of K-oriented elliptic curves $\varphi : (E, \iota) \to (E', \iota')$ is an isogeny $\varphi : E \to E'$ such that $\iota' = \varphi_*(\iota)$; we call this a K-oriented isogeny. A K-oriented isogeny is a K-*isomorphism* if it is an isomorphism of the underlying curves.

For a fixed imaginary quadratic order $\mathfrak{O} \subseteq K$, we consider the collection of all $\mathfrak{O}$-oriented curves and define the following set:

$$\mathcal{S}_{\mathfrak{O}}(p) = \{(E, \iota) \mid (E, \iota) \text{ is an } \mathfrak{O}\text{-oriented curve}\} / \sim,$$

where two oriented curves are equivalent if they are K-isomorphic.

Here we recall the following conditions for the set $\mathcal{S}_{\mathfrak{O}}(p)$ to be non-empty.

Proposition 3 ([Onu21, Proposition 3.2]). *The set $\mathcal{S}_{\mathfrak{O}}(p)$ is not empty if and only if p does not split in K and does not divide the conductor of $\mathfrak{O}$.*

When $\mathcal{S}_{\mathfrak{O}}(p)$ is non-empty, the set of invertible $\mathfrak{O}$-ideals acts on it. Specifically, let $\mathfrak{a}$ be an such an ideal and $(E, \iota_E) \in \mathcal{S}_{\mathfrak{O}}(p)$, then

$$\mathfrak{a} \star (E, \iota_E) := (E_{\mathfrak{a}}, \iota_{E_{\mathfrak{a}}}),$$

where $E_{\mathfrak{a}}$ is the codomain of the isogeny $\phi_{\mathfrak{a}}$ whose kernel is $E[\mathfrak{a}] := \cap_{a \in \mathfrak{a}} \ker \iota_E(a)$ and $\iota_{E_{\mathfrak{a}}}$ is the induced orientation on $E_{\mathfrak{a}}$ by $\phi_{\mathfrak{a}}$. Principal $\mathfrak{O}$-ideals act trivially on (E, ι_E), therefore this action induces an action of $\mathrm{Cl}(\mathfrak{O})$ on $\mathcal{S}_{\mathfrak{O}}(p)$. It was shown in [Onu21] that this is action is free and it has one or two orbits.

2.3   New Isogeny Representation in Higher Dimensions

An isogeny representation is a way to *effectively* represent the isogeny so that there is an *efficient* algorithm for evaluating the isogeny on given points. Common representations include rational maps, isogeny chains, and kernel representation. However, these methods are no longer compact or efficient when the degree d of the isogeny is a large prime and the kernel points are defined over a large degree extension field of $\mathbb{F}_p$.

The Deuring correspondence allows us to efficiently represent such isogenies with their corresponding ideals in maximal quaternion orders, this is call the *ideal representation*. This, however, reveals the endomorphism rings for both the domain and codomain curve. To remedy the situation, Leroux in [Ler22a] introduced another representation called the *suborder representation* which is not strictly an isogeny representation but satisfies a weaker definition as introduced in [CII+23] and requires to reveal the endomorphism ring of the domain curve.

Finally, Robert [Rob22] suggested to use the techniques used in SIDH attacks [CD23, MMP+23, Rob23] to obtain a new isogeny representation, by embedding the desired isogeny between supersingular elliptic curves into an isogeny between abelian varieties of higher dimension. While not named as such in Robert's paper, we refer to it as *high dimension representation* in our paper. This new representation doesn't reveal the endomorphism rings and is much more efficient than suborder representation. It consists only of evaluation of the isogeny to be represented on points of smooth order, and in the right setting it can be pretty easy to compute. While used destructively at first, it has been recently used constructively for building various protocols [DLRW23, Ler23, BMP23, DMS23]. For a detailed account of of the "old" isogeny representations, like the kernel or ideal representation, see [Ler22b]. In what follows, we explain in more details the idea of *high dimension representation* in dimension 2. The main result behind this representation is Kani's Lemma [Kan97] that we present below as Lemma 4.

Lemma 4 (Kani). *Let us consider a commutative diagram of isogenies between principally polarized abelian varieties of dimension g*

$$\begin{array}{ccc} A' & \xrightarrow{\varphi'} & B' \\ \psi \uparrow & & \uparrow \psi' \\ A & \xrightarrow{\varphi} & B \end{array}$$

where φ and φ' are a-isogenies and ψ and ψ' are b-isogenies for integers a, b. The isogeny $F : A \times B' \longrightarrow B \times A'$ given in matrix notation by

$$F := \begin{pmatrix} \varphi & \widetilde{\psi'} \\ -\psi & \widetilde{\varphi'} \end{pmatrix}$$

is a d-isogeny between abelian varieties of dimension $2g$ with $d = a + b$, for the product polarisations.

If $\ker \widetilde{\varphi} \cap \ker \psi' = \{0\}$, the kernel of F is

$$\ker(F) = \{(\widetilde{\varphi}(x), \psi'(x)) \mid x \in B[d]\}.$$

Similarly, if $\ker \varphi \cap \ker \psi = \{0\}$, then

$$\ker(\widetilde{F}) = \{(\varphi(x), \psi(x)) \mid x \in A[d]\}.$$

The commutative diagram in Lemma 4 is often called as an isogeny diamond. Following the notations introduced in [Ler23], we call a *2dim-representation* of an isogeny $\varphi : A \to B$ between two elliptic curves A, B any data from which the isogeny F obtained by applying Lemma 4 with $g = 1$ can be computed efficiently. The idea is that φ can be recovered from F by pre-composition with any embedding $A \to A \times B'$ that acts as the identity on A, and post-composition with the canonical projection $B \times A' \to B$.

To represent the orientation of our SCALLOP-HD group action in Sect. 4.1, we will use the 2dim-representation of an endomorphism with a commutative diagram obtained from two commuting endomorphisms.

Remark 5. One could also embed the isogeny φ in isogenies between abelian varieties in dimension 4 or 8, as discussed for the SQISignHD protocol in [DLRW23]. The higher the dimension, the easier it is to generate the isogeny diamond, however, the complexity of computing isogenies between abelian varieties scales exponentially with the dimension. This is why it is generally better to use the smallest possible dimension. In SQISignHD, it is argued that dimension 2 isogenies do not provide a clear advantage over the original SQISign scheme [DFKL+20] due to the complexity to set-up the isogeny diamond, which is the main reason why SQISignHD works with dimension 4 and dimension 8. In our case, thanks to the idea of using isogeny diamond built from commuting endomorphisms, we will be able to work dimension 2 to achieve better efficiency.

3   Group Action in Isogeny-Based Cryptography

Informally, a group action is a map of the form $\star : G \times X \to X$, where G is a group and X is a set, such that for any $g_1, g_2 \in G$ and any $x \in X$, we have

$$g_1 \star (g_2 \star x) = (g_1 g_2) \star X.$$

We revisit here the concepts of effective group action (EGA) and restricted effective group action (REGA) from [ADFMP20], which capture the essence of two types of group actions used in isogeny-based cryptography. To clarify the distinction between the two and align with subsequent discussions, we exclude details concerning the set X — specifically, membership testing, unique representation, and the existence of the origin in X.

Definition 6. *(EGA) A group action $(G, X, \star)$ is effective if the following properties are satisfied:*

1. *The group G is finite and there exist efficient (PPT) algorithms for:*
   (a) *Membership testing, i.e., to decide if a given bit string represents a valid group element in G.*
   (b) *Equality testing, i.e., to decide if two bit strings represent the same group element in G.*
   (c) *Sampling, i.e., to sample an element g from a distribution $\mathcal{D}_G$ on G.*
   (d) *Operation, i.e., to compute gh for any $g, h \in G$.*
   (e) *Inversion, i.e., to compute g^{-1} for any $g \in G$.*
2. *There exists an efficient algorithm that given (some bit-string representation of) any $g \in G$ and any $x \in X$, outputs $g \star x$.*

Definition 7. *(REGA) Let $(G, X, \star)$ be a group action and let $\mathbf{g} = \{g_1, \ldots, g_n\}$ be a (not necessarily minimal) generating set for G. The action is said to be $\mathbf{g}$-restricted effective if the following properties are satisfied:*

1. *G is finite and $n = \mathsf{poly}(\log |G|)$.*
2. *There exists an efficient algorithm that given any $i \in [n]$ and any bit string representation of $x \in X$, outputs $g_i \star x$ and $g_i^{-1} \star x$.*

Existing instantiation of this definition from isogenies are all based on the ideal class group action. Specifically, it's the action of $\mathrm{Cl}(\mathfrak{O})$ on $\mathcal{S}_{\mathfrak{O}}(p)$ for some imaginary quadratic $\mathfrak{O}$ as defined in Sect. 2.2. This action can be made a REGA immediately by choosing a generating set $\mathbf{g} = \{\mathfrak{l}_1, \ldots, \mathfrak{l}_n\}$, where each $\mathfrak{l}_i$ is a prime ideal of small norm. To further convert this action into an EGA, challenges arise in sampling elements from a distribution $\mathcal{D}_G$ on G, and computing the action $g \star x$ for $g \in G$ sampled from $\mathcal{D}_G$ and $x \in X$. In this paper, we restrict our interest to the uniform distribution $\mathcal{U}_G$.

In [BKV19], Beullens, Kleinjung, and Vercauteren laid out a general strategy to turn the class group action from a REGA to an EGA as follows:

1. **Offline phase:**
   1.1 *Class group computation* - Compute a generator $\mathfrak{g}$ of the class group $\mathrm{Cl}(\mathfrak{O})$, which is possible because generically $\mathrm{Cl}(\mathfrak{O})$ is cyclic.
   1.2 *Construct the lattice of relations $\mathcal{L}$* - This lattice is generated by the column vectors of the following matrix

$$\begin{pmatrix} 1 & 0 & 0 & \ldots & 0 & 0 \\ 0 & 1 & 0 & \ldots & 0 & 0 \\ 0 & 0 & 1 & \ldots & 0 & 0 \\ \vdots & \vdots & \vdots & \ddots & \vdots & \vdots \\ 0 & 0 & 0 & \ldots & 1 & 0 \\ r_1 & r_2 & r_3 & \ldots & r_n & \#\mathrm{Cl}(\mathfrak{O}) \end{pmatrix},$$

where $r_i's$ are integers such that $[\mathfrak{l}_i] = [\mathfrak{g}^{r_i}]$.

1.3 *Lattice reduction* - Compute a reduced basis of $\mathcal{L}$ suitable for solving approximate-CVP.

2. **Online phase:**

2.1 *Solve approximate-CVP* - Given $\mathfrak{g}^e \in \mathrm{Cl}(\mathfrak{O})$, solve approximate-CVP to find a decomposition $\mathfrak{g}^e = \prod_{i=1}^{i=n} \mathfrak{l}_i^{e_i}$ with small exponents.

2.2 *Group action evaluation* - Compute the action $(\prod_{i=1}^{i=n} \mathfrak{l}_i^{e_i}) \star (E, \iota_E)$ for $(E, \iota_E) \in \mathcal{S}_\mathfrak{O}(p)$.

This strategy allowed Beullens, Kleinjung and Vercauteren to extend the REGA behind the CSIDH key exchange [CLM+18] to an EGA, leading to the construction of the signature scheme CSI-FiSh. They worked with the imaginary quadratic order $\mathbb{Z}[\sqrt{-p}]$ which has a discriminant of 154 digits. The primary challenge for them was computing the class group $\mathrm{Cl}(\mathbb{Z}[\sqrt{-p}])$, and the remaining steps were efficient, essentially due to the fact that they could use a relatively small n and consequently, a lattice with rather small dimension. However, their method can't be scaled for bigger prime p due to the infeasibility of the class group computations.

To address this, SCALLOP [DFFK+23] proposed the use of a distinct class of quadratic orders of the form $\mathfrak{O} = \mathbb{Z}[f\sqrt{-d}]$, where f is a large prime and d is a small positive integer. While this sidesteps the class group computation challenges as discussed in Sect. 2.2 and enhances scalability, it introduces representation complexities for the set elements—oriented curves (E, ι_E). In order to achieve an efficient representation, an generator of $\mathfrak{O}$ of smooth norm should be found, constraining the choice of f and yielding a class group with a non-smooth size. Consequently, the second step of precomputation—computing the lattice of relation—remains subexponential in time due to the need to solve discrete logarithms in groups with subexponential order sizes. Moreover, SCALLOP demands more computations to perform the group action, rendering it much slower than CSI-FiSh.

The security of CSIDH, CSI-FiSh and SCALLOP relies on the hardness of the vectorization problem. Abstractly, for a transitive group action, this problem is defined as follows.

Problem 8. (Vectorization) Given $x, y \in X$, find $g \in G$ such that $y = g \star x$.

According to [Wes22, Proposition 3], the fastest known generic classically method to solve the vectorization problem associated to the group action has complexity $l^{O(1)} |D_\mathfrak{O}|^{1/4}$ where l denotes the length of the input. In the setting of SCALLOP, this is $\log(p + |D_\mathfrak{O}|)^{O(1)} \min(p^{1/2}, f^{1/2})$ [DFFK+23, Section 4].

The main quantum approach to solve the vectorization problem is given by Kuperberg's abelian hidden-shift algorithm [Kup05] and descendants, where the hidden "shift" corresponds to the secret group element g given x and $y = g \star x$. Even though it is known to take subexponential time $L[1/2]$, determining the precise quantum cost for concrete group actions appears difficult. Since 2020, a series of papers [BLMP19,BS20,Pei20,CSCDJRH22] has been studying the quantum security of CSIDH, with some authors claiming that CSIDH-512 and CSIDH-1024 fall far short of reaching NIST security level 1. Instead, [BS20] recommended that the CSIDH prime p should be upgraded to at least 2260 or 5280 bits, according to what they named as *aggressive* and *conservative* modes, respectively. [CSCDJRH22] recommended to use a CSIDH prime of 4096 bits for the level 1 security and 6144 bits for level 2. These analyses, together with the desire of obtaining EGAs from isogenies, have spurred the motivation to improve the scaling of isogeny-based group actions to larger sizes. Since the known quantum attacks work essentially the same for all CRS-style group actions, we will also model the security of SCALLOP using the analyses for CSIDH. Specifically, this means we match the size of the class group $\#\mathrm{Cl}(\mathfrak{O})$ with that of CSIDH to estimate the quantum security level of SCALLOP. In this line of research, CSI-FiSh was only able to scale to achieve the security level of CSIDH-512, and SCALLOP managed to scale to achieve the security level of CSIDH-1024.

4   2dim-Representation of Orientations and Endomorphisms

In this section, we introduce a new representation called 2dim-representation of orientations and endomorphisms. Since representing an endomorphism θ amounts to representing any $\theta + n \in \mathbb{Z}[\theta]$, representing orientations and endomorphisms are essentially the same thing in different languages. Therefore, even though the results in this section are mostly stated with respect to orientations, they apply to endomorphisms as well.

In Sect. 4.1, we introduce the definition of our 2dim-representation for orientations and discuss how to recover the orientation from the 2dim-representation, then in Sect. 4.2, we show that any orientation (endomorphism) admits a 2dim-representation that can be computed in polynomial time. Finally, in Sect. 4.3, we conclude with a formula that computes the $\mathrm{Cl}(\mathfrak{O})$-action on the set $\mathcal{S}_{\mathfrak{O}}(p)$ with set elements given by 2dim-representations.

While our 2dim-representation is introduced to represent orientations appearing in SCALLOP-HD, this technique also has other applications in isogeny-based cryptography.

4.1   2dim-Representation

Let (E, ι_E) be an $\mathfrak{O}$-oriented supersingular elliptic curve. Motivated by the idea of 2dim representation of isogenies, we introduce the following definition.

Definition 9. *Let $\mathfrak{O}$ be an imaginary quadratic order with discriminant $D_{\mathfrak{O}}$ and odd conductor f. Given an $\mathfrak{O}$-oriented supersingular elliptic curve (E, ι_E), take any $\omega \in \mathfrak{O}$ such that $\mathfrak{O} = \mathbb{Z}[\omega]$ and define $\omega_E := \iota_E(\omega)$. Let $\beta \in \mathfrak{O}$ such that $n(\omega) + n(\beta) = 2^e$ and $\gcd(n(\beta), n(\omega)) = 1$. Let P, Q be a basis of $E[2^e]$. Then the tuple $(E, \omega, \beta, P, Q, \omega_E(P), \omega_E(Q))$ is called a 2dim-representation of (E, ι_E).*

Given a 2dim-representation $(E, \omega, \beta, P, Q, \omega_E(P), \omega_E(Q))$ of (E, ι_E), let $\beta_E := \iota_E(\beta)$, we immediately have the following isogeny diamond.

$$E \xrightarrow{\hat{\omega}_E} E$$
$$\beta_E \uparrow \qquad \beta_E \uparrow$$
$$E \xrightarrow{\hat{\omega}_E} E.$$

From here, we can define an isogeny $F_E : E^2 \to E^2$ by the matrix

$$F_E := \begin{pmatrix} \hat{\omega}_E & \hat{\beta}_E \\ -\beta_E & \omega_E \end{pmatrix}.$$

And as discussed in Sect. 2.3, if $\ker \omega_E \cap \ker \beta_E = \{0\}$, then

$$\ker F_E = \{(\omega_E(R), \beta_E(R)) \mid R \in E[2^e]\}.$$

Since β is a translated scalar multiplication of ω_E, knowing the evaluation of ω_E on $E[2^e]$ suffices to compute $\ker F_E$, and to compute the endomorphism ω_E.

4.2 Computing a 2dim-Representation

Now, we explain how to compute a 2dim-representation for an $\mathfrak{O}$-orientation when the discriminant $D_{\mathfrak{O}}$ is equal to 5 mod 8.

Proposition 10. *Let $\mathfrak{O}$ be an imaginary quadratic order of discriminant equal to 5 mod 8, then any $(E, \iota_E) \in \mathcal{S}_{\mathfrak{O}}(p)$ admits a 2dim-representation as in Definition 9.*

Proof. To prove this result, it suffices to show that we can always find $e \in \mathbb{N}, \omega, \beta \in \mathfrak{O}$ such that

$$\mathfrak{O} = \mathbb{Z}[\omega], \quad \gcd(n(\omega), n(\beta)) = 1, \quad n(\omega) + n(\beta) = 2^e.$$

Using the explicit representation of $\mathfrak{O}$ given in Sect. 2.2, $\omega = x + \frac{D_{\mathfrak{O}} + \sqrt{D_{\mathfrak{O}}}}{2}$ and $\beta = y + z \frac{D_{\mathfrak{O}} + \sqrt{D_{\mathfrak{O}}}}{2}$ for some integers x, y, z. Therefore, the last condition above translates to finding an integer solution to the following equation:

$$x^2 + D_{\mathfrak{O}} x + \frac{D_{\mathfrak{O}}(D_{\mathfrak{O}} - 1)}{4} + y^2 + D_{\mathfrak{O}} yz + \frac{D_{\mathfrak{O}}(D_{\mathfrak{O}} - 1)}{4} z^2 = 2^e. \quad (1)$$

Rewriting Eq. (1) and multiplying both sides by 4 gives rise to the following:

$$(2x + D_{\mathfrak{O}})^2 + (2y + D_{\mathfrak{O}} z)^2 = 2^{e+2} + D_{\mathfrak{O}}(z^2 + 1). \quad (2)$$

This equation can be solved efficiently by taking a random z and trying to express $2^{e+2} + D_{\mathfrak{O}}(1 + z^2)$ as a sum of two-squares with Cornacchia's algorithm. When e is large enough, we will be able to try enough z that one will give a solution. No matter what value of z we choose, we see that $2^{e+2} + D_{\mathfrak{O}}(1 + z^2)$ is either equal to 1 mod 4 or 2 times a number that is equal to 1 mod 4. As all numbers that can be written as a sum of two squares satisfy this constraint, we see that there is no obstacle there. Moreover, when $D_{\mathfrak{O}} = 5$ mod 8, we can see that the norm of $\omega = x + \frac{D_{\mathfrak{O}} + \sqrt{D_{\mathfrak{O}}}}{2}$ is always odd. Thus, $n(\omega)$ and $n(\beta)$ are coprime since they sum to a power of 2. □

We now detail the resolution of Eq. (2) with the OrientDiamondDim2 algorithm. The name suggests this algorithm is for building an isogeny diamond for a 2dim-representation of an orientation. Proposition 12 shows that such a diamond can be constructed in polynomial time. We also consider a constant C that is an implicit parameter of OrientDiamondDim2.

Algorithm 1. OrientDiamondDim2($D_{\mathfrak{O}}$)

Input: An imaginary quadratic order $\mathfrak{O}$ with discriminant $D_{\mathfrak{O}} \equiv 5 \bmod 8$.
Output: $\omega, \beta \in \mathfrak{O}$ such that $\mathfrak{O} = \mathbb{Z}[\omega]$, $n(\omega)+n(\beta)$ is a 2-power and $\gcd(n(\beta), n(\omega)) = 1$.

1: Let e be the smallest integer such that $2^{e+2} > C(\log|D_{\mathfrak{O}}|)|D_{\mathfrak{O}}|$.
2: Set $x := 0$, $y := 0$.
3: **for** $z \in [1, \lfloor\sqrt{\frac{2^{e+1}}{|D_{\mathfrak{O}}|}} - 1\rfloor]$ **do**
4:    $M := 2^{e+2} + D_{\mathfrak{O}}(z^2 + 1)$.
5:    **if** M is a prime such that $M \equiv 1 \bmod 4$ or $M = 2M'$ where M' is a prime such that $M' \equiv 1 \bmod 4$ **then**
6:       Use Cornacchia's algorithm to find X, Y such that $X^2 + Y^2 = M$ and X is odd.
7:       Set $x = (X - D_{\mathfrak{O}})/2$ and $y = (Y - zD_{\mathfrak{O}})/2$.
8:       **break**
9:    **end if**
10: **end for**
11: **if** $x = 0$ and $y = 0$ **then**
12:    Return $\perp$.
13: **end if**
14: $\omega := x + \frac{D_{\mathfrak{O}}+\sqrt{D_{\mathfrak{O}}}}{2}$, $\beta := y + z\frac{D_{\mathfrak{O}}+\sqrt{D_{\mathfrak{O}}}}{2}$.
15: **return** ω, β.

The complexity statement on Algorithm 1 only holds assuming some plausible heuristic regarding the distribution of number of the form $2^e + D(1 + z^2)$ that we state below as Heuristic 11.

Heuristic 11. Let $e, D_{\mathfrak{O}}$ be as in Algorithm 1. If $D_{\mathfrak{O}} = 5 \bmod 8$, and z are sampled as random integers then the integers $2^{e+2} + D_{\mathfrak{O}}(1 + z^2)$ behave like random integers of the same size that are either congruent to 1 mod 4 or equal to 2 times an integer that is equal to 1 modulo 4.

Proposition 12. *Assuming Heuristic 11, and $D_{\mathfrak{O}} = 5 \bmod 8$, OrientDiamond Dim2 is correct, runs in $O\left(\text{poly}\left(C\log(|D_{\mathfrak{O}}|)\right)\right)$, and there exists a constant C' such that the computation has succeeded with probability at least:*

$$1 - (1 - C'/\log(|D_{\mathfrak{O}}|))^{\sqrt{C\log(D_{\mathfrak{O}})}}.$$

Proof. The correctness of Algorithm 1 follows from the observation that the outputs ω, β will always satisfy that $\mathfrak{O} = \mathbb{Z}[\omega], \gcd(n(\omega), n(\beta)) = 1$ and $n(\omega) +$

$n(\beta) = 2^e$. In particular, M is either congruent to 1 mod 4 or equal to 2 times an integer that is congruent to 1 mod 4 depending on the parity of z, then at least one of X, Y is odd. In either cases, both $X - D_{\mathfrak{D}}$ and $Y - zD_{\mathfrak{D}}$ will be even.

The complexity follows from the fact that we perform $O(\sqrt{C \log(|D_{\mathfrak{D}})|}$ iteration of the loop and that the operations required inside each iteration are logarithmic in $|D_{\mathfrak{D}}|$. The integers M have size $C(\log |D_{\mathfrak{D}}|)|D_{\mathfrak{D}}|$ and we assume that they behave like random integers under Heuristic 11, therefore there is a constant C' such that either $M/2$ or M is prime with probability higher than $C'/(\log |D_{\mathfrak{D}}|)$. The bound on the success probability follows directly from there. □

Remark 13. We choose to work with isogenies in dimension 2 of degree $N = 2^e$ for efficiency of computing such isogenies in practice, and we later choose p such that 2^e-torsion is defined over $\mathbb{F}_{p^2}$ in the set up of SCALLOP-HD. However, our definition for *2dim*-representation and OrientDiamondDim2 easily generalizes to general degree N. Explicitly, it suffices to require that

$$n(\omega) + n(\beta) = N$$

in Definition 9, and to solve the equation

$$(2x + D_{\mathfrak{D}})^2 + (2y + D_{\mathfrak{D}}z)^2 = 4N + D_{\mathfrak{D}}(z^2 + 1)$$

to find ω, β. This equation can be solved similarly except that one needs to impose a different congruence condition on $D_{\mathfrak{D}}$ with respect to that of N to ensure that the right hand side is a sum of two squares with non-negligible probability. One particular interesting case is when N is chosen to be powersmooth as in this case the torsion subgroup $E[N]$ can be effectively represented. Despite the condition that $D_{\mathfrak{D}} \equiv 5 \mod 8$ in Proposition 10, this remark justifies our claim that every orientation and endomorphism can be effectively represented by an isogeny in between abelian surfaces.

Remark 14. By choosing N to be powersmooth, our *2dim*-representation can be applied to [HW23, Algorithm 1] to replace the isogeny computations in dimension 8 with computations in dimension 2, improving its efficiency.

4.3   Class Group Action Evaluation

Let $[\mathfrak{a}] \in \mathrm{Cl}(\mathfrak{D})$ where $\mathfrak{a}$ is an integral $\mathfrak{D}$-ideal such that $\gcd(n(\mathfrak{a}), 2) = 1$. We now explain how to calculate the group action introduced in Sect. 2.2 in the context of the *2dim*-representation.

Let $(E, \omega, \beta, P, Q, \omega_E(P), \omega_E(Q))$ be a *2dim*-representation of (E, ι_E), to calculate a *2dim*-representation for $(E_{\mathfrak{a}}, \iota_{E_{\mathfrak{a}}})$, we can keep the same ω and β. Since $\gcd(n(\mathfrak{a}), 2) = 1$, $\{\phi_{\mathfrak{a}}(P), \phi_{\mathfrak{a}}(Q)\}$ form a basis of $E_{\mathfrak{a}}[2^e]$. By definition,

$$\iota_{E_{\mathfrak{a}}}(\phi_{\mathfrak{a}}(P, Q)) = \frac{1}{n(\mathfrak{a})}\phi_{\mathfrak{a}} \circ \omega_E \circ \hat{\phi}_{\mathfrak{a}}(\phi_{\mathfrak{a}}(P, Q)) = \phi_{\mathfrak{a}}(\omega_E(P, Q)).$$

Let $\{R, S\}$ be a basis for $E_{\mathfrak{a}}[2^e]$, such as the one computed by a deterministic algorithm that computes a basis. Given $P, Q, \omega_E(P), \omega_E(Q) \in E[2^e]$, to compute $\iota_{E_{\mathfrak{a}}}(\omega)(R)$ and $\iota_{E_{\mathfrak{a}}}(\omega)(S)$, we first write R, S as linear combinations of $\phi_{\mathfrak{a}}(P)$ and $\phi_{\mathfrak{a}}(Q)$, then compute $\iota_{E_{\mathfrak{a}}}(\omega)(R)$ and $\iota_{E_{\mathfrak{a}}}(\omega)(S)$ from $\iota_{E_{\mathfrak{a}}}(\phi_{\mathfrak{a}}(P)) = \phi_{\mathfrak{a}}(\omega(P))$ and $\iota_{E_{\mathfrak{a}}}(\phi_{\mathfrak{a}}(Q)) = \phi_{\mathfrak{a}}(\omega(Q))$.

5   SCALLOP-HD Group Action

In this section, we introduce SCALLOP-HD, an effective group action (EGA). SCALLOP-HD builds on SCALLOP by using the same group action, i.e., $\mathrm{Cl}(\mathfrak{O})$ acts on $\mathcal{S}_{\mathfrak{O}}(p)$ for $\mathfrak{O} = \mathbb{Z}[f\sqrt{-d}]$. However, SCALLOP-HD deviates from SCALLOP by representing the set elements differently. Precisely, SCALLOP-HD uses the 2dim-representation for $(E, \iota_E) \in \mathcal{S}_{\mathfrak{O}}(p)$. It turns out that this choice significantly simplifies the group action computation, and removes some of the constraints on parameter choices, which essentially is due to the fact that we no longer need to find a generator of $\mathfrak{O}$ of smooth norm, removing the trade-off between the smoothness of the generator norm and the group size $\#\mathrm{Cl}(\mathfrak{O})$. As has been mentioned before, SCALLOP-HD has better scalability and has the potential of being more efficient.

5.1   Outline of SCALLOP-HD

It is clear from Sect. 3 that to introduce an EGA using the class group action, one needs to

- specify the group and the set,
- convert the action into a REGA by choosing the set **g** as in Definition 7,
- and derive an EGA following the stragety outlined in Sect. 3.

To define the group action, we start with choosing the field characteristic p and the quadratic order $\mathfrak{O}$, they determine the group $\mathrm{Cl}(\mathfrak{O})$ and the set $\mathcal{S}_{\mathfrak{O}}(p)$. When making these choices, there are two aspects one needs to take into consideration – first, from a security point of view, the vectorization problem of the action should be hard; second, from an efficiency point of view, p should be of a particular form so that the torsion points involved in subsequent calculations are defined over $\mathbb{F}_{p^2}$, and additionally $\mathfrak{O}$ should be an order for which $\#\mathrm{Cl}(\mathfrak{O})$ is as smooth as possible for an efficient generation of the lattice of relation $\mathcal{L}$ (Sect. 3). In SCALLOP-HD, each element (E, ι_E) will be given using the 2dim-representation, and we also specify the relevant parameters ω, β as a part of the group action definition. We discuss the details in Sect. 5.2.

To perform the group action, it's essential to possess an element from the set $\mathcal{S}_{\mathfrak{O}}(p)$. Acquiring this element, given our choice of $\mathfrak{O}$, isn't straightforward. We introduce the SetUpCurveHD algorithm in Sect. 5.3 specifically for this purpose.

Once the group action is set up, we proceed in the conventional manner to convert it into a REGA. Let $\{\ell_1, \ldots, \ell_n\}$ be the first n odd primes that split in $\mathfrak{O}$ for $n = O(\log f)$, then we choose the set **g** to consist of the ideals $\{\mathfrak{l}_1, \ldots, \mathfrak{l}_k\}$

with $\mathfrak{l}_i$ being one of the prime ideal above ℓ_i. To further convert the REGA to an EGA, the offline phase is discussed in Sect. 5.4 and the online phase is discussed in Sect. 5.5.

5.2   Set Up the Group Action

In this section, we explicit various choice of parameters for setting up the group action.

Choice of the Quadratic Order. Let $\mathfrak{O}_0 = \mathbb{Z}[\sqrt{-d}]$ be an imaginary quadratic order of class number equal to 1 and discriminant equal to $d = 5 \bmod 8$, as in SCALLOP, we choose $\mathfrak{O}$ to be of the form $\mathbb{Z} + f\mathfrak{O}_0$ for a large prime f. The size of f will be determined by the target security level. For the efficient precomputation of the lattice of relations (elaborated further in Sect. 5.4), we want to ensure that $\#\mathrm{Cl}(\mathfrak{O}) = f - \left(\frac{-d}{f}\right)$ is as smooth as possible. Such a prime integer f can be found efficiently in polynomial time by generating random smooth integers and see whether they are of the form $f - \left(\frac{-d}{f}\right)$.

Choosing the Field Characteristic p. To ensure that the set $\mathcal{S}_{\mathfrak{O}}(p)$ is non-empty, we need to choose p that does not split in $\mathfrak{O}$ and does not divide the conductor f according to Proposition 3. Moreover, the form of p is determined by the torsion subgroups needed. To efficiently represent the orientation, we require that 2^e-torsion is defined over $\mathbb{F}_{p^2}$. For efficient computation of the group action, we also require to have the $\prod_{1 \le i \le n} \ell_i$-torsion defined over $\mathbb{F}_{p^2}$. These conditions on torsion points amounts to selecting a prime of the form:

$$p = c2^e \prod_{i=1}^{n} \ell_i \pm 1,$$

where c is a small cofactor.

Representing the Orientation. Recall that a *2*dim-representation of an orientation is given by the tuple $(E, \omega, \beta, P, Q, \omega_E(P), \omega_E(Q))$. Once we have fixed $\mathfrak{O}$ from the previous discussion, we can determine the integer e and $\omega, \beta \in \mathfrak{O}$ for instance using the OrientDiamondDim2 algorithm.

In SCALLOP-HD group action, ω, β will be part of public parameters, therefore, they can be omitted from the orientation representation. Furthermore, we can use a deterministic algorithm that computes a basis of $E[2^e]$ for any curve E, this way we omit P, Q from the representation to make it even compacter. That being said, in the actual application of SCALLOP-HD group action, the orientation representation will be of the form $(E, \omega_E(P), \omega_E(Q))$.

5.3   Set Up a Starting Curve

The computation of one $\mathfrak{O}$-oriented curve is necessary to set-up the scheme. This starting curve can be used to generate every other oriented curve by applying the group action. Concretely, computing one 2dim-representation for a $\mathfrak{D}$-oriented curve means the following: compute any f-isogeny starting from an $\mathfrak{D}_0$-oriented curve E_0 and evaluate it on a basis of $E_0[2^e]$.

For this, we propose to revisit SetUpCurve [DFFK+23, Algorithm 1] as our setting remains very similar to SCALLOP. Since the conductor f is a big prime, we cannot hope to compute any isogeny of degree f directly. The trick behind SetUpCurve is to use an endomorphism of norm fS where S is a smooth integer and to express the f isogeny as the composition of this endomorphism and an isogeny of degree S. Such endomorphisms can be found with the FullRepresent-Integer [DFLLW23, Algorithm 1] as soon as $fS \approx p$. Since our ultimate goal is to evaluate the orientation on the 2^e torsion, the best option would be to take S coprime to 2, and with our choice of prime characteristic, we would have $S = \prod_i \ell_i$. Unfortunately, since $2^e \approx f^2$, we have $f \prod_i \ell_i \approx p/f$. This means that we must include other factors in S to reach the desired size. The only remaining available torsion is the power of 2. Since $2^{e/2} \approx f$, we should have $f 2^{e/2} \prod_i \ell_i \approx p$. This means that we will be able to find endomorphisms of norm $\ell_1^h f 2^{e/2} \prod_{i>1} \ell_i$ for some small exponent h. In that case, we can circumvent the fact that S is not coprime to 2 by using a trick presented in [DLRW23, Sect. 5.4] to cut the computation of the 2-dimensional isogeny in two, which allows us to divide by two the torsion requirement. For the group action computation, we prefer to use the full 2^e-torsion because the computation is more direct, but for the set-up of the scheme it is not a problem to sacrifice a bit of efficiency. The idea we just outlined gives the algorithm SetUpCurveHD that we describe below.

We start with an element $(E_0, \iota_0) \in \mathcal{S}_{\mathfrak{D}_0}(p)$. Let $\mathcal{O}_0$ be a maximal quaternion order such that $\mathrm{End}(E_0) \cong \mathcal{O}_0$, and we can fix an explicit isomorphism $\rho_0 : \mathcal{O}_0 \hookrightarrow \mathrm{End}(E_0)$, we write ω_0 for $\iota_0(\sqrt{-d})$. Then, the orientation ι_0 is derived from the inclusion $\mathfrak{D}_0 \subseteq \mathcal{O}_0$ and the isomorphism ρ_0.

Proposition 15. *SetUpCurveHD is correct and terminates in $O(\mathrm{cpoly}(\log(p)))$.*

Proof. To prove correctness, we need to verify that the output $(E, (R, S))$ is a correct 2dim-representation of an element in $\mathcal{S}_{\mathfrak{D}}(p)$. Let us assume that the verification made in the loop passed. We will start by proving correctness under that assumption, then we will justify why the verification always passes.

When the verification passes, it means that there exists $\omega_E \in \mathrm{End}(E)$ of same norm and trace as ω. Thus, $\mathbb{Z}[\omega_E] \cong \mathbb{Z}[\omega] = \mathfrak{D}$, and sending ω to ω_E defines a $\mathfrak{D}$-orientation ι_E on E (we explain later in the proof why this is an optimal embedding of $\mathfrak{D}$ into $\mathrm{End}(E)$). Moreover, $R, S = \omega_E(P, Q)$ for a deterministic basis $\{P, Q\}$ of $E[2^e]$. Therefore, $(E, (R, S)) = (E, \omega_E(P, Q))$ is a valid 2dim-representation of $(E, \iota_E) \in \mathcal{S}_{\mathfrak{D}}(p)$.

Now, let us justify that there always is an i that passes the verification. The element $\gamma \in \mathcal{O}_0$ provides us with a principal ideal $\mathcal{O}_0\gamma$, whose corresponding isogeny $\rho_0(\varphi_\gamma)$ is an endomorphism of E_0. Moreover, we have that (up to composing with some isomorphisms if necessary) $\varphi_\gamma = \psi' \circ \varphi \circ \varphi_f$ where $\varphi_f : E_0 \to E$ has degree f, $\varphi : E \to E'$ has degree ℓ_1^{h-1} and $\psi' : E' \to E_0$ has degree $2^{e/2} \prod_i \ell_i$. By [DFFK+23, Proposition 16], E is an $\mathfrak{D}$-orientable curve

---

Algorithm 2. SetUpCurveHD(p, f)

Input: p, f, e, ω, β as defined in Sect. 5.2 and $\mathfrak{O}_0, (E_0, \iota_0)$ as defined above.

Output: A 2dim-representation for $(E, \iota_E) \in \mathcal{S}_{\mathfrak{O}}(p)$ where $\mathfrak{O} = \mathbb{Z} + f\mathfrak{O}_0$.

1: Set h such that $\ell_1^h > p/(f2^{e/2} \prod_{i>1} \ell_i)$ and compute $\gamma \in \mathcal{O}_0$ of norm $f2^{e/2} \ell_1^h \prod_{i>1} \ell_i$ with FullRepresentInteger. Repeat that, until $\mathcal{O}_0\langle \gamma, f \rangle$ do not commute with ω_0.

2: Compute the isogeny $\psi : E_0 \to E'$ of degree $2^{e/2} \prod_i \ell_i$ corresponding to the ideal $\mathcal{O}_0\langle \bar{\gamma}, 2^{e/2} \prod_i \ell_i \rangle$.

3: Compute P_0, Q_0 a basis of $E_0[2^e]$ and compute $R_0, S_0 = \iota(P_0, Q_0)$.

4: Compute the points $P_0, Q_0, R_0, S_0 = \rho_0(\gamma)(P_0, Q_0, R_0, S_0)$.

5: Make the list $(\varphi_i : E' \to E_i)_{1 \le i \le m}$ with $m = (\ell_1 + 1)\ell_1^{h-2}$ of all isogenies of degree ℓ_1^{h-1} from E'.

6: **for** $i \in [1, m]$: **do**

7:    Compute $P_i, Q_i, R_i, S_i = ([(\ell_1^h \prod_{i>1} \ell_i)^{-1} \bmod 2^{e/2}])\varphi_i \circ \psi(P_0, Q_0, R_0, S_0)$.

8:    Compute $R_i, S_i = [f](R_i, S_i)$.

9:    Try to use P_i, Q_i, R_i, S_i to build two isogenies $F_1 : E_i^2 \to C$ and $\hat{F}_2 : E_i^2 \to C$.

10:   If it works, check that $F = F_2 \circ F_1$ is a dimension 2 representation for endomorphisms $\omega_{E_i}, \beta_{E_i}$.

11:   If yes, verify that $\text{tr}(\omega_{E_i}), n(\omega_{E_i})$ is the same as $\text{tr}(\omega), n(\omega)$. If yes, break from the loop.

12: **end for**

13: Set $E = E_i$, and compute a deterministic basis P, Q of $E[2^e]$.

14: Use F to compute $R, S = \omega_E(P, Q)$.

15: **return** $(E, (R, S))$.

---

unless φ_f corresponds to one of the $1 + \left(\frac{d_0}{f}\right)$ horizontal f-isogenies of domain E_0. Let us assume for now that it is not. The endomorphism $\omega_E = \iota_E(\omega)$ is equal to $[x] + \varphi_f \circ \omega_0 \circ \hat{\varphi}_f$. By design, the ideal $\langle \bar{\gamma}, 2^{e/2} \prod_i \ell_i \rangle$ corresponds to the isogeny $\hat{\psi}'$. Thus, we have that the isogeny ψ computed in Step 2, is the isogeny $\hat{\psi}'$. Then, if we take the index i_0 such that $\varphi_{i_0} = \hat{\varphi}$, we get that E_{i_0} is the curve E that we are looking for. Then, it can be verified that P_{i_0}, Q_{i_0} is equal to $[2^{e/2}]\varphi_f(P_0, Q_0)$, so it is a basis of $E_{i_0}[2^{e/2}]$. It can also be verified that the equality $R_{i_0}, S_{i_0} = \varphi_f \circ \omega_0 \circ \hat{\varphi}_f(P_{i_0}, Q_{i_0})$. From there, the image points $\omega_E(P_{i_0}, Q_{i_0})$ and $\beta_E(P_{i_0}, Q_{i_0})$ can be recovered, and this is enough to build the two isogenies $\hat{F}_2$ and F_1 as described in [DLRW23, Appendix A.4]. Then, F is the correct endomorphism on E^2 constructed from isogeny diamond formed by ω_E and β_E, and so the check for norm and trace equality will pass.

To finish the proof of correctness, we simply need to prove that the case where φ_f might be one of the bad isogenies cannot happen. In that case, we have that φ_f is one of the horizontal isogenies and since $\mathfrak{O}_0$ has class number one, this means that φ_f commutes with ω_0 which is equivalent to the fact that ideal corresponding to φ_f commutes with ω_0. Since this ideal is exactly equal to $\mathcal{O}_0\langle \gamma, f \rangle$, this situation is prevented from happening.

Regarding complexity, we have $\ell_1^{h-1} < p/(f2^{e/2} \prod_i \ell_i)$ and since we have $f = O(2^{e/2})$, the loop is repeated at most $O(c)$ times. The computations over the quaternions are in $O(\mathsf{poly}(\log(p)))$. Then, since we have the explicit isomorphism ρ_0, we can compute ψ and evaluate $\rho_0(\gamma)$ over the 2^e-torsion in $O(\mathsf{poly}(\log(p)))$ (remember that the 2^e-torsion is defined over $\mathbb{F}_{p^2}$ and $2^e < p$). Then, the computation of each φ_i is in $O(\mathsf{poly}(\log(p)))$ and computing s_i and checking the trace has $O(\mathsf{poly}(\log(p)))$ complexity with the CheckTrace algorithm introduced in [Ler22a]. Computing the norm can be done very similarly with the same complexity. This proves the result. □

5.4 Offline Phase

The remaining operations required to be done in the precomputation are exactly the same as in SCALLOP. First, we need to generate the relation lattice associated to the ideal basis $(\mathfrak{l}_i)_{1 \le i \le n}$. Second, we need to find a reduced basis of this lattice. These operations can be done exactly as explained in [DFFK+23]. The lattice of relations is generated by solving some discrete logarithms in the class group. Then, the reduced basis is found using standard lattice reduction techniques.

The only real difference between SCALLOP and our new construction is the complexity of those operations. In particular, with our choice of quadratic order, the generation of the lattice of relations takes polynomial time. Indeed, the choice of f ensures that the class group has order $f - \left(\frac{-d}{f}\right)$ with a polynomial smoothness bound. This means that the Pohlig-Hellman method succeeds in solving discrete logarithm in polynomial time and so the full lattice of relations can be generated in polynomial time (whereas it has subexponential complexity in general). Unfortunately, the complexity of the basis reductions remains superpolynomial, which means that the overall complexity of the precomputation is still superpolynomial. However, as explained in [DFFK+23], for modest parameter sizes, the dimension of the relation lattice can be taken quite small and so a nearly-optimal basis can be found efficiently in practice.

5.5 Online Phase

We now describe precisely an algorithm GroupAction to perform the group action for SCALLOP-HD given an ideal $\mathfrak{a} = \prod_{1 \le i \le n} \mathfrak{l}_i^{e_i}$ where $\mathfrak{l}_i$ is an ideal of norm ℓ_i. In GroupAction below, we restrict to the case $\mathfrak{a} = \prod_i \mathfrak{l}_i$ to simplify the exposition as the generic algorithm simply consists in several executions of the sub-algorithm for $\prod_i \mathfrak{l}_i$.

Proposition 16. *Algorithm 3 GroupAction is correct and runs in*

$$\tilde{O}\left(\mathsf{poly}\left(\log(p)\log(f)n\right)\sqrt{\max_{1 \le i \le n} \ell_i}\right).$$

Proof. Let us start by proving correctness. Since $\omega, \beta \in \mathfrak{O}$ we have that the endomorphisms $\omega_E, \iota_E(\beta)$ commutes and since we have $2^e = n(\omega) + n(\beta)$, by Lemma 4, the 2^e-isogeny $F_E : E^2 \to E^2$ is correctly computed from its kernel.

Algorithm 3. GroupAction($(E, \iota_E), \mathfrak{a}$)

Input: p, f, e, ω, β as defined in Section 5.2, 2dim-representation $(E, \omega_E(P), \omega_E(Q))$ of (E, ι_E), and an ideal $\mathfrak{a} = \prod_{1 \le i \le n} \mathfrak{l}_i$, where each $\mathfrak{l}_i$ is an ideal of odd prime norm ℓ_i

Output: 2dim-representation of $\mathfrak{a} \star (E, \iota_E) = (E_{\mathfrak{a}}, \iota_{E_{\mathfrak{a}}})$

1: Compute a deterministic basis P, Q of $E[2^e]$.
2: Set x_β, y_β the values in $\mathbb{Z}$ such that $\beta = x_\beta + y_\beta \omega$.
3: Compute $F : E^2 \to E^2$ the 2^e-isogeny of kernel generated by $(\omega_E(P), [x_\beta]P + [y_\beta]\omega_E(P)), (\omega_E(Q), [x_\beta]Q + [y_\beta]\omega_E(Q))$.
4: Compute the value λ_i such that $\mathfrak{l}_i = \mathfrak{O}\langle \omega - \lambda_i, \ell_i \rangle$.
5: **for** $i \in [1, \dots, n]$ **do**
6:    Let P_i, Q_i be a basis of ℓ_i in $E[\ell_i]$.
7:    Compute $(\star, U_i) = F(0_E, P_i)$ and $(\star, V_i) = F(0_E, Q_i)$.
8:    Set R_i as one point of order ℓ_i among $\{[\mathrm{tr}(\omega) - \lambda_i]P_i - U_i, [\mathrm{tr}(\omega) - \lambda_i]Q_i - V_i\}$.
9: **end for**
10: Compute $\varphi_{\mathfrak{a}} : E \to E_{\mathfrak{a}}$, the isogeny of kernel $G_{\mathfrak{a}} = \bigcap_{1 \le i \le n} \langle R_i \rangle$.
11: Compute a deterministic basis R, S of $E_{\mathfrak{a}}[2^e]$.
12: Compute $\iota_{E_{\mathfrak{a}}}(\omega)(R)$ and $\iota_{E_{\mathfrak{a}}}(\omega)(S)$ using $\varphi_{\mathfrak{a}}(\omega_E(P))$ and $\varphi_{\mathfrak{a}}(\omega_E(Q))$.
13: **return** $E_{\mathfrak{a}}, \iota_{E_{\mathfrak{a}}}(\omega)(R), \iota_{E_{\mathfrak{a}}}(\omega)(S)$.

Then, we have that $F(0, R) = (\star, \omega_E(R))$ for any point R. Thus, we do have $U_i = \omega_E(P_i), V_i = \omega_E(Q_i)$ for each $1 \le i \le n$. The kernel of $\omega_E - \lambda_i$ is equal to $(\hat{\omega}_E - \lambda_i)(E[\ell_i])$ and since $\hat{\omega}_E = [\mathrm{tr}(\omega)] - \omega_E$, the point R_i computed is a generator of $\ker(\omega_E - \lambda_i) = \ker \varphi_{\mathfrak{l}_i} = \ker \varphi_{\mathfrak{a}} \cap E[\ell_i]$. Thus, the computation of $\varphi_{\mathfrak{a}}$ is correct, and the computation of the 2dim-representation of $\mathfrak{a} \star (E, \iota_E)$ is correct by the formulas given in Sect. 4.3. The last step is merely changing the evaluation to the deterministic basis using linear algebra.

Regarding the complexity, the 2^e-isogeny F_E can be computed evaluated in $O\left(\mathsf{poly}\left(\log(p)e\right)\right) = O\left(\mathsf{poly}\left(\log(p)\log(f)\right)\right)$. Then, since the points of $E[\ell_i]$ are defined over $\mathbb{F}_{p^2}$, the cost to compute the bases P_i, Q_i and to compute U_i, V_i through evaluation of F is $O\left(\mathsf{poly}\left(\log(p)\log(f)n\right)\right)$.

Finally, using the $\sqrt{\text{élu}}$ formulas introduced in [BDFLS20], it is possible to compute the isogeny $\varphi_{\mathfrak{a}}$ of norm $\prod_{1 \le i \le n} \ell_i$ in $\tilde{O}\left(\mathsf{poly}\left(\log(p)n\right)\sqrt{\max_{1 \le i \le n} \ell_i}\right)$. This proves the result. $\qquad\square$

5.6 Implementation Results

In this section, we report on our preliminary proof-of-concept implementation of SCALLOP-HD in SageMath [The23], which can be found at:

https://github.com/isogeny-scallophd/scallophd

·

Order and Relation Lattice. We computed suitable choices of $\mathfrak{O}$ and reduced bases of its associated lattice of relations, for sizes of $D_{\mathfrak{O}}$ up to 4096 bits, which is twice the size of the largest provided SCALLOP instantiation. The lattice of relations can easily be found for even larger sizes; however, increasing sizes of $D_{\mathfrak{O}}$

and therefore $h(\mathfrak{O})$ warrant the use of growing lattice dimensions, which (due to the superpolynomial asymptotic growth in cost) eventually renders either the lattice-reduction step or the online phase prohibitively costly.

In all parameter sets, we use fundamental discriminant $D_K = -11$, which is congruent to 5 modulo 8 as required. The conductor f was chosen as a random prime of the form $f = 2^k m + 1$ with m a small odd integer, such that f is split in $\mathbb{Q}(\sqrt{D_K})$. Hence the class group is cyclic of order $2^k m$, which makes the required discrete logarithms in the class group particularly easy to compute.[2] As a generating set of the class group, we consider the first n prime integers ℓ_i which split in $\mathfrak{O}$ and, for each of them, let $\mathfrak{l}_i = (\ell_i, f\sqrt{D_\mathfrak{O}} - m_i)$ where m_i is the smallest non-negative integer such that $\mathfrak{l}_i$ is a prime ideal of norm ℓ_i. The reduced relation lattices for these parameter sets can be computed in no more than a few core-hours per parameter set, almost all of which is spent on running the BKZ lattice-reduction algorithm.

Starting Curve. We then computed starting curves for the chosen parameters using a KLPT-based approach using the implementation of [EPSV23]. This is practically easier than using SetUpCurveHD (Algorithm 2) for lack of sufficiently general genus-2 isogeny libraries, but presumably slower: Computing the starting curve took about 2 single-core hours for a 512-bit discriminant with $n = 74$ as in CSIDH-512, and about 85 single-core hours for a 1024-bit discriminant with $n = 100$. (We stress again that these timings are for a naïve implementation of the setup phase and can be improved a lot.)

Computing the Action. Finally, our implementation of the SCALLOP-HD group action itself relies heavily on the SageMath implementation of dimension-2 isogenies provided by [DMPR23]. Although it is hard to compare our Sage-Math implementation to the C++ implementation of SCALLOP, our preliminary results seem to indicate that SCALLOP-HD can at least compete: For the 512-bit parameter set, a single group-action evaluation averages around 88 s on an Intel Alder Lake CPU core clocked at 2.1 GHz, compared to around 42 s for SCALLOP on the same hardware configuration. For the 1024-bit parameter set, a single group-action evaluation averages around 19 min, compared to around 15 min for SCALLOP. However, profiling data reveals that the 2-dimensional isogenies used in SCALLOP-HD are in fact relatively cheap, accounting for only about a third of the total computational effort: Most of the time is spent on "traditional" elliptic-curve arithmetic, which can therefore be expected to benefit from very significant speedups using well-known standard optimization techniques and implementation tricks for genus-1 arithmetic which have not been incorporated into SageMath. We are thus optimistic that a more optimized

---

[2] We note that Kuperberg's quantum algorithm works by first reducing to cyclic groups of two-power order, hence this group structure cannot be fundamentally weaker against Kuperberg's algorithm than a random cyclic group of similar size. See for instance [Pan21, §2.6.3].

SCALLOP-HD implementation will be able to outperform SCALLOP by a comfortable margin as the security level grows.

6   Some Remarks on Security

The security of SCALLOP-HD is identical to that of SCALLOP because the group action has the same exact structure. In this section, we take the opportunity to discuss the impact of recent developments from the papers [CII+23, CV23] on the security of SCALLOP and SCALLOP-HD.

In [DFFK+23], one proposed method to attack SCALLOP is to compute the ideal corresponding to the isogeny φ_f of degree f connecting the $\mathfrak{O}_0$-oriented curve E_0 with the $\mathfrak{O}$-oriented curve E. In [CII+23], a polynomial-time quantum algorithm is introduced to perform that computation when there is an efficient way to evaluate this f-isogeny on points of powersmooth order. Since the endomorphism ω_E can be written as $d + \varphi_f \circ \omega_0 \circ \hat{\varphi}_f$ for some integer d and $\omega_0 \in \mathrm{End}(E_0)$, the security of SCALLOP then reduces to the following question:

Can we use the effective orientation ω_E revealed in SCALLOP(-HD) to evaluate φ_f?

As far as we know, the answer to this question is no (at least not in polynomial time). In fact, the problem of evaluating the descending isogeny φ_f was already discussed in [DFFK+23, Sect. 7] even though the algorithm from [CII+23] didn't exist at the time. The discussion presented in [DFFK+23, Sect. 7] is still relevant and justifies why evaluating φ_f from ω_E appears hard. One possible way to reduce the search space introduced in [DFFK+23, Sect. 7] would be to use nontrivial self-pairings (i.e. pairing such that $e(P, P)$ is not 1). However, there are no known self-pairings in the context of SCALLOP(-HD) and some negative results regarding the existence of these objects were even recently shown in [CHM+23].

Recently, [CV23] introduced a generalization of the "lollipop method" to recover an isogeny from a partial torsion information. More concretely, it targets the following setting. Let $\varphi : E_0 \to E$ be an isogeny of degree f and P, Q be a basis of $E_0[N]$ for some big enough integer N. The goal is to recover φ from the knowledge of T, S where T, S is a basis of $E[N]$ equal to $X \cdot \varphi(P, Q)$ for some secret matrix X contained in some subset of $GL_2(\mathbb{Z}/N\mathbb{Z})$. Typically, [CV23] targets the case where X is diagonal, but they introduce a generic framework that can handle a broader variety of families of Xs. The fact that X is unknown is the main obstacle to apply the usual isogeny recovery attacks or the attack from [CII+23]. The paper [CV23] shows how to overcome this obstacle when the parameters d, N, p allow the existence (and efficient computation) of an endomorphism $\rho \in \mathrm{End}(E_0)$ satisfying various constraints.

Below, we try to apply this attack to recover the isogeny φ_f using the knowledge of the orientation. In particular, we will have a look at the case where X is diagonal. Indeed, when taking N as a product of split primes in $\mathfrak{O}_0$, P, Q to be two generators of the eigenspaces of ω_0 in $E_0[N]$ and T, S generators of the eigenspaces of $\omega_E \in E[N]$, we are exactly in the desired setting where the unknown matrix is diagonal (since eigenspaces of ω_0 are mapped to eigenspaces of ω_E by φ_f).

When N is powersmooth, the points P, Q, T, S can be computed in polynomial time by evaluating ω_0 and ω_E, and solving some discrete logarithms. The method introduced in [CD23] works by computing a non-trivial endomorphism $\rho = \kappa \circ \sigma$ such that $[\varphi_f]_*\sigma$ can be computed efficiently, the matrix of the action of ρ in the basis P, Q commutes with the matrix X and $\deg \kappa \leq N^2/f^2$. When those conditions are satisfied, it can be shown that the image of the isogeny $\psi = [\sigma]_*\varphi_f \circ \kappa \circ \hat{\varphi}_f$ on T, S can be computed exactly, allowing for its efficient computation with higher dimensional isogenies. In a number of cases, this is enough to recover φ_f directly, but not always. In the setting of SCALLOP-HD, this is not necessarily new information if the endomorphism $\hat{\psi} \circ [\varphi_f]_*\sigma$ belongs to $\iota_E(\mathfrak{O})$. On the other hand, when it does not, then we obtain a full quaternion suborder of $\mathrm{End}(E)$ in that matter, and that might be enough to evaluate φ_f with an adaptation of [Ler22a, Algorithm 5] and then, we can apply the attack from [CII+23].

Thus, the question becomes: can we find such an endomorphism ρ satisfying all the previous constraints? While we do not know how to prove formally that the answer is always no, we provide examples where we can prove that finding a suitable ρ is impossible.

As far as we know, there are essentially three types of isogenies σ for which we have an efficient way to compute the push-forward $[\varphi_f]_*\sigma$:

1. The identity.
2. The Frobenius.
3. Horizontal isogenies (used in the group action).

Let us consider the case where σ is the identity. We want to find $\rho \in \mathrm{End}(E_0)$ that acts as a diagonal matrix on the subgroups generated by P and Q. As we explained before, we have an attack if we can find $\rho \notin \mathbb{Z}[\omega_0]$ (otherwise we don't learn anything new).

Let $\mathcal{O}_0$ be a quaternion maximal order isomorphic to $\mathrm{End}(E_0)$ and I, J, the two left $\mathcal{O}_0$-ideals of norm N corresponding to the subgroups generated by P and Q under the Deuring correspondence. Then, ρ will act as a diagonal matrix on the two subgroups if and only if it is contained inside the quaternion order $\mathcal{O} = (\mathbb{Z} + I) \cap (\mathbb{Z} + J)$ which is an Eichler order of level N^2. This is a lattice of volume equal to Cp^2N^4 for some small constant C. And this means the four successive minimas $\lambda_1, \lambda_2, \lambda_3, \lambda_4$ satisfy

$$p^2 N^4 \leq \lambda_1\lambda_2\lambda_3\lambda_4 \leq 16\,Cp^2\,N^4 \tag{3}$$

However, since $\mathbb{Z}[\omega_0]$ is contained inside $\mathcal{O}$ by design, and $\mathfrak{O}_0$ is a quadratic order of very small discriminant, we know that the two first successive minimas are 1 and $n(\omega_0)$ (assuming that ω_0 is the element of smallest norm in $\mathbb{Z}[\omega_0] \setminus \mathbb{Z}$, which we can do without any loss of generality). Moreover, since $\omega_0 \in \mathcal{O}$, we can always multiply any element by ω_0, this means that we must have $\lambda_4 \leq n(\omega_0)\lambda_3$, and so we can deduce that $\lambda_3 \geq pN^2$. This means that the smallest element ρ

we can expect to find in $\mathcal{O} \setminus \mathbb{Z}[i]$ has norm greater than pN^2. But, to make the attack work, we need that $N^2 > f^2 \deg \rho$. These two conditions are clearly not compatible, and this means that there is no hope to find a suitable ρ to make the attack work in this setting.

Let us now consider the case where σ is the Frobenius isogeny. When $\mathcal{O}_0$ contains j (which we can assume since the class number of $\mathfrak{O}_0$ is 1 and it has been shown in [CPV20] that the only $\mathfrak{O}_0$-oriented is $\mathbb{F}_p$-rational when p is big enough), finding ρ when σ is the Frobenius implies that ρ is contained inside $\mathcal{O} \cap \mathcal{O}_0 j$. It can be verified that the successive minimum of this lattice are small linear combinations of $p, p\omega_0, Nj, N\omega_0 j$ and thus the solutions outside of $\mathbb{Z}[i]$ have norm bigger than N^2. Thus, it is once again not possible to find ρ with $N^2 > f^2 \deg \rho$. A similar reasoning can be applied to prove that a suitable endomorphism ρ cannot be found when σ is an $\mathfrak{O}_0$-horizontal isogeny.

Thus, we have proven that the lollipop method cannot be applied to the setting of SCALLOP-HD when considering the torsion information revealed by the orientation on the points whose order is a product of split primes.

The same reasoning cannot be applied if we consider inert primes. Indeed, in that case, the matrix will probably not be diagonal. However, this also means that we don't really know what kind of matrix is required for the endomorphism ρ. Thus, it seems hard to use the lollipop method in that case.

7   Conclusion and Future Work

SCALLOP-HD represents the progression of a series of efforts to enhance the scalability of EGAs based on isogenies. Beginning with CSI-FiSh, which established the foundational strategy and gave a notable example, there was a significant challenge in computing larger class groups. SCALLOP then built upon the work of CSI-FiSh by overcoming this limitation, but still needed superpolynomial time for generating the lattice of relations. SCALLOP-HD takes this advancement a step further, making precomputation polynomial-time except for the lattice reduction phase. Indeed, this renders SCALLOP-HD the first member in the CSI-FiSh family whose practical bottleneck equals the asymptotic bottleneck of the construction, indicating that a fundamentally different approach may be required to achieve further progress.

SCALLOP-HD is heavily based on the SCALLOP group action [DFFK+23]. The main difference stems from the way the orientation is computed. In SCALLOP, an effective orientation is obtained from an endomorphism of smooth degree, whereas in SCALLOP-HD, an effective orientation is obtained from a 2dim-representation of an arbitrary degree endomorphism. The relaxation of the constraint on the degree of the endomorphism is the main advantage of SCALLOP-HD as it improves scalability and simplifies the group action computation at the cost of requiring the computation of a 2^e-isogeny between abelian variety of dimension 2.

The 2dim-representation technique we developed in order to represent set elements in SCALLOP-HD is interesting in its own right. It has already seen applications in [Ler23] and Remark 14, bringing down the dimension needed to compute the isogenies between abelian varieties from 4 or 8 to 2. The main remaining problem is to engineer an efficient and side-channel resistant implementation of SCALLOP-HD. This is a non-trivial task due to the need for isogeny computation in higher dimension. The state of the art on this matter was recently improved by [DMPR23], which is a great leap in the right direction, but algorithms for dimension-2 isogenies still haven't reached the level of maturity required for serious cryptographic implementation work. In the end, we are optimistic that the efficiency of SCALLOP-HD's group-action computation will outperform that of SCALLOP.

Acknowledgements. The first author would like to thank Christophe Petit for helpful feedback. Mingjie Chen is supported by EPSRC through grant number EP/V011324/1. Thanks to Giacomo Pope and Damien Robert for their help in debugging some corner cases of the 2-dimensional isogeny implementation.

References

[ADFMP20] Alamati, N., De Feo, L., Montgomery, H., Patranabis, S.: Cryptographic group actions and applications. In: Moriai, S., Wang, H. (eds.) ASIACRYPT 2020. LNCS, vol. 12492, pp. 411–439. Springer, Cham (2020). https://doi.org/10.1007/978-3-030-64834-3_14

[BDFLS20] Bernstein, D.J., De Feo, L., Leroux, A., Smith, B.: Faster computation of isogenies of large prime degree. Open Book Ser. 4(1), 39–55 (2020)

[BDK+23] Beullens, W., Dobson, S., Katsumata, S., Lai, Y.-F., Pintore, F.: Group signatures and more from isogenies and lattices: generic, simple, and efficient. Des Codes Cryptogr. 1–60 (2023)

[BKP20] Beullens, W., Katsumata, S., Pintore, F.: Calamari and Falafl: logarithmic (linkable) ring signatures from isogenies and lattices. In: Moriai, S., Wang, H. (eds.) ASIACRYPT 2020. LNCS, vol. 12492, pp. 464–492. Springer, Cham (2020). https://doi.org/10.1007/978-3-030-64834-3_16

[BKV19] Beullens, W., Kleinjung, T., Vercauteren, F.: CSI-FiSh: efficient isogeny based signatures through class group computations. In: Galbraith, S.D., Moriai, S. (eds.) ASIACRYPT 2019. LNCS, vol. 11921, pp. 227–247. Springer, Cham (2019). https://doi.org/10.1007/978-3-030-34578-5_9

[BLMP19] Bernstein, D.J., Lange, T., Martindale, C., Panny, L.: Quantum circuits for the CSIDH: optimizing quantum evaluation of isogenies. In: Ishai, Y., Rijmen, V. (eds.) EUROCRYPT 2019. LNCS, vol. 11477, pp. 409–441. Springer, Cham (2019). https://doi.org/10.1007/978-3-030-17656-3_15

[BMP23] Basso, A., Maino, L., Pope, G.: FESTA: fast encryption from supersingular torsion attacks. Cryptology ePrint Archive (2023)

[BS16] Biasse, J.F., Song, F.: Efficient quantum algorithms for computing class groups and solving the principal ideal problem in arbitrary degree number fields, pp. 893–902 (2016)

[BS20] Bonnetain, X., Schrottenloher, A.: Quantum security analysis of CSIDH. In: Canteaut, A., Ishai, Y. (eds.) EUROCRYPT 2020. LNCS, vol. 12106, pp. 493–522. Springer, Cham (2020). https://doi.org/10.1007/978-3-030-45724-2_17

[CD23] Castryck, W., Decru, T.: An efficient key recovery attack on SIDH. In: Hazay, C., Stam, M. (eds.) EUROCRYPT 2023. LNCS, vol. 14008, pp. 423–447. Springer, Heidelberg (2023). https://doi.org/10.1007/978-3-031-30589-4_15

[CHM+23] Castryck, W., Houben, M., Merz, S.P., Mula, M., Buuren, S.V., Vercauteren, F.: Weak instances of class group action based cryptography via self-pairings. In: Handschuh, H., Lysyanskaya, A. (eds.) CRYPTO 2023. LNCS, vol. 14083, pp. 762–792. Springer, Heidelberg (2023). https://doi.org/10.1007/978-3-031-38548-3_25

[CII+23] Chen, M., Imran, M., Ivanyos, G., Kutas, P., Leroux, A., Petit, C.: Hidden stabilizers, the isogeny to endomorphism ring problem and the cryptanalysis of pSIDH. Cryptology ePrint Archive, Paper 2023/779 (2023). https://eprint.iacr.org/2023/779

[CK20] Colò, L., Kohel, D.: Orienting supersingular isogeny graphs. J. Math. Cryptol. 14(1), 414–437 (2020)

[CLM+18] Castryck, W., Lange, T., Martindale, C., Panny, L., Renes, J.: CSIDH: an efficient post-quantum commutative group action. In: Peyrin, T., Galbraith, S. (eds.) ASIACRYPT 2018. LNCS, vol. 11274, pp. 395–427. Springer, Cham (2018). https://doi.org/10.1007/978-3-030-03332-3_15

[CPV20] Castryck, W., Panny, L., Vercauteren, F.: Rational isogenies from irrational endomorphisms. In: Canteaut, A., Ishai, Y. (eds.) EUROCRYPT 2020. LNCS, vol. 12106, pp. 523–548. Springer, Cham (2020). https://doi.org/10.1007/978-3-030-45724-2_18

[CS20] Cozzo, D., Smart, N.P.: Sashimi: cutting up CSI-FiSh secret keys to produce an actively secure distributed signing protocol. In: Ding, J., Tillich, J.-P. (eds.) PQCrypto 2020. LNCS, vol. 12100, pp. 169–186. Springer, Cham (2020). https://doi.org/10.1007/978-3-030-44223-1_10

[CSCDJRH22] Chávez-Saab, J., Chi-Domínguez, J.-J., Jaques, S., Rodríguez-Henríquez, F.: The SQALE of CSIDH: sublinear Vélu quantum-resistant isogeny action with low exponents. J. Cryptogr. Eng. 12(3), 349–368 (2022)

[CV23] Castryck, W., Vercauteren, F.: A polynomial time attack on instances of M-SIDH and FESTA. In: Guo, J., Steinfeld, R. (eds.) ASIACRYPT. LNCS, vol. 14444, pp. 127–156. Springer, Heidelberg (2023). https://doi.org/10.1007/978-981-99-8739-9_5

[DFFK+23] Feo, L.D., et al.: SCALLOP: scaling the CSI-FiSh. In: Boldyreva, A., Kolesnikov, V. (eds.) PKC. LNCS, vol. 13940, pp. 345–375. Springer, Heidelberg (2023). https://doi.org/10.1007/978-3-031-31368-4_13

[DFK+23] Feo, L.D., et al.: SCALLOP: scaling the CSI-FiSh. Cryptology ePrint Archive, Paper 2023/058 (2023). https://eprint.iacr.org/archive/2023/058/20230303:083840

[DFKL+20] De Feo, L., Kohel, D., Leroux, A., Petit, C., Wesolowski, B.: SQISign: compact post-quantum signatures from quaternions and isogenies. In: Moriai, S., Wang, H. (eds.) ASIACRYPT 2020. LNCS, vol. 12491, pp. 64–93. Springer, Cham (2020). https://doi.org/10.1007/978-3-030-64837-4_3

[DFLLW23] De Feo, L., Leroux, A., Longa, P., Wesolowski, B.: New algorithms for the Deuring correspondence: towards practical and secure SQISign signatures. In: Hazay, C., Stam, M. (eds.) EUROCRYPT 2023. LNCS, vol. 14008, pp. 659–690. Springer, Heidelberg (2023). https://doi.org/10.1007/978-3-031-30589-4_23

[DFM20]   De Feo, L., Meyer, M.: Threshold schemes from isogeny assumptions. In: Kiayias, A., Kohlweiss, M., Wallden, P., Zikas, V. (eds.) PKC 2020. LNCS, vol. 12111, pp. 187–212. Springer, Cham (2020). https://doi.org/10.1007/978-3-030-45388-6_7

[DLRW23] Dartois, P., Leroux, A., Robert, D., Wesolowski, B.: SQISignHD: new dimensions in cryptography. Cryptology ePrint Archive (2023)

[DMPR23] Dartois, P., Maino, L., Pope, G., Robert, D.: An algorithmic approach to $(2,2)$-isogenies in the theta model and applications to isogeny-based cryptography. IACR Cryptology ePrint Archive 2023/1747 (2023). https://eprint.iacr.org/2023/1747

[DMS23]   Decru, T., Maino, L., Sanso, A.: Towards a quantum-resistant weak verifiable delay function. Cryptology ePrint Archive (2023)

[EPSV23] Eriksen, J.K., Panny, L., Sotáková, J., Veroni, M.: Deuring for the people: supersingular elliptic curves with prescribed endomorphism ring in general characteristic. In: LuCaNT 2023 (2023). https://eprint.iacr.org/2023/106

[HM89]   Hafner, J.L., McCurley, K.S.: A rigorous subexponential algorithm for computation of class groups. J. Am. Math. Soc. **2**, 837–850 (1989)

[HW23]   Herlédan Le Merdy, A., Wesolowski, B.: The supersingular endomorphism ring problem given one endomorphism. Cryptology ePrint Archive, Paper 2023/1448 (2023). https://eprint.iacr.org/2023/1448

[Kan97]   Kani, E.: The number of curves of genus two with elliptic differentials. J. für die reine und angewandte Mathematik (Crelles J.) **1997**, 93–122 (1997)

[KLLQ23] Katsumata, S., Lai, Y.F., LeGrow, J.T., Qin, L.: CSI-Otter: Isogeny-based (partially) blind signatures from the class group action with a twist. In: Handschuh, H., Lysyanskaya, A. (eds.) CRYPTO 2023. LNCS, vol. 14083, pp. 729–761. Springer, Heidelberg (2023). https://doi.org/10.1007/978-3-031-38548-3_24

[Koh96]   Kohel, D.R.: Endomorphism rings of elliptic curves over finite fields. PhD thesis, University of California, Berkeley (1996)

[Kup05]   Kuperberg, G.: A subexponential-time quantum algorithm for the dihedral hidden subgroup problem. SIAM J. Comput. **35**(1), 170–188 (2005)

[Ler22a] Leroux, A.: A new isogeny representation and applications to cryptography. In: Agrawal, S., Lin, D. (eds.) ASIACRYPT 2022. LNCS, vol. 13792, pp. 3–35. Springer, Heidelberg (2022). https://doi.org/10.1007/978-3-031-22966-4_1

[Ler22b] Leroux, A.: Quaternion Algebra and isogeny-based cryptography. PhD thesis, Ecole doctorale de l'Institut Polytechnique de Paris (2022)

[Ler23]   Leroux, A.: Verifiable random function from the Deuring correspondence and higher dimensional isogenies. Cryptology ePrint Archive (2023)

[LR22]   Leroux, A., Roméas, M.: Updatable encryption from group actions. Cryptology ePrint Archive (2022)

[MMP+23] Maino, L., Martindale, C., Panny, L., Pope, G., Wesolowski, B.: A direct key recovery attack on SIDH. In: Hazay, C., Stam, M. (eds.) EUROCRYPT 2023. LNCS, vol. 14008, pp. 448–471. Springer, Heidelberg (2023). https://doi.org/10.1007/978-3-031-30589-4_16

[Onu21]   Onuki, H.: On oriented supersingular elliptic curves. Finite Fields App. **69** (2021)

[Pan21] Panny, L.: Cryptography on Isogeny Graphs. PhD thesis, Technische Universiteit Eindhoven (2021)

[Pei20] Peikert, C.: He gives C-Sieves on the CSIDH. In: Canteaut, A., Ishai, Y. (eds.) EUROCRYPT 2020. LNCS, vol. 12106, pp. 463–492. Springer, Cham (2020). https://doi.org/10.1007/978-3-030-45724-2_16

[Rob22] Robert, D.: Evaluating isogenies in polylogarithmic time. Cryptology ePrint Archive (2022)

[Rob23] Robert, D.: Breaking SIDH in polynomial time. In: Hazay, C., Stam, M. (eds.) EUROCRYPT 2023. LNCS, vol. 14008, pp. 472–503. Springer, Heidelberg (2023). https://doi.org/10.1007/978-3-031-30589-4_17

[The23] The Sage Developers. SageMath, the Sage Mathematics Software System (version 10.2) (2023)

[Wat69] Waterhouse, W.C.: Abelian varieties over finite fields. In: Annales scientifiques de l'École normale supérieure, vol. 2, pp. 521–560 (1969)

[Wes22] Wesolowski, B.: Orientations and the supersingular endomorphism ring problem. In: Dunkelman, O., Dziembowski, S. (eds.) EUROCRYPT 2022. LNCS, vol. 13277, pp. 345–371. Springer, Heidelberg (2022). https://doi.org/10.1007/978-3-031-07082-2_13

New Proof Systems and an OPRF from CSIDH

Cyprien Delpech de Saint Guilhem(ID) and Robi Pedersen$^{(\boxtimes)}$(ID)

COSIC, KU Leuven, Kasteelpark Arenberg 10 Bus 2452, 3001 Leuven, Belgium
robi.pedersen@protonmail.com

Abstract. Isogeny computations in CSIDH (Asiacrypt 2018) are described using a commutative group $\mathcal{G}$ acting on the set of supersingular elliptic curves. The commutativity property gives CSIDH enough flexibility to allow the creation of many cryptographic primitives and protocols. Nevertheless, these operations are limited and more complex applications have not yet been proposed.

When calling the composition of two group elements of $\mathcal{G}$ *addition*, our goal in this work is to explore exponentiation, multiplication with public elements, and multiplication between secret elements of this group. We first introduce a two-party interactive protocol for multiplication of secret group elements. Then, we explore zero-knowledge proofs of these different arithmetic operations. We present two types of approaches, using either standard sigma protocols or the MPC-in-the-Head paradigm. Most of our proofs need a trusted setup, which can be removed in the MPC-in-the-Head setting using cut-and-choose techniques. We conclude this work by presenting an oblivious pseudorandom function based on our new framework, that is competitive with current state-of-the-art designs.

Keywords: Isogeny-based cryptography · CSIDH · Zero-knowledge proofs · MPC-in-the-Head · Cryptographic Protocols · OPRF

1 Introduction

Isogeny-based assumptions are one of a few promising candidates for quantum-resistant cryptography. Even after the recent break of SIKE and SIDH [21,52,59] and related schemes, protocols based on different security assumptions, such as CSIDH [22] and SQISign [29], remain viable alternatives for isogeny-based constructions. The former has shown a lot of versatility over the past few years and many protocols have been based on its flexibility, such as signatures [13,28,33] and public-key encryption [37,54], oblivious transfer [6,51], oblivious pseudorandom functions [17,42], distributed protocols [4,5,13–15,23,26,30] and many more [1,2,32].

CSIDH-based schemes can be described via a group $\mathcal{G}$ acting on a set $\mathcal{E}$ as

$$\star : \mathcal{G} \times \mathcal{E} \to \mathcal{E}\,.$$

Given $(E, \mathfrak{a} \star E) \in \mathcal{E}^2$, where $\mathfrak{a} \in \mathcal{G}$, it is computationally infeasible to learn $\mathfrak{a}$. Here, $\mathcal{E}$ is the set of supersingular elliptic curves over a prime field $\mathbb{F}_p$ with some

© International Association for Cryptologic Research 2024
Q. Tang and V. Teague (Eds.): PKC 2024, LNCS 14603, pp. 217–251, 2024.
https://doi.org/10.1007/978-3-031-57725-3_8

specified endomorphism ring. There is no defined operation on the elements of $\mathcal{E}$. The only flexibility allowing the construction of protocols comes from $\mathcal{G}$, the ideal-class group $\mathrm{cl}(\mathcal{O})$ of an order $\mathcal{O}$ in $\mathbb{Q}(\sqrt{-p})$, which is commutative, among other properties. This allows to easily build a Diffie–Hellman scheme between two parties, with secret-public key pairs $(\mathfrak{a}, \mathfrak{a} \star E)$ and $(\mathfrak{b}, \mathfrak{b} \star E)$, respectively, by each using the other's public key to compute $\mathfrak{a} \star (\mathfrak{b} \star E) = \mathfrak{a}\mathfrak{b} \star E = \mathfrak{b} \star (\mathfrak{a} \star E)$. This is exactly the operation underlying the Diffie–Hellman key exchange scheme from Castryck et al. [22].

Expressed in terms of a public generator $\langle \mathfrak{g} \rangle \subseteq \mathcal{G}$, let $\mathfrak{a} = \mathfrak{g}^a$ and $\mathfrak{b} = \mathfrak{g}^b$, then this Diffie–Hellman scheme amounts to the *addition* of elements in the exponent of $\mathfrak{g}$, i.e. $\mathfrak{g}^a \star (\mathfrak{g}^b \star E) = \mathfrak{g}^{a+b} \star E$, which we can compute from the knowledge of a and $\mathfrak{g}^b \star E$, even without knowing b. On the other hand, it is hard to compute $\mathfrak{g}^{a+b} \star E$ from the knowledge of $\mathfrak{g}^a \star E$ and $\mathfrak{g}^b \star E$ only [22]. *Multiplication* in the exponent of the group generator, on the other hand, does not straightforwardly follow in the same way. In fact, there is no direct way to compute $\mathfrak{g}^{ab} \star E$ from knowledge of a and $\mathfrak{g}^b \star E$, let alone from the knowledge of $\mathfrak{g}^a \star E$ and $\mathfrak{g}^b \star E$; this extends to exponentiation.

The possibility of using more complex arithmetic operations in the exponent of the generator is what makes the discrete logarithm setting so versatile. The goal of this work is to extend the flexibility of CSIDH-based schemes to also incorporate these operations and hopefully allow to construct protocols that appear out of reach with the current toolbox. We note that these new operations come with new hard problems. These problems also can be used to construct new zero-knowledge protocols based on them, which are explored in this work.

Our Contributions. We extend the current isogeny-based group action toolbox with the possibility of performing squaring and (scalar) multiplications in the exponent of a public class group generator $\mathfrak{g}$ acting on elliptic curves. If this generator is public, we can define the group action using the group in the exponent of the group generator. Assuming $\langle \mathfrak{g} \rangle = \mathcal{G}$ of order N, this group action looks like

$$[\,] : \mathbb{Z}/N\mathbb{Z} \times \mathcal{E} \to \mathcal{E}$$
$$(a, E) \mapsto [a]E = \mathfrak{g}^a \star E.$$

Table 1 presents a brief overview of the different arithmetic operations we define on isogenies. In order to draw some parallels to the discrete log (DLOG) setting, we define $\mathcal{H}$ to be a group in which the discrete logarithm problem is hard. We can describe operations in the DLOG setting as a group $\mathcal{D}$ acting on $\mathcal{H}$ with $\star : \mathcal{D} \times \mathcal{H} \to \mathcal{H}$ as $\mathfrak{a} \star h \mapsto h^{\mathfrak{a}}$. The DLOG assumption implies that it is hard to find $\mathfrak{a} \in \mathcal{D}$, given $(h, h^{\mathfrak{a}})$. If $\mathcal{D}$ is generated by a fixed $\mathfrak{g} \in \mathcal{D}$ and $\#\mathcal{D} = M$, we can also define the group action $[\,] : \mathbb{Z}_M \times \mathcal{H} \to \mathcal{H}$, such that $[a]h \mapsto \mathfrak{g}^a \star h = h^{\mathfrak{g}^a}$. Note that we do not assume the discrete logarithm problem to be hard in $\mathcal{D}$.

After introducing some background in Sect. 2, we start Sect. 3 by introducing new hardness assumptions related to these new operations. We show how they can be reduced to known problems in the literature. We then discuss two-party

Table 1. Arithmetic operations for the discrete logarithm and isogeny settings. We show how to compute operations given the minimal amount of secret information, and indicate the minimum number of secrets necessary to do so. For better illustration, we abuse notation by using the same letters for elements in $\mathcal{G}$ and $\mathcal{D}$, as well as in $\mathbb{Z}_N$ and $\mathbb{Z}_M$. In both cases, we assume $\mathfrak{a}$ and $\mathfrak{b}$ to be secret and c and e to be public scalars. We identify $\mathfrak{a} = \mathfrak{g}^a$ and $\mathfrak{b} = \mathfrak{g}^b$, and assume $\mathfrak{a} \star E$, $\mathfrak{b} \star E$, $h^\mathfrak{a}$, $h^\mathfrak{b}$ to be public.

	Isogenies	Discrete logarithm	Secrets
Addition	$\mathfrak{a} \star (\mathfrak{b} \star E) = \mathfrak{b} \star (\mathfrak{a} \star E) = \mathfrak{a}\mathfrak{b} \star E$ $= [a][b]E = [b][a]E = [a+b]E$	$(h^\mathfrak{a})^\mathfrak{b} = (h^\mathfrak{b})^\mathfrak{a} = h^{\mathfrak{a}\mathfrak{b}} =$ $(h^{g^a})^{g^b} = (h^{g^b})^{g^a} = h^{g^{a+b}}$	1
Scalar Mult.	$\mathfrak{a}^c \star E = [ca]E$	$h^{\mathfrak{a}^c} = h^{g^{ca}}$	1
Exponentiation	$\mathfrak{g}^{\mathfrak{a}^e} \star E = [a^e]E$	$h^{g^{a^e}}$	1
Multiplication	$\mathfrak{a}^b \star E = \mathfrak{b}^a \star E = [ab]E$	$h^{\mathfrak{a}^b} = h^{\mathfrak{b}^a} = h^{g^{ab}}$	2

protocols for multiplications of the type $[ab]E = \mathfrak{g}^{ab} \star E$, where one party knows a, and the other b, without revealing those elements. We note that interactive protocols of this type need a trusted setup, which we also introduce.

In Sect. 4, we then present zero-knowledge proof systems for the languages defined by our newly proposed hardness assumptions. These protocols allow for example to prove that some tuples, such as $(E, [a]E, [b]E, [ab]E)$ or $(e, E, [a]E, [a^e]E)$ are well-formed. We achieve this in two ways, either with standard sigma protocols, or using MPC-in-the-Head (MPCitH). These proofs are competitive with protocols proving correct structure of additive tuples, i.e. tuples of the form $(E, [a]E, [b]E, [a+b]E)$ as they were presented by Cozzo and Smart [26]. Again, our protocols rely on a trusted setup. In the MPCitH protocols, however, we can remove the trusted setup by using the "cut-and-choose" technique [47]. We show that proofs of multiplication and exponentiation are reminiscent of pairings in elliptic curve cryptography, although without the advantage of public verifiability.

We conclude this work by introducing a new post-quantum secure oblivious pseudo-random function (OPRF) in Sect. 5, based on the new tools presented in this work. Our OPRF relies on a trusted setup which can be removed using a pre-processing protocol based on OT extensions [6,48,49], and relies on a new hardness assumption, which we motivate well. Compared to the state-of-the-art of post-quantum OPRFs, our protocol has very competitive computational and communication cost, even for conservative security parameters, and is round-optimal. Furthermore, we can extend our construction to a verifiable OPRF.

Related Work. Boneh, Kogan and Woo [17] introduced the first two OPRF constructions based on isogenies, one based on SIDH and one on CSIDH assumptions. Although the SIDH-based OPRF was first broken by Basso et al. [9] and later SIDH itself [21,52,59], a new design by Basso [8] solves both of these problems, at the cost of working with much larger parameters. Independently, Heimberger et al. modified the CSIDH-based OPRF of Boneh et al. to also work in the restricted effective group action setting [42] (where canonical representation of class group elements is not possible [2]), while also decreasing the computational and communication cost of the protocol. On the downside, this protocol has a much higher round complexity.

Independently of this work, Joux [45] proposed MPC-in-the-head protocols to decrease the soundness error of the CSI-FiSh identification protocol [16]. While we are also considering MPC-in-the-head protocols, we note that there is no direct overlap between this work and theirs, as we are introducing new types of identification schemes.

2   Background

Notation. We let λ denote the computational security parameter. A function $f(x)$ is *negligible* if for any constant c, there exists x_0 such that for all $x > x_0$, we have $f(x) < x^{-c}$. We write $\mathbb{Z}_N = \mathbb{Z}/N\mathbb{Z}$ and $[n] = \{1, \ldots, n\}$.

2.1   Isogeny-Based Cryptography

Isogenies are surjective morphisms between elliptic curves. Endomorphisms are isogenies from elliptic curves to themselves. The endomorphisms of an elliptic curve E, together with the zero-map, define a ring under addition and composition. For supersingular elliptic curves over $\mathbb{F}_p$, the ring of $\mathbb{F}_p$-rational endomorphisms is isomorphic to an order $\mathcal{O}$ in the quadratic imaginary field $\mathbb{Q}(\sqrt{-p})$.

Separable isogenies are uniquely determined by their kernel, which can be expressed as a finite group of points on the domain. A straightforward way to generate such a group of points is via the kernel of ideals $\mathfrak{a} \in \mathcal{O}$, then $E[\mathfrak{a}] = \{P \in E(\overline{\mathbb{F}_p}) \mid \forall \alpha \in \mathfrak{a} : \alpha(P) = \infty\}$ defines the kernel of an isogeny $E \to \mathfrak{a} \star E := E/E[\mathfrak{a}]$. We can interpret elements in the ideal-class group $\mathrm{cl}(\mathcal{O})$ as acting on the set of supersingular elliptic curves over $\mathbb{F}_p$ whose $\mathbb{F}_p$-rational endomorphism ring is isomorphic to $\mathcal{O}$. We denote this set as $\mathcal{E}$ and write the action as $\star :$ $\mathrm{cl}(\mathcal{O}) \times \mathcal{E} \to \mathcal{E}$. We note that this action is free and transitive. As a shorthand, we will simply refer to ideals in the class groups as isogenies. If the class group is cyclic and a generator $\mathfrak{g}$ is known and fixed, we can write the group action using the exponent notation introduced in [16],

$$[\ ] : \mathbb{Z}_N \times \mathcal{E} \to \mathcal{E}$$
$$(a, E) \mapsto [a]E = \mathfrak{g}^a \star E,$$

where $N = \#\mathrm{cl}(\mathcal{O})$.[1] Note that $\mathbb{Z}_N$ defines the group in the exponent of the generator $\mathfrak{g}$, e.g. consecutive actions amount to the addition of the elements in $\mathbb{Z}_N$, e.g. $[a]([b]E) = \mathfrak{g}^a \star (\mathfrak{g}^b \star E) = \mathfrak{g}^{a+b} \star E = [a+b]E$.

It is important to note that the class number N is generally a composite number. This implies that the coefficients in the exponent are defined over a

---

[1] We assume $\mathrm{cl}(\mathcal{O})$ to be cyclic. While not always the case, we can work in a cyclic subgroup of a non-cyclic class group. With high probability, such large cyclic subgroups exist [24]. For the rest of this work, we assume that N is not a smooth number.

ring, rather than a field as is commonly the case in cryptographic constructions. While this does not really impact addition, we have to be more careful when talking about multiplication, especially concerning elements that do not have a multiplicative inverse.

Throughout this work, we consider supersingular elliptic curves defined over some prime field $\mathbb{F}_p$. For efficiency reasons (see [22]), p is chosen to have the form $p = 4 \prod_{i=1}^{n} \ell_i - 1$, where $\ell_1, \ldots, \ell_{n-1}$ are the $n - 1$ smallest distinct odd primes and $\ell_n > \ell_{n-1}$ is the smallest possible prime that makes p a prime as well. By this choice, the ideal $\ell_i \mathcal{O}$ always splits into a prime ideal $\mathfrak{l}_i$ and its conjugate $\bar{\mathfrak{l}}_i$, defining an isogeny of degree ℓ_i or its dual. Now, the consecutive computation of many small isogenies of these prime degrees allows to compute isogenies of large degree efficiently, even if the class group structure is unknown. However, translating any arbitrary isogeny, e.g. $\mathfrak{g}^a$ into small prime degree isogenies, requires knowing the relation lattice between the different elements $\mathfrak{l}_1, \ldots, \mathfrak{l}_n$. Then arbitrary elements can be reduced modulo this lattice to yield efficiently computable isogenies, although the actual efficiency depends on how short the basis of the relation lattice is. The class group structure and a short relation lattice have been computed for the CSIDH-512 parameter set [16] (where $\log p \approx 512$). Higher parameter sets can be computed in polynomial time on a quantum computer [50] or with the approach outlined by De Feo et al. [27], but the reduction of the relation lattices are less efficient. A workaround for higher parameter sets can be found in [56]. Throughout this work, we assume that uniform sampling and canonical representations of elements as powers of a generator are possible and efficient. Most notably, this allows to construct efficient signatures that do not need rejection sampling [28], such as CSI-FiSh [16].

In the ID-protocol underlying CSI-FiSh, a prover proves knowledge of a secret element s connecting two elliptic curves E_0 and $E_1 = [s]E_0$, which is a witness for the following hard problem.

Problem 1 (Group action inverse problem (GAIP)). Given a pair of elliptic curves $(E_0, E_1) \in \mathcal{E}^2$, find $s \in \mathbb{Z}_N$, such that $[s]E_0 = E_1$.

To prove knowledge of s, the prover commits to a curve $E_b = [b]E_0$ for a random $b \leftarrow \mathbb{Z}_N$, then upon receiving a challenge $c \leftarrow \{0, 1\}$, returns $r = b - cs$. Finally, the verifier accepts the proof only if $[r]E_c = E_s$.

2.2   Zero-Knowledge Proofs

Let X and W be sets, and let $\mathcal{R} : X \times W \rightarrow \{0, 1\}$ be a relation defining the language $\mathcal{L} = \{x \in X : \exists w \in W \text{ with } \mathcal{R}(x, w) = 1\}$. First introduced by Goldwasser, Micali and Rackoff, interactive proofs are two-party protocols where a prover P convinces a verifier V that, given $x \in X$, it knows a witness $w \in W$ such that $\mathcal{R}(x, w) = 1$ [41]. Sigma protocols are protocols that execute in three rounds, in which the prover first sends a commitment value b to V, who then issues a challenge c. The prover responds to the challenge with r. After a verification step, the verifier then either accepts or rejects the proof. In order to be secure, such an interactive proof must be *complete* and *sound*. Completeness implies that if $\mathcal{R}(x, w) = 1$, the honest verifier accepts the proof, while soundness requires that a malicious prover cannot make an honest verifier accept a proof for a relation $\mathcal{R}(x', w') = 0$, up to negligible probability. The stronger notion of *2-special soundness* requires the existence of a PPT algorithm (the extractor), which, given two accepting transcripts for the same commitment b, but with different challenges $c \neq c'$, is able to extract a witness w. Optionally, interactive proofs can also be *(honest verifier) zero-knowledge*, which implies that a (honest) verifier cannot extract any information about the witness w from the transcript of the protocol. This last property can be proven by building a simulator that can produce a protocol transcript that is indistinguishable from a real one, without the knowledge of w.

Definition 1 (Completeness). *A sigma protocol between parties P, V is complete for the relation $\mathcal{R}$, if for all $\mathcal{R}(x, w) = 1$, V outputs* True.

Definition 2 (Special soundness). *A sigma protocol between parties P, V is special sound, if there exists a PPT extractor* Ext, *which for any $x \in \mathcal{L}$, when given two valid protocol transcripts (b, c, r) and (b, c', r'), can extract $w \in W$, such that $\mathcal{R}(x, w) = 1$.*

Definition 3 (Zero-knowledge). *A sigma protocol between parties P, V is zero-knowledge, if there exists a PPT simulator* Sim, *which for any $x \in \mathcal{L}$ can generate a transcript (b, c, r) of the protocol, indistinguishable from a real transcript of the protocol, without knowledge of w.*

MPC-in-the-Head. First proposed by Ishai, Kushilevitz, Ostrovsky and Sahai in 2007, the MPC-in-the-Head (MPCitH) framework is a recent construction for zero-knowledge proof systems using secure multiparty computation (MPC) [44].

To prove a relation $\mathcal{R}(x, w) = 1$, the prover simulates "in its head" the execution of an n-party protocol which verifies the witness. To this end, the prover samples random tapes for each party, gives them their share w_i of the witness, and simulates their communication and internal states according to the MPC protocol. With the random tape r_i, the witness share w_i, and all the incoming messages, the prover can save the internal view of party P_i. After receiving commitments to each of these views, the verifier selects a subset at random which the prover has to open. The verifier then checks for each opened views that the incoming and outgoing messages are consistent with each other, and that the local computations have been performed correctly and finally, if the execution of the MPC protocol yields $\mathcal{R}(x, w) = 1$. Based on this, the verifier accepts or rejects the proof.

This work focuses on MPCitH proofs built from MPC protocols that use additive secret-sharing and that are secure against passive corruptions. Assuming ideal commitments, this implies that the resulting proof system is zero-knowledge when the verifier opens $n - 1$ of the committed views, and it has soundness error $1/n$, since the prover can successfully guess the verifier's challenge and cheat on one out of the n views. More formally, the MPC protocol Π should satisfy the following definition of privacy, with $t = n - 1$.

Definition 4 (t-privacy [44]). *Let $1 \leq t < n$. We say that Π realizes f with t-privacy if there is a PPT simulator Sim such that for any inputs $x, w_1, \ldots, w_n$ and every set of corrupted players $T \subseteq \{1, \ldots, n\}$, where $|T| \leq t$, the joint view $\mathsf{View}_T(x, w_1, \ldots, w_n)$ of players in T is indistinguishable from $\mathsf{Sim}(T, x, (w_i)_{i \in T}, f_T(x, w_1, \ldots, w_n))$.*

We refer the reader to previous works on MPCitH for the formal security statements of generic proofs built within this paradigm and for the reduction of the soundness error using repetition [44, 47].

The Cut-and-choose Technique. The cut-and-choose method is used to provide security against malicious adversaries. When a single party has to generate commitments to sets of correlated randomness, but is not trusted to do so honestly, they are asked to provide commitments to additional sets of randomness. Then, the other member(s) of the computation will randomly "cut and choose" some of the commitments that the generator must open to demonstrate their honesty. Since the generating party does not know in advance which commitments will be "cut", and which will be "chosen" for the computation, this serves as a probabilistic test for the correctness of the unopened sets of randomness.

In the case of MPCitH argument systems, using the cut-and-choose technique was first proposed by Katz, Kolesnikov and Wang to enable the use of MPC protocols with a witness-independent pre-processing phase [47]. Concretely, the idea is that, before simulating the views of the parties during the MPC protocol, the prover commits to m executions of the pre-processing generation, of which the verifier cuts $m - \tau$ in order to verify that they were correctly computed. If the prover has cheated on $c \in [m]$ of these executions, then the probability that the cut-and-choose technique fails to uncover this is $\binom{m-c}{m-\tau} / \binom{m}{m-\tau}$.

For each of the τ executions chosen after the cut, the prover has probability $1/n$ of successfully cheating if the pre-processed data is honest, and has probability 1 otherwise. Accounting for the c executions with dishonest pre-processing, this implies that the Prover has probability $1/n^{\tau-c}$ of successfully cheating in the online phase of the MPC protocol.

In summary, MPCitH proof systems based on the cut-and-choose technique have the following soundness error formula [11, Theorem 2]:

$$\epsilon_{\mathsf{CnC}}(m, n, \tau) = \max_{0 \leq c \leq \tau} \left\{ \frac{\binom{m-c}{m-\tau}}{\binom{m}{m-\tau} \cdot n^{\tau-c}} \right\}.$$

Furthermore, they require that the prover pre-computes m copies of the correlated randomness and that the verifier re-computes $m - \tau$ of them.

Non-interactive MPCitH Proofs. Generic MPCitH proof systems are always public-coin and secure in the honest-verifier setting. Therefore, the proof systems constructed in the original 3-round framework of Ishai et al. [44] can be transformed into non-interactive zero-knowledge proofs of knowledge, and therefore digital signature schemes, using the generic Fiat–Shamir transform [35]. The

MPCitH proof systems constructed in the cut-and-choose framework introduced by Katz et al. are usually 5-round protocols (or sometimes more) and can also be made non-interactive using recent techniques [10, 46, 47].

3   Towards Multiplication from Addition

This section introduces our toolbox to construct the protocols that follow in later sections. We start with the functionality to generate trusted tuples and show how this can be used by two parties to multiply their secrets.

3.1   Tuple Generation Functionality

In 1991, Beaver introduced a method to securely compute the product of two secret values using a pre-computed triple of *random* secret values $B = (x, y, z)$ such that $z = xy$ [12]. When the elements of Beaver triples are additively secret-shared between multiple parties, it allows them to compute the product of two other secret-shared values, say a and b, by first opening masked values and then constructing the product $c = ab$ using only local linear operations.

More precisely, let $(a_i, b_i, x_i, y_i, z_i)$ be the additive shares that party P_i has of (a, b, x, y, xy), respectively. By revealing their shares $\alpha_i = a_i - x_i$ and $\beta_i = b_i - y_i$, the parties can each compute the values $\alpha = \sum_i \alpha_i = a - x$ and $\beta = \sum_i \beta_i = b - y$.[2] Since x and y are random, this does not reveal information about a and b. Then, the parties can locally compute their additive share of $c = a \cdot b$ by setting

$$c_i = \alpha y_i + \beta x_i + z_i + \begin{cases} \alpha\beta & \text{if } i = n, \\ 0 & \text{otherwise,} \end{cases}$$

It now follows that $\sum_{i=1}^{n} c_i = \alpha y + \beta x + xy + \alpha\beta = (\alpha + x)(\beta + y) = ab$. We can explicitly write the secret-shared triple as

$$B = (\text{id}; (x_1, \ldots, x_n), (y_1, \ldots, y_n), (z_1, \ldots, z_n)) \in \{0, 1\}^* \times (\mathbb{Z}_N^n)^3, \quad (1)$$

with $\sum_{i=1}^{n} z_i = (\sum_{i=1}^{n} x_i)(\sum_{i=1}^{n} y_i)$, and where $\text{id} \in \{0, 1\}^*$ is a unique identifier. We call *view* the set of shares or elements that a party has knowledge of. In general multi-party protocols as described above, the view of party P_i is given by $View_{P_i}(B) = (\text{id}; x_i, y_i, z_i)$.

Multiplying Group Elements. We show how to use Beaver triples of the type (1), when we want to compute the product of two secret-shared values a and b in $\mathbb{Z}_N$. Again, let $\alpha = a - x$ and $\beta = b - y$ and assume they are given to each of the n parties, as if they had been opened. Now,

$$[ab]E = \left[\left(\alpha + \sum_{i=1}^{n} x_i\right)\left(\beta + \sum_{i=1}^{n} y_i\right)\right]E$$

$$= \left[\alpha\beta + \alpha \sum_{i=1}^{n} y_i + \beta \sum_{i=1}^{n} x_i + \sum_{i=1}^{n} z_i\right]E$$

$$= [\alpha y_1 + \beta x_1 + z_1] \cdots [\alpha y_n + \beta x_n + z_n + \alpha\beta]E,$$

---

[2] We note that all operations are operations in $\mathbb{Z}_N$, i.e. should be read modulo N.

and parties can compute $[ab]E$ by each P_i computing the action $[\alpha y_i + \beta x_i + z_i]$ in a round-robin fashion, using only their knowledge of α, β and $View_{P_i}(B)$. The final action $[\alpha\beta]E$ is computed by P_n (but could in fact be computed by any party). We summarize the round-robin steps in Fig. 1.

MPC multiplication protocol for $P_i(\alpha, \beta, x_i, y_i, z_i)$

---

1 : from P_{i-1} receive F_{i-1} (P_1 receives $F_0 = E_0$)

2 : if $i < n$ then

3 : $F_i \leftarrow [\beta x_i + \alpha y_i + z_i]F_{i-1}$

4 :   send F_i to P_{i+1}

5 : if $i = n$ then

6 : $F_n \leftarrow [\alpha\beta + \beta x_n + \alpha y_n + z_n]F_{n-1}$

7 :   Broadcast(F_n)

Fig. 1. Round-robin step in the multiplication protocol for n parties.

This protocol is only passively secure, i.e. a correct output is only guaranteed if all parties behave according to the instructions of the protocol. In order to make this protocol actively secure, we introduce zero-knowledge proofs later in Sect. 4, which parties can append to their messages to prove that their computations have been indeed performed correctly. But this protocol is even more versatile: we further show in Sect. 4, how it can be used to create MPCitH proof systems in order to prove correct multiplication by a party that knows a and b.

Note that the way that α and β are communicated to the parties varies with each of those protocols. Sometimes, they will be generated and shared by the parties themselves as in the protocol above, sometimes by an external dealer (e.g. for MPCitH protocols where the Prover can deal α and β to the parties as global inputs, see Sects. 2.2 and 4.4)

Tuple Generation Functionality. Equation (1) is just an example of a Beaver triple sharing, in this case for n-party multiplication with passive security. Throughout this work, we will need more general *tuples*, which will look different depending on the arithmetic operation to be performed or the assumptions about the adversaries. In particular, we will sometimes need extra elements, such as specific elliptic curves, as part of the tuples. These different shapes and structures will be introduced in the relevant sections. We now define the generalized functionality used in this work to represent these tuples, and parties' access to them. What *valid* means, will depend on the context and be introduced whenever needed.

Definition 5 (Tuple generation functionality). *Let T be an algorithm that generates* valid *tuples of a predetermined type for a set of parties $\mathcal{P} = \{P_1, \ldots, P_n\}$. On input id by party P, if $P \notin \mathcal{P}$, T returns $\perp$. If no such tuple* *exists, $\mathcal{T}$ generates a new tuple B with identifier* id. *In either case, if $P \in \mathcal{P}$, $\mathcal{T}$ returns $View_P(B)$.*

In the simplest case, we will assume that $\mathcal{T}$ is a trusted party, and that the parties engaging in protocols needing such tuples have black-box access to $\mathcal{T}$. In some cases (e.g. for MPCitH) however, we can use the *cut-and-choose* technique to let the prover generate them (see Sect. 2.2). We note that these tuples are independent of the secret pair to be masked and as such, can be precomputed.

3.2 Two-Party Multiplication Protocol

Suppose we have two parties P_a and P_b, which using their respective secrets $a, b \in \mathbb{Z}_N$ want to compute $[ab]E_0$, where E_0 is a specific starting curve. We describe an interactive 2-party protocol between P_a and P_b to compute $[ab]E_0$ together, using precomputed tuples by a trusted third party $\mathcal{T}$. The generated tuples have the following form

$$B = (\mathsf{id}; x, y, z_a, z_b) \in \{0,1\}^* \times \mathbb{Z}_N^4,$$
$$View_{P_a}(B) = (\mathsf{id}, x, z_a), \quad \text{and} \quad View_{P_b}(B) = (\mathsf{id}, y, z_b).$$

with $z_a + z_b = xy$. Inspired by traditional MPC protocols, the parties first secret-share their inputs a and b with each other as $\alpha = a - x$ and $\beta = b - y$ and then combine these sharings with secret information to compute partial curves, which can be used to each reconstruct the desired curve $[ab]E_0$. As such, we can also see this protocol as an interactive Diffie–Hellman key exchange. Figure 2 details this joint multiplication protocol for two parties, which uses a tuple B of the aforementioned form as input. The evaluation of this protocol costs 2 group actions per player (performed in parallel), which is only twice the cost of the Diffie–Hellman protocol of Castryck et al. [22].[3]

Theorem 1. *The protocol of Fig. 2 is correct and private.*

Proof. **Correctness:** This follows from the structure of the tuple.

Privacy: Let $\mathcal{S}_b$ be a simulator interacting with the party P_a. Whenever P_a requests a new tuple, $\mathcal{S}_b$ generates $B = (\mathsf{id}; x, y, z_a, z_b)$ and sends $View_{P_a}(B)$ to P_a. Upon reception of the output curve E_{out}, $\mathcal{S}_b$ first samples $\beta \leftarrow \mathbb{Z}_N$ and sends it to P_a in the first round. In the second round, $\mathcal{S}_b$ computes $E_b = [-(\alpha\beta + \beta x + z_a)]E_{\mathrm{out}}$ and sends it to P_a. The transcript generated by $\mathcal{S}_b$ is indistinguishable from real transcripts, as both the real and simulated β are uniformly random in $\mathbb{Z}_N$ and both $E_b = [r]E_{\mathrm{out}}$, for some r uniformly random in $\mathbb{Z}_N$. The simulator $\mathcal{S}_a$ interacting with P_b works exactly the same. □

---

[3] We can remove the symmetry of this protocol and make e.g. party P_a only compute E_a, then send it to P_b, which computes the output $[ab]E$. Then, each party only has to perform a single group action, while also reducing the communication cost between the parties. Still, the total cost of the protocol remains 2 group actions.

$$B = (\mathrm{id}; x, y, z_a, z_b)$$

$P_a : a, x, z_a$ .... $P_b : b, y, z_b$

$\alpha = a - x$ $\xrightarrow{\quad\alpha\quad}$ $\xleftarrow{\quad\beta\quad}$ $\beta = b - y$

$E_a = [\beta x + z_a]E$ $\xrightarrow{\quad E_a\quad}$ $\xleftarrow{\quad E_b\quad}$ $E_b = [\alpha y + z_b]E$

return .... **return**

$[\alpha\beta + \beta x + z_a]E_b$ .... $[\alpha\beta + \alpha y + z_b]E_a$

Fig. 2. Passively secure 2-party multiplication protocol from additive secret sharing, using a trusted tuple B as input.

4 Zero-Knowledge Proof Systems

In this section, we present zero-knowledge proof systems for different arithmetic operations in $\mathbb{Z}_N$. Among other applications, these will allow us to augment the passively secure protocol from the previous section to active security. We distinguish proofs along two dimensions: the relation that they prove (addition, scalar multiplication, exponentiation or secret multiplication) and the paradigm that they follow (from computational assumptions or from MPC-in-the-Head).

4.1 Languages and Security Assumptions

We consider the following languages, with $E, E', E_i, E'_i \in \mathcal{E}$, $a, b, c_i \in \mathbb{Z}_N$ and $e_i \in \mathbb{N}$:

$$\mathcal{L}_k^{\mathrm{Add}} = \left\{ ((E_i, E'_i)_{i=1,\dots,k}, a) : \bigwedge_{i=1}^{k} E'_i = [a]E_i \right\} \tag{2}$$

$$\mathcal{L}_k^{\mathrm{Scal}} = \left\{ ((E_i, E'_i, c_i)_{i=1,\dots,k}, a) : \bigwedge_{i=1}^{k} E'_i = [c_i a]E_i \right\} \tag{3}$$

$$\mathcal{L}^{\mathrm{Exp}} = \left\{ (([a]E, E', e), a) : E' = [a^e]E \right\} \tag{4}$$

$$\mathcal{L}^{\mathrm{Mult}} = \left\{ (([a]E, [b]E, E'), (a, b)) : E' = [ab]E \right\} \tag{5}$$

A zero-knowledge protocol for $\mathcal{L}_k^{\mathrm{Add}}$ already exists [26], while a version of $\mathcal{L}_k^{\mathrm{Scal}}$ was proposed in [4], but with $c_1 = 1$ fixed. Both languages coincide for $c_1 = \cdots = c_k = 1$, thus $\mathcal{L}_k^{\mathrm{Add}}$ can be seen as a special case of $\mathcal{L}_k^{\mathrm{Scal}}$. We can see that $\mathcal{L}_1^{\mathrm{Add}}$ is exactly the language underlying the ID protocol of CSI-FiSh outlined in Sect. 2.1, with GAIP (Problem 1) the associated security assumption. For $\mathcal{L}_2^{\mathrm{Add}}$, the underlying assumption corresponds to the computational Diffie–Hellman problem.

Problem 2 (Computational Diffie-Hellman problem (CDH) [22,25,60]). Given $(E, [a]E, F)$, where $a \in \mathbb{Z}_N$ and $E, F \in \mathcal{E}$, compute $[a]F$.

We can define similar computational problems when looking at scalar multipli-cation, i.e. for $\mathcal{L}_1^{\mathrm{Scal}}$, we can define

Problem 3 (Scalar-CDH [7,34]). Given $(c, E, [a]E)$ where $c, a \in \mathbb{Z}_N$ and $E \in \mathcal{E}$, compute $[ca]E$.

For our purposes, these assumptions cover the hardness of executing additions or scalar multiplications with unknown secrets. Increasing k would define more hardness assumptions but will not be relevant in this work. Instead, we introduce the following new assumptions, which also cover exponentiation and multiplica-tion, i.e. are related to $\mathcal{L}^{\mathrm{Mult}}$ and $\mathcal{L}^{\mathrm{Exp}}$.[4]

Problem 4 (Exp-CDH). Given $(E, [a]E, e)$, where $e \in \mathbb{N}$, $a \in \mathbb{Z}_N$ and $E \in \mathcal{E}$, compute $[a^e]E$.

Problem 5 (Mult-CDH). Given $(E, [a]E, [b]E)$, where $a, b \in \mathbb{Z}_N$ and $E \in \mathcal{E}$, compute $[ab]E$.

In the full version of the paper, we show that the following reductions hold when N is odd. This condition is guaranteed by choosing $p \equiv 3 \bmod 4$ [22].

$$\mathrm{CDH} \equiv \mathrm{Scalar\text{-}CDH} \leq \mathrm{Exp\text{-}CDH} \equiv \mathrm{Mult\text{-}CDH} \leq \mathrm{GAIP}\,. \tag{6}$$

Note that following from [39,53,61], CDH and GAIP are equivalent under quan-tum reductions, implying that the hardness of all problems in this section col-lapse to the quantum hardness of GAIP.

4.2 Addition and Scalar Multiplication

In this section, we present the more general version of the protocol first intro-duced by Atapoor et al. [4]. This protocol is a proof system for the general scalar multiplication language $\mathcal{L}_k^{\mathrm{Scal}}$, but a proof system for $\mathcal{L}_k^{\mathrm{Add}}$ can be obtained as discussed above. These protocols have furthermore been proven secure in the QROM [4,13]. We note that the latter proof can straightforwardly be extended to the case $c_1 \neq 1$. We summarize the protocol in Fig. 3. We note that the soundness error is $2^{-\lambda}$. Throughout this section, we define the cryptographic hash function $\mathsf{H} : \{0,1\}^* \to \{0,1\}^\lambda$, where λ is a given security parameter.

Cost. The computational cost of the protocol is $k\lambda$ group actions, for both the proof and also for the verification part, neglecting other costs, such as $\mathbb{Z}_N$-arithmetic and hash computations.

---

[4] We emphasize that the notation in [34] deviates from ours, as e.g. squaring in [34] is related to computing $[2a]E$ from $(E, [a]E)$, which we call doubling.

Scal.Prove$_\lambda(a, X)$

Input: Secret a, set $X = \{(E_i, E_i', c_i)\}_{i=1,\ldots,k}$, s.t. $E_i, E_i' \in \mathcal{E}$ and $\{c_1, \ldots, c_k\}$ an exceptional set modulo N, security parameter λ.
Output: A proof π for the language $\mathcal{L}_k^{\mathrm{Scal}}$.

1. For $j = 1, \ldots, \lambda$:
   (a) $b_j \leftarrow \mathbb{Z}_N$
   (b) For $i = 1, \ldots, k$, compute $\hat{E}_{i,j} = [c_i b_j] E_i$
2. $d_1 \ldots d_\lambda = \mathsf{H}(X, \{\hat{E}_{i,j}\}_{i=1,\ldots,m}^{j=1,\ldots,k}) \in \{0,1\}^\lambda$
3. For $j = 1, \ldots, \lambda$, compute $r_j = b_j - d_j a$.
4. Return $\pi = ((d_1, \ldots, d_\lambda), (r_1, \ldots, r_\lambda))$.

Scal.Verify(X, π)

Input: Statement $X = \{(E_i, E_i', c_i)\}_{i=1,\ldots,k}$, proof $\pi = ((d_1, \ldots, d_\lambda), (r_1, \ldots, r_\lambda))$.
Output: accept or reject

1. For $j = 1, \ldots, \lambda$:
   – If $d_j = 0$, then let $\hat{E}_{i,j} = [c_i r_j] E_i$ for $i = 1, \ldots, k$,
   – If $d_j = 1$, then let $\hat{E}_{i,j} = [c_i r_j] E_i'$ for $i = 1, \ldots, k$.
2. Return $(d_1, \ldots, d_k) \overset{?}{=} \mathsf{H}(X, \{\hat{E}_{i,j}\}_{i=1,\ldots,m}^{j=1,\ldots,k})$.

Fig. 3. Non-interactive zero-knowledge proof and verification for the language $\mathcal{L}_k^{\mathrm{Scal}}$. (A set is exceptional modulo N, if the pairwise difference between any two elements is invertible in $\mathbb{Z}_N$. This ensures extractability for any challenge.)

Example. As an application example, with $c_1 = c_2 = 1$, this protocol can be used to prove that four elliptic curves constitute a well-formed "Diffie-Hellman tuple", i.e. $(E, [a]E, [b]E, [a+b]E) \in \mathcal{L}_2^{\mathrm{Add}}$ without revealing the secrets a and b, an observation that was initially proposed by Cozzo and Smart [26]. In the case where $[a]E$ and $[b]E$ are public elements, a prover needs to know only one of the secrets. Assuming for example that the prover knows a and $[b]E$, it can prove correctness of the tuple via

$$\pi \leftarrow \mathsf{Scal.Prove}_\lambda(a, \{(E, [a]E), ([b]E, [a+b]E)\}),$$

where, for conciseness, we drop the c_i factor in the case where $c_i = 1$.

4.3   Multiplication with Trusted Setup

We use the scalar multiplication protocol from the previous section to create a protocol for general multiplication. This means that we assume a prover knowing $a, b \in \mathbb{Z}_N$ wants to prove that a tuple $(E, [a]E, [b]E, [ab]E) \in \mathcal{L}^{\mathrm{Mult}}$. The high level idea is that we can prove this in a way similar to the approach explained in Sect. 3.1. Initially, the prover discloses $\alpha = a - x$ and $\beta = b - y$ and computes the action of $[ab]E = [(\alpha + x)(\beta + y)]E$ consecutively as $[\alpha\beta][\beta x][\alpha y][xy]E$. In order to prove that the individual actions have been computed correctly, the prover

---

Mult.Prove$_\lambda(s, B_P)$

Input: Secret pair $s = (a, b)$, tuple $B_P = View_P(B) = (\text{id}, x, y, M_x, M_y, M_{xy})$.
Output: A proof π for the language $\mathcal{L}^{\text{Mult}}$.

1. Set $\alpha = a - x$ and $\beta = b - y$.
2. Compute $E_1 = [\alpha y]M_z$ and $\pi_1 = \text{Scal.Prove}_\lambda(y, \{(E_0, M_y), (M_{xy}, E_1, \alpha)\})$.
3. Compute $E_2 = [\beta x]E_1$ and $\pi_2 = \text{Scal.Prove}_\lambda(x, \{(E_0, M_x), (E_1, E_2, \beta)\})$.
4. Return $\pi = ((E_1, E_2), (\pi_1, \pi_2), (\alpha, \beta))$

Mult.Verify(X, B_V, π)

Input: Proof $\pi = ((E_1, E_2), (\pi_1, \pi_2), (\alpha, \beta))$ of statement $X = (E, E_a, E_b, E_{ab})$,
tuple $B_V = (M_x, M_y, M_{xy}) = View_V(B)$ of committed triple.
Output: accept or reject

1. Verify, if $[\alpha]M_x \stackrel{?}{=} E_a$, $[\beta]M_y \stackrel{?}{=} E_b$ and $[\alpha\beta]E_2 \stackrel{?}{=} E_{ab}$.
2. Check Scal.Verify$(\{(E_0, M_y), (M_{xy}, E_1, \alpha)\}, \pi_1)$ and
   Scal.Verify$(\{(E_0, M_x), (E_1, E_2, \beta)\}, \pi_2)$.
3. Accept if all verifications succeed, otherwise reject.

Fig. 4. Non-interactive zero-knowledge proof and verification for the language $\mathcal{L}^{\text{Mult}}$ in the additive secret sharing case.

uses Scal.Prove at each step. As a reference for these proofs, the prover further needs commitments to the shares

$$M_x = [x]E_0, \quad M_y = [y]E_0, \quad M_{xy} = [xy]E_0.$$

Then, in order to prove correct execution of e.g. the action $F' = [\alpha y]F$, the prover runs Scal.Prove$_\lambda(y, \{(E_0, M_y), (F, F', \alpha)\})$. Using this idea, we show a protocol for the language $\mathcal{L}^{\text{Mult}}$ in Fig. 4. In order to guarantee that the commitments M_x, M_y, M_z have the correct structure, we assume that they are generated by the functionality $\mathcal{T}$ of Definition 5. We require the tuples to have the form

$$B = (\text{id}; x, y, M_x, M_y, M_{xy}) \in \{0, 1\}^* \times \mathbb{Z}_N^2 \times \mathcal{E}^3, \tag{7}$$

with M_x, M_y, M_{xy} as above, such that the prover has full access to the elements, but only the M_i are public, i.e. accessible to the verifiers. We define their views as $View_P(B) = B$ and $View_V(B) = (\text{id}; M_x, M_y, M_{xy})$.

Theorem 2. *The algorithms Mult.Prove and Mult.Verify realize a non-interactive zero-knowledge proof of knowledge for the language $\mathcal{L}^{Mult}$.*

Proof. **Completeness.** After correct execution of the protocol, we have

$$[\alpha]M_x = [a - x][x]E_0 = [a]E_0, \quad [\beta]M_y = [b - y][y]E_0 = [b]E_0,$$
$$\text{and } [\alpha\beta]E_2 = [\alpha\beta + \beta y + \alpha x + xy]E_0 = [ab]E_0.$$

Furthermore, since $M_y = [y]E_0$ and $E_1 = [\alpha y]M_z$, as well as $M_x = [x]E_0$ and $E_2 = [\beta x]E_0$, both the verifications of π_1 and π_2 will succeed.

Soundness. Soundness of the full protocol is directly related to the soundness of Scal.Prove$_\lambda$ and Scal.Verify. We note that the extractor in either invocation of Scal.Prove allows the extraction of x or y, respectively. The secrets can then be recovered as $a = \alpha + x$ or $b = \beta + y$. The total soundness error is $2^{-\lambda}$, given by the maximal soundness error of the different Scal.Prove subalgorithms.

Zero-Knowledge. Zero-knowledge of our protocol immediately follows from the zero-knowledge property of Scal.Prove and the theorem of sequential composition for zero-knowledge [40, Theorem 9]. □

Remark 1. Similarly to Fig. 4, using Scal.Prove allows us to make protocols like Fig. 2 actively secure. It suffices to attach a proof that the correct x or y has been used. To this end, the trusted tuples would also need to contain the curves M_x and M_y, which are accessible by both parties (but not M_{xy}). These commitments also give parties the possibility to verify the received α and β, by testing whether $[\alpha]M_x \overset{?}{=} E_a$ and $[\beta]M_y \overset{?}{=} E_b$.

Cost. In Fig. 4, the prover computes a total of $2 + 4\lambda$ group actions and the verifier $3 + 4\lambda$. This is about twice the cost of proving correctness of DH-tuples in $\mathcal{L}_2^{\mathrm{Add}}$ using Scal.Prove, or verifying them using Scal.Verify.

Exponentiation with Trusted Setup. A similar idea to multiplication with Beaver triples can be used in order to prove elements in $\mathcal{L}^{\mathrm{Exp}}$, e.g. compute powers of a secret $a \in \mathbb{Z}_N$, such as $[a^e]E_0$, for some $e \in \mathbb{N}$. In the full version of this paper, we also introduce protocols for squaring and cubing, which can be combined to arbitrary exponents using a square-and-multiply approach.

4.4 MPC-in-the-Head Protocols

In this section, we propose alternative proofs of correct multiplication, using the MPCitH technique. These proofs again use tuples which have auxiliary elliptic curves in them. If these tuples are generated by a trusted third party, such as in Definition 5, then the protocols in this section outperform the protocols presented previously, which also use such a trusted setup. But another advantage of the MPCitH technique is that we can use the cut-and-choose approach to remove the trusted third party. This results in slightly slower, but still competitive protocols that do not require a trusted setup.

4.4.1 Multiplication-in-the-Head with Trusted Setup.
For the protocol in this section, we initially assume the existence of a trusted third party $\mathcal{T}$, accessible by both prover and verifier, to generate random sharings of tuples of the type

$$B = (\mathsf{id}; (x_i, y_i, z_i)_{i \in [n]}, M_x, M_y) \in \{0,1\}^* \times \mathbb{Z}_N^{3n} \times \mathcal{E}^2$$

for n parties, where $M_x = [x]E_0$, $M_y = [y]E_0$ and $\sum_{i=1}^{n} x_i = x$, $\sum_{i=1}^{n} y_i = y$ and $\sum_{i=1}^{n} z_i = xy$. Whenever the prover queries a new tuple, we let $\mathcal{T}$ respond with $B_P = (\mathrm{id}; (x_i, y_i, z_i)_{i \in [n]})$; when the verifier queries $\mathcal{T}$ for an existing tuple with identifier id, we let $\mathcal{T}$ respond with $B_V = (\mathrm{id}; M_x, M_y)$ if id exists, and with $\perp$ otherwise. As part of the proof, we assume that the prover can give the verifier access to tuples of the form $B_i = (\mathrm{id}; x_i, y_i, z_i)$. Once in possession of $(x_i, y_i, z_i)_{i \in [n]}$, the prover distributes these values among the n parties, together with the public values $\alpha = a - x$ and $\beta = b - y$. In the same way as in Fig. 1 (with the round-robin communication), the parties jointly compute $F_n = [ab]E_0$. We denote the joint execution of parties $P_1, \ldots, P_n$ as $\mathsf{MultITH}_n(\alpha, \beta, B_P)$.

To construct an interactive proof of knowledge from this MPC protocol, the prover commits to the views of the n parties (i.e. to their inputs and the messages they received) as well as the public values α and β. We denote party i's view as $\mathcal{V}_i = (B_i, F_{i-1}, F_i)$. In order to commit to these views, the prover samples secret values $\mu_i \leftarrow \{0, 1\}^\lambda$ and computes the commitments $C_i = \mathcal{C}(\mathcal{V}_i, \mu_i)$. After receiving the commitments, the verifier responds with a random challenge $c \in [n]$ which determines the party whose view the prover *does not* open. The prover therefore sends the set of $n - 1$ views $\{\mathcal{V}_i\}_{i \in [n] \setminus \{c\}}$ for which the verifier checks that (1) F_i has been correctly computed from F_{i-1} using α, β and B_i; (2) the views are consistent with each other, i.e. if for all pairs $\{i, i+1\} \not\ni c$, whether F_i contained in $\mathcal{V}_i$ is consistent with F_i contained in $\mathcal{V}_{i+1}$; (3a) in the case $c \neq 1$, the initial curve F_0 is equal to E_0 and (3b) in the case $c \neq n$, the final curve F_n implied by $\mathcal{V}_n$ is equal to the expected outcome E_{ab} of the protocol.

As the challenge space from which c is sampled has size only n, this MPCitH protocol has soundness error $1/n$ (see also Sect. 2.2) and must be repeated $\tau = \lceil \lambda / \log_2 n \rceil$ times to achieve soundness error $2^{-\lambda}$. (See also Sect. 2.2 for the transformation into a non-interactive argument system.)

Theorem 3. *Assuming ideal commitments, the protocol in Fig. 5 is an interactive and honest-verifier zero-knowledge proof of knowledge for the language $\mathcal{L}^{Mult}$ with soundness error $1/n$.*

Proof. **Completeness:** The code in Fig. 1 computes $E_n = [ab]E_0$ via

$$E_n = \left[\alpha\beta + \beta\sum_{i=1}^{n} x_i + \alpha\sum_{i=1}^{n} y_i + \sum_{i=1}^{n} z_i\right]E_0 = [\alpha\beta + \beta x + \alpha y + xy]E_0.$$

We note that the checks in step 8 uniquely fix $\alpha = a - x$ and $\beta = b - y$.

Special Soundness: Let c and c' be two different challenges and let $(\mathfrak{C}, c, \mathfrak{R})$ and $(\mathfrak{C}, c', \mathfrak{R}')$ be two accepting transcripts, where $\mathfrak{C} = (\{C_i\}_{i \in [n]}, \alpha, \beta)$ and $\mathfrak{R} = (\{\mathcal{V}_i, \mu_i\}_{i \in [n] \setminus \{c\}})$. By the binding property of the idealised commitment scheme, we have that $B_i = B'_i$ for all $i \in [n]$, since C_c is verified as a valid commitment for $\mathcal{V}'_c$ in $\mathfrak{R}'$. Thus, the extractor can reconstruct x and y from $\{B_i\}_{i \in [n] \setminus \{c\}} \cup \{B'_c\}$ and recover a and b from α and β respectively.

As discussed in Sect. 2.2, standard techniques then show that this protocol has soundness error $1/n$ if executed once, and $1/n^\tau$ if repeated τ times.

Input: Secret pair $s = (a, b)$, statement $X = \{[a]E_0, [b]E_0, [ab]E_0\}$,
   security parameter λ.
Output: accept or reject whether $X \in \mathcal{L}^{\mathrm{Mult}}$.

Prover:
 1. Query $\mathcal{T}$ for tuple $B_P = (\mathsf{id}, (x_i, y_i, z_i)_{i \in [n]})$.
 2. Execute $(\mathcal{V}_1, \ldots, \mathcal{V}_n) \leftarrow \mathsf{MultITH}_n(\alpha, \beta, B_P)$,
    with $\alpha = a - x$ and $\beta = b - y$.
 3. For $i = 1, \ldots, n$, sample $\mu_i \leftarrow \{0, 1\}^\lambda$ and commit to $C_i = \mathcal{C}(\mathcal{V}_i, \mu_i)$.
    Send $\{C_1, \ldots, C_n\}$ to the verifier as well as α and β.
Verifier:
 4. Sample a challenge $c \in [n]$ uniformly at random and send c to the prover.
Prover:
 5. Send $\{\mathcal{V}_i, \mu_i\}_{i \in [n] \setminus \{c\}}$.

Verifier:
 6. Check that all $\mathcal{V}_i$, for $i \in [n] \setminus \{c\}$, contain the same id.
 7. Query $\mathcal{T}$ with id for tuple $B_V = (\mathsf{id}, (M_x, M_y))$.
 8. Check $[\alpha]M_x \overset{?}{=} E_a$ and $[\beta]M_y \overset{?}{=} E_b$.
 9. Check the commitments $C_i \overset{?}{=} \mathcal{C}(\mathcal{V}_i, \mu_i)$, for $i \in [n] \setminus \{c\}$.
 10. If $c \neq 1$, verify that $F_0 \overset{?}{=} E_0$, where $F_0 \in \mathcal{V}_1$.
 11. If $c \neq n$, verify that $F_n \overset{?}{=} E_{ab}$ and that $F_n \overset{?}{=} [\alpha\beta + \beta x_n + \alpha y_n + z_n]F_{n-1}$, where
     $F_{n-1}, F_n \in \mathcal{V}_n$ and $x_n, y_n, z_n \in B_n$.
 12. For $i \in [n-1] \setminus \{c\}$,
    (a) verify that $F_i = [\beta x_i + \alpha y_i + z_i]F_{i-1}$ for $F_{i-1}, F_i \in \mathcal{V}_i$ and $x_i, y_i, z_i \in B_i$.
    (b) if $c \neq i + 1$, verify that $F_i \in \mathcal{V}_i$ is equal to $F_{i-1} \in \mathcal{V}_{i-1}$.
 13. If all checks succeed, return accept, otherwise reject.

Fig. 5. Interactive ZK proof for $\mathcal{L}^{\mathrm{Mult}}$ using MPC-in-the-Head with trusted party.

Zero-Knowledge: The simulator $\mathcal{S}$ plays the role of the prover (without knowing a or b), of the trusted third party, and of the challenge generation in order to output a transcript that is indisguishable from one made with a valid witness. (Note that the argument below is equivalent to proving the $(n-1)$-privacy of the protocol of Fig. 1.)

First, $\mathcal{S}$ samples α and β at random. As the third party $\mathcal{T}$, it then creates a new tuple by sampling all x_i, y_i, z_i at random, for $i \in [n]$ and setting $M_x = [-\alpha]E_a, M_y = [-\beta]E_b$, and creating a random id.

Next, $\mathcal{S}$ samples $c \in [n]$ at random on behalf of an honest verifier. Since α and β contain no information about a and b, and the simulated triple is not correct, computing F_i honestly, for $i \in [n]$, will not produce $F_n = E_{ab}$ as expected by the verifier. Instead, the simulator computes F_i for $1 \leq i < c$ "forwards", as per the protocol, but computes F_i for $c \leq i \leq n$ "backwards" from $F_n = E_{ab}$, ensuring that the chain results in the correct final curve. Thus:

$$
F_i = \begin{cases}
[\beta x_i + \alpha y_i]F_{i-1} & 1 \leq i < c \\
[-\beta x_{i+1} - \alpha y_{i+1}]F_{i+1} & c \leq i < n - 1 \\
[-\alpha\beta - \beta x_n - \alpha y_n]E_n & i = n - 1,
\end{cases}
$$

where $F_0 = E_0$.

The simulator can now set $\mathcal{V}_i = (\mathrm{id}, x_i, y_i, F_{i-1}, F_i)$, sample μ_i as per the protocol, and compute the set of commitments $\{C_i\}$. This gives the transcript $(\{C_i\}_{i \in [n]}, \alpha, \beta, c, \{\mathcal{V}_i, \mu_i\}_{i \in [n] \setminus \{c\}})$ as the final output of $\mathcal{S}$.

Correctness: The simulated transcript will verify since $[\alpha]M_x = E_a$ and $[\beta]M_y = E_b$ by construction; $F_n = E_{ab}$ by construction of F_{n-1}; all of the F_i curves, for $i \neq c$, satisfy the right relation.

Indistinguishability: Since x and y are uniformly generated by $\mathcal{T}$ in the protocol, sampling α and β directly in the simulation is perfectly indistinguishable. By the same argument, the curves M_x and M_y of the simulated tuple are distributed identically to an honest tuple, since in addition the idealised commitment perfectly hides x_c and y_c from the Verifier, who therefore cannot recover x and y. Within the MPC protocol, the only inconsistency is the computation of F_c which Verifier cannot detect since x_c and y_c are hidden by the commitment scheme. □

Cost. In Fig. 1, each party computes one isogeny computation. The prover runs this protocol τ times for n parties, resulting in a total computational cost of $n\tau = n\lceil \lambda / \log_2 n \rceil$ for the prover. The verifier on the other hand has to verify the steps in Fig. 1 for $n - 1$ parties and compute 2τ further isogeny computations in step 8 of the protocol, resulting in the total $(n + 1)\tau$. By choosing $n = 3$, we optimize with respect to the total cost of the proof and verification. In that case, the prover computes approximately 1.89λ isogenies, and the verifier 2.52λ.[5] We note that this cost is competitive with proofs of DH-tuples, which cost 2λ in proof and in verification costs, see Sect. 4.2.

Scalar-in-the-Head. Since scalar operations on additively-shared secret values are linear, they can be computed locally by parties in MPC protocols. Similarly, for public c and secret a, an MPCitH prover can secret-share $a = \sum_{i \in [n]} a_i$ and have every party compute $[ca_i]E_{i-1}$ and pass it on to the next one in the same round-robin fashion as the multiplication protocol. This will clearly result in $E_n = [ca]E_0$. Furthermore, since the verifier sees that every MPC party used the public value c, there is no trusted helper required here.

4.4.2 Exponentiation-in-the-Head with Trusted Setup.

Proving Exponentiation with MPCitH works along the same idea as multiplication. For exponentiation to the power e, we need tuples of the type

$$B = \left(\mathrm{id}; (x_i^{(k)})_{i \in [n]}^{k \in [e]}, M_x\right) \in \{0,1\}^* \times (\mathbb{Z}_N)^{e \cdot n} \times \mathcal{E}, \tag{8}$$

where $M_x = [x]E_0$. The shares are defined, such that $\sum_{i=1}^n x_i^{(k)} = x^k$. The trusted third party $\mathcal{T}$ sends $\mathrm{View}_P(B) = \left(\mathrm{id}; (x_i^{(k)})_{i \in [n]}^{k \in [e]}\right)$ to the prover and

---

[5] Alternatively, $n = 4$, leads to the higher average of 2.00λ for the prover and the slightly lower average of 2.50λ for the verifier.

MPC exponentiation protocol for $P_i(\alpha, x_i^{(1)}, \ldots, x_i^{(e)})$

---

1 : from P_{i-1} receive F_{i-1} (P_1 receives $F_0 = E_0$)

2 : **if** $i < n$ **then**

3 : $F_i \leftarrow \left[\sum_{k=1}^{e} \binom{e}{k} \alpha^{e-k} x_i^{(k)} \right] F_{i-1}$

4 :   send F_i to P_{i+1}

5 : **if** $i = n$ **then**

6 : $F_n \leftarrow \left[\alpha^e + \sum_{k=1}^{e} \binom{e}{k} \alpha^{e-k} x_i^{(k)} \right] F_{i-1}$

7 :   Broadcast(F_n)

Fig. 6. MPC pseudocode for exponentiation

MPC polynomial evaluation protocol for $P_i(\alpha, f, x_i^{(1)}, \ldots, x_i^{(d)})$

---

1 : from P_{i-1} receive F_{i-1} (P_1 receives $F_0 = E_0$)

2 : **if** $i < n$ **then**

3 : $F_i \leftarrow \left[\sum_{e=1}^{d} \sum_{k=1}^{e} f_k \binom{e}{k} \alpha^{e-k} x_i^{(k)} \right] F_{i-1}$

4 :   send F_i to P_{i+1}

5 : **if** $i = n$ **then**

6 : $F_n \leftarrow \left[\left(f_0 + \sum_{e=1}^{d} \alpha^e \right) + \sum_{e=1}^{d} \sum_{k=1}^{e} \binom{e}{k} \alpha^{e-k} x_i^{(k)} \right] F_{i-1}$

7 :   Broadcast(F_n)

Fig. 7. MPC pseudocode for polynomial evaluation

$\text{View}_V(B) = (\text{id}; M_x)$ to the verifier. The prover distributes the values $(x_i^{(k)})^{k \in [e]}$ to each party P_i, together with $\alpha = a - x$. We describe the MPC protocol in Fig. 6, which we denote $\text{ExpITH}_n^e(\alpha, B_P)$. The interactive proof of knowledge can be found in the full version of this paper. We note that, in contrast to the approach from Sect. 4.3, this cost is independent of the exponent e.

4.4.3 Polynomial Evaluation In-the-Head with Trusted Setup. The exponentiation protocol from the previous section can be extended to the case where multiple parties want to evaluate a public polynomial on a shared input.

Let $f(x) = \sum_{k=0}^{d} f_k x^k$; then we can see that $[f(x)]E$ can be evaluated on a shared x, using the consecutive application of exponentiations. This can be achieved with the same trusted setup as for exponentiation, see Equation (8). We summarize the MPC protocol in Fig. 7. The full zero-knowledge protocol follows straightforwardly from the exponentiation protocol in the full paper.

4.4.4   Removing the Trusted Helper with Cut-and-choose. We now show how the cut-and-choose technique can be used to remove the trusted helper in our multiplication (and exponentiation) protocols. The idea is that the prover now generates the structured tuple instead of the helper. However, the verifier must also be convinced that the elements in this tuple are well formed, such as e.g. $z = xy$ or $M_x = [x]E_0$. This can be achieved with the cut-and-choose method described in Sect. 2.2: the prover precomputes and commits to a large amount m of these tuples and is then challenged to open $m - \tau$ of them. Afterwards, the verifier can check that they have the desired structure.

The prover then runs the proof using the τ undisclosed tuples, also convincing the verifier that the proof statement is correct. These proofs are computed by running $\mathsf{MultITH}_n$ or ExpITH_n^e, respectively, for each of the τ tuples. If all of these checks succeed for appropriate choices of m and τ, the verifier is convinced of the truth of the statement up to a negligible error probability.

We present the protocol for $\mathcal{L}^{\mathrm{Mult}}$ in Fig. 8. The protocol for $\mathcal{L}^{\mathrm{Exp}}$ can be built with the exact same tools and can be found in the full version of the paper.

Theorem 4. *Assuming ideal commitments, the protocol in Fig. 8 is an interactive and honest-verifier zero-knowledge proof of knowledge for the language $\mathcal{L}^{\mathrm{Mult}}$ with soundness error $\epsilon_{\mathsf{CnC}}(m, n, \tau)$.*

Proof. **Correctness:** It is clear that correctly formed tuples pass the verification conditions for $j \in \mathcal{I}$. For each execution $j \in [m] \setminus \mathcal{I}$, correctness follows from the correctness of $\mathsf{MultITH}$.

Special soundness: By the same argument as for Theorem 3, for a given j, the extractor can obtain x^j and y^j by using a malicious prover's accepting responses to two different party challenges c^j and c'^j. By also rewinding the prover back to the commitment of the pre-processing data, and obtaining a third accepting transcript with a different opening of τ datasets, the extractor can ensure that the (x^j, y^j, z^j) tuple used above is a valid multiplication tuple.

Zero-knowledge: To ouput an indistinguishable transcript, the simulator $\mathcal{S}$ first samples $\mathcal{I}$ at random and then generates honest secret-sharings $(\{x_i\}_{[n]}, \{y_i\}_{[n]}, \{z_i\}_{[n]}, M_x, M_y)_j$ for $j \in \mathcal{I}$. For the remaining $j \in [m] \setminus \mathcal{I}$, $\mathcal{S}$ does as for Theorem 3 by sampling α^j and β^j at random and setting $M_x^j = [-\alpha^j]E_a$ and $M_y^j = [-\beta^j]E_b$. It then falsifies the round-robin computation of F_n^j in the same way: by sampling the challenge c^j at random, and computing F_{c-1}^j "forwards" from E_0 and F_c^j "backwards" from E_{ab}. Since x_c^j, y_c^j, z_c^j remain hidden from the Verifier, and since there is no commitment as in the protocol with trusted setup, no other simulation is necessary.

Correctness: Here, F_n^j will equal the correct curves by construction and the views will be consistent due to the "forward" and "backward" computations.

Indistinguishability: The public values α^j and β^j are sampled at random, which means they are distributed identically to the protocol, assuming that the Verifier has no knowledge of x^j, y^j, z^j. Similarly, M_x^j and M_y^j are distributed identically to an honest tuple. The idealised commitments perfectly hide x_c^j, y_c^j, z_c^j from the

---

Input: Secret pair $s = (a, b)$, statement $X = \{[a]E_0, [b]E_0, [ab]E_0\}$,
   security parameter λ.
Output: accept or reject whether $X \in \mathcal{L}^{\mathrm{Mult}}$.

Prover:
1. Generate the secret-shared pre-processing data:

$$\left\{ \left(\{x_i\}_{[n]}, \{y_i\}_{[n]}, \{z_i\}_{[n]}, M_x, M_y \right)_j \right\}_{j=[m]}.$$

2. Commit to the pre-processed data for each party and to the curves M_x^j, M_y^j for each copy $j \in [m]$, and send the commitments to the verifier.

Verifier:
3. Sample a random subset $\mathcal{I} \subset [m]$ of size $m - \tau$ and send $\mathcal{I}$ to the prover.

Prover:
4. For each $j \in [m] \setminus \mathcal{I}$, Execute $(\mathcal{V}_1^j, \ldots, \mathcal{V}_n^j) \leftarrow \mathsf{MultITH}_n(\alpha^j, \beta^j, (x, y, z)^j)$,
   with $\alpha^j = a - x^j$ and $\beta^j = b - y^j$.
5. For $j \in [m] \setminus \mathcal{I}$ and $i \in [n]$, sample $\mu_i^j \leftarrow \{0, 1\}^\lambda$ and commit to $C_i^j = \mathcal{C}(\mathcal{V}_i^j, \mu_i^j)$.
   Send $(\{C_1^j, \ldots, C_n^j\}, \alpha^j, \beta^j)_{j=[m] \setminus \mathcal{I}}$ to the verifier, as well as and the opening of
   $(\{x_i\}_{[n]}, \{y_i\}_{[n]}, \{z_i\}_{[n]}, M_x, M_y)_{j \in \mathcal{I}}$.

Verifier:
6. Sample challenges $c^j \in [n]$, for $j \in [m] \setminus \mathcal{I}$ uniformly at random and send $\{c^j\}$ to the prover.

Prover:
7. Send $\{\mathcal{V}_i^j, \mu_i^j\}_{i \in [n] \setminus \{c\}, j \in [m] \setminus \mathcal{I}}$.

Verifier:
8. For $j \in \mathcal{I}$, verify if the commitments to $(\{x_i\}_{[n]}, \{y_i\}_{[n]}, \{z_i\}_{[n]}, M_x, M_y)_j$ open correctly and are correctly formed.
9. For all $j \in [M] \setminus \mathcal{I}$, perform the same verifications as in Figure 5.
10. If all checks succeed, return **accept**, otherwise **reject**.

Fig. 8. Interactive ZK proof for $\mathcal{L}^{\mathrm{Mult}}$ using MPCitH without trusted party.

Verifier, so the perfect secrecy of the additive secret-sharing scheme implies the perfect zero-knowledge of the protocol. □

Cost. In the protocol of Fig. 8, the prover computes a total of $2m + n\tau$ isogenies, $2m$ when generating the tuples and $n\tau$ when running the MultITH protocol. The verifier checks $2(m - \tau)$ of these tuples and verifies the protocol using another $(n + 1)\tau$ isogenies, yielding the total $2m + (n - 1)\tau$.

The computational costs of the protocols introduced in this section depend on the choices of m and τ, which themselves are determined by the equation established in Sect. 2.2. Using numerical techniques, we found that choosing $n = 3$ always minimizes these costs. In particular we can find, that for the multiplication protocol, the prover has to approximately compute 4.96λ isogenies and the verifier 4.25λ.

4.4.5   Cost Overview. We summarize the costs of the protocols introduced throughout this section in Table 2.

Table 2. Number of isogeny computations of the prover and verifier for the protocols introduced in this work. The costs are given in terms of the security parameter λ, to ensure a soundness error of $2^{-\lambda}$. We further indicate, if the protocols need a trusted setup or not and which type of statements they are proving. We note that $\mathsf{Scal.Prove}_{k=1}$ coincides with the binary CSI-FiSh ID-protocol. The subscripts $\mathcal{T}$ and cnc indicate the protocol versions with trusted setup and cut-and-choose, respectively. We also note that the cost for $\mathsf{ExpITH}_{\mathcal{T}}$ and ExpITH_{cnc} are the same as for the respective polynomial evaluation protocols described in Sect. 4.4.3.

	Prover cost	Verifier cost	Trusted Party	Statement type
$\mathsf{Scal.Prove}_{k=1}$	λ	λ	No	$(E, [s]E)$
$\mathsf{Scal.Prove}_{k=2}$	2λ	2λ	No	$(E, [a]E, [b]E, [a+b]E)$
$\mathsf{Mult.Prove}$	4λ	4λ	Yes	
$\mathsf{MultITH}_{\mathcal{T}}$	1.89λ	2.52λ	Yes	$(E, [a]E, [b]E, [ab]E)$
$\mathsf{MultITH}_{cnc}$	4.96λ	4.25λ	No	
$\mathsf{Exp.Prove}$	$\lfloor \log_2 e \rfloor 6\lambda$	$\lfloor \log_2 e \rfloor 6\lambda$	Yes	
$\mathsf{ExpITH}_{\mathcal{T}}$	1.89λ	1.89λ	Yes	$(e, [a]E, [a^e]E)$
ExpITH_{cnc}	3.52λ	3.52λ	No	

4.5   New Signatures

To give an idea of the applications we can build with the tools from this section, we introduce two examples of signature schemes, based on proofs of scalar multiplication and multiplication, respectively. The ideas behind these signature schemes are loosely based on the schemes of Boneh, Lynn and Shacham [18] (BLS) and of Zhang, Safavi-Naini and Susilo [62] (ZSS). The original schemes, proposed in the discrete logarithm setting, produce particularly short signatures and are verified using elliptic curve pairings, neither of which is the case here.

Rather, we present the signatures as instructive examples on how (scalar) multiplication proofs can be used to prove statements reminiscent of pairings in elliptic curve cryptography. The underlying observation is that statements of the language $\mathcal{L}^{\mathrm{Mult}}$, e.g. tuples of the form $(E, [a]E, [b]E, [ab]E)$ have a similar feel to pairing-based verification equations of the type $e([a]P, [b]P) = e(P, [ab]P)$. The caveats with respect to this interpretation are plentiful, however. As an example, elliptic curve points and the codomain of pairings both form groups, and operations in these groups are often crucial to allow verification, a perk that the elliptic curve set $\mathcal{E}$ doesn't benefit from. Furthermore, while pairing equations can be performed using public elements, in our setting, we always need the prover to generate these publicly verifiable proofs first.

With this in mind, we present our signatures in Fig. 9. The first scheme uses a proof for the language $\mathcal{L}_2^{\mathrm{Scal}}$, while the latter uses proofs for $\mathcal{L}^{\mathrm{Mult}}$. We note

Keygen(pp)
1. Sample $s \leftarrow \mathbb{Z}_N$ and compute $E_s = [s]E_0$.
2. Return $(sk, pk) = (s, E_s)$.

Scal-Sign(m, s)
1. Compute $\sigma = [sH(m)]E_0$.
2. Construct a $\mathcal{L}_2^{\text{Scal}}$-proof π for the statement $((E_0, E_s), (E_0, \sigma, H(m)))$.
3. Return σ, π.

Mult-Sign(m, s)
1. Compute $\sigma = \left[\frac{1}{s+H(m)}\right]E_0$ and $F = [H(m)]E_s$.
2. Construct a $\mathcal{L}^{\text{Mult}}$-proof π for the statement $(E_0, \sigma, F, [1]E_0)$.
3. Return σ, π.

Scal-Verify(m, E_s, σ, π)
1. Compute $H(m)$ and verify $(H(m), E_s, \sigma)$ using π.
2. If verification succeeds, return True, otherwise False.

Mult-Verify(m, E_s, σ, π)
1. Compute $F = [H(m)]E_s$ and verify σ using π.
2. If verification succeeds, return True, otherwise False.

Fig. 9. Two signature schemes using proofs of scalar multiplication or multiplication.

that any of the appropriate proof systems introduced in this work can be used. For both cases, we define the hash function $H : \{0, 1\}^* \to \mathbb{Z}_N$.

Security of these schemes immediately follows from the security of the proof schemes they employ. We note however, that in the multiplicative signature, for the element $s + H(m)$ to be invertible, we would need to assume that N is prime, so that $\mathbb{Z}_N$ is a field, since in any ring, the "allowed" values for $H(m)$ would reveal information about s.

While the signatures in this section do not outperform the current state-of-the-art isogeny-based signature schemes (see Table 2 for reference), we hope that this inspires more research into other potential applications of the tools presented in this work.

5 An Oblivious Pseudo-random Function

We finish our work by introducing an oblivious pseudo-random function based on the tools developed throughout the last sections.

An oblivious pseudo-random function (OPRF) is a protocol between a client C and a server S. The server has a secret key k defining a function $F_k(\cdot)$. The client has a secret input m, on which it wants to evaluate this function. The goal of an OPRF is for the client to receive the evaluation $F_k(m)$ without learning anything about k, while the server doesn't learn anything, i.e. neither the input m, nor the output $F_k(m)$. A *verifiable* OPRF further allows the client to verify that the server has indeed correctly used its secret k towards the computation of $F_k(x)$.

In our case, we assume the secret key of the server to be a polynomial $f(x)$, represented in terms of the polynomial coefficients $k = (f_0, f_1, \ldots, f_d)$, where

$d = \deg f$. On input a message m, we define the OPRF evaluation to be the function $F_k(m) = [f(m)]E_0$, for some starting curve E_0.

The idea behind the OPRF is that two parties engage in a polynomial evaluation protocol similar to the idea in Sect. 4.4.3. A major difference here, is that the polynomial coefficients are not public, but rather secrets of the server. As a result, they also have to be hidden. Therefore the parties jointly have to evaluate terms of the type $[f_j m^j]E$ with f_j and m hidden. The resulting protocol is therefore rather a blend of the multiplication and exponentiation protocols introduced previously. To compute terms of this type, we assume that there is a functionality $\mathcal{T}$ that generates the following kind of tuples:

$$B = (\mathsf{id}; x, \{y_j\}^{j \in [d]}, (\widetilde{z_C}, \widetilde{z_S}), \{(z_C^{(j,k)}, z_S^{(j,k)})\}_{k \in [j-1]}^{j \in [d]}), \qquad (9)$$

$$\mathrm{View}_C(B) = (\mathsf{id}; x, \widetilde{z_C}, \{z_C^{(j,k)}\}_{k \in [j-1]}^{j \in [d]}),$$

$$\mathrm{View}_S(B) = (\mathsf{id}, \{y_j\}^{j \in [d]}, \widetilde{z_S}, \{z_S^{(j,k)}\}_{k \in [j-1]}^{j \in [d]}),$$

such that[6]

$$z_C^{(j,k)} + z_S^{(j,k)} = y_j x^k \quad \text{and} \quad \widetilde{z_C} + \widetilde{z_S} = \sum_{j=1}^{d} y_j x^j.$$

We present our construction in Fig. 10 and discuss its security in the theorem below. Some of the security properties of our OPRF will depend on properties of the polynomial f. We outline the necessary restrictions as part of the proof and defer the discussion about concrete instantiations of f to Sect. 5.1.

Theorem 5. *The protocol in Fig. 10 satisfies the security requirements of an OPRF, i.e. correctness, hiding against a malicious client, hiding against a malicious server, binding and one-more unpredictability.*

Proof. We omit the full definition of the security properties of an OPRF here, and refer the reader to [17,38,55] more details.

Correctness: By summing the action of the client and of the server, it can be quickly verified that the action on E_0 is given by

$$f_0 + \widetilde{z_S} + \widetilde{z_C} + \sum_{j=1}^{d}(f_j \alpha^j + \beta_j x^j) + \sum_{j=1}^{d} \sum_{k=1}^{j-1} \binom{j}{k} \alpha^{j-k}\left(z_S^{(j,k)} + z_C^{(j,k)} + \beta_j x^k\right).$$

By plugging in the definitions of Equation (9) as well as the fact that $\beta_j + y_j = f_j$, this simplifies to

$$f_0 + \sum_{j=1}^{d} f_j \left(\alpha^j + \sum_{k=1}^{j-1} \binom{j}{k} \alpha^{j-k} x^k + x^j\right),$$

---

[6] Note that we could as well have defined the tuples to contain $\{(z_C^{(j,k)}, z_S^{(j,k)})\}_{k \in [j]}^{j \in [d]}$. Since in our protocol, the coefficients of terms where $j = k$ is always 1, we can summarize all of these terms in $\widetilde{z_C}$ and $\widetilde{z_S}$, which leads to a smaller trusted setup by reducing the amount of such terms by $d - 1$.

Input: Secret key $k = (f_0, f_1, \ldots, f_d) \in \mathbb{Z}_N^{d+1}$ held by the server S, secret input $m \in \mathbb{Z}_N^*$ by the client C. Shared tuple B as in equation (9).
Output: Evaluation $F_k(m) = [f(m)]E_0$.

Client:
1. Compute $\alpha = m - x$ and send it to the server.

Server:
2. For $j = 1, \ldots, d$, compute $\beta_j = f_j - y_j$.
3. Compute

$$E_S = \left[f_0 + \widetilde{zs} + \sum_{j=1}^{d} f_j \alpha^j + \sum_{j=1}^{d} \sum_{k=1}^{j-1} \binom{j}{k} \alpha^{j-k} z_S^{(j,k)} \right] E_0 \,.$$

4. Send $(\beta_1, \ldots, \beta_d)$ and E_S it to the client.

Client:
5. Return

$$\left[\widetilde{zc} + \sum_{j=1}^{d} \beta_j x^j + \sum_{j=1}^{d} \sum_{k=1}^{j-1} \binom{j}{k} \alpha^{j-k} \left(\beta_j x^k + z_C^{(j,k)} \right) \right] E_S \,.$$

Fig. 10. Oblivious pseudo-random function based on joint polynomial evaluation.

which is the expression $\sum_{j=0}^{d} f_j (\alpha + x)^j = f(m)$.

Hiding against malicious server: It is clear that α information-theoretically hides m: as the functionality $\mathcal{T}$, the simulator samples B uniformly at random from the different sets and sends $\mathrm{View}_S(B)$ to the server. Then, as the client, it samples $\alpha \leftarrow \mathbb{Z}_N$ and send it to the server. This simulation is perfectly indistinguishable from the real execution of the protocol.

Hiding against malicious client: To prove this, we show that the malicious client has a negligible advantage in the hiding game. After receiving α from the adversary, the challenger samples $b \leftarrow \{0, 1\}$. Then,

– if $b = 0$, it computes $\beta_j^{(0)} = f_j - y_j$ for $j = 1, \ldots, d$ and

$$r^{(0)} = f_0 + \widetilde{zs} + \sum_{j=1}^{d} f_j \alpha^j + \sum_{j=1}^{d} \sum_{k=1}^{j-1} \binom{j}{k} \alpha^{j-k} z_S^{(e,k)},$$

– if $b = 1$, it samples $r^{(1)} \leftarrow \mathbb{Z}_N$ and $\beta_j^{(1)} \leftarrow \mathbb{Z}_N$ for $j = 1, \ldots, d$.

In either case, the server sends $(\beta_1^{(b)}, \ldots, \beta_d^{(b)})$ and $E_S^{(b)} = [r^{(b)}]E_0$ to the client. The adversary then outputs $b' \in \{0, 1\}$ and wins the game if $b' = b$. It is clear that $(\beta_1^{(1)}, \ldots, \beta_d^{(1)})$ and $(\beta_1^{(0)}, \ldots, \beta_d^{(0)})$ follow perfectly indistinguishable distributions as f_j and y_j are unknown to the adversary. Similarly, $r^{(0)}$ and $r^{(1)}$ should be indistinguishable, but we note, that in the first case, the adversary can evaluate the OPRF correctly and receive $[f(m)]E_0$ after applying its half of the action. Now, due to the freeness of the group action, the adversary will still not be able to distinguish both cases, as long as the output distribution of the polynomial $f(m)$ is indistinguishable from uniform. We note that this is an important restriction when we are working in rings. In particular, since the client's queries are hidden, a malicious client could only send inputs in a subgroup of $\mathbb{Z}_N$, which it could easily distinguish from a random $r^{(1)}$. We therefore have to assume that we are working in a subgroup of the class group of prime order if we want to protect against malicious clients. For semi-honest clients, we emphasize that this restriction is not necessary.

Binding: Due to the freeness of the group action, we only have a collision, if $f(m) = f(m')$. The OPRF is binding, if f is collision-resistant.

One-more unpredictability: We assume the adversary $\mathcal{A}$ has oracle access to an OPRF oracle, which on input m outputs $[f(m)]E_0$. After r evaluations of the OPRF, the adversary has knowledge of

$$(m_1, [f(m_1)]E_0), \ldots, (m_r, [f(m_r)]E_0).$$

The client breaks one-more security by finding a pair $m^*, [f(m^*)]E_0$, where $m^* \notin \{m_1, \ldots, m_r\}$. The hardness of this again depends on the polynomial f. We discuss these restrictions in Sect. 5.1. □

5.1   Choosing the Polynomial

The first restriction from Theorem 5, is that we have to work in a prime order subgroup of the class group to guarantee security against a malicious adversary. So, throughout this section, we assume that we are working in a prime order subgroup of the class group and that $\mathbb{Z}_N$ constitutes a field. In the proof of Theorem 5, we also found the following restrictions on f:

1. f has output distribution indistinguishable from uniform,
2. f is collision-resistant,
3. the one-more unpredictability problem is hard.

From Eq. (9), we see that polynomials of high degree lead to a higher communication and storage cost in terms of tuples. We can easily count that the number of elements in the tuple B is $3 + d^2$. As a further restriction, we therefore add, that

4. f has small degree.

It is immediately clear that the first two restrictions can be achieved by permutation polynomials, i.e. a bijective polynomial $f : \mathbb{Z}_N \to \mathbb{Z}_N$. Any linear polynomial already fits the bill here, but unfortunately, linear polynomials turn out to not be secure against quantum adversaries. If $d = 1$, the output is a multiplication with an offset, i.e. $[f_0 + f_1 m]E_0$. In the reduction from GAIP to Parallelization outlined by Galbraith et al. [39], the authors show that access to an oracle, which on input m outputs $[f_1 m]E$ is sufficient to recover f_1. It is clear that this breaks one-more-unpredictability.

For $d = 2$, permutation polynomials only exist over fields with characteristic 2, which contradicts the premise that N is a prime. Thankfully, when going to $d = 3$, if $p \equiv 2 \pmod 3$, any polynomial of the form $f(m) = a(m+b)^3 + c$ with $a \neq 0$ is a permutation polynomial [31]. We do however note that heuristically, a polynomial of degree 2 (with non-zero coefficients) is also enough. In a field, using a quadratic polynomial satisfies the binding property, since for every $f(m)$, there exists *at most* a second input that evaluates to $f(m)$ (this follows from the fact that $f(m) = f(m')$ is an equation of degree 2 and therefore admits at most two solutions). Similarly, since at least half of $\mathbb{Z}_N$ is covered by the outputs of f (with each element reached at most twice), we can also guarantee the hiding property against a malicious client.

So, we have found polynomials that fit our bill, assuming the one-more unpredictability problem is hard. Let us first rephrase the latter as a game, where the adversary $\mathcal{A}$ against one-more unpredictability has oracle access to an OPRF oracle $\mathcal{O}$, which on input m, outputs $[f(m)]E_0$. After polynomially many queries, $\mathcal{A}$ outputs (m^*, E^*) with m^* not previously queried to $\mathcal{O}$, and wins the game, if $E^* = [f(m^*)]E_0$. We first start by noticing that our assumption reduces to (Scalar-)CDH, i.e. access to such an oracle, allows us to find $[f(m^*)]E_0$ as follows (for simplicity, we outline the case $d = 2$, while other cases work analogously):

1. Query $\mathcal{O}$ on $m \in \{-1, 0, 1\}$ to get $[f_0]E_0$, $[f_0 + f_1 + f_2]E_0$ and $[f_0 - f_1 + f_2]E_0$.
2. Use the CDH-oracle to build $[f_1 + f_2]E_0$ and $[-f_1 + f_2]E_0$ from these by subtraction of $[f_0]E_0$, then build $[2f_1]E_0$ and $[2f_2]E_0$ from addition and subtraction.
3. For any message m^*, compute $m^*/2$ and $(m^*)^2/2$ and call the Scalar-CDH oracle to compute $[f_1 m^*]E_0$ and $[f_2 (m^*)^2]E_0$.
4. Finally, compute and output $[f_0 + f_1 m^* + f_2 (m^*)^2]E_0 = [f(m^*)]E_0$.

Showing the converse is less trivial, however. Assuming oracle access to an OPRF-oracle, which on input m gives us the output $[f(m)]E_0$ does not give us much to work with, when we want to use this to break some assumption. As a result, we have to rely on a more heuristic argumentation to convince ourselves that it is hard for $\mathcal{A}$ to win the game. To this end, let's view our map as follows.

$$\mathbb{Z}_N \longrightarrow \mathbb{Z}_N \longrightarrow \mathcal{E}$$
$$m \longmapsto f(m) \longmapsto [f(m)]E_0$$

The adversary interacting with $\mathcal{O}$ chooses m and learns $[f(m)]E_0$, thus the left and the right hand side of our map. We can argue that from both of these sides, the adversary is not able to infer any information about $f(m)$. We already know from the proof of Theorem 5 that by choosing m, we can't learn anything about $f(m)$ as long as it has output indistinguishable from uniform. Furthermore, inferring anything about $f(m)$ from $[f(m)]E_0$ contradicts the assumptions of a cryptographic group action being one-way and unpredictable. This last sentence has to be taken with a large grain of salt, as this argument would also apply in the case where $f(m)$ is a linear function, which we have proven to be insufficient, and allowing the extraction of the secret. However, linear functions define instances of the hidden subgroup problem, while non-linear (non-monomial) polynomials ostensibly do not. As a result, none of the standard attacks from the literature seem to be applicable to our problem, from which we conjecture that it is a hard problem. With this, we leave further scrutiny of our security assumption as an open problem for future research.

5.2   Adding Verifiability

We discuss how to turn our OPRF into a verifiable OPRF. The idea is similar to protocols like the one in Fig. 4, where we add elliptic curves to the honestly generated tuples B and use Scal.Prove in order to convince the verifier that the computation has been done as instructed.

To this end, we define the server's public key as $\{P_j = [f_j]E_0\}_{j=0,\dots,d}$ and we need to add the following publicly visible elements to the trusted tuple

$$\widetilde{M} = [\widetilde{z_S}]E_0, \ \{M^{(j,k)} = [z_S^{(j,k)}]E_0\}_{k\in[j-1]}^{j\in[d]}.$$

Then the server computes the different additions in Step 3 of Fig. 10 consecutively, starting from its public key, and appends a proof of correct computation. The server steps then become

$$\left[\alpha^j f_j\right]_{j\in[d]} \left[\binom{j}{k}\alpha^{j-k} z_S^{(j,k)}\right]_{k\in[j-1]}^{j\in[d]} \left[\widetilde{z_S}\right] P_0 \,,$$

with appended proofs at each step, that the correct witness was used with the correct factor from a curve E_{i-1} to E_i, e.g.

$$\text{Scal.Prove}_\lambda \left(z_S^{(j,k)}, \{(E_0, M^{(j,k)}), (E_{i-1}, E_i, \binom{j}{k}\alpha^{j-k})\}, \right) \,.$$

All the proofs are sent to the client, which verifies them and finally computes its own action, to get the OPRF output $[f(m)]E_0$.

5.3   Comparison to the Literature

We end this section by comparing the cost of our OPRF with CSIDH-based (and other isogeny-based) OPRFs in the literature. The first CSIDH-based OPRF was introduced by Boneh et al. [17] and is based on a Naor-Reingold PRF, where the server and the client engage in λ $\binom{2}{1}$-oblivious transfers. Note that this initial design is based on the OT by Lai et al. [51] which requires a trusted setup. Follow-up work by Heimberger et al. [42] improves the protocol of Boneh et al. by reducing its round-complexity and presents a new OPRF protocol without trusted setup, and which also works when the class group is unknown. We summarize the different protocols and their relative costs in Table 3, and compare polynomial degrees $d = 2$ and 3 of our design.

In our protocol, a malicious client comes at no extra communication or computational cost to the semi-honest case and our number of rounds is optimal, even in the verifiable case. The non-verifiable version of our protocol strongly outperforms the other protocols from the literature in terms of computation and communication costs, by at least two orders of magnitude. Even when we add verifiability, which hasn't been done before in the CSIDH setting, our protocol still outperforms the designs of Boneh et al. [17] and only has about twice the computational cost of the semi-honest protocol by Heimberger et al. [42], while still being round-optimal and having lower communication cost.

Remark 2. For completeness, we would also like to note that an isogeny-based OPRF has recently been proposed by Basso [8] in the M-SIDH (masked torsion point) setting of Fouotsa, Moriya and Petit [36]. Basso's work introduces a round-optimal verifiable OPRF based on a trusted setup, with a total communication cost of approximately $60\lambda \log p + 87\lambda^2$. Due to the point masking procedure of M-SIDH, the prime is chosen to be 8868 bits long to achieve NIST level I security. A comparison with our protocol in terms of theoretical costs is not directly possible, as Basso's works with isogenies over $\mathbb{F}_{p^2}$ and with operations such as scalar multiplication and pushing through of points. The author foregoes a direct analysis of the computational complexity. Furthermore, the quantum security of CSIDH in relation to NIST level I is not completely settled yet [19,57], so that it is hard to define the same security level in both settings. However, we note that even with the most conservative estimate of a 4096-bit prime for level I security, the communication cost of our OPRF outperforms Basso's by a factor 8 in the verifiable case (4.6, if $d = 3$), and by a factor 122 in the non-verifiable case (81, if $d = 3$). We point the interested reader to [42, Section 8] for a more thorough comparison of current post-quantum OPRF designs and to [20] for a more general overview of OPRF designs.

5.4 Removing the Trusted Setup

Generating trusted tuples of the form required by our protocol can be seen as an arithmetic computation over $\mathbb{Z}_N$. When $\mathbb{Z}_N$ is a field, this can be efficiently realized, even with malicious security, using multi-party protocols. In particular, the MASCOT protocol of Keller, Orsini and Scholl [49] enables this, using only oblivious transfer (OT) as a public-key primitive. The particular advantage of using OT as the fundamental primitive is that, with symmetric-key OT extension techniques, a large number of tuples can be produced using a small number of OT instances [43,48]. Furthermore, isogeny-based OT constructions exist [3,6,51].

OPRF is a useful tool for larger protocols, such as private set intersection; see Rindal and Schoppmann [58, Section 4] for the standard construction of a PSI protocol from an OPRF. Application to PSI means that larger numbers of OPRF calls are required. In the case of private contact discovery, one party may need to make hundreds of thousands of OPRF calls. In this scenario, the amortization offered by MASCOT brings a tremendous advantage to reduce the number of

Table 3. Comparison of the OPRFs by Boneh et al. [17] and Heimberger et al. [42] with our protocol in Fig. 10 and the verifiable OPRF from Sect. 5.2, both for the polynomial degrees $d = 2, 3$. The computational cost is expressed in the amount of group actions to be performed. *In Sect. 5.4, we discuss how the trusted setup can be removed for our protocol. We note that this increases the total computational and communication costs as outlined in that section.

Source	Malicious Client	Verifiable	Number of Rounds	Total Computational cost	Total Communication cost	No Trusted Setup	Without Class Group
[42]	X	X	$2\lambda + 2$	$3\lambda + 3$	$(3\lambda + 2)\log p$	✓	✓
[17]	X	X	2	$5\lambda + 2$	$(2\lambda + 1)\log p + 2\lambda^2$	X	X
	✓	X	4	$11\lambda + 2$	$(5\lambda + 1)\log p + 5\lambda^2$	X	X
$d = 2$	✓	X	2	2	$6\log p$	X*	X
$d = 3$	✓	X	2	2	$9\log p$	X*	X
$d = 2$	✓	✓	2	$8\lambda + 4$	$(2\lambda + \frac{17}{2})\log p + 4\lambda$	X	X
$d = 3$	✓	✓	2	$14\lambda + 7$	$(\frac{7}{2}\lambda + \frac{29}{2})\log p + 7\lambda$	X	X

base OT executions that are necessary. For 128-bit fields, the MASCOT protocol for two parties, with full malicious security, can reach throughputs of up to 4,800 triples per second over a 1 Gbit/s network [49]. To this throughput cost we must add a one-time setup cost to execute the base-OTs required for the OT extension. Keller, Orsini and Scholl's extension protocol requires λ base OTs [48] and Badrinarayanan et al.'s isogeny-based OT protocol requires 5 isogeny computations [6], thus totalling a one-time cost of 5λ isogeny computations.

After the setup, each triple generated by the symmetric OT extension protocol is sufficient to construct one multiplication tuple for our trusted setups. When $d = 2$, we require four multiplications to construct the tuple of Eq. (9) which implies that throughputs upwards of 1,000 tuples per second could be acheived. For 256-bit fields, we estimate that this would be reduced by a factor of 1/4, yielding a throughput of 250–300 tuples per second, and for $d = 3$ still about half of that.

Acknowledgments. The authors would like to thank Karim Baghery, Steven Galbraith, Yi-Fu Lai, Emmanuela Orsini, Nigel Smart and Frederik Vercauteren for helpful discussions regarding the contents of this work. This work was supported in part by the European Research Council (ERC) under the European Union's Horizon 2020 research and innovation programme (grant agreement ISOCRYPT - No. 101020788) and by CyberSecurity Research Flanders with reference number VR20192203. Cyprien Delpech de Saint Guilhem is a Junior FWO Postdoctoral Fellow under project 1266123N.

References

1. Abdalla, M., Eisenhofer, T., Kiltz, E., Kunzweiler, S., Riepel, D.: Password-authenticated key exchange from group actions. In: Dodis, Y., Shrimpton, T. (eds.) CRYPTO 2022, Part II. LNCS, vol. 13508, pp. 699–728. Springer, Heidelberg (2022). https://doi.org/10.1007/978-3-031-15979-4_24
2. Alamati, N., De Feo, L., Montgomery, H., Patranabis, S.: Cryptographic group actions and applications. In: Moriai, S., Wang, H. (eds.) ASIACRYPT 2020, Part II. LNCS, vol. 12492, pp. 411–439. Springer, Heidelberg (2020). https://doi.org/10.1007/978-3-030-64834-3_14
3. Alamati, N., Montgomery, H., Patranabis, S., Sarkar, P.: Two-round adaptively secure MPC from isogenies, LPN, or CDH. In: Tibouchi, M., Wang, H. (eds.) ASIACRYPT 2021, Part II. LNCS, vol. 13091, pp. 305–334. Springer, Heidelberg (2021). https://doi.org/10.1007/978-3-030-92075-3_11
4. Atapoor, S., Baghery, K., Cozzo, D., Pedersen, R.: CSI-SharK: CSI-FiSh with sharing-friendly keys. In: Simpson, L., Baee, M.A.R. (eds.) ACISP 2023. Lecture Notes in Computer Science, vol. 13915, pp. 471–502. Springer (2023). https://doi.org/10.1007/978-3-031-35486-1_21
5. Atapoor, S., Baghery, K., Cozzo, D., Pedersen, R.: Practical robust DKG protocols for CSIDH. In: Tibouchi, M., Wang, X. (eds.) ACNS 2023, Part II. Lecture Notes in Computer Science, vol. 13906, pp. 219–247. Springer (2023). https://doi.org/10.1007/978-3-031-33491-7_9
6. Badrinarayanan, S., Masny, D., Mukherjee, P., Patranabis, S., Raghuraman, S., Sarkar, P.: Round-optimal oblivious transfer and MPC from computational CSIDH. In: Boldyreva, A., Kolesnikov, V. (eds.) PKC 2023, Part I. LNCS, vol. 13940, pp. 376–405. Springer, Heidelberg (2023). https://doi.org/10.1007/978-3-031-31368-4_14
7. Baghery, K., Cozzo, D., Pedersen, R.: An isogeny-based ID protocol using structured public keys. In: Paterson, M.B. (ed.) 18th IMA International Conference on Cryptography and Coding. LNCS, vol. 13129, pp. 179–197. Springer, Heidelberg (2021). https://doi.org/10.1007/978-3-030-92641-0_9
8. Basso, A.: A post-quantum round-optimal oblivious PRF from isogenies. Cryptology ePrint Archive, Report 2023/225 (2023). https://eprint.iacr.org/2023/225
9. Basso, A., Kutas, P., Merz, S.P., Petit, C., Sanso, A.: Cryptanalysis of an oblivious PRF from supersingular isogenies. In: Tibouchi, M., Wang, H. (eds.) ASIACRYPT 2021, Part I. LNCS, vol. 13090, pp. 160–184. Springer, Heidelberg (2021). https://doi.org/10.1007/978-3-030-92062-3_6
10. Baum, C., Delpech de Saint Guilhem, C., Kales, D., Orsini, E., Scholl, P., Zaverucha, G.: Banquet: short and fast signatures from AES. In: Garay, J. (ed.) PKC 2021, Part I. LNCS, vol. 12710, pp. 266–297. Springer, Heidelberg (2021). https://doi.org/10.1007/978-3-030-75245-3_11
11. Baum, C., Nof, A.: Concretely-efficient zero-knowledge arguments for arithmetic circuits and their application to lattice-based cryptography. In: Kiayias, A., Kohlweiss, M., Wallden, P., Zikas, V. (eds.) PKC 2020, Part I. LNCS, vol. 12110, pp. 495–526. Springer, Heidelberg (2020). https://doi.org/10.1007/978-3-030-45374-9_17
12. Beaver, D.: Efficient multiparty protocols using circuit randomization. In: Feigenbaum, J. (ed.) CRYPTO 1991. LNCS, vol. 576, pp. 420–432. Springer, Heidelberg (1992). https://doi.org/10.1007/3-540-46766-1_34

13. Beullens, W., Disson, L., Pedersen, R., Vercauteren, F.: CSI-RAShi: distributed key generation for CSIDH. In: Cheon, J.H., Tillich, J.P. (eds.) Post-Quantum Cryptography - 12th International Workshop, PQCrypto 2021, pp. 257–276. Springer, Heidelberg (2021). https://doi.org/10.1007/978-3-030-81293-5_14

14. Beullens, W., Dobson, S., Katsumata, S., Lai, Y.F., Pintore, F.: Group signatures and more from isogenies and lattices: generic, simple, and efficient. In: Dunkelman, O., Dziembowski, S. (eds.) EUROCRYPT 2022, Part II. LNCS, vol. 13276, pp. 95–126. Springer, Heidelberg (2022). https://doi.org/10.1007/978-3-031-07085-3_4

15. Beullens, W., Katsumata, S., Pintore, F.: Calamari and Falafl: logarithmic (linkable) ring signatures from isogenies and lattices. In: Moriai, S., Wang, H. (eds.) ASIACRYPT 2020, Part II. LNCS, vol. 12492, pp. 464–492. Springer, Heidelberg (2020). https://doi.org/10.1007/978-3-030-64834-3_16

16. Beullens, W., Kleinjung, T., Vercauteren, F.: CSI-FiSh: efficient isogeny based signatures through class group computations. In: Galbraith, S.D., Moriai, S. (eds.) ASIACRYPT 2019, Part I. LNCS, vol. 11921, pp. 227–247. Springer, Heidelberg (2019). https://doi.org/10.1007/978-3-030-34578-5_9

17. Boneh, D., Kogan, D., Woo, K.: Oblivious pseudorandom functions from isogenies. In: Moriai, S., Wang, H. (eds.) ASIACRYPT 2020, Part II. LNCS, vol. 12492, pp. 520–550. Springer, Heidelberg (2020). https://doi.org/10.1007/978-3-030-64834-3_18

18. Boneh, D., Lynn, B., Shacham, H.: Short signatures from the Weil pairing. J. Cryptol. 17(4), 297–319 (2004). https://doi.org/10.1007/s00145-004-0314-9

19. Bonnetain, X., Schrottenloher, A.: Quantum security analysis of CSIDH. In: Canteaut, A., Ishai, Y. (eds.) EUROCRYPT 2020, Part II. LNCS, vol. 12106, pp. 493–522. Springer, Heidelberg (2020). https://doi.org/10.1007/978-3-030-45724-2_17

20. Casacuberta, S., Hesse, J., Lehmann, A.: Sok: oblivious pseudorandom functions. In: 7th IEEE European Symposium on Security and Privacy, EuroS&P 2022, Genoa, Italy, June 6-10, 2022, pp. 625–646. IEEE (2022). https://doi.org/10.1109/EUROSP53844.2022.00045

21. Castryck, W., Decru, T.: An efficient key recovery attack on SIDH. In: Hazay, C., Stam, M. (eds.) EUROCRYPT 2023, Part V. LNCS, vol. 14008, pp. 423–447. Springer, Heidelberg (2023). https://doi.org/10.1007/978-3-031-30589-4_15

22. Castryck, W., Lange, T., Martindale, C., Panny, L., Renes, J.: CSIDH: an efficient post-quantum commutative group action. In: Peyrin, T., Galbraith, S. (eds.) ASIACRYPT 2018, Part III. LNCS, vol. 11274, pp. 395–427. Springer, Heidelberg (2018). https://doi.org/10.1007/978-3-030-03332-3_15

23. Chung, K.M., Hsieh, Y.C., Huang, M.Y., Huang, Y.H., Lange, T., Yang, B.Y.: Group signatures and accountable ring signatures from isogeny-based assumptions. Cryptology ePrint Archive, Report 2021/1368 (2021). https://eprint.iacr.org/2021/1368

24. Cohen, H., Lenstra, H.W.: Heuristics on class groups of number fields. In: Jager, H. (ed.) Number Theory Noordwijkerhout 1983. LNM, vol. 1068, pp. 33–62. Springer, Heidelberg (1984). https://doi.org/10.1007/BFb0099440

25. Couveignes, J.M.: Hard homogeneous spaces. Cryptology ePrint Archive, Report 2006/291 (2006). https://eprint.iacr.org/2006/291

26. Cozzo, D., Smart, N.P.: Sashimi: cutting up CSI-FiSh secret keys to produce an actively secure distributed signing protocol. In: Ding, J., Tillich, J.P. (eds.) Post-Quantum Cryptography - 11th International Conference, PQCrypto 2020, pp. 169–186. Springer, Heidelberg (2020). https://doi.org/10.1007/978-3-030-44223-1_10

27. De Feo, L., et al.: SCALLOP: scaling the CSI-FiSh. In: Boldyreva, A., Kolesnikov, V. (eds.) PKC 2023, Part I. LNCS, vol. 13940, pp. 345–375. Springer, Heidelberg (2023). https://doi.org/10.1007/978-3-031-31368-4_13

28. De Feo, L., Galbraith, S.D.: SeaSign: compact isogeny signatures from class group actions. In: Ishai, Y., Rijmen, V. (eds.) EUROCRYPT 2019, Part III. LNCS, vol. 11478, pp. 759–789. Springer, Heidelberg (2019). https://doi.org/10.1007/978-3-030-17659-4_26

29. De Feo, L., Kohel, D., Leroux, A., Petit, C., Wesolowski, B.: SQISign: compact post-quantum signatures from quaternions and isogenies. In: Moriai, S., Wang, H. (eds.) ASIACRYPT 2020, Part I. LNCS, vol. 12491, pp. 64–93. Springer, Heidelberg (2020). https://doi.org/10.1007/978-3-030-64837-4_3

30. De Feo, L., Meyer, M.: Threshold schemes from isogeny assumptions. In: Kiayias, A., Kohlweiss, M., Wallden, P., Zikas, V. (eds.) PKC 2020, Part II. LNCS, vol. 12111, pp. 187–212. Springer, Heidelberg (2020). https://doi.org/10.1007/978-3-030-45388-6_7

31. Dickson, L.E.: Linear Groups: With an Exposition of the Galois Field Theory, vol. 6. BG Teubner (1901)

32. Eaton, E., Jao, D., Komlo, C., Mokrani, Y.: Towards post-quantum key-updatable public-key encryption via supersingular isogenies. In: AlTawy, R., Hülsing, A. (eds.) SAC 2021. LNCS, vol. 13203, pp. 461–482. Springer, Heidelberg (2022). https://doi.org/10.1007/978-3-030-99277-4_22

33. El Kaafarani, A., Katsumata, S., Pintore, F.: Lossy CSI-FiSh: efficient signature scheme with tight reduction to decisional CSIDH-512. In: Kiayias, A., Kohlweiss, M., Wallden, P., Zikas, V. (eds.) PKC 2020, Part II. LNCS, vol. 12111, pp. 157–186. Springer, Heidelberg (2020). https://doi.org/10.1007/978-3-030-45388-6_6

34. Felderhoff, J.: Hard homogenous spaces and commutative supersingular isogeny based diffie-hellman. Ecole polytechnique; ENS de Lyon, Internship Report, LIX (2019)

35. Fiat, A., Shamir, A.: How to prove yourself: practical solutions to identification and signature problems. In: Odlyzko, A.M. (ed.) CRYPTO 1986. LNCS, vol. 263, pp. 186–194. Springer, Heidelberg (1987). https://doi.org/10.1007/3-540-47721-7_12

36. Fouotsa, T.B., Moriya, T., Petit, C.: M-SIDH and MD-SIDH: countering SIDH attacks by masking information. In: Hazay, C., Stam, M. (eds.) EUROCRYPT 2023, Part V. LNCS, vol. 14008, pp. 282–309. Springer, Heidelberg (2023). https://doi.org/10.1007/978-3-031-30589-4_10

37. Fouotsa, T.B., Petit, C.: SimS: a simplification of SiGamal. In: Cheon, J.H., Tillich, J.P. (eds.) Post-Quantum Cryptography - 12th International Workshop, PQCrypto 2021, pp. 277–295. Springer, Heidelberg (2021). https://doi.org/10.1007/978-3-030-81293-5_15

38. Freedman, M.J., Ishai, Y., Pinkas, B., Reingold, O.: Keyword search and oblivious pseudorandom functions. In: Kilian, J. (ed.) TCC 2005. LNCS, vol. 3378, pp. 303–324. Springer, Heidelberg (2005). https://doi.org/10.1007/978-3-540-30576-7_17

39. Galbraith, S., Panny, L., Smith, B., Vercauteren, F.: Quantum equivalence of the DLP and CDHP for group actions. Math. Cryptology 1(1), 40–44 (2021)

40. Goldreich, O.: On expected probabilistic polynomial-time adversaries: a suggestion for restricted definitions and their benefits. In: Vadhan, S.P. (ed.) TCC 2007. LNCS, vol. 4392, pp. 174–193. Springer, Heidelberg (2007). https://doi.org/10.1007/978-3-540-70936-7_10

41. Goldwasser, S., Micali, S., Rackoff, C.: The knowledge complexity of interactive proof systems. SIAM J. Comput. 18(1), 186–208 (1989)

42. Heimberger, L., Meisingseth, F., Hennerbichler, T., Ramacher, S., Rechberger, C.: OPRFs from isogenies: designs and analysis. Cryptology ePrint Archive, Paper 2023/639 (2023). https://eprint.iacr.org/2023/639
43. Ishai, Y., Kilian, J., Nissim, K., Petrank, E.: Extending oblivious transfers efficiently. In: Boneh, D. (ed.) CRYPTO 2003. LNCS, vol. 2729, pp. 145–161. Springer, Heidelberg (2003). https://doi.org/10.1007/978-3-540-45146-4_9
44. Ishai, Y., Kushilevitz, E., Ostrovsky, R., Sahai, A.: Zero-knowledge proofs from secure multiparty computation. SIAM J. Comput. **39**(3), 1121–1152 (2009). https://doi.org/10.1137/080725398
45. Joux, A.: MPC in the head for isomorphisms and group actions. Cryptology ePrint Archive, Paper 2023/664 (2023). https://eprint.iacr.org/2023/664
46. Kales, D., Zaverucha, G.: An attack on some signature schemes constructed from five-pass identification schemes. In: Krenn, S., Shulman, H., Vaudenay, S. (eds.) CANS 20. LNCS, vol. 12579, pp. 3–22. Springer, Heidelberg (2020). https://doi.org/10.1007/978-3-030-65411-5_1
47. Katz, J., Kolesnikov, V., Wang, X.: Improved non-interactive zero knowledge with applications to post-quantum signatures. In: Lie, D., Mannan, M., Backes, M., Wang, X. (eds.) ACM CCS 2018, pp. 525–537. ACM Press (2018). https://doi.org/10.1145/3243734.3243805
48. Keller, M., Orsini, E., Scholl, P.: Actively secure OT extension with optimal overhead. In: Gennaro, R., Robshaw, M.J.B. (eds.) CRYPTO 2015, Part I. LNCS, vol. 9215, pp. 724–741. Springer, Heidelberg (2015). https://doi.org/10.1007/978-3-662-47989-6_35
49. Keller, M., Orsini, E., Scholl, P.: MASCOT: faster malicious arithmetic secure computation with oblivious transfer. In: Weippl, E.R., Katzenbeisser, S., Kruegel, C., Myers, A.C., Halevi, S. (eds.) ACM CCS 2016, pp. 830–842. ACM Press (2016). https://doi.org/10.1145/2976749.2978357
50. Kitaev, A.Y.: Quantum measurements and the abelian stabilizer problem. Electron. Colloquium Comput. Complex. **TR96-003** (1996). https://eccc.weizmann.ac.il/eccc-reports/1996/TR96-003/index.html
51. Lai, Y.F., Galbraith, S.D., Delpech de Saint Guilhem, C.: Compact, efficient and UC-secure isogeny-based oblivious transfer. In: Canteaut, A., Standaert, F.X. (eds.) EUROCRYPT 2021, Part I. LNCS, vol. 12696, pp. 213–241. Springer, Heidelberg (2021). https://doi.org/10.1007/978-3-030-77870-5_8
52. Maino, L., Martindale, C., Panny, L., Pope, G., Wesolowski, B.: A direct key recovery attack on SIDH. In: Hazay, C., Stam, M. (eds.) EUROCRYPT 2023, Part V. LNCS, vol. 14008, pp. 448–471. Springer, Heidelberg (2023). https://doi.org/10.1007/978-3-031-30589-4_16
53. Montgomery, H., Zhandry, M.: Full quantum equivalence of group action DLog and CDH, and more. In: Agrawal, S., Lin, D. (eds.) ASIACRYPT 2022, Part I. LNCS, vol. 13791, pp. 3–32. Springer, Heidelberg (2022). https://doi.org/10.1007/978-3-031-22963-3_1
54. Moriya, T., Onuki, H., Takagi, T.: SiGamal: a supersingular isogeny-based PKE and its application to a PRF. In: Moriai, S., Wang, H. (eds.) ASIACRYPT 2020, Part II. LNCS, vol. 12492, pp. 551–580. Springer, Heidelberg (2020). https://doi.org/10.1007/978-3-030-64834-3_19
55. Naor, M., Pinkas, B.: Oblivious transfer and polynomial evaluation. In: Vitter, J.S., Larmore, L.L., Leighton, F.T. (eds.) Proceedings of the Thirty-First Annual ACM Symposium on Theory of Computing, May 1–4, 1999, Atlanta, Georgia, USA, pp. 245–254. ACM (1999). https://doi.org/10.1145/301250.301312

56. Page, A., Robert, D.: Introducing clapoti(s): evaluating the isogeny class group action in polynomial time (2023). https://eprint.iacr.org/2023/1766
57. Peikert, C.: He gives C-sieves on the CSIDH. In: Canteaut, A., Ishai, Y. (eds.) EUROCRYPT 2020, Part II. LNCS, vol. 12106, pp. 463–492. Springer, Heidelberg (2020). https://doi.org/10.1007/978-3-030-45724-2_16
58. Rindal, P., Schoppmann, P.: VOLE-PSI: fast OPRF and circuit-PSI from vector-OLE. In: Canteaut, A., Standaert, F.X. (eds.) EUROCRYPT 2021, Part II. LNCS, vol. 12697, pp. 901–930. Springer, Heidelberg (2021). https://doi.org/10.1007/978-3-030-77886-6_31
59. Robert, D.: Breaking SIDH in polynomial time. In: Hazay, C., Stam, M. (eds.) EUROCRYPT 2023, Part V. LNCS, vol. 14008, pp. 472–503. Springer, Heidelberg (2023). https://doi.org/10.1007/978-3-031-30589-4_17
60. Rostovtsev, A., Stolbunov, A.: Public-Key cryptosystem based on isogenies. Cryptology ePrint Archive, Report 2006/145 (2006). https://eprint.iacr.org/2006/145
61. Wesolowski, B.: Orientations and the supersingular endomorphism ring problem. In: Dunkelman, O., Dziembowski, S. (eds.) EUROCRYPT 2022, Part III. LNCS, vol. 13277, pp. 345–371. Springer, Heidelberg (2022). https://doi.org/10.1007/978-3-031-07082-2_13
62. Zhang, F., Safavi-Naini, R., Susilo, W.: An efficient signature scheme from bilinear pairings and its applications. In: Bao, F., Deng, R., Zhou, J. (eds.) PKC 2004. LNCS, vol. 2947, pp. 277–290. Springer, Heidelberg (2004). https://doi.org/10.1007/978-3-540-24632-9_20

Lattices and Applications

On Structure-Preserving Cryptography and Lattices

Dennis Hofheinz[1], Kristina Hostáková[1], Roman Langrehr[1]([⊠]),
and Bogdan Ursu[2]

[1] Department of Computer Science, ETH Zurich, Zurich, Switzerland
{hofheinz,kristina.hostakova,roman.langrehr}@inf.ethz.ch
[2] Consensys, Fort Worth, USA
bogdan.ursu@consensys.net

Abstract. The Groth-Sahai proof system is a highly efficient pairing-based proof system for a specific class of group-based languages. Cryptographic primitives that are compatible with these languages (such that we can express, e.g., that a ciphertext contains a valid signature for a given message) are called "structure-preserving". The combination of structure-preserving primitives with Groth-Sahai proofs allows to prove complex statements that involve encryptions and signatures, and has proved useful in a variety of applications. However, so far, the concept of structure-preserving cryptography has been confined to the pairing setting.

In this work, we propose the first framework for structure-preserving cryptography in the lattice setting. Concretely, we

- define "structure-preserving sets" as an abstraction of (typically noisy) lattice-based languages,
- formalize a notion of generalized structure-preserving encryption and signature schemes (capturing a number of existing lattice-based encryption and signature schemes),
- construct a compatible zero-knowledge argument system that allows to argue about lattice-based structure-preserving primitives,
- offer a lattice-based construction of verifiably encrypted signatures in our framework.

Along the way, we also discover a new and efficient *strongly* secure lattice-based signature scheme. This scheme combines Rückert's lattice-based signature scheme with the lattice delegation strategy of Agrawal et al., which yields more compact and efficient signatures.

We hope that our framework provides a first step towards a modular and versatile treatment of cryptographic primitives in the lattice setting.

Keywords: Structure-preserving cryptography · lattice-based cryptography · public-key cryptography

1 Introduction

Structure-Preserving Cryptography. Groth-Sahai (GS) proofs [34] are practical non-interactive zero-knowledge (NIZK) proof systems for a very general class of group-based languages. Essentially, GS proofs allow to argue in zero-knowledge about the

---

B. Ursu—Author based in Zurich, Switzerland and work carried out during the author's time at ETH Zurich.

© International Association for Cryptologic Research 2024
Q. Tang and V. Teague (Eds.): PKC 2024, LNCS 14603, pp. 255–287, 2024.
https://doi.org/10.1007/978-3-031-57725-3_9

satisfiability of systems of equations over groups that may involve exponentiation, of course group operations, and even pairing operations. When used in conjunction with "suitably algebraic" group-based cryptographic primitives (like encryption or signature schemes), GS proofs allow to efficiently prove complex statements like "This ciphertext contains an electronic passport for John Smith that is certified by a government authority."[1] In comparison to a generic approach (with, say, a generic NIZK system for NP [26]), such a "native" approach is significantly more practical.

"Suitably algebraic" cryptographic primitives are called *structure-preserving* [2, 32] (or, in a slightly different formulation, *automorphic* [28]). Numerous examples of structure-preserving signature (e.g., [1–3,19,20,33]) and public-key encryption schemes (e.g., [15,23,25,37]), as well as other primitives (e.g., [12,50]) are known, based on different computational assumptions, and having different efficiency and security features.

All of these building blocks can be combined, and GS proofs can be used to argue about such combinations efficiently. However, so far, the paradigm of structure-preserving relies on a particular algebraic setting (of pairing-friendly cyclic groups), and it is unclear whether a similar modular combination of cryptographic primitives is also possible over other domains.[2]

This Work: Structure-Preserving Cryptography over Lattices. In this work, we initiate the study of structure-preserving cryptography over lattices. We put forward suitable definitions of structure-preserving signature and encryption schemes, and present a suitable NIZK system for proving statements about combinations of these primitives. Hence, in short, our core contributions are

- a suitable definition of lattice-based structure-preserving cryptographic primitives (including the modeling of a number of existing signature and encryption schemes according to this definition),
- a suitable zero-knowledge argument system that allows to show statements about lattice-based structure-preserving primitives,
- as an application (and to demonstrate the usefulness of our approach), a modular lattice-based protocol for verifiably encrypted signatures.

As we will explain, our notion of lattice-based structure-preserving primitives is not quite as universal as in the GS setting. This allows us to model a large class of primitives, but also asks for some degree of compatibility among the used primitives. We still believe that our abstract framework is a step towards plug-and-play lattice-based cryptography. Indeed, one benefit of our approach is modularity: It is true that the security

---

[1] Such a combination has been suggested before (e.g., [10,11,13]), but GS proofs allow a much more general treatment, and a broader class of languages and potential applications.

[2] Of course, dedicated protocols for concrete tasks (such as identity escrow [35] or verifiable encryption [16]) exist also based on other assumptions. Also, very efficient lattice-based commit-and-prove protocols for general classes of languages exist in the random oracle model [40]. However, nothing comparable to the full "structure-preserving cryptography" paradigm (that ensures a non-interactive and conceptually simple plug-and-play combination of different primitives) exists in other algebraic settings.

analysis for each lattice-based component (i.e., signature or encryption scheme) needs to keep track of noise growth and failure probabilities. However, due to our interface, this analysis needs to be done only once *per component*, not once for every possible *combination of components*.

Contribution 1: A Definition of Lattice-Based Structure-Preserving Primitives. First, we cannot use or easily adapt existing (group-based) definitions of structure-preserving primitives: with computations over lattices, there is no equivalent of "exponentiation" or "pairing". Besides, typically lattice-based ciphertexts or signatures often feature a "noise term", which may grow with operations on these values. Once the noise term becomes too large, decryption or verification becomes unreliable. Hence, operations on these values are limited in a quantitative way, and this limitation should be reflected in a definition of structure-preserving cryptography.

Since lattice-based cryptographic constructions usually work over the ring $\mathbb{Z}_q$ (for a suitable integer q), it is tempting to call the solutions to arbitrary systems of linear equations over $\mathbb{Z}_q$, possibly with boundaries on norms (to accommodate noise terms), structure-preserving. Unfortunately, we do not know how to instantiate a proof system for such general sets in the standard model.[3]

So instead of trying to match the group-based definition, we start from scratch with a relatively simple definition of "structure-preserving sets" modelling exactly the noise terms of lattice-based cryptography. We present a standard-model non-interactive proof system for these sets, and aim to interpret signatures and ciphertexts (or, rather, the randomness of ciphertexts) as structure-preserving sets. To express more powerful statements in terms of structure-preserving sets, we additionally require our structure-preserving signature and encryption schemes to allow for suitable homomorphic operations (that, e.g., allow to verify a signature inside an encryption scheme).

Fortunately, we discover that several existing signature and encryption schemes satisfy our definitions. Examples include Regev encryption [45] and its dual variant [30], the GSW leveled homomorphic encryption scheme [31], and the signature schemes of Boyen [14] and Rückert [46].[4]

At this point, the mentioned required compatibility among used primitives is crucial: we unfortunately cannot combine arbitrary lattice-based structure-preserving encryption and signature schemes. Essentially, we require that the encryption scheme allows to homomorphically verify an encrypted signature. This allows to combine, e.g., the GSW FHE scheme with all of the mentioned signature schemes; alternatively, we can combine any additively homomorphic scheme (such as Regev's scheme or its dual variant) with Rückert's scheme or its mentioned new and more compact variant, but *not* with Boyen's scheme.

Contribution 2: A Compatible NIZK Argument System. To allow arguing about combinations of encryption and signature schemes, we also introduce an analogue of GS

---

[3] We note that in the random oracle model, very efficient such proof systems exist [24,42].

[4] Rückert's scheme uses the "Bonsai trees" lattice delegation method of [18]. As an aside, we also make explicit a vastly more compact version of Rückert's scheme that uses the more compact lattice delegation strategy of [5]. While this modification entails no significant technical complications, it may be worthwhile to point out.

proofs. In our case, we use the LWE-based NIZK system of Libert et al. [36] as a basis. This proof system is based upon a Σ-protocol [21] for proving that an LWE encryption contains a certain value. (That Σ-protocol is later converted to a NIZK system by applying the Fiat-Shamir transform [27] in the standard model, with a correlation-intractable hash function). To suit our needs, however, we need to generalize this proof system to structure-preserving sets (i.e., to statements that are valid "up to noise"). This requires a more careful analysis, and in particular a liberal use of rejection sampling [38].

We should emphasize that we are interested in a standard-model proof system. Indeed, while our application does not require this, we would like to be able to argue about encrypted *proofs* (and thus achieve the "nestable" property of Groth-Sahai proofs). If proof verification involves random oracle queries, this is not possible transparently. We should note, however, that our proof system supports only linear languages, while its verification itself is not linear. Hence, nesting proofs of our proof system is only possible when using leveled homomorphic encryption schemes (that allow to verify even a nonlinear encrypted proof through homomorphic evaluation). We leave open the construction of a lattice-based proof system for a language that includes its own verification.

Contribution 3: Lattice-Based Verifiably Encrypted Signatures. Finally, we demonstrate the usefulness of our approach using the setting of verifiably encrypted signatures [7,13,29,47]. Concretely, we show how to combine lattice-based structure-preserving signature and an encryption schemes to obtain a scheme that allows to prove that a given ciphertext contains an encryption of a valid signature for given (publicly known) message. While generic constructions (e.g., using lattice-based zero-knowledge for NP [43]) for this task are possible, and very efficient techniques for related problems exist in the random oracle world [24,42], it appears that our protocol is the first non-generic (i.e., at least somewhat efficient) lattice-based verifiably encrypted signature scheme in the standard model.

More Related Work. As already mentioned, there is a very successful line of work [8, 24,40,41] that aims at practical (non-interactive) zero-knowledge proofs from lattices in the random oracle model. The supported languages are very general and include typical "noisy linear" languages, as crucial for many lattice-based schemes. Conceptually, these schemes are commit-and-prove schemes, much like Groth-Sahai proofs.

On the other hand, the use of random oracles appears inherent. For instance, the scheme from [40] is obtained by using the Fiat-Shamir transform on a suitable Σ-protocol. Unlike in our setting, these Σ-protocols do not appear to satisfy the requirements for the use of correlation-intractable hash functions as replacements for random oracles. Still, when one is not interested in nesting proofs (and if one accepts random oracles), then these protocols appear to be excellent replacements for our proof system.

1.1 Technical Overview

We now take a closer look at our framework. Our first step will be to define *structure-preserving sets*, an abstraction of "noise terms" that are omnipresent in lattice-based cryptography.

Structure-Preserving Sets. We call a set $S \subseteq \mathbb{Z}_q^d$ *structure-preserving* if there is a ("noise") distribution $\mathcal{D}$ such that

- $\mathcal{D}$ "smudges" elements from S in the sense that for any $\mathbf{s}, \mathbf{s}' \in S$ and $\mathbf{d} \leftarrow \mathcal{D}$, the values $\mathbf{s} + \mathbf{d}$ and $\mathbf{s}' + \mathbf{d}$ are statistically close.[5]
- Smudging with $\mathcal{D}$ preserves (non-)membership in S, in the sense that for $\overline{S} = \mathbb{Z}_q^d \setminus S$, we have that $S + \operatorname{supp}(\mathcal{D})$ and $\overline{S} + \operatorname{supp}(\mathcal{D})$ are disjoint.[6] This condition guarantees that the smudging process is non-trivial.

The set of short-norm vectors is structure-preserving according to (the non-oversimplified version of) this definition. But structure-preserving sets also cover more complex cases, such as the set of vectors close to a given vector, (the union of) intervals, or the cartesian product of structure-preserving sets. In essence, we only require that a structure-preserving set is "non-trivially smudgeable".

Jumping ahead, structure-preserving sets will be used to model, e.g., the "raw" (i.e., un-rounded) verification output of signature schemes. This verification output only encodes a bit (the verification verdict), but may need to be smudged for further processing to avoid leakage about the signature. In fact, we now proceed to (informally) define structure-preserving signature and encryption schemes.

Structure-Preserving Signatures. A (lattice-based) signature scheme is called structure-preserving for a family $\mathcal{F}$ of functions if each verification key vk and message msg defines an $f \in \mathcal{F}$ such that a given signature σ is valid if and only if $f(\sigma) \in S$ for a (fixed) structure-preserving set S.[7] We will be particularly interested in families $\mathcal{F}$ of *linear* functions, since such $\mathcal{F}$ will allow for (non-generic) zero-knowledge proofs. This is also the reason for the need to smudge f's output: existing lattice-based signature schemes usually postprocess the result of a linear operation with a rounding step obtain the verification verdict bit. Instead of this rounding step, we require that $f(\sigma) \in S$.

We show that Rückert's signature scheme [46] is structure-preserving for a linear $\mathcal{F}$, and that Boyen's signature scheme [14] is structure-preserving for an $\mathcal{F}$ that contains linear functions and functions computed by low-depth Boolean circuits. Additionally, we present a more compact variant of Rückert's scheme (that is also strongly secure and structure-preserving for a linear $\mathcal{F}$). This new scheme is retrieved by replacing the "Bonsai trees" lattice delegation method of [18] with the more compact lattice delegation strategy of [5].

Structure-Preserving Encryption. We say that a (lattice-based) encryption scheme is structure-preserving if ciphertexts are of the form

$$\mathsf{ct} = \mathbf{B}\mathbf{r} + g(\mathsf{msg})$$

---

[5] This is an oversimplification. In particular, for, e.g., the set of short vectors S to be structure-preserving, we need a slightly more relaxed definition. Our actual definition involves rejection sampling and actually only requires "closeness in a significant portion of cases".

[6] Again, this oversimplifies. We really only require this for almost all vectors of $\overline{S}$ and a large enough subset of $\operatorname{supp}(\mathcal{D})$.

[7] Our actual definition also considers signatures which carry "tags" which can be used to pre-process messages prior to verifying (but whose publication does not harm security).

for a matrix $\mathbf{B} \in \mathbb{Z}_q^{d \times r}$, $\mathbf{r} \in S$ for a structure-preserving set S, and an invertible and additively homomorphic "message encoding function" g.[8] Intuitively, we require that $\mathbf{r} \in S$ to be able to argue about "valid encryptions" (for which the encrypted message is uniquely determined).

For our applications, it will also be beneficial if the scheme is $\mathcal{F}$-homomorphic, in the sense that $\mathsf{ct} = \mathbf{Br} + g(\mathsf{msg})$ allows to efficiently compute $\mathsf{ct}' = \mathbf{Br}' + g(f(\mathsf{msg}))$ for any $f \in \mathcal{F}$ (possibly at the price of a larger noise).

We observe that Regev's encryption scheme [45], its dual variant [30], and the GSW leveled homomorphic encryption scheme [31] fit our framework (for linear functions, resp. low-depth circuits). While itself not technically involved, this provides a helpful uniform way to reason about these schemes.

A Zero-Knowledge Protocol for Encrypted Structure-Preserving Sets. Our last ingredient is a suitable (lattice-based, non-interactive) zero-knowledge proof system that allows to argue about structure-preserving primitives (and in particular structure-preserving sets). More concretely, we start with a Σ-protocol that shows that a given ciphertext (from an arbitrary structure-preserving encryption scheme) encrypts an element $\mathsf{msg} \in S$ from a structure-preserving set S.

This Σ-protocol is derived from a Σ-protocol due to Libert et al. [36] for proving equality of encrypted messages (where the used encryption scheme is a variant [6] of Regev encryption). The basic protocol of [36] (following Schnorr's blueprint [49]) proceeds as follows. Say that we want to show that a given ciphertext ct is an encryption of 0.[9] The prover P then starts by sending a fresh 0-encryption ct_0 to the verifier V. Then V chooses to either open ct_0 or $\mathsf{ct}_0 + \mathsf{ct}$ (by sending the random coins of that ciphertext).

Soundness follows from the fact that if ct is not a 0-encryption, then at least one of the two ciphertexts ct_0 and $\mathsf{ct}_0 + \mathsf{ct}$ encrypts a nonzero value. (Of course, to obtain a negligible soundness error, the above protocol will have to be repeated). Zero-knowledge follows from the fact that if one knows in advance which ciphertext is opened, one can program ct_0 such that the to-be-opened ciphertext surely encrypts 0.

In our setting, we want to prove that ct encrypts some $\mathbf{s} \in S$ (without revealing $\mathbf{s}$). Since S is a structure-preserving set, we can smudge $\mathbf{s}$ with a suitable smudging vector $\mathbf{d} \leftarrow \mathcal{D}$. When we set up ct_0 as an encryption of such a $\mathbf{d}$, we obtain that

– opening ct_0 reveals only a smudging value $\mathbf{d}$, and
– opening $\mathsf{ct}_0 + \mathsf{ct}$ reveals a smudged value $\mathbf{s} + \mathbf{d}$, which is (almost) statistically independent of $\mathbf{s}$.

Hence, using a similar strategy as in [36], we obtain zero-knowledge. Moreover, since smudging preserves (non-)membership in S, we obtain soundness (after sufficiently many repetitions). The actual proof is more involved than this overview, of course, largely because of the already mentioned rejection sampling necessary for statistical closeness.

---

[8] We also define the notion of a "noise level" of a ciphertext which we ignore in this overview.

[9] Since the used homomorphic encryption scheme is homomorphic, we can reduce proving equality of ciphertexts to proving 0-encryptions.

We only briefly mention that our protocol is compatible with recent standard-model techniques [17,43] to transform Σ-protocols in the lattice setting into non-interactive zero-knowledge (NIZK) proofs. We use a sophisticated variant [36] of this approach[10] that even achieves unbounded simulation-soundness for specific classes of Σ-protocols. In the end, we obtain a NIZK argument system for encrypted structure-preserving sets.

From Structure-Preserving sets to Structure-Preserving Primitives. As an application (and to demonstrate the usefulness of our proof system), we construct a verifiably encrypted signature (VES [7,13,29,47]) scheme. Intuitively, in a VES scheme, a dedicated signer hands out *encrypted signatures* (i.e., signatures generated using the signer's secret key, and encrypted under the public key of a designated "adjudicator"). Such encrypted signatures also contain a NIZK proof of validity (i.e., of the fact that the given ciphertext really contains a valid signature for a given message). In case of a conflict, however, the adjudicator can extract (by decrypting) a "proper" (i.e., non-simulatable) signature from a given encrypted signature. VES schemes are useful, e.g., in contract signing applications [7,13].

Using our framework, a lattice-based VES scheme can be obtained generically from a structure-preserving signature scheme, a structure-preserving encryption scheme with compatible message space (and such that it allows to homomorphically verify signatures), and our zero-knowledge proof system for (encrypted) structure-preserving sets. These primitives are combined in a straightforward way. Perhaps the most interesting part of this construction is the fact that it suffices to prove that an encrypted value comes from a structure-preserving set. Indeed, to prove that a given encryption contains a valid signature, we (a) first homomorphically verify that signature inside the encryption, and (b) then prove that the result corresponds to an "accept". Recall that by our definition of structure-preserving signatures, this means proving membership in a structure-preserving set.

Our formal proof is similar to a proof for an existing VES scheme by Fuchsbauer [29] that uses pairing-based structure-preserving cryptography.

1.2 Roadmap

After recalling some notation and standard building blocks in Sect. 2, we present our definition of structure-preserving sets in Sect. 3. Building on this definition, we proceed with our notions of structure-preserving signatures (Sect. 4) and structure-preserving encryption schemes (Sect. 5). We identify and construct example schemes in Sect. 4.1 and 5.1 and more in the full version. Our Σ-protocol for (encrypted) structure-preserving sets appears in Sect. 6, followed by its conversion to a NIZK proof system in Section 7. The VES application follows in Section 8 where we also discuss its efficiency.

---

[10] One important advantage of [36] is that it only requires the homomorphic evaluation of a low-depth circuit in the computation of the CI-Hash function from [43].

2   Preliminaries

2.1   Notation

A function f is *negligible* if for every polynomial $p(\cdot)$, there exists an $n_0 \in \mathbb{N}$ such that for every $n > n_0$ it holds that $f(n) < \frac{1}{p(n)}$. We write negl to denote an arbitrary negligible function. Let X and Y be two probability distributions over a domain Ω. The *statistical distance* between X and Y is defined as $\Delta(X, Y) := \frac{1}{2} \sum_{\omega \in \Omega} |\Pr[X = \omega] - \Pr[Y = \omega]|$. We say that two ensembles $\{X_n\}_{n \in \mathbb{N}}$ and $\{Y_n\}_{n \in \mathbb{N}}$ of distributions are *statistically indistinguishable*, denoted as $\{X_n\}_{n \in \mathbb{N}} \approx_s \{Y_n\}_{n \in \mathbb{N}}$, if $\Delta(X_n, Y_n) = \mathrm{negl}(n)$. We say that two ensembles $\{X_n\}_{n \in \mathbb{N}}$ and $\{Y_n\}_{n \in \mathbb{N}}$ of distributions are *computationally indistinguishable*, denoted as $\{X_n\}_{n \in \mathbb{N}} \approx_c \{Y_n\}_{n \in \mathbb{N}}$, if for every probabilistic polynomial time (PPT) adversary $\mathcal{A}$, we have $|\Pr[\mathcal{A}(X_n) = 1] - \Pr[\mathcal{A}(Y_n) = 1]| = \mathrm{negl}(n)$.

Let S be a finite set. Then by $x \leftarrow_{\mathrm{R}} S$ we mean that x was sampled from the uniform distribution over S. For a probability distribution $\mathcal{D}$ on S we denoted the support by $\mathrm{supp}(\mathcal{D}) \subseteq S$.

Let $\mathbf{x} \in \mathbb{R}^n$ be a column vector. The x_i, for $i \in \{1, \dots, n\}$ denotes the i-th coordinate of $\mathbf{x}$. The ℓ_2-*norm* of $\mathbf{x}$ is defined as $\|\mathbf{x}\| := \sqrt{\sum_{i=1}^{n} x_i^2}$. The ℓ_2 *norm of a matrix* $\mathbf{M} \in \mathbb{R}^{n \times m}$ is defined as $\|\mathbf{M}\| = \sup_{\mathbf{x} \in \mathbb{R}^m, \mathbf{x} \neq 0} \frac{\|\mathbf{M}\mathbf{x}\|}{\|\mathbf{x}\|}$. We denote $\overline{\mathbf{M}}$ the Gram-Schmidt orthogonalization of the matrix $\mathbf{M}$.

For two sets $A, B \subseteq \mathbb{Z}_q^n$, we define the sets $A \setminus B, A + B, A - B \subseteq \mathbb{Z}_q^n$ as follows:

$$A \setminus B := \{x \mid x \in A \land x \notin B\},$$
$$A + B := \{(a_1 + b_1, \dots, a_n + b_n) \mid (a_1, \dots, a_n) \in A, (b_1, \dots, b_n) \in B\},$$
$$A - B := \{(a_1 - b_1, \dots, a_n - b_n) \mid (a_1, \dots, a_n) \in A, (b_1, \dots, b_n) \in B\}.$$

If $A = \emptyset$ or $B = \emptyset$, then we define $A + B := \emptyset$ and $A - B := \emptyset$.

We use $B_\delta(S) := \{\mathbf{v} \in \mathbb{Z}_q^n \mid (\min_{\mathbf{s} \in S, \mathbf{x} \in \mathbb{Z}^n} \|\mathbf{v} - \mathbf{s} + q\mathbf{x}\|) \leq \delta\}$ to denote the closed δ-ball around a set of vectors $S \subseteq \mathbb{Z}_q^n$.

We write $H \leq G$ to denote that H is a subgroup of a group G.

We say that a function $f: X \to Y$ is *invertible* if there exists a function $f^{-1}: Y \to X \cup \{\bot\}$ such that (i) f^{-1} is efficiently computable, (ii) for every $x \in X$ it holds $f^{-1}(f(x)) = x$, and (iii) for every $y \in Y \setminus \mathrm{Img}(f)$ it holds $f^{-1}(y) = \bot$.

2.2   Lattices

Let us recall various basic lattice notions and hardness problems that we need in later sections of this work.

Let $\mathbf{\Sigma} \in \mathbb{R}^{n \times n}$ be a symmetric positive-definite matrix, and $\mathbf{c} \in \mathbb{R}^n$. Then the *Gaussian function* on $\mathbb{R}^n$ is defined as $\rho_{\mathbf{\Sigma}}(\mathbf{x}) := \exp\{-\pi \mathbf{x}^\top \mathbf{\Sigma}^{-1} \mathbf{x}\}$. The function extends to sets in the usual way. That is, for any countable set $A \subset \mathbb{R}^n$, $\rho_{\mathbf{\Sigma}}(A) := \sum_{\mathbf{x} \in A} \rho_{\mathbf{\Sigma}}(\mathbf{x})$. Moreover, for every countable set $A \subset \mathbb{R}^n$ and any $\mathbf{x} \in A$, the *discrete Gaussian function* is defined by $\rho_{A, \mathbf{\Sigma}}(\mathbf{x}) := \frac{\rho_{\mathbf{\Sigma}}(\mathbf{x})}{\rho_{\mathbf{\Sigma}}(A)}$ and we denote the corresponding *discrete Gaussian distribution* as $\mathcal{D}_{A, \mathbf{\Sigma}}$. If $\mathbf{\Sigma} = \sigma^2 \cdot \mathbf{I}_n$, where $\mathbf{I}_n$ is the $n \times n$ identity matrix, we denote the Gaussian function as ρ_σ, the discrete Gaussian function as $\rho_{A,\sigma}$ and the discrete Gaussian distribution as $\mathcal{D}_{A,\sigma}$ for short. We will make use of the following tail bound for the discrete Gaussian distribution for $\mathbb{Z}^n$.

Lemma 2.1 ([39, **Lemma 4.4**]). *For any* $k > 1$ *we have* $\mathrm{Pr}_{\mathbf{x} \leftarrow \mathcal{D}_{\mathbb{Z}^n,\sigma}}[\|\mathbf{x}\| > k\sigma\sqrt{n}] < k^n e^{\frac{n}{2}(1-k^2)}$.

Let $\mathbf{B} \in \mathbb{R}^{m \times n}$ be a matrix with linearly independent columns $\mathbf{b}_1, \ldots, \mathbf{b}_n \in \mathbb{R}^m$ for $m \geq n$. The m-dimensional *lattice* Λ with lattice basis $\mathbf{B}$ is defined as $\Lambda = \{\mathbf{y} \in \mathbb{R}^m \mid \exists \mathbf{s} \in \mathbb{Z}^n, \mathbf{y} = \mathbf{Bs}\}$. The *dual lattice* of Λ is defined as $\Lambda^* := \{\mathbf{z} \in \mathbb{R}^m \mid \forall \mathbf{y} \in \Lambda, \mathbf{z}^\top\mathbf{y} \in \mathbb{Z}\}$. For $q \geq 2$ and a matrix $\mathbf{A} \in \mathbb{Z}_q^{n \times m}$ we define two m-dimensional integer lattices $\Lambda^\perp(\mathbf{A}) := \{\mathbf{x} \in \mathbb{Z}^m \mid \mathbf{Ax} = 0 \mod q\}$ and $\Lambda(\mathbf{A}) = \{\mathbf{y} \in \mathbb{Z}^m \mid \exists \mathbf{s} \in \mathbb{Z}^n, \mathbf{A}^\top\mathbf{s} = \mathbf{y} \mod q\}$.

Definition 2.2 (Learning With Errors). *Let* q, m, n *be positive integers and* χ *be a probability distribution on* $\mathbb{Z}$. *The* $\mathsf{LWE}_{m,n,q,\chi}$ *problem is to distinguish the following two distributions:* $\{(\mathbf{A}, \mathbf{b}) \mid (\mathbf{A}, \mathbf{b}) \leftarrow_{\mathrm{R}} \mathbb{Z}_q^{n \times m} \times \mathbb{Z}_q^m\}$ *and* $\{(\mathbf{A}, \mathbf{b}) \mid \mathbf{A} \leftarrow_{\mathrm{R}} \mathbb{Z}_q^{n \times m}, \mathbf{s} \leftarrow_{\mathrm{R}} \mathbb{Z}_q^n, \mathbf{e} \leftarrow \chi^m, \mathbf{b} := \mathbf{A}^\top\mathbf{s} + \mathbf{e}\}$.

Definition 2.3 (LWE with short secrets). *Let* q, m, n *be positive integers and* χ *be a probability distribution on* $\mathbb{Z}$. *The* $\mathsf{SSLWE}_{m,n,q,\chi}$ *problem is to distinguish the following two distributions:* $\{(\mathbf{A}, \mathbf{b}) \mid (\mathbf{A}, \mathbf{b}) \leftarrow_{\mathrm{R}} \mathbb{Z}_q^{n \times m} \times \mathbb{Z}_q^m\}$ *and* $\{(\mathbf{A}, \mathbf{b}) \mid \mathbf{A} \leftarrow_{\mathrm{R}} \mathbb{Z}_q^{n \times m}, \mathbf{s} \leftarrow \chi^n, \mathbf{e} \leftarrow \chi^m, \mathbf{b} := \mathbf{A}^\top\mathbf{s} + \mathbf{e}\}$.

Definition 2.4 (Short Integer Solution). *Let* q, m, n *be positive integers,* $\mathbf{A} \in \mathbb{Z}_q^{n \times m}$ *and* $\beta \in \mathbb{R}$. *The* $\mathsf{SIS}_{m,n,q,\beta}$ *problem in* ℓ_2 *norm is to find a non-zero vector* $\mathbf{x} \in \mathbb{Z}^m$ *such that* $\mathbf{Ax} = 0 \mod q$ *and* $\|\mathbf{x}\| \leq \beta$.

Definition 2.5 (Inhomogeneous Short Integer Solution). *Let* q, m, n *be positive integers,* $\mathbf{A} \in \mathbb{Z}_q^{n \times m}$, $\mathbf{y} \in \mathbb{Z}_q^n$ *and* $\beta \in \mathbb{R}$. *The* $\mathsf{ISIS}_{m,n,q,\beta}$ *problem in* ℓ_2 *norm is to find a non-zero vector* $\mathbf{x} \in \mathbb{Z}^m$ *such that* $\mathbf{Ax} = \mathbf{y} \mod q$ *and* $\|\mathbf{x}\| \leq \beta$.

Remark 2.6. When the $\mathsf{SIS}_{m,n,q,\beta}$ problem is hard, the $\mathsf{ISIS}_{m,n,q,\beta'}$ problem is hard as well where β' is only slightly larger than β.

We will use the following variant of the Rejection Sampling Lemma by Lyubashevsky to "smudge" small noise – despite working with a polynomial modulus – by rejection sampling.

Lemma 2.7 ([39, **Theorem 4.6**]). *For all* $T \in \mathbb{N}$ *and* $\sigma \geq T\sqrt{n}$ *there exists a constant* M *such that for all* $\mathbf{v} \in \mathbb{Z}^n$ *with* $\|\mathbf{v}\| \leq T$ *the distribution*

$$\mathbf{d} \leftarrow \mathcal{D}_{\mathbb{Z}^n,\sigma}, \mathbf{z} := \mathbf{v} + \mathbf{d}, \ \mathrm{Output:} \begin{cases} \mathbf{z} & \mathrm{with\,prob.}\ \min\left(\frac{\rho_{\mathbb{Z}^n,\sigma}(\mathbf{z})}{M\rho_{\mathbb{Z}^n,\sigma}(\mathbf{d})}, 1\right) \\ \bot & \mathrm{otherwise} \end{cases}$$

is within statistical distance $1/(M2^n)$ *of*

$$\mathbf{d} \leftarrow \mathcal{D}_{\mathbb{Z}^n,\sigma}, \ \mathrm{Output:} \begin{cases} \mathbf{d} & \mathrm{with\,prob.}\ 1/M \\ \bot & \mathrm{otherwise} \end{cases}.$$

2.3   Cryptographic Primitives

We first recall the definition of a gap Σ-protocol and a trapdoor gap Σ-protocol. Our definitions are adapted from the work of Libert et al. [36] which in turn closely follow the definitions put forward by Canetti et al. [17].

Definition 2.8 (Gap Σ-protocol). *Let $\mathcal{L} = (\mathcal{L}_{zk}, \mathcal{L}_{sound})$ be a language associated with two NP relations $\mathcal{R}_{zk}, \mathcal{R}_{sound}$ s.t. $\mathcal{L}_{zk} \subseteq \mathcal{L}_{sound}$ (i.e., $\mathcal{L}$ is a gap language).*

Let $\mathsf{Setup}(1^\lambda, \mathcal{L})$ be an algorithm that takes an unary encoded security parameter $\lambda \in \mathbb{N}$ and a language description $\mathcal{L}$ as input and outputs a common reference string crs. An interactive proof system $\Pi = (\mathsf{Setup}, \mathsf{P}, \mathsf{V})$ in the common reference string model is a Gap Σ-protocol for $\mathcal{L}$ if it has the following 3-move form, where $\mathsf{crs} \leftarrow \mathsf{Setup}(1^\lambda, \mathcal{L})$, x is a statement and w is a witness:

Prover $\mathsf{P} = (\mathsf{P}_1, \mathsf{P}_2)$	*Verifier* V
$\mathtt{Input}: (\mathsf{crs}, x, w)$	$\mathtt{Input}: (\mathsf{crs}, x)$
$(\mathsf{a}, \mathsf{st}) \leftarrow \mathsf{P}_1(\mathsf{crs}, x, w)$ $\xrightarrow{\ \mathsf{a}\ }$	
$\xleftarrow{\ \mathsf{Chal}\ }$	$\mathsf{Chal} \leftarrow_{\mathtt{R}} \mathcal{C}$
$\mathsf{z} \leftarrow \mathsf{P}_2(\mathsf{st}, \mathsf{a}, \mathsf{Chal})$ $\xrightarrow{\ \mathsf{z}\ }$	
	$b \leftarrow \mathsf{V}(\mathsf{crs}, x, \mathsf{a}, \mathsf{Chal}, \mathsf{z})$ $\mathtt{Output}: b$

and the following properties holds:

Completeness: *If $(x, w) \in \mathcal{R}_{zk}$ and both P and V follow the protocol, then V accepts with probability $1 - \mathsf{negl}(\lambda)$. Formally, for every $(x, w) \in \mathcal{R}_{zk}$, we have*

$$\Pr \left[\mathsf{V}(\mathsf{crs}, x, \mathsf{a}, \mathsf{Chal}, \mathsf{z}) = 1 \; \middle| \; \begin{array}{c} \mathsf{crs} \leftarrow \mathsf{Setup}(1^\lambda, \mathcal{L}), \\ (\mathsf{a}, \mathsf{st}) \leftarrow \mathsf{P}_1(\mathsf{crs}, x, w), \\ \mathsf{Chal} \leftarrow_{\mathtt{R}} \mathcal{C}, \mathsf{z} \leftarrow \mathsf{P}_2(\mathsf{st}, \mathsf{a}, \mathsf{Chal}) \end{array} \right] \geq 1 - \mathsf{negl}(\lambda).$$

Special zero-knowledge: *There exists a PPT simulator ZKSim such that for any $\mathsf{crs} \in \mathsf{Setup}(1^\lambda, \mathcal{L})$, any $(x, w) \in \mathcal{R}_{zk}$ and any challenge $\mathsf{Chal} \in \mathcal{C}$, the following distributions are computationally indistinguishable:*

$$\{(\mathsf{a}, \mathsf{Chal}, \mathsf{z}) \mid (\mathsf{a}, \mathsf{z}) \leftarrow \mathsf{ZKSim}(\mathsf{crs}, x, \mathsf{Chal})\} \approx_c$$
$$\{(\mathsf{a}, \mathsf{Chal}, \mathsf{z}) \mid (\mathsf{a}, \mathsf{st}) \leftarrow \mathsf{P}_1(\mathsf{crs}, x, w), \mathsf{z} \leftarrow \mathsf{P}_2(\mathsf{st}, \mathsf{a}, \mathsf{Chal})\}.$$

Special soundness: *For any CRS $\mathsf{crs} \in \mathsf{Setup}(1^\lambda, \mathcal{L})$, any $x \notin \mathcal{L}_{sound}$, and any first prover's message a, there exists at most one challenge $\mathsf{Chal} = f(\mathsf{crs}, x, \mathsf{a}) \in \mathcal{C}$ for which there exists a valid prover's reply z, i.e., $\mathsf{V}(\mathsf{crs}, x, \mathsf{a}, \mathsf{Chal}, \mathsf{z}) = 1$. The function f is called the* bad challenge function *of Π.*

Definition 2.9 (Trapdoor gap Σ-protocol). *Let $\mathcal{L} = (\mathcal{L}_{zk}, \mathcal{L}_{sound})$ be a language associated with two NP relations $\mathcal{R}_{zk}, \mathcal{R}_{sound}$, s.t. $\mathcal{L}_{zk} \subseteq \mathcal{L}_{sound}$. A gap Σ-protocol $\Pi = (\mathsf{Setup}, \mathsf{P}, \mathsf{V})$ for $\mathcal{L}$ with a bad challenge function f is a* trapdoor gap Σ-protocol *if there exist PPT algorithms $(\mathsf{TrapSetup}, \mathsf{BadChallenge})$ with the following syntax:*

$\mathsf{TrapSetup}(1^\lambda, \mathcal{L}, \tau_\mathcal{L})$: *Given public parameters* par, *language* $\mathcal{L}$ *and a membership trapdoor* $\tau_\mathcal{L}$ *for the language* $\mathcal{L}_{\mathsf{sound}}$ *as input, it outputs a CRS* crs *and a trapdoor* $\tau_\Sigma \in \{0,1\}^{\ell_\tau}$ *for some* $\ell_\tau(\lambda)$;
$\mathsf{BadChallenge}(\tau_\Sigma, \mathsf{crs}, x, \mathsf{a})$: *Given a trapdoor* τ_Σ, *a CRS* crs, *a statement* x *and a first prover message* a *as input, it outputs a challenge* Chal;

and satisfying the following properties:

CRS indistinguishability: *For any trapdoor* $\tau_\mathcal{L}$ *for the language* $\mathcal{L}_{\mathsf{sound}}$, *the following distributions are computationally indistinguishable*

$$\{\mathsf{crs} \mid \mathsf{crs} \leftarrow \mathsf{Setup}(1^\lambda, \mathcal{L})\} \approx_c \{\mathsf{crs} \mid \mathsf{crs} \leftarrow \mathsf{TrapSetup}(1^\lambda, \mathcal{L}, \tau_\mathcal{L})\}.$$

Correctness: *There exists a language-specific trapdoor* $\tau_\mathcal{L}$ *s.t. for any instance* $x \notin \mathcal{L}_{\mathsf{sound}}$, *all pairs* $(\mathsf{crs}, \tau_\Sigma) \in \mathsf{TrapSetup}(1^\lambda, \mathcal{L}, \tau_\mathcal{L})$ *and any first prover message* a, *we have* $\mathsf{BadChallenge}(\tau_\Sigma, \mathsf{crs}, x, \mathsf{a}) = f(\mathsf{crs}, x, \mathsf{a})$.

Let us now recall the definition of a Non-Interactive Zero Knowledge (NIZK) proof. We closely follow the definition given by Libert et al. [36].

Definition 2.10 (NIZK). *Let* $\mathcal{L} = (\mathcal{L}_{\mathsf{zk}}, \mathcal{L}_{\mathsf{sound}})$ *be a language associated with two NP relations* $\mathcal{R}_{\mathsf{zk}}$, $\mathcal{R}_{\mathsf{sound}}$, *such that* $\mathcal{L}_{\mathsf{zk}} \subseteq \mathcal{L}_{\mathsf{sound}}$ *and statements are of bit-length* N. *A non-interactive zero-knowledge (NIZK) argument system* Π *for a language* $\mathcal{L}$ *consists of three PPT algorithms* $(\mathsf{Setup}, \mathsf{P}, \mathsf{V})$ *with the following syntax:*

$\mathsf{Setup}(1^\lambda, \mathcal{L}, \tau_\mathcal{L})$: *Given an unary encoded security parameter* λ, *a language* $\mathcal{L}$ *and a membership testing trapdoor* $\tau_\mathcal{L}$ *for* $\mathcal{L}$ *as input, it outputs a CRS* crs.
$\mathsf{P}(\mathsf{crs}, x, w)$: *Given a CRS* crs, *a statement* $x \in \{0,1\}^N$, *and a witness* w *as input, the proving algorithm outputs a proof* π.
$\mathsf{V}(\mathsf{crs}, x, \pi)$: *Given a CRS* crs, *a statement* $x \in \{0,1\}^N$, *and a proof* π *as input, the verification algorithm outputs a decision bit.*

Moreover, Π *should satisfy the following properties.*

Completeness: *For any* $(x, w) \in \mathcal{R}_{\mathsf{zk}}$, *any* $|\mathsf{b}| \in \{0,1\}^*$ *and any membership testing trapdoor* $\tau_\mathcal{L}$ *for* $\mathcal{L}$, *we have*

$$\Pr[\mathsf{V}(\mathsf{crs}, x, \pi) = 1 \mid \mathsf{crs} \leftarrow \mathsf{Setup}(1^\lambda, \mathcal{L}, \tau_\mathcal{L}), \pi \leftarrow \mathsf{P}(\mathsf{crs}, x, w)] \geq 1 - \mathsf{negl}(\lambda).$$

Soundness: *For any* $x \in \{0,1\}^N \setminus \mathcal{L}_{\mathsf{sound}}$, *any membership testing trapdoor* $\tau_\mathcal{L}$ *for* $\mathcal{L}$ *and any PPT prover* P^*, *we have*

$$\Pr[\mathsf{V}(\mathsf{crs}, x, \pi) = 1 \mid \mathsf{crs} \leftarrow \mathsf{Setup}(1^\lambda, \mathcal{L}, \tau_\mathcal{L}), \pi \leftarrow \mathsf{P}^*(\mathsf{crs}, x)] \leq \mathsf{negl}(\lambda).$$

Zero-Knowledge: *There is a PPT simulator* $(\mathsf{Sim}_0, \mathsf{Sim}_1)$ *such that for any PPT adversary* $\mathcal{A}$, *we have that for all trapdoors* $\tau_\mathcal{L}$:

$$| \Pr[1 \leftarrow \mathcal{A}^{\mathcal{O}_\mathsf{P}(\mathsf{crs},\cdot,\cdot)}(\mathsf{crs}) \mid \mathsf{crs} \leftarrow \mathsf{Setup}(1^\lambda, \mathcal{L}, \tau_\mathcal{L})]$$
$$- \Pr[1 \leftarrow \mathcal{A}^{\mathcal{O}_\mathsf{Sim}(\mathsf{crs}, \tau_{\mathsf{zk}}, \cdot, \cdot)}(\mathsf{crs}) \mid (\mathsf{crs}, \tau_{\mathsf{zk}}) \leftarrow \mathsf{Sim}_0(1^\lambda, \mathcal{L})]| \leq \mathsf{negl}(\lambda),$$

where $\mathcal{O}_\mathsf{P}(\mathsf{crs}, x, w)$ *outputs* $\bot$ *if* $(x, w) \notin \mathcal{R}_{\mathsf{zk}}$ *and* $\pi \leftarrow \mathsf{P}(\mathsf{crs}, x, w)$ *otherwise, and* $\mathcal{O}_\mathsf{Sim}(\mathsf{crs}, \tau_{\mathsf{zk}}, x, w)$ *outputs* $\bot$ *if* $(x, w) \notin \mathcal{R}_{\mathsf{zk}}$ *and* $\mathsf{Sim}_1(\mathsf{crs}, \tau_{\mathsf{zk}}, x)$ *otherwise.*

Finally we recall the standard definition for digital signature and a public key encryption scheme.

Definition 2.11 (Digital Signature). *A digital signature scheme Σ for a message space $\mathcal{M}$ and signature space $\mathbb{S}$ consist of three PPT algorithms* (KeyGen, Sign, Ver) *with the following syntax*

KeyGen(1^λ): *Given an unary encoded security parameter λ as input, it outputs a verification key* vk *and a signing key* sk.
Sign(sk, msg): *Given a signing key* sk *and a message* msg $\in \mathcal{M}$ *as input, it outputs a signature* sig $\in \mathbb{S}$.
Ver(vk, msg, sig): *Given a verification key* vk, *a message* msg $\in \mathcal{M}$ *and a signature* sig $\in \mathbb{S}$ *as input, it outputs* 1 *(indicating a valid signature) or* 0 *(indicating an invalid signature).*

A digital signature scheme $\Sigma = $ (KeyGen, Sign, Ver) *is* correct, *if for every message* msg $\in \mathcal{M}$, *we have*

$$| \Pr[\text{Ver}(\text{vk}, \text{msg}, \text{sig}) = 1 \mid (\text{vk}, \text{sk}) \leftarrow \text{KeyGen}(1^\lambda), \text{sig} \leftarrow \text{Sign}(\text{sk}, \text{msg})]|$$
$$\geq 1 - \text{negl}(\lambda).$$

Definition 2.12 (Public-Key Encryption). *A public key encryption scheme Π for a message space $\mathcal{M}$ consist of three PPT algorithms* (KeyGen, Enc, Dec) *with the following syntax*

KeyGen(1^λ): *Given an unary encoded security parameter λ as input, it outputs a public key* pk *and a secret key* sk.
Enc(pk, msg): *Given a public key* pk *and a message* msg $\in \mathcal{M}$ *as input, it outputs a ciphertext* ct.
Dec(sk, ct): *Given a secret key* sk *and a ciphertext* ct *as input, it outputs a message* msg $\in \mathcal{M}$ *or* $\perp$ *(indicating a failure).*

A PKE scheme $\Pi = $ (KeyGen, Enc, Dec) *is* correct, *if for every* msg $\in \mathcal{M}$, *we have*

$$| \Pr[\text{Dec}(\text{sk}, \text{ct}) = \text{msg} \mid (\text{pk}, \text{sk}) \leftarrow \text{KeyGen}(1^\lambda), \text{ct} \leftarrow \text{Enc}(\text{pk}, \text{msg})]| \geq 1 - \text{negl}(\lambda).$$

3 Structure-Preserving Sets

The first building block in our framework is the notion of a structure-preserving set, which is a crucial tool in capturing the defining characteristics of a specific family of lattice-based signatures, encryption schemes and NIZKs which are compatible with each other. The properties that lead to such structure-preserving cryptographic primitives are described in later sections.

Let q be a large prime. A structure-preserving set S is a special subset of $\mathbb{Z}_q^d$ that can be rerandomized to obtain a rerandomized set $S' = S + D$ (where D is a set which contains the rerandomizing terms). Given a vector $\mathbf{s} \in S$, we can rerandomize $\mathbf{s}$ to obtain $\mathbf{s}' \in S + D$. The structure-preserving property of S ensures that given $\mathbf{s}'$, one is able to check whether the original vector $\mathbf{s} \in \mathbb{Z}_q^d$ belonged to S or whether it lied outside of S. In particular, vector $\mathbf{s}'$ allows to check membership of the original $\mathbf{s}$, but it hides its original value.

Definition 3.1 (Uniformly Structure-Preserving Set). *We say that a set* $S \subseteq \mathbb{Z}_q^d$ *is* uniformly structure-preserving *if (i) there exists a subset* $D \subseteq \mathbb{Z}_q^d$ *such that for all messages* $\mathbf{s}, \mathbf{s}' \in S$

$$\boxed{\mathbf{d} \leftarrow_R D, \quad \text{Output:}\, \mathbf{s} + \mathbf{d}} \approx_s \boxed{\mathbf{d} \leftarrow_R D, \quad \text{Output:}\, \mathbf{s}' + \mathbf{d}}$$

(ii) for $\overline{S} := \mathbb{Z}_q^d \setminus S$ *it holds that* $(S + D) \cap (\overline{S} + D) = \emptyset$, *and the membership problem for* D *and* $S + D$ *are easy and we can efficiently sample uniformly at random from* D. *We call the maximal statistical distance between the first two boxed distributions the* structure-preserving error.

To provide some intuition about the introduced notion, let us demonstrate the definition of a concrete example that we use later in the paper. Namely, we show that cosets of subgroups are uniformly structure-preserving.

Example 3.2 (Cosets of subgroups). Every coset S of an additive subgroup $G \leq \mathbb{Z}_q^d$ is uniformly structure-preserving.

Proof. By definition of a coset, all the sets $S_{\mathbf{s}} = \{\mathbf{s} + \mathbf{d} \mid \mathbf{d} \in G\}$ (for $\mathbf{s} \in S$) are the same set S again. Thus by picking $D := G$, we get that for all $\mathbf{s}, \mathbf{s}' \in S$, $\mathbf{s} + \mathbf{d}$ and $\mathbf{s}' + \mathbf{d}$ for $\mathbf{d} \leftarrow_R D$ are identically distributed. Hence the first part of the definition is satisfied and the structure-preserving error is 0.

For $\mathbf{x} \in \mathbb{Z}_q^d \setminus S$, we know that $\mathbf{x} \in S'$ for $S' \neq S$ being another coset of G. Thus for every $\mathbf{d} \in G$, we have $\mathbf{x} + \mathbf{d} \in S'$. Since different cosets are disjoint, the second part of the definition is satisfied as well. □

Remark 3.3. The above example, in particular, implies that

1. all additive subgroups of $\mathbb{Z}_q^d$ are uniformly structure-preserving; and
2. all singleton sets are uniformly structure-preserving, because they are cosets of the trivial subgroup $\{\mathbf{0}\}$.

In order to define lattice-based structure-preserving signatures and encryptions, we will need a more generic definition of a structure-preserving set. Namely, we do not want to restrict ourselves to $\mathbf{d}$ being sampled uniformly at random, but from any distribution on $\mathbb{Z}_q^d$. Looking ahead, since we work with lattice-based primitives, we are particularly interested in Gaussian distributions. Along with the change of distribution for $\mathbf{d}$, we generalize the definition by loosening some of its condition. At a high level, in both the first and the second part of the definition, we allow for small errors with some probability.

Definition 3.4 (Structure-Preserving Set). *We say that a set* $S \subseteq \mathbb{Z}_q^d$ *is* structure-preserving *with noise growth* δ *if there exists an efficiently sampleable probability distribution* $\mathcal{D}$ *on* $\mathbb{Z}_q^d$, *a constant* $\alpha \in (0, 1]$, *that we will call the* no-abort constant, *and a function* success $: S \times S \times \mathrm{supp}(\mathcal{D}) \to (0, 1]$, *that we will call the* no-abort function, *such that (i) for all messages* $\mathbf{s}, \mathbf{s}' \in S$

$$
\begin{array}{|l|}
\hline
\mathbf{d} \leftarrow \mathcal{D} \\[4pt]
\text{Output:} \begin{cases} \mathbf{s} + \mathbf{d} & \text{with prob.} \\ & \text{success}(\mathbf{s}, \mathbf{s}', \mathbf{d}) \\ \bot & \text{otherwise} \end{cases} \\
\hline
\end{array}
\quad \approx_s \quad
\begin{array}{|l|}
\hline
\mathbf{d} \leftarrow \mathcal{D} \\[4pt]
\text{Output:} \begin{cases} \mathbf{s}' + \mathbf{d} & \text{with prob. } \alpha \\ \bot & \text{otherwise} \end{cases} \\
\hline
\end{array}
$$

and (ii) there exists a set $D' \subseteq \mathbb{Z}_q^d$, that we will call the smudging set, such that $\Pr_{\mathbf{d} \leftarrow \mathcal{D}}[\mathbf{d} \in D'] \geq 1 - \mathsf{negl}(\lambda)$ for a negligible function negl, and for $\overline{S}_\delta := \mathbb{Z}_q^d \setminus B_\delta(S)$, it holds that $(S + D') \cap (\overline{S}_\delta + D') = \emptyset$. Moreover, the membership problem for D' and $(S + D')$ are easy.[11] We call negl the soundness error.

It is easy to see that uniformly structure-preserving sets are special cases of structure-preserving sets.

Lemma 3.5. Let S be an uniformly structure-preserving set. Then S is a structure-preserving set with noise growth 0 and soundness error 0.

Proof. By setting $\mathcal{D}$ to be the uniform distribution on D, success to be the constant function 1, $\alpha := 1$ and $D' = D$, we directly obtain that S is a structure-preserving with noise growth 0 and soundness error 0. □

Let us provide an example of a structure-preserving set which is not uniformly structure-preserving.

Example 3.6 (Close vectors). Every set $S \subseteq \mathbb{Z}_q^d$ where $S - S$ is T-bounded (i.e., $S - S \subseteq B_T(\{0\})$) is structure-preserving with noise growth $4Td + 1$, when d grows polynomially with the security parameter.

Proof. Pick $\mathcal{D} := \mathcal{D}_{\mathbb{Z}^d, \sigma}$ with $\sigma := T\sqrt{d}$. For all $\mathbf{s}, \mathbf{s}' \in S$, by Lemma 2.7, the distribution that outputs $\mathbf{s} - \mathbf{s}' + \mathbf{d}$ for $\mathbf{d} \leftarrow \mathcal{D}_{\mathbb{Z}^d, \sigma}$ with probability $\text{success}(\mathbf{s}, \mathbf{s}', \mathbf{d}) := \min\left(\frac{\rho_{\mathbb{Z}^d, \sigma}(\mathbf{s} - \mathbf{s}' + \mathbf{d})}{M \rho_{\mathbb{Z}^d, \sigma}(\mathbf{d})}, 1 \right)$ is statistically close to outputting $\mathbf{d} \leftarrow \mathcal{D}_{\mathbb{Z}^d, \sigma}$ with probability $\alpha := 1/M$ for a constant M. By adding $\mathbf{s}'$ to the output of these two distributions, we get that the first condition for a structure-preserving set is satisfied.

Pick $D' := B_{2Td}(\{0\})$ as smudging set. By the tail bound for Gaussian distributions (Lemma 2.1) we have $\Pr_{\mathbf{d} \leftarrow \mathcal{D}_{\mathbb{Z}^d, \sigma}}[\|\mathbf{d}\| > 2Td] < 2^d e^{\frac{-3d}{2}} = \left(2e^{-3/2}\right)^d < \frac{1}{2^d}$, which shows that this choice is valid. For $\mathbf{x} \in \overline{S}_\delta := \mathbb{Z}_q^d \setminus B_{4Td+1}(S)$ and $\mathbf{d} \in D'$ we have $\mathbf{x} + \mathbf{d} \in \mathbb{Z}_q^d \setminus B_{2Td}(S)$. On the other hand, for $\mathbf{s} \in S$ we have $\mathbf{s} + \mathbf{d} \in B_{2Td}(S)$. This implies that $(S + D') \cap (\overline{S}_\delta + D') = \emptyset$ which is the second condition for a structure-preserving set. □

Remark 3.7. This example, in particular, implies that sets of small vectors are structure-preserving. Namely, let $S \subseteq \mathbb{Z}_q^d$ be a T-bounded set. Then by triangular inequality, $S - S$ is $2T$-bounded and hence S structure-preserving with noise growth $8Td + 1$.

Next, we show that structure-preserving sets are closed under the cartesian product.

---

[11] The membership problem for S does not need to be easy.

Example 3.8. When $S_1 \subseteq \mathbb{Z}_q^{d_1}$ is a structure-preserving set with noise growth δ_1 and $S_2 \subseteq \mathbb{Z}_q^{d_2}$ is a structure-preserving set with noise growth δ_2, then $S_1 \times S_2 \subseteq \mathbb{Z}_q^{d_1+d_2}$ is structure-preserving with noise $\max\{\delta_1, \delta_2\}$.

Proof. Let $\mathcal{D}_1, \text{success}_1, \alpha_1$ be the distribution, abort function and abort constant that make S_1 a structure-preserving set with noise δ_1 and $\mathcal{D}_2, \text{success}_2, \alpha_2$ be the distribution, abort function and abort constant that make S_2 a structure-preserving set with noise δ_2. Then the distribution $\mathcal{D}_1 \times \mathcal{D}_2$ with the success function

$$\text{success}((\mathbf{m}_1, \mathbf{m}_2), (\mathbf{m}_1', \mathbf{m}_2'), \mathbf{d}) := \text{success}_1(\mathbf{m}_1, \mathbf{m}_1', \mathbf{d}) \cdot \text{success}_2(\mathbf{m}_2, \mathbf{m}_2', \mathbf{d})$$

and success probability constant $\alpha := \alpha_1 \alpha_2$ makes the set $S_1 \times S_2$ structure-preserving with noise $\max\{\delta_1, \delta_2\}$. $\quad\square$

We complete this section with an alternative formulation of the structure-preserving set property that is easier to use in some of the proofs.

Lemma 3.9. *For a structure-preserving set S with noise growth δ and smudging set D' we have $S + D' - D' \subseteq B_\delta(S)$.*

Proof. We prove this Lemma by contradiction. Suppose there exist $\mathbf{s} \in S$ and $\mathbf{d}, \mathbf{d}' \in \mathcal{D}$ such that $\mathbf{x} := \mathbf{s} + \mathbf{d} - \mathbf{d}' \notin B_\delta(S)$, i.e. $\mathbf{x} \in \overline{S}_\delta := \mathbb{Z}_q^d \setminus B_\delta(S)$. But then

$$S + D' \ni \mathbf{s} + \mathbf{d} = \mathbf{x} + \mathbf{d}' \in \overline{S}_\delta + D',$$

which is in contradiction to part (ii) of Definition 3.4. $\quad\square$

4 Lattice-Based Structure-Preserving Signatures

A lattice-based structure-preserving signature (SPS) scheme Σ expresses its verification algorithm in the framework of structure-preserving sets. Namely, a signature σ can be split into two separate parts $\sigma = (\text{core}, \text{tag})$. In order to verify that σ is valid, the Σ verification algorithm checks whether $f(\text{core})$ belongs to a structure-preserving set S. The function f is publicly computable from tag, along with public verification key vk and the message m.

The requirement to use tag arises from specific properties of known lattice-based SPS schemes. The tag is publicly samplable and, for example, it could be a random string. At a technical level, the tag is usually required in all known lattice-based signatures that satisfy strong-unforgeability, and can remain unused in some schemes that are only existentially-unforgeable.

Definition 4.1 (Lattice SPS). *A lattice-based $\mathcal{F}$-structure-preserving signature Σ for a family $\mathcal{F}$ of functions $f : \mathbb{S} \to \mathbb{Z}_q^{d'}$ is a digital signature with signature space $\mathbb{S} \times \mathbb{T}$ where for every verification key vk, every message msg and every signature $(\text{core}, \text{tag}) \in \mathbb{S} \times \mathbb{T}$*

$$\text{Ver}(\text{vk}, \text{msg}, (\text{core}, \text{tag})) = 1 \iff f(\text{core}) \in S$$

where $f \in \mathcal{F}$ and $S \subseteq \mathbb{Z}_q^{d'}$ are derived from vk, msg *and* tag. *Furthermore, S is a structure-preserving set. Finally, we require that tags are publicly samplable. That is, there exists an algorithm* TagGen *that, given the verification key* vk *and a message* m *generates a tag* tag *that has the same distribution as the tag part of the signatures generate with the signing algorithm.*

$(\text{vk}, \text{sk}) \leftarrow_R \text{KeyGen}(1^\lambda)$	$\mathcal{O}_{\text{sign}}(m)$:
$Q := \emptyset$	sig $\leftarrow_R$ Sign(sk, msg)
$(m^\star, \text{sig}^\star) \leftarrow_R \mathcal{A}^{\mathcal{O}_{\text{sign}}}(\text{vk})$	$\boxed{Q \leftarrow Q \cup \{m\}}$
$b \leftarrow \text{Ver}'(\text{vk}, m^\star, \text{sig}^\star)$	
$\boxed{\textbf{return } b \wedge m^\star \notin Q}$	$\boxed{Q \leftarrow Q \cup \{(m, \text{sig})\}}$
$\boxed{\textbf{return } b \wedge (m^\star, \text{sig}^\star) \notin Q}$	**return** sig
	Ver$'(\text{vk}, m, \text{sig} = (\text{core}, \text{tag}))$:
	return $(f(\text{core}) \in B_{\delta_S}(S))$

Fig. 1. Security experiment for $\boxed{\text{SPS-EUF-CMA}}$ and $\boxed{\text{SPS-sEUF-CMA}}$ security of lattice-based structure-preserving signatures.

Remark 4.2. Since we do not require the membership problem for the sets S to be easy, this definition does not give immediately rise to an alternative verification procedure.

We are particularly interested in the cases where $\mathcal{F}$ is the set of linear functions or the set of functions that can be computed by bounded-depth Boolean circuits after encoding the signature as a binary string.

For structure-preserving signatures we require a slightly stronger security notion (defined below) than standard (strong) existential unforgeability under chosen message attacks ((s)EUF-CMA). Compared to (s)EUF-CMA, we relax the verification of the forged signature as follows: Instead of requiring that the forged signature sig $=$ (core, tag) satisfies $f(\text{core}) \in S$, we only require $f(\text{core}) \in B_{\delta_S}(S)$.

Definition 4.3 (SPS-(s)EUF-CMA). *We call a structure-preserving signature scheme* (KeyGen, Sign, Ver) SPS-EUF-CMA *or* SPS-sEUF-CMA-*secure, if every PPT adversary can win the respective game in Fig. 1 with at most negligible probability.*

4.1 SPS Instantiation

Examples of structure-preserving signatures are Boyen's signature scheme [14], Rückert's signature scheme [46] and a new scheme, that combines the advantages of these two schemes. Namely, it achieves strong unforgeablity and has a simpler verification (because it does not need the non-zero signature check). Furthermore, it is more efficient (due to shorter signatures) than Rückert's scheme. We only show that the new scheme satisfies Definition 4.1 here and present the remaining details in the full version.

As a prerequisite, we state some facts that are needed in the signature scheme description, and define and construct chameleon hash functions.

Fact 1 ([14, **Fact 5**]). *There is a PPT algorithm* TrapGen *that, on input the security parameter* λ, *an odd prime* $q = \mathrm{poly}(\lambda)$, *and two integers* $n = \Theta(\lambda)$ *and* $m \geq 6n \log q$, *outputs a matrix* $\mathbf{A} \in \mathbb{Z}_q^{n \times m}$ *statistically close to uniform, and a basis* $\mathbf{T_A}$ *for* $\Lambda^{\perp}(\mathbf{A})$ *such that* $\|\bar{\mathbf{T}}_{\mathbf{A}}\| \leq \tilde{\Theta}(\sqrt{m}) \leq L$ *with overwhelming probability. We assume* $L = \tilde{\Omega}(\sqrt{m})$.

Fact 2 ([14, **Lemma 22**]). *For a security parameter* λ, *let* $q = \mathrm{poly}(\lambda)$ *be an odd prime,* $n = \Theta(\lambda)$, $m \geq 6n \log q$, $L = \tilde{\Omega}(\sqrt{m})$ *and* $\sigma \geq L\omega(\sqrt{\log m})$. *Then there exist a PPT algorithm* SamplePre *that on input a Gaussian parameter* σ, *a modulus* q, *a matrix* $\mathbf{F} := [\mathbf{A}|\mathbf{B}] \leftarrow_{\mathrm{R}} \mathbb{Z}_q^{n \times 2m}$, *and a basis* $\mathbf{T_A} \subset \Lambda^{\perp}(\mathbf{A})$ *of norm* $\|\bar{\mathbf{T}}_{\mathbf{A}}\| \leq L$, *and a vector* $\mathbf{u}$, *outputs* $\mathbf{d} \in \Lambda^{\perp}(\mathbf{F})$ *from the distribution* $\mathcal{D}_{\mathbb{Z}^m, \sigma}$ *conditioned on* $\mathbf{Fd} = \mathbf{u}$.

Fact 3 ([4, **Section 4.2**]). *Given matrices* $\mathbf{A}, \mathbf{B} \in \mathbb{Z}_q^{n \times m}$, $\mathbf{B}$ *needs to have rank* n, *a short basis* $\mathbf{T_B}$ *for* $\mathbf{B}$ *and a short matrix* $\mathbf{R} \in \mathbb{Z}_q^{m \times m}$, *one can compute efficiently a short basis* $\mathbf{T_F}$ *for* $\mathbf{F} := (\mathbf{A}|\mathbf{AR} + \mathbf{B})$ *with* $\|\widetilde{\mathbf{T}_{\mathbf{F}}}\| \leq \|\widetilde{\mathbf{T}_{\mathbf{B}}}\|(\|\mathbf{R}\| + 1)$.

Definition 4.4 (Chameleon hash function). *A chameleon hash function with message space* $\mathcal{M}$ *and hash space* $\mathcal{N}$ *consists of an efficiently sampable distribution* $\mathcal{R}$ *on some randomness space* R *and two PPT algorithms* (GenCH, TrapColl) *with the following syntax*

GenCH(1^{λ})**:** *Given an unary encoded security parameter* λ *as input, it outputs an efficiently computable chameleon hash function* ch $: \mathcal{M} \times R \rightarrow \mathcal{N}$ *and a trapdoor* τ.

TrapColl($\tau, m \in \mathcal{M}, r \in R, m^* \in \mathcal{M}$)**:** *Given the trapdoor* τ *for a chameleon hash function* ch, *two messages* m, m^* *and one randomness* r *this algorithm outputs* r^* *such that* ch$(m, r) = $ ch(m^*, r^*) *and* r^* *is distributed according to* $\mathcal{R}$.

The security property we require for chameleon hash functions is *collision resistance*. That is, for every PPT adversary $\mathcal{A}$, the following probability is negligible

$$\Pr[(\mathrm{ch}, \tau) \leftarrow_{\mathrm{R}} \mathsf{GenCH}, (m, r, m^*, r^*) \leftarrow_{\mathrm{R}} \mathcal{A}(1^{\lambda}, \mathrm{ch}) : \mathrm{ch}(m, r) = \mathrm{ch}(m^*, r^*)$$
$$\wedge (m, r) \neq (m^*, r^*)].$$

An example of a chameleon hash function based on the SIS assumption is by [18]. It has message space $\mathcal{M} := \{0, 1\}^k$ and randomness space $R := \{\mathbf{r} \in \mathbb{Z}^m \mid \|\mathbf{r}\| < s\sqrt{m}\}$ with a tail-truncated discrete Gaussian distribution $\mathcal{D}_{R,s}$ where $s = L \cdot \omega(\sqrt{\log m})$ and n, m, and L are as in Fact 1. It works as follows:

GenCH(1^{λ}) samples $\mathbf{A}_0 \leftarrow_{\mathrm{R}} \mathbb{Z}_q^{n \times k}$ and $\mathbf{A}_1 \in \mathbb{Z}_q^{n \times m}$ with short basis $\mathbf{S}$ using TrapGen. Output $\mathbf{A} := (\mathbf{A}_0 | \mathbf{A}_1)$ to describe the chameleon hash function

$$\mathrm{ch}_{\mathbf{A}} : \{0, 1\}^k \times R \rightarrow \mathbb{Z}_q^n$$

$$(\mathbf{m}, \mathbf{r}) \mapsto \mathbf{A} \cdot \begin{pmatrix} \mathbf{m} \\ \mathbf{r} \end{pmatrix}$$

TrapColl($\tau, \mathbf{m} \in \mathcal{M}, \mathbf{r} \in R, \mathbf{m}^* \in \mathcal{M}$) samples and outputs a vector $\mathbf{r}^*$ according to (a distribution statistically close to) $\mathcal{D}_{R,s}$ condition on $\mathrm{ch}_{\mathbf{A}}(\mathbf{m}^*, \mathbf{r}^*) = \mathrm{ch}_{\mathbf{A}}(\mathbf{m}, \mathbf{r})$ using Fact 2.

Lemma 4.5 ([18, **Lemma 4.1**]). *The above chameleon hash function is collision-resistant under the* $\mathsf{SIS}_{m,n,q,\beta}$ *problem where* $\beta := \sqrt{k + 4s^2 m}$.

The ISIS-based signature scheme requires a chameleon hash function (GenCH, TrapColl) with message space $\mathcal{M}$, randomness space R and hash space $\mathcal{N} = \{0,1\}^\ell$ and is described as follows:

KeyGen(1^λ): Given unary encoded security parameter λ as input, proceed as follows:
1. Execute the TrapGen algorithm to obtain a matrix $\mathbf{A} \in \mathbb{Z}_q^{n \times m}$ and a basis $\mathbf{T_A} \in \Lambda^\top(\mathbf{A})$ such that $\|\bar{\mathbf{T}}_\mathbf{A}\| \leq L$.
2. Sample $\mathbf{y} \leftarrow_\mathsf{R} \mathbb{Z}_q^n$, $(\mathbf{C}_0, \ldots, \mathbf{C}_\ell) \leftarrow_\mathsf{R} \mathbb{Z}_q^{n \times m} \times \ldots, \mathbb{Z}_q^{n \times m}$.
3. Sample $(\mathsf{ch}, \tau) \leftarrow_\mathsf{R} \mathsf{GenCH}(1^\lambda)$.
4. Output $\mathsf{vk} := (\mathbf{A}, \mathbf{C}_0, \ldots, \mathbf{C}_\ell, \mathbf{y}, \mathsf{ch})$ and $\mathsf{sk} := \mathbf{T_A}$.

Sign($\mathsf{sk}, \mathsf{msg}$): Given a signing key $\mathsf{sk} = \mathbf{T_A}$ and a message $\mathsf{msg} \in \mathcal{M}$ as input proceed as follows:
1. Sample $r \leftarrow \mathcal{R}$ and set $\mathsf{msg}' := \mathsf{ch}(\mathsf{msg}, r)$.
2. Compute $\mathbf{C}_\mathsf{msg} := \mathbf{C}_0 + \sum_{i=1}^\ell \mathsf{msg}_i' \mathbf{C}_i$ and set $\mathbf{F}_\mathsf{msg} := [\mathbf{A} \mid \mathbf{C}_\mathsf{msg}] \in \mathbb{Z}_q^{n \times 2m}$.
3. Execute the algorithm SamplePre on $\mathbf{F}_\mathsf{msg}$, $\mathbf{T_A}$ and $\sigma \geq 2L\omega(\sqrt{\log m})$ to obtain a short non-zero random point $\mathbf{d}$ with $\mathbf{F}_\mathsf{msg}\mathbf{d} = \mathbf{y}$.
4. Output the signature $\mathsf{sig} := (\mathsf{core} = \mathbf{d}, \mathsf{tag} = r)$.

Ver($\mathsf{vk}, \mathsf{msg}, \mathsf{sig}$): Given a verification key $\mathsf{vk} = (\mathbf{A}, \mathbf{C}_0, \ldots, \mathbf{C}_\ell, \mathbf{y}, \mathsf{ch})$, a message $\mathsf{msg} \in \mathcal{M}$ and signature $\mathsf{sig} = (\mathbf{d} \in \mathbb{Z}_q^{2m}, r)$ as input, set $\mathsf{msg}' := \mathsf{ch}(\mathsf{msg}, r)$ and output 1 if (1) $\|\mathbf{d}\| \leq \sqrt{2m} \cdot \sigma$ and (2) $[\mathbf{A} \mid \mathbf{C}_0 + \sum_{i=1}^\ell \mathsf{msg}_i' \mathbf{C}_i]\mathbf{d} = \mathbf{y} \mod q$. Otherwise, output 0.

Lemma 4.6. *The ISIS-based signature scheme from above is a SPS scheme.*

Proof. A signature sig is of the form $(\mathsf{core}, \mathsf{tag}) = (\mathbf{d}, r)$. Clearly, these tags are publicly samplable.

According to definition Definition 4.1, what remains to show is that the signature verification can be expressed as $f(\mathsf{core}) \in S$ for some function $f : \mathbb{Z}_q^{2m} \to \mathbb{Z}_q^{d'}$ and some set $S \subseteq \mathbb{Z}_q^{d'}$ which is structure-preserving. Both the function f and the set S might depend on the message being signed, the verification key and the public parameters of the scheme. We show that the signature verification can be expressed as two checks of the type $f_i(\mathsf{core}) \in S_i$ ($i \in \{1,2\}$). These check can then be combined to a single check by setting $f(\mathsf{core}) := (f_1(\mathsf{core}), f_2(\mathsf{core}))$ and $S := S_1 \times S_2$. The set S is structure-preserving when S_1 and S_2 are structure-preserving by Example 3.8.

The first check is $\|\mathsf{core}\| \leq \sqrt{2m} \cdot \sigma$, i.e., that core is a small vector. For this, we can set $n_1' := 2m$ and

$$f_1(\mathsf{core}) := \mathsf{core}, \quad \text{and} \quad S_1 := \{\mathbf{x} \in \mathbb{Z}_q^{2m} \mid \|\mathbf{x}\| \leq \sqrt{2m} \cdot \sigma\} = B_{\sqrt{2m} \cdot \sigma}(\{0\}).$$

By triangular inequality, we have that $S_1 - S_1 \subseteq B_{2\sqrt{2m} \cdot \sigma}(\{0\})$. By Remark 3.7, we can conclude that S_1 is structure-preserving with noise growth $16m\sigma + 1$.

For the second check, we can set $n_2' := n$ and

$$f_2(\mathsf{core}) := \left[\mathbf{A} \,\middle|\, \mathbf{C}_0 + \sum_{i=1}^\ell \mathsf{msg}_i \mathbf{C}_i\right] \mathsf{core} \quad \text{and} \quad S_2 := \{\mathbf{y}\} \subset \mathbb{Z}_q^n.$$

Note that the function f_2 is defined by the message and the verification key. Moreover, S_2 is a singleton set and hence by Remark 3.3 and Lemma 3.5, we know that it is structure-preserving with noise growth 0.   □

We prove SPS-sEUF-CMA-security of our scheme in the full version.

5   Lattice-Based Structure-Preserving Encryption

Our notion of a structure-preserving encryption (SPE) captures the common properties of known lattice-bases encryption schemes which are compatible with efficient lattice-based sigma protocols and NIZKs that prove statements about ciphertexts. In particular, the randomness space needs to be a structure-preserving set (Definition 3.4) and ciphertexts are of the form $ct = \mathbf{B}_\alpha r + g_\alpha(msg)$, where $\mathbf{B}_\alpha$ is a public matrix depending on the message dimension α, and g_α is an invertible encoding function.

In addition, SPE needs to satisfy a series of technical properties on the noise, which provides bounds on the noise levels. This is a crucial property that allows for compatibility with the sigma protocols in later sections.

Definition 5.1 (Lattice SPE). *A PKE scheme* (KeyGen, Enc, Dec) *is a lattice-based structure-preserving encryption scheme if it satisfies the following properties:*

– *It has message space $\mathcal{M}^*$ for some base set $\mathcal{M}$. That is, we can encrypt arbitrary dimensional vectors of some base set $\mathcal{M}$. The ciphertexts will reveal the dimensions of the vectors.*
– *Public key: The public key implicitly defines matrices $(\mathbf{B}_\alpha \in \mathbb{Z}_q^{d(\alpha) \times r(\alpha)})_{\alpha \in \mathbb{N}_+}$ and efficiently sampleable distribution $(\mathcal{R}_\alpha)_{\alpha \in \mathbb{N}_+}$ such that $r \leftarrow \mathcal{R}_\alpha$ lies with overwhelming probability in a structure-preserving set $R_\alpha \subseteq \mathbb{Z}_q^r$. The parameter α denotes the dimension of the message, i.e. to encrypt a message $msg \in \mathcal{M}^\alpha$ we will use $\mathbf{B}_\alpha$ and $\mathcal{R}_\alpha$.*
– *Message encoding: The public key implicitly defines for every $\alpha \in \mathbb{N}_+$ an additively homomorphic invertible function $g_\alpha \colon \mathcal{M}^\alpha \to \mathbb{Z}_q^{d(\alpha)}$ such that Enc is equivalent to an algorithm that samples a vector $r \leftarrow \mathcal{R}_\alpha$ and outputs $ct = \mathbf{B}_\alpha r + g_\alpha(msg)$.*
– *Noise Levels: There exists a polynomial time algorithm NoiseLevel(sk, ct) that computes a noise level $\nu \in \mathbb{N}_0$ for each ciphertext and satisfies the following:*
  • *Initial noise level: For every security parameter λ there is a constant $\nu_{init} \in \mathbb{N}_0$ such that for every key pair (pk, sk) in the range of KeyGen(1^λ) and every ciphertext ct in the range of Enc(pk, msg) for a message $msg \in \mathcal{M}^\alpha$ we have NoiseLevel(sk, ct) $\leq \nu_{init}$.*
  • *Maximum noise level: For every security parameter λ there is a constant $\nu_{max} \geq 2\nu_{init}$ such that for every key pair (pk, sk) in the range of KeyGen(1^λ) and every ciphertext $ct = \mathbf{B}_\alpha r + g_\alpha(msg)$ with NoiseLevel(sk, ct) $\leq \nu_{max}$ we have Dec(sk, ct) = msg.*
  • *Symmetry: For every secret key sk and ciphertext ct*

$$NoiseLevel(sk, ct) = NoiseLevel(sk, -ct).$$

- *Subadditivity: For every secret key* sk *and any two ciphertexts* $\mathsf{ct}_1, \mathsf{ct}_2$ *with* $\mathsf{NoiseLevel}(\mathsf{sk}, \mathsf{ct}_1), \mathsf{NoiseLevel}(\mathsf{sk}, \mathsf{ct}_2) \leq \nu_{\max}/2$ *satisfy*

$$\mathsf{NoiseLevel}(\mathsf{sk}, \mathsf{ct}_1 + \mathsf{ct}_2) \leq \mathsf{NoiseLevel}(\mathsf{sk}, \mathsf{ct}_1) + \mathsf{NoiseLevel}(\mathsf{sk}, \mathsf{ct}_2).$$

- *Boundedness: For every security parameter* λ *there exists an efficiently computable function* $\mathsf{MaxNoiseLevel} : \mathbb{N}_0 \to \mathbb{N}_0$ *such that for every message dimension* α *and vector* $\mathbf{r}$ *of suitable length*

$$\|\mathbf{r}\| < \delta \to \mathsf{NoiseLevel}(\mathsf{sk}, \mathbf{B}_\alpha \mathbf{r} + g_\alpha(\mathbf{0})) \leq \mathsf{MaxNoiseLevel}(\delta)$$

holds with overwhelming probability over the choice of the secret key sk. *We will later require in Sect. 6 that* $\mathsf{MaxNoiseLevel}$ *is small for small inputs.*

Definition 5.2. *We say that a lattice-based SPE scheme is* $\mathcal{F}$-homomorphic for a family *of functions* $\mathcal{F}$ *if for all* $f \in \mathcal{F}$, $f : \mathcal{M}^{\alpha_{\mathsf{in}}} \to \mathcal{M}^{\alpha_{\mathsf{out}}}$ *when there exists a maximum noise level* $\nu_{\mathsf{in}} \geq \nu_{\mathsf{init}}$ *and a deterministic polynomial time algorithm* Eval_f *that takes* pk *and a ciphertext* $\mathsf{ct} = \mathbf{B}_{\alpha_{\mathsf{in}}} \mathbf{r} + g_{\alpha_{\mathsf{in}}}(\mathsf{msg})$ *that encrypts a* α_{in}-*dimensional message* msg *under* pk *with noise level* $\mathsf{NoiseLevel}(\mathsf{sk}, \mathsf{ct}) \leq \nu_{\mathsf{in}}$. *It outputs a new ciphertext* $\mathbf{B}_{\alpha_{\mathsf{out}}} \mathbf{r}_f + g_{\alpha_{\mathsf{out}}}(f(\mathsf{msg}))$ *with* $\mathbf{r}_f \in R_f$, *where* R_f *is a structure-preserving set with noise growth* δ_{R_f} *such that every ciphertext* $\mathsf{ct} = \mathbf{B}_{\alpha_{\mathsf{out}}} \mathbf{r} + g_{\alpha_{\mathsf{out}}}(\mathsf{msg})$ *with* $\mathbf{r} \in B_{\delta_{R_f}}(R_f)$ *and* $\mathsf{msg} \in \mathcal{M}^{\alpha_{\mathsf{out}}}$ *has* $\mathsf{NoiseLevel}(\mathsf{sk}, \mathsf{ct}) \leq \nu_{\max}$.

We further require that there is a deterministic polynomial time algorithm $\mathsf{Eval}_f^{\mathsf{rand}}$ that takes the public key pk and $\mathbf{r} \in R$ and outputs $\mathbf{r}_f$ such that

$$\mathbf{B}_{\alpha_{\mathsf{out}}} \mathbf{r}_f + g(f(\mathsf{msg})) = \mathsf{Eval}_f(\mathsf{pk}, \mathbf{B}_{\alpha_{\mathsf{in}}} \mathbf{r} + g(\mathsf{msg}))$$

Note that every SPE scheme is linearly homomorphic. In more detail, given two ciphertexts $\mathsf{ct}_1 = \mathbf{B}_\alpha \mathbf{r}_1 + g_\alpha(\mathsf{msg}_1)$ and $\mathsf{ct}_2 = \mathbf{B}_\alpha \mathbf{r}_2 + g_\alpha(\mathsf{msg}_2)$ with $\mathsf{NoiseLevel}(\mathsf{sk}, \mathsf{ct}_1), \mathsf{NoiseLevel}(\mathsf{sk}, \mathsf{ct}_2) \leq \nu_{\max}/2$, the ciphertext $\mathsf{Eval}_+(\mathsf{pk}, \mathsf{ct}_1, \mathsf{ct}_2) := \mathsf{ct}_1 + \mathsf{ct}_2$ is a valid ciphertext for $\mathsf{msg}_1 + \mathsf{msg}_2$ with randomness $\mathsf{Eval}_f^{\mathsf{rand}}(\mathsf{pk}, \mathbf{r}_1, \mathbf{r}_2) := \mathbf{r}_1 + \mathbf{r}_2$, since g_α is additively homomorphic. This can be extended to linear functions (with sufficiently small coefficients) of multiple ciphertexts.

5.1 SPE Instantiation

Examples of SPE schemes are Regev's encryption scheme, the Dual Regev encryption scheme and the GSW encryption scheme. We only prove that Regev's scheme is a SPE scheme here and present the proof for the remaining two schemes in the full version.

As Regev's original scheme [45] allows to encrypt a single bit only, we recall its variant, put forward by Peikert et al. [44], that allows to encrypt messages from the message space $\mathcal{M} = \mathbb{Z}_p$ for p s.t. $\frac{q}{p}$ is sufficiently large. We assume that $q = p^k$, for a sufficiently large $k \in \mathbb{N}$, and we denote $c := \frac{q}{p} = p^{k-1}$. In addition to the LWE modulus q, the scheme is parametrized by a dimension n, number of samples $m \geq n \log q$ and an error distribution $\chi = \mathcal{D}_{\mathbb{Z},\sigma}$. We recall this scheme with $\alpha = 1$. To encrypt a higher-dimensional message $(\mathsf{msg}_1, \ldots, \mathsf{msg}_\alpha)^\top \in \mathcal{M}^\alpha$, we encrypt each component individually, i.e. generate $\mathsf{ct}_i = \mathsf{Enc}(\mathsf{pk}, \mathsf{msg}_i)$ for $i \in \{1, \ldots, \alpha\}$ and chain the ciphertext together, i.e. $\mathsf{ct}^\top = (\mathsf{ct}_1^\top, \ldots, \mathsf{ct}_\alpha^\top)$.

KeyGen(1^λ): Sample $\mathbf{A} \leftarrow_R \mathbb{Z}_q^{n \times m}$, $\mathbf{s} \leftarrow_R \mathbb{Z}_q^n$ and $\mathbf{e} \leftarrow \chi^m$. Output the secret key sk $:= \mathbf{s}$ and the public key pk $= (\mathbf{A}, \mathbf{s}^\top \mathbf{A} + \mathbf{e}^\top) \in \mathbb{Z}_q^{n \times m} \times \mathbb{Z}_q^{1 \times m}$.

Enc(pk, msg): Parse pk as $(\mathbf{A}, \mathbf{x})$. Sample $\mathbf{z} \leftarrow_R \{-1, 0, 1\}^m$ and compute $\mathbf{c}_0 := \mathbf{A}\mathbf{z} \in \mathbb{Z}_q^n$ and $c_1 := \mathbf{x}\mathbf{z} + c \cdot \mathsf{msg} \in \mathbb{Z}_q$. Then output the ciphertext ct $:= (\mathbf{c}_0, c_1) \in \mathbb{Z}_q^n \times \mathbb{Z}_q$.

Dec(sk, ct): Parse ct as $(\mathbf{c}_0, c_1)$ and set $\mathbf{s} :=$ sk. Compute $d := c_1 - \mathbf{s}^\top \mathbf{c}_0 \in \mathbb{Z}_q$ and output $x \in \mathbb{Z}_p$, such that $d - c \cdot x \mod q$ is closest to 0.

Lemma 5.3. *Regev's encryption scheme is a lattice-based SPE scheme.*

Proof. For a public key pk $= (\mathbf{A}, \mathbf{x}) \in \mathbb{Z}_q^{n \times m} \times \mathbb{Z}_q^{1 \times m}$, dimension α, and a message msg $\in \mathcal{M}^\alpha$, let us define the matrix $\mathbf{B} \in \mathbb{Z}_q^{\alpha(n+1) \times \alpha m}$ and the function $g_\alpha : \mathcal{M}^\alpha \to \mathbb{Z}_q^{\alpha(n+1)}$ as follows :

$$
\mathbf{B} := \mathbf{I}_\alpha \otimes \begin{pmatrix} \mathbf{A} \\ \mathbf{x} \end{pmatrix} = \begin{pmatrix} \mathbf{A} \\ \mathbf{x} \\ & \ddots \\ & & \mathbf{A} \\ & & \mathbf{x} \end{pmatrix}, \quad g_\alpha \begin{pmatrix} \mathsf{msg}_1 \\ \vdots \\ \mathsf{msg}_\alpha \end{pmatrix} := \begin{pmatrix} \mathbf{0} \\ c \cdot \mathsf{msg}_1 \\ \vdots \\ \mathbf{0} \\ c \cdot \mathsf{msg}_\alpha \end{pmatrix}.
$$

Let $\mathcal{R}$ be the uniform distribution over $R := \{-1, 0, 1\}^{\alpha m}$. Clearly, $\mathbf{r} \leftarrow \mathcal{R}$ lies in R with probability 1. We need to show that R is a structure-preserving set. $R = \{-1, 0, 1\}^{\alpha m} \subseteq \mathbb{Z}_q^{\alpha m}$ is a $\sqrt{\alpha m}$-bounded set which, by Remark 3.7, implies that R is structure-preserving with noise growth $\delta_R := 8m + 1$.

As a next set, we need to argue that g is invertible and additively homomorphic. Let $g_\alpha^{-1} : \mathrm{Img}(g_\alpha) \to \mathbb{Z}_p$ be a function that on input $\mathbf{y} = (\mathbf{0}^\top, y_1, \ldots, \mathbf{0}^\top, y_\alpha)^\top \in \mathrm{Img}(g_\alpha)$, outputs $\mathbf{x} \in \mathbb{Z}_p^\alpha$, such that $y_i - cx_i \mod q = 0$ for all $i \in \{1, \ldots, \alpha\}$. It is easy to see that g^{-1} is the inverse of g. It is easy to see that g_α is additively homorphic, because it is composed of additively homomorphic functions.

Furthermore, we need to prove that the encryption algorithm is equivalent to sampling $\mathbf{r} \leftarrow \mathcal{R}_\alpha$ and computing $\mathbf{B}_\alpha \mathbf{r} + g_\alpha(\mathsf{msg})$. For msg $\in \mathbb{Z}_p^\alpha$ and $\mathbf{r} \leftarrow \mathcal{R}_\alpha$, we have, for $\mathbf{r}^\top = (\mathbf{r}_1^\top, \ldots, \mathbf{r}_\alpha^\top)$ with $\mathbf{r}_i \in \mathbb{Z}_q^m$,

$$
\mathbf{B}_\alpha \mathbf{r} + g_\alpha(\mathsf{msg}) = \begin{pmatrix} \mathbf{A}\mathbf{r}_1 \\ \mathbf{x}\mathbf{r}_1 + c \cdot \mathsf{msg}_1 \\ \vdots \\ \mathbf{A}\mathbf{r}_\alpha \\ \mathbf{x}\mathbf{r}_\alpha + c \cdot \mathsf{msg}_\alpha \end{pmatrix} = \begin{pmatrix} \mathsf{ct}_1 \\ \vdots \\ \mathsf{ct}_\alpha \end{pmatrix} = \mathsf{ct}
$$

which shows that this procedure indeed gives us a well-distributed ciphertext.

Finally, we need to prove that the existence of the NoiseLevel(sk, ct) algorithm. Let us define NoiseLevel(sk, ct) as follows: Parse ct as $(\mathsf{ct}_1, \ldots, \mathsf{ct}_\alpha)$ and each ct_i as $(\mathbf{c}_{i,0}, c_{i,1})$ and set $\mathbf{s} :=$ sk. Compute $d_i := c_{1,i} - \mathbf{s}^\top \mathbf{c}_{i,0} \in \mathbb{Z}_q$ and $\nu_i := |d_i - c \cdot \mathrm{Dec}(\mathsf{sk}, \mathsf{ct}_i)|$. Output $\max_{1 \leq i \leq \alpha} \nu_i$.

To show that this definition satisfies the desired properties, it suffices to prove it for dimension $\alpha = 1$, because all these properties only talk about upper bounds[12] of the noise level and the noise level of a ciphertext for $\alpha > 1$ is simply the maximum of the noise levels of the ciphertexts for each component of the message.

To show boundedness, define $\mathsf{MaxNoiseLevel}(\delta) := 2\sigma\sqrt{m}\delta$. Then, for $\|\mathbf{z}\| < \delta$, we have

$$\mathsf{NoiseLevel}(\mathsf{sk}, \mathsf{ct} = (\mathbf{Az}, ((\mathbf{s}^\top \mathbf{A} + \mathbf{e}^\top)\mathbf{z} + c\mathsf{msg})) = |\mathbf{e}^\top \mathbf{z}| \overset{(1)}{\le} \|\mathbf{e}\|\|\mathbf{z}\| \overset{(2)}{\le} 2\sigma\sqrt{m}\delta,$$

where inequality (1) follows from the Cauchy-Schwartz inequality and inequality (2) follows from the Gaussian tail bound (Lemma 2.1).

The maximal initial noise level is $\nu_{\mathsf{init}} := 2\sigma m$: An honestly generated ciphertext has randomness $\mathbf{z} \in \{0, 1\}^m$ and thus $\|\mathbf{z}\| \le \sqrt{m}$. Plugging this in the $\mathsf{MaxNoiseLevel}$ function yields the desired bound.

The maximum noise level is $\nu_{\mathsf{max}} := \lceil c/2 \rceil$, because then for a ciphertext $\mathsf{ct} = (c_0, c_1)$ for msg, the value $d := c_1 - \mathbf{s}^\top \mathbf{c_0}$ deviates at most by $\lceil c/2 \rceil$ from $c\mathsf{msg}$ and so the Dec algorithm will round to msg.

The Symmetry property of $\mathsf{NoiseLevel}$ follows immediately from the definition and the subadditivity property follows immediately from the triangle inequality. $\square$

6 Σ-Protocol Constructions

In this section, we describe a generalization of the sigma protocols in [36] that, at a high level, allow to prove that the value encrypted in an SPE scheme belongs to a structure-preserving set S (up to an additional inherent error that comes from the noises of the encryption scheme and the structure-preserving set S).

More formally, we construct a trapdoor gap Σ-protocol that can prove for a lattice-based SPE scheme $\Pi = (\mathsf{KeyGen}, \mathsf{Enc}, \mathsf{Dec}^\star)$ that a ciphertext encrypts a message $\mathsf{msg} \in S$ where S is a structure-preserving set with noise growth δ and $B_\delta(S) \subseteq \mathcal{M}^\alpha$. Let:

- α be the dimension of the message in the ciphertext
- $\mathbf{B}_\alpha \in \mathbb{Z}_q^{d(\alpha) \times r(\alpha)}$ be the matrix defined by the public key for messages of length α,
- g_α be the message encoding function for messages of length α,
- R_α be the randomness space with maximum noise level ν_R (i.e. for all $\mathbf{r} \in R_\alpha$ and messages msg we have $\mathsf{NoiseLevel}(\mathsf{sk}, \mathbf{B}_\alpha \mathbf{r} + g_\alpha(\mathsf{msg})) \le \nu_R$). We also require R_α to be structure-preserving with noise growth δ_R using the distribution $\mathcal{D}_R$, smudging set D'_R, no-abort function $\mathsf{success}_R$ and no-abort constant α_R.
- S be a structure-preserving set with noise growth δ using distribution $\mathcal{D}$, smudging set D'_S with $S, D'_S, S + D'_S \subseteq \mathcal{M}$, no-abort function success and no-abort constant α,
- $\mathbf{r}' \in R_\alpha$ be an arbitrary fixed element of R_α,
- and $\mathsf{msg}' \in S$ be an arbitrary fixed element of S.

---

[12] Note that the symmetry property is equivalent to $\mathsf{NoiseLevel}(\mathsf{sk}, \mathsf{ct}) \le \mathsf{NoiseLevel}(\mathsf{sk}, -\mathsf{ct})$.

- And assume that the parameters of the SPE scheme are selected such that

$$\nu_{\mathsf{init}} + \nu_R + \mathsf{MaxNoiseLevel}(\delta_R) < \nu_{\mathsf{max}}/2. \tag{1}$$

We construct a gap Σ-protocol for:

$$\mathcal{L}_{\mathsf{zk}} = \{\mathbf{B}_\alpha \mathbf{r} + g_\alpha(\mathsf{msg}) \mid \mathbf{r} \in R_\alpha, \mathsf{msg} \in S\}$$
$$\mathcal{L}_{\mathsf{sound}} = \{\mathsf{ct} \mid \mathsf{NoiseLevel}(\mathsf{sk}, \mathsf{ct}) \le 2 \cdot \nu_{\mathsf{init}} + \nu_R + 2 \cdot \mathsf{MaxNoiseLevel}(\delta_R),$$
$$\mathsf{Dec}(\mathsf{sk}, \mathsf{ct}) \in B_\delta(S)\}$$

From the SPE definition we get $\mathcal{L}_{\mathsf{zk}} \subseteq \mathcal{L}_{\mathsf{sound}}$.

The language is described by the modulus q, the matrix $\mathbf{B}_\alpha$ and the structure-preserving sets R_α and S and the message encoding function g_α. The Setup algorithm will output as crs simply the language description, i.e. $\mathsf{crs} = (q, \mathbf{B}_\alpha, R_\alpha, S, g_\alpha)$. The membership testing trapdoor for the language is the secret key sk of the structure-preserving encryption scheme and TrapSetup will simply output as trapdoor this secret key, i.e. $\tau_\Sigma = \mathsf{sk}$. The definition of the prover and verifier can be found in Fig. 2.

Prover $\mathsf{P} = (\mathsf{P}_1, \mathsf{P}_2)$	Verifier V
Input: $(\mathsf{crs} = (q, \mathbf{B}_\alpha, R_\alpha, S, g_\alpha),$ $x = \mathbf{Br} + g(\mathsf{msg}), w = \mathbf{r})$	Input: $(\mathsf{crs} = (q, \mathbf{B}_\alpha, R_\alpha, S, g_\alpha), x)$

$\mathbf{r}_R \leftarrow \mathcal{D}_R$; $m_S \leftarrow \mathcal{D}_S$
$\mathsf{a} := \mathbf{B}_\alpha \mathbf{r}_R + g_\alpha(m_S)$

$\xrightarrow{\ \mathsf{a}\ }$

$\xleftarrow{\ \mathsf{Chal}\ }$ $\mathsf{Chal} \leftarrow_{\mathsf{R}} \{0, 1\}$

if Chal $= 0$ **then**
$\quad \mathsf{z} := \mathbf{r}_R$
else
$\quad \mathsf{z} := \mathbf{r} + \mathbf{r}_R$
$\theta_1 := \mathsf{success}_R(\mathbf{r}, \mathsf{Chal} \cdot \mathbf{r}' + (1 - \mathsf{Chal}) \cdot \mathbf{r}, \mathbf{r}_R)$
Abort with probability $1 - \theta_1$
$\theta_2 := \mathsf{success}_S(\mathsf{msg}, \mathsf{Chal} \cdot \mathsf{msg}' + (1 - \mathsf{Chal}) \cdot \mathsf{msg}, m_S)$
Abort with probability $1 - \theta_2$

$\xrightarrow{\ \mathsf{z}\ }$

if Chal $= 0$ **then**
$\quad$ Output: $\mathsf{z} \in D'_R \wedge g_\alpha^{-1}(\mathsf{a} - \mathbf{Bz}) \in D'_S$
else
$\quad$ Output: $\mathsf{z} \in R_\alpha + D'_R \wedge g_\alpha^{-1}(\mathsf{a} + x - \mathbf{Bz}) \in S + D'_S$

Fig. 2. The interaction between Prover and Verifier in our Σ-protocol.

Theorem 6.1. *The above construction is a trapdoor gap Σ-protocol for* $(\mathcal{L}_{\mathsf{zk}}, \mathcal{L}_{\mathsf{sound}})$.

Proof. **Completeness:** Suppose that $r_R \in D'_R$ and $m_S \in D'_S$. Both of these events happens with overwhelming probability by the second part of the structure-preserving set definition. Given this, it is easy to verify that the protocol accepts for both $\mathsf{Chal} = 0$ and $\mathsf{Chal} = 1$ when $x \in \mathcal{L}_{\mathsf{zk}}$.

Special Soundness: Suppose that for a statement x and a first flow message a there exist responses z_0 and z_1 that an honest verifier accepts for challenge $\mathsf{Chal} = 0$ resp. $\mathsf{Chal} = 1$. Then

$$z_0 \in D'_R \tag{2}$$

$$z_1 \in D'_R + R_\alpha \tag{3}$$

$$g_\alpha^{-1}(\mathsf{a} - \mathbf{B}_\alpha z_0) \in D'_S \tag{4}$$

$$g_\alpha^{-1}(x + \mathsf{a} - \mathbf{B}_\alpha z_1) \in D'_S + S \tag{5}$$

holds. By subtracting Eq. (4) from Eq. (5) and using the additive homomorphism of g_α, we get

$$g_\alpha^{-1}(x + \mathsf{a} - \mathbf{B}_\alpha z_1 - (\mathsf{a} - \mathbf{B}_\alpha z_0)) = g_\alpha^{-1}(x - \mathbf{B}_\alpha(z_1 - z_0)) \in S + D'_S - D'_S \subseteq B_\delta(S),$$

where the last relation follows using Lemma 3.9. Since we also have $z_1 - z_0 \in R_\alpha + D'_R - D'_R \subseteq B_{\delta_R}(R_\alpha)$ (again using Lemma 3.9) this proves $x \in \{\mathbf{B}_\alpha r + g_\alpha(\mathsf{msg}) \mid r \in B_{\delta_R}(R_\alpha), \mathsf{msg} \in B_\delta(S)\} \subseteq \{\mathsf{ct} \mid \mathsf{NoiseLevel}(\mathsf{sk}, \mathsf{ct}) \leq \nu_R + \mathsf{MaxNoiseLevel}(\delta_R), \mathsf{Dec}(\mathsf{sk}, \mathsf{ct}) \in B_\delta(S)\} \subseteq \mathcal{L}_{\mathsf{sound}}$. For the first subset relationship we use that we can write $r = r' + y$ with $r' \in R_\alpha$ and $\|y\| \leq \delta_R$ since $r \in B_{\delta_R}(R_\alpha)$. The statement then follows from using $\mathsf{NoiseLevel}(\mathsf{sk}, \mathbf{B}_\alpha r' + g_\alpha(\mathsf{msg})) \leq \nu_R$, $\mathsf{NoiseLevel}(\mathsf{sk}, \mathbf{B}_\alpha y) \leq \mathsf{MaxNoiseLevel}(\delta_R)$ (boundedness property of the NoiseLevel function) and combining this with the subadditivity property of the NoiseLevel function, which we can use due to Eq. (1).

Special Zero-Knowledge: We show that there exists a zero-knowledge simulator, that outputs statistically close transcripts and has statistically close aborting behavior as the real protocol. The simulator ZKSim works as follows on input $(\mathsf{crs} = (q, \mathbf{B}_\alpha, R_\alpha, S, g_\alpha), x \in \mathcal{L}_{\mathsf{zk}}, \mathsf{Chal}^\star \in \{0, 1\})$:

1. Sample $r_R^\star \leftarrow \mathcal{D}_R$; $m_S^\star \leftarrow \mathcal{D}$.
2. Compute $\mathsf{a}^\star := \mathbf{B}_\alpha r_R^\star + \mathsf{Chal}^\star(\mathbf{B}_\alpha r' + g_\alpha(\mathsf{msg}') - x) + g_\alpha(m_S^\star)$.
3. Compute $z^\star := r_R^\star + \mathsf{Chal}^\star \cdot r'$.
4. Abort with probability $1 - \alpha_R$.
5. Abort with probability $1 - \alpha$.
6. Output $(\mathsf{a}^\star, z^\star)$.

For $x \in \mathcal{L}_{\mathsf{zk}}$, we have $x = \mathbf{B}_\alpha r + g_\alpha(\mathsf{msg})$ for $r \in R_\alpha$ and $\mathsf{msg} \in S$.

First, we will focus on the case $\mathsf{Chal}^\star = 0$. In the real protocol, the randomness r_R of the first flow a is sampled from $\mathcal{D}_R$ and the protocol continues with probability $\theta_1 := \mathsf{success}_R(r, r, r_R)$. The zero-knowledge simulator samples the first flow randomness from the same distribution, but continues with probability α_R. We use now that R_α is a structure-preserving set. By plugging in r and r (in the role of s and s') in the first part of the structure-preserving set definition, we get that the distribution of the first flow randomness in the real and the simulated protocol is statistically close.

Similarly, the distribution of the message part of the first flow is $\mathcal{D}$ both in the real protocol and the simulated one, but the real protocol continues with probability $\theta_2 := \mathsf{success}(\mathsf{msg}, \mathsf{msg}, m_S)$ while the simulated one continues with probability α. By using that S is a structure-preserving and plugging in msg and msg (in the role of s and s') in the first part of the definition, it follows that the distribution of the first flow message in real and the simulated protocol is statistically close.

Next, we will discuss the remaining case $\mathsf{Chal}^\star = 1$. In the real protocol, the randomness part $\mathbf{r}_R$ of the first flow a is sampled again from $\mathcal{D}_R$ and the protocol continues with probability $\theta_1 := \mathsf{success}_R(\mathbf{r}, \mathbf{r}', \mathbf{r}_R)$. The simulated protocol samples $\mathbf{r}_R^\star \leftarrow \mathcal{D}_R$ and uses $\mathbf{r}_R^\star + \mathbf{r}' - \mathbf{r}$ as randomness and continues with probability α_R. We use again that R_α is a structure-preserving set, but plug in $\mathbf{r}$ and $\mathbf{r}'$ in the first part of the structure-preserving set definition. This gives us that outputting $\mathbf{r} + \mathbf{r}_R$ with probability $\mathsf{success}_R(\mathbf{r}, \mathbf{r}', \mathbf{r}_R)$ is statistically close to outputting $\mathbf{r}_R^\star + \mathbf{r}'$ with probability α_R.

The message part of the first flow is m_S, sampled from $\mathcal{D}$ in the real protocol and the protocol aborts with probability $\mathsf{success}(\mathsf{msg}, \mathsf{msg}', m_S)$. The simulator samples $m_S^\star \leftarrow \mathcal{D}$ and uses $\mathsf{msg}' - \mathsf{msg} + m_S^\star$ as message part of the first flow. Furthermore, the simulator aborts with probability α. Using that S is a structure-preserving set and plugging in msg and msg' in the first part of the definition, we get that these two distributions are also statistically close.

Putting this together, we see that the simulated first flow is statistically close to an honest first flow. And the third flow outputted by ZKSim is always the correct third flow with respect to the first flow and challenge, so ZKSim is a correct simulator. Furthermore, the zero knowledge simulator only aborts with a constant probability, so the real protocol also aborts only with constant probability.

Correctness of BadChallenge: We show that the following BadChallenge algorithm outputs for any $x \notin \mathcal{L}_{\mathsf{sound}}$ a bad challenge. The BadChallenge algorithm proceeds on input $(\tau_\Sigma = \mathsf{sk}, \mathsf{crs}, x, \mathsf{a})$ as follows:

1. If $\mathsf{NoiseLevel}(\mathsf{sk}, \mathsf{a}) > \nu_{\mathsf{init}} + \mathsf{MaxNoiseLevel}(\delta_R) \vee \mathsf{Dec}(\mathsf{sk}, \mathsf{a}) \notin D_S'$, output $\mathsf{Chal} = 1$ (indicating that the prover cannot finish the protocol for $\mathsf{Chal} = 0$).
2. Otherwise, if $\mathsf{NoiseLevel}(\mathsf{sk}, x + \mathsf{a}) > \nu_{\mathsf{init}} + \nu_R + \mathsf{MaxNoiseLevel}(\delta_R) \vee \mathsf{Dec}(\mathsf{sk}, x + \mathsf{a}) \notin S + D_S'$, output $\mathsf{Chal} = 0$.
3. Otherwise, output $\bot$.

First, assume that $\mathsf{NoiseLevel}(\mathsf{sk}, \mathsf{a}) > \nu_{\mathsf{init}} + \mathsf{MaxNoiseLevel}(\delta_R)$ or $\mathsf{Dec}(\mathsf{a}) \notin D_S'$ holds. Then a can not be written as $\mathsf{a} = \mathbf{B}_\alpha \mathbf{r}_R + g_\alpha(m_S)$ with $\mathbf{r}_R \in D_R', m_S \in D_S'$ because then it would have both of the above properties. In this scenario there is no third flow that would make the Verifier accept for $\mathsf{Chal} = 0$, so the BadChallenge correctly returns 0.

Second, assume that $\mathsf{NoiseLevel}(\mathsf{sk}, x + \mathsf{a}) > \nu_{\mathsf{init}} + \nu_R + \mathsf{MaxNoiseLevel}(\delta_R)$ or $\mathsf{Dec}(x + \mathsf{a}) \notin S + D_S'$ holds. Then $x + \mathsf{a}$ can not be written as $x + \mathsf{a} = \mathbf{B}_\alpha \mathbf{r} + g_\alpha(\mathsf{msg})$ with $\mathbf{r} \in R_\alpha + D_R', \mathsf{msg} \in S + D_S'$ because then it would have both of the above properties. In this scenario there is no third flow that would make the Verifier accept for $\mathsf{Chal} = 1$, so the $\mathsf{BadChallenge}$ correctly returns 1 (if the first case does not apply as well).

Finally, assume that neither of the two cases above applies. Then

$$
\begin{aligned}
\mathsf{NoiseLevel}(\mathsf{sk}, x) &= \mathsf{NoiseLevel}(\mathsf{sk}, x + \mathsf{a} - \mathsf{a}) \\
&\leq \mathsf{NoiseLevel}(\mathsf{sk}, x + \mathsf{a}) + \mathsf{NoiseLevel}(\mathsf{sk}, -\mathsf{a}) \\
&= \mathsf{NoiseLevel}(\mathsf{sk}, x + \mathsf{a}) + \mathsf{NoiseLevel}(\mathsf{sk}, \mathsf{a}) \\
&\leq 2 \cdot \nu_{\mathsf{init}} + \nu_R + 2 \cdot \mathsf{MaxNoiseLevel}(\delta_R).
\end{aligned}
$$

The inequality follows from subadditivity of the $\mathsf{NoiseLevel}$-function which we can use due to Eq. (1). This guarantees that

$$
\mathsf{Dec}(\mathsf{sk}, x) = \mathsf{Dec}(\mathsf{sk}, x + \mathsf{a}) - \mathsf{Dec}(\mathsf{sk}, \mathsf{a}) \in S + D'_S - D'_S \subseteq B_\delta(S)
$$

which shows that $x \in \mathcal{L}_{\mathsf{sound}}$, in contradiction to our initial assumption. □

7 Lattice-Based Structure-Preserving NIZK Arguments

Definition 7.1 (SPNIZK). *Let S be a structure-preserving set with noise growth δ and SPE be a structure-preserving public key encryption scheme with message space $\mathcal{M}^\alpha$ and randomness distribution $\mathcal{R}_\alpha$, where $\mathbf{r} \leftarrow_{\mathrm{R}} \mathcal{R}$ lies with overwhelming probability in a structure-preserving set $R_\alpha \subseteq \mathbb{Z}_q^r$ with noise growth δ_R. A NIZK argument system $(\mathsf{Gen}_{\mathsf{par}}, \mathsf{Gen}_{\mathcal{L}}, \mathsf{P}, \mathsf{V})$ is a structure-preserving NIZK (SPNIZK) argument with respect to S and SPE if for any $(\mathsf{pk}, \cdot) \leftarrow \mathsf{SPE.Setup}(1^\lambda)$, encryption randomness $\mathbf{r} \leftarrow_{\mathrm{R}} \mathcal{R}$ and $m \in S$, SPNIZK supports the following functionality:*

- *$\mathsf{ProveMembershipS}_S(\mathsf{crs}, \mathsf{pk}, m, \mathsf{ct}, \mathbf{r})$ outputs a proof π that ct encrypts a message m which belongs to the structure-preserving set S.*
- *$\mathsf{VerifyMembershipS}_S(\mathsf{crs}, \mathsf{pk}, \mathsf{ct}, \pi)$ verifies that ct indeed encrypts a message m which belongs to the structure-preserving set S.*

As in Definition 2.10, the SPNIZK must satisfy completeness, computational soundness, and zero-knowledge. Moreover, we require our SPNIZK argument system to satisfy unbounded simulation soundness [22,48]. We refer the reader to the full version for the definition of these properties.

Due to lack of space, we defer to the full version an instantiation of Definition 7.1 with unbounded simulation soundness and multi-theorem zero-knowledge. Our instantiation is obtained by compiling the sigma protocol from Sect. 6 into an SPNIZK argument using the Fiat-Shamir transformation. As mentioned in Sect. 1, we implement the used hash function with a correlation-intractable hash function in this.

8 Verifiably Encrypted Signatures (VES)

Using a verifiable encrypted signature (VES), a signer can encrypt a signature under the public key of a trusted-third party (the *adjudicator*) and then generate a proof that the ciphertext encrypts a valid signature for a known message.

The main application of VES is online contract signing, in which two parties Alice and Bob agree on a contract by using the help of a trusted third party called an adjudicator. Alice and Bob start the protocol by producing a VES Ω_{Alice}, Ω_{Bob} on the agreed contract m, using the public key apk of the adjudicator. Upon receipt of the VES Ω_{Alice}, Ω_{Bob}, both Alice and Bob reveal the unencrypted versions $\sigma_{\text{Alice}}, \sigma_{\text{Bob}}$ of their signatures, agreeing to the contract. If any one of the parties, for example Bob, refuses to release his signature σ_{Bob}, Alice can contact the adjudicator and ask them to extract σ_{Bob} from Ω_{Bob}. This prevents Bob from not completing the protocol and using σ_{Alice} to negotiate a better contract elsewhere.

We recall the formal definition of VES in the full version. We discuss it here only informally. A VES is a tuple of PPT algorithms $(\text{Kg}, \text{AdjKg}, \text{Sig}, \text{Vf}, \text{Create}, \text{VesVf})$, where Kg, Sig and Vf are defined similarly to a digital signature scheme. AdjKg generates a key pair (apk, ask) for the adjudicator, Create computes a VES on a given message, and VesVf allows to verify that a given VES is a encryption of a valid signature on a given message. In addition to completeness, VES is required to satisfy four security properties: unforgeability, abuse freeness, extractability and opacity.

Unforgeability guarantees that no PPT adversary given the public key and oracle access Create and Adj, is able to compute a VES Ω for a message m that they have never queried to its oracles. Abuse freeness requires that no malicious, PPT adjudicator with access to a Create oracle is able to output a valid VES for a message that they have never queried. Extractability requires that no malicious signer which can create their own vk and is granted oracle access to Adj is able to efficiently output a valid VES Ω, from which the Adj algorithm is unable to extract a valid signature. Opacity requires that no PPT adversary, given public keys vk and apk and oracle access to Create and Adj, can return a valid signature σ^* for some message m^*, provided it has not queried Adj on m^*.

8.1 The VES Construction

We are now ready to show how to use our notions of structure-preserving signatures, encryptions and NIZK arguments to obtain verifiably encrypted signatures. Our construction is given in Fig. 3 and informally discussed below.

The starting point of our construction is any structure-preserving SPS (see Definition 4.1), over a modulus q. Recall that signatures are tuples $\sigma = (\text{core}, \text{tag})$, which consist of a vector core $\in \mathbb{Z}_q^\gamma$ and a public string tag $\in \{0,1\}^\varsigma$. To compute a VES Ω, we encrypt the core part of the signature core and obtain a ciphertext ct^1. The public tag is not encrypted, and is revealed together with ct^1 as part of Ω.

If we stop at this point, the verifier has no way of checking if core is valid, as it is only given in its encrypted form. Therefore, we now want to convince the verifier that the ciphertexts encrypt a vector core that is part of a valid signature. To this end, we first compute efficiently the structure-preserving set and function (S, f) that correspond to signature verification in the sense of Definition 4.1. Note that in our notation, f is a function that takes γ inputs and outputs a vector in $\mathbb{Z}_q^\tau$. We then compute ciphertexts ct^2 that correspond to homomorphic evaluation using function f over ct^1. Then, we use our SPNIZK argument to compute a proof π that ct^2 actually encrypts a vector that belongs to the structure-preserving set S. The resulting VES is hence $\Omega = (\text{ct}^1, \pi, \text{tag})$.

Table 1. The table indicates which of the SPE schemes can be combined with which SPS scheme to obtain VES.

	Our ISIS-based signature scheme	Rückert's scheme	Boyen's scheme
Regev	✓	✓	✗
Dual Regev	✓	✓	✗
GSW	✓	✓	✓

We can combine an SPE scheme with an SPS scheme if the SPE scheme is $\mathcal{F}$-homomorphic where $\mathcal{F}$ is the set of all functions f that can appear in the signature verification procedure in the sense of Definition 4.1. Table 1 summarizes which SPE scheme can be combined with which SPS scheme.

Verification is now straightforward. Namely, we recompute (S, f) using vk, m and the public tag, and check that the SPNIZK proof π is indeed valid. Finally, adjudication is performed by simply decrypting ciphertexts ct^1 and revealing the vector core.

We refer the reader to the full version for the security proof and for a discussion on parameters. For the rest of this section, we discuss the efficiency considerations of our VES scheme.

8.2 Efficiency Considerations

Let λ be the security parameter. Then SPE has dimension $n' = \lambda$ and modulus $q' = \mathrm{poly}(\lambda)$. The CI-Hash of [43] is implemented using GSW encryption. The decryption algorithm of SPE must be expressible as an NC_1 circuit of depth $\mathcal{O}(\log \lambda)$—which is the case with the schemes analysed in this paper. Such an NC_1 circuit can be translated to a branching program of size $\mathcal{O}(\mathrm{poly}(\lambda))$, and the GSW parameters are $q = \mathrm{poly}(\lambda) = q'\mathrm{poly}(\lambda)$ and $n = \lambda^{c-o(1)}$, where c is a constant that depends on the SPE decryption circuit. The output of the CI hash function consists of m bits, where $m = n\lceil \log(q) \rceil$. In addition, the compiler for obtaining an unbounded simulation-sound NIZK also contains the ciphertexts of a generalised lossy encryption scheme—and the entire construction requires a $\theta(\lambda)$ number of parallel repetitions.

While this machinery might sound daunting relative to pairing-based NIZK systems, the NIZK presented here remains the most efficient lattice-based construction which is secure in the standard model (for proving membership to structure-preserving sets). There are several reasons for this:

1. The CI-Hash requires homomorphic encryption, but no bootstrapping is required since SPE decryption circuits have low depth $c_{\mathsf{Dec}} \cdot \kappa_{\mathsf{SPE}}$, where κ_{SPE} is the size of SPE ciphertexts and c_{Dec} is a small constant $c_{\mathsf{Dec}} \leq 44$ (for example using the results of [9]).
2. It avoids expensive Karp reductions, which would be necessary if one used general purpose NIZKs such as the one of [43].

The standard model NIZK incurs a significant overhead when compared to the usage of lattice NIZKs in the ROM, which is why the proposed NIZK is only semi-efficient.

Generic Construction of a Verifiable Encrypted Signature Scheme VES based on any Structure-Preserving Signature SPS

VES.Kg(1^λ):
  Return (vk, sk) $\leftarrow_R$ SPS.KeyGen(1^λ).

VES.Sig(sk, m):
  Return $\sigma \leftarrow_R$ SPS.Sign(sk, m).

VES.Ver(vk, m, σ):
  Return (SPS.Ver(vk, m, σ) $\stackrel{?}{=} 1$).

VES.AdjKg(1^λ):
  Return (apk, ask) $\leftarrow_R$ SPE.KeyGen(1^λ).

VES.Create(sk, apk, m):
  $\sigma = $ (core, tag) $\leftarrow_R$ SPS.Sig(sk, m) $\in \mathbb{Z}_q^\gamma \times \{0,1\}^\varsigma$
  $\mathbf{r}^1 \leftarrow_R \mathcal{R}_\gamma$
  $\mathsf{ct}^1 \leftarrow$ SPE.Enc(apk, core; $\mathbf{r}^1$)
  $(S, f) \leftarrow$ ComputeSPSetsAndFunctions(vk, m, tag)
  val $\leftarrow f(\mathsf{core}) \in \mathbb{Z}_q^\tau$
  $\mathsf{ct}^2 \leftarrow$ Eval$_f$(apk, ct^1)
  $\mathbf{r}^2 \leftarrow$ Eval$_f^{\mathsf{rand}}$(apk, $\mathbf{r}^1$)
  $\pi \leftarrow_R$ SPNIZK.ProveMembershipS$_S$(crs, apk, val, ct^2, $\mathbf{r}^2$)
  Return $\Omega \leftarrow (\mathsf{ct}^1, \pi, \mathsf{tag})$

VES.VesVf(apk, vk, Ω, m):
  Parse Ω as $(\mathsf{ct}^1, \pi, \mathsf{tag})$
  $(S, f) \leftarrow$ ComputeSPSetsAndFunctions(vk, m, tag)
  $\mathsf{ct}^2 \leftarrow$ Eval$_f$(apk, ct^1)
  If SPNIZK.VerifyMembershipS$_S$(crs, apk, ct^2, π) $= 0$, then return 0
    Else, return 1

VES.Adj(ask, apk, vk, Ω, m):
  Parse Ω as $(\mathsf{ct}^1, \pi, \mathsf{tag})$
  $(S, f) \leftarrow$ ComputeSPSetsAndFunctions(vk, m, tag)
  $\mathsf{ct}^2 \leftarrow$ Eval$_f$(apk, ct^1)
  If SPNIZK.VerifyMembershipS$_S$(crs, apk, ct^2, π) $= 0$, then return $\perp$
  $\mathsf{core}_i \leftarrow$ SPE.Dec(ask, ct_i^1)
  Return $\sigma = $ (core, tag)

Fig. 3. A verifiably-encrypted signature (VES) scheme (Kg, AdjKg, Sig, Vf, Create, VesVf). SPS denotes a structure-preserving signature scheme, while SPE is a lattice-based structure-preserving encryption. SPNIZK is a structure-preserving NIZK argument for SPE, allowing to prove that encryptions encode plaintexts that belong to a structure-preserving set S.

For this reason, we do not provide more detailed efficiency comparisions with random-oracle implementations. At the same time, we note that a gap can also be observed between the Groth-Sahai NIZK and Fiat-Shamir compilations of more restricted sigma protocols that only lead to secure NIZKs in the ROM. Nevertheless, such a gap in the group setting appears to be smaller than in the lattice case.

References

1. Abe, M., Chase, M., David, B., Kohlweiss, M., Nishimaki, R., Ohkubo, M.: Constant-size structure-preserving signatures: generic constructions and simple assumptions. In: Wang, X., Sako, K. (eds.) ASIACRYPT 2012. LNCS, vol. 7658, pp. 4–24. Springer, Heidelberg (2012). https://doi.org/10.1007/978-3-642-34961-4_3
2. Abe, M., Fuchsbauer, G., Groth, J., Haralambiev, K., Ohkubo, M.: Structure-preserving signatures and commitments to group elements. In: Rabin, T. (ed.) CRYPTO 2010. LNCS, vol. 6223, pp. 209–236. Springer, Heidelberg (2010). https://doi.org/10.1007/978-3-642-14623-7_12
3. Abe, M., Groth, J., Haralambiev, K., Ohkubo, M.: Optimal structure-preserving signatures in asymmetric bilinear groups. In: Rogaway, P. (ed.) CRYPTO 2011. LNCS, vol. 6841, pp. 649–666. Springer, Heidelberg (2011). https://doi.org/10.1007/978-3-642-22792-9_37
4. Agrawal, S., Boneh, D., Boyen, X.: Efficient lattice (H)IBE in the standard model. In: Gilbert, H. (ed.) EUROCRYPT 2010. LNCS, vol. 6110, pp. 553–572. Springer, Heidelberg (2010). https://doi.org/10.1007/978-3-642-13190-5_28
5. Agrawal, S., Boneh, D., Boyen, X.: Lattice basis delegation in fixed dimension and shorter-ciphertext hierarchical IBE. In: Rabin, T. (ed.) CRYPTO 2010. LNCS, vol. 6223, pp. 98–115. Springer, Heidelberg (2010). https://doi.org/10.1007/978-3-642-14623-7_6
6. Applebaum, B., Cash, D., Peikert, C., Sahai, A.: Fast cryptographic primitives and circular-secure encryption based on hard learning problems. In: Halevi, S. (ed.) CRYPTO 2009. LNCS, vol. 5677, pp. 595–618. Springer, Heidelberg (2009). https://doi.org/10.1007/978-3-642-03356-8_35
7. Asokan, N., Shoup, V., Waidner, M.: Optimistic fair exchange of digital signatures. In: Nyberg, K. (ed.) EUROCRYPT 1998. LNCS, vol. 1403, pp. 591–606. Springer, Heidelberg (1998). https://doi.org/10.1007/BFb0054156
8. Attema, T., Lyubashevsky, V., Seiler, G.: Practical product proofs for lattice commitments. In: Micciancio, D., Ristenpart, T. (eds.) CRYPTO 2020, Part II. LNCS, vol. 12171, pp. 470–499. Springer, Cham (2020). https://doi.org/10.1007/978-3-030-56880-1_17
9. Beame, P.W., Cook, S.A., Hoover, H.J.: Log depth circuits for division and related problems. In: 25th Annual Symposium on Foundations of Computer Science 1984, pp. 1–6 (1984). https://doi.org/10.1109/SFCS.1984.715894
10. Belenkiy, M., Chase, M., Kohlweiss, M., Lysyanskaya, A.: P-signatures and noninteractive anonymous credentials. In: Canetti, R. (ed.) TCC 2008. LNCS, vol. 4948, pp. 356–374. Springer, Heidelberg (2008). https://doi.org/10.1007/978-3-540-78524-8_20
11. Bellare, M., Micciancio, D., Warinschi, B.: Foundations of group signatures: formal definitions, simplified requirements, and a construction based on general assumptions. In: Biham, E. (ed.) EUROCRYPT 2003. LNCS, vol. 2656, pp. 614–629. Springer, Heidelberg (2003). https://doi.org/10.1007/3-540-39200-9_38
12. Blazy, O., Chevalier, C.: Structure-preserving smooth projective hashing. In: Cheon, J.H., Takagi, T. (eds.) ASIACRYPT 2016, Part II. LNCS, vol. 10032, pp. 339–369. Springer, Heidelberg (2016). https://doi.org/10.1007/978-3-662-53890-6_12

13. Boneh, D., Gentry, C., Lynn, B., Shacham, H.: Aggregate and verifiably encrypted signatures from bilinear maps. In: Biham, E. (ed.) EUROCRYPT 2003. LNCS, vol. 2656, pp. 416–432. Springer, Heidelberg (2003). https://doi.org/10.1007/3-540-39200-9_26

14. Boyen, X.: Lattice mixing and vanishing trapdoors: a framework for fully secure short signatures and more. In: Nguyen, P.Q., Pointcheval, D. (eds.) PKC 2010. LNCS, vol. 6056, pp. 499–517. Springer, Heidelberg (2010). https://doi.org/10.1007/978-3-642-13013-7_29

15. Camenisch, J., Haralambiev, K., Kohlweiss, M., Lapon, J., Naessens, V.: Structure preserving CCA secure encryption and applications. In: Lee, D.H., Wang, X. (eds.) ASIACRYPT 2011. LNCS, vol. 7073, pp. 89–106. Springer, Heidelberg (2011). https://doi.org/10.1007/978-3-642-25385-0_5

16. Camenisch, J., Shoup, V.: Practical verifiable encryption and decryption of discrete logarithms. In: Boneh, D. (ed.) CRYPTO 2003. LNCS, vol. 2729, pp. 126–144. Springer, Heidelberg (2003). https://doi.org/10.1007/978-3-540-45146-4_8

17. Canetti, R., et al.: Fiat-Shamir: from practice to theory. In: Charikar, M., Cohen, E. (eds.) 51st ACM STOC, pp. 1082–1090. ACM Press (2019). https://doi.org/10.1145/3313276.3316380

18. Cash, D., Hofheinz, D., Kiltz, E., Peikert, C.: Bonsai trees, or how to delegate a lattice basis. In: Gilbert, H. (ed.) EUROCRYPT 2010. LNCS, vol. 6110, pp. 523–552. Springer, Heidelberg (2010). https://doi.org/10.1007/978-3-642-13190-5_27

19. Cathalo, J., Libert, B., Yung, M.: Group encryption: non-interactive realization in the standard model. In: Matsui, M. (ed.) ASIACRYPT 2009. LNCS, vol. 5912, pp. 179–196. Springer, Heidelberg (2009). https://doi.org/10.1007/978-3-642-10366-7_11

20. Chase, M., Kohlweiss, M.: A new hash-and-sign approach and structure-preserving signatures from DLIN. In: Visconti, I., De Prisco, R. (eds.) SCN 2012. LNCS, vol. 7485, pp. 131–148. Springer, Heidelberg (2012). https://doi.org/10.1007/978-3-642-32928-9_8

21. Cramer, R., Damgård, I., Schoenmakers, B.: Proofs of partial knowledge and simplified design of witness hiding protocols. In: Desmedt, Y.G. (ed.) CRYPTO 1994. LNCS, vol. 839, pp. 174–187. Springer, Heidelberg (1994). https://doi.org/10.1007/3-540-48658-5_19

22. De Santis, A., Di Crescenzo, G., Ostrovsky, R., Persiano, G., Sahai, A.: Robust non-interactive zero knowledge. In: Kilian, J. (ed.) CRYPTO 2001. LNCS, vol. 2139, pp. 566–598. Springer, Heidelberg (2001). https://doi.org/10.1007/3-540-44647-8_33

23. ElGamal, T.: A public key cryptosystem and a signature scheme based on discrete logarithms. In: Blakley, G.R., Chaum, D. (eds.) CRYPTO 1984. LNCS, vol. 196, pp. 10–18. Springer, Heidelberg (1985). https://doi.org/10.1007/3-540-39568-7_2

24. Esgin, M.F., Nguyen, N.K., Seiler, G.: Practical exact proofs from lattices: new techniques to exploit fully-splitting rings. In: Moriai, S., Wang, H. (eds.) ASIACRYPT 2020, Part II. LNCS, vol. 12492, pp. 259–288. Springer, Cham (2020). https://doi.org/10.1007/978-3-030-64834-3_9

25. Faonio, A., Fiore, D., Herranz, J., Ràfols, C.: Structure-preserving and re-randomizable RCCA-secure public key encryption and its applications. In: Galbraith, S.D., Moriai, S. (eds.) ASIACRYPT 2019, Part III. LNCS, vol. 11923, pp. 159–190. Springer, Cham (2019). https://doi.org/10.1007/978-3-030-34618-8_6

26. Feige, U., Lapidot, D., Shamir, A.: Multiple non-interactive zero knowledge proofs based on a single random string (extended abstract). In: 31st FOCS, pp. 308–317. IEEE Computer Society Press (1990). https://doi.org/10.1109/FSCS.1990.89549.

27. Fiat, A., Shamir, A.: How to prove yourself: practical solutions to identification and signature problems. In: Odlyzko, A.M. (ed.) CRYPTO 1986. LNCS, vol. 263, pp. 186–194. Springer, Heidelberg (1987). https://doi.org/10.1007/3-540-47721-7_12

28. Fuchsbauer, G.: Automorphic signatures and applications. Ph.D. thesis. ENS Paris and Universite Paris 7 (2011). https://www.di.ens.fr/fuchsbau/ThesisFuchsbauer.pdf

29. Fuchsbauer, G.: Commuting signatures and verifiable encryption. In: Paterson, K.G. (ed.) EUROCRYPT 2011. LNCS, vol. 6632, pp. 224–245. Springer, Heidelberg (2011). https://doi.org/10.1007/978-3-642-20465-4_14

30. Gentry, C., Peikert, C., Vaikuntanathan, V.: Trapdoors for hard lattices and new cryptographic constructions. In: Ladner, R.E., Dwork, C. (eds.) 40th ACM STOC, pp. 197–206. ACM Press (2008). https://doi.org/10.1145/1374376.1374407.

31. Gentry, C., Sahai, A., Waters, B.: Homomorphic encryption from learning with errors: conceptually-simpler, asymptotically-faster, attribute-based. In: Canetti, R., Garay, J.A. (eds.) CRYPTO 2013, Part I. LNCS, vol. 8042, pp. 75–92. Springer, Heidelberg (2013). https://doi.org/10.1007/978-3-642-40041-4_5

32. Groth, J.: Optimal structure-preserving signatures (invited talk). In: Boyen, X., Chen, X. (eds.) ProvSec 2011. LNCS, vol. 6980, p. 1. Springer, Heidelberg (2011). https://doi.org/10.1007/978-3-642-24316-5_1

33. Groth, J.: Simulation-sound NIZK proofs for a practical language and constant size group signatures. In: Lai, X., Chen, K. (eds.) ASIACRYPT 2006. LNCS, vol. 4284, pp. 444–459. Springer, Heidelberg (2006). https://doi.org/10.1007/11935230_29

34. Groth, J., Sahai, A.: Efficient non-interactive proof systems for bilinear groups. In: Smart, N. (ed.) EUROCRYPT 2008. LNCS, vol. 4965, pp. 415–432. Springer, Heidelberg (2008). https://doi.org/10.1007/978-3-540-78967-3_24

35. Kilian, J., Petrank, E.: Identity escrow. In: Krawczyk, H. (ed.) CRYPTO 1998. LNCS, vol. 1462, pp. 169–185. Springer, Heidelberg (1998). https://doi.org/10.1007/BFb0055727

36. Libert, B., Nguyen, K., Passelègue, A., Titiu, R.: Simulation-sound arguments for LWE and applications to KDM-CCA2 security. In: Moriai, S., Wang, H. (eds.) ASIACRYPT 2020, Part I. LNCS, vol. 12491, pp. 128–158. Springer, Cham (2020). https://doi.org/10.1007/978-3-030-64837-4_5

37. Libert, B., Peters, T., Qian, C.: Structure-preserving chosen-ciphertext security with shorter verifiable ciphertexts. In: Fehr, S. (ed.) PKC 2017, Part I. LNCS, vol. 10174, pp. 247–276. Springer, Heidelberg (2017). https://doi.org/10.1007/978-3-662-54365-8_11

38. Lyubashevsky, V.: Fiat-Shamir with aborts: applications to lattice and factoring-based signatures. In: Matsui, M. (ed.) ASIACRYPT 2009. LNCS, vol. 5912, pp. 598–616. Springer, Heidelberg (2009). https://doi.org/10.1007/978-3-642-10366-7_35

39. Lyubashevsky, V.: Lattice signatures without trapdoors. In: Pointcheval, D., Johansson, T. (eds.) EUROCRYPT 2012. LNCS, vol. 7237, pp. 738–755. Springer, Heidelberg (2012). https://doi.org/10.1007/978-3-642-29011-4_43

40. Lyubashevsky, V., Nguyen, N.K., Seiler, G.: Practical lattice-based zero-knowledge proofs for integer relations. In: Ligatti, J., Ou, X., Katz, J., Vigna, G. (eds.) ACM CCS 2020, pp. 1051–1070. ACM Press (2020). https://doi.org/10.1145/3372297.3417894

41. Lyubashevsky, V., Nguyen, N.K., Seiler, G.: Shorter lattice-based zero-knowledge proofs via one-time commitments. In: Garay, J.A. (ed.) PKC 2021, Part I. LNCS, vol. 12710, pp. 215–241. Springer, Cham (2021). https://doi.org/10.1007/978-3-030-75245-3_9

42. Lyubashevsky, V., Nguyen, N.K., Seiler, G.: SMILE: set membership from ideal lattices with applications to ring signatures and confidential transactions. In: Malkin, T., Peikert, C. (eds.) CRYPTO 2021, Part II. LNCS, vol. 12826, pp. 611–640. Springer, Cham (2021). https://doi.org/10.1007/978-3-030-84245-1_21

43. Peikert, C., Shiehian, S.: Noninteractive zero knowledge for np from (plain) learning with errors. In: Boldyreva, A., Micciancio, D. (eds.) CRYPTO 2019, Part I. LNCS, vol. 11692, pp. 89–114. Springer, Cham (2019). https://doi.org/10.1007/978-3-030-26948-7_4

44. Peikert, C., Vaikuntanathan, V., Waters, B.: A framework for efficient and composable oblivious transfer. In: Wagner, D. (ed.) CRYPTO 2008. LNCS, vol. 5157, pp. 554–571. Springer, Heidelberg (2008). https://doi.org/10.1007/978-3-540-85174-5_31

45. Regev, O.: On lattices, learning with errors, random linear codes, and cryptography. In: Gabow, H.N., Fagin, R. (eds.) 37th ACM STOC, pp. 84–93. ACM Press (2005). https://doi.org/10.1145/1060590.1060603.
46. Rückert, M.: Strongly unforgeable signatures and hierarchical identity-based signatures from lattices without random oracles. In: Sendrier, N. (ed.) PQCrypto 2010. LNCS, vol. 6061, pp. 182–200. Springer, Heidelberg (2010). https://doi.org/10.1007/978-3-642-12929-2_14
47. Rückert, M., Schröder, D.: Security of verifiably encrypted signatures and a construction without random oracles. In: Shacham, H., Waters, B. (eds.) Pairing 2009. LNCS, vol. 5671, pp. 17–34. Springer, Heidelberg (2009). https://doi.org/10.1007/978-3-642-03298-1_2
48. Sahai, A.: Non-malleable non-interactive zero knowledge and adaptive chosen- ciphertext security. In: 40th FOCS, pp. 543–553. IEEE Computer Society Press (1999). https://doi.org/10.1109/SFFCS.1999.814628
49. Schnorr, C.P.: Efficient identification and signatures for smart cards. In: Brassard, G. (ed.) CRYPTO 1989. LNCS, vol. 435, pp. 239–252. Springer, New York (1990). https://doi.org/10.1007/0-387-34805-0_22
50. Zhang, T., Wu, H., Chow, S.S.M.: Structure-preserving certificateless encryption and its application. In: Matsui, M. (ed.) CT-RSA 2019. LNCS, vol. 11405, pp. 1–22. Springer, Cham (2019). https://doi.org/10.1007/978-3-030-12612-4_1

Tagged Chameleon Hash from Lattices and Application to Redactable Blockchain

Yiming Li[1,2] and Shengli Liu[1,2(✉)]

[1] Department of Computer Science and Engineering, Shanghai Jiao Tong University,
Shanghai 200240, China
{lym_sjtu,slliu}@sjtu.edu.cn
[2] State Key Laboratory of Cryptology, P.O. Box 5159, Beijing 100878, China

Abstract. Chameleon hash (CH) is a trapdoor hash function. Generally it is hard to find collisions, but with the help of a trapdoor, finding collisions becomes easy. CH plays an important role in converting a conventional blockchain to a redactable one. However, most of existing CH schemes are too weak to support redactable blockchains. The currently known CH schemes serving for redactable blockchains have the best security of so-called "full collision resistance (f-CR)", but they are built either in the random oracle model or rely on heavy tools like the simulation-sound extractable non-interactive zero-knowledge (SSE-NIZK) proof system. Moreover, up to now there is no CH scheme with post-quantum f-CR security in the standard model. Therefore, no CH can support redactable blockchains in a post-quantum way without relying on random oracles.

In this paper, we introduce a variant of CH, namely tagged chameleon hash (tCH). Tagged chameleon hash takes a tag into hash evaluations and collision finding algorithms. We define two security notions for tCH, restricted collision resistance (r-CR) and full collision resistance (f-CR), and prove the equivalence between r-CR and f-CR when tCH works in the one-time tag mode. We propose a tCH scheme from lattices without using any NIZK proof, and prove that its restricted collision resistance is reduced to the Short Integer Solution (SIS) assumption in the standard model. We also show how to apply tCH to a blockchain in one-time tag mode so that the blockchain can be compiled to a redactable one. Our tCH scheme provides the first post-quantum solution for redactable blockchains, without resorting to random oracles or NIZK proofs. Besides, we also construct a more efficient tCH scheme with r-CR tightly reduced to SIS in the random oracle model, which may be of independent interest.

Keywords: Tagged chameleon hash · Lattice-based cryptography · Redactable blockchain

1 Introduction

The chameleon hash (CH) was first introduced by Krawczyk and Rabin [25] and it can be seen as a trapdoor collision resistant hash function. Informally,

© International Association for Cryptologic Research 2024
Q. Tang and V. Teague (Eds.): PKC 2024, LNCS 14603, pp. 288–320, 2024.
https://doi.org/10.1007/978-3-031-57725-3_10

a CH is associated with a public parameter pp and a trapdoor td. With pp, one can efficiently evaluate the hash value for any given message, and with td, one can efficiently find collisions for any target hash value. The fundamental security requirement of a chameleon hash, namely the collision resistance, assures that any adversary cannot find collisions without the knowledge of td. Since its introduction, chameleon hash has developed different security notions, serving for a wide range of applications. There are mainly four kinds of security notions for CH, as we summarized below.

Weak Collision Resistance. The weak collision resistance (w-CR) for CH is the basic security requirement formalized in [25] and it assures the infeasibility of finding a collision $(h^*, m^*, r^*, m'^*, r'^*)$ s.t. $m^* \neq m'^*$ but $h^* = \mathsf{Hash}(m^*; r^*) = \mathsf{Hash}(m'^*; r'^*)$ without the trapdoor. The w-CR CH is often used to construct chameleon signatures [25] and lift non-adaptively secure signatures to adaptively secure ones [23, 28, 31]. However, most of CH schemes with w-CR suffer from a so-called key-exposure problem, that is, anyone can recover the trapdoor after seeing only one collision with two different messages. A sequence of works [4, 10, 11] have identified this problem and proposed different CHs with key-exposure freeness. However, such CHs are still insufficient for the security requirements asked from more complicated applications.

Enhanced Collision Resistance. The enhanced collision resistance (e-CR) was first proposed by Ateniese et al. [3] as a strengthening of the weak collision resistance. It assures the infeasibility of finding a collision $(h^*, m^*, r^*, m'^*, r'^*)$ if no collision for this specific h^* has ever been revealed to the adversary before. A chameleon hash with e-CR was suggested to construct a redactable blockchain [3, 24, 38], but in fact, e-CR is still not strong enough to deal with attacks on a redactable blockchain system as we will discuss later.

Standard Collision Resistance. The standard collision resistance (s-CR) was introduced by Camenisch et al. [9] and it assures the infeasibility of finding a collision $(h^*, m^*, r^*, m'^*, r'^*)$ if no collision involving the target message m^* has ever been revealed to the adversary before. A CH with s-CR can be used to construct sanitizable signatures [9] and redactable blockchains. However, s-CR is still insufficient for the security requirements asked by a redactable blockchain.

Full Collision Resistance. The full collision resistance (f-CR) was introduced by Derler, Samelin and Slamanig [13] as a combination of e-CR and s-CR[1]. It assures the infeasibility of finding a collision $(h^*, m^*, r^*, m'^*, r'^*)$ if no collision for the target hash-message pair (h^*, m^*) has ever been revealed to the adversary before. To the best of our knowledge, f-CR is the strongest one among all security notions of a chameleon hash, and it is adequate for most of the applications of chameleon hash, especially for redactable blockchain.

Redactable blockchain is an important application of a chameleon hash and it has high requirements for CH. Recall that blockchain was originally designed

---

[1] According to [13], e-CR and s-CR are incomparable, which means that neither e-CR implies s-CR nor s-CR implies e-CR.

to satisfy immutability, i.e., the infeasibility of tampering the messages stored in the blocks. However, rigid immutability might not be friendly for healthy developments of blockchains. For example, once some illegal or malicious information is stored in blocks, it is hardly to be erased any more. In fact, the European General Data Protection Regulation (GDPR) has suggested the "right to be forgotten". Therefore, researches on technical tools for changing or deleting sensitive information stored in blocks draw more attentions in the academic society. This yields the so-called *redactable* blockchain. In a redactable blockchain, immutability becomes flexible in the sense that a trusted regulation party (or multi-parties) can use a trapdoor to redact the chain by rewriting blocks in the chain according to the well-accepted regulation rules. We refer readers to [3] for more discussions about the necessity of a redactable blockchain.

Given the concept of redactable blockchain, how to do the redactions in a secure and controlled way has become a critical problem to be solved. As summarized by [39], there are four mechanisms to achieve redactable blockchains, that is, the consensus-based, chameleon hash-based, mate-transaction-based, and pruning-based. For the consensus-based mechanisms, redactions are performed by on-chain voting, like the hard fork and [14,36]; for the mate-transaction-based mechanisms, redactions are triggered by a special transaction called the mate-transaction, like [16,17,34]; for the pruning-based mechanisms, redactions are made by pruning transactions or blocks when some conditions are satisfied, like [27,35]. Ateniese et al. [3] suggested to construct redactable blockchains with the help of CH, that is, the chameleon hash-based redactable blockchains. In this paper, we focus on this type of redaction mechanism.

Below we briefly describe the suggestion of constructing a redactable blockchain from a chameleon hash in [3] and show the security requirements of CH.

Redactable Blockchain from CH. A conventional blockchain can be converted to a redactable one by replacing one of the hash functions used to construct blocks with a chameleon one [3]. Let $\mathcal{H} = (\mathsf{Setup}, \mathsf{Hash}, \mathsf{Adapt})$ be a chameleon hash, where the setup algorithm is used to generate the public parameter and trapdoor, i.e., $(pp, td) \leftarrow \mathsf{Setup}(1^\kappa)$, the hash algorithm is used to evaluate the hash value for a given message with some randomness, i.e., $h \leftarrow \mathsf{Hash}(m; r)$, and the adaptation algorithm is used to find a collision with td, i.e., $r' \leftarrow \mathsf{Adapt}(td, h, m, r, m')$ s.t. $h = \mathsf{Hash}(m; r) = \mathsf{Hash}(m'; r')$.

For a CH-based redactable blockchain, a trusted regulation party is granted to generate $(pp, td) \leftarrow \mathsf{Setup}(1^\kappa)$ and then publish pp. A miner collects the message m, evaluates $h \leftarrow \mathsf{Hash}(m; r)$, constructs a valid block B containing the triple (h, m, r) as well as other information required, and finally appends it to the blockchain. When an adaptation is required from m to m' in some block B^2, the trusted authority computes $r' \leftarrow \mathsf{Adapt}(td, h, m, r, m')$, replaces (m, r) stored in B with (m', r') while keeping other information unchanged, and finally publishes the redacted block. In this way, we obtain a redactable blockchain.

---

[2] Here, adaptations are only allowed for blocks considered to be settled in the redactable blockchain system.

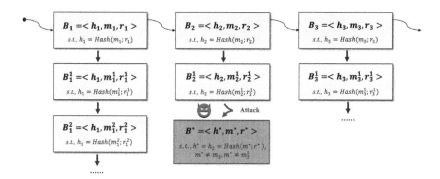

Fig. 1. Possible attack on redactions in a redactable blockchain. The adversary sees all grey blocks and tries to create the red one. The blocks link to a chain in the way that previous hash value h_i constitutes a part of message m_{i+1} in the next block. The down-arrows in dark-blue denote authorized adaptations done by the trusted regulation party and the arrow in red denotes an attack. (Color figure online)

Security Requirements of CH in Redactable Blockchain. In a redactable blockchain, each block B_j records information of (h_j, m_j, r_j) and we denote it by $B_j = \langle h_j, m_j, r_j \rangle$. Adaptations for block B_j result in multiple new adapted blocks $\{B_j^i = \langle h_j, m_j^i, r_j^i \rangle\}_{i \in [n_j]}$ s.t. $h_j = \mathsf{Hash}(m_j; r_j) = \mathsf{Hash}(m_j^i; r_j^i)$ for $i \in [n_j]$. Now we consider the adversary's attack on redactions in a redactable blockchain. The adversary sees all original blocks $B_1, B_2, B_3, \cdots$ and all corresponding adapted blocks $\{B_1^i\}_{i \in [n_1]}, \{B_2^i\}_{i \in [n_2]}, \{B_3^i\}_{i \in [n_3]}, \cdots$, where each $n_j = \mathsf{poly}(\kappa)$ denotes the number of adaptations for block B_j. The aim of an adversary is to redact the chain by adapting some block $B_j = \langle h_j, m_j, r_j \rangle$ to a new one $B^* = \langle h^*, m^*, r^* \rangle$ s.t. $h^* = h_j = \mathsf{Hash}(m_j; r_j) = \mathsf{Hash}(m^*; r^*)$, where m^* is the adapted message satisfying $m^* \notin \{m_j\} \cup \{m_j^i\}_{i \in [n_j]}$, in other words, (h^*, m^*) is fresh w.r.t. B_j and $\{B_j^i\}_{i \in [n_j]}$. Note that we do not exclude the possibility that m^* belongs to $\{m_{j'}\} \cup \{m_{j'}^i\}_{i \in [n_{j'}]}$ with $j \neq j'$. See Fig. 1.

Obviously, to make sure that the adversary succeeds in redacting blocks with negligible probability, it suffices for a chameleon hash to be full collision resistant. In contrast, e-CR and s-CR are not sufficient. Firstly, the adversary can obtain multiple adapted blocks $\{B_j^i = \langle h_j, m_j^i, r_j^i \rangle\}_{i \in [n_j]}$ for the target hash value $h_j = h^*$, so, e-CR is not enough for CH. Secondly, the adversary may obtain some adapted block $B_{j'}^i = \langle h_{j'}, m^*, r_{j'}^i \rangle$ with $j \neq j'$, and hence s-CR is not enough either.

To the best of our knowledge, only a CH with f-CR security is sufficient to the security requirements of a redactable blockchain. However, existing CH schemes with f-CR [12,13] are all generic constructions relying on some heavy building blocks like the simulation-sound extractable non-interactive zero knowledge (SSE-NIZK) proof system [13]. Besides, almost all instantiations of CH with f-CR security are based on pairings or the discrete logarithm (DL) assumption, and hence are not secure against quantum adversaries. The only known post-quantum instantiation is based on the learning parity with noise (LPN) assumption in the random oracle (RO) model [12]. Then a natural question arises:

"*Can we construct a post-quantum chameleon hash function serving for a redactable blockchain in the standard model (especially without relying on a NIZK proof system)?*"

In this paper, we provide a new approach to this problem. We take into considerations some nice properties of a redactable blockchain so that the security requirements for CH can be weakened. That makes possible simpler constructions of CH serving for a secure redactable blockchain. In more details, we have the following three observations for a CH-based redactable blockchain.

- **Observation 1.** Each settled block can be uniquely indexed by a unique identifier τ (like the timestamp, the hash value of its previous block or its position in the chain). Taking τ into account results in blocks of the form $B = \langle \tau, h, m, r \rangle$.
- **Observation 2.** Each block has a chameleon hash value h and identifier τ, and adaptations towards that block keep h and τ unchanged. Together with observation 1, we know that each tag τ is uniquely bound with one block (and hence the chameleon hash value h).
- **Observation 3.** All adaptations towards a specific block are made with fresh messages. In a redactable blockchain, this can be easily accomplished by appending a unique (e.g. increasing) counter value to the adapted message.

Now we additionally take τ as input for chameleon hash evaluations and adaptations, and this results in a new variant of CH, namely the *tagged CH* (tCH). Next we consider the full collision resistance for a tagged CH. The adversary can see many tuples (τ, h, m, r) as well as their adaptations (τ, h, m', r'), where m is the original message and m' is the adapted message s.t. $h = \mathsf{Hash}(\tau, m; r) = \mathsf{Hash}(\tau, m'; r')$. Let $\mathcal{Q}$ record tuples (τ, h, m) and the adapted tuples (τ, h, m'). The adversary wins if it finally comes up with a forgery $(\tau^*, h^*, m^*, r^*, m'^*, r'^*)$ such that

$$h^* = \mathsf{Hash}(\tau^*, m^*; r^*) = \mathsf{Hash}(\tau^*, m'^*; r'^*),\ m^* \neq m'^*,\ (\tau^*, h^*, m^*) \notin \mathcal{Q}. \quad (1)$$

Obviously, the full collision resistance of tCH is sufficient for a redactable blockchain. But actually, the three observations can help to change the security requirements of tCH to a weaker variant. Note that in (1.1), we have

$$(\tau^*, h^*, m^*) \notin \mathcal{Q}$$
$$\Leftrightarrow \left((\tau^*, h^*, m^*) \notin \mathcal{Q} \wedge (\tau^*, \cdot, m'^*) \notin \mathcal{Q} \right) \vee \left((\tau^*, h^*, m^*) \notin \mathcal{Q} \wedge (\tau^*, \cdot, m'^*) \in \mathcal{Q} \right)$$
$$\Leftrightarrow \left((\tau^*, \cdot, m^*) \notin \mathcal{Q} \wedge (\tau^*, \cdot, m'^*) \notin \mathcal{Q} \right) \vee \left((\tau^*, \cdot, m^*) \notin \mathcal{Q} \wedge (\tau^*, h^*, m'^*) \in \mathcal{Q} \right),$$

where $(\tau^*, \cdot, m'^*) \notin \mathcal{Q}$ means that there exists no h such that $(\tau^*, h, m'^*) \in \mathcal{Q}$, while $(\tau^*, \cdot, m'^*) \in \mathcal{Q}$ means that there exists an h such that $(\tau^*, h, m'^*) \in \mathcal{Q}$. Here "$\Leftarrow$" holds obviously, and "$\Rightarrow$" holds due to the observation 2. By observation 2, for any adapted blocks with $(\tau^*, h^*, \cdot, \cdot)$ we know that τ^* is uniquely bound with h^*, so $(\tau^*, h^*, m^*) \notin \mathcal{Q} \Rightarrow (\tau^*, \cdot, m^*) \notin \mathcal{Q}$ and $(\tau^*, \cdot, m'^*) \in \mathcal{Q} \Rightarrow (\tau^*, h^*, m'^*) \in \mathcal{Q}$ (otherwise, τ^* corresponds to both h^* and some $h \neq h^*$ in the blockchain system, which is impossible).

Define a predicate Valid as $\mathsf{Valid}(\tau^*, h^*, m^*, m'^*) = 1$ if $\big((\tau^*, \cdot, m^*) \notin \mathcal{Q} \wedge (\tau^*, \cdot, m'^*) \notin \mathcal{Q}\big) \vee \big((\tau^*, \cdot, m^*) \notin \mathcal{Q} \wedge (\tau^*, h^*, m'^*) \in \mathcal{Q}\big)$. Now (1.1) becomes:

$$h^* = \mathsf{Hash}(\tau^*, m^*; r^*) = \mathsf{Hash}(\tau^*, m'^*; r'^*),\ m^* \neq m'^*,\ \mathsf{Valid}(\tau^*, h^*, m^*, m'^*) = 1.$$

According to observation 2 again, it is reasonable to assume that there do not exist $(\tau, h, \cdot)$ and $(\tau, h'', \cdot)$ with $h \neq h''$ among those tuples and adapted tuples contained in $\mathcal{Q}$. Furthermore, according to observation 3, we can require that all adapted messages w.r.t. a block (and hence a unique τ) are distinct.

Hence for redactable blockchain, we arrive at a security requirement for tCH which is weaker than the full collision resistance. We call such a security requirement *restricted collision resistance* since it has more restrictions on adversaries compared with the full one (see Fig. 3 for their formal definitions). Now the problem can be simplified as follows.

"Can we construct a post-quantum tagged chameleon hash function with restricted collision resistance in the standard model (especially without relying on a NIZK proof system)?"

1.1 Our Contributions

In this paper, we answer the above question in the affirmative and have made the following three contributions.

New Concept of Tagged Chameleon Hash (tCH). We introduce a new primitive, named tagged chameleon hash (tCH), which additionally takes as input a tag τ for hash evaluations and adaptations. We provide two CR security notions for our tCH. One is the full collision resistance (f-CR) and the other is the restricted collision resistance (r-CR). The full collision resistance is defined similar to that of a tag-free CH [13]. That is, it is infeasible to find $(\tau^*, h^*, m^*, r^*, m'^*, r'^*)$ s.t. $m^* \neq m'^*$ and $h^* = \mathsf{Hash}(\tau^*, m^*; r^*) = \mathsf{Hash}(\tau^*, m'^*; r'^*)$ even if the adversary sees many adaptation outputs r' by issuing queries (τ, h, m, r, m') of its choice. The only limitation is that (τ^*, h^*, m^*) does not appear in its queries. Restricted collision resistance is weaker than the full one in the sense that the adversary's behaviors and winning conditions are further restricted. Meanwhile, we also require *statistical indistinguishability* from tCH which asks that the hash value and randomness are statistically close to the adapted ones.

We show that if tCH works in the one-time tag mode, the two CR security notions are equivalent to each other. Here the one-time tag mode requires that each invocation of hash evaluation takes a fresh and distinct tag as input.

Constructions of tCH from Lattices. We provide two constructions of tCH from lattices and prove their r-CR security.

- Our first tCH construction achieves the restricted collision resistance in the standard model. The restricted collision resistance of our tCH is tightly reduced to the SIS assumption and the pseudorandomness of a pseudorandom function (PRF). Given the LWE-based PRFs like [5], our construction yields the first r-CR secure tCH from LWE and SIS in the standard model.
- Our second tCH construction achieves the restricted collision resistance in the random oracle model. It is more efficient than the first one and is tightly reduced to the SIS assumption.

According to the relation between f-CR and r-CR, both of our two tCHs can provide security guarantee as good as f-CR when working in the one-time tag mode. We stress that our tCH schemes are free of NIZK proof systems.

Application of tCH in Redactable Blockchain. Each settled block can be uniquely indexed by a unique identifier τ in the redactable blockchain. So different blocks have distinct identifiers τ. When a tCH is applied to the blockchain, we can take τ as the tag of tCH to compute hash values for messages stored in blocks, and hence each hash value (for a settled block) is computed from a distinct tag. Note that, adaptations are made only for those settled blocks. In this way, the tCH already works in the one-time tag mode for the redactable blockchain. Therefore, our tCH schemes with restricted collision resistance serve for redactable blockchains perfectly.

1.2   Related Works

Chameleon Hash. Krawczyk and Rabin [25] proposed two CH constructions with w-CR based on the claw-free trapdoor permutations [22] and the Pedersen's commitment scheme [32] respectively. Chen, Zhang and Kim [11] proposed the first key-exposure free CH from the computational Diffie-Hellman (CDH) assumption based on the gap Diffie-Hellman (GDH) group. Ateniese and de Medeiros [4] also proposed several key-exposure free CHs from various assumptions like the RSA and the discrete logarithm (DL) assumptions. Later in 2017, Ateniese et al. [3] proposed a generic way to lift a CH from w-CR to e-CR with helps of a CPA secure public key encryption (PKE) and a true-simulation extractable non-interactive zero knowledge (tSE-NIZK) proof system. Ateniese et al. [3] instantiated the generic construction from the decisional Diffie-Hellman assumption in the random oracle model, and from k-linear assumption in the standard model, respectively. Since then, several efficient CH schemes with e-CR have been proposed from various assumptions. Khalili, Dakhilalian and Susilo [24] proposed two CHs with e-CR: one is constructed by combining a weak CH with Groth-Sahai NIZK proof and Cramer-Shoup PKE, and the other is constructed with the ZK-SNARKs. Wu, Ke and Du [38] gave two CH schemes from the lattice-based assumptions in the generic group model (GGM) and in the random oracle model (ROM), respectively. As for s-CR, Camenisch et al. [9] proposed an s-CR secure CH based on the one-more RSA assumption in the random oracle model. Recently, Derler, Samelin and Slamanig [13] suggested f-CR as a more desirable security notion for a CH, and proposed a generic construction of a f-CR secure CH with building blocks a CPA secure PKE and a simulation-sound extractable non-interactive zero knowledge (SSE-NIZK) proof. Derler, Samelin and Slamanig [13] provided instantiations of the generic construction based on the DDH assumption in ROM, and based on the symmetric external Diffie-Hellman (SXDH) assumption in the standard model, respectively. Later, Deler et al. [12] proposed a relatively simpler generic f-CR secure CH construction with building blocks a non-interactive commitment scheme and also an SSE-NIZK. Deler et al. [12] instantiated the generic construction from the DL assumption in ROM, and from the LPN assumption in ROM, respectively.

1.3 Technique Overview

In this subsection, we provide high-level ideas of our tCH constructions from lattices. We propose two tCH schemes: one is in the standard model and the other is in the random oracle model. Both of our tCHs are constructed and proved following a partitioning proof strategy, which has been used in designing advanced signatures and public-key encryptions [6,7,37]. To do the "partitioning", our tCH in the standard model uses a pseudorandom function (PRF) and homomorphic evaluation techniques [6–8,20], while our tCH in the ROM relies on the re-programmable property of random oracles.

Here we provide a brief description of our tCH in the standard model. The public parameter pp consists of a random matrix $\mathbf{A} \in \mathbb{Z}_q^{n \times m}$, a PRF's secret key $\mathbf{k}$ (only used for the security proof), and random matrices $\mathbf{A}_1, \ldots, \mathbf{A}_k, \hat{\mathbf{A}}_1, \ldots, \hat{\mathbf{A}}_h \in \mathbb{Z}_q^{n \times w}$ (which will be used for embedding $\mathbf{k}$ and messages to be hashed in the security proof). The master trapdoor mtd is set as a trapdoor $\mathbf{T_A}$ of $\mathbf{A}$ s.t. $\mathbf{T_A}$ is small and $\mathbf{A} \cdot \mathbf{T_A} = 0^{n \times m}$.

To hash a message $\mathbf{m} = (m_1, \ldots, m_h) \in \{0,1\}^h$ w.r.t. a tag τ, we first sample $\mathbf{y}$ uniformly at random, and then construct a circuit $C[\tau \| \mathbf{m}, \mathbf{y}](\cdot)$ s.t. $C[\tau \| \mathbf{m}, \mathbf{y}](\mathbf{k})$ returns 1 if $\mathsf{PRF}(\mathbf{k}, \tau \| \mathbf{m}) = \mathbf{y}$, and returns 0 otherwise. We further construct a matrix $\mathbf{F} := [\mathbf{A} | \mathbf{A}_{\mathsf{prf}}] \in \mathbb{Z}_q^{n \times (m+w)}$ from pp, $\mathbf{m}$ and τ, where $\mathbf{A}_{\mathsf{prf}}$ is generated through homomorphic evaluations on $C[\tau \| \mathbf{m}, \mathbf{y}](\cdot)$ with $\mathbf{A}_1, \ldots, \mathbf{A}_k$. The hash value is computed as $\mathbf{h} := \mathbf{F} \cdot \mathbf{e}$ with $\mathbf{e} \in \mathbb{Z}^{m+w}$ a short integer vector sampled from the discrete Gaussian distribution; the randomness r includes $\mathbf{e}$, $\mathbf{y}$ and other randomnesses used to generate $\mathbf{F}$.

To find a collision r' towards $(\tau, \mathbf{h}, \mathbf{m}, r, \mathbf{m}')$ so that $(\tau, \mathbf{m}, r)$ and $(\tau, \mathbf{m}', r')$ both hash to $\mathbf{h}$, we first construct $\mathbf{F}' := [\mathbf{A} | \mathbf{A}'_{\mathsf{prf}}]$ from pp, τ and $\mathbf{m}'$. Then we can find a short integer vector $\mathbf{e}'$ s.t. $\mathbf{h} = \mathbf{F}' \cdot \mathbf{e}'$ with the help of $\mathbf{T_A}$ through trapdoor delegation [33] and preimage sampling [19].

Now we are ready to sketch the security proof. In the security experiment of r-CR, adversary $\mathcal{A}$ can make multiple adaptation queries and for each query $(\tau_i, \mathbf{h}_i, \mathbf{m}_i, r_i, \mathbf{m}'_i)$, the challenger responds $\mathcal{A}$ with a randomness r'_i s.t. $\mathbf{h}_i = \mathsf{Hash}(\tau_i, \mathbf{m}_i; r_i) = \mathsf{Hash}(\tau_i, \mathbf{m}'_i; r'_i)$. Then in the challenge phase, $\mathcal{A}$ submits its forgery $(\tau^*, \mathbf{h}^*, \mathbf{m}^*, r^*, \mathbf{m}'^*, r'^*)$ and it wins if $\mathbf{h}^* = \mathsf{Hash}(\tau^*, \mathbf{m}^*; r^*) = \mathsf{Hash}(\tau^*, \mathbf{m}'^*; r'^*)$, $\mathbf{m}'^* \neq \mathbf{m}^*$ and $\mathsf{Valid}(\tau^*, \mathbf{h}^*, \mathbf{m}^*, \mathbf{m}'^*) = 1$. The reduction algorithm

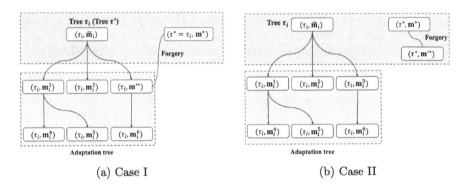

(a) Case I   (b) Case II

Fig. 2. A partition on tag-message pairs: those in blue dashed boxes with $\mathsf{PRF}(\mathbf{k}, \tau\|\mathbf{m}) = \mathbf{y}$, and those in red dashed boxes with $\mathsf{PRF}(\mathbf{k}, \tau\|\mathbf{m}) \neq \mathbf{y}$. Here "$(\tau, \mathbf{m}_i) \to (\tau, \mathbf{m}_j)$" with arrows in dark-blue means an adaptation from tuple $(\tau, \mathbf{m}_i)$ to $(\tau, \mathbf{m}_j)$ made by the challenger during the adaptation query phase; "$(\tau^*, \mathbf{m}^*) \sim (\tau^*, \mathbf{m}'^*)$" means the forgery tuples submitted by the adversary. (Color figure online)

can embed a SIS problem instance into the random matrix $\mathbf{A}$, but then there are two problems to be solved.

- **Problem I:** Since $\mathbf{A}$ is a SIS instance now, the trapdoor $\mathbf{T_A}$ of $\mathbf{A}$ is unknown to the reduction algorithm. In this case, how to find a collision for $(\tau_i, \mathbf{h}_i, \mathbf{m}_i, r_i, \mathbf{m}'_i)$ without $\mathbf{T_A}$ upon the adversary's adaptation queries?
- **Problem II:** How does the reduction algorithm derive a valid solution to the SIS problem when $\mathcal{A}$ successfully finds a valid collision?

For expression simplicity, let's introduce some facts for tCH first. Consider all valid adaptation queries $\{(\tau_i, \mathbf{h}_i, \mathbf{m}_i, r_i, \mathbf{m}'_i)\}$ submitted by $\mathcal{A}$ in the r-CR security experiment, where τ_i is bound to a unique $\mathbf{h}_i$ and $\mathsf{Hash}(\tau_i, \mathbf{m}_i; r_i) = \mathbf{h}_i$. Then all valid adaptation queries constitute a sequence of trees. Let τ_i index the trees. Tree τ_i has a root $(\tau_i, \tilde{\mathbf{m}}_i)$ which is NOT an adapted tuple, and all non-root nodes $\{(\tau_i, \mathbf{m}'_i)\}$ in the tree are adapted from their parent nodes. For $\mathcal{A}$'s forgery $(\tau^*, \mathbf{h}^*, \mathbf{m}^*, r^*, \mathbf{m}'^*, r'^*)$, it requires that $(\tau^*, \mathbf{m}^*)$ never appears in adaptation queries, so $(\tau^*, \mathbf{m}^*)$ does not belong to any adaptation tree. The other tuple $(\tau^*, \mathbf{m}'^*)$ either lies in some adaptation tree τ_i (Case I), or does not belong to any adaptation tree (Case II). See Fig. 2 for a demonstration.

Now let us see how to solve the above two problems. We give an adaptive partition of all tag-and-message tuples $\{(\tau_i, \mathbf{m}_i), (\tau_i, \mathbf{m}'_i)\}$ in adaptation queries and tuples $(\tau^*, \mathbf{m}^*), (\tau^*, \mathbf{m}'^*)$ in the forgery according to whether $\mathsf{PRF}(\mathbf{k}, \tau\|\mathbf{m}) = \mathbf{y}$, where $\mathbf{y}$ is a randomness included in r.

- For the root node $(\tau_i, \tilde{\mathbf{m}}_i)$ in each tree (say tree τ_i), its corresponding $\tilde{\mathbf{y}}_i$ is chosen by the adversary who knows nothing about $\mathsf{PRF}(\mathbf{k}, \tau_i\|\tilde{\mathbf{m}}_i)$. Then $\mathsf{PRF}(\mathbf{k}, \tau_i\|\tilde{\mathbf{m}}_i) \neq \tilde{\mathbf{y}}_i$ due to the pseudorandomness of PRF, and hence $C[\tau_i\|\tilde{\mathbf{m}}_i, \tilde{\mathbf{y}}_i](\mathbf{k}) = 0$.

- For those non-root nodes in tree τ_i, they must be adapted tuples $(\tau_i, \mathbf{m}'_i)$. We choose $\mathbf{y}'_i$ s.t. $\mathbf{y}'_i = \mathsf{PRF}(\mathbf{k}, \tau_i \| \mathbf{m}'_i)$ and hence $C[\tau_i \| \mathbf{m}'_i, \mathbf{y}'_i](\mathbf{k}) = 1$.
- For the node $(\tau^*, \mathbf{m}^*)$ in the forgery, it is submitted by the adversary and does not belong to any adaptation tree, so $\mathsf{PRF}(\mathbf{k}, \tau^* \| \mathbf{m}^*) \neq \mathbf{y}^*$ and hence $C[\tau^* \| \mathbf{m}^*, \mathbf{y}^*](\mathbf{k}) = 0$ due to the pseudorandomness of PRF.
- For the node $(\tau^*, \mathbf{m}'^*)$ in the forgery, we consider two cases.
  - **Case I:** $(\tau^*, \mathbf{m}'^*)$ lies in some tree τ_i. Then it can be a root with $\mathsf{PRF}(\mathbf{k}, \tau^* \| \mathbf{m}'^*) \neq \mathbf{y}'^*$ and $C[\tau^* \| \mathbf{m}'^*, \mathbf{y}'^*](\mathbf{k}) = 0$, or an adapted tuple with $\mathsf{PRF}(\mathbf{k}, \tau^* \| \mathbf{m}'^*) = \mathbf{y}'^*$ and $C[\tau^* \| \mathbf{m}'^*, \mathbf{y}'^*](\mathbf{k}) = 1$.
  - **Case II:** $(\tau^*, \mathbf{m}'^*)$ does not belong to any adaptation tree. Then $\mathsf{PRF}(\mathbf{k}, \tau^* \| \mathbf{m}'^*) \neq \mathbf{y}'^*$ and $C[\tau^* \| \mathbf{m}'^*, \mathbf{y}'^*](\mathbf{k}) = 0$ due to the pseudorandomness of PRF.

In conclusion, for those adapted tuples $\{(\tau_i, \mathbf{m}'_i)\}$, they all satisfy $C[\tau_i \| \mathbf{m}'_i, \mathbf{y}'_i](\mathbf{k}) = 1$, see nodes in blue dashed boxes in Fig. 2. In Case I, we have $(\tau^*, \mathbf{m}^*)$ and $(\tau^* = \tau_i, \tilde{\mathbf{m}}_i)$ s.t. $C[\tau^* \| \mathbf{m}^*, \mathbf{y}^*](\mathbf{k}) = C[\tau^* \| \tilde{\mathbf{m}}_i, \tilde{\mathbf{y}}_i](\mathbf{k}) = 0$. In Case II, we have $(\tau^*, \mathbf{m}^*)$ and $(\tau^*, \mathbf{m}'^*)$ s.t. $C[\tau^* \| \mathbf{m}^*, \mathbf{y}^*](\mathbf{k}) = C[\tau^* \| \mathbf{m}'^*, \mathbf{y}'^*](\mathbf{k}) = 0$. See nodes in red dashed boxes in Fig. 2.

To implement the partitioning strategy, we embed the PRF's key $\mathbf{k}$ in $\mathbf{A}_i$, that is, we generate $\mathbf{A}_i := \mathbf{AR}_i + k_i \mathbf{G}$ instead of $\mathbf{A}_i \xleftarrow{\$} \mathbb{Z}_q^{n \times w}$, where $\mathbf{R}_i \in \mathbb{Z}_q^{m \times w}$ is a randomly chosen short matrix and $\mathbf{G} \in \mathbb{Z}_q^{n \times w}$ is the gadget matrix [28]. This change is statistically indistinguishable to $\mathcal{A}$ due to the leftover hash lemma. For each adaptation query $(\tau_i, \mathbf{h}_i, \mathbf{m}_i, r_i, \mathbf{m}'_i)$, we compute $\mathbf{y}'_i := \mathsf{PRF}(\mathbf{k}, \tau_i \| \mathbf{m}'_i)$ instead of $\mathbf{y}'_i \xleftarrow{\$} \{0,1\}^y$, and these two ways of generating $\mathbf{y}'_i$ are computationally indistinguishable due to the pseudorandomness of PRF. Then $C[\tau_i \| \mathbf{m}'_i, \mathbf{y}'_i](\mathbf{k}) = 1$ and we have $\mathbf{F}'_i := [\mathbf{A} | \mathbf{A}'_{\mathsf{prf},i}] = [\mathbf{A} | \mathbf{AR}'_{\mathsf{prf},i} + C[\tau_i \| \mathbf{m}'_i, \mathbf{y}'_i](\mathbf{k}) \cdot \mathbf{G}] = [\mathbf{A} | \mathbf{AR}'_{\mathsf{prf},i} + \mathbf{G}]$ through homomorphic evaluations. Note that $\mathbf{F}'_i \cdot [-\mathbf{R}'^\top_{\mathsf{prf},i} | \mathbf{I}^\top]^\top = \mathbf{G}$, and hence $\mathbf{R}'_{\mathsf{prf},i}$ is a gadget trapdoor [28] for $\mathbf{F}'_i$. Given the gadget trapdoor $\mathbf{R}'_{\mathsf{prf},i}$, the reduction can also generate a delegated trapdoor for $\mathbf{F}'_i$ efficiently [28], and then find a collision for $(\tau_i, \mathbf{h}_i, \mathbf{m}_i, r_i, \mathbf{m}'_i)$ with the help of the delegated trapdoor. This solves the problem I. Then for the problem II, as we analyzed before, there exist $(\tau^*, \mathbf{m}^*)$ (the forgery tuple) and some $(\tau^*, \bar{\mathbf{m}})$ s.t. $C[\tau^* \| \mathbf{m}^*, \mathbf{y}^*](\mathbf{k}) = 0$ and $C[\tau^* \| \bar{\mathbf{m}}, \bar{\mathbf{y}}](\mathbf{k}) = 0$. Hence we have $\mathbf{F}^* = [\mathbf{A} | \mathbf{A}^*_{\mathsf{prf}}] = [\mathbf{A} | \mathbf{AR}^*_{\mathsf{prf}} + C[\tau^* \| \mathbf{m}^*, \mathbf{y}^*](\mathbf{k}) \cdot \mathbf{G}] = [\mathbf{A} | \mathbf{AR}^*_{\mathsf{prf}} + 0 \cdot \mathbf{G}]$ and $\bar{\mathbf{F}} = [\mathbf{A} | \bar{\mathbf{A}}_{\mathsf{prf}}] = [\mathbf{A} | \mathbf{A}\bar{\mathbf{R}}_{\mathsf{prf}} + C[\tau^* \| \bar{\mathbf{m}}, \bar{\mathbf{y}}](\mathbf{k}) \cdot \mathbf{G}] = [\mathbf{A} | \mathbf{A}\bar{\mathbf{R}}_{\mathsf{prf}} + 0 \cdot \mathbf{G}]$ due to homomorphic evaluations. If $\mathcal{A}$ wins, it holds that $\mathbf{h}^* = [\mathbf{A} | \mathbf{AR}^*_{\mathsf{prf}}] \cdot \mathbf{e}^* = [\mathbf{A} | \mathbf{A}\bar{\mathbf{R}}_{\mathsf{prf}}] \cdot \bar{\mathbf{e}}$, and then $\mathbf{A} \cdot ([\mathbf{I} | \mathbf{R}^*_{\mathsf{prf}}] \mathbf{e}^* - [\mathbf{I} | \bar{\mathbf{R}}_{\mathsf{prf}}] \bar{\mathbf{e}}) = 0^{n \times m}$. The short vector $\mathbf{v} := ([\mathbf{I} | \mathbf{R}^*_{\mathsf{prf}}] \mathbf{e}^* - [\mathbf{I} | \bar{\mathbf{R}}_{\mathsf{prf}}] \bar{\mathbf{e}})$ serves as a solution to the SIS problem.

There is a subtlety in above SIS solution $\mathbf{v}$ in the reduction. For valid solution, we have to make sure that $\mathbf{v} \neq 0^m$. To this end, we construct those $\mathbf{F}$ as $[\mathbf{A} | \mathbf{A}_{\mathsf{prf}} + \sum_i m_i \hat{\mathbf{A}}_i]$ with public parameters $\hat{\mathbf{A}}_i = \mathbf{A}\hat{\mathbf{R}}_i$. This change does not influence the correctness and the partitioning strategy. We refer readers to Subsect. 4.1 for a more detailed description.

We note that, by replacing the homomorphic evaluations related algorithms with random oracles, namely $\mathbf{F} := [\mathbf{A} | \mathsf{H}(\mathbf{A}, \tau \| \mathbf{m})]$ and H is a hash function modeled as a random oracle, we obtain a tCH in the ROM. To see this, the re-programmable properties of random oracles can also play the role of implementing the partition strategy, and hence the above reduction still holds.

2   Preliminaries

Notations. In this paper, column vectors are denoted by bold lower-case letters like $\mathbf{x}$ and the i-th component of $\mathbf{x}$ is denoted by x_i. Specifically, let 0^k denote the k-dimensional zero vector $(0, 0, \ldots, 0)^\top \in \mathbb{Z}_q^k$. For two bit strings $\mathbf{x}_1 \in \{0,1\}^n$ and $\mathbf{x}_2 \in \{0,1\}^m$, let $\mathbf{x}_1 \| \mathbf{x}_2 \in \{0,1\}^{n+m}$ denote the concatenation of $\mathbf{x}_1$ and $\mathbf{x}_2$. Matrices are denoted by bold upper-case letters like $\mathbf{A}$ and the i-th column of $\mathbf{A}$ is denoted by $\mathbf{a}_i$. The transpose of $\mathbf{A}$ is denoted by $\mathbf{A}^\top$. Let $\mathbf{I}_k \in \{0,1\}^{k \times k}$ denote the k-dimensional identity matrix. For matrices $\mathbf{A} \in \mathbb{Z}_q^{n \times m}$ and $\mathbf{B} \in \mathbb{Z}_q^{k \times s}$, denote by $\mathbf{A} \otimes \mathbf{B}$ the Kronecker product of $\mathbf{A}$ and $\mathbf{B}$. For a vector $\mathbf{x} = (x_1, x_2, \ldots, x_n)^\top \in \mathbb{Z}^n$, let $\|\mathbf{x}\| := (\sum_{i \in [n]} x_i^2)^{\frac{1}{2}}$ denote the ℓ_2 norm of $\mathbf{x}$. For a matrix $\mathbf{A} = (\mathbf{a}_1, \mathbf{a}_2, \ldots, \mathbf{a}_m) \in \mathbb{Z}^{n \times m}$ with $\mathbf{a}_i \in \mathbb{Z}^n$, let $\|\mathbf{A}\| := \max_{i \in [m]} \|\mathbf{a}_i\|$ denote the ℓ_2 norm of $\mathbf{A}$, $\tilde{\mathbf{A}}$ denote the Gram-Schmidt orthogonalization of $\mathbf{A}$, and $s_1(\mathbf{A}) := \max_{\|\mathbf{x}\|=1} \|\mathbf{A}\mathbf{x}\|$ the largest singular value of $\mathbf{A}$.

For an integer $n \in \mathbb{N}$, let $[n]$ denote the finite set $\{1, 2, \ldots, n\}$. For a distribution (or a random variable) X, let $x \leftarrow X$ denote the process of sampling x according to X. For a finite set $\mathcal{X}$, let $x \xleftarrow{\$} \mathcal{X}$ denote the process of sampling x from $\mathcal{X}$ uniformly at random.

Let κ denote the security parameter and $\mathsf{poly}(\kappa)$ denote the polynomial function. An algorithm is efficient if it runs in $\mathsf{poly}(\kappa)$-time. Let $\mathsf{negl} : \mathbb{N} \to \mathbb{R}$ denote the negligible function, i.e., for any polynomial $\mathsf{poly}(n)$, there exists an $n' \in \mathbb{N}$ s.t. for all $n > n'$, $\mathsf{negl}(n) < 1/\mathsf{poly}(n)$. For a primitive XX and a security notion YY, we denote by $\mathsf{Exp}_{\mathsf{XX},\mathcal{A}}^{\mathsf{YY}}(\kappa) \Rightarrow b$ a security experiment interacting with adversary $\mathcal{A}$ and returning a bit b. Furthermore, we denote by $\mathsf{Adv}_{\mathsf{XX},\mathcal{A}}^{\mathsf{YY}}(\kappa)$ the advantage of $\mathcal{A}$ in $\mathsf{Exp}_{\mathsf{XX},\mathcal{A}}^{\mathsf{YY}}(\kappa)$, and define $\mathsf{Adv}_{\mathsf{XX}}^{\mathsf{YY}}(\kappa) := \max_{\mathsf{PPT}\mathcal{A}} \mathsf{Adv}_{\mathsf{XX},\mathcal{A}}^{\mathsf{YY}}(\kappa)$.

Let X and Y be two random variables over support $\mathcal{S}$, then the statistical distance between X and Y is defined by $\mathsf{SD}(X, Y) = 1/2 \cdot \sum_{s \in \mathcal{S}} |\Pr[X = s] - \Pr[Y = s]|$. We say that X and Y are statistically indistinguishable and denote it by $X \approx_s Y$ if $\mathsf{SD}(X, Y) \leq \mathsf{negl}(\kappa)$. If $\mathsf{SD}(X, Y) = 0$, then X and Y has the same distribution and we denote it by $X \equiv Y$.

Definition 1 (Average min-entropy [15]). *Let X and Y be two random variables. The min-entropy of X is defined as $\mathsf{H}_\infty(X) := -\log(\max_x \Pr[X = x])$. The average min-entropy of X given Y is defined as $\tilde{\mathsf{H}}_\infty(X \mid Y) := -\log[\mathbb{E}_{y \leftarrow Y} (\max_x \Pr[X = x \mid Y = y])]$.*

Lemma 1 ([15]). *Let X, Y be two random variables and Y has at most 2^ℓ possible values, then $\tilde{\mathsf{H}}_\infty(X|Y) \geq \mathsf{H}_\infty(X) - \ell$.*

2.1   Lattice Background

Let k, n, m, q be positive integers. Given n $(n \leq m)$ linearly independent basis vectors $\mathbf{a}_1, \ldots, \mathbf{a}_n \in \mathbb{R}^m$, construct a matrix $\mathbf{A} \in \mathbb{R}^{n \times m}$ as $\mathbf{A}^\top := (\mathbf{a}_1, \ldots, \mathbf{a}_n)$. Define the m-dimensional lattice generated by $\mathbf{A}$ as $\Lambda(\mathbf{A}) := \{\mathbf{y} \in \mathbb{R}^m \mid \mathbf{y} = \mathbf{A}^\top \mathbf{x}, \mathbf{x} \in \mathbb{Z}^n\}$. We also define the following m-dimensional q-ary integer lattices: $\Lambda_q(\mathbf{A}) := \{\mathbf{y} \in \mathbb{Z}^m \mid \mathbf{y} = \mathbf{A}^\top \mathbf{x} \mod q, \mathbf{x} \in \mathbb{Z}_q^n\}$; $\Lambda_q^\perp(\mathbf{A}) := \{\mathbf{x} \in \mathbb{Z}^m \mid \mathbf{A}\mathbf{x} = \mathbf{0}^n \mod q\}$. For any vector $\mathbf{u} \in \mathbb{Z}_q^n$, define the coset (or shifted lattice) $\Lambda_q^{\mathbf{u}}(\mathbf{A}) := \{\mathbf{x} \in \mathbb{Z}^m \mid \mathbf{A}\mathbf{x} = \mathbf{u} \mod q\}$.

Definition 2 (Discrete Gaussian distribution). *The Gaussian function with parameter s and center $\mathbf{c} \in \mathbb{R}^n$ is defined as $\rho_{s,\mathbf{c}} : \mathbb{R}^n \to \mathbb{R}$, $\rho_{s,\mathbf{c}}(\mathbf{x}) := \exp(-\pi \|\mathbf{x} - \mathbf{c}\|^2/s^2)$. For a countable set $\mathcal{S} \subset \mathbb{R}^n$, the discrete Gaussian distribution $D_{\mathcal{S},s,\mathbf{c}}$ parameterized with s and $\mathbf{c}$ is defined as $D_{\mathcal{S},s,\mathbf{c}}(\mathbf{x}) := \rho_{s,\mathbf{c}}(\mathbf{x})/\sum_{\mathbf{x} \in \mathcal{S}} \rho_{s,\mathbf{c}}(\mathbf{x})$ for $\mathbf{x} \in \mathcal{S}$ and $D_{\mathcal{S},s,\mathbf{c}}(\mathbf{x}) := 0$ for $\mathbf{x} \notin \mathcal{S}$. Usually, s is omitted when $s = 1$ and $\mathbf{c}$ is omitted if $\mathbf{c} = \mathbf{0}$.*

Lemma 2 (Randomness extraction [1,19]). *Let q, n, m be positive integers s.t. q is a prime and $m \geq 3n \log q$. Then:*

- *If $\mathbf{A} \xleftarrow{\$} \mathbb{Z}_q^{n \times m}$, $\mathbf{s} \xleftarrow{\$} \{1, -1\}^m$ and $\mathbf{u} \xleftarrow{\$} \mathbb{Z}_q^n$, then $\mathsf{SD}((\mathbf{A}, \mathbf{As}), (\mathbf{A}, \mathbf{u})) \leq 2^{-n}$.*
- *If $\mathbf{A} \xleftarrow{\$} \mathbb{Z}_q^{n \times m}$, $\mathbf{s} \leftarrow D_{\mathbb{Z}^m, \gamma}$ with Gaussian parameter $\gamma \geq \omega(\sqrt{\log m})$ and $\mathbf{u} \xleftarrow{\$} \mathbb{Z}_q^n$, then $\mathsf{SD}((\mathbf{A}, \mathbf{As}), (\mathbf{A}, \mathbf{u})) \leq 2^{-n}$.*

In this paper, we consider two types of lattice trapdoors. Let q, n, m be integers and define $w := n\lceil \log q \rceil$. Firstly, for a matrix $\mathbf{A} \in \mathbb{Z}_q^{n \times m}$, we consider a non-singular square matrix $\mathbf{T}_\mathbf{A} \in \mathbb{Z}_q^{m \times m}$ of short integer vectors such that $\mathbf{A}\mathbf{T}_\mathbf{A} = \mathbf{0}^{n \times m} \mod q$, and call it a trapdoor of $\mathbf{A}$. We also consider the G-trapdoor (gadget trapdoor) proposed by Micciancio and Peikert [28]. A G-trapdoor for a matrix $\mathbf{A} \in \mathbb{Z}_q^{n \times m}$ is a matrix $\mathbf{R} \in \mathbb{Z}^{(m-w) \times w}$ s.t. $\mathbf{A} \cdot [-\mathbf{R}^\top | \mathbf{I}_w^\top]^\top = \mathbf{G}$, where $\mathbf{G} \in \mathbb{Z}_q^{n \times w}$ is the gadget matrix (see Definition 3). Clearly, if $\mathbf{A} = [\bar{\mathbf{A}} | \bar{\mathbf{A}}\mathbf{R} + \mathbf{G}]$, then $\mathbf{R}$ is the G-trapdoor for $\mathbf{A}$. Below we recall some definitions and lemmas related to afore-mentioned two trapdoors.

Lemma 3 (Trapdoor generation [2]). *Let q, n, m be positive parameters s.t. q is odd, $q \geq 3$ and $m = O(n \log q)$. There exists a PPT algorithm $\mathsf{TrapGen}(1^n, 1^m, q)$ that outputs matrices $\mathbf{A} \in \mathbb{Z}_q^{n \times m}$ and $\mathbf{T}_\mathbf{A} \in \mathbb{Z}^{m \times m}$ s.t. the distribution of $\mathbf{A}$ is statistically close to a uniform rank n matrix in $\mathbb{Z}_q^{n \times m}$ and matrix $\mathbf{T}_\mathbf{A}$ is a trapdoor for $\mathbf{A}$ satisfying $\mathbf{A}\mathbf{T}_\mathbf{A} = \mathbf{0}^{n \times m}$, $\|\tilde{\mathbf{T}}_\mathbf{A}\| \leq O(\sqrt{n \log q})$ and $\|\mathbf{T}_\mathbf{A}\| \leq O(n \log q)$ with all but 2^{-n} probability.*

Lemma 4 (Preimage sampling [19]). *Let q, n, m, γ be positive parameters s.t. $q \geq 2$. Let $\mathbf{A} \in \mathbb{Z}_q^{n \times m}$ be a matrix with a trapdoor $\mathbf{T}_\mathbf{A} \in \mathbb{Z}^{m \times m}$. Let $\gamma \geq \|\tilde{\mathbf{T}}_\mathbf{A}\| \cdot \omega(\sqrt{\log m})$. For any $\mathbf{u} \in \mathbb{Z}_q^n$, there exists a PPT algorithm $\mathsf{SamplePre}(\mathbf{A}, \mathbf{T}_\mathbf{A}, \mathbf{u}, \gamma)$ that outputs $\mathbf{s} \in \mathbb{Z}_q^m$ with distribution statistically close to $D_{\Lambda_q^{\mathbf{u}}(\mathbf{A}), \gamma}$.*

Lemma 5 (Trapdoor delegation [33]**).** *Let* $q, n, m, m', \bar{m}$ *be positive parameters and* $\bar{m} = m + m'$. *Let* $\mathbf{A} \in \mathbb{Z}_q^{n \times m}$ *and* $\mathbf{A}' \in \mathbb{Z}_q^{n \times m'}$ *be matrices and* $\mathbf{T_A} \in \mathbb{Z}^{m \times m}$ *be a trapdoor for* $\mathbf{A}$. *There exists a deterministic polynomial-time algorithm* TrapDel$([\mathbf{A}|\mathbf{A}'], \mathbf{T_A})$ *that outputs a trapdoor* $\mathbf{T_{A|A'}} \in \mathbb{Z}_q^{\bar{m} \times \bar{m}}$ *for the matrix* $[\mathbf{A}|\mathbf{A}']$. *Besides, it holds that* $\|\tilde{\mathbf{T}}_{\mathbf{A|A'}}\| = \|\tilde{\mathbf{T}}_{\mathbf{A}}\|$.

Definition 3 (Gadget matrix [28]**).** *For any integer modulus* q, *the gadget vector over* $\mathbb{Z}_q$ *is defined as* $\mathbf{g}^\top := (1, 2, 4, \ldots, 2^{\lceil \log q \rceil - 1}) \in \mathbb{Z}_q^{1 \times \lceil \log q \rceil}$. *Let* $w := n \lceil \log q \rceil$, *the gadget matrix* $\mathbf{G}$ *with full row rank is defined as:*

$$\mathbf{G} = \mathbf{I}_n \otimes \mathbf{g}^\top = \begin{pmatrix} \mathbf{g}^\top & 0 & 0 & 0 \\ 0 & \mathbf{g}^\top & 0 & 0 \\ \vdots & \vdots & \ddots & \vdots \\ 0 & 0 & 0 & \mathbf{g}^\top \end{pmatrix} \in \mathbb{Z}_q^{n \times w}.$$

Lemma 6 (G-to-Basis [28]**).** *Let* n, m, q *be positive integers and define* $w := n \lceil \log q \rceil$. *Let* $\mathbf{A} \in \mathbb{Z}_q^{n \times m}$ *be a matrix with a G-trapdoor* $\mathbf{R} \in \mathbb{Z}^{(m-w) \times w}$. *There exists a PPT algorithm* GtoBasis$(\mathbf{R})$ *that returns a trapdoor* $\mathbf{T_A} \in \mathbb{Z}^{m \times m}$ *of* $\mathbf{A}$. *Moreover, the trapdoor* $\mathbf{T_A}$ *satisfies* $\|\tilde{\mathbf{T}}_{\mathbf{A}}\| \leq \sqrt{5}(s_1(\mathbf{R}) + 1)$.

We recall in Lemma 7 the results of homomorphic evaluations established by a sequence of works [6–8, 20] . Lemma 8 provides two statistically indistinguishable methods to generate $(\mathbf{A}, \mathbf{h}, \mathbf{e})$ s.t. $\mathbf{h} = \mathbf{A}\mathbf{e}$, where $\mathbf{h}$ follows the uniform distribution and $\mathbf{e}$ is short.

Lemma 7 (Homomorphic evaluation [6–8,20]**).** *Let* q, n, m, ℓ *and* k *be positive integers and define* $w := n \lceil \log q \rceil$. *Let* $\mathbf{G} \in \mathbb{Z}_q^{n \times w}$ *be the gadget matrix. Given a NAND boolean circuit* $C : \{0,1\}^\ell \to \{0,1\}^k$ *with circuit depth* d, *vector* $\mathbf{x} = (x_1, \ldots, x_\ell)^\top \in \{0,1\}^\ell$, *and matrices* $\mathbf{A} \in \mathbb{Z}_q^{n \times m}$, $(\mathbf{A}_i \in \mathbb{Z}_q^{n \times w})_{i \in [\ell]}$ *and* $(\mathbf{R}_i \in \{\pm 1\}^{m \times w})_{i \in [\ell]}$, *there exist two efficient deterministic algorithms.*

- *Algorithm* Eval$_{pub}(C, \mathbf{A}, (\mathbf{A}_i)_{i \in [\ell]})$ *takes as inputs the circuit* C *and matrices* $\mathbf{A}$, $(\mathbf{A}_i)_{i \in [\ell]}$, *and outputs a matrix* $\mathbf{A}_C \in \mathbb{Z}_q^{n \times kw}$.
- *Algorithm* Eval$_{prv}(C, \mathbf{A}, \mathbf{x}, (\mathbf{R}_i)_{i \in [\ell]})$ *takes as inputs the circuit* C, *matrix* $\mathbf{A}$, *vector* $\mathbf{x}$ *and matrices* $(\mathbf{R}_i)_{i \in [\ell]}$, *and outputs a matrix* $\mathbf{R}_C \in \mathbb{Z}^{m \times kw}$.

Homomorphism. *If* $\mathbf{A}_i = \mathbf{A}\mathbf{R}_i + x_i \cdot \mathbf{G} \in \mathbb{Z}_q^{n \times w}$ *for all* $i \in [\ell]$, $\mathbf{A}_C \leftarrow$ Eval$_{pub}(C, \mathbf{A}, (\mathbf{A}_i)_{i \in [\ell]})$ *and* $\mathbf{R}_C \leftarrow$ Eval$_{prv}(C, \mathbf{A}, \mathbf{x}, (\mathbf{R}_i)_{i \in [\ell]})$, *then we have* $\mathbf{A}_C = \mathbf{A}\mathbf{R}_C + C(\mathbf{x}) \otimes \mathbf{G}$, *where* $s_1(\mathbf{R}_C) \leq O(4^d \cdot m^{\frac{3}{2}})$. *Particularly, when* C *is in the circuit class* NC^1, *i.e.,* C *is of depth* $d = c \log \ell$ *for some constant* c, *we have* $s_1(\mathbf{R}_C) \leq O(\ell^{2c} \cdot m^{\frac{3}{2}})$.

Lemma 8 ([19]**).** *Let* n, m, q *be integers and* $\gamma > 2\sqrt{n \log q}$, *then for all but negligible probability over* $(\mathbf{A}, \mathbf{T_A}) \leftarrow$ TrapGen$(1^n, 1^m, q)$, *it holds that*

$$\{(\mathbf{A}, \mathbf{h}, \mathbf{e}) \mid \mathbf{h} \xleftarrow{\$} \mathbb{Z}_q^n, \mathbf{e} \leftarrow \text{SamplePre}(\mathbf{A}, \mathbf{T_A}, \mathbf{h}, \gamma)\} \approx_s$$
$$\{(\mathbf{A}, \mathbf{h}, \mathbf{e}) \mid \mathbf{e} \leftarrow D_{\mathbb{Z}^m, \gamma}, \mathbf{h} := \mathbf{A}\mathbf{e}\}.$$

2.2   Computational Assumption

Definition 4 (The SIS assumption). *Let q, n, m be positive integers and β be a positive real. The (homogeneous) short integer solution (SIS) assumption $\mathsf{SIS}_{n,q,\beta,m}$ states that for any PPT adversary $\mathcal{A}$, its advantage satisfies:*

$$\mathsf{Adv}^{\mathsf{SIS}}_{[n,q,\beta,m],\mathcal{A}}(\kappa) := \Pr\left[\mathcal{A}(\mathbf{A}) \to \mathbf{e} : \mathbf{Ae} = 0^n \wedge \mathbf{e} \neq 0^m \wedge \|\mathbf{e}\| \leq \beta\right] \leq \mathsf{negl}(\kappa),$$

where $\mathbf{A} \xleftarrow{\$} \mathbb{Z}_q^{n \times m}$ and $0^n = (0, \ldots, 0)^\top \in \mathbb{Z}_q^n$.

Lemma 9 (The hardness of SIS [19,29,30]). *For any $m = \mathsf{poly}(n)$ and any sufficiently large $q \geq \beta \cdot \mathsf{poly}(n)$, solving $\mathsf{SIS}_{n,q,\beta,m}$ with non-negligible probability is at least as hard as solving the decisional approximate shortest vector problem GapSVP_γ and the approximate shortest independent vector problem SIVP_γ in the worst case with overwhelming probability, for some $\gamma = \beta \cdot \mathsf{poly}(n)$.*

Since GapSVP and SIVP are well-studied worst-case hard problems on lattices, the reduction from GapSVP and SIVP to SIS in Lemma 9 makes the SIS assumption a widely-accepted post-quantum assumption.

2.3   Pseudorandom Function

Definition 5 (Pseudorandom function family [21]). *A pseudorandom function family $\mathsf{PRF} := \{F : \mathcal{K} \times \mathcal{X} \to \mathcal{Y}\}$ is equipped with two polynomial time algorithms $(\mathsf{Setup}, \mathsf{PRF})$ defined below.*

- $\mathsf{Setup}(1^\kappa)$ *takes as input the security parameter $\kappa \in \mathbb{N}$ and outputs a public parameter pp.*
- $\mathsf{PRF}(pp, k, x)$ *takes as inputs the public parameter pp, key $k \in \mathcal{K}$ and message $x \in \mathcal{X}$, and outputs $y \in \mathcal{Y}$. For simplicity, we will omit pp and just write it as $\mathsf{PRF}(k, x)$ when the context is clear.*

Pseudorandomness. *Let $\mathsf{RF} : \mathcal{X} \to \mathcal{Y}$ be a truly random function. For any PPT adversary $\mathcal{A}$, its advantage satisfies $\mathsf{Adv}^{pse}_{\mathsf{PRF},\mathcal{A}}(\kappa) := \big| \Pr[\mathcal{A}^{\mathcal{O}_{\mathsf{PRF}}(\cdot)}(pp) \Rightarrow 1] - \Pr[\mathcal{A}^{\mathcal{O}_{\mathsf{RF}}(\cdot)}(pp) \Rightarrow 1] \big| \leq \mathsf{negl}(\kappa)$, where $pp \leftarrow \mathsf{Setup}(1^\kappa)$, $k \xleftarrow{\$} \mathcal{K}$, oracle $\mathcal{O}_{\mathsf{PRF}}(x)$ returns $\mathsf{PRF}(pp, k, x)$ and oracle $\mathcal{O}_{\mathsf{RF}}(x)$ returns $\mathsf{RF}(x)$.*

3   Tagged Chameleon Hash

In this section, we propose a new primitive named tagged chameleon hash (tCH), which is characterized by four algorithms, the setup algorithm, hash algorithm, adapt algorithm and check algorithm. The setup algorithm generates public parameters pp along with a trapdoor td. The hash algorithm is a randomized one used for evaluating the hash value of a message m w.r.t. a tag τ and it outputs a randomness r serving as the witness of hashing relation among h, m and τ. For simplicity, we just call h the hash value of (τ, m, r). Given (τ, h, m, r, m'), where

$$\mathsf{Exp}^{fcr}_{\mathsf{tCH},\mathcal{A}}(\kappa):$$
  $(pp, td) \leftarrow \mathsf{Setup}(1^\kappa), \mathcal{Q}_{\mathsf{Adapt}} := \emptyset$
  $(\tau^*, h^*, m^*, r^*, m'^*, r'^*) \leftarrow \mathcal{A}^{\mathcal{O}_{\mathsf{Adapt}}(\cdots\cdots)}(pp)$
  If $\mathsf{Check}(\tau^*, h^*, m^*, r^*) = \mathsf{Check}(\tau^*, h^*, m'^*, r'^*) = 1$
  $\wedge m^* \neq m'^* \wedge (\tau^*, h^*, m^*) \notin \mathcal{Q}_{\mathsf{Adapt}}$, return 1
  Otherwise, return 0

$\mathcal{O}_{\mathsf{Adapt}}(\tau, h, m, r, m')$: // m' is the adapted message
  If $\mathsf{Check}(pp, \tau, h, m, r) = 0$, return $\perp$
  $r' \leftarrow \mathsf{Adapt}(td, \tau, h, m, r, m')$
  If $r' \neq \perp$, $\mathcal{Q}_{\mathsf{Adapt}} := \mathcal{Q}_{\mathsf{Adapt}} \cup \{(\tau, h, m), (\tau, h, m')\}$
  Return r'

$$\mathsf{Exp}^{rcr}_{\mathsf{tCH},\mathcal{A}}(\kappa):$$
  $(pp, td) \leftarrow \mathsf{Setup}(1^\kappa), \mathcal{Q}_{\mathsf{Adapt}} := \emptyset$
  $(\tau^*, h^*, m^*, r^*, m'^*, r'^*) \leftarrow \mathcal{A}^{\mathcal{O}_{\mathsf{Adapt}}(\cdots\cdots)}(pp)$
  If $\mathsf{Check}(\tau^*, h^*, m^*, r^*) = \mathsf{Check}(\tau^*, h^*, m'^*, r'^*) = 1$
  $\wedge m^* \neq m'^* \wedge \mathsf{Valid}(\tau^*, h^*, m^*, m'^*) = 1$, return 1
  Otherwise, return 0

$\mathsf{Valid}(\tau^*, h^*, m^*, m'^*)$:
  If $(\tau^*, \cdot, m^*) \notin \mathcal{Q}_{\mathsf{Adapt}} \wedge (\tau^*, h^*, m'^*) \in \mathcal{Q}_{\mathsf{Adapt}}$, return 1
  If $(\tau^*, \cdot, m^*) \notin \mathcal{Q}_{\mathsf{Adapt}} \wedge (\tau^*, \cdot, m'^*) \notin \mathcal{Q}_{\mathsf{Adapt}}$, return 1
  Otherwise, return 0

$\mathcal{O}_{\mathsf{Adapt}}(\tau, h, m, r, m')$: // m' is the adapted message
  If $\mathsf{Check}(pp, \tau, h, m, r) = 0$, return $\perp$
  If $\exists (\tau, h'', m) \in \mathcal{Q}_{\mathsf{Adapt}} \wedge h'' \neq h$, return $\perp$
  // τ is uniquely bound with hash value h
  If $\exists (\tau, \cdot, m') \in \mathcal{Q}_{\mathsf{Adapt}}$, return $\perp$
  // m' is a fresh message w.r.t τ
  $r' \leftarrow \mathsf{Adapt}(td, \tau, h, m, r, m')$
  If $r' \neq \perp$, $\mathcal{Q}_{\mathsf{Adapt}} := \mathcal{Q}_{\mathsf{Adapt}} \cup \{(\tau, h, m), (\tau, h, m')\}$
  Return r'

Fig. 3. Experiments $\mathsf{Exp}^{fcr}_{\mathsf{tCH},\mathcal{A}}$ and $\mathsf{Exp}^{rcr}_{\mathsf{tCH},\mathcal{A}}$ defining f-CR and r-CR for tCH.

h is the hash value of (τ, m, r) and m' is a new message, the adapt algorithm uses the trapdoor td to find a randomness r' so that (τ, m, r) and (τ, m', r') collide at the same hash value h. The check algorithm is used to decide whether h is the hash value of a tag-message-randomness triple (τ, m, r). For a tCH, we define the statistical indistinguishability, and provide two security notions: one is the full collision resistance (f-CR) defined following [13], and the other is a weaker one named the restricted collision resistance (r-CR). We show that when tCH works in the one-time tag mode, f-CR and r-CR are equivalent.

Definition 6 (Tagged chameleon hash). *Let $\mathcal{M}$ be the message space and $\mathcal{T}$ be the tag space. A tagged chameleon hash (tCH) tCH consists of four polynomial time algorithms* $\mathsf{tCH} = (\mathsf{Setup}, \mathsf{Hash}, \mathsf{Adapt}, \mathsf{Check})$ *defined as follows.*

- $\mathsf{Setup}(1^\kappa)$ *takes as input the security parameter $\kappa \in \mathbb{N}$ and returns a public parameter pp and a trapdoor td.*
- $\mathsf{Hash}(pp, \tau, m)$ *takes as inputs the public parameter pp, a tag $\tau \in \mathcal{T}$ and a message $m \in \mathcal{M}$, and returns a hash value h and a randomness r.*
- $\mathsf{Adapt}(td, \tau, h, m, r, m')$ *takes as inputs the trapdoor td, a tag $\tau \in \mathcal{T}$, a hash value h, a message $m \in \mathcal{M}$, a randomness r and a fresh target message $m' \in \mathcal{M}$, and returns a new randomness r'.*
- $\mathsf{Check}(pp, \tau, h, m, r)$ *takes as inputs the public parameter pp, a tag $\tau \in \mathcal{T}$, a hash value h, a message $m \in \mathcal{M}$ and a randomness r, and returns a decision bit $b \in \{0, 1\}$.*

For expression simplicity, we will sometimes omit the "pp" part in the inputs of Hash and Check, and just write them as $\mathsf{Hash}(\tau, m)$ and $\mathsf{Check}(\tau, h, m, r)$ respectively when the context is clear.

- **Correctness.** *For all tag* $\tau \in \mathcal{T}$ *and messages* $m, m' \in \mathcal{M}$, *for all* $(pp, td) \leftarrow$ Setup(1^κ), $(h, r) \leftarrow$ Hash(pp, τ, m) *and* $r' \leftarrow$ Adapt(td, τ, h, m, r, m'), *we have*

$$\Pr\left[\mathsf{Check}(pp, \tau, h, m, r) = \mathsf{Check}(pp, \tau, h, m', r') = 1\right] \geq 1 - \mathsf{negl}(\kappa).$$

- **Statistical Indistinguishability.** *For all tag* $\tau \in \mathcal{T}$ *and messages* $m, m' \in \mathcal{M}$, *and for* $(pp, td) \leftarrow$ Setup(1^κ), *it holds that*

$$\{(h, r) \mid (h, r) \leftarrow \mathsf{Hash}(pp, \tau, m)\}$$
$$\approx_s \{(h, r) \mid (h, r') \leftarrow \mathsf{Hash}(pp, \tau, m'), r \leftarrow \mathsf{Adapt}(td, \tau, h, m', r', m)\}.$$

- **Full collision resistance (f-CR).** *For any PPT adversary* $\mathcal{A}$, *its advantage satisfies* $\mathsf{Adv}^{fcr}_{\mathsf{tCH}, \mathcal{A}}(\kappa) := \Pr[\mathsf{Exp}^{fcr}_{\mathsf{tCH}, \mathcal{A}}(\kappa) \Rightarrow 1] \leq \mathsf{negl}(\kappa)$, *where the experiment* $\mathsf{Exp}^{fcr}_{\mathsf{tCH}, \mathcal{A}}$ *is described in Fig. 3 (left).*
- **Restricted collision resistance (r-CR).** *For any PPT adversary* $\mathcal{A}$, *its advantage satisfies* $\mathsf{Adv}^{rcr}_{\mathsf{tCH}, \mathcal{A}}(\kappa) := \Pr[\mathsf{Exp}^{rcr}_{\mathsf{tCH}, \mathcal{A}}(\kappa) \Rightarrow 1] \leq \mathsf{negl}(\kappa)$, *where the experiment* $\mathsf{Exp}^{rcr}_{\mathsf{tCH}, \mathcal{A}}$ *is described in Fig. 3 (right).*

One-time tag mode for tCH. In this paper, we consider a special working mode for tagged chameleon hash, where every invocation of hash evaluation takes as input a distinct tag. The special working mode is named *one-time tag mode*. Note that in a tCH-based redactable blockchain, tCH just works in this mode when setting the unique identifier of the block (like the timestamp, hash value of its previous block, or its position in the chain) as its tag.

Definition 7 (One-time tag mode). *A tCH scheme* tCH = (Setup, Hash, Adapt, Check) *works in the one-time tag mode if any* $Q = \mathsf{poly}(\kappa)$ *invocations of* Hash(pp, τ_i, m_i) *with* $i \in [Q]$, *we have* $\tau_k \neq \tau_j$ *for any* $k, j \in [Q]$ *and* $k \neq j$.

Next we show that f-CR is equivalent to r-CR in the one-time tag mode. It is easy to see that f-CR implies r-CR. As for the other direction, we show in Theorem 1 that r-CR implies f-CR when a tCH works in the one-time tag mode.

Theorem 1. *If a tagged chameleon hash* tCH *satisfies the restricted collision resistance, then it also satisfies the full collision resistance when it is used in the one-time tag mode. More precisely, for any PPT adversary* $\mathcal{A}$, *it holds that*

$$\mathsf{Adv}^{fcr}_{\mathsf{tCH}, \mathcal{A}}(\kappa) \leq \mathsf{Adv}^{rcr}_{\mathsf{tCH}}(\kappa).$$

A high-level idea of proof for Theorem 1 has been described in the introduction, and see our full version [26] for the detailed proof.

Remark. Ateniese and de Medeiros considered a chameleon hash with labels (abbrv., labeled CH) in [4]. Our tCH and labeled CH both take an extra tag/label as input, but they have different syntax, security notions and applications.

- Syntax difference. Labeled CH involves an additional algorithm IForge, which generates (m'', r'') given a collision pair (τ, h, m, r, m', r') s.t. $h = \mathsf{Hash}(\tau, m''; r'') = \mathsf{Hash}(\tau, m'; r') = \mathsf{Hash}(\tau, m; r)$. In other words, anyone who obtains a collision for (τ, h) can freely generate a new collision for the same (τ, h). In contrast, our tCH can find a collision only with a secret trapdoor.

- Security difference. Labeled CH requires a weaker security named the key-exposure freeness, which assures the infeasibility of finding a collision $(\tau^*, h^*, m^*, r^*, m'^*, r'^*)$ when no collision for the specific τ^* has been revealed. In contrast, our CR/fCR allows the adversary to see polynomial collisions for the same target tag.
- Application difference. Labeled CH is usually used to construct chameleon signature and it is not secure enough to be used in a redactable blockchain. Note that adversaries in a redactable blockchain may obtain multiple collisions towards one (τ, h). With labeled CH, any one is able to create collisions for (τ, h) using algorithm lForge, and then redactable blockchain becomes insecure. In contrast, our tCH with f-CR security (or r-CR security in one-time tag mode) serves for the security requirement from a redactable blockchain.

4   Lattice-Based Tagged Chameleon Hash

In this section, we propose two tCH constructions satisfying the restricted collision resistance based on the SIS assumption. In Subsect. 4.1, we propose a tCH construction in the standard model. In Subsect. 4.2, we provide another tCH scheme with tight security in the random oracle model.

4.1   tCH in the Standard Model

In this subsection, we propose a tCH construction from lattices, namely tCH, in the standard model.

First we introduce the building blocks and some notations used in our tCH construction. Let n, q, m be positive integers, and define $w := n\lceil \log q \rceil$.

- A pseudorandom function $\mathsf{PRF} = (\mathsf{PRF.Setup}, \mathsf{PRF})$ with key space $\{0,1\}^k$, input space $\{0,1\}^x$ and output space $\{0,1\}^y$.
- Define a circuit $C[\mathbf{x}, \mathbf{y}] : \{0,1\}^k \to \{0,1\}$ w.r.t. PRF as below, where $\mathbf{x} \in \{0,1\}^x$ and $\mathbf{y} \in \{0,1\}^y$ are hard-wired to the circuit.

$$C[\mathbf{x}, \mathbf{y}](\mathbf{k}) = \begin{cases} 1 & \text{if } \mathsf{PRF}(\mathbf{k}, \mathbf{x}) = \mathbf{y}, \\ 0 & \text{otherwise.} \end{cases} \tag{2}$$

Our tCH construction tCH is given in Fig. 4.

Parameter setting. Parameters of our tCH construction include the security parameter κ, the dimension parameters k, x, y, t, h, the SIS parameters n, m, q, β and the Gaussian parameter γ. Define $w := n\lceil \log q \rceil$. The afore-mentioned parameters are required to satisfy the following conditions simultaneously.

- Let $k, x, y, t, h = \mathsf{poly}(\kappa)$ be positive integers and $x = t + h + k$.
- Let n, q, m, β be positive parameters, $n, m, \beta, q = \mathsf{poly}(\kappa)$ and $\beta \cdot \mathsf{poly}(n) \le q$ so that the SIS problem is hard according to Lemma 9.
- Let $\gamma \ge O(\kappa^c) \cdot \omega(\sqrt{m+w})$ with some constant c and $\gamma \ge O(n \log q) \cdot \omega(\sqrt{m+w})$ so that Lemma 4 can be applied.

$(pp, td) \leftarrow \mathsf{Setup}(1^\kappa)$.

1. Generate $pp_{\mathsf{prf}} \leftarrow \mathsf{PRF}.\mathsf{Setup}(1^\kappa)$.
2. Generate $(\mathbf{A}, \mathbf{T_A}) \leftarrow \mathsf{TrapGen}(1^n, 1^m, q)$ with $\mathbf{A} \in \mathbb{Z}_q^{n \times m}$.
3. For $i \in [k]$, sample $\mathbf{A}_i \xleftarrow{\$} \mathbb{Z}_q^{n \times w}$. For $i \in [h]$, sample $\hat{\mathbf{A}}_i \xleftarrow{\$} \mathbb{Z}_q^{n \times w}$.
4. Return $pp := (pp_{\mathsf{prf}}, \mathbf{A}, \{\mathbf{A}_i\}_{i \in [k]}, \{\hat{\mathbf{A}}_i\}_{i \in [h]})$ and $td := (pp, \mathbf{T_A})$.

$(\mathbf{h}, r) \leftarrow \mathsf{Hash}(pp, \tau \in \{0,1\}^t, \mathbf{m} \in \{0,1\}^h)$.

1. Parse $pp = (pp_{\mathsf{prf}}, \mathbf{A}, \{\mathbf{A}_i\}_{i \in [k]}, \{\hat{\mathbf{A}}_i\}_{i \in [h]})$ and $\mathbf{m} = (m_1, \ldots, m_h)$.
2. Sample $\mathbf{z} \xleftarrow{\$} \{0,1\}^\kappa$ and set $\mathbf{x} := \tau \|\mathbf{m}\| \mathbf{z} \in \{0,1\}^x$.
3. Sample $\mathbf{y} \xleftarrow{\$} \{0,1\}^y$ and construct the circuit $C[\mathbf{x}, \mathbf{y}]$ as defined by (2).
4. Compute $\mathbf{C}_{\mathsf{prf}} \leftarrow \mathsf{Eval}_{pub}(C[\mathbf{x}, \mathbf{y}](\cdot), \mathbf{A}, \{\mathbf{A}_i\}_{i \in [k]})$ and $\mathbf{B}_{\mathsf{prf}} := \sum_{i \in [h]} m_i \hat{\mathbf{A}}_i$.
5. Compute $\mathbf{A}_{\mathsf{prf}} := \mathbf{C}_{\mathsf{prf}} + \mathbf{B}_{\mathsf{prf}}$.
6. Sample $\mathbf{e} = (\mathbf{e}_1, \mathbf{e}_2) \leftarrow D_{\mathbb{Z}^{m+w}, \gamma}$ with $\mathbf{e}_1 \in \mathbb{Z}_q^m$ and $\mathbf{e}_2 \in \mathbb{Z}_q^w$ s.t. $\mathbf{e}_2 \neq 0^w$.
7. Return $\mathbf{h} := [\mathbf{A}|\mathbf{A}_{\mathsf{prf}}] \cdot \mathbf{e} \in \mathbb{Z}_q^n$ and $r := (\mathbf{z}, \mathbf{y}, \mathbf{e})$.

$r' \leftarrow \mathsf{Adapt}(td, \tau \in \{0,1\}^t, \mathbf{h}, \mathbf{m} \in \{0,1\}^h, r, \mathbf{m}' \in \{0,1\}^h)$.

1. Parse $td = (pp, \mathbf{T_A})$, $pp = (pp_{\mathsf{prf}}, \mathbf{A}, \{\mathbf{A}_i\}_{i \in [k]}, \{\hat{\mathbf{A}}_i\}_{i \in [h]})$, $\mathbf{m}' = (m_1', \ldots, m_h')$.
2. If $\mathsf{Check}(pp, \tau, \mathbf{h}, \mathbf{m}, r) = 0$, return $\bot$. Otherwise, continue.
3. Sample $\mathbf{z}' \xleftarrow{\$} \{0,1\}^\kappa$ and $\mathbf{y}' \xleftarrow{\$} \{0,1\}^y$.
4. Set $\mathbf{x}' := \tau \|\mathbf{m}'\| \mathbf{z}' \in \{0,1\}^x$ and construct $C[\mathbf{x}', \mathbf{y}']$ as defined by (2).
5. Compute $\mathbf{C}_{\mathsf{prf}}' \leftarrow \mathsf{Eval}_{pub}(C[\mathbf{x}', \mathbf{y}'](\cdot), \mathbf{A}, \{\mathbf{A}_i\}_{i \in [k]})$ and $\mathbf{B}_{\mathsf{prf}}' := \sum_{i \in [h]} m_i' \hat{\mathbf{A}}_i$.
6. Compute $\mathbf{A}_{\mathsf{prf}}' := \mathbf{C}_{\mathsf{prf}}' + \mathbf{B}_{\mathsf{prf}}'$. Delegate $\mathbf{T}_{\mathbf{A}|\mathbf{A}_{\mathsf{prf}}'} \leftarrow \mathsf{TrapDel}([\mathbf{A}|\mathbf{A}_{\mathsf{prf}}'], \mathbf{T_A})$.
7. Sample $\mathbf{e}' = (\mathbf{e}_1', \mathbf{e}_2') \leftarrow \mathsf{SamplePre}([\mathbf{A}|\mathbf{A}_{\mathsf{prf}}'], \mathbf{T}_{\mathbf{A}|\mathbf{A}_{\mathsf{prf}}'}, \mathbf{h}, \gamma)$ with $\mathbf{e}_1' \in \mathbb{Z}_q^m$ and $\mathbf{e}_2' \in \mathbb{Z}_q^w$ s.t. $\mathbf{e}_2' \neq 0^w$.
8. Return $r' := (\mathbf{z}', \mathbf{y}', \mathbf{e}')$.

$0/1 \leftarrow \mathsf{Check}(pp, \tau \in \{0,1\}^t, \mathbf{h}, \mathbf{m} \in \{0,1\}^h, r)$.

1. Parse $pp = (pp_{\mathsf{prf}}, \mathbf{A}, \{\mathbf{A}_i\}_{i \in [k]}, \{\hat{\mathbf{A}}_i\}_{i \in [h]})$, $\mathbf{m} = (m_1, \ldots, m_h)$ and $r = (\mathbf{z}, \mathbf{y}, \mathbf{e})$.
2. Set $\mathbf{x} := \tau \|\mathbf{m}\| \mathbf{z} \in \{0,1\}^x$ and construct $C[\mathbf{x}, \mathbf{y}]$ as defined by (2).
3. Compute $\mathbf{C}_{\mathsf{prf}} \leftarrow \mathsf{Eval}_{pub}(C[\mathbf{x}, \mathbf{y}](\cdot), \mathbf{A}, \{\mathbf{A}_i\}_{i \in [k]})$ and $\mathbf{B}_{\mathsf{prf}} := \sum_{i \in [h]} m_i \hat{\mathbf{A}}_i$.
4. Compute $\mathbf{A}_{\mathsf{prf}} := \mathbf{C}_{\mathsf{prf}} + \mathbf{B}_{\mathsf{prf}}$.
5. Parse $\mathbf{e} = (\mathbf{e}_1, \mathbf{e}_2)$ with $\mathbf{e}_1 \in \mathbb{Z}_q^m$ and $\mathbf{e}_2 \in \mathbb{Z}_q^w$. If $\mathbf{h} = [\mathbf{A}|\mathbf{A}_{\mathsf{prf}}] \cdot \mathbf{e}$, $\|\mathbf{e}\| \leq \gamma \sqrt{m+w}$ and $\mathbf{e}_2 \neq 0^w$, return 1; otherwise, return 0.

Fig. 4. Tagged chameleon hash tCH in the standard model.

- Let $m = O(n \log q)$ and $\gamma \cdot O(\kappa^c) \cdot \sqrt{m+w} \leq \beta$ with some constant c to serve for our security proof.

Theorem 2. *Let* PRF *be a pseudorandom function. Given parameters described above, construction* tCH *in Fig. 4 is a tagged chameleon hash if the* $\mathsf{SIS}_{n,q,\beta,m}$ *assumption holds. Furthermore, restricted collision resistance of* tCH *is tightly reduced to the SIS assumption and the pseudorandomness of* PRF:

$$\Pr[\mathsf{Exp}_{\mathsf{tCH},\mathcal{A}}^{rcr}(\kappa) \Rightarrow 1] \leq \mathsf{Adv}_{[n,q,\beta,m]}^{\mathsf{SIS}}(\kappa) + 2\mathsf{Adv}_{\mathsf{PRF}}^{pse}(\kappa) + 2^{-O(\kappa)}.$$

Correctness of tCH. It follows directly from Lemma 5 (trapdoor delegation), Lemma 4 (preimage sampling) and Lemma 7 (homomorphic evaluation), and we omit the proof of it here.

Proof of statistical indistinguishability for tCH. We prove that, given tag τ and messages $\mathbf{m}, \mathbf{m}'$, the distribution of $(\mathbf{h}, r)$ generated by Hash is statistically close to that generated by Hash-then-Adapt.

First consider the distribution of $(\mathbf{h}, r)$ generated by Hash, i.e., $(\mathbf{h}, r) \leftarrow$ Hash$(\tau, \mathbf{m})$. It follows the distribution D_H defined below:

$$D_\mathsf{H} := \left\{ (\mathbf{h}, r = (\mathbf{z}, \mathbf{y}, \mathbf{e})) \;\middle|\; \begin{array}{l} \mathbf{z} \xleftarrow{\$} \{0,1\}^\kappa, \mathbf{y} \xleftarrow{\$} \{0,1\}^y, \\ \mathbf{e} \leftarrow D_{\mathbb{Z}^{m+w}, \gamma}, \mathbf{h} = [\mathbf{A}|\mathbf{A}_\mathsf{prf}] \cdot \mathbf{e} \end{array} \right\},$$

where $\mathbf{A}_\mathsf{prf}$ is deterministically computed from $\tau, \mathbf{m}$, the public parameters $(\mathbf{A}, \{\mathbf{A}_i\}_{i \in [k]}, \{\hat{\mathbf{A}}_i\}_{i \in [h]})$ and uniformly chosen $\mathbf{z}, \mathbf{y}$ (see algorithm Hash in Fig. 4).

Next consider the distribution of $(\mathbf{h}, r)$ generated by Hash-then-Adapt, i.e., first $(\mathbf{h}, r' = (\mathbf{z}', \mathbf{y}', \mathbf{e}')) \leftarrow$ Hash$(\tau, \mathbf{m}')$ and then $r \leftarrow$ Adapt$(td, \tau, \mathbf{h}, \mathbf{m}', r', \mathbf{m})$. It follows the distribution $D_\mathsf{H\&A}$ defined below:

$$D_\mathsf{H\&A} := \left\{ (\mathbf{h}, r = (\mathbf{z}, \mathbf{y}, \mathbf{e})) \;\middle|\; \begin{array}{l} \mathbf{z}, \mathbf{z}' \xleftarrow{\$} \{0,1\}^\kappa, \; \mathbf{y}, \mathbf{y}' \xleftarrow{\$} \{0,1\}^y, \; \mathbf{e}' \leftarrow D_{\mathbb{Z}^{m+w}, \gamma}, \\ \mathbf{h} := [\mathbf{A}|\mathbf{A}'_\mathsf{prf}] \cdot \mathbf{e}', \mathbf{e} \leftarrow \mathsf{SamplePre}([\mathbf{A}|\mathbf{A}_\mathsf{prf}], \mathbf{T}_{\mathbf{A}|\mathbf{A}_\mathsf{prf}}, \mathbf{h}, \gamma) \end{array} \right\}$$

where $\mathbf{A}_\mathsf{prf}$ is computed in the same way as above, and $\mathbf{A}'_\mathsf{prf}$ is generated similar to $\mathbf{A}_\mathsf{prf}$ but with $\mathbf{m}', \mathbf{z}'$ and $\mathbf{y}'$.

First we show that $\mathbf{h} := [\mathbf{A}|\mathbf{A}'_\mathsf{prf}] \cdot \mathbf{e}'$ in $D_\mathsf{H\&A}$ is statistically close to the uniform distribution over $\mathbb{Z}_q^n$. Note that

$$\mathbf{h} := [\mathbf{A}|\mathbf{A}'_\mathsf{prf}] \cdot \mathbf{e}' = \mathbf{A}\mathbf{e}'_1 + \mathbf{A}'_\mathsf{prf}\mathbf{e}'_2 \approx_s \mathbf{u}' + \mathbf{A}'_\mathsf{prf}\mathbf{e}'_2 \equiv \mathbf{u},$$

where $\mathbf{u}', \mathbf{u} \xleftarrow{\$} \mathbb{Z}_q^n$, $\mathbf{e}' = (\mathbf{e}'_1 \| \mathbf{e}'_2) \leftarrow D_{\mathbb{Z}^{m+w}, \sigma}$, $\mathbf{e}'_1 \in \mathbb{Z}_q^m$ and $\mathbf{e}'_2 \in \mathbb{Z}_q^w$. The "$\approx_s$" follows from Lemma 2 and "$\equiv$" follows from the uniformity of $\mathbf{u}'$. Therefore, it holds that $D_\mathsf{H\&A} \approx_s D'_\mathsf{H\&A}$, where

$$D'_\mathsf{H\&A} := \left\{ (\mathbf{h}, r = (\mathbf{z}, \mathbf{y}, \mathbf{e})) \;\middle|\; \begin{array}{l} \mathbf{z} \xleftarrow{\$} \{0,1\}^\kappa, \mathbf{y} \xleftarrow{\$} \{0,1\}^y, \mathbf{h} \xleftarrow{\$} \mathbb{Z}_q^n, \\ \mathbf{e} \leftarrow \mathsf{SamplePre}([\mathbf{A}|\mathbf{A}_\mathsf{prf}], \mathbf{T}_{\mathbf{A}|\mathbf{A}_\mathsf{prf}}, \mathbf{h}, \gamma) \end{array} \right\}$$

Then according to Lemma 8, $D_\mathsf{H} \approx_s D'_\mathsf{H\&A}$. Therefore, $D_\mathsf{H} \approx_s D_\mathsf{H\&A}$ by triangle inequality and this proves the statistical indistinguishability of tCH. □

Proof of restricted collision resistance for tCH. We define a sequence of hybrid games $\mathsf{G}_0 \sim \mathsf{G}_4$, where G_0 is identical to $\mathsf{Exp}^{rcr}_{\mathsf{tCH}, \mathcal{A}}(\kappa)$ defined in Fig. 3. We show that G_i and G_{i-1} are indistinguishable for all $i \in [4]$, and in G_4, the adversary wins with negligible probability. The differences between adjacent games are highlighted in blue. Assume that $\mathcal{A}$ makes at most Q adaptation queries.

Game G_0. Game G_0 is identical to $\mathsf{Exp}^{rcr}_{\mathsf{tCH}, \mathcal{A}}(\kappa)$ defined by Fig. 3.

0. The challenger $\mathcal{C}$ initializes set $\mathcal{Q}_\mathsf{Adapt} := \emptyset$.
1. During the setup phase, the challenger $\mathcal{C}$ proceeds as follows.
   - Generate $pp_\mathsf{prf} \leftarrow \mathsf{PRF.Setup}(1^\kappa)$.
   - Generate $(\mathbf{A}, \mathbf{T}_\mathbf{A}) \leftarrow \mathsf{TrapGen}(1^n, 1^m, q)$.
   - Sample $\mathbf{A}_i \xleftarrow{\$} \mathbb{Z}_q^{n \times w}$ for $i \in [k]$. Sample $\hat{\mathbf{A}}_i \xleftarrow{\$} \mathbb{Z}_q^{n \times w}$ for $i \in [h]$.

 – $pp := (pp_{\mathsf{prf}}, \mathbf{A}, \{\mathbf{A}_i\}_{i \in [k]}, \{\hat{\mathbf{A}}_i\}_{i \in [h]})$, $td := (pp, \mathbf{T_A})$ and send pp to $\mathcal{A}$.

2. Upon an adaptation query $(\tau, \mathbf{h}, \mathbf{m}, r, \mathbf{m}')$ from $\mathcal{A}$, $\mathcal{C}$ proceeds as follows.

 – If $\exists$ $(\tau, \mathbf{h}'', \mathbf{m}) \in \mathcal{Q}_{\mathsf{Adapt}} \wedge \mathbf{h}'' \neq \mathbf{h}$, or $\exists$ $(\tau, \cdot, \mathbf{m}') \in \mathcal{Q}_{\mathsf{Adapt}}$, or $\mathsf{Check}(\tau,$ $\mathbf{h}, \mathbf{m}, r) = 0$ holds, return $\perp$; otherwise, continue.

 – Sample $\mathbf{z}' \xleftarrow{\$} \{0,1\}^{\kappa}$ and set $\mathbf{x}' := \tau \| \mathbf{m}' \| \mathbf{z}'$.

 – Sample $\mathbf{y}' \xleftarrow{\$} \{0,1\}^y$ and construct $C[\mathbf{x}', \mathbf{y}']$ as defined by (2).

 – $\mathbf{C}'_{\mathsf{prf}} \leftarrow \mathsf{Eval}_{pub}(C[\mathbf{x}', \mathbf{y}'](\cdot), \mathbf{A}, \{\mathbf{A}_i\}_{i \in [k]})$ and $\mathbf{B}'_{\mathsf{prf}} := \sum_{i \in [h]} m'_i \hat{\mathbf{A}}_i$.

 – Set $\mathbf{A}'_{\mathsf{prf}} := \mathbf{C}'_{\mathsf{prf}} + \mathbf{B}'_{\mathsf{prf}}$. Delegate $\mathbf{T}_{\mathbf{A}|\mathbf{A}'_{\mathsf{prf}}} \leftarrow \mathsf{TrapDel}([\mathbf{A}|\mathbf{A}'_{\mathsf{prf}}], \mathbf{T_A})$.

 – $\mathbf{e}' = (\mathbf{e}'_1, \mathbf{e}'_2) \leftarrow \mathsf{SamplePre}([\mathbf{A}|\mathbf{A}'_{\mathsf{prf}}], \mathbf{T}_{\mathbf{A}|\mathbf{A}'_{\mathsf{prf}}}, \mathbf{h}, \gamma)$ s.t. $\mathbf{e}'_2 \neq 0^w$.

 – Send $r' := (\mathbf{z}', \mathbf{y}', \mathbf{e}')$ to $\mathcal{A}$ and $\mathcal{Q}_{\mathsf{Adapt}} := \mathcal{Q}_{\mathsf{Adapt}} \cup \{(\tau, \mathbf{h}, \mathbf{m}), (\tau, \mathbf{h}, \mathbf{m}')\}$.

3. On receiving the forgery $(\tau^*, \mathbf{h}^*, \mathbf{m}^*, r^*, \mathbf{m}'^*, r'^*)$, $\mathcal{C}$ makes the following checks, and returns 0 if any of them fails. Otherwise, $\mathcal{C}$ returns 1.

 – Check if $\mathsf{Check}(\tau^*, \mathbf{h}^*, \mathbf{m}^*, r^*) = \mathsf{Check}(\tau^*, \mathbf{h}^*, \mathbf{m}'^*, r'^*) = 1$.

 – Check if $\mathbf{m}^* \neq \mathbf{m}'^*$ and $\mathsf{Valid}(\tau^*, \mathbf{h}^*, \mathbf{m}^*, \mathbf{m}'^*) = 1$.

By definition, we have $\Pr[\mathsf{G}_0 \Rightarrow 1] = \Pr[\mathsf{Exp}^{rcr}_{\mathsf{tCH}, \mathcal{A}}(\kappa) \Rightarrow 1]$.

Game G_1. Game G_1 is similar to G_0 except for the generation of $\mathbf{y}'$ in the adaptation query phase. In G_0, $\mathbf{y}'$ is sampled uniformly at random for each adaptation query. In G_1, $\mathbf{y}'$ is computed by PRF, i.e., $\mathbf{y}' \leftarrow \mathsf{PRF}(\mathbf{k}, \mathbf{x}')$, where key $\mathbf{k} \xleftarrow{\$} \{0,1\}^k$ is sampled in the setup phase.

$1'$. During the setup phase, the challenger $\mathcal{C}$ proceeds as follows.

 – Generate $pp_{\mathsf{prf}} \leftarrow \mathsf{PRF.Setup}(1^{\kappa})$ and sample $\mathbf{k} \xleftarrow{\$} \{0,1\}^k$.

 – Generate $(\mathbf{A}, \mathbf{T_A}) \leftarrow \mathsf{TrapGen}(1^n, 1^m, q)$.

 – Sample $\mathbf{A}_i \xleftarrow{\$} \mathbb{Z}_q^{n \times w}$ for $i \in [k]$. Sample $\hat{\mathbf{A}}_i \xleftarrow{\$} \mathbb{Z}_q^{n \times w}$ for $i \in [h]$.

 – $pp := (pp_{\mathsf{prf}}, \mathbf{A}, \{\mathbf{A}_i\}_{i \in [k]}, \{\hat{\mathbf{A}}_i\}_{i \in [h]})$, $td := (pp, \mathbf{T_A})$ and send pp to $\mathcal{A}$.

$2'$. Upon an adaptation query $(\tau, \mathbf{h}, \mathbf{m}, r, \mathbf{m}')$ from $\mathcal{A}$, $\mathcal{C}$ proceeds as follows.

 – If $\exists$ $(\tau, \mathbf{h}'', \mathbf{m}) \in \mathcal{Q}_{\mathsf{Adapt}} \wedge \mathbf{h}'' \neq \mathbf{h}$, or $\exists$ $(\tau, \cdot, \mathbf{m}') \in \mathcal{Q}_{\mathsf{Adapt}}$, or $\mathsf{Check}(\tau,$ $\mathbf{h}, \mathbf{m}, r) = 0$ holds, return $\perp$; otherwise, continue.

 – Sample $\mathbf{z}' \xleftarrow{\$} \{0,1\}^{\kappa}$ and set $\mathbf{x}' := \tau \| \mathbf{m}' \| \mathbf{z}'$.

 – Compute $\mathbf{y}' \leftarrow \mathsf{PRF}(\mathbf{k}, \mathbf{x}')$ and construct $C[\mathbf{x}', \mathbf{y}']$ as defined by (2).

 – $\mathbf{C}'_{\mathsf{prf}} \leftarrow \mathsf{Eval}_{pub}(C[\mathbf{x}', \mathbf{y}'](\cdot), \mathbf{A}, \{\mathbf{A}_i\}_{i \in [k]})$ and $\mathbf{B}'_{\mathsf{prf}} := \sum_{i \in [h]} m'_i \hat{\mathbf{A}}_i$.

 – Set $\mathbf{A}'_{\mathsf{prf}} := \mathbf{C}'_{\mathsf{prf}} + \mathbf{B}'_{\mathsf{prf}}$. Delegate $\mathbf{T}_{\mathbf{A}|\mathbf{A}'_{\mathsf{prf}}} \leftarrow \mathsf{TrapDel}([\mathbf{A}|\mathbf{A}'_{\mathsf{prf}}], \mathbf{T_A})$.

 – $\mathbf{e}' = (\mathbf{e}'_1, \mathbf{e}'_2) \leftarrow \mathsf{SamplePre}([\mathbf{A}|\mathbf{A}'_{\mathsf{prf}}], \mathbf{T}_{\mathbf{A}|\mathbf{A}'_{\mathsf{prf}}}, \mathbf{h}, \gamma)$ s.t. $\mathbf{e}'_2 \neq 0^w$.

 – Send $r' := (\mathbf{z}', \mathbf{y}', \mathbf{e}')$ to $\mathcal{A}$ and $\mathcal{Q}_{\mathsf{Adapt}} := \mathcal{Q}_{\mathsf{Adapt}} \cup \{(\tau, \mathbf{h}, \mathbf{m}), (\tau, \mathbf{h}, \mathbf{m}')\}$.

Lemma 10. *Games G_1 and G_2 are computationally indistinguishable due to the pseudorandomness of* PRF, *i.e.,* $| \Pr[\mathsf{G}_1 \Rightarrow 1] - \Pr[\mathsf{G}_2 \Rightarrow 1]| \leq \mathsf{Adv}^{pse}_{\mathsf{PRF}}(\kappa) + 2^{-O(\kappa)}$.

Proof of Lemma 10 (sketch). Note that $\mathbf{z}' \xleftarrow{\$} \{0,1\}^{\kappa}$ is sampled uniformly at random for each adaptation query, then all $\mathbf{x}' = \tau \| \mathbf{m}' \| \mathbf{z}'$ constructed for the adaptation queries are different from each other with probability $1 - 2^{-O(\kappa)}$. Now according to the pseudorandomness of PRF, we know that the distribution of

$\mathbf{y}' \xleftarrow{\$} \{0,1\}^y$ is computationally indistinguishable from that of $\mathbf{y}' \leftarrow \mathsf{PRF}(\mathbf{k}, \mathbf{x}')$ and this proves Lemma 10.   □

Game G_2. Game G_2 is similar to G_1 except for the generations of $\{\mathbf{A}_i\}_{i\in[k]}$ and $\{\hat{\mathbf{A}}_i\}_{i\in[h]}$ in the setup phase, and the computations of $\mathbf{A}'_{\mathsf{prf}}$ in the adaptation query phase. In G_1, $\mathbf{A}_i \xleftarrow{\$} \mathbb{Z}_q^{n\times w}$ and $\hat{\mathbf{A}}_i \xleftarrow{\$} \mathbb{Z}_q^{n\times w}$ are sampled uniformly at random in the setup phase, and $\mathbf{A}'_{\mathsf{prf}}$ is computed by Eval_{pub} from $\mathbf{A}_i$'s and $\hat{\mathbf{A}}_i$'s when answering each adaptation query. In G_2, $\mathbf{A}_i$ and $\hat{\mathbf{A}}_i$ are computed by $\mathbf{A}_i := \mathbf{A}\mathbf{R}_i + k_i\mathbf{G}$ and $\hat{\mathbf{A}}_i := \mathbf{A}\hat{\mathbf{R}}_i$ with $\mathbf{R}_i \xleftarrow{\$} \{\pm 1\}^{m\times w}$ and $\hat{\mathbf{R}}_i \xleftarrow{\$} \{\pm 1\}^{m\times w}$ in the setup phase, and $\mathbf{A}'_{\mathsf{prf}} := \mathbf{A}\mathbf{R}'_{\mathsf{prf}} + \mathbf{G}$ when answering each adaptation query with $\mathbf{R}'_{\mathsf{prf}}$ computed by Eval_{prv} from $\mathbf{R}_i$'s and $\hat{\mathbf{R}}_i$'s.

$1''$. During the setup phase, the challenger $\mathcal{C}$ proceeds as follows.

- Generate $pp_{\mathsf{prf}} \leftarrow \mathsf{PRF.Setup}(1^\kappa)$ and sample $\mathbf{k} \xleftarrow{\$} \{0,1\}^k$.
- Generate $(\mathbf{A}, \mathbf{T_A}) \leftarrow \mathsf{TrapGen}(1^n, 1^m, q)$.
- Sample $\mathbf{R}_i \xleftarrow{\$} \{\pm 1\}^{m\times w}$ and set $\mathbf{A}_i := \mathbf{A}\mathbf{R}_i + k_i\mathbf{G}$ for $i \in [k]$. Sample $\hat{\mathbf{R}}_i \xleftarrow{\$} \{\pm 1\}^{m\times w}$ and set $\hat{\mathbf{A}}_i := \mathbf{A}\hat{\mathbf{R}}_i$ for $i \in [h]$.
- $pp := (pp_{\mathsf{prf}}, \mathbf{A}, \{\mathbf{A}_i\}_{i\in[k]}, \{\hat{\mathbf{A}}_i\}_{i\in[h]})$, $td := (pp, \mathbf{T_A})$ and send pp to $\mathcal{A}$.

$2''$. Upon an adaptation query $(\tau, \mathbf{h}, \mathbf{m}, r, \mathbf{m}')$ from $\mathcal{A}$, $\mathcal{C}$ proceeds as follows.

- If $\exists (\tau, \mathbf{h}'', \mathbf{m}) \in \mathcal{Q}_{\mathsf{Adapt}} \wedge \mathbf{h}'' \neq \mathbf{h}$, or $\exists (\tau, \cdot, \mathbf{m}') \in \mathcal{Q}_{\mathsf{Adapt}}$, or $\mathsf{Check}(\tau, \mathbf{h}, \mathbf{m}, r) = 0$ holds, return $\perp$; otherwise, continue.
- Sample $\mathbf{z}' \xleftarrow{\$} \{0,1\}^\kappa$ and set $\mathbf{x}' := \tau\|\mathbf{m}'\|\mathbf{z}'$.
- Compute $\mathbf{y}' \leftarrow \mathsf{PRF}(\mathbf{k}, \mathbf{x}')$ and construct $C[\mathbf{x}', \mathbf{y}']$ as defined by (2).
- $\mathbf{S}'_{\mathsf{prf}} \leftarrow \mathsf{Eval}_{prv}(C[\mathbf{x}', \mathbf{y}'](\cdot), \mathbf{A}, \mathbf{k}, \{\mathbf{R}_i\}_{i\in[k]})$ and $\mathbf{P}'_{\mathsf{prf}} := \sum_{i\in[h]} m'_i\hat{\mathbf{R}}_i$.
- Set $\mathbf{R}'_{\mathsf{prf}} := \mathbf{S}'_{\mathsf{prf}} + \mathbf{P}'_{\mathsf{prf}}$ and $\mathbf{A}'_{\mathsf{prf}} := \mathbf{A}\mathbf{R}'_{\mathsf{prf}} + \mathbf{G}$. Delegate $\mathbf{T}_{\mathbf{A}|\mathbf{A}'_{\mathsf{prf}}} \leftarrow \mathsf{TrapDel}([\mathbf{A}|\mathbf{A}'_{\mathsf{prf}}], \mathbf{T_A})$.
- $\mathbf{e}' = (\mathbf{e}'_1, \mathbf{e}'_2) \leftarrow \mathsf{SamplePre}([\mathbf{A}|\mathbf{A}'_{\mathsf{prf}}], \mathbf{T}_{\mathbf{A}|\mathbf{A}'_{\mathsf{prf}}}, \mathbf{h}, \gamma)$ s.t. $\mathbf{e}'_2 \neq 0^w$.
- Send $r' := (\mathbf{z}', \mathbf{y}', \mathbf{e}')$ to $\mathcal{A}$ and $\mathcal{Q}_{\mathsf{Adapt}} := \mathcal{Q}_{\mathsf{Adapt}} \cup \{(\tau, \mathbf{h}, \mathbf{m}), (\tau, \mathbf{h}, \mathbf{m}')\}$.

Lemma 11. *Games G_1 and G_2 are statistically indistinguishable and* $|\Pr[\mathsf{G}_1 \Rightarrow 1] - \Pr[\mathsf{G}_2 \Rightarrow 1]| \leq 2^{-O(\kappa)}$.

Proof of Lemma 11. For each $i \in [k]$, we have

$$\mathbf{A}_i := \mathbf{A}\mathbf{R}_i + k_i\mathbf{G} \text{ (in } \mathsf{G}_2) \approx_s \mathbf{U}_i + k_i\mathbf{G} \equiv \mathbf{U}'_i =: \mathbf{A}_i \text{ (in } \mathsf{G}_1) ,$$

where $\mathbf{R}_i \xleftarrow{\$} \{\pm 1\}^{m\times w}$ and $\mathbf{U}_i, \mathbf{U}'_i \xleftarrow{\$} \mathbb{Z}_q^{n\times w}$. The "$\approx_s$" follows from Lemma 2 (randomness extraction) and the triangle inequality. The "$\equiv$" holds due to the uniformity of $\mathbf{U}_i$. Similarly, we can prove that the distribution of $\{\hat{\mathbf{A}}_i\}_{i\in[h]}$ in G_1 is statistically indistinguishable from that of $\{\hat{\mathbf{A}}_i\}_{i\in[h]}$ in G_2 by

$$\hat{\mathbf{A}}_i := \mathbf{A}\hat{\mathbf{R}}_i \text{ (in } \mathsf{G}_2) \approx_s \mathbf{U}_i =: \hat{\mathbf{A}} \text{ (in } \mathsf{G}_1) ,$$

where $\mathbf{R}_i \xleftarrow{\$} \{\pm 1\}^{m \times w}$ and $\mathbf{U}_i \xleftarrow{\$} \mathbb{Z}_q^{n \times w}$.

Next we show that $\mathbf{A}'_{\mathsf{prf}}$ computed by Eval_{pub} from $\mathbf{A}_i$'s and $\hat{\mathbf{A}}_i$'s in G_1 is identical to that computed by Eval_{prv} from $\mathbf{R}_i$'s and $\hat{\mathbf{R}}_i$'s in G_2. Given $\mathbf{A}_i = \mathbf{AR}_i + k_i \mathbf{G}$ for $i \in [k]$, we have $\mathbf{C}'_{\mathsf{prf}} := \mathbf{AS}'_{\mathsf{prf}} + C[\mathbf{x}',\mathbf{y}'](\mathbf{k}) \cdot \mathbf{G} = \mathbf{AS}'_{\mathsf{prf}} + \mathbf{G}$ with $\mathbf{C}'_{\mathsf{prf}} \leftarrow \mathsf{Eval}_{pub}(C[\mathbf{x}',\mathbf{y}'](\cdot), \mathbf{A}, \{\mathbf{A}_i\}_{i \in [k]})$ and $\mathbf{S}'_{\mathsf{prf}} \leftarrow \mathsf{Eval}_{prv}(C[\mathbf{x}',\mathbf{y}'](\cdot), \mathbf{A}, \mathbf{k}, \{\mathbf{R}_i\}_{i \in [k]})$ due to Lemma 7 (homomorphic evaluation) and the fact that $\mathbf{y}' = \mathsf{PRF}(\mathbf{k},\mathbf{x}')$. Besides, given $\hat{\mathbf{A}}_i = \mathbf{A}\hat{\mathbf{R}}_i$, we have $\mathbf{B}'_{\mathsf{prf}} := \sum_{i \in [h]} m'_i \hat{\mathbf{A}}_i = \mathbf{A} \sum_{i \in [h]} m'_i \hat{\mathbf{R}}_i = \mathbf{AP}'_{\mathsf{prf}}$. Then it holds that $\mathbf{A}'_{\mathsf{prf}} := \mathbf{C}'_{\mathsf{prf}} + \mathbf{B}'_{\mathsf{prf}} = \mathbf{AS}'_{\mathsf{prf}} + \mathbf{G} + \mathbf{AP}'_{\mathsf{prf}} = \mathbf{AR}'_{\mathsf{prf}} + \mathbf{G}$ with $\mathbf{R}'_{\mathsf{prf}} = \mathbf{S}'_{\mathsf{prf}} + \mathbf{P}'_{\mathsf{prf}}$. This completes the proof.   □

Game G_3. Game G_3 is similar to G_2 except for the generation of the trapdoor $\mathbf{T}_{\mathbf{A}|\mathbf{A}'_{\mathsf{prf}}}$ in the adaptation query phase. In G_2, $\mathbf{T}_{\mathbf{A}|\mathbf{A}'_{\mathsf{prf}}}$ is delegated from $\mathbf{T}_{\mathbf{A}}$. In G_3, $\mathbf{T}_{\mathbf{A}|\mathbf{A}'_{\mathsf{prf}}}$ is generated from a G-trapdoor of $[\mathbf{A}|\mathbf{A}'_{\mathsf{prf}}]$.

2'''. Upon an adaptation query $(\tau, \mathbf{h}, \mathbf{m}, r, \mathbf{m}')$ from $\mathcal{A}$, $\mathcal{C}$ proceeds as follows.

- If $\exists (\tau, \mathbf{h}'', \mathbf{m}) \in \mathcal{Q}_{\mathsf{Adapt}} \wedge \mathbf{h}'' \neq \mathbf{h}$, or $\exists (\tau, \cdot, \mathbf{m}') \in \mathcal{Q}_{\mathsf{Adapt}}$, or $\mathsf{Check}(\tau, \mathbf{h}, \mathbf{m}, r) = 0$ holds, return $\bot$; otherwise, continue.
- Sample $\mathbf{z}' \xleftarrow{\$} \{0,1\}^\kappa$ and set $\mathbf{x}' := \tau \| \mathbf{m}' \| \mathbf{z}'$.
- Compute $\mathbf{y}' \leftarrow \mathsf{PRF}(\mathbf{k}, \mathbf{x}')$ and construct $C[\mathbf{x}', \mathbf{y}']$ as defined by (2).
- $\mathbf{S}'_{\mathsf{prf}} \leftarrow \mathsf{Eval}_{prv}(C[\mathbf{x}', \mathbf{y}'](\cdot), \mathbf{A}, \mathbf{k}, \{\mathbf{R}_i\}_{i \in [k]})$ and $\mathbf{P}'_{\mathsf{prf}} := \sum_{i \in [h]} m'_i \hat{\mathbf{R}}_i$.
- Set $\mathbf{R}'_{\mathsf{prf}} := \mathbf{S}'_{\mathsf{prf}} + \mathbf{P}'_{\mathsf{prf}}$ and $\mathbf{A}'_{\mathsf{prf}} := \mathbf{AR}'_{\mathsf{prf}} + \mathbf{G}$. Generate $\mathbf{T}_{\mathbf{A}|\mathbf{A}'_{\mathsf{prf}}} \leftarrow \mathsf{GtoBasis}(\mathbf{R}'_{\mathsf{prf}})$.
- $\mathbf{e}' = (\mathbf{e}'_1, \mathbf{e}'_2) \leftarrow \mathsf{SamplePre}([\mathbf{A}|\mathbf{A}'_{\mathsf{prf}}], \mathbf{T}_{\mathbf{A}|\mathbf{A}'_{\mathsf{prf}}}, \mathbf{h}, \gamma)$ s.t. $\mathbf{e}'_2 \neq 0^w$.
- Send $r' := (\mathbf{z}', \mathbf{y}', \mathbf{e}')$ to $\mathcal{A}$ and $\mathcal{Q}_{\mathsf{Adapt}} := \mathcal{Q}_{\mathsf{Adapt}} \cup \{(\tau, \mathbf{h}, \mathbf{m}), (\tau, \mathbf{h}, \mathbf{m}')\}$.

Lemma 12. *Games G_2 and G_3 are statistically indistinguishable and $|\Pr[\mathsf{G}_2 \Rightarrow 1] - \Pr[\mathsf{G}_3 \Rightarrow 1]| \leq 2^{-\kappa}$.*

Proof of Lemma 12. Note that the changes in G_3 only influence the sampling of $\mathbf{e}'$ during the adaptation query phase, then it suffices to show that the distribution of $\mathbf{e}'$ in G_3 is identical to that in G_2. In G_2, $\mathbf{T}_{\mathbf{A}|\mathbf{A}'_{\mathsf{prf}}}$ is delegated from $\mathbf{T}_{\mathbf{A}}$ and of norm $\|\tilde{\mathbf{T}}_{\mathbf{A}|\mathbf{A}'_{\mathsf{prf}}}\| = \|\tilde{\mathbf{T}}_{\mathbf{A}}\| \leq O(\sqrt{n \log q})$ according to Lemma 5 (trapdoor delegation). Together with Lemma 4 (preimage sampling) and the parameter setting that $\gamma > O(\sqrt{n \log q}) \cdot \omega(\sqrt{m + w})$, the vector $\mathbf{e}'$ sampled in G_2 follows the distribution $D_{\Lambda_q^{\mathbf{h}}(\mathbf{A}), \gamma}$. In G_3, we have $\mathbf{A}'_{\mathsf{prf}} = \mathbf{AR}'_{\mathsf{prf}} + \mathbf{G}$, and hence $\mathbf{R}'_{\mathsf{prf}}$ is a G-trapdoor for $[\mathbf{A}|\mathbf{A}'_{\mathsf{prf}}]$ according to [28]. Then according to Lemma 6 (G-to-basis), $\mathbf{T}_{\mathbf{A}|\mathbf{A}'_{\mathsf{prf}}}$ generated from the G-trapdoor $\mathbf{R}'_{\mathsf{prf}}$ is also a trapdoor for $[\mathbf{A}|\mathbf{A}'_{\mathsf{prf}}]$ with norm $\|\tilde{\mathbf{T}}_{\mathbf{A}|\mathbf{A}'_{\mathsf{prf}}}\| = \sqrt{5}(s_1(\mathbf{R}'_{\mathsf{prf}}) + 1) \leq O(\kappa^c)$ for some constant c. Together with Lemma 4 (preimage sampling) and the parameter setting that $\gamma \geq O(\kappa^c) \cdot \omega(\sqrt{m + w})$, the vector $\mathbf{e}'$ sampled in G_3 also follows the distribution $D_{\Lambda_q^{\mathbf{h}}(\mathbf{A}), \gamma}$. This completes the proof.   □

Game G_4. Game G_4 is similar to G_3 except for the generation of $\mathbf{A}$ in the setup phase. In G_3, $\mathbf{A}$ is generated by algorithm $(\mathbf{A}, \mathbf{T}_{\mathbf{A}}) \leftarrow \mathsf{TrapGen}(1^n, 1^m, q)$. In G_4, $\mathbf{A} \xleftarrow{\$} \mathbb{Z}_q^{n \times m}$ is sampled uniformly at random.

$1'''$. During the setup phase, the challenger $\mathcal{C}$ proceeds as follows.

- Generate $pp_{\mathsf{prf}} \leftarrow \mathsf{PRF.Setup}(1^\kappa)$ and sample $\mathbf{k} \stackrel{\$}{\leftarrow} \{0,1\}^k$.
- Sample $\mathbf{A} \stackrel{\$}{\leftarrow} \mathbb{Z}_q^{n \times m}$.
- Sample $\mathbf{R}_i \stackrel{\$}{\leftarrow} \{\pm 1\}^{m \times w}$ and set $\mathbf{A}_i := \mathbf{A}\mathbf{R}_i + k_i\mathbf{G}$ for $i \in [k]$. Sample $\hat{\mathbf{R}}_i \stackrel{\$}{\leftarrow} \{\pm 1\}^{m \times w}$ and set $\hat{\mathbf{A}}_i := \mathbf{A}\hat{\mathbf{R}}_i$ for $i \in [h]$.
- $pp := (pp_{\mathsf{prf}}, \mathbf{A}, \{\mathbf{A}_i\}_{i \in [k]}, \{\hat{\mathbf{A}}_i\}_{i \in [h]})$, $td := (pp, \perp)$ and send pp to $\mathcal{A}$.

Lemma 13. *Games* G_3 *and* G_4 *are statistically indistinguishable and* $|\Pr[\mathsf{G}_3 \Rightarrow 1] - \Pr[\mathsf{G}_4 \Rightarrow 1]| \leq 2^{-\kappa}$.

Lemma 13 holds directly from Lemma 3 (trapdoor generation).

Next we show that any PPT adversary $\mathcal{A}$ wins in G_4 with negligible probability. To do this, we classify the adversaries into two types, $\mathcal{A}^{(I)}$ and $\mathcal{A}^{(II)}$.

- **Type I:** $\mathcal{A}^{(I)}$ finally submits a forgery $(\tau^*, \mathbf{h}^*, \mathbf{m}^*, r^*, \mathbf{m}'^*, r'^*)$ satisfying the first Valid condition, i.e., $(\tau^*, \cdot, \mathbf{m}^*) \notin \mathcal{Q}_{\mathsf{Adapt}} \wedge (\tau^*, \mathbf{h}^*, \mathbf{m}^*) \in \mathcal{Q}_{\mathsf{Adapt}}$.
- **Type II:** $\mathcal{A}^{(II)}$ finally submits a forgery $(\tau^*, \mathbf{h}^*, \mathbf{m}^*, r^*, \mathbf{m}'^*, r'^*)$ satisfying the second Valid condition, i.e., $(\tau^*, \cdot, \mathbf{m}^*) \notin \mathcal{Q}_{\mathsf{Adapt}} \wedge (\tau^*, \cdot, \mathbf{m}'^*) \notin \mathcal{Q}_{\mathsf{Adapt}}$.

Next we show in Lemma 14 that $\mathcal{A}^{(I)}$ and $\mathcal{A}^{(II)}$ hardly win in G_4.

Lemma 14. *For any PPT adversary* $\mathcal{A}^{(T)}$ *with* $T \in \{I, II\}$, *it holds that* $\Pr[\mathsf{G}_4 \Rightarrow 1] \leq \mathsf{Adv}_{\mathsf{PRF}}^{pse}(\kappa) + \mathsf{Adv}_{[n,q,\beta,m]}^{\mathsf{SIS}}(\kappa) + 2^{-\kappa}$.

Proof of Lemma 14. We consider $\mathcal{A}^{(I)}$ and $\mathcal{A}^{(II)}$ separately.

First, we prove that if there exists a PPT $\mathcal{A}^{(I)}$ that wins in G_4, then we construct a PPT algorithm $\mathcal{B}^{(I)}$ to solve the SIS problem.

Algorithm $\mathcal{B}^{(I)}$. Given an SIS instance $\mathbf{A} \in \mathbb{Z}_q^{n \times m}$, $\mathcal{B}^{(I)}$ aims to obtain a non-zero short vector $\mathbf{v} \in \mathbb{Z}_q^m$ s.t. $\mathbf{A}\mathbf{v} = \mathbf{0}^n$. It proceeds as follows.

0. The algorithm $\mathcal{B}^{(I)}$ initializes sets $\mathcal{Q}_{\mathsf{Adapt}} := \emptyset$ and $\mathcal{Q}_r := \emptyset$.
1. During the setup phase, the challenger $\mathcal{B}^{(I)}$ proceeds as follows.
   - Generate $pp_{\mathsf{prf}} \leftarrow \mathsf{PRF.Setup}(1^\kappa)$ and sample $\mathbf{k} \stackrel{\$}{\leftarrow} \{0,1\}^k$.
   - Sample $\mathbf{R}_i \stackrel{\$}{\leftarrow} \{\pm 1\}^{m \times w}$ and set $\mathbf{A}_i := \mathbf{A}\mathbf{R}_i + k_i\mathbf{G}$ for $i \in [k]$. Sample $\hat{\mathbf{R}}_i \stackrel{\$}{\leftarrow} \{\pm 1\}^{m \times w}$ and set $\hat{\mathbf{A}}_i := \mathbf{A}\hat{\mathbf{R}}_i$ for $i \in [h]$. (Note that $\mathbf{A}$ is the SIS instance.)
   - Send $pp = (pp_{\mathsf{prf}}, \mathbf{A}, \{\mathbf{A}_i\}_{i \in [k]}, \{\hat{\mathbf{A}}_i\}_{i \in [h]})$ to $\mathcal{A}^{(I)}$.
2. Upon an adaptation query $(\tau, \mathbf{h}, \mathbf{m}, r, \mathbf{m}')$ from $\mathcal{A}^{(I)}$, $\mathcal{B}^{(I)}$ proceeds as follows.
   - If $\exists (\tau, \mathbf{h}'', \mathbf{m}) \in \mathcal{Q}_{\mathsf{Adapt}} \wedge \mathbf{h}'' \neq \mathbf{h}$, or $\exists (\tau, \cdot, \mathbf{m}') \in \mathcal{Q}_{\mathsf{Adapt}}$, or $\mathsf{Check}(\tau, \mathbf{h}, \mathbf{m}, r) = 0$ holds, return $\perp$; otherwise, continue.
   - Sample $\mathbf{z}' \stackrel{\$}{\leftarrow} \{0,1\}^\kappa$ and set $\mathbf{x}' := \tau \| \mathbf{m}' \| \mathbf{z}'$.
   - Compute $\mathbf{y}' \leftarrow \mathsf{PRF}(\mathbf{k}, \mathbf{x}')$ and construct $C[\mathbf{x}', \mathbf{y}']$ as defined by (2).
   - $\mathbf{S}'_{\mathsf{prf}} \leftarrow \mathsf{Eval}_{prv}(C[\mathbf{x}', \mathbf{y}'](\cdot), \mathbf{A}, \mathbf{k}, \{\mathbf{R}_i\}_{i \in [k]})$ and $\mathbf{P}'_{\mathsf{prf}} := \sum_{i \in [h]} m'_i \hat{\mathbf{R}}_i$.

- Set $\mathbf{R}'_{prf} := \mathbf{S}'_{prf} + \mathbf{P}'_{prf}$ and $\mathbf{A}'_{prf} := \mathbf{AR}'_{prf} + \mathbf{G}$. Generate $\mathbf{T}_{\mathbf{A}|\mathbf{A}'_{prf}} \leftarrow$ GtoBasis($\mathbf{R}'_{prf}$).
- $\mathbf{e}' = (\mathbf{e}'_1, \mathbf{e}'_2) \leftarrow$ SamplePre($[\mathbf{A}|\mathbf{A}'_{prf}], \mathbf{T}_{\mathbf{A}|\mathbf{A}'_{prf}}, \mathbf{h}, \gamma$) s.t. $\mathbf{e}'_2 \neq 0^w$.
- Send $r' := (\mathbf{z}', \mathbf{y}', \mathbf{e}')$ to $\mathcal{A}^{(I)}$. Set $\mathcal{Q}_{Adapt} := \mathcal{Q}_{Adapt} \cup \{(\tau, \mathbf{h}, \mathbf{m}), (\tau, \mathbf{h}, \mathbf{m}')\}$ and $\mathcal{Q}_r := \mathcal{Q}_r \cup \{(\tau, \mathbf{h}, \mathbf{m}, r), (\tau, \mathbf{h}, \mathbf{m}', r')\}$.
3. Upon a forgery tuple $(\tau^*, \mathbf{h}^*, \mathbf{m}^*, r^*, \mathbf{m}'^*, r'^*)$, if $\mathcal{A}^{(I)}$ wins, it holds that $\mathbf{m}^* \neq \mathbf{m}'^*$, Check($\tau^*, \mathbf{h}^*, \mathbf{m}^*, r^*$) = Check($\tau^*, \mathbf{h}^*, \mathbf{m}'^*, r'^*$) = 1 and $(\tau^*, \cdot, \mathbf{m}^*) \notin \mathcal{Q}_{Adapt} \wedge (\tau^*, \mathbf{h}^*, \mathbf{m}'^*) \in \mathcal{Q}_{Adapt}$. Find $(\tau^*, \mathbf{h}^*, \bar{\mathbf{m}}) \in \mathcal{Q}_{Adapt}$ s.t. $(\tau^*, \mathbf{h}^*, \bar{\mathbf{m}}, \bar{r}) \in \mathcal{Q}_r$, Check($\tau^*, \mathbf{h}^*, \bar{\mathbf{m}}, \bar{r}$) = 1 and $\bar{\mathbf{m}}$ is never queried to $\mathcal{O}_{Adapt}$ as the adapted message w.r.t. tag τ^*. Then $\mathcal{B}^{(I)}$ computes a SIS solution as follows.
   - Parse $\bar{r} = (\bar{\mathbf{z}}, \bar{\mathbf{y}}, \bar{\mathbf{e}})$ and $r^* = (\mathbf{z}^*, \mathbf{y}^*, \mathbf{e}^*)$.
   - Set $\bar{\mathbf{x}} := \tau^* \| \bar{\mathbf{m}} \| \bar{\mathbf{z}}$ and $\mathbf{x}^* := \tau^* \| \mathbf{m}^* \| \mathbf{z}^*$. Construct $C[\bar{\mathbf{x}}, \bar{\mathbf{y}}]$ and $C[\mathbf{x}^*, \mathbf{y}^*]$.
   - $\bar{\mathbf{C}}_{prf} \leftarrow \mathsf{Eval}_{pub}(C[\bar{\mathbf{x}}, \bar{\mathbf{y}}](\cdot), \mathbf{A}, \{\mathbf{A}_i\}_{i\in[k]})$ and $\bar{\mathbf{B}}_{prf} := \sum_{i\in[h]} \bar{m}_i \hat{\mathbf{A}}_i$.
   - $\bar{\mathbf{S}}_{prf} \leftarrow \mathsf{Eval}_{prv}(C[\bar{\mathbf{x}}, \bar{\mathbf{y}}](\cdot), \mathbf{A}, k, \{\mathbf{R}_i\}_{i\in[k]})$ and $\bar{\mathbf{P}}_{prf} := \sum_{i\in[h]} \bar{m}_i \hat{\mathbf{R}}_i$.
   - Set $\bar{\mathbf{A}}_{prf} := \bar{\mathbf{C}}_{prf} + \bar{\mathbf{B}}_{prf}$ and $\bar{\mathbf{R}}_{prf} := \bar{\mathbf{S}}_{prf} + \bar{\mathbf{P}}_{prf}$.
   - $\mathbf{C}^*_{prf} \leftarrow \mathsf{Eval}_{pub}(C[\mathbf{x}^*, \mathbf{y}^*](\cdot), \mathbf{A}, \{\mathbf{A}_i\}_{i\in[k]})$ and $\mathbf{B}^*_{prf} := \sum_{i\in[h]} m^*_i \hat{\mathbf{A}}_i$.
   - $\mathbf{S}^*_{prf} \leftarrow \mathsf{Eval}_{prv}(C[\mathbf{x}^*, \mathbf{y}^*](\cdot), \mathbf{A}, k, \{\mathbf{R}_i\}_{i\in[k]})$ and $\mathbf{P}^*_{prf} := \sum_{i\in[h]} m^*_i \hat{\mathbf{R}}_i$.
   - Set $\mathbf{A}^*_{prf} := \mathbf{C}^*_{prf} + \mathbf{B}^*_{prf}$ and $\mathbf{R}^*_{prf} := \mathbf{S}^*_{prf} + \mathbf{P}^*_{prf}$.
   - Compute and return $\mathbf{v} := [\mathbf{I}_m | \mathbf{R}^*_{prf}] \cdot \mathbf{e}^* - [\mathbf{I}_m | \bar{\mathbf{R}}_{prf}] \cdot \bar{\mathbf{e}}$ to its own challenger.

We show the existence of tuple $(\tau^*, \mathbf{h}^*, \bar{\mathbf{m}}) \in \mathcal{Q}_{Adapt}$ in step 3. The adversary may issue multiple adaptation queries centered around $(\tau^*, \mathbf{h}^*)$, but there must be a root tuple $(\tau^*, \mathbf{h}^*, \bar{\mathbf{m}}, \bar{r})$ such that all other tuples $(\tau^*, \mathbf{h}^*, \cdot, \cdot)$ are adapted from it directly or indirectly. According to the specification of $\mathcal{O}_{Adapt}$, all the target new messages w.r.t. τ^* are different from the root message $\bar{\mathbf{m}}$. Consequently, tuple $(\tau^*, \mathbf{h}^*, \bar{\mathbf{m}}, \bar{r})$ satisfies $(\tau^*, \mathbf{h}^*, \bar{\mathbf{m}}, \bar{r}) \in \mathcal{Q}_r$, Check($\tau^*, \mathbf{h}^*, \bar{\mathbf{m}}, \bar{r}$) = 1 and $\bar{\mathbf{m}}$ is never queried to $\mathcal{O}_{Adapt}$ as the adapted message w.r.t. τ^*.

Next we show that $\mathbf{v}$ is a valid solution to the SIS problem. Note that $(\tau^*, \cdot, \mathbf{m}^*) \notin \mathcal{Q}_{Adapt}$ is never queried to the adaptation oracle, then nothing about PRF($\mathbf{k}, \mathbf{x}^*$) with $\mathbf{x}^* = \tau^* \| \mathbf{m}^* \| \mathbf{z}^*$ is revealed to $\mathcal{A}^{(I)}$. For $\mathbf{y}^*$ chosen by $\mathcal{A}^{(I)}$, $\mathbf{y}^* = $ PRF($\mathbf{k}, \mathbf{x}^*$) hardly holds due to the pseudorandomness of PRF. Then with overwhelming probability, $C[\mathbf{x}^*, \mathbf{y}^*](\mathbf{k}) = 0$ and

$$\mathbf{A}^*_{prf} = \mathbf{AR}^*_{prf} + C[\mathbf{x}^*, \mathbf{y}^*](\mathbf{k}) \cdot \mathbf{G} = \mathbf{AR}^*_{prf} + 0 \cdot \mathbf{G} = \mathbf{AR}^*_{prf}.$$

Besides, since $(\tau^*, \mathbf{h}^*, \bar{\mathbf{m}}) \in \mathcal{Q}_{Adapt}$ and $\bar{\mathbf{m}}$ is never queried to $\mathcal{Q}_{Adapt}$ as a target new message under tag τ^* before, we know that $(\tau^*, \mathbf{h}^*, \bar{\mathbf{m}}, \bar{r})$ is generated by $\mathcal{A}^{(I)}$ itself and PRF($\mathbf{k}, \bar{\mathbf{x}}$) with $\bar{\mathbf{x}} = \tau^* \| \bar{\mathbf{m}} \| \bar{\mathbf{z}}$ is never obtained by $\mathcal{A}^{(I)}$. Through an analogous analysis, we know that with overwhelming probability,

$$\bar{\mathbf{A}}_{prf} = \mathbf{A}\bar{\mathbf{R}}_{prf} + C[\bar{\mathbf{x}}, \bar{\mathbf{y}}](\mathbf{k}) \cdot \mathbf{G} = \mathbf{A}\bar{\mathbf{R}}_{prf} + 0 \cdot \mathbf{G} = \mathbf{A}\bar{\mathbf{R}}_{prf}.$$

Furthermore, since Check($\tau^*, \mathbf{h}^*, \mathbf{m}^*, r^*$) = Check($\tau^*, \mathbf{h}^*, \bar{\mathbf{m}}, \bar{r}$) = 1, we have

$$[\mathbf{A}|\mathbf{A}^*_{prf}] \cdot \mathbf{e}^* = \mathbf{h}^* = [\mathbf{A}|\bar{\mathbf{A}}_{prf}] \cdot \bar{\mathbf{e}} \Leftrightarrow [\mathbf{A}|\mathbf{AR}^*_{prf}] \cdot \mathbf{e}^* - [\mathbf{A}|\mathbf{A}\bar{\mathbf{R}}_{prf}] \cdot \bar{\mathbf{e}} = 0^n$$

$$\Leftrightarrow \mathbf{A} \underbrace{([\mathbf{I}_m|\mathbf{R}^*_{prf}] \cdot \mathbf{e}^* - [\mathbf{I}_m|\bar{\mathbf{R}}_{prf}] \cdot \bar{\mathbf{e}})}_{=:\mathbf{v}\in\mathbb{Z}_q^m} = 0^n,$$

where $\mathbf{e}^* = (\mathbf{e}_1^*, \mathbf{e}_2^*)$, $\|\mathbf{e}^*\| \le \gamma\sqrt{m+w}$, $\mathbf{e}_2^* \ne 0^w$, $\bar{\mathbf{e}} = (\bar{\mathbf{e}}_1, \bar{\mathbf{e}}_2)$, $\|\bar{\mathbf{e}}\| \le \gamma\sqrt{m+w}$ and $\bar{\mathbf{e}}_2 \ne 0^w$. Together with our parameter setting that $\gamma \cdot O(\kappa^c) \cdot \sqrt{m+w} \le \beta$, we have $\|\mathbf{v}\| \le O(\kappa^c) \cdot \gamma\sqrt{m+w} \le \beta$ for some constant c.

It remains to show that $\mathbf{v} = ([\mathbf{I}_m|\mathbf{R}_{\mathsf{prf}}^*] \cdot \mathbf{e}^* - [\mathbf{I}_m|\bar{\mathbf{R}}_{\mathsf{prf}}] \cdot \bar{\mathbf{e}}) \ne 0^m$. Denote by $\mathbf{r}_i^*$ (resp., $\bar{\mathbf{r}}_i$, $\mathbf{s}_i^*$, $\mathbf{p}_i^*$ and $\{\hat{\mathbf{r}}_{j,i}\}_{j\in[h]}$) the i-th column of $\mathbf{R}_{\mathsf{prf}}^*$ (resp., $\bar{\mathbf{R}}_{\mathsf{prf}}$, $\mathbf{S}_{\mathsf{prf}}^*$, $\mathbf{P}_{\mathsf{prf}}^*$ and $\{\hat{\mathbf{R}}_j\}_{j\in[h]}$), and $e_{2,i}^*$ the i-th item of $\mathbf{e}_2^*$. Recall that $\mathbf{r}_i^* = \mathbf{s}_i^* + \mathbf{p}_i^* = \mathbf{s}_i^* + \sum_{j\in[h]} m_j^* \hat{\mathbf{r}}_{j,i}$. Since $(\tau^*, \cdot, \mathbf{m}^*) \notin \mathcal{Q}_{\mathsf{Adapt}}$ and $(\tau^*, \mathbf{h}^*, \bar{\mathbf{m}}) \in \mathcal{Q}_{\mathsf{Adapt}}$, we know that $\bar{\mathbf{m}} \ne \mathbf{m}^*$ and hence there must exist some index $\iota \in [h]$ s.t. $\bar{m}_\iota \ne m_\iota^*$. W.l.o.g., let $\bar{m}_\iota = 0$ and $m_\iota^* = 1$. Besides, since $\mathbf{e}_2^* \ne 0^w$, there must exist some index $\nu \in [w]$ s.t. $e_{2,\nu}^* \ne 0$. Now we show that $\mathbf{v} = 0^m$ holds with negligible probability. Note that

$$\mathbf{v} = \mathbf{e}_1^* + \mathbf{R}_{\mathsf{prf}}^* \mathbf{e}_2^* - \bar{\mathbf{e}}_1 - \bar{\mathbf{R}}_{\mathsf{prf}} \bar{\mathbf{e}}_2 = 0^m$$
$$\Leftrightarrow \hat{\mathbf{r}}_{\iota,\nu} = \underbrace{(\bar{\mathbf{e}}_1 + \bar{\mathbf{R}}_{\mathsf{prf}} \bar{\mathbf{e}}_2 - \mathbf{e}_1^* - \sum_{i\ne\nu} \mathbf{r}_i^* e_{2,i}^*)/e_{2,\nu}^* - \mathbf{s}_\nu^* - \sum_{j\ne\iota} m_j^* \hat{\mathbf{r}}_{j,\nu}}_{=:W}. \quad (3)$$

Recall that $\hat{\mathbf{r}}_{\iota,\nu}$ is sampled uniformly from $\{1, -1\}^m$ and the only information of $\hat{\mathbf{r}}_{\iota,\nu}$ revealed to $\mathcal{A}^{(I)}$ is $\mathbf{u} = \mathbf{A}\hat{\mathbf{r}}_{\iota,\nu} \in \mathbb{Z}_q^n$. Together with Lemma 1 and the parameter setting that $m \ge O(n\log q)$, $\tilde{\mathbf{H}}_\infty(\hat{\mathbf{r}}_{\iota,\nu}|\mathbf{u}) \ge \mathbf{H}_\infty(\hat{\mathbf{r}}_{\iota,\nu}) - n\log q = m - n\log q \ge \kappa$ and $\hat{\mathbf{r}}_{\iota,\nu}$ still has high entropy. Further since "W" in Eq. (3) is independent of $\hat{\mathbf{r}}_{\iota,\nu}$, we have $\hat{\mathbf{r}}_{\iota,\nu} = W$ with probability $2^{-\kappa}$. Then Eq. (3) holds with a negligible probability and $\mathbf{v} = 0^m$ holds with negligible probability.

Now we have proved that $\mathbf{v}$ is a valid solution for SIS and $\Pr[\mathsf{G}_4 \Rightarrow 1|\mathcal{A}^{(I)}] \le \mathsf{Adv}_{\mathsf{PRF}}^{pse}(\kappa) + \mathsf{Adv}_{[n,q,\beta,m]}^{\mathsf{SIS}}(\kappa) + 2^{-\kappa}$.

Next, we prove that if there exists a PPT $\mathcal{A}^{(II)}$ that wins in G_4, then we construct a PPT algorithm $\mathcal{B}^{(II)}$ to solve the SIS problem. The algorithm $\mathcal{B}^{(II)}$ is similar to $\mathcal{B}^{(I)}$ except for the step 3, as described below.

3. Upon a forgery tuple $(\tau^*, \mathbf{h}^*, \mathbf{m}^*, r^*, \mathbf{m}'^*, r'^*)$, if $\mathcal{A}^{(II)}$ wins, it holds that $\mathbf{m}^* \ne \mathbf{m}'^*$, $\mathsf{Check}(\tau^*, \mathbf{h}^*, \mathbf{m}^*, r^*) = \mathsf{Check}(\tau^*, \mathbf{h}^*, \mathbf{m}'^*, r'^*) = 1$ and $(\tau^*, \cdot, \mathbf{m}^*) \notin \mathcal{Q}_{\mathsf{Adapt}} \wedge (\tau^*, \cdot, \mathbf{m}'^*) \notin \mathcal{Q}_{\mathsf{Adapt}}$. Then $\mathcal{B}^{(II)}$ computes a SIS solution as follows.
   - Parse $r^* = (\mathbf{z}^*, \mathbf{y}^*, \mathbf{e}^*)$ and $r'^* = (\mathbf{z}'^*, \mathbf{y}'^*, \mathbf{e}'^*)$. Set $\mathbf{x}^* := \tau^* \|\mathbf{m}^*\| \mathbf{z}^*$ and $\mathbf{x}'^* := \tau^* \|\mathbf{m}'^*\| \mathbf{z}'^*$. Construct $C[\mathbf{x}^*, \mathbf{y}^*]$ and $C[\mathbf{x}'^*, \mathbf{y}'^*]$.
   - $\mathbf{C}_{\mathsf{prf}}^* \leftarrow \mathsf{Eval}_{pub}(C[\mathbf{x}^*, \mathbf{y}^*](\cdot), \mathbf{A}, \{\mathbf{A}_i\}_{i\in[k]})$ and $\mathbf{B}_{\mathsf{prf}}^* := \sum_{i\in[h]} m_i^* \hat{\mathbf{A}}_i$.
   - $\mathbf{S}_{\mathsf{prf}}^* \leftarrow \mathsf{Eval}_{prv}(C[\mathbf{x}^*, \mathbf{y}^*](\cdot), \mathbf{A}, \mathbf{k}, \{\mathbf{R}_i\}_{i\in[k]})$ and $\mathbf{P}_{\mathsf{prf}}^* := \sum_{i\in[h]} m_i^* \hat{\mathbf{R}}_i$.
   - Set $\mathbf{A}_{\mathsf{prf}}^* := \mathbf{C}_{\mathsf{prf}}^* + \mathbf{B}_{\mathsf{prf}}^*$ and $\mathbf{R}_{\mathsf{prf}}^* := \mathbf{S}_{\mathsf{prf}}^* + \mathbf{P}_{\mathsf{prf}}^*$.
   - $\mathbf{C}_{\mathsf{prf}}'^* \leftarrow \mathsf{Eval}_{pub}(C[\mathbf{x}'^*, \mathbf{y}'^*](\cdot), \mathbf{A}, \{\mathbf{A}_i\}_{i\in[k]})$ and $\mathbf{B}_{\mathsf{prf}}'^* := \sum_{i\in[h]} m_i'^* \hat{\mathbf{A}}_i$.
   - $\mathbf{S}_{\mathsf{prf}}'^* \leftarrow \mathsf{Eval}_{prv}(C[\mathbf{x}'^*, \mathbf{y}'^*](\cdot), \mathbf{A}, \mathbf{k}, \{\mathbf{R}_i\}_{i\in[k]})$ and $\mathbf{P}_{\mathsf{prf}}'^* := \sum_{i\in[h]} m_i'^* \hat{\mathbf{R}}_i$.
   - Set $\mathbf{A}_{\mathsf{prf}}'^* := \mathbf{C}_{\mathsf{prf}}'^* + \mathbf{B}_{\mathsf{prf}}'^*$ and $\mathbf{R}_{\mathsf{prf}}'^* := \mathbf{S}_{\mathsf{prf}}'^* + \mathbf{P}_{\mathsf{prf}}'^*$.
   - Compute and return $\mathbf{v} := [\mathbf{I}_m|\mathbf{R}_{\mathsf{prf}}^*] \cdot \mathbf{e}^* - [\mathbf{I}_m|\mathbf{R}_{\mathsf{prf}}'^*] \cdot \mathbf{e}'^*$ to its challenger.

Then we show that $\mathbf{v}$ is a valid solution to the SIS problem. Note that $(\tau^*, \cdot, \mathbf{m}^*) \notin \mathcal{Q}_{\mathsf{Adapt}}$ and $(\tau^*, \cdot, \mathbf{m}'^*) \notin \mathcal{Q}_{\mathsf{Adapt}}$ are not queried to the adaptation oracle, so nothing about $\mathsf{PRF}(\mathbf{k}, \mathbf{x}^*)$ and $\mathsf{PRF}(\mathbf{k}, \mathbf{x}'^*)$ with $\mathbf{x}^* = \tau^* \|\mathbf{m}^*\| \mathbf{z}^*$

and $\mathbf{x}'^* = \tau^* \| \mathbf{m}'^* \| \mathbf{z}'^*$, has ever been revealed to $\mathcal{A}^{(II)}$, and hence $\mathsf{PRF}(\mathbf{k}, \mathbf{x}^*)$ and $\mathsf{PRF}(\mathbf{k}, \mathbf{x}'^*)$ are pseudorandom due to the pseudorandomness of PRF. As a consequence, neither $\mathbf{y}^* = \mathsf{PRF}(\mathbf{k}, \mathbf{x}^*)$ nor $\mathbf{y}'^* = \mathsf{PRF}(\mathbf{k}, \mathbf{x}'^*)$ holds except for negligible probability, where $\mathbf{y}^*$ and $\mathbf{y}'^*$ are chosen by $\mathcal{A}^{(II)}$, and this leads to $C[\mathbf{x}^*, \mathbf{y}^*](\mathbf{k}) = 0$ and $C[\mathbf{x}'^*, \mathbf{y}'^*](\mathbf{k}) = 0$. Therefore,

$$\mathbf{A}_{\mathsf{prf}}^* = \mathbf{A}\mathbf{R}_{\mathsf{prf}}^* + C[\mathbf{x}^*, \mathbf{y}^*](\mathbf{k}) \cdot \mathbf{G} = \mathbf{A}\mathbf{R}_{\mathsf{prf}}^* + 0 \cdot \mathbf{G} = \mathbf{A}\mathbf{R}_{\mathsf{prf}}^*$$
$$\mathbf{A}_{\mathsf{prf}}'^* = \mathbf{A}\mathbf{R}_{\mathsf{prf}}'^* + C[\mathbf{x}'^*, \mathbf{y}'^*](\mathbf{k}) \cdot \mathbf{G} = \mathbf{A}\mathbf{R}_{\mathsf{prf}}'^* + 0 \cdot \mathbf{G} = \mathbf{A}\mathbf{R}_{\mathsf{prf}}'^*.$$

Through an analogous analysis as before, $\mathbf{v} := [\mathbf{I}_m | \mathbf{R}_{\mathsf{prf}}^*] \cdot \mathbf{e}^* - [\mathbf{I}_m | \mathbf{R}_{\mathsf{prf}}'^*] \cdot \mathbf{e}'^*$ is a valid SIS solution with overwhelming probability. Now we obtain $\Pr[\mathsf{G}_4 \Rightarrow 1 | \mathcal{A}^{(II)}] \leq \mathsf{Adv}_{\mathsf{PRF}}^{pse}(\kappa) + \mathsf{Adv}_{[n,q,\beta,m]}^{\mathsf{SIS}}(\kappa) + 2^{-\kappa}.$ □

From Lemma 14, we have

$$\Pr[\mathsf{G}_4 \Rightarrow 1] = \Pr[\mathsf{G}_4 \Rightarrow 1 | \mathcal{A}^{(I)}] \Pr[\mathcal{A}^{(I)}] + \Pr[\mathsf{G}_4 \Rightarrow 1 | \mathcal{A}^{(II)}] \Pr[\mathcal{A}^{(II)}]$$
$$\leq \mathsf{Adv}_{\mathsf{PRF}}^{pse}(\kappa) + \mathsf{Adv}_{[n,q,\beta,m]}^{\mathsf{SIS}}(\kappa) + 2^{-O(\kappa)}. \tag{4}$$

Finally combining Lemmas 10, 11, 12, 13 and (4), it holds that

$$\Pr[\mathsf{Exp}_{\mathsf{tCH}, \mathcal{A}}^{rcr}(\kappa) \Rightarrow 1]$$
$$\leq \big| \Pr[\mathsf{G}_0 \Rightarrow 1] - \Pr[\mathsf{G}_1 \Rightarrow 1] \big| + \big| \Pr[\mathsf{G}_1 \Rightarrow 1] - \Pr[\mathsf{G}_2 \Rightarrow 1] \big|$$
$$+ \big| \Pr[\mathsf{G}_2 \Rightarrow 1] - \Pr[\mathsf{G}_3 \Rightarrow 1] \big| + \big| \Pr[\mathsf{G}_3 \Rightarrow 1] - \Pr[\mathsf{G}_4 \Rightarrow 1] \big| + \Pr[\mathsf{G}_4 \Rightarrow 1]$$
$$\leq \mathsf{Adv}_{[n,q,\beta,m]}^{\mathsf{SIS}}(\kappa) + 2\mathsf{Adv}_{\mathsf{PRF}}^{pse}(\kappa) + 2^{-O(\kappa)}. \tag{5}$$

By (5), it is easy to see that the r-CR security of tCH can be tightly reduced to the SIS assumption and the pseudorandomness of PRF. Given the concrete PRF schemes [5], our tCH enjoys r-CR based on the SIS and LWE assumptions. ∎

4.2 tCH with Tight Security in ROM

In this subsection, we provide another lattice-based tCH construction, namely tCH′, with r-CR security proved in the random oracle model. Compared with tCH in Fig. 4, our second tCH construction replaces the underlying homomorphic evaluations and PRF with a hash function (which is modeled as a random oracle), and hence achieves better efficiency and tightness. Let $\mathsf{H} : \mathbb{Z}_q^{n \times m} \times \{0,1\}^x \to \mathbb{Z}_q^{n \times w}$ be a hash function. Our tCH scheme tCH′ is given in Fig. 5.

Parameter setting. Parameters of tCH′ include the security parameter κ, the dimension parameters x, t, h, the SIS parameters n, m, q, β and the Gaussian parameter γ. Define $w = n\lceil \log q \rceil$. The afore-mentioned parameters are required to satisfy the following restrictions simultaneously.

- Let $x, t, h = \mathsf{poly}(\kappa)$ be positive integers and $x = t + h + \kappa$.
- Let n, q, m, β be positive parameters, $n, m, \beta, q = \mathsf{poly}(\kappa)$ and $\beta \cdot \mathsf{poly}(n) \leq q$ so that the SIS problem is hard according to Lemma 9.

$(pp, td) \leftarrow \mathsf{Setup}(1^\kappa)$.

1. Generate $(\mathbf{A}, \mathbf{T_A}) \leftarrow \mathsf{TrapGen}(1^n, 1^m, q)$ with $\mathbf{A} \in \mathbb{Z}_q^{n \times m}$.
2. Return $pp := \mathbf{A}$ and $td := (pp, \mathbf{T_A})$.

$(\mathbf{h}, r) \leftarrow \mathsf{Hash}(pp, \tau \in \{0,1\}^t, \mathbf{m} \in \{0,1\}^h)$.

1. Parse $pp = \mathbf{A}$.
2. Sample $\mathbf{z} \xleftarrow{\$} \{0,1\}^\kappa$ and set $\mathbf{x} := \tau \|\mathbf{m}\| \mathbf{z} \in \{0,1\}^x$.
3. Compute $\mathbf{A}_h = H(\mathbf{A}, \mathbf{x})$ with $\mathbf{A}_h \in \mathbb{Z}_q^{n \times w}$.
4. Sample $\mathbf{e} = (\mathbf{e}_1, \mathbf{e}_2) \leftarrow D_{\mathbb{Z}^{m+w}, \gamma}$ with $\mathbf{e}_1 \in \mathbb{Z}_q^m$ and $\mathbf{e}_2 \in \mathbb{Z}_q^w$ s.t. $\mathbf{e}_2 \neq 0^w$.
5. Return $\mathbf{h} = [\mathbf{A}|\mathbf{A}_h] \cdot \mathbf{e} \in \mathbb{Z}_q^n$ and $r = (\mathbf{z}, \mathbf{e})$.

$r' \leftarrow \mathsf{Adapt}(td, \tau \in \{0,1\}^t, \mathbf{h}, \mathbf{m} \in \{0,1\}^h, r, \mathbf{m}' \in \{0,1\}^h)$.

1. Parse $td = (pp, \mathbf{T_A})$ and $pp = \mathbf{A}$.
2. If $\mathsf{Check}(pp, \tau, \mathbf{h}, \mathbf{m}, r) = 0$, return $\bot$. Otherwise, continue.
3. Sample $\mathbf{z}' \xleftarrow{\$} \{0,1\}^\kappa$ and set $\mathbf{x}' := \tau \|\mathbf{m}'\| \mathbf{z}' \in \{0,1\}^x$.
4. Compute $\mathbf{A}_h' = H(\mathbf{A}, \mathbf{x}')$ with $\mathbf{A}_h' \in \mathbb{Z}_q^{n \times w}$.
5. Delegate $\mathbf{T}_{\mathbf{A}|\mathbf{A}_h'} \leftarrow \mathsf{TrapDel}([\mathbf{A}|\mathbf{A}_h'], \mathbf{T_A})$.
6. Sample $\mathbf{e}' = (\mathbf{e}_1', \mathbf{e}_2') \leftarrow \mathsf{SamplePre}([\mathbf{A}|\mathbf{A}_h'], \mathbf{T}_{\mathbf{A}|\mathbf{A}_h'}, \mathbf{h}, \gamma)$ with $\mathbf{e}_1' \in \mathbb{Z}_q^m$ and $\mathbf{e}_2' \in \mathbb{Z}_q^w$ s.t. $\mathbf{e}_2' \neq 0^w$.
7. Return $r' = (\mathbf{z}', \mathbf{e}')$.

$0/1 \leftarrow \mathsf{Check}(pp, \tau \in \{0,1\}^t, \mathbf{h}, \mathbf{m} \in \{0,1\}^h, r)$.

1. Parse $pp = \mathbf{A}$ and $r = (\mathbf{z}, \mathbf{e})$. Set $\mathbf{x} := \tau \|\mathbf{m}\| \mathbf{z} \in \{0,1\}^x$.
2. Compute $\mathbf{A}_h = H(\mathbf{A}, \mathbf{x})$ with $\mathbf{A}_h \in \mathbb{Z}_q^{n \times w}$.
3. Parse $\mathbf{e} = (\mathbf{e}_1, \mathbf{e}_2)$ with $\mathbf{e}_1 \in \mathbb{Z}_q^m$ and $\mathbf{e}_2 \in \mathbb{Z}_q^w$. If $\mathbf{h} = [\mathbf{A}|\mathbf{A}_h] \cdot \mathbf{e}$, $\|\mathbf{e}\| \leq \gamma\sqrt{m+w}$ and $\mathbf{e}_2 \neq 0^w$, return 1; otherwise, return 0.

Fig. 5. Tagged chameleon hash tCH' in the random oracle model.

- Let $\gamma \geq \omega(\sqrt{m(m+w)})$ so that Lemma 4 can be applied.
- Let $m = O(n \log q)$ and $2\gamma\sqrt{m(m+w)} \leq \beta$ to serve for our security proof.

Theorem 3. *Let* $\mathsf{H} : \mathbb{Z}_q^{n \times m} \times \{0,1\}^x \rightarrow \mathbb{Z}_q^{n \times w}$ *be a hash function modeled as a random oracle. Given parameters described above, construction* tCH' *in Fig. 5 is a tagged chameleon hash if the* $\mathsf{SIS}_{n,q,\beta,m}$ *assumption holds. Furthermore, restricted collision resistance of* tCH' *enjoys tight security:*

$$\Pr[\mathsf{Exp}_{\mathsf{tCH}',\mathcal{A}}^{rcr}(\kappa) \Rightarrow 1] \leq \mathsf{Adv}_{[n,q,\beta,m]}^{\mathsf{SIS}}(\kappa) + 2^{-O(\kappa)}.$$

The correctness of tCH' follows directly from Lemma 5 (trapdoor delegation) and Lemma 4 (preimage sampling). Proofs of statistical indistinguishability and restricted collision resistance for tCH' are similar to those for tCH, and we provide them in our full version [26].

5   Application of tCH to the Redactable Blockchain

In this section, we show how to apply our tCH in constructing redactable blockchain. In Subsect. 5.1, we introduce some notations of a redactable blockchain. In Subsect. 5.2, we show how to redact a blockchain with a tCH. In Subsect. 5.3, we provide a security analysis of our redactable blockchain.

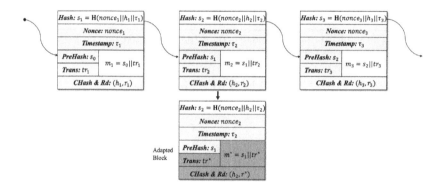

Fig. 6. An illustration of a redactable blockchain from tCH. All parts with light-grey background constitutes a block. Parts with white background are conceptual and shown for better presentation. Blocks link to a chain in a way that a previous hash value s_{i-1} for block B_{i-1} is stored in the "PreHash" part of block B_i. Take an adaptation from tr_2 to tr^* as an example, the corresponding hash-randomness pair (h_2, r_2) will be changed accordingly to (h_2, r^*), where r^* is computed by Adapt of tCH. The changed parts in the adapted block are decorated with dark-grey background. The down-arrow in dark-blue denotes the authorized adaptation done by the trusted regulation party. (Color figure online)

5.1   Redactable Blockchain

We follow notations of blockchain and redactable blockchain introduced in [3, 18]. According to [3], a redactable block uses two hash functions, one is a cryptographic hash and the other is a chameleon hash. Now we replace the chameleon hash with our tCH, and additionally introduce a unique identifier (like the timestamp, previous hash or position of the block in the chain) into each block to serve as the "tag τ" of tCH. See Fig. 6 for a pictorial presentation.

Let $H : \{0,1\}^* \to \mathbb{N}$ be a cryptographic hash function and $\mathsf{tCH} = (\mathsf{Setup}, \mathsf{Hash}, \mathsf{Adapt}, \mathsf{Check})$ be a tCH. In a redactable blockchain, each block B is of the form

$$B = \langle nonce, \tau, \underbrace{s, tr}_{m}, (h, r) \rangle,$$

where $nonce \in \mathbb{N}$ denotes the nonce value, $\tau \in \{0,1\}^t$ denotes a unique identifier, $s \in \mathbb{N}$ is a hash value computed by H, $tr \in \{0,1\}^x$ denotes the information stored in a block, (h, r) is a hash-randomness pair computed by Hash from $m :=$ $(s \| tr) \in \{0,1\}^h$ w.r.t. τ, i.e., $(h, r) \leftarrow \mathsf{Hash}(\tau, m)$. We say that a block B is valid if $\mathsf{ValidRB}_q^D(B) = 1$ with

$$\mathsf{ValidRB}_q^D(B) := \big(H(nonce \| h \| \tau) < D\big) \wedge \big(\mathsf{Check}(\tau, h, m, r) = 1\big) \wedge \big(nonce < q\big),$$

where $D \in \mathbb{N}$ is the block's difficulty level and $q \in \mathbb{N}$ denotes the maximum allowed number of hash queries in a round.

Algorithm 1: Blockchain Redacting Algorithm

Input: The public parameter and trapdoor (pp, td) of tCH.
      A blockchain $\mathcal{C}$ with $\mathsf{len}(\mathcal{C}) = n$.
      A sequence of target indices $\mathcal{I} = (\iota_1, \ldots, \iota_k) \subseteq [n]$.
      A sequence of target messages $\mathcal{M} = (tr^*_{\iota_1}, \ldots, tr^*_{\iota_k})$.
Output: A redacted blockchain $\mathcal{C}'$ with $\mathsf{len}(\mathcal{C}') = n$

1   **for** $i = 1, \ldots, n$ **do**
2   **if** $i \in \mathcal{I}$ **then**
3   Parse the i-th block B_i of $\mathcal{C}$ as $B_i = \langle nonce_i, \tau_i, s_i, tr_i, (h_i, r_i) \rangle$;
4   Compute $r^*_i \leftarrow \mathsf{Adapt}(td, \tau_i, h_i, s_i \| tr_i, r_i, s_i \| tr^*_i)$;
5   Set $B^*_i := \langle nonce_i, \tau_i, s_i, tr^*_i, (h_i, r^*_i) \rangle$;
6   Set $\mathcal{C} := \mathcal{C}^{\lceil n-i+1} \| B^*_i \| {}^{i\rceil}\mathcal{C}$;

7   **return** $\mathcal{C}$

A redactable blockchain $\mathcal{C}$ is a sequence of valid blocks. The head of chain $\mathcal{C}$, denoted by $\mathsf{head}(\mathcal{C})$, is the rightmost block in it. The length of chain $\mathcal{C}$, denoted by $\mathsf{len}(\mathcal{C})$, is the number of blocks contained in it. Let $\mathcal{C} = \varepsilon$ if chain $\mathcal{C}$ is empty. Any chain $\mathcal{C}'$ with head $\mathsf{head}(\mathcal{C}') = \langle nonce', \tau', s', tr', (h', r') \rangle$ can be extended to a longer one by appending a new valid block $B = \langle nonce, \tau, s, tr, (h, r) \rangle$ satisfying $s = \mathsf{H}(nonce' \| h' \| \tau')$, and then the head of the extended chain $\mathcal{C} = \mathcal{C}' \| B$ is changed to $\mathsf{head}(\mathcal{C}) = B$. In case $\mathcal{C}' = \varepsilon$, any valid block B can append to it.

For a chain $\mathcal{C}$ with length $\mathsf{len}(\mathcal{C}) = n$ and any nonnegative integer $k \leq n$, we denote by $\mathcal{C}^{\lceil k}$ the chain resulting from removing the k rightmost blocks of $\mathcal{C}$, and denote by ${}^{k\rceil}\mathcal{C}$ the chain resulting from removing the k leftmost blocks of $\mathcal{C}$.

5.2   Redacting Blocks

In this subsection, we provide a blockchain redacting algorithm to redact blocks. Let n, k be positive integers s.t. $k \leq n$. The algorithm takes as inputs the public parameter and trapdoor of a tagged chameleon hash tCH, a blockchain $\mathcal{C}$ of length n, k target indices that represent the positions of blocks in $\mathcal{C}$ to be redacted, and k corresponding adapted messages for blocks to be redacted, and finally returns a redacted blockchain $\mathcal{C}'$. The detailed description is given in Algorithm 1.

5.3   Security Analysis

In this subsection, we provide a security analysis for the resulting redactable blockchain given a tCH with r-CR security. Note that tCH works in the one-time tag mode in the redactable blockchain since the tCH hash value w.r.t. each settled block is computed with a unique tag and authorized adaptations are made only for those settled blocks. Then f-CR of tCH is equivalent to r-CR according to Theorem 1. Therefore, all we need to do is to prove that the redactable blockchain is secure as long as tCH has f-CR security.

As we described in Subsect. 5.1, each block B in the chain is of the form $B = \langle nonce, \tau, s, tr, (h, r) \rangle$. For expression simplicity, we only consider the tCH-related parts of each block and briefly write B as $B = \langle \tau, h, m, r \rangle$ (note that $m = s \| tr$). Recall that in a redactable blockchain system, the adversary sees all original blocks $B_1, B_2, B_3, \cdots$ and adapted blocks $\{B_1^i\}_{i \in [n_1]}, \{B_2^i\}_{i \in [n_2]}, \{B_3^i\}_{i \in [n_3]}$, $\cdots$, where each $n_j = \mathsf{poly}(\kappa)$ denotes the number of adaptations for block B_j. The aim of an adversary is to redact the chain by adapting some block $B_j = \langle \tau_j, h_j, m_j, r_j \rangle$ to a new one $B^* = \langle \tau_j, h_j, m^*, r^* \rangle$, such that $h_j = \mathsf{Hash}(\tau_j, m_j; r_j) = \mathsf{Hash}(\tau_j, m^*; r^*)$ and $m^* \notin \{m_j\} \cup \{m_j^i\}_{i \in [n_j]}$ w.r.t. those B_j and $\{B_j^i\}_{i \in [n_j]}$.

We show that if there exists an adversary $\mathcal{A}$ performing the above attack successfully, then we can break the full collision resistance of tCH. If $\mathcal{A}$ wins, it must hold that $h_j = \mathsf{Hash}(\tau_j, m_j; r_j) = \mathsf{Hash}(\tau_j, m^*; r^*)$ and m^* is fresh w.r.t. (τ_j, h_j). In this case, we find a tuple $(\tau_j, h_j, m^*, r^*, m_j, r_j)$ s.t. $h_j = \mathsf{Hash}(\tau_j, m_j; r_j) = \mathsf{Hash}(\tau_j, m^*; r^*)$ and (τ_j, h_j, m^*) is fresh, and hence break the f-CR of tCH.

Therefore, the security of the resulting redactable blockchain is reduced to the f-CR security of tCH. Given the equivalence of f-CR and r-CR in the scenario of redactable blockchain, we know that, the redactable blockchain is secure as long as the underlying tCH has r-CR security.

Finally with Theorems 2 and 3, both our tCHs in Subsect. 4.1 and Subsect. 4.2 can serve as secure compilers converting a conventional blockchain to a redactable one.

Acknowledgements. We would like to thank the reviewers for their valuable comments. The authors are partially sponsored by Guangdong Major Project of Basic and Applied Basic Research under Grant No. 2019B030302008, National Natural Science Foundation of China under Grant No. 61925207 and the National Key R&D Program of China under Grant No. 2022YFB2701500.

References

1. Agrawal, S., Boneh, D., Boyen, X.: Efficient lattice (H)IBE in the standard model. In: Gilbert, H. (ed.) EUROCRYPT 2010. LNCS, vol. 6110, pp. 553–572. Springer, Heidelberg (2010). https://doi.org/10.1007/978-3-642-13190-5_28
2. Alwen, J., Peikert, C.: Generating shorter bases for hard random lattices. In: STACS, pp. 75–86 (2009)
3. Ateniese, G., Magri, B., Venturi, D., Andrade, E.R.: Redactable blockchain - or - rewriting history in bitcoin and friends. In: EuroS&P, pp. 111–126 (2017)
4. Ateniese, G., de Medeiros, B.: On the key exposure problem in chameleon hashes. In: Blundo, C., Cimato, S. (eds.) SCN 2004. LNCS, vol. 3352, pp. 165–179. Springer, Heidelberg (2005). https://doi.org/10.1007/978-3-540-30598-9_12
5. Banerjee, A., Peikert, C., Rosen, A.: Pseudorandom functions and lattices. In: Pointcheval, D., Johansson, T. (eds.) EUROCRYPT 2012. LNCS, vol. 7237, pp. 719–737. Springer, Heidelberg (2012). https://doi.org/10.1007/978-3-642-29011-4_42

6. Boneh, D., et al.: Fully key-homomorphic encryption, arithmetic circuit ABE and compact garbled circuits. In: Nguyen, P.Q., Oswald, E. (eds.) EUROCRYPT 2014. LNCS, vol. 8441, pp. 533–556. Springer, Heidelberg (2014). https://doi.org/10.1007/978-3-642-55220-5_30

7. Boyen, X., Li, Q.: Towards tightly secure lattice short signature and ID-based encryption. In: Cheon, J.H., Takagi, T. (eds.) ASIACRYPT 2016. LNCS, vol. 10032, pp. 404–434. Springer, Heidelberg (2016). https://doi.org/10.1007/978-3-662-53890-6_14

8. Brakerski, Z., Vaikuntanathan, V.: Lattice-based FHE as secure as PKE. In: ITCS (2014). https://doi.org/10.1145/2554797.2554799

9. Camenisch, J., Derler, D., Krenn, S., Pöhls, H.C., Samelin, K., Slamanig, D.: Chameleon-hashes with ephemeral trapdoors – and applications to invisible sanitizable signatures. In: Fehr, S. (ed.) PKC 2017. LNCS, vol. 10175, pp. 152–182. Springer, Heidelberg (2017). https://doi.org/10.1007/978-3-662-54388-7_6

10. Chen, X., Tian, H., Zhang, F., Ding, Y.: Comments and improvements on key-exposure free chameleon hashing based on factoring. In: Lai, X., Yung, M., Lin, D. (eds.) Inscrypt 2010. LNCS, vol. 6584, pp. 415–426. Springer, Heidelberg (2011). https://doi.org/10.1007/978-3-642-21518-6_29

11. Chen, X., Zhang, F., Kim, K.: Chameleon hashing without key exposure. In: Zhang, K., Zheng, Y. (eds.) ISC 2004. LNCS, vol. 3225, pp. 87–98. Springer, Heidelberg (2004). https://doi.org/10.1007/978-3-540-30144-8_8

12. Derler, D., Krenn, S., Samelin, K., Slamanig, D.: Fully collision-resistant chameleon-hashes from simpler and post-quantum assumptions. In: Galdi, C., Kolesnikov, V. (eds.) SCN 2020. LNCS, vol. 12238, pp. 427–447. Springer, Cham (2020). https://doi.org/10.1007/978-3-030-57990-6_21

13. Derler, D., Samelin, K., Slamanig, D.: Bringing order to chaos: the case of collision-resistant chameleon-hashes. In: Kiayias, A., Kohlweiss, M., Wallden, P., Zikas, V. (eds.) PKC 2020. LNCS, vol. 12110, pp. 462–492. Springer, Cham (2020). https://doi.org/10.1007/978-3-030-45374-9_16

14. Deuber, D., Magri, B., Thyagarajan, S.A.K.: Redactable blockchain in the permissionless setting. In: IEEE Symposium on Security and Privacy, pp. 124–138 (2019). https://doi.org/10.1109/SP.2019.00039

15. Dodis, Y., Reyzin, L., Smith, A.: Fuzzy extractors: how to generate strong keys from biometrics and other noisy data. In: Cachin, C., Camenisch, J.L. (eds.) EUROCRYPT 2004. LNCS, vol. 3027, pp. 523–540. Springer, Heidelberg (2004). https://doi.org/10.1007/978-3-540-24676-3_31

16. Dorri, A., Kanhere, S.S., Jurdak, R.: MOF-BC: a memory optimized and flexible blockchain for large scale networks. Future Gener. Comput. Syst. **92**, 357–373 (2019). https://doi.org/10.1016/J.FUTURE.2018.10.002

17. Florian, M., Henningsen, S.A., Beaucamp, S., Scheuermann, B.: Erasing data from blockchain nodes. In: EuroS&P. pp. 367–376 (2019). https://doi.org/10.1109/EUROSPW.2019.00047

18. Garay, J., Kiayias, A., Leonardos, N.: The bitcoin backbone protocol: analysis and applications. In: Oswald, E., Fischlin, M. (eds.) EUROCRYPT 2015. LNCS, vol. 9057, pp. 281–310. Springer, Heidelberg (2015). https://doi.org/10.1007/978-3-662-46803-6_10

19. Gentry, C., Peikert, C., Vaikuntanathan, V.: Trapdoors for hard lattices and new cryptographic constructions. In: STOC, pp. 197–206 (2008)

20. Gentry, C., Sahai, A., Waters, B.: Homomorphic encryption from learning with errors: conceptually-simpler, asymptotically-faster, attribute-based. In: Canetti, R., Garay, J.A. (eds.) CRYPTO 2013. LNCS, vol. 8042, pp. 75–92. Springer, Heidelberg (2013). https://doi.org/10.1007/978-3-642-40041-4_5

21. Goldreich, O., Goldwasser, S., Micali, S.: How to construct random functions (extended abstract). In: FOCS, pp. 464–479. IEEE Computer Society (1984)

22. Goldwasser, S., Micali, S., Rivest, R.L.: A digital signature scheme secure against adaptive chosen-message attacks. SIAM J. Comput. (2) (1988). https://doi.org/10.1137/0217017

23. Hohenberger, S., Waters, B.: Short and stateless signatures from the RSA assumption. In: Halevi, S. (ed.) CRYPTO 2009. LNCS, vol. 5677, pp. 654–670. Springer, Heidelberg (2009). https://doi.org/10.1007/978-3-642-03356-8_38

24. Khalili, M., Dakhilalian, M., Susilo, W.: Efficient chameleon hash functions in the enhanced collision resistant model. Inf. Sci. 155–164 (2020)

25. Krawczyk, H., Rabin, T.: Chameleon signatures. In: Proceedings of the Network and Distributed System Security Symposium. NDSS 2000, San Diego, California, USA (2000). https://www.ndss-symposium.org/ndss2000/chameleon-signatures/

26. Li, Y., Liu, S.: Tagged chameleon hash from lattice and application to redactable blockchain. ePrint (2023). https://eprint.iacr.org/2023/774

27. Matzutt, R., Kalde, B., Pennekamp, J., Drichel, A., Henze, M., Wehrle, K.: How to securely prune bitcoin's blockchain. In: IFIP Networking Conference, pp. 298–306 (2020). https://ieeexplore.ieee.org/document/9142720

28. Micciancio, D., Peikert, C.: Trapdoors for lattices: simpler, tighter, faster, smaller. In: Pointcheval, D., Johansson, T. (eds.) EUROCRYPT 2012. LNCS, vol. 7237, pp. 700–718. Springer, Heidelberg (2012). https://doi.org/10.1007/978-3-642-29011-4_41

29. Micciancio, D., Peikert, C.: Hardness of SIS and LWE with small parameters. In: Canetti, R., Garay, J.A. (eds.) CRYPTO 2013. LNCS, vol. 8042, pp. 21–39. Springer, Heidelberg (2013). https://doi.org/10.1007/978-3-642-40041-4_2

30. Micciancio, D., Regev, O.: Worst-case to average-case reductions based on gaussian measures. In: FOCS. IEEE Computer Society (2004). https://doi.org/10.1109/FOCS.2004.72

31. Pan, J., Wagner, B.: Short identity-based signatures with tight security from lattices. In: Cheon, J.H., Tillich, J.-P. (eds.) PQCrypto 2021 2021. LNCS, vol. 12841, pp. 360–379. Springer, Cham (2021). https://doi.org/10.1007/978-3-030-81293-5_19

32. Pedersen, T.P.: Non-interactive and information-theoretic secure verifiable secret sharing. In: Feigenbaum, J. (ed.) CRYPTO 1991. LNCS, vol. 576, pp. 129–140. Springer, Heidelberg (1992). https://doi.org/10.1007/3-540-46766-1_9

33. Peikert, C.: Bonsai trees (or, arboriculture in lattice-based cryptography). IACR Cryptology ePrint Archive (2009). http://eprint.iacr.org/2009/359

34. Puddu, I., Dmitrienko, A., Capkun, S.: μchain: how to forget without hard forks. IACR Cryptology ePrint Archive, p. 106 (2017). http://eprint.iacr.org/2017/106

35. Pyoung, C.K., Baek, S.J.: Blockchain of finite-lifetime blocks with applications to edge-based IoT. IEEE Internet Things J. 7(3), 2102–2116 (2020). https://doi.org/10.1109/JIOT.2019.2959599

36. Thyagarajan, S.A.K., Bhat, A., Magri, B., Tschudi, D., Kate, A.: Reparo: Publicly verifiable layer to repair blockchains. In: Borisov, N., Diaz, C. (eds.) FC 2021. LNCS, vol. 12675, pp. 37–56. Springer, Heidelberg (2021). https://doi.org/10.1007/978-3-662-64331-0_2

37. Tsabary, R.: Fully secure attribute-based encryption for t-CNF from LWE. In: Boldyreva, A., Micciancio, D. (eds.) CRYPTO 2019. LNCS, vol. 11692, pp. 62–85. Springer, Cham (2019). https://doi.org/10.1007/978-3-030-26948-7_3

38. Wu, C., Ke, L., Du, Y.: Quantum resistant key-exposure free chameleon hash and applications in redactable blockchain. Inf. Sci. 438–449 (2021)

39. Zhang, D., Le, J., Lei, X., Xiang, T., Liao, X.: Exploring the redaction mechanisms of mutable blockchains: a comprehensive survey. Int. J. Intell. Syst. **36**(9), 5051–5084 (2021). https://doi.org/10.1002/INT.22502

Diffie Hellman and Applications

Laconic Branching Programs
from the Diffie-Hellman Assumption

Sanjam Garg[1], Mohammad Hajiabadi[2], Peihan Miao[3], and Alice Murphy[2(✉)]

[1] NTT Research and UC Berkeley, Berkeley, USA
`sanjamg@berkeley.edu`
[2] University of Waterloo, Waterloo, Canada
`{mdhajiabadi,anlmurph}@uwaterloo.ca`
[3] Brown University, Providence, USA
`peihan_miao@brown.edu`

Abstract. Laconic cryptography enables secure two-party computation (2PC) on unbalanced inputs with asymptotically-optimal communication in just two rounds of communication. In particular, the receiver (who sends the first-round message) holds a long input and the sender (who sends the second-round message) holds a short input, and the size of their communication to securely compute a function on their joint inputs only grows with the size of the sender's input and is independent of the receiver's input size. The work on laconic oblivious transfer (OT) [Cho et al. CRYPTO 2017] and laconic private set intersection (PSI) [Alamati et al. TCC 2021] shows how to achieve secure laconic computation for OT and PSI from the Diffie-Hellman assumption.

In this work, we push the limits further and achieve laconic branching programs from the Diffie-Hellman assumption. In particular, the receiver holds a large branching program P and the sender holds a short input x. We present a two-round 2PC protocol that allows the receiver to learn x iff $P(x) = 1$, and nothing else. The communication only grows with the size of x and the depth of P, and does not further depend on the size of P.

Keywords: Laconic cryptography · unbalanced secure computation · branching programs

1 Introduction

Suppose a server holds a *large* set of elements Y (which could be exponentially large) that can be represented as a polynomial-sized branching program P, that is, $y \in Y$ iff $P(y) = 1$. The server would like to publish a *succinct* digest of Y such that any client who holds a *small* set X can send a *short* message to the server to allow her to learn the set intersection $X \cap Y$ but nothing beyond that.

This is a special case of the secure two-party computation (2PC) [Yao86] problem, where two mutually distrustful parties, each holding a private input

© International Association for Cryptologic Research 2024
Q. Tang and V. Teague (Eds.): PKC 2024, LNCS 14603, pp. 323–355, 2024.
https://doi.org/10.1007/978-3-031-57725-3_11

x and y respectively, would like to jointly compute a function f over their private inputs without revealing anything beyond the output of the computation. Garbled circuits [Yao86] together with oblivious transfer (OT) [Rab81,Rab05] enables 2PC for any function f with two rounds of communication: one message from the *receiver* to the *sender* and another message from the sender back to the receiver. This approach achieves the optimal round complexity; nevertheless, it requires the communication complexity to grow with the size of f. In particular, if we represent f as a Boolean circuit, then the communication grows with the number of gates in the circuit, which grows at least with the size of the inputs x and y. For unbalanced input lengths (i.e., $|x| \gg |y|$ or $|x| \ll |y|$), *is it possible to make the communication only grow with the shorter input and independent of the longer input?*

Long Sender Input. When the sender has a long input, i.e. $|x| \gg |y|$, we can use fully homomorphic encryption (FHE) [Gen09] to achieve communication that only grows with the receiver's input length $|y|$ plus the output length. This technique works for any function but can only be based on variants of the learning with errors (LWE) assumption [GSW13]. For simpler functions that can be represented by a branching program, in particular, if the sender holds a private large branching program P and the receiver holds a private short input y, the work of Ishai and Paskin [IP07] illustrates how to construct 2PC for $P(y)$ where the communication only grows with $|y|$ and the *depth* of P, and does not further depend on the size of P. Their construction is generic from a primitive called *rate-1 OT*, which can be built based on a variety of assumptions such as DCR, DDH, QR, and LWE assumptions with varying efficiency parameters [IP07,DGI+19, GHO20,CGH+21]. In this setting, there are works in secure BP evaluation for applications in machine learning and medicine [BPSW07,BFK+09,KNL+19, CDPP22]. Our results concern the dual setting, in which the receiver has the longer input and is the party that learns the output. Moreover, this should be achieved in only two rounds of communication.

Long Receiver Input. When the receiver has a long input, i.e. $|x| \ll |y|$, a recent line of work on *laconic cryptography* [CDG+17,QWW18,DGGM19,ABD+21, ALOS22] focuses on realizing secure 2PC with asymptotically-optimal communication in two rounds. In particular, the receiver has a large input and the size of her protocol message only depends on the security parameter and not her input size. The second message (sent by the sender) as well as the sender's computation may grow with the size of the sender's input, but should be independent of the receiver's input size.

In this dual setting, the work of Quach, Wee, and Wichs [QWW18] shows how to realize laconic 2PC for general functionalities using LWE. Regarding laconic 2PC for simpler functions from assumptions other than LWE, much less is known compared to the setting of long sender inputs.

The work of Cho et al. [CDG+17] introduced the notion of laconic oblivious transfer (laconic OT), where the receiver holds a large input $D \in \{0, 1\}^n$, the sender holds an input $(i \in [n], m_0, m_1)$, and the two-round protocol allows the receiver to learn $(i, m_{D[i]})$ and nothing more. The communication complexity as well as the sender's computation only grow with the security parameter and is independent of the size of D. Besides LWE [QWW18], laconic OT can be built from DDH, CDH, and QR [CDG+17, DG17].[1] Recent work [ABD+21, ALOS22] extends the functionality to laconic private set intersection (laconic PSI), where the sender and receiver each holds a private set of elements X and Y respectively ($|X| \ll |Y|$), and the two-round protocol allows the receiver to learn the set intersection $X \cap Y$ and nothing more. The communication complexity and the sender's computational complexity are both independent of $|Y|$. Laconic PSI can be built from CDH/LWE [ABD+21] or pairings [ALOS22].

Both laconic OT and laconic PSI can be viewed as special cases of a branching program. Recall that in the setting of long sender input, where a sender has a large branching program, we have generic constructions from rate-1 OT, which can be built from various assumptions. However, in the dual setting of long receiver input, we no longer have such a generic construction. Laconic OT *seems* to be a counterpart building block in the dual setting, but it does *not* give us laconic branching programs. Given the gap between the two settings, we ask the following question:

Can we achieve laconic branching programs from assumptions other than LWE?

This diversifies the set of assumptions from which laconic MPC can be realized. It also increases our understanding of how far each assumption allows us to expand the functionality, which helps in gaining insights into the theoretical limits of the assumptions themselves.

1.1   Our Results

We answer the above question in the affirmative. In particular, as a natural counterpart to the aforementioned setting of long sender input, when the receiver holds a private large branching program BP and the sender holds a private short input x, we construct a two-round 2PC protocol allowing the receiver to learn x iff BP(x) = 1, and nothing else. The communication only grows with $|x|$ and the *depth* of BP, and does not further depend on the size of BP. Furthermore, the sender's computation also only grows with $|x|$ and the depth of BP. The receiver's computation grows with the number of BP nodes and the number of root-to-leaf paths. Our construction is based on anonymous hash encryption schemes [BLSV18], which can in turn be based on CDH/LWE [DG17, BLSV18].

Sender Security. We achieve what we call *weak sender security* which says if BP(x) = 0, then no information about x is leaked; else, there are no privacy guarantees for x. A stronger security requirement would be that in the latter case, the

---

[1] Importantly, in laconic OT, the receiver's second-phase computation time should have at most a polylog dependence on $|D|$. This can be achieved in the laconic OT setting because the index i is known to the receiver. In other settings, such as laconic PSI, this cannot be realized (without pre-processing) because *not* probing a particular database entry leaks information about the sender's input.

receiver only learns $BP(x)$, and no other information about x. Unfortunately, realizing strong sender security is too difficult in light of known barriers: it generically implies a notion called *private laconic OT* [CDG+17, DGI+19]. Private laconic OT is laconic OT in which the index i chosen by the sender is also kept hidden from the receiver. The only existing construction of private laconic OT with polylogarithmic communication uses techniques from laconic secure function evaluation and is based on LWE [QWW18]. In particular, it is not known if private laconic OT can be realized using Diffie-Hellman assumptions.

Strong sender security allows one to achieve *laconic PSI cardinality*, a generalization of laconic PSI. In the PSI cardinality problem, the receiver learns only the size of the intersection and nothing about the intersection set itself. Strong sender security for a receiver with a large set S and a sender with a single element x would allow the receiver to *only* learn whether or not $x \in S$. This immediately implies laconic PSI cardinality by having the sender send a second-round protocol message for each element in its set. Laconic PSI cardinality generically implies private laconic OT, establishing a barrier. The same barriers prevented [DKL+23] from building laconic PSI cardinality. We can get laconic PSI as an application of our results (and other applications discussed below), but our results do not allow us to realize laconic PSI cardinality. More specifically, after receiving the second-round message from the sender, the receiver in our protocol works by checking which path in their BP tree (if any) decrypts to "accept". If there is an accepting path, then $BP(x) = 1$, where x is the sender's input. But this reveals the value of x since the receiver knows which path resulted in acceptance.

Applications. Our laconic branching program construction directly implies laconic OT and laconic PSI, as their functionalities can be represented as branching programs. Moreover, we can capture other functionalities not considered by previous work, such as private-set unions (PSU). A branching program for PSU can be obtained by making local changes to a branching program for PSI. (See Sect. 5.) This demonstrates the versatility of our approach, giving a unifying construction for all these functionalities. In contrast, the accumulator-based PSI constructions in [ABD+21, ALOS22, DKL+23] are crucially tied to the PSI setting, and do not seem to extend to the PSU setting. This is because the sender's message to the receiver only provides enough information to indicate which element (if any) in the receiver's set is also held by the sender. In essence, only the index of this element within the receiver's set needs to be conveyed in the sender's message. In the PSU setting, on the other hand, there could be elements in the union that do not exist in the receiver's set. So, the sender's message needs to contain more information than an index. If the sender's element is not in the receiver's set, the receiver needs to be able to recover the sender's element from the message.

Our techniques can be used in unbalanced PSI where the receiver holds a large set (possibly of exponential size) that can be represented as a branching program. For instance, a recent work by Garimella et al. [GRS22] introduced the notion of *structure-aware PSI* where one party's (potentially large) set Y is publicly known to have a certain structure. As long as the publicly known structure can be represented as a branching program, our techniques can be used to achieve a two-round fuzzy-matching PSI protocol where the communication only grows with the size of the smaller set $|X|$ and the *depth* of the branching program, and does not further depend on $|Y|$, which could potentially be *exponentially* large.

2 Technical Overview

Our constructions are based on hash encryption (HE) schemes [DG17,BLSV18]. An HE scheme, parameterized by $n = n(\lambda)$ (where λ is the security parameter), consists of a hash function $\mathsf{Hash}(\mathsf{pp}, \cdot) : \{0,1\}^n \to \{0,1\}^\lambda$ and associated HEnc and HDec functions. One can encrypt n pairs of plaintexts $\mathbf{m} := (m_{i,b})$ (for $i \in [n]$ and $b \in \{0,1\}$) with respect to $h := \mathsf{Hash}(\mathsf{pp}, z)$ to get $\mathsf{cth} \leftarrow \mathsf{HEnc}(h, \mathbf{m})$.[2] The ciphertext cth is such that given z, one may recover $(m_{1,z_1}, \ldots, m_{n,z_n})$ from cth, while maintaining semantic security for $(m_{i,1-z_i})$ even in the presence of z. HE can be realized using CDH/LWE [DG17,BLSV18].

Consider a simple example where the receiver R has a depth-one BP on bits (see Definition 3 for branching programs) where the root node encodes index $i^* \in [n]$ and its left child encodes accept ($b_0 := \mathsf{acpt}$) and its right child encodes reject ($b_1 := \mathsf{rjct}$). This BP evaluates an input x by checking the bit value at index i^*. If $x[i^*] = 0$, then the value of left child is output: $b_0 = \mathsf{acpt}$. If $x[i^*] = 1$, then the value of right child is output: $b_1 = \mathsf{rjct}$. As a starting point, suppose R only wants to learn if $\mathsf{BP}(x) = 1$, where x is the sender's input. The receiver hashes $h := \mathsf{Hash}(\mathsf{pp}, (i^*, b_0, b_1))$, padding the input if necessary, and sends h to the sender, S. S has the following circuit $\mathsf{F}[x]$ with their input x hardwired: on input (j, q_0, q_1), $\mathsf{F}[x]$ outputs $q_{x[j]}$. S garbles $\mathsf{F}[x]$ to get a garbled circuit $\widetilde{\mathsf{F}}$ and corresponding labels $(\mathsf{lb}_{i,b})$. S uses the hash value, h, from R to compute $\mathsf{cth} \leftarrow \mathsf{HEnc}(h, (\mathsf{lb}_{i,b}))$. Finally, S sends $(\widetilde{\mathsf{F}}, \mathsf{cth})$ to R. The receiver, given her hash pre-image value $z := (i^*, \mathsf{acpt}, \mathsf{rjct})$ can only recover $(\mathsf{lb}_{i,z[i]})$, allowing her in turn to learn $\mathsf{F}[x](z)$ from the garbled circuit, outputting either accept ($\mathsf{BP}(x) = 1$) or reject ($\mathsf{BP}(x) = 0$).

Beyond Depth 1. Next, consider the BP of depth 2 in Fig. 1 held by the receiver, R. Each internal node encodes an index, $\mathsf{rot}, \mathsf{lft}, \mathsf{rgt} \in [n]$. The four leaves have values with variables $(b_{00}, b_{01}, b_{10}, b_{11})$. For $i, j \in \{0,1\}$, $b_{ij} \in \{\mathsf{acpt}, \mathsf{rjct}\}$. Suppose $x[\mathsf{rot}] = 0$, where x is the sender's input, so the root-leaf path induced by $\mathsf{BP}(x)$ first goes left. If the sender, S, 'by some miracle' knows the hash value $h_0 := \mathsf{Hash}(\mathsf{pp}, (\mathsf{lft}, b_{00}, b_{01}))$, he can, as above, send a garbled circuit for $\mathsf{F}[x]$ and an HE ciphertext wrt h_0 of the underlying labels, allowing R to evaluate $\mathsf{F}[x](\mathsf{lft}, b_{00}, b_{01})$. But S does not know the value of h_0, nor does he know whether the first move is left or right, because the BP is hidden from S. Moreover, R cannot send both $h_0 := \mathsf{Hash}(\mathsf{pp}, (\mathsf{lft}, b_{00}, b_{01}))$ and $h_1 := \mathsf{Hash}(\mathsf{pp}, (\mathsf{rgt}, b_{10}, b_{11}))$ because (a) there will be a size blowup (the communication will grow with the size, and not the depth, of the BP), and (b) R will learn more information than

---

[2] HEnc also takes the public parameter pp as input, but we omit it here for brevity.

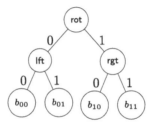

Fig. 1. Depth 2 BP example

necessary because S does not know *a priori* whether the induced computation travels left or right, so he has to encrypt the labels under both h_0 and h_1. But encrypting the labels $(\mathsf{lb}_{i,b})$ under both h_0 and h_1 will allow the receiver to recover two labels for an index on which $(\mathsf{lft}, b_{00}, b_{01})$ and $(\mathsf{rgt}, b_{10}, b_{11})$ differ, destroying garbled-circuit security.

Fixing Size Blow-Up via Deferred Encryption. We fix the above issue via deferred encryption techniques [DG17, BLSV18, GHMR18, ABD+21], allowing the sender to defer the HE encryptions of $(\mathsf{lb}_{i,b})$ labels to the receiver herself at decryption time! To enable this technique, the receiver further hashes (h_0, h_1) such that during decryption, the receiver, through the evaluation of a garbled circuit, will obtain an HE encryption of $(\mathsf{lb}_{i,b})$ labels with respect to $h_{x[\mathsf{rot}]}$, where $(\mathsf{lb}_{i,b})$ and (h_0, h_1) are as above. To do this, we have to explain how the receiver further hashes down h_0 and h_1, and how she can later perform deferred encryption. First, the receiver R computes the hash value $\mathsf{hr} := \mathsf{Hash}(\mathsf{pp}, (h_0, h_1, \mathsf{rot}))$, and sends hr to S. Next the sender $S(x)$ garbles $\mathsf{F}[x]$ to get $(\widetilde{\mathsf{F}}, \mathsf{lb}_{i,b})$ as above. Then, he forms a circuit $\mathsf{G}[x, (\mathsf{lb}_{i,b})]$ with x and $(\mathsf{lb}_{i,b})$ hardwired, which on an input (h'_0, h'_1, u) outputs $\mathsf{HEnc}(h'_{x_u}, (\mathsf{lb}_{i,b}))$. The sender garbles $\mathsf{G}[x, (\mathsf{lb}_{i,b})]$ to get $(\widetilde{\mathsf{G}}, (\mathsf{lb}'_{i,b}))$. Before proceeding, let us consider R's perspective. If R is given $\widetilde{\mathsf{G}}$ and the labels $(\mathsf{lb}'_{i,z'[i]})$, where $z' := (h_0, h_1, \mathsf{rot})$, she can evaluate $\widetilde{\mathsf{G}}$ on these labels, which will in turn release an HE encryption of labels $(\mathsf{lb}_{i,b})$ under $h_{x_{\mathsf{rot}}}$, as desired. To ensure R only gets the $(\mathsf{lb}'_{i,z'[i]})$ labels, S encrypts the $\{\mathsf{lb}'_{i,b}\}$ labels under hr, and sends the resulting HE ciphertext cth', as well as $\widetilde{\mathsf{F}}$ and $\widetilde{\mathsf{G}}$ to R. From cth' and $z' := (h_0, h_1, \mathsf{rot})$, R can only recover the labels $(\mathsf{lb}'_{i,z'[i]})$, as desired.

How Can the Receiver Decrypt? The receiver will evaluate $\widetilde{\mathsf{G}}$ on the decrypted $(\mathsf{lb}'_{i,z'[i]})$ labels, releasing an HE encryption cth of $(\mathsf{lb}_{i,b})$ labels under $h_{x_{\mathsf{rot}}}$. The receiver does not know whether cth is encrypted under h_0 or h_1, so she tries to decrypt with respect to the pre-images of both hash values and checks which one (if any) is valid. However, this results in the following security issue: an HE scheme is not guaranteed to hide the underlying hash value with respect to which an HE ciphertext was made. For example, imagine an HE scheme where $\mathsf{HEnc}(h, (m_{i,b}))$ appends h to the ciphertext. Employing such an HE scheme (which is semantically secure) in the above construction will signal to the receiver if cth' was encrypted under h_0 or h_1, namely the bit value of $x[\mathsf{rot}]$. This breaks sender security if $\mathsf{BP}(x) = 0$. Moreover, even if the HE encryption scheme is anonymous in the sense of hiding h, decrypting an h_b-formed HE encryption under the pre-image of h_{1-b} may result in $\perp$, or in junk labels that do not work on $\tilde{\mathsf{F}}$. We use the same technique as in [ABD+21] of using anonymous hash encryption and garbled circuits to resolve this issue.

Signalling the Correct Output of F. In the above examples, $\mathsf{F}[x]$ outputs either acpt or rjct, indicating if $\mathsf{BP}(x)$ equals 1 or 0, respectively. But, in the desired functionality, $\mathsf{F}[x]$ outputs x if $\mathsf{BP}(x) = 1$. We cannot simply modify $\mathsf{F}[x]$ to output x if $q_{x_j} = \mathsf{acpt}$ since in that case if the receiver evaluates $\tilde{\mathsf{F}}$ on junk labels she will not be able to tell the difference between the junk output and x. Similar to [ABD+21], we address this problem by having S include a signal value in the ciphertext and in their message to R. Then we can modify $\mathsf{F}[x]$ to output x and the decrypted signal value. The receiver compares this output signal value with the true value. If they are equal, R knows that output x is not junk.

Handling Unbalanced Branching Programs. The above discussion can be naturally extended to the balanced BP setting, wherein we have a full binary tree of depth d. When the BP is unbalanced, like our BPs for PSI and PSU, the above approach does not work, because the sender does not know *a priori* which branches stop prematurely. We solve this issue via the following technique. We design the circuit G to work in two modes: normal mode (as explained above) and halting mode, which is triggered when its input signals a leaf node. In halting mode, the circuit G will release its hardwired input x, assuming the halt is an accept. Executing the above blueprint requires striking a delicate balance to have both correctness and security.

Comparison with [ABD+21]. At a high level, the garbled-circuit-based laconic PSI construction of [ABD+21] is an ad hoc and specific instantiation of our general methodology. In particular, for a receiver with $m = 2^k$ elements (for $k := \mathsf{polylog}(\lambda)$), the construction of [ABD+21] builds a full binary tree of depth k, with the m elements appearing sorted in the leaves, Merkle hashed all the way up in a specific way. In particular, the pre-image of each node's hash value is comprised of its two children's hashes as well as some additional encoded information about its sub-tree, enabling an evaluator, with an input x, to make a deterministic left-or-right downward choice at each intermediate node. This is a very specific BP instantiation of PSI, where the intermediate BP nodes, instead of running index predicates (e.g., going left/right if the ith bit is $0/1$), they run full-input predicates $\Phi : x \mapsto \{0, 1\}$, where Φ is defined based on the left sub-tree of the node. Our approach, on the other hand, handles branching programs for index predicates, and we subsume the results of [ABD+21] as a special case. In particular, we show how to design simple index-predicate BPs for PSI, PSU, and wildcard matching, the latter two problems are not considered by [ABD+21].

In summary, our construction generalizes and simplifies the approach of [ABD+21], getting much more mileage out of the garbled-circuit based approach. For example, [ABD+21] builds a secure protocol for a specific PSI-based

BP which is in fact a decision tree: namely, the in-degree of all internal nodes is one. On the other hand, we generalize this concept to handle all decision trees and even the broader class of branching programs, in which the in-degree of intermediates nodes can be greater than one. Moreover, we introduce some new techniques (e.g., for handling unbalanced BPs) that may be of independent interest.

Comparison with [DGGM19]. The work of Döttling, Garg, Goyal, and Malavolta [DGGM19] builds laconic conditional disclosure of secrets (CDS) involving a sender holding an NP instance x and a message m, and a receiver holding x and a potential witness w for x. If $R(x, w) = 1$, where R is the corresponding relation R, the receiver learns m; else, the receiver learns no information about m. They show how to build two-round laconic CDS protocols from CDH/LWE with polylogarithmic communication and polylogarithmic sender computation. The CDS setting is incomparable to ours. The closest resemblance is to think of x, the BP input, as the NP instance, and of the BP as the NP witness w. But then under CDS, the input x is not kept hidden from the receiver. In particular, it is not even clear whether laconic CDS implies laconic PSI.

3 Preliminaries

Throughout this work, λ denotes the security parameter. $\mathsf{negl}(\lambda)$ denotes a negligible function in λ, that is, a function that vanishes faster than any inverse polynomial in λ.

For $n \in \mathbb{N}$, $[n]$ denotes the set $\{1, \ldots, n\}$. If $x \in \{0,1\}^n$ then the bits of x can be indexed as $x[i] := x_i$ for $i \in [n]$, where $x = x_1 \ldots x_n$ (note that indexing begins at 1, not 0). $x := y$ is used to denote the assignment of variable x to the value y. If $\mathcal{A}$ is a deterministic algorithm, $y \leftarrow \mathcal{A}(x)$ denotes the assignment of the output of $\mathcal{A}(x)$ to variable y. If $\mathcal{A}$ is randomized, $y \xleftarrow{\$} \mathcal{A}(x)$ is used. If S is a (finite) set, $x \xleftarrow{\$} S$ denotes the experiment of sampling uniformly at random an element x from S. If D is a distribution over S, $x \xleftarrow{\$} D$ denotes the element x sampled from S according to D. If D_0, D_1 are distributions, we say that D_0 is statistically (resp. computationally) indistinguishable from D_1, denoted by $D_0 \approx_s D_1$ (resp. $D_0 \stackrel{c}{\equiv} D_1$), if no unbounded (resp. PPT) adversary can distinguish between the distributions except with probability at most $\mathsf{negl}(\lambda)$.

If Π is a two-round two-party protocol, then $(\mathsf{m}_1, \mathsf{m}_2) \leftarrow \mathsf{tr}^\Pi(x_0, x_1, \lambda)$ denotes the protocol transcript, where x_i is party P_i's input for $i \in \{0, 1\}$. For $i \in \{0, 1\}$, $(x_i, r_i, \mathsf{m}_1, \mathsf{m}_2) \leftarrow \mathsf{view}_i^\Pi(x_0, x_1, \lambda)$ denotes P_i's "view" of the execution of Π, consisting of their input, random coins, and the protocol transcript.

Definition 1 (Computational Diffie-Hellman). *Let $\mathcal{G}(\lambda)$ be an algorithm that outputs $(\mathbb{G}, p, g)$ where $\mathbb{G}$ is a group of prime order p and g is a generator of the group. The CDH assumption holds for generator $\mathcal{G}$ if for all PPT adversaries $\mathcal{A}$*

$$\Pr\left[g^{a_1 a_2} \leftarrow \mathcal{A}(\mathbb{G}, p, g, g^{a_1}, g^{a_2}) : \begin{array}{c} (\mathbb{G}, p, g) \leftarrow \mathcal{G}(\lambda) \\ a_1, a_2 \xleftarrow{\$} \mathbb{Z}_p \end{array}\right] \leq \mathsf{negl}(\lambda).$$

Definition 2 (Learning with Errors). *Let $q, k \in \mathbb{N}$ where $k \in \mathsf{poly}(\lambda)$, $\mathbf{A} \in \mathbb{Z}_q^{k \times n}$ and $\beta \in \mathbb{R}$. For any $n = \mathsf{poly}(k \log q)$, the LWE assumption holds if for every PPT algorithm $\mathcal{A}$ we have*

$$|\Pr[1 \leftarrow \mathcal{A}(\mathbf{A}, \mathbf{sA} + \mathbf{e})] - \Pr[1 \leftarrow \mathcal{A}(\mathbf{A}, \mathbf{y})]| \leq \mathsf{negl}(\lambda)$$

for $\mathbf{s} \xleftarrow{\$} \{0,1\}^k$, $\mathbf{e} \xleftarrow{\$} D_{\mathbb{Z}^n, \beta}$ and $\mathbf{y} \xleftarrow{\$} \{0,1\}^n$, where $D_{\mathbb{Z}^n, \beta}$ is some error distribution.

The following definitions related to branching programs are modified from [IP07].

Definition 3 (Branching Program (BP)). *A (deterministic) branching program over the input domain $\{0,1\}^\lambda$ and output domain $\{0,1\}$ is defined by a tuple (V, E, T, Val) where:*

- *$G := (V, E)$ is a directed acyclic graph of depth d.*
- *Two types of nodes partition V:*
  - *Interior nodes: Have outdegree 2.[3] The root node, denoted $v_1^{(0)}$, has indegree 0.*
  - *Terminal/leaf nodes: Have outdegree 0. T denotes the set of terminal nodes. Leaf nodes are labeled as $T = \{u_1, \ldots, u_{|T|}\}$. Each $u_i \in T$ encodes a value in $\{0,1\}$.*
- *For every non-root node $u \in V \setminus \{v_1^{(0)}\}$ there exists a path from $v_1^{(0)}$ to u.*
- *Each node in V encodes a value in $[\lambda]$. These values are stored in the array Val such that for all $v \in V$, $\mathsf{Val}[v] = i$ for some $i \in [\lambda]$.*
- *The elements of the edge set E are formatted as an ordered tuple (v, v', b) indicating a directed edge from $v \in V$ to $v' \in V$ with label $b \in \{0,1\}$. If $b = 0$ (resp. $b = 1$), v' is the left (resp. right) child of v.*

BP Evaluation. The output of a branching program is defined by the function $\mathsf{BP} : \{0,1\}^\lambda \to \{0,1\}$, which on input $x \in \{0,1\}^\lambda$ outputs a bit. Evaluation of BP (see Fig. 2, right, and relevant function definitions below) follows the unique path in G induced by x from the root $v_1^{(0)}$ to a leaf node $u \in T$. The output of BP is the value encoded in u, $\mathsf{Val}[u]$.

- $\Gamma : V \setminus T \times \{0,1\} \to V$ takes as input an internal node v and a bit b and outputs v's left child if $b = 0$ and v's right child if $b = 1$.
- $\mathsf{Eval}_{\mathsf{int}} : V \setminus T \times \{0,1\}^\lambda \to V$ takes as input an interior node v and a string of length λ and outputs either v's left or right child ($\Gamma(v, 0)$ or $\Gamma(v, 1)$, respectively). See Fig. 2, left.
- $\mathsf{Eval}_{\mathsf{leaf}} : T \to \{0,1\}$ takes as input a terminal node $u \in T$ and outputs the value $\mathsf{Val}[u]$.

---

[3] We assume no nodes have outdegree 1 since such nodes can be removed from the BP w.l.o.g.

$\mathsf{Eval_{int}}(v, x)$:	$\mathsf{BP}(x)$:
$i \leftarrow \mathsf{Val}[v]$	$v \leftarrow v_1^{(0)}$
If $x[i] = 0$ then return $\Gamma(v, 0)$	While $v \notin T$ do $v \leftarrow \mathsf{Eval_{int}}(v, x)$
Else return $\Gamma(v, 1)$	$y \leftarrow \mathsf{Eval_{leaf}}(v)$
	Return y

Fig. 2. Interior node evaluation function $\mathsf{Eval_{int}}$ and BP evaluation function BP.

Definition 4 (Layered BP). *A BP of depth d is layered if the node set V can be partitioned into $d + 1$ disjoint levels $V = \bigcup_{i=0}^{d} V^{(i)}$, such that $V^{(0)} = \{v_1^{(0)}\}$, $V^{(d)} = T$, and for every edge $e = (u, v)$ we have $u \in V^{(i)}$, $v \in V^{(i+1)}$ for some level $i \in \{0, \ldots, d\}$. We refer to $V^{(i)}$ as the i-th level of the BP, or the level at depth i. Nodes on level i are labelled from leftmost to rightmost: $V^{(i)} = \{v_1^{(i)}, \ldots, v_{|V^{(i)}|}^{(i)}\}$.*

We require that all branching programs in this work are layered.

4   Semi-honest Laconic 2PC with Branching Programs

Our construction uses hash encryption schemes with garbled circuits. The following definitions are taken directly from [ABD+21].

Definition 5 (Hash Encryption [DG17,BLSV18]). *A hash encryption scheme $\mathsf{HE} = (\mathsf{HGen}, \mathsf{Hash}, \mathsf{HEnc}, \mathsf{HDec})$ and associated security notions are defined as follows.*

- $\mathsf{HGen}(1^\lambda, n)$: *Takes as input a security parameter 1^λ and an input size n and outputs a hash key pp.*
- $\mathsf{Hash}(\mathsf{pp}, z)$: *Takes as input a hash key pp and $z \in \{0,1\}^n$, and deterministically outputs $h \in \{0,1\}^\lambda$.*
- $\mathsf{HEnc}(\mathsf{pp}, h, \{m_{i,b}\}_{i \in [n], b \in \{0,1\}}; \{r_{i,b}\})$: *Takes as input a hash key pp, a hash output h, messages $\{m_{i,b}\}$ and randomness $\{r_{i,b}\}$, and outputs $\{\mathsf{cth}_{i,b}\}_{i \in [n], b \in \{0,1\}}$, (written concisely as $\{\mathsf{cth}_{i,b}\}$). Each ciphertext $\mathsf{cth}_{i,b}$ is computed as $\mathsf{cth}_{i,b} = \mathsf{HEnc}(\mathsf{pp}, h, m_{i,b}, (i, b); r_{i,b})$, where we have overloaded the HEnc notation.*
- $\mathsf{HDec}(z, \{\mathsf{cth}_{i,b}\})$: *Takes as input a hash input z and $\{\mathsf{cth}_{i,b}\}$ and outputs n messages $(m_1, \ldots, m_n)$. Correctness is required such that for the variables above, $(m_1, \ldots, m_n) = (m_{1,z[1]}, \ldots, m_{n,z[n]})$.*
- **Semantic Security:** *Given $z \in \{0,1\}^n$, no adversary can distinguish between encryptions of messages made to indices $(i, \bar{z}_i)$. For any PPT $\mathcal{A}$, sampling $\mathsf{pp} \xleftarrow{\$} \mathsf{HGen}(1^\lambda, n)$, if $(z, \{m_{i,b}\}, \{m'_{i,b}\}) \xleftarrow{\$} \mathcal{A}(\mathsf{pp})$ and if $m_{i,z[i]} = m'_{i,z[i]}$ for all $i \in [n]$, then $\mathcal{A}$ cannot distinguish between $\mathsf{HEnc}(\mathsf{pp}, h, \{m_{i,b}\})$ and $\mathsf{HEnc}(\mathsf{pp}, h, \{m'_{i,b}\})$, where $h \leftarrow \mathsf{Hash}(\mathsf{pp}, z)$.*
- **Anonymous Semantic Security:** *For a random $\{m_{i,b}\}$ with equal rows (i.e., $m_{i,0} = m_{i,1}$), the output of $\mathsf{HEnc}(\mathsf{pp}, h, \{m_{i,b}\})$ is pseudorandom even*

in the presence of the hash input. Formally, for any $z \in \{0,1\}^n$, sampling $\mathsf{pp} \overset{\$}{\leftarrow} \mathsf{HGen}(1^\lambda, n)$, $h \leftarrow \mathsf{Hash}(\mathsf{pp}, z)$, *and sampling* $\{m_{i,b}\}$ *uniformly at random with the same rows, then* $v := (\mathsf{pp}, z, \mathsf{HEnc}(\mathsf{pp}, h, \{m_{i,b}\}))$ *is indistinguishable from another tuple in which we replace the hash-encryption component of* v *with a random string.*

The following results are from [BLSV18, GGH19].

Lemma 1. *Assuming CDH/LWE there exists anonymous hash encryption schemes, where* $n = 3\lambda$ *(i.e.,* $\mathsf{Hash}(\mathsf{pp}, \cdot) \colon \{0,1\}^{3\lambda} \mapsto \{0,1\}^\lambda$ *).*[4] *Moreover, the hash function* Hash *satisfies robustness in the following sense: for any input distribution on* z *which samples at least* 2λ *bits of* z *uniformly at random,* $(\mathsf{pp}, \mathsf{Hash}(\mathsf{pp}, z))$ *and* (pp, u) *are statistically close, where* $\mathsf{pp} \overset{\$}{\leftarrow} \mathsf{HGen}(1^\lambda, 3\lambda)$ *and* $u \overset{\$}{\leftarrow} \{0,1\}^\lambda$.

We also review garbled circuits and the anonymous property, as defined in [BLSV18].

Definition 6 (Garbled Circuits). *A garbling scheme for a class of circuits* $\mathcal{C} := \{\mathsf{C} \colon \{0,1\}^n \mapsto \{0,1\}^m\}$ *consists of* $(\mathsf{Garb}, \mathsf{Eval}, \mathsf{Sim})$ *satisfying the following.*

- *Correctness: For all* $\mathsf{C} \in \mathcal{C}$, $\mathsf{m} \in \{0,1\}^n$, $\Pr[\mathsf{Eval}(\widetilde{\mathsf{C}}, \{\mathsf{lb}_{i,\mathsf{m}[i]}\}) = \mathsf{C}(\mathsf{m})] = 1$, *where* $(\widetilde{\mathsf{C}}, \{\mathsf{lb}_{i,b}\}) \overset{\$}{\leftarrow} \mathsf{Garb}(1^\lambda, \mathsf{C})$.
- *Simulation Security: For any* $\mathsf{C} \in \mathcal{C}$ *and* $\mathsf{m} \in \{0,1\}^n$: $(\widetilde{\mathsf{C}}, \{\mathsf{lb}_{i,\mathsf{m}[i]}\}) \overset{c}{\equiv}$ $\mathsf{Sim}(1^\lambda, \mathsf{C}, \mathsf{C}(\mathsf{m}))$, *where* $(\widetilde{\mathsf{C}}, \{\mathsf{lb}_{i,b}\}) \overset{\$}{\leftarrow} \mathsf{Garb}(1^\lambda, \mathsf{C})$.
- *Anonymous Security*[5] *[BLSV18]: For any* $\mathsf{C} \in \mathcal{C}$, *if the output of* $\mathsf{C}(x)$ *for* $x \in \{0,1\}^n$ *is uniformly random, then the output of* $\mathsf{Sim}(1^\lambda, \mathsf{C}, y)$ *is pseudorandom.*

Lemma 2 ([BLSV18]). *Anonymous garbled circuits can be built from one-way functions.*

Hash Encryption Notation. We assume $\mathsf{Hash}(\mathsf{pp}, \cdot) \colon \{0,1\}^n \mapsto \{0,1\}^\lambda$, where $n = 3\lambda$. $\{\mathsf{lb}_{i,b}\}$ denotes a sequence of pairs of labels, where $i \in [n]$ and $b \in \{0,1\}$. For $r := \{r_{i,b}\}$, $\mathsf{HEnc}(\mathsf{pp}, h, \{\mathsf{lb}_{i,b}\}; r)$ denotes ciphertexts $\{\mathsf{cth}_{i,b}\}$, where $\mathsf{cth}_{i,b} = \mathsf{HEnc}(\mathsf{pp}, h, \mathsf{lb}_{i,b}, (i,b); r_{i,b})$. We overload notation as follows. $\{\mathsf{lb}_i\}$ denotes a sequence of 3λ elements. For $r := \{r_{i,b}\}$, $\mathsf{HEnc}(\mathsf{pp}, h, \{\mathsf{lb}_i\}; r)$ denotes a hash encryption where both plaintext rows are $\{\mathsf{lb}_i\}$; namely, ciphertexts $\{\mathsf{cth}_{i,b}\}$, where $\mathsf{cth}_{i,b} = \mathsf{HEnc}(\mathsf{pp}, h, \{m_{i,b}\}; r_{i,b})$ and $m_{i,0} = m_{i,1} = \mathsf{lb}_i$, for all i.

Definition 7 (BP-2PC Functionality). *We define the evaluation of a branching program in the two-party communication setting (BP-2PC) to be a two-round protocol between a receiver* R *and a sender* S *such that:*

---

[4] The CDH construction of [BLSV18] satisfies a weaker notion of anonymity, in which only some part of the ciphertext is pseudorandom. But for ease of presentation, we keep the notion as is.

[5] Called *blind* garbled circuits in [BLSV18].

- R holds a branching program BP *with evaluation function* BP : $\{0,1\}^\lambda \to \{0,1\}$ *and* S *holds a string* id $\in \{0,1\}^\lambda$. *In the first round of the protocol,* R *sends the message* m_1 *to* S. *In the second round* S *sends* m_2 *to* R.
- **Correctness:** *If* BP(id) = 1, *then* R *outputs* id. *Otherwise,* R *outputs* $\bot$.
- **Computational (resp., statistical) receiver security:** *BP-2PC achieves receiver security if for all* id $\in \{0,1\}^\lambda$, *and all pairs of branching programs* BP_0, BP_1 *we have that* $\mathsf{view}_S^{\mathsf{BP}}\text{-}2PC(BP_0, \mathsf{id}, \lambda) \approx \mathsf{view}_S^{\mathsf{BP}}\text{-}2PC(BP_1, \mathsf{id}, \lambda)$. *If the distributions are computationally (resp., statistically) indistinguishable then we have computational (resp., statistical) security.*
- **Computational (resp., statistical) sender security:** *BP-2PC achieves sender security if for all branching programs* BP, *and all pairs* $\mathsf{id}_0, \mathsf{id}_1 \in \{0,1\}^\lambda$ *with* $BP(\mathsf{id}_0) = 0 = BP(\mathsf{id}_1)$, *we have that* $\mathsf{view}_R^{\mathsf{BP}}\text{-}2PC(BP, \mathsf{id}_0, \lambda) \approx \mathsf{view}_R^{\mathsf{BP}}\text{-}2PC(BP, \mathsf{id}_1, \lambda)$. *If the distributions are computationally (resp. statistically) indistinguishable, we have computational (resp. statistical) security.*

4.1   The BP-2PC Construction

In this section, we give a construction for a BP-2PC protocol, inspired by laconic OT techniques [CDG+17, ABD+21]. Construction 1 uses hash encryption and garbling schemes. A high-level overview is as follows.

1. The receiver party R hashes their branching program in a 'specific way' from the leaf level up to the root. R then sends the message $m_1 = (d_m, h_{root})$ to the sender, where d_m is the maximum BP depth and h_{root} is the hash value of the root node of the hashed BP.
2. The sender party S gets the message $m_1 = (d_m, h_{root})$ and garbles one circuit for every possible level of the hash tree, (i.e., generates d_m garbled circuits). S starts with the leaf level and garbles circuit F (Fig. 3). F takes as input a leaf node value and two random strings. If the leaf node value is 1, F outputs the hardcoded sender element id and a random, fixed, signal string r. Otherwise, F outputs two random strings (id', r'). Then for every level from the leaf parents to the root, S garbles the circuit V (also in Fig. 3). Each V garbled by the sender has the labels of the previously generated garbled circuit hardcoded. After garbling, S computes a hash encryption of the root-level garbled circuit labels using the hash image h_{root}. Finally, S sends $m_2 := (\widetilde{C}_{d_m}, \ldots, \widetilde{C}_0, \{\mathsf{cth}_{i,b}^{(0)}\}, r)$ to R, where $\widetilde{C}_w$ is the garbled circuit associated with level w, $\{\mathsf{cth}_{i,b}^{(0)}\}$ is the encryption of the labels for $\widetilde{C}_0$, and r is the signal value.
3. For all root-to-leaf paths through the BP, R runs DecPath (Fig. 3, bottom) on m_2 searching for the path that will decrypt to a signal value equal to r from m_2. On input a path pth and m_2, DecPath outputs a pair $(\mathsf{id}_{pth}, r_{pth})$ to R. If $r_{pth} = r$, then R takes id_{pth} to be S's element.

Construction 1 (BP-2PC). *We require the following ingredients for the two-round, two-party communication BP construction.*

1. *An anonymous and robust hash encryption scheme* $\mathsf{HE} = (\mathsf{HGen}, \mathsf{Hash}, \mathsf{HEnc},$ $\mathsf{HDec})$, *where* $\mathsf{Hash}(\mathsf{pp}, \cdot): \{0,1\}^{3\lambda} \mapsto \{0,1\}^{\lambda}$.
2. *An anonymous garbling scheme* $\mathsf{GS} = (\mathsf{Garb}, \mathsf{Eval}, \mathsf{Sim})$.
3. *Circuits* F, V, *and procedure* $\mathsf{DecPath}$, *defined in Fig. 3.*

 The receiver holds a-potentially unbalanced-branching program BP *of depth* $d \leq \lambda + 1$ *as defined in Definition 3. The sender has a single element* $\mathsf{id} \in \{0,1\}^{\lambda}$. $\mathsf{BP}\text{-}\mathsf{2PC} := (\mathsf{GenCRS}, \mathsf{R}_1, \mathsf{S}, \mathsf{R}_2)$ *is a triple of algorithms built as follows.*

 $\mathsf{GenCRS}(1^{\lambda})$: *Return* $\mathsf{crs} \xleftarrow{\$} \mathsf{HGen}(1^{\lambda}, 3\lambda)$.

 $\mathsf{R}_1(\mathsf{crs}, BP)$: BP *has terminal node set* $T = \{u_1, \ldots, u_{|T|}\}$. *Nodes in level* $0 \leq w \leq d$ *are labelled from leftmost to rightmost:* $V^{(w)} = \{v_1^{(w)}, \ldots, v_{|V^{(w)}|}^{(w)}\}$.

- *Parse* $\mathsf{crs} := \mathsf{pp}$. *The receiver creates a hashed version of* BP, *beginning at the leaf level: For* $j \in [|T|]$, *sample* $x_j, x_j' \xleftarrow{\$} \{0,1\}^{\lambda}$ *and compute* $h_j^{(d)} \leftarrow \mathsf{Hash}(\mathsf{pp}, (\mathsf{Val}[u_j]^{\times \lambda}, x_j, x_j'))$. $\mathsf{Val}[u_j]^{\times \lambda}$ *indicates that* $\mathsf{Val}[u_j]$ *is copied* λ *times to obtain either the all zeros or all ones string of length* λ.
  The remaining levels are hashed from level $d - 1$ *up to* 0 *(the root):*
  1. *For* w *from* $d - 1$ *to* 0, $|V^{(w)}|$ *nodes are added to level* w. *The hash value of each node is the hash of the concatenation of its left child, right child, and the index encoded in the current node. Formally: For* $j \in [|V^{(w)}|]$, *set* $h_j^{(w)} \leftarrow \mathsf{Hash}(\mathsf{pp}, (h_{2j-1}^{(w+1)}, h_{2j}^{(w+1)}, \mathsf{Val}[v_j^{(w)}]))$, *where* $\mathsf{Val}[v_j^{(w)}]$ *is the value of the bit encoded in the* j*-th node of level* w. *If needed, padding is added so that* $\|\mathsf{Val}[v_j^{(w)}]\| = \lambda$.
  2. *Let* $\mathsf{m}_1 := (\mathsf{d_m}, \mathsf{h_{root}})$, *where* $\mathsf{d_m} = \lambda + 1$ *is the maximum tree depth and* $\mathsf{h_{root}} := h_1^{(0)}$ *is the root hash value. For all* $i \in [|T|]$, $w \in \{0, \ldots, d\}$, *and* $j \in [|V^{(w)}|]$, *set* $\mathsf{st} := (\{x_i\}, \{x_i'\}, \{v_j^{(w)}\})$. *Send* m_1 *to* S.

$\mathsf{S}(\mathsf{crs}, \mathsf{id}, \mathsf{m}_1)$:

- *Parse* $\mathsf{m}_1 := (\mathsf{d_m}, \mathsf{h_{root}})$ *and* $\mathsf{crs} := \mathsf{pp}$. *Sample* $r, \mathsf{id}', r' \xleftarrow{\$} \{0,1\}^{\lambda}$ *and padding* $\mathsf{pad} \xleftarrow{\$} \{0,1\}^{2(n-1)}$. *Let* $\mathsf{C_{d_m}} := \mathsf{F}[\mathsf{id}, \mathsf{id}', r, r']$ *(Fig. 3). Garble* $(\widetilde{\mathsf{C}}_{\mathsf{d_m}}, \{\mathsf{lb}_{i,b}^{(\mathsf{d_m})}\})$ $\xleftarrow{\$} \mathsf{Garb}(\mathsf{C_{d_m}})$. *For* w *from* $\mathsf{d_m} - 1$ *to* 0 *do:*
  1. *Sample random* $\boldsymbol{r}_w$ *and let* $\mathsf{C}_w := \mathsf{V}[\mathsf{pp}, \mathsf{id}, \{\mathsf{lb}_{i,b}^{(w+1)}\}, \boldsymbol{r}_w, r, \mathsf{id}', r', \mathsf{pad}]$.
  2. *Garble* $(\widetilde{\mathsf{C}}_w, \{\mathsf{lb}_{i,b}^{(w)}\}) \xleftarrow{\$} \mathsf{Garb}(\mathsf{C}_w)$.
- *Let* $\{\mathsf{cth}_{i,b}^{(0)}\} \xleftarrow{\$} \mathsf{HEnc}(\mathsf{pp}, \mathsf{h_{root}}, \{\mathsf{lb}_{i,b}^{(0)}\})$.
- *Send* $\mathsf{m}_2 := (\widetilde{\mathsf{C}}_{\mathsf{d_m}}, \ldots, \widetilde{\mathsf{C}}_0, \{\mathsf{cth}_{i,b}^{(0)}\}, r)$ *to* R_2.

$\mathsf{R}_2(\mathsf{crs}, \mathsf{st}, \mathsf{m}_2)$: *Parse* $\mathsf{st} := (\{x_i\}, \{x_i'\}, \{v_j^{(w)}\})$ *and* $\mathsf{m}_2 := (\widetilde{\mathsf{C}}_{\mathsf{d_m}}, \ldots, \widetilde{\mathsf{C}}_0, \{\mathsf{cth}_{i,b}^{(0)}\},$ $r)$. $\forall$ *leaves* $u \in T$, *let* $\mathsf{pth}_u := ((\mathsf{Val}[u]^{\times \lambda}, x, x'), \ldots, \mathsf{h_{root}})$ *be the root to leaf* u *path in* BP. *Let* ℓ *be the length of* pth_u *and let*

$$(\mathsf{id}_u, r_u) \leftarrow \mathsf{DecPath}(\mathsf{pth}_u, \widetilde{\mathsf{C}}_{\mathsf{d_m}}, \ldots, \widetilde{\mathsf{C}}_0, \{\mathsf{cth}_{i,b}^{(0)}\}).$$

If $r_u = r$, *then output* id_u *and halt. If for all* $u \in T$, $r_u \neq r$, *then output* $\bot$.

Circuit $F[\text{id}, \text{id}', r, r'](v, x, x')$:	Circuit $V[\text{pp}, \text{id}, \{\text{lb}_{i,b}\}, r, r, \text{id}', r', \text{pad}](a, b, c)$:
HARDWIRED: Target identity id, signal value r, and random strings id', r'.	HARDWIRED: Hash public parameter pp, target identity id, labels $\{\text{lb}_{i,b}\}$, HEnc randomness r, signal value r, random strings id', r', and padding pad.
OPERATION: Return $$\begin{cases} \{\text{id}, r\} & \text{if } v = 1^\lambda \\ \{\text{id}', r'\} & \text{otherwise} \end{cases}$$	OPERATION: If $a = 1^\lambda$ then return $\{\text{id}, r, \text{pad}\}$ If $a = 0^\lambda$ then return $\{\text{id}', r', \text{pad}\}$ Else set $h_1 \leftarrow a$, $h_2 \leftarrow b$, $i \leftarrow c$ and return $$\{\text{cth}_{i,b}\} \leftarrow \begin{cases} \text{HEnc}(\text{pp}, h_1, \{\text{lb}_{i,b}\}; r) & \text{if } \text{id}[i] = 0 \\ \text{HEnc}(\text{pp}, h_2, \{\text{lb}_{i,b}\}; r) & \text{otherwise} \end{cases}$$

Procedure $\text{DecPath}(\text{pth}, \text{m}_2)$:

INPUT: A leaf-root path pth of length $\ell \leq d$ and tuple $\text{m}_2 := (\widetilde{\mathsf{C}}_{\text{d}_\text{m}}, \dots, \widetilde{\mathsf{C}}_0, \{\text{cth}_{i,b}^{(0)}\}, r)$.

OPERATION: 1. Parse

$$\text{pth} := (\underbrace{(\text{Val}[v^{(\ell)}]^{\times \lambda}, x, x')}_{z_\ell}, \underbrace{(h^{(\ell)}, h'^{(\ell)}, \text{Val}[v^{(\ell-1)}])}_{z_{\ell-1}}, \dots, \underbrace{(h^{(1)}, h'^{(1)}, \text{Val}[v^{(0)}])}_{z_0}, h_{\text{root}}).$$

2. For w from 0 to $\ell - 1$ do:
   (a) Let $\{\text{lb}_i^{(w)}\} \leftarrow \text{HDec}(z_w, \{\text{cth}_{i,b}^{(w)}\})$. (b) Set $\{\text{cth}_{i,b}^{(w+1)}\} \leftarrow \text{Eval}(\widetilde{\mathsf{C}}_w, \{\text{lb}_i^{(w)}\})$.
3. Let $\{\text{lb}_i^{(\ell)}\} \leftarrow \text{HDec}(z_\ell, \{\text{cth}_{i,b}^{(\ell)}\})$.
4. Let $\{\text{id}_{\text{pth}}, r_{\text{pth}}, \text{pad}\} \leftarrow \text{Eval}(\widetilde{\mathsf{C}}_\ell, \{\text{lb}_i^{(\ell)}\})$ and return $(\text{id}_{\text{pth}}, r_{\text{pth}})$.

Fig. 3. Circuits F, V and procedure DecPath for construction 1. Circuits based on those in Table 1 of [ABD+21].

R_2 must run DecPath on every root-to-leaf path. R_2 is written above as if there is a unique path from the root to each leaf. But since we allow nodes to have in-degree > 1, a leaf may be reachable from more than one path. In such a case, the path iteration in R_2 should be modified so that all paths are explored.

Communication Costs. The first message m_1 is output by R_1 and sent to S. m_1 consists of the maximum depth d_m and the hash digest h_{root}, which are $O(\log \lambda)$ and λ bits, respectively. So the receiver's communication cost is $\text{poly}(\text{d}_\text{m}, \lambda)$, and since we assume $\text{d}_\text{m} = \lambda + 1$, this is $\text{poly}(\text{d}_\text{m}, \lambda)$. Next, m_2 is output by S and sent to R_2. m_2 consists of $\widetilde{\mathsf{C}}_0$, $\widetilde{\mathsf{C}}_i$ for $i \in [\text{d}_\text{m}]$, $\{\text{cth}_{i,b}^{(0)}\}_{i \in [n], b \in \{0,1\}}$, and r. So the sender's communication cost grows with $\text{poly}(\lambda, \text{d}_\text{m}, |\text{id}|)$, which is $\text{poly}(\lambda)$.

Computation Costs. R_1: performs $|V|$ Hash evaluations and samples $2|T|$ random strings of length λ. S: samples $\text{poly}(\lambda, \text{d}_\text{m})$ random bits, garbles an F circuit, garbles d_m V circuits, and performs a hash encryption of 6λ garbled labels. The sender's computation cost is $\text{poly}(\lambda, \text{d}_\text{m})$. R_2: runs DecPath for every root-leaf path. Each iteration of DecPath requires at most $\text{d}_\text{m} + 1$ HDec and GS.Eval evaluations. In total, R's computation cost is $O(\lambda, \text{d}_\text{m}, |V|, |\text{PTH}|)$, where $|\text{PTH}|$

is the total number of root-to-leaf paths in the BP. So we require $|V|$ and $|\mathsf{PTH}|$ to be $\mathsf{poly}(\lambda)$.

Lemma 3. *Construction 1 is correct in the sense that (1) if* $\mathsf{BP}(\mathsf{id}) = 1$*, then with overwhelming probability* R_2 *outputs* id *and (2) if* $\mathsf{BP}(\mathsf{id}) = 0$*, then with overwhelming probability* R_2 *outputs* $\perp$*.*

Theorem 1. *If* HE *is an anonymous and robust hash encryption (defined in Lemma 1), and* GS *is an anonymous garbling scheme, then the* BP*-2PC protocol of Construction 1 provides statistical security for the receiver and semi-honest security for the sender.*

The proofs of Lemma 3 and Theorem 1 are in Sects. 6 and 7, respectively.

5 Applications

Construction 1 can be used to realize multiple functionalities by reducing the desired functionality to an instance of BP-2PC. One step of the reductions involves constructing a branching program based on a set of bit strings.

At a high level, SetBP (Fig. 4) creates a branching program for a set of elements $S := \{x_1, \ldots, x_m\}$ in three main steps. For concreteness, suppose the goal is to use this BP for a private set intersection.

First, for every prefix $a \in \{\epsilon\} \cup \{0,1\} \cup \{0,1\}^2 \cup \cdots \cup \{0,1\}^\lambda$ of the elements in S, a node v_a is added to the set of nodes V. If $a \in S$, then the value encoded in v_a is set to 1; this is an 'accept' leaf. If $|a| < \lambda$, then the encoded value is set to $|a| + 1$. When the BP is being evaluated on some input, $|a| + 1$ will indicate the bit following prefix a. Next, edges are created between the BP levels. For $|a| < \lambda$, if for $b \in \{0,1\}$, node $v_{a\|b}$ exists in V, then a b-labelled edge is added from v_a to $v_{a\|b}$. For $b \in \{0,1\}$, if $v_{a\|b} \notin V$, then node $v_{a\|b}$ is added to V with an encoded bit 0. This is a 'reject' leaf. Then a b-labelled edge is added from v_a to $v_{a\|b}$. Finally, the BP is pruned. If two sibling leaves are both encoded with the same value, they are deleted and their parent becomes a leaf encoding that same value.

The definition below generalizes this concept by allowing us to capture both PSI and PSI via an indicator bit b_{pth}. In the description above, b_{pth} is set to 1 for the PSI setting. For PSU we set $b_{\mathsf{pth}} = 0$.

Construction 2 (Set to branching program). *Figure 4 defines a procedure to create a branching program from an input set* S*.* $\mathsf{SetBP}(S, b_{\mathsf{pth}})$ *takes as input a set* $S := \{x_1, \ldots, x_m\}$ *of m strings, all of length* λ *and a bit* b_{pth} *and outputs a tuple* (V, E, T, Val) *defining a branching program. The output BP is such that if* $x \in S$*, then* $\mathsf{BP}(x) = b_{\mathsf{pth}}$*, and if* $x \notin S$*, then* $\mathsf{BP}(x) = 1 - b_{\mathsf{pth}}$*.*

Procedure SetBP *runs in time* $O(\lambda|S|)$*. In particular, when* $|S| = \mathsf{poly}(\lambda)$*,* SetBP *generates the BP in time* $O(\mathsf{poly}(\lambda))$*. The output BP has depth* $d \leq \lambda + 1$ *and the number of nodes is* $2d + 1 \leq |V| \leq 2^{d+1} - 1$*. Evaluation of* $\mathsf{BP}(x)$ *for arbitrary* $x \in \{0,1\}^\lambda$ *takes time* $O(\mathsf{poly}(\lambda))$*.*

Procedure SetBP(S, b_{pth}):
$\{x_1, \ldots, x_m\} \leftarrow S$; $\lambda \leftarrow |x_1|$; $V, E, T \leftarrow \emptyset$
$V \leftarrow V \cup \{v_\epsilon\}$; $\mathsf{Val}[v_\epsilon] \leftarrow 1$ ▷ set root node
For $1 \leq i \leq \lambda$ do ▷ add a node for every prefix of length i in S
  For $1 \leq j \leq m$ do
    $a \leftarrow x_j[1..i]$; $V \leftarrow V \cup \{v_a\}$
    If $|a| = \lambda$ then $\mathsf{Val}[v_a] \leftarrow b_{\mathsf{pth}}$; $T \leftarrow T \cup \{v_a\}$ ▷ accept leaves
    Else $\mathsf{Val}[v_a] \leftarrow |a| + 1$
For all $v_a \in V$ s.t. $|v_a| < \lambda$ do ▷ adding edges from v_a to children
  For $b \in \{0, 1\}$ do
    If $\exists\, v_{a\|b} \in V$ then $E \leftarrow E \cup \{(v_a, v_{a\|b}, b)\}$
    Else
      $V \leftarrow V \cup \{v_{a\|b}\}$; $\mathsf{Val}[v_{a\|b}] \leftarrow 1 - b_{\mathsf{pth}}$ ▷ reject leaves
      $E \leftarrow E \cup \{(v_a, v_{a\|b}, b)\}$; $T \leftarrow T \cup \{v_{a\|b}\}$
▷ Pruning: if a node has 2 leaf children with value b_{pth}, delete
  the children and change parent value to b_{pth}.
While $\exists\, v_a \in V$ s.t. $v_{a\|b} \in T \wedge \mathsf{Val}[v_{a\|b}] = b_{\mathsf{pth}}$ for $b \in \{0, 1\}$ do
  $\mathsf{Val}[v_a] \leftarrow b_{\mathsf{pth}}$; $T \leftarrow T \cup \{v_a\}$
  $V \leftarrow V \setminus \{v_{a\|0}, v_{a\|1}\}$; $E \leftarrow E \setminus \{(v_a, v_{a\|b}, b) \mid b \in \{0, 1\}\}$
Return (V, E, T, Val)

Fig. 4. Procedure for constructing a BP from a set of m λ-bit strings. See Construction 2. Based on a description in [CGH+21].

BP Evaluation Runtime: Recall the BP evaluation algorithm in Fig. 2. Each loop iteration moves down the tree one level. The number of iterations is at most the tree depth, which is $\leq \lambda + 1$ for a BP created in Fig. 4. Each iteration takes constant time, so evaluation of $\mathsf{BP}(x)$ for any $x \in \{0, 1\}^\lambda$ takes time $O(\mathsf{poly}(\lambda))$.

5.1 Private Set Intersection (PSI)

Assume a sender party has a set $S_S = \{\mathsf{id}\}$ where $\mathsf{id} \in \{0, 1\}^\lambda$ and a receiver has a polynomial-sized set $S_R \subset \{0, 1\}^\lambda$. In this setting, we define PSI as follows.

Definition 8 (Private set Intersection (PSI) functionality with $|S_S|$ = 1). *Let Π be a two-party communication protocol. Let R be the receiver holding set $S_R \subset \{0, 1\}^\lambda$ and let S be the sender holding singleton set $S_S = \{\mathsf{id}\}$, with $\mathsf{id} \in \{0, 1\}^\lambda$. Π is a PSI protocol if the following hold after it is executed.*

- *Correctness: R learns $S_R \cap \{\mathsf{id}\}$ if and only if $\mathsf{id} \in S_R$.*
- *Receiver security: Π achieves receiver security if $\forall \mathsf{id} \in \{0, 1\}^\lambda$, and all pairs $S_{R0}, S_{R1} \subset \{0, 1\}^\lambda$ we have that $\mathsf{view}_S^\Pi(S_{R0}, \mathsf{id}, \lambda) \approx \mathsf{view}_S^\Pi(S_{R1}, \mathsf{id}, \lambda)$. If the distributions are computationally (resp., statistically) indistinguishable then we have computational (resp., statistical) security.*

- **Sender security:** Π achieves sender security if $\forall \lambda \in \mathbb{N}$, $S_R \subset \{0,1\}^\lambda$, and all pairs $\mathsf{id}_0, \mathsf{id}_1 \in \{0,1\}^\lambda \setminus S_R$ we have that $\mathsf{view}_R^{\Pi}(S_R, \mathsf{id}_0, \lambda) \approx \mathsf{view}_R^{\Pi}(S_R, \mathsf{id}_1, \lambda)$. If the distributions are computationally (resp., statistically) indistinguishable then we have computational (resp., statistical) security.

The PSI functionality can be achieved by casting it as an instance of BP-2PC:

1. R runs $\mathsf{SetBP}(S_R, 1)$ (Fig. 4) to generate a branching program $\mathsf{BP}_{\mathsf{psi}}$ such that $\mathsf{BP}_{\mathsf{psi}}(x) = 1$ if $x \in S_R$ and $\mathsf{BP}_{\mathsf{psi}}(x) = 0$ otherwise.
2. R and S run BP-2PC with inputs $\mathsf{BP}_{\mathsf{psi}}$ and id, respectively. By construction of BP-2PC:

$$\begin{cases} R \text{ learns } \mathsf{id} & \text{if } \mathsf{BP}_{\mathsf{psi}}(\mathsf{id}) = 1 \implies \mathsf{id} \in S_R \\ R \text{ does not learn } \mathsf{id} & \text{if } \mathsf{BP}_{\mathsf{psi}}(\mathsf{id}) = 0 \implies \mathsf{id} \notin S_R \end{cases},$$

which satisfies the PSI correctness condition and security follows from the security of Construction 1 for BP-2PC.

The computation and communication costs of the receiver and sender do not depend on $|S_R|$. If the receiver holds a polynomial-sized BP describing a set S_R of exponential size, then this PSI protocol can run in polynomial time.[6]

5.2   Private Set Union (PSU)

As before, assume the sender has a singleton set $S_S = \{\mathsf{id}\}$ where $\mathsf{id} \in \{0,1\}^\lambda$ and the receiver has a set S_R. In this setting, we define PSU as follows.

Definition 9 (Private set union (PSU) functionality with $|S_S| = 1$).
Let Π be a two-party communication protocol. Let R be the receiver holding set $S_R \subset \{0,1\}^\lambda$ and let S be the sender holding singleton set $S_S = \{\mathsf{id}\}$, with $\mathsf{id} \in \{0,1\}^\lambda$. Π is a PSU protocol if the following hold after execution of the protocol.

- **Correctness:** R learns $S_R \cup \{\mathsf{id}\}$.
- **Receiver security:** Π achieves receiver security if $\forall \mathsf{id} \in \{0,1\}^\lambda$, and all pairs $S_{R0}, S_{R1} \subset \{0,1\}^\lambda$ we have that $\mathsf{view}_S^{\Pi}(S_{R0}, \mathsf{id}, \lambda) \approx \mathsf{view}_S^{\Pi}(S_{R1}, \mathsf{id}, \lambda)$. If the distributions are computationally (resp., statistically) indistinguishable then we have computational (resp., statistical) security.
- **Sender security:** Π achieves sender security if $\forall S_R \subset \{0,1\}^\lambda$, and all pairs $\mathsf{id}_0, \mathsf{id}_1 \in S_R$ we have that $\mathsf{view}_R^{\Pi}(S_R, \mathsf{id}_0, \lambda) \approx \mathsf{view}_R^{\Pi}(S_R, \mathsf{id}_1, \lambda)$. If the distributions are computationally (resp., statistically) indistinguishable then we have computational (resp., statistical) security.

The PSU functionality can be achieved by casting it as an instance of BP-2PC:

---

[6] This assumes R already has the polynomial-sized BP and does not have to build it from their exponential-sized set S_R.

1. R runs $\mathsf{SetBP}(S_\mathsf{R}, 0)$ (Fig. 4) to generate a branching program BP_psu such that $\mathsf{BP}_\mathrm{psu}(x) = 1$ if $x \notin S_\mathsf{R}$ and $\mathsf{BP}_\mathrm{psu}(x) = 0$ otherwise.
2. R and S run BP-2PC with inputs BP_psu and id, respectively. By construction of BP-2PC:

$$\begin{cases} R \text{ learns id} & \text{if } \mathsf{BP}_\mathrm{psu}(\mathsf{id}) = 1 \implies \mathsf{id} \notin S_\mathsf{R} \\ R \text{ does not learn id} & \text{if } \mathsf{BP}_\mathrm{psu}(\mathsf{id}) = 0 \implies \mathsf{id} \in S_\mathsf{R} \end{cases},$$

which satisfies the PSU correctness condition and security follows from the security of Construction 1 for BP-2PC.

The computation and communication costs of the receiver and sender do not depend on $|S_\mathsf{R}|$. If the receiver holds a polynomial-sized BP describing a set S_R of exponential size, then this PSU protocol can run in polynomial time.[7]

5.3 Wildcards

Definition 10 (Wildcard). *In a bit string a wildcard, denoted by an asterisk* *, is used in place of a bit to indicate that its position may hold either bit value. In particular, the wildcard character replaces only a single bit, not a string. (E.g. $00* = \{000, 001\}$ and $**0 = \{000, 010, 100, 110\}$.)*

SetBP in Fig. 4 creates a branching program based on a set that does not contain strings with wildcards. Figure 5 presents a modified version called SetBP^* which creates a BP based on a singleton set containing a string with wildcard elements. Using SetBP^* instead of SetBP in the constructions for PSI and PSU above allows the receiver's set to contain wildcards.

SetBP^* runs in $O(\lambda)$ time. The resulting BP has depth $\overline{k}$, or $\lambda - k$, where k is the number of wildcard indices, and will contain $2\overline{k} + 1$ nodes, where $\overline{k} \leq \lambda$ is the number of non-wildcard indices. Since the depth leaks the number of wildcards in x, the receiver's message m_1 to the sender in Construction 1 contains the maximum depth d_m, instead of the true depth.

Overview of SetBP^*. SetBP^* (Fig. 5) starts by forming an ordered ascending list of all indices of x without wildcards. Then it loops over each of these indices. A node is added to the BP for every prefix of x ending with an explicit (as opposed to *) bit value. Each node value is set to the index of the next non-wildcard bit in x. The node representing the final non-wildcard index is given value b_pth. For example, if $x = 0*1*0$, then we add prefix nodes $v_\epsilon, v_0, v_{0*1}, v_{0*1*0}$, (where v_ϵ is the root), and set their values to $1, 3, 5, b_\mathsf{pth}$, respectively.

Each iteration adds an edge from the previous prefix node to the one just created. This edge is labelled with the bit value at the current non-wildcard index. Continuing with the example, in the iteration that node v_{0*1} is created, an edge from v_0 to v_{0*1} is added with label 1. Since S_R only contains one element, we also create a $1 - b_\mathsf{pth}$ leaf representing the prefix of the current interior node

---

[7] This assumes R already has the polynomial-sized BP and does not have to build it from their exponential-sized set S_R.

Procedure SetBP*(S, b_{pth}):

$x \leftarrow S$; $\lambda \leftarrow |x|$; $V, E, T \leftarrow \emptyset$; $\overline{\mathsf{WC}} \leftarrow \{i \mid x[i] \neq *\}$; $\overline{k} \leftarrow |\overline{\mathsf{WC}}|$

If $x[1] \neq *$ then $V \leftarrow V \cup \{v_\epsilon\}$; $\mathsf{Val}[v_\epsilon] \leftarrow 1$

If $x[1] = *$ then $V \leftarrow V \cup \{v_\epsilon\}$; $\mathsf{Val}[v_\epsilon] \leftarrow \overline{\mathsf{WC}}[1]$

For $1 \leq i \leq \overline{k}$ do

$\quad j \leftarrow \overline{\mathsf{WC}}[i]$; $a \leftarrow x[1..j]$; $V \leftarrow V \cup \{v_a\}$

$\quad$ If $i = \overline{k}$ then $\mathsf{Val}[v_a] \leftarrow b_{\mathsf{pth}}$; $T \leftarrow T \cup \{v_a\}$

$\quad$ Else $\mathsf{Val}[v_a] \leftarrow \overline{\mathsf{WC}}[i+1]$

$\quad a_{prev} \leftarrow x[1..\overline{\mathsf{WC}}[i-1]]$; $E \leftarrow E \cup \{(v_{a_{prev}}, v_a, x[j])\}$

$\quad a' \leftarrow x[1..(j-1)] \| (1 - x[j])$; $V \leftarrow V \cup \{v_{a'}\}$; $T \leftarrow T \cup \{v_{a'}\}$

$\quad \mathsf{Val}[v_{a'}] \leftarrow 1 - b_{\mathsf{pth}}$; $E \leftarrow E \cup \{(v_{a_{prev}}, v_{a'}, 1 - x[j])\}$

Return (V, E, T, Val)

Fig. 5. Procedure for constructing a BP from a singleton set with a λ-bit string with wildcards. See Construction 2 and Sect. 5.3.

with the final bit flipped. An edge labelled with this flipped bit is also added from the previous node. In the example, v_{0*0} is created with value $1 - b_{\mathsf{pth}}$ and edge $(v_{0*}, v_{0*0}, 0)$ is added. Once all non-wildcard indices of x have been considered, the BP is returned. If $|S_\mathsf{R}| > 1$, SetBP* can be run multiple times to add more leaf nodes to the BP. After the first SetBP* run, the zero-set initialization of V, E, T should be omitted.

5.4 Fuzzy Matching

A fuzzy match [GRS22] in our PSI setting refers to the inclusion of an element $x \in S_\mathsf{R}$ in the intersection $S_\mathsf{R} \cap S_\mathsf{S}$ if S_S contains an element that is δ-close to x. The receiver sets a distance threshold δ, which defines an ℓ_∞ ball of radius δ around all points in S_R. If an element in S_S falls within any of these balls, it counts as a match and the point in S_R at the center of this ball will be included in the intersection set. Construction 1 can be used for PSI with fuzzy matches defined with the ℓ_∞-norm as the distance metric (as considered in the structure-aware PSI [GRS22]). This may be accomplished if the receiver's BP can be modified with the addition of wildcards to allow any BP input within an ℓ_∞ ball centred at a point of S_R to be accepted as a fuzzy match.

6 Proof of Lemma 3

Proof. (*Condition (1):* BP(id) $= 1 \Rightarrow$ R_2 outputs id w.o.p.)

Claim 1: When DecPath is evaluated on the correct path, it will output (id, r).

Proof of claim 1: Consider the root-to-leaf path of length ℓ induced by the evaluation of BP(id). By hypothesis BP(id) $= 1$, so the path leaf node encodes the value 1. For concreteness, suppose the induced path has the leftmost leaf of the BP, $u_1 \in T$, as the leaf endpoint. With this in mind, denote the path as,

$$\mathsf{pth}[u_1] := (\underbrace{(1^\lambda, x_1, x_1')}_{z_\ell}, \underbrace{(h_1^{(\ell)}, h_2^{(\ell)}, \mathsf{Val}[v_1^{(\ell-1)}])}_{z_{\ell-1}}, \ldots, \underbrace{(h_1^{(1)}, h_2^{(1)}, \mathsf{Val}[v_1^{(0)}])}_{z_0}, h_{\mathsf{root}}).$$

(1)

For the remainder of the proof, node labels v will be identified with their encoded values $\mathsf{Val}[v]$ to save space. Let $(\mathsf{id}_{u_1}, r_{u_1}) \leftarrow \mathsf{DecPath}(\mathsf{pth}[u_1], \widetilde{\mathsf{C}}_{\mathsf{d_m}}, \ldots, \widetilde{\mathsf{C}}_0, \{\mathsf{cth}_{i,b}^{(0)}\})$, where $\widetilde{\mathsf{C}}_{\mathsf{d_m}}, \ldots, \widetilde{\mathsf{C}}_0, \{\mathsf{cth}_{i,b}^{(0)}\}$ are defined as in the construction. Then it suffices to show that $r_{u_1} = r$. Consider an arbitrary iteration $w \in \{0, \ldots, \ell - 2\}$ of the loop in step 2 of DecPath:

2. (a) $\{\mathsf{lb}_i^{(w)}\} \leftarrow \mathsf{HDec}(z_w, \{\mathsf{cth}_{i,b}^{(w)}\})$

$\quad \leftarrow \mathsf{HDec}((h_1^{(w+1)}, h_2^{(w+1)}, v_1^{(w)}), \mathsf{HEnc}(\mathsf{pp}, h_1^{(w)}, \{\mathsf{lb}_{i,b}^{(w)}\}; \boldsymbol{r}_w))$

$\quad \leftarrow \mathsf{HDec}((h_1^{(w+1)}, h_2^{(w+1)}, v_1^{(w)}), \mathsf{HEnc}(\mathsf{pp}, \mathsf{Hash}(\mathsf{pp}, (h_1^{(w+1)}, h_2^{(w+1)}, v_1^{(w)})), \{\mathsf{lb}_{i,b}^{(w)}\}; \boldsymbol{r}_w))$

Since the two terms indicated are equal, the labels $\{\mathsf{lb}_i^{(w)}\}$ output by HDec are the subset of $\{\mathsf{lb}_{i,b}^{(w)}\}$ corresponding to the bits of $z_w := (h_1^{(w+1)}, h_2^{(w+1)}, v_1^{(w)})$. More precisely, $\mathsf{lb}_{i,0}^{(w)} := \mathsf{lb}_{i,z_w[i]}^{(w)}$ and $\mathsf{lb}_{i,1}^{(w)} := \mathsf{lb}_{i,z_w[i]}^{(w)}$ for all $i \in [n]$.

2. (b) $\{\mathsf{cth}_{i,b}^{(w+1)}\} \leftarrow \mathsf{Eval}(\widetilde{\mathsf{C}}_w, \{\mathsf{lb}_i^{(w)}\})$.

$\quad \{\mathsf{cth}_{i,b}^{(w+1)}\} \leftarrow \mathsf{V}[\mathsf{pp}, \mathsf{id}, \{\mathsf{lb}_{i,b}^{(w+1)}\}, \boldsymbol{r}_w, r, \mathsf{id}', r', \mathsf{pad}](h_1^{(w+1)}, h_2^{(w+1)}, v_1^{(w)})$

$\quad \{\mathsf{cth}_{i,b}^{(w+1)}\} \leftarrow \mathsf{HEnc}(\mathsf{pp}, \underbrace{h_1^{(w+1)}}_{=\mathsf{Hash}(\mathsf{pp}, (h_1^{(w+2)}, h_2^{(w+2)}, v_1^{(w+1)}))}, \{\mathsf{lb}_{i,b}^{(w+1)}\}; \boldsymbol{r}_w)$

(2)

The first input $h_1^{(w+1)}$ is used in the input to HEnc because $\mathsf{pth}[u_1]$ was defined to have the leftmost leaf as an endpoint. In other words, travelling from the root, $\mathsf{pth}[u_1]$ always progresses to the left child.

In the final iteration of the loop, when $w = \ell - 1$, the steps expanded above remain the same except for Eq. 2. When $w = \ell - 1$, Eq. 2 is instead

$$\{\mathsf{cth}_{i,b}^{(\ell)}\} \leftarrow \mathsf{HEnc}(\mathsf{pp}, \underbrace{h_1^{(\ell)}}_{=\mathsf{Hash}(\mathsf{pp}, (1^\lambda, x_1, x_1'))}, \{\mathsf{lb}_{i,b}^{(\ell)}\}; \boldsymbol{r}_{\ell-1}).$$

With this in mind, the final two steps of DecPath are as follows.

3. $\{\mathsf{lb}_i^{(\ell)}\} \leftarrow \mathsf{HDec}(z_\ell, \{\mathsf{cth}_{i,b}^{(\ell)}\})$

$\quad \{\mathsf{lb}_i^{(\ell)}\} \leftarrow \mathsf{HDec}((1^\lambda, x_1, x_1'), \mathsf{HEnc}(\mathsf{pp}, \mathsf{Hash}(\mathsf{pp}, (1^\lambda, x_1, x_1')), \{\mathsf{lb}_{i,b}^{(\ell)}\}))$

Since the two terms indicated above are equal, the labels $\{\mathsf{lb}_i^{(\ell)}\}$ output by HDec are the subset of labels $\{\mathsf{lb}_{i,b}^{(\ell)}\}$ used in the input to HEnc, where the subset corresponds to the bits of $z_\ell = (1^\lambda, x_1, x_1')$.

4. $\{\mathsf{id}_{u_1}, r_{u_1}, \mathsf{pad}\} \leftarrow \mathsf{Eval}(\widetilde{C}_\ell, \{\mathsf{lb}_i^{(\ell)}\})$

$$\{\mathsf{id}_{u_1}, r_{u_1}, \mathsf{pad}\} \leftarrow \mathsf{V}[\mathsf{pp}, \mathsf{id}, \{\mathsf{lb}_{i,b}^{(\ell+1)}\}, \boldsymbol{r}_\ell, r, \mathsf{id}', r', \mathsf{pad}](1^\lambda, x_1, x_1')$$

$$\{\mathsf{id}_{u_1}, r_{u_1}, \mathsf{pad}\} \leftarrow \{\mathsf{id}_{u_1} \leftarrow \mathsf{id}, r_{u_1} \leftarrow r, \text{ and } \mathsf{pad} \xleftarrow{\$} \{0,1\}^{2(n-1)}\}$$

Then return $(\mathsf{id}_{u_1}, r_{u_1})$ to the receiver. The first input to V is 1^λ, so the tuple $(\mathsf{id}_{u_1}, r_{u_1})$ is equal to (id, r).

The receiver compares r_{u_1} from DecPath with r in m_2. Since these strings are equal, the receiver takes id_{u_1} output from DecPath as the sender's element. Hence, the receiver learns id when $\mathsf{BP}(\mathsf{id}) = 1$, completing the proof of claim 1.

In the above, we made use of the correctness properties of garbled circuit evaluation and HE decryption. These guarantees give us that $\Pr[\mathsf{id}_{u_1} = \mathsf{id} \wedge r_{u_1} = r \mid (\mathsf{id}_{u_1}, r_{u_1}) \leftarrow \mathsf{DecPath}(\mathsf{pth}[u_1], \mathsf{m}_2)] = 1$ when $\mathsf{pth}[u_1]$ is the correct path through the BP. In order for the correctness condition (1) to be met, it must also be true that there does not exist any other path $\mathsf{pth}[u'] \neq \mathsf{pth}[u_1]$ such that $r_{u'} = r$ where $(\mathsf{id}_{u'}, r_{u'}) \leftarrow \mathsf{DecPath}(\mathsf{pth}[u'], \mathsf{m}_2)$. In other words, there must not exist an incorrect path that decrypts the correct signal value r.

Claim 2: With at most negligible probability, there exists an incorrect path that when input to DecPath, decrypts to the correct signal value r.

Proof of claim 2: To show that occurs with negligible probability, consider running DecPath on an incorrect path $\mathsf{pth}[u'] \neq \mathsf{pth}[u_1]$. Let $\mathsf{pth}[u_1]$ and $\mathsf{pth}[u']$ have lengths ℓ and ℓ', respectively where $1 \leq \ell, \ell' \leq d$. Suppose these paths are equal at level $\alpha - 1$ and differ at level α onward, for some $\alpha \in \{0, \ldots, \min\{\ell, \ell'\}\}$. Suppose $u_1 \in T$ is the leftmost leaf, as above, and $u' \in T \setminus \{u_1\}$ is the leaf endpoint of $\mathsf{pth}[u']$. Let these paths be given by the following.

$$\mathsf{pth}[u_1] := (\underbrace{(u_1^{(\ell) \times \lambda}, x_1, x_1')}_{z_\ell}, \underbrace{(h_1^{(\ell)}, h_2^{(\ell)}, v^{(\ell-1)})}_{z_{\ell-1}}, \ldots, \underbrace{(h_1^{(\alpha+1)}, h_2^{(\alpha+1)}, v_1^{(\alpha)})}_{z_\alpha}, \quad (3)$$

$$\underbrace{(h_1^{(\alpha)}, h_2^{(\alpha)}, v_1^{(\alpha-1)})}_{z_{\alpha-1}}, \ldots, \underbrace{(h_1^{(1)}, h_2^{(1)}, v_1^{(0)})}_{z_0}, \mathsf{h}_{\mathsf{root}})$$

$$\mathsf{pth}[u'] := (\underbrace{(u'^{(\ell') \times \lambda}, x, x')}_{z'_{\ell'}}, \underbrace{(h^{(\ell')}, h'^{(\ell')}, v^{(\ell'-1)})}_{z'_{\ell'-1}}, \ldots, \underbrace{(h_3^{(\alpha+1)}, h_4^{(\alpha+1)}, v_2^{(\alpha)})}_{z'_\alpha}, \quad (4)$$

$$\underbrace{(h_1^{(\alpha)}, h_2^{(\alpha)}, v_1^{(\alpha-1)})}_{z'_{\alpha-1}}, \ldots, \underbrace{(h_1^{(1)}, h_2^{(1)}, v_1^{(0)})}_{z'_0}, \mathsf{h}_{\mathsf{root}}).$$

Since $\mathsf{pth}[u']$ differs from the correct path at level α, the steps of $\mathsf{DecPath}(\mathsf{pth}[u'], \mathsf{m}_2)$ and $\mathsf{DecPath}(\mathsf{pth}[u_1], \mathsf{m}_2)$ will be identical until loop iteration $w = \alpha$. Consider iteration $w = \alpha - 1$ of $\mathsf{DecPath}(\mathsf{pth}[u'], \mathsf{m}_2)$:

2. (a) $\{\mathsf{lb}_i'^{(\alpha)}\} \leftarrow \mathsf{HDec}(z_\alpha', \{\mathsf{cth}_{i,b}^{(\alpha)}\})$

$\leftarrow \mathsf{HDec}((h_3^{(\alpha+1)}, h_4^{(\alpha+1)}, v_2^{(\alpha)}), \mathsf{HEnc}(\mathsf{pp}, h_1^{(\alpha)}, \{\mathsf{lb}_{i,b}^{(\alpha)}\}; r_{\alpha-1}))$

$\leftarrow \mathsf{HDec}((h_3^{(\alpha+1)}, h_4^{(\alpha+1)}, v_2^{(\alpha)}), \mathsf{HEnc}(\mathsf{pp}, (h_1^{(\alpha+1)}, h_2^{(\alpha+1)}, v_1^{(\alpha)}), \{\mathsf{lb}_{i,b}^{(\alpha)}\}; r_{\alpha-1})).$

Since the indicated terms are equal, the $\{\mathsf{lb}_i^{(\alpha-1)}\}$ labels output are the labels of circuit $\widetilde{C}_{\alpha-1}$ corresponding to the bits of $z_{\alpha-1}'$.

2. (b) $\{\mathsf{cth}_{i,b}^{(\alpha)}\} \leftarrow \mathsf{Eval}(\widetilde{C}_{\alpha-1}, \{\mathsf{lb}_i^{(\alpha-1)}\})$

$\leftarrow \mathsf{V}[\mathsf{pp}, \mathsf{id}, \{\mathsf{lb}_{i,b}^{(\alpha)}\}, r_{\alpha-1}, r, \mathsf{id}', r', \mathsf{pad}](h_1^{(\alpha)}, h_2^{(\alpha)}, v_1^{(\alpha-1)})$

$\leftarrow \mathsf{HEnc}(\mathsf{pp}, h_1^{(\alpha)}, \{\mathsf{lb}_{i,b}^{(\alpha)}\}; r_{\alpha-1}).$

In the last line, $h_1^{(\alpha)}$ is used in the hash encryption due to the assumption that the correct path has the leftmost leaf as an endpoint, meaning $\mathsf{id}[v_1^{(\alpha+1)}] = 0.$[8] Next, the $w = \alpha$ iteration of the loop proceeds as follows.

2. (a) $\{\mathsf{lb}_i'^{(\alpha)}\} \leftarrow \mathsf{HDec}(z_\alpha', \{\mathsf{cth}_{i,b}^{(\alpha)}\})$

$\leftarrow \mathsf{HDec}((h_3^{(\alpha+1)}, h_4^{(\alpha+1)}, v_2^{(\alpha)}), \mathsf{HEnc}(\mathsf{pp}, h_1^{(\alpha)}, \{\mathsf{lb}_{i,b}^{(\alpha)}\}; r_{\alpha-1}))$

$\leftarrow \mathsf{HDec}((h_3^{(\alpha+1)}, h_4^{(\alpha+1)}, v_2^{(\alpha)}), \mathsf{HEnc}(\mathsf{pp}, (h_1^{(\alpha+1)}, h_2^{(\alpha+1)}, v_1^{(\alpha)}), \{\mathsf{lb}_{i,b}^{(\alpha)}\}; r_{\alpha-1})).$

The two indicated terms are not equal. Decrypting an HE ciphertext with an incorrect hash preimage produces an output containing no PPT-accessible information about the encrypted plaintext. For this reason, a prime was added above to the LHS labels to differentiate them from the labels encrypted on the RHS. Thus $\{\mathsf{lb}_i'^{(\alpha)}\}$ provides no information about $\{\mathsf{lb}_{i,b}^{(\alpha)}\}$.

2. (b) $\{\mathsf{cth}_{i,b}^{(\alpha+1)}\} \leftarrow \mathsf{Eval}(\widetilde{C}_\alpha, \{\mathsf{lb}_i'^{(\alpha)}\}).$

Note that $\{\mathsf{lb}_i'^{(\alpha)}\}$ are *not* labels of $\widetilde{C}_\alpha$, and certainly not a subset of those labels corresponding to a meaningful input. So the output $\{\mathsf{cth}_{i,b}^{(\alpha+1)}\}$ is a meaningless set of strings, not a ciphertext.

For w from α to ℓ', every HDec operation will output $\{\mathsf{lb}_i'^{(w)}\}$ which are *not* circuit labels for $\widetilde{C}_w$ and every evaluation $\mathsf{Eval}(\widetilde{C}_w, \{\mathsf{lb}_i'^{(w)}\})$ will output strings with no relation to $\widetilde{C}_w$. In step 4, $\{\mathsf{id}_{u'}, r_{u'}, \mathsf{pad}\} \leftarrow \mathsf{Eval}(\widetilde{C}_{\ell'}, \{\mathsf{lb}_i'^{(\ell')}\})$ is computed. Since $\{\mathsf{lb}_i'^{(\ell')}\}$ are not labels, the evaluation output is meaningless. In particular, the tuple $(\mathsf{id}_{u'}, r_{u'})$ output to R_2 contains no PPT-accessible information about (id, r). Hence $\Pr[r_{u'} = r] \le 2^{-\lambda} + \mathsf{negl}(\lambda)$. By assumption on the size of BP, there are a polynomial number of root-to-leaf paths, thus by the

---

[8] It is straightforward to change the proof to apply to cases of different correct paths.

union bound the probability that any incorrect root-to-path causes DecPath to output r is,

$$\Pr[\exists\, u \in T \setminus \{u_1\} \text{ s.t. } r_u = r \mid (\mathsf{id}_u, r_u) \leftarrow \mathsf{DecPath}(\mathsf{pth}[u], \mathsf{m}_2)] \leq \frac{\mathsf{poly}(\lambda)}{2^\lambda} + \mathsf{negl}(\lambda).$$

The probability that R_2 outputs id when $\mathsf{BP}(\mathsf{id}) = 1$ is the probability that none of the incorrect paths output a signal value equal to r:

$$\Pr\left[\mathsf{R}_2 \text{ outputs id} \mid \mathsf{BP}(\mathsf{id}) = 1\right] \geq 1 - \frac{\mathsf{poly}(\lambda)}{2^\lambda} - \mathsf{negl}(\lambda).$$

Thus proving claim 2 and correctness condition (1).

(*Condition (2)*: $\mathsf{BP}(\mathsf{id}) = 0 \Rightarrow \mathsf{R}_2$ outputs $\bot$ w.o.p.) In the proof of Theorem 1 we will show that when $\mathsf{BP}(\mathsf{id}) = 0$,

$$(\widetilde{\mathsf{C}}_{\mathsf{d}_m}, \ldots, \widetilde{\mathsf{C}}_0, \{\mathsf{cth}_{i,b}^{(0)}\}, r) \overset{c}{\equiv} (\widetilde{\mathsf{C}}'_{\mathsf{d}_m}, \ldots, \widetilde{\mathsf{C}}'_0, \{\mathsf{cth}_{i,b}'^{(0)}\}, r'), \tag{5}$$

where all primed values are sampled uniformly random. On the LHS, the circuits all have r hardcoded, while the RHS is independent of r. So, for all fixed $u \in T$,

$$\Pr\left[r_u = r \mid (\mathsf{id}_u, r_u) \leftarrow \mathsf{DecPath}(\mathsf{pth}[u], (\widetilde{\mathsf{C}}'_{\mathsf{d}_m}, \ldots, \widetilde{\mathsf{C}}'_0, \{\mathsf{cth}_{i,b}'^{(0)}\}, r'))\right] \leq \frac{1}{2^\lambda},$$

where $\mathsf{pth}[u]$ denotes the path from the root to leaf u. By assumption on the size of BP, there are a polynomial number of root-to-leaf paths, thus by the union bound the probability that any root-to-leaf paths decrypt to output r is,

$$\Pr\left[\exists\, u \in T \text{ s.t. } r_u = r \mid (\mathsf{id}_u, r_u) \leftarrow \mathsf{DecPath}(\mathsf{pth}[u], (\widetilde{\mathsf{C}}'_{\mathsf{d}_m}, \ldots, \widetilde{\mathsf{C}}'_0, \{\mathsf{cth}_{i,b}'^{(0)}\}, r'))\right]$$
$$\leq \frac{\mathsf{poly}(\lambda)}{2^\lambda}.$$

By Eq. 5, we must also have that the analogous probability for inputs $(\widetilde{\mathsf{C}}_{\mathsf{d}_m}, \ldots, \widetilde{\mathsf{C}}_0, \{\mathsf{cth}_{i,b}^{(0)}\}, r)$ is computationally indistinguishable. Thus,

$$\Pr\left[\exists\, u \in T \text{ s.t. } r_u = r \mid (\mathsf{id}_u, r_u) \leftarrow \mathsf{DecPath}(\mathsf{pth}[u], (\widetilde{\mathsf{C}}_{\mathsf{d}_m}, \ldots, \widetilde{\mathsf{C}}_0, \{\mathsf{cth}_{i,b}^{(0)}\}, r))\right]$$
$$\leq \frac{\mathsf{poly}(\lambda)}{2^\lambda} + \mathsf{negl}(\lambda).$$

If R_2 receives r_u from DecPath s.t. $r_u = r$, then R_2 outputs id_u. It follows that,

$$\Pr\left[\mathsf{R}_2 \text{ outputs } \bot \mid \mathsf{BP}(\mathsf{id}) = 0\right] \geq 1 - \frac{\mathsf{poly}(\lambda)}{2^\lambda} - \mathsf{negl}(\lambda),$$

which completes the proof of Lemma 3.   □

7   Proof of Theorem 1

*Proof (**Theorem** 1 **receiver security proof**).* Note that node labels will be identified with their encoded values to save space. Following Definition 7, for any pair (BP_0, BP_1) consider the distribution below for $i \in \{0, 1\}$.

$$\text{view}_S^{BP}\text{-2PC}(BP_i, \text{id}, \lambda) = (\text{id}, r_S, m_1, m_2)$$

$$= (\text{id}, r_S, (d_m, h_{\text{root}_i}), (\widetilde{C}_{d_m}, \ldots, \widetilde{C}_0, \text{HEnc}(pp, h_{\text{root}_i}, \{lb_{i,b}^{(0)}\}), r)),$$

where r_S are the sender's random coins, h_{root_i} is the root hash, and d_m is the maximum depth of branching program BP_i. Since both BPs have security parameter λ, both will have $d_m = \lambda + 1$. Let d_i be the depth of BP_i.

Robustness of HE implies that for all $pp \xleftarrow{\$} \text{HGen}(1^\lambda, 3\lambda)$ and $u \in T$, the distribution $(pp, \text{Hash}(pp, (u^\lambda, x, x')))$, where $x, x' \xleftarrow{\$} \{0, 1\}^\lambda$, is statistically close to $(pp, h_\$)$ where $h_\$ \xleftarrow{\$} \{0, 1\}^\lambda$. Hence $\text{Hash}(pp, (u^\lambda, x, x'))$ statistically hides u. At level d_i, BP_i will have at least two leaf nodes with the same parent. Let u_1, u_2 be two such leaves and let $v^{(d_i - 1)}$ be the parent. Node $v^{(d_i - 1)}$ will then have hash value,

$$h^{(d_i - 1)} \leftarrow \text{Hash}(pp, (h_1^{(d_i)}, h_2^{(d_i)}, v^{(d_i - 1)}))$$

$$\leftarrow \text{Hash}(pp, (\text{Hash}(pp, (u_1^\lambda, x_1, x_1')), \text{Hash}(pp, (u_2^\lambda, x_2, x_2')), v^{(d_i - 1)})).$$

Since $h_1^{(d_i)}$ and $h_2^{(d_i)}$ are both statistically close to uniform, we have that $h^{(d_i - 1)}$ is also statistically close to uniform. Continuing up the tree in this way, we see that the root hash h_{root_i} is also indistinguishable from random. Thus $h_{\text{root}_0} \approx_s h_{\text{root}_1}$, which gives us $\text{view}_S^{BP}\text{-2PC}(BP_0, \text{id}, \lambda) \approx_s \text{view}_S^{BP}\text{-2PC}(BP_1, \text{id}, \lambda)$.   □

*Proof (**Theorem** 1 **sender security proof**).*
Sender security will be proved through a sequence of indistinguishable hybrids in two main steps. First, all garbled circuits in the sender's message m_2 are replaced one at a time with simulated circuits. Then m_2 is switched to random.

Sender security only applies when $BP(\text{id}) = 0$, so this will be assumed for the proof. For concreteness, suppose the path induced on the BP by evaluating id has the leftmost leaf as an endpoint. In particular, let

$$\text{pth} := (\underbrace{(\text{Val}[v_1^{(\ell)}]^{\times \lambda}, x_1, x_1')}_{z_\ell}, \underbrace{(h_1^{(\ell)}, h_2^{(\ell)}, \text{Val}[v_1^{(\ell-1)}])}_{z_{\ell-1}}, \ldots, \underbrace{(h_1^{(1)}, h_2^{(1)}, \text{Val}[v_1^{(0)}])}_{z_0}, h_{\text{root}})$$

$$(6)$$

be the leaf-root path induced on the hashed BP by evaluation of id, where ℓ is the path length and d is the BP depth.[9] Since $BP(\text{id}) = 0$, the terminal node encodes value 0, i.e., $\text{Val}[v_1^{(\ell)}] = 0$. We let $h_{\text{root}} \leftarrow \text{Hash}(pp, z_0)$ and $h_1^{(i)} \leftarrow \text{Hash}(pp, z_i)$ for all $1 \le i \le \ell$, where the z_i values are defined as in Eq. 6. To save space, often

---

[9] We assume $\ell \ge 1$. If the receiver's BP has depth 0, then two dummy leaves can be introduced as root children.

node labels v will be identified with their encoded index values $\mathsf{Val}[v]$ and the padding superscript will be omitted from leaf node values.

Hyb$_0$: [Fig. 6 left] The sender's message $\mathsf{m}_2 := (\widetilde{C}_{\mathsf{d_m}}, \ldots, \widetilde{C}_0, \{\mathsf{cth}_{i,b}^{(0)}\}, r)$ is formed as described in the construction.

Hyb$_1$: [Fig. 6 right] All circuits are simulated. The circuits are simulated so that if R runs $\mathsf{DecPath}$ on pth with simulated circuits, then every step occurs, from the view of R, as it would in **Hyb$_0$**. This requires knowledge of pth and the correct sequence of hash preimages $z_\ell, \ldots, z_0$, where $z_\ell = (0^\lambda, x_1, x_1')$ and $z_j = (h_1^{(j+1)}, h_2^{(j+1)}, v_1^{(j)})$ for $j \in \{0, \ldots, \ell - 1\}$. By assumption of pth, every evaluation $\mathsf{Eval}(\widetilde{C}_j, \{\mathsf{lb}_i^{(j)}\})$, where $\{\mathsf{lb}_i^{(j)}\} \leftarrow \mathsf{HDec}(z_j, \{\mathsf{cth}_{i,b}^{(j)}\})$, done in $\mathsf{DecPath}$ for $j \in \{0, \ldots, \ell - 1\}$ will output ciphertexts $\mathsf{HEnc}(\mathsf{pp}, h_1^{(j+1)}, \{\mathsf{lb}_{i,b}^{(j+1)}\}; r_j)^{10}$. Moreover, evaluation of $\mathsf{Eval}(\widetilde{C}_\ell, \{\mathsf{lb}_i^{(\ell)}\})$ outputs $\{\mathsf{id}', r', \mathsf{pad}\}$ for random $\mathsf{id}', r' \xleftarrow{\$} \{0,1\}^\lambda$ and $\mathsf{pad} \xleftarrow{\$} \{0,1\}^{2(n-1)}$. Simulating circuits $\widetilde{C}_\ell, \ldots, \widetilde{C}_0$ is straightforward.

To simulate circuits $\widetilde{C}_{\mathsf{d_m}}, \ldots, \widetilde{C}_{\ell+1}$ note that none of these circuits can be used by R in $\mathsf{DecPath}$ to obtain a meaningful output. Only this behaviour needs to be mimicked. To this end, we define "ghost" values $z_{\mathsf{d_m}}, \ldots, z_{\ell+1}$ with their associated hash values. The deepest is defined to be uniformly random: $z_{\mathsf{d_m}} \xleftarrow{\$} \{0,1\}^{3\lambda}$. Then for $j \in \{\mathsf{d_m} - 1, \ldots, \ell + 1\}$ define,

Hyb$_0$:	**Hyb$_1$:**
$r, r', \mathsf{id}' \xleftarrow{\$} \{0,1\}^\lambda$	$r, r', \mathsf{id}' \xleftarrow{\$} \{0,1\}^\lambda$; $\mathsf{pad} \xleftarrow{\$} \{0,1\}^{2(n-1)}$
$\mathsf{pad} \xleftarrow{\$} \{0,1\}^{2(n-1)}$	$z_{\mathsf{d_m}} \xleftarrow{\$} \{0,1\}^{3\lambda}$; $(\widetilde{C}_{\mathsf{d_m}}, \{\mathsf{lb}_i^{(\mathsf{d_m})}\}) \xleftarrow{\$} \mathsf{Sim}(\mathsf{F}, \{\mathsf{id}', r'\})$
$C_{\mathsf{d_m}} := \mathsf{F}[\mathsf{id}, \mathsf{id}', r, r']$	For $0 \le w \le \mathsf{d_m} - 1$ sample random r_w
$(\widetilde{C}_{\mathsf{d_m}}, \{\mathsf{lb}_{i,b}^{(\mathsf{d_m})}\}) \xleftarrow{\$} \mathsf{Garb}(C_{\mathsf{d_m}})$	For i from $\mathsf{d_m} - 1$ down to $\ell + 1$ do
For w from $\mathsf{d_m} - 1$ to 0 do	$\quad v'^{(i)} \xleftarrow{\$} \{0,1\}^\lambda$; $h'^{(i+1)} \leftarrow \mathsf{Hash}(\mathsf{pp}, z_{i+1})$
$\quad$ Sample random r_w	$\quad z_i := (h'^{(i+1)}, h'^{(i+1)}, v'^{(i)})$
$\quad C_w := \mathsf{V}[\mathsf{pp}, \mathsf{id}, \{\mathsf{lb}_{i,b}^{(w+1)}\}, r_w,$	For w from $\mathsf{d_m} - 1$ down to $\ell + 1$ do
$\qquad r, \mathsf{id}', r', \mathsf{pad}]$	$\quad \{\mathsf{cth}_{i,b}^{(w+1)}\} \leftarrow \mathsf{HEnc}(\mathsf{pp}, h'^{(w+1)}, \{\mathsf{lb}_{i,b}^{(w+1)}\}; r_w)$
$\quad (\widetilde{C}_w, \{\mathsf{lb}_{i,b}^{(w)}\}) \xleftarrow{\$} \mathsf{Garb}(C_w)$	$\quad (\widetilde{C}_w, \{\mathsf{lb}_i^{(w)}\}) \xleftarrow{\$} \mathsf{Sim}(\mathsf{V}, \{\mathsf{cth}_{i,b}^{(w+1)}\})$
$\{\mathsf{cth}_{i,b}^{(0)}\} \xleftarrow{\$} \mathsf{HEnc}(\mathsf{pp}, h_{\mathsf{root}}, \{\mathsf{lb}_{i,b}^{(0)}\})$	$(\widetilde{C}_\ell, \{\mathsf{lb}_i^{(\ell)}\}) \xleftarrow{\$} \mathsf{Sim}(\mathsf{V}, \{\mathsf{id}', r', \mathsf{pad}\})$
$\mathsf{m}_2 := (\widetilde{C}_{\mathsf{d_m}}, \ldots, \widetilde{C}_0, \{\mathsf{cth}_{i,b}^{(0)}\}, r)$	For w from $\ell - 1$ down to 0 do
Return m_2	$\quad \{\mathsf{cth}_{i,b}^{(w+1)}\} \leftarrow \mathsf{HEnc}(\mathsf{pp}, h_1^{(w+1)}, \{\mathsf{lb}_i^{(w+1)}\}; r_w)$
	$\quad (\widetilde{C}_w, \{\mathsf{lb}_i^{(w)}\}) \xleftarrow{\$} \mathsf{Sim}(\mathsf{V}, \{\mathsf{cth}_{i,b}^{(w+1)}\})$
	$\{\mathsf{cth}_i^{(0)}\} \xleftarrow{\$} \mathsf{HEnc}(\mathsf{pp}, h_{\mathsf{root}}, \{\mathsf{lb}_i^{(0)}\})$
	Return $\mathsf{m}_2 := (\widetilde{C}_{\mathsf{d_m}}, \ldots, \widetilde{C}_0, \{\mathsf{cth}_{i,b}^{(0)}\}, r)$

Fig. 6. Hyb$_0$ and Hyb$_1$ for the proof of Theorem 1.

---

[10] The use of $h_1^{(j+1)}$ in HEnc is from the assumption that pth has the leftmost leaf as an endpoint and hence the first hash input is always used in the V encryption. In the general case, this hash value would be changed accordingly.

$$h'^{(j)} := \mathsf{Hash}(\mathsf{pp}, (\overbrace{\underbrace{h'^{(j+1)}}_{\mathsf{Hash}(\mathsf{pp}, z_{j+1})}, h'^{(j+1)}, v'^{(j)}}^{z_j}))$$

where $v'_j \xleftarrow{\$} \{0,1\}^\lambda$. In this way, two-thirds of the z_j preimage is uniformly random which allows us to invoke the HE robustness property. Moreover, the z_j values create a chain of preimages similar to the z_j values for $0 \leq j \leq \ell - 1$.

Lemma 4. *Hybrids* $\mathbf{Hyb}_0$ *and* $\mathbf{Hyb}_1$ *are computationally indistinguishable.*

For $p - 1 < \ell$:

$$\underbrace{\widetilde{\mathsf{C}}_{\mathsf{d}_\mathsf{m}}, \widetilde{\mathsf{C}}_{\mathsf{d}_\mathsf{m}-1}}_{\mathsf{Garb(F)}}, \dots\dots\dots\dots\dots\dots, \underbrace{\widetilde{\mathsf{C}}_{\ell+1}, \quad \widetilde{\mathsf{C}}_\ell, \quad \widetilde{\mathsf{C}}_{\ell-1}, \dots, \widetilde{\mathsf{C}}_p}_{\mathsf{Garb}(\mathsf{V}[\mathsf{pp},\mathsf{id},\{\mathsf{lb}^{(w+1)}_{i,b}\},r_w,r,\mathsf{id}',r',\mathsf{pad}])}, \underbrace{\widetilde{\mathsf{C}}_{p-1}, \dots, \widetilde{\mathsf{C}}_0}_{\mathsf{Sim}(\mathsf{V},\mathsf{HEnc}(h^{(w+1)}_1,\{\mathsf{lb}^{(w+1)}_i\};r_w))}$$

For $p - 1 = \ell$:

$$\underbrace{\widetilde{\mathsf{C}}_{\mathsf{d}_\mathsf{m}}, \widetilde{\mathsf{C}}_{\mathsf{d}_\mathsf{m}-1}}_{\mathsf{Garb(F)}}, \dots\dots\dots\dots\dots\dots, \underbrace{\widetilde{\mathsf{C}}_{p=\ell+1}, \widetilde{\mathsf{C}}_{p-1=\ell}}_{\mathsf{Garb}(\mathsf{V}[''])}, \underbrace{\widetilde{\mathsf{C}}_{\ell-1}}_{\mathsf{Sim}(\mathsf{V},\{\mathsf{id}',r',\mathsf{pad}\})}, \dots\dots\dots\dots, \underbrace{\widetilde{\mathsf{C}}_0}_{\mathsf{Sim}(\mathsf{V},\mathsf{HEnc}(''))}$$

For $p - 1 > \ell$:

$$\underbrace{\widetilde{\mathsf{C}}_{\mathsf{d}_\mathsf{m}}}_{\mathsf{Garb(F)}}, \underbrace{\widetilde{\mathsf{C}}_{\mathsf{d}_\mathsf{m}-1}, \dots, \widetilde{\mathsf{C}}_p}_{\mathsf{Garb}(\mathsf{V}[''])}, \underbrace{\widetilde{\mathsf{C}}_{p-1}, \dots\dots\dots, \widetilde{\mathsf{C}}_{\ell+1}}_{\mathsf{Sim}(\mathsf{V},\mathsf{HEnc}(h'^{(w+1)},\{\mathsf{lb}^{(w+1)}_i\}))}, \quad \underbrace{\widetilde{\mathsf{C}}_\ell}_{\mathsf{Sim}(\mathsf{V},\{'' \})}, \underbrace{\widetilde{\mathsf{C}}_{\ell-1}, \dots\dots\dots, \widetilde{\mathsf{C}}_0}_{\mathsf{Sim}(\mathsf{V},\mathsf{HEnc}(''))}$$

Fig. 7. Method of generating circuits in $\mathbf{Hyb}_{1.p}$ depending on the value of $p-1$ relative to the value of ℓ. Use of $h^{(w+1)}_1$ in HEnc on the LHS is from the assumption that pth has the leftmost leaf as an endpoint. $''$ is the ditto symbol.

$\mathbf{Hyb}_2$: Sample m_2 at random.

Lemma 5. *Hybrids* $\mathbf{Hyb}_1$ *and* $\mathbf{Hyb}_2$ *are computationally indistinguishable.*

If m_2 is pseudorandom to the receiver, then m_2 created with some id_0 is computationally indistinguishable from m_2 created with some other id_1. Therefore we have $\mathsf{view}^{\mathsf{BP}}_R\text{-}\mathsf{2PC}(\mathsf{BP}, \mathsf{id}_0, \lambda) \stackrel{c}{\equiv} \mathsf{view}^{\mathsf{BP}}_R\text{-}\mathsf{2PC}(\mathsf{BP}, \mathsf{id}_1, \lambda)$, hence the above two lemmas establish computational sender security.

7.1 Proof of Lemma 4

To prove that $\mathbf{Hyb}_0 \stackrel{c}{\equiv} \mathbf{Hyb}_1$, we define a chain of $\mathsf{d}_\mathsf{m}+1$ hybrids between $\mathbf{Hyb}_0$ and $\mathbf{Hyb}_1$. Then we prove each game hop is indistinguishable.

$\mathbf{Hyb}_{1.p}$ *for* $0 \leq p \leq \mathsf{d}_\mathsf{m}$ *(Fig. 8):* Let pth be as in Eq. 6 and recall we assume that $\mathsf{Val}[v^{(\ell)}_1] = 0$. In $\mathbf{Hyb}_{1.p}$ circuits $\widetilde{\mathsf{C}}_0, \dots, \widetilde{\mathsf{C}}_{p-1}$ are simulated and circuits $\widetilde{\mathsf{C}}_p, \dots, \widetilde{\mathsf{C}}_{\mathsf{d}_\mathsf{m}}$ are honestly generated (as in $\mathbf{Hyb}_0$). In $\mathbf{Hyb}_{1.0}$, all circuits are generated honestly[11] and in $\mathbf{Hyb}_{1.d_m}$ all circuits are simulated except for $\widetilde{C}_{d_m}$. The way a particular circuit $\widetilde{C}_i$ for $i \leq p-1$ is simulated depends on if $i < \ell$, $i = \ell$, or $i > \ell$, where ℓ is the length of path induced by id. These differences are shown in Fig. 7. As in $\mathbf{Hyb}_1$, simulating circuits $\widetilde{C}_{\ell+1}, \ldots, \widetilde{C}_{d_m-1}$ is done using ciphertexts created with "ghost" z values.

$\mathbf{Hyb}_{1.p}$:

$r, \mathsf{id}', r' \xleftarrow{\$} \{0,1\}^\lambda$; $\mathsf{pad} \xleftarrow{\$} \{0,1\}^{2(n-1)}$; $z_{d_m} \xleftarrow{\$} \{0,1\}^{3\lambda}$; $\forall 0 \leq w \leq d_m$ sample random r_w

For i from $d_m - 1$ to $\ell+1$ do $\triangleright$ Generate "ghost" hash inputs for levels below pth

$\quad v'^{(i)} \xleftarrow{\$} \{0,1\}^\lambda$; $z_i := (h'^{(i+1)}, h'^{(i+1)}, v'^{(i)})$

$(\widetilde{C}_{d_m}, \{\mathsf{lb}_{i,b}^{(d_m)}\}) \xleftarrow{\$} \mathsf{Garb}(\mathsf{F}[\mathsf{id},\mathsf{id}',r,r'])$; $\{\mathsf{lb}_i^{(d_m)}\} := \{\mathsf{lb}_{i,z_{d_m}[i]}^{(d_m)}\}$

For w from $d_m - 1$ to p do $(\widetilde{C}_w, \{\mathsf{lb}_{i,b}^{(w)}\}) \xleftarrow{\$} \mathsf{Garb}(\mathsf{V}[\mathsf{pp},\mathsf{id}, \{\mathsf{lb}_{i,b}^{(w+1)}\}, r_w, r, \mathsf{id}', r', \mathsf{pad}])$

$\{\mathsf{lb}_i^{(p)}\} := \{\mathsf{lb}_{i,z_p[i]}^{(p)}\}$ $\triangleright$ Final set of honest labels

If $p - 1 \geq \ell$ then $\triangleright$ If circuits at, or below, pth leaf level are simulated

$\quad$ If $p - 1 > \ell$ then for $p-1$ to $\ell+1$ do $\triangleright$ Below pth leaf level

$\qquad \{\mathsf{cth}_{i,b}^{(w+1)}\} \leftarrow \mathsf{HEnc}(\mathsf{pp}, h'^{(w+1)}, \{\mathsf{lb}_i^{(w+1)}\}; r_w)$; $(\widetilde{C}_w, \{\mathsf{lb}_i^{(w)}\}) \xleftarrow{\$} \mathsf{Sim}(\mathsf{V}, \{\mathsf{cth}_{i,b}^{(w+1)}\})$

$\quad (\widetilde{C}_\ell, \{\mathsf{lb}_i^{(\ell)}\}) \xleftarrow{\$} \mathsf{Sim}(\mathsf{V}, \{\mathsf{id}', r', \mathsf{pad}\})$ $\triangleright$ At pth leaf level

$\quad$ For w from $\ell - 1$ to 0 do $\triangleright$ From interior pth nodes to root

$\qquad \{\mathsf{cth}_{i,b}^{(w+1)}\} \leftarrow \mathsf{HEnc}(\mathsf{pp}, h_1^{(w+1)}, \{\mathsf{lb}_i^{(w+1)}\}; r_w)$; $(\widetilde{C}_w, \{\mathsf{lb}_i^{(w)}\}) \xleftarrow{\$} \mathsf{Sim}(\mathsf{V}, \{\mathsf{cth}_{i,b}^{(w+1)}\})$

Else $\triangleright$ If all circuits at, and below, pth leaf level are honest

$\quad$ For w from $p - 1$ to 0 do

$\qquad \{\mathsf{cth}_{i,b}^{(w+1)}\} \leftarrow \mathsf{HEnc}(\mathsf{pp}, h_1^{(w+1)}, \{\mathsf{lb}_i^{(w+1)}\}; r_w)$; $(\widetilde{C}_w, \{\mathsf{lb}_i^{(w)}\}) \xleftarrow{\$} \mathsf{Sim}(\mathsf{V}, \{\mathsf{cth}_{i,b}^{(w+1)}\})$

$\{\mathsf{cth}_{i,b}^{(0)}\} \xleftarrow{\$} \mathsf{HEnc}(\mathsf{pp}, h_{\mathsf{root}}, \{\mathsf{lb}_i^{(0)}\})$

Return $\mathsf{m}_2 := (\widetilde{C}_{d_m}, \ldots, \widetilde{C}_0, \{\mathsf{cth}_{i,b}^{(0)}\}, r)$

Fig. 8. $\mathbf{Hyb}_{1.p}$ for $0 \leq p \leq d_m$. The last $p+1$ circuits in $\mathbf{Hyb}_{1.p}$ are generated honestly and the remainder are simulated. See Lemma 4.

Lemma 6. $\mathbf{Hyb}_0 \overset{c}{\equiv} \mathbf{Hyb}_{1.0}$ *and* $\mathbf{Hyb}_1 \overset{c}{\equiv} \mathbf{Hyb}_{1.d_m}$.

Proof. First we will prove $\mathbf{Hyb}_0 \overset{c}{\equiv} \mathbf{Hyb}_{1.0}$ (Fig. 6 and Fig. 8). In both hybrids all circuits are honestly generated, but they differ in two ways. The first is in how the labels $\{\mathsf{lb}_i^{(d_m)}\}$ are formed. Both hybrids generate the tuple $(\widetilde{C}_{d_m}, \{\mathsf{lb}_{i,b}^{(d_m)}\}) \xleftarrow{\$} \mathsf{Garb}$ $(\mathsf{F}[\mathsf{id},\mathsf{id}',r,r'])$ but $\mathbf{Hyb}_{1.0}$ additionally does $\{\mathsf{lb}_i^{(d_m)}\} := \{\mathsf{lb}_{i,z_{d_m}[i]}^{(d_m)}\}$. If $\ell < d_m$, then z_{d_m} is random. In that case, $\mathsf{Eval}(\widetilde{C}_{d_m}, \{\mathsf{lb}_{i,z_{d_m}[i]}^{(d_m)}\})$ will return $\{\mathsf{id}', r'\}$ w.o.p. If $\ell = d_m$ then $z_{d_m} := (0^\lambda, x_1, x_1')$ and so $\mathsf{Eval}(\widetilde{C}_{d_m}, \{\mathsf{lb}_{i,z_{d_m}[i]}^{(d_m)}\})$ will return $\{\mathsf{id}', r'\}$ with probability 1. Hence the difference between the sets of labels is indistinguishable by the $\mathsf{BP}(\mathsf{id}) = 0$ assumption.

---

[11] When $p = 0$, $\mathbf{Hyb}_{1.p}$ is defined so that circuits $\widetilde{C}_0, \ldots, \widetilde{C}_{-1}$ are simulated, which we define to mean that no circuits are simulated.

The second difference between $\mathbf{Hyb}_0$ and $\mathbf{Hyb}_{1.0}$ is in how $\{\mathsf{cth}_{i,b}^{(0)}\}$ is formed. In $\mathbf{Hyb}_0$ we define $\{\mathsf{cth}_{i,b}^{(0)}\} \stackrel{\$}{\leftarrow} \mathsf{HEnc}(\mathsf{pp}, \mathsf{h}_{\mathsf{root}}, \{\mathsf{lb}_{i,b}^{(0)}\})$. While $\mathbf{Hyb}_{1.0}$ does $\{\mathsf{cth}_{i,b}^{(0)}\}$ $\stackrel{\$}{\leftarrow} \mathsf{HEnc}(\mathsf{pp}, \mathsf{h}_{\mathsf{root}}, \{\mathsf{lb}_i^{(0)}\})$, where $\{\mathsf{lb}_i^{(0)}\} := \{\mathsf{lb}_{i,z_0[i]}^{(0)}\}$. Since $\mathsf{h}_{\mathsf{root}} \leftarrow \mathsf{Hash}(\mathsf{pp}, z_0)$, by semantic security of hash encryption we have that $\mathsf{HEnc}(\mathsf{pp}, \mathsf{h}_{\mathsf{root}}, \{\mathsf{lb}_i^{(0)}\}) \stackrel{c}{\equiv}$ $\mathsf{HEnc}(\mathsf{pp}, \mathsf{h}_{\mathsf{root}}, \{\mathsf{lb}_{i,b}^{(0)}\})$, completing the proof of $\mathbf{Hyb}_0 \stackrel{c}{\equiv} \mathbf{Hyb}_{1.0}$.

Next we prove $\mathbf{Hyb}_1 \stackrel{c}{\equiv} \mathbf{Hyb}_{1.d_m}$. In $\mathbf{Hyb}_1$ (Fig. 6) all circuits are simulated. In $\mathbf{Hyb}_{1.d_m}$ (Fig. 8) all circuits except for $\widetilde{\mathsf{C}}_{d_m}$ are simulated. The hybrids are the same after constructing $\widetilde{\mathsf{C}}_{d_m}$ and its labels. So, either hybrid can be simulated with r, the induced path pth, and $(\widetilde{\mathsf{C}}_{d_m}, \{\mathsf{lb}_i^{(d_m)}\})$. For brevity, let $(\widetilde{\mathsf{C}}, \{\mathsf{lb}_i\})$ and $(\widetilde{\mathsf{C}}', \{\mathsf{lb}_i'\})$ denote the distribution of $(\widetilde{\mathsf{C}}_{d_m}, \{\mathsf{lb}_i^{(d_m)}\})$ in $\mathbf{Hyb}_1$ and $\mathbf{Hyb}_{1.0}$, respectively. Then $(\widetilde{\mathsf{C}}, \{\mathsf{lb}_i\}) \stackrel{\$}{\leftarrow} \mathsf{Sim}(\mathsf{F}, \{\mathsf{id}', r'\})$ for random $\mathsf{id}', r' \stackrel{\$}{\leftarrow} \{0,1\}^\lambda$. In $\mathbf{Hyb}_{1.0}$, letting $\mathsf{C}_{d_m} := \mathsf{F}[\mathsf{id}, \mathsf{id}', r, r']$ for random r, we have $(\widetilde{\mathsf{C}}', \{\mathsf{lb}_{i,b}\}) \stackrel{\$}{\leftarrow} \mathsf{Garb}(\mathsf{C}_{d_m})$ and $\{\mathsf{lb}_i'\} := \{\mathsf{lb}_{i,z_{d_m}[i]}\}$, where $z_{d_m} \stackrel{\$}{\leftarrow} \{0,1\}^{3\lambda}$ if $\ell < d_m$ and $z_{d_m} := (\mathsf{Val}[v_1^{(d_m)}]^{\times \lambda}, x_1, x_1')$ otherwise, where $\mathsf{Val}[v_1^{(d_m)}]^{\times \lambda} = 0^\lambda$. By garbling simulation security $(\widetilde{\mathsf{C}}', \{\mathsf{lb}_i'\}) \stackrel{c}{\equiv} \mathsf{Sim}(\mathsf{F}, \mathsf{C}_{d_m}(z_{d_m})) \stackrel{c}{\equiv} \mathsf{Sim}(\mathsf{F}, \{\mathsf{id}', r'\})$. If $\ell < d_m$ and z_{d_m} is random, then $\mathsf{C}_{d_m}(z_{d_m}) = \{\mathsf{id}, r\}$ with probability $2^{-\lambda}$. If $\ell = d_m$ and $z_{d_m} := (0^\lambda, x_1, x_1')$ then $\mathsf{C}_{d_m}(z_{d_m}) = \{\mathsf{id}', r'\}$ with probability 1. Thus, $(r, \mathsf{pth}, \widetilde{\mathsf{C}}, \{\mathsf{lb}_i\}) \stackrel{c}{\equiv} (r, \mathsf{pth}, \widetilde{\mathsf{C}}', \{\mathsf{lb}_i'\})$, proving $\mathbf{Hyb}_1 \stackrel{c}{\equiv} \mathbf{Hyb}_{1.0}$ and completing the proof of Lemma 6. $\qquad\square$

Lemma 7. *For all* $p \in \{0, \ldots, d_m - 1\}$, $\mathbf{Hyb}_{1.p} \stackrel{c}{\equiv} \mathbf{Hyb}_{1.p+1}$.

Proof. First, consider the circuits created in either hybrid:

$$\mathbf{Hyb}_{1.p} : \overbrace{\widetilde{\mathsf{C}}_{d_m}, \ldots, \widetilde{\mathsf{C}}_{p+1}, \widetilde{\mathsf{C}}_p}^{\mathsf{Garb}}, \overbrace{\widetilde{\mathsf{C}}_{p-1}, \ldots, \widetilde{\mathsf{C}}_0}^{\mathsf{Sim}}$$

$$\mathbf{Hyb}_{1.p+1} : \underbrace{\widetilde{\mathsf{C}}_{d_m}, \ldots, \widetilde{\mathsf{C}}_{p+1}}_{\mathsf{Garb}}, \underbrace{\widetilde{\mathsf{C}}_p, \widetilde{\mathsf{C}}_{p-1}, \ldots, \widetilde{\mathsf{C}}_0}_{\mathsf{Sim}}$$

$\widetilde{\mathsf{C}}_{d_m}, \{\mathsf{lb}_{i,b}^{(d_m)}\}, \ldots, \widetilde{\mathsf{C}}_{p+1}, \{\mathsf{lb}_{i,b}^{(p+1)}\}$ are the same in both hybrids. They differ only in the distribution of $(\widetilde{\mathsf{C}}_p, \{\mathsf{lb}_i^{(p)}\})$; it is generated honestly in $\mathbf{Hyb}_{1.p}$ and simulated in $\mathbf{Hyb}_{1.p+1}$. There are three possible ways $(\widetilde{\mathsf{C}}_p, \{\mathsf{lb}_i^{(p)}\})$ can be simulated in $\mathbf{Hyb}_{1.p+1}$ depending on the value of p relative to ℓ (see Fig. 7, but note that it shows $\mathbf{Hyb}_{1.p}$, not $\mathbf{Hyb}_{1.p+1}$). First, if $p < \ell$, then $(\widetilde{\mathsf{C}}_p, \{\mathsf{lb}_i^{(p)}\})$ is simulated using a hash encryption of $\{\mathsf{lb}_i^{(p+1)}\}$ with z_{p+1}. If $p = \ell$, then $(\widetilde{\mathsf{C}}_p, \{\mathsf{lb}_i^{(p)}\})$ is simulated using random output since $\mathsf{BP}(\mathsf{id}) = 0$. Finally, if $p > \ell$, then $(\widetilde{\mathsf{C}}_p, \{\mathsf{lb}_i^{(p)}\})$ is simulated using a hash encryption of $\{\mathsf{lb}_i^{(p+1)}\}$ using "ghost" value z_{p+1}. We will prove that in each case it holds that $(\widetilde{\mathsf{C}}_p, \{\mathsf{lb}_i^{(p)}\})_{\mathbf{Hyb}_{1.p}} \stackrel{c}{\equiv} (\widetilde{\mathsf{C}}_p, \{\mathsf{lb}_i^{(p)}\})_{\mathbf{Hyb}_{1.p+1}}$.

1. If $p < \ell$:

$$\mathbf{Hyb}_{1.p} : \begin{cases} (\widetilde{\mathsf{C}}_p, \{\mathsf{lb}_{i,b}^{(p)}\}) \xleftarrow{\$} \mathsf{Garb}(V[\mathsf{pp}, \mathsf{id}, \{\mathsf{lb}_{i,b}^{(p+1)}\}, \boldsymbol{r}_p, r, \mathsf{id}', r', \mathsf{pad}]) \\ \{\mathsf{lb}_i^{(p)}\} := \{\mathsf{lb}_{i,z_p[i]}^{(p)}\} \quad \text{where } z_p = (h_1^{(p+1)}, h_2^{(p+1)}, v_1^{(p)}) \end{cases}$$

$$\mathbf{Hyb}_{1.p+1} : \begin{cases} \{\mathsf{cth}_{i,b}^{(p+1)}\} \leftarrow \mathsf{HEnc}(\mathsf{pp}, h_1^{(p+1)}, \{\mathsf{lb}_i^{(p+1)}\}; \boldsymbol{r}_p) \\ (\widetilde{\mathsf{C}}_p, \{\mathsf{lb}_i^{(p)}\}) \xleftarrow{\$} \mathsf{Sim}(V, \{\mathsf{cth}_{i,b}^{(p+1)}\}) \end{cases} \tag{7}$$

By simulation security of garbled circuits,

$$(\widetilde{\mathsf{C}}_p, \{\mathsf{lb}_i^{(p)}\})_{\mathbf{Hyb}_{1.p}} \overset{c}{\equiv} \mathsf{Sim}(V, \mathsf{C}_p(z_p))$$
$$\overset{c}{\equiv} \mathsf{Sim}(V, \mathsf{HEnc}(\mathsf{pp}, h_1^{(p+1)}, \{\mathsf{lb}_{i,b}^{(p+1)}\}; \boldsymbol{r}_p)). \tag{8}$$

The use of $h_1^{(p+1)}$ in Eq. 8 is due to the assumption that the path induced by id has the leftmost node as its terminal node. So by definition of C_p, its hardwired labels $\{\mathsf{lb}_{i,b}^{(p+1)}\}$ will be encrypted under $h_1^{(p+1)}$. Equation 8 is identical to the RHS of Eq. 7, and thus when $p > \ell$ we have $(\widetilde{\mathsf{C}}_p, \{\mathsf{lb}_i^{(p)}\})_{\mathbf{Hyb}_{1.p}} \overset{c}{\equiv} (\widetilde{\mathsf{C}}_p, \{\mathsf{lb}_i^{(p)}\})_{\mathbf{Hyb}_{1.p+1}}$.

2. If $p = \ell$:

$$\mathbf{Hyb}_{1.p} : \begin{cases} (\widetilde{\mathsf{C}}_p, \{\mathsf{lb}_{i,b}^{(p)}\}) \xleftarrow{\$} \mathsf{Garb}(V[\mathsf{pp}, \mathsf{id}, \{\mathsf{lb}_{i,b}^{(p+1)}\}, \boldsymbol{r}_p, r, \mathsf{id}', r', \mathsf{pad}]) \\ \{\mathsf{lb}_i^{(p)}\} := \{\mathsf{lb}_{i,z_p[i]}^{(p)}\} \quad \text{where } z_p = (0^\lambda, x_1, x_1') \end{cases}$$

$$\mathbf{Hyb}_{1.p+1} : \begin{cases} (\widetilde{\mathsf{C}}_p, \{\mathsf{lb}_i^{(p)}\}) \xleftarrow{\$} \mathsf{Sim}(V, \{\mathsf{id}', r', \mathsf{pad}\}) \\ \text{where } \mathsf{id}', r' \xleftarrow{\$} \{0,1\}^\lambda ; \mathsf{pad} \xleftarrow{\$} \{0,1\}^{2(n-1)} \end{cases} \tag{9}$$

By simulation security of garbled circuits,

$$(\widetilde{\mathsf{C}}_p, \{\mathsf{lb}_i^{(p)}\})_{\mathbf{Hyb}_{1.p}} \overset{c}{\equiv} \mathsf{Sim}(V, \mathsf{C}_p(z_p)) \overset{c}{\equiv} \mathsf{Sim}(V, \{\mathsf{id}', r', \mathsf{pad}\}). \tag{10}$$

When $p = \ell$, $z_p = (0^\lambda, x_1, x_1')$ which causes $\mathsf{C}_p(z_p)$ to output a random ID and signal string. So, the RHS of Eq. 10 is identical to the first line of Eq. 9. Thus if $p = \ell$, we have $(\widetilde{\mathsf{C}}_p, \{\mathsf{lb}_i^{(p)}\})_{\mathbf{Hyb}_{1.p}} \overset{c}{\equiv} (\widetilde{\mathsf{C}}_p, \{\mathsf{lb}_i^{(p)}\})_{\mathbf{Hyb}_{1.p+1}}$.

3. If $p > \ell$:

$$\mathbf{Hyb}_{1.p} : \begin{cases} (\widetilde{\mathsf{C}}_p, \{\mathsf{lb}_{i,b}^{(p)}\}) \xleftarrow{\$} \mathsf{Garb}(V[\mathsf{pp}, \mathsf{id}, \{\mathsf{lb}_{i,b}^{(p+1)}\}, \boldsymbol{r}_p, r, \mathsf{id}', r', \mathsf{pad}]) \\ \{\mathsf{lb}_i^{(p)}\} := \{\mathsf{lb}_{i,z_p[i]}^{(p)}\} \quad \text{where } z_p = (h'^{(p+1)}, h'^{(p+1)}, v'^{(p)}) \end{cases}$$

$$\mathbf{Hyb}_{1.p+1} : \begin{cases} \{\mathsf{cth}_{i,b}^{(p+1)}\} \leftarrow \mathsf{HEnc}(\mathsf{pp}, h'^{(p+1)}, \{\mathsf{lb}_i^{(p+1)}\}; \boldsymbol{r}_p) \\ (\widetilde{\mathsf{C}}_p, \{\mathsf{lb}_i^{(p)}\}) \xleftarrow{\$} \mathsf{Sim}(V, \{\mathsf{cth}_{i,b}^{(p+1)}\}) \\ \text{where } h'^{(p+1)} \leftarrow \mathsf{Hash}(\mathsf{pp}, z_{p+1}) \text{ is pseudorandom} \end{cases} \tag{11}$$

Consider evaluating $\widetilde{C}_p$ on labels $\{\mathsf{lb}_{i,z_p[i]}^{(p)}\}$ as in $\mathbf{Hyb}_{1.p}$:

$$\mathsf{Eval}(\widetilde{C}_p, \{\mathsf{lb}_{i,z_p[i]}^{(p)}\}) = \mathsf{V}[\mathsf{pp}, \mathsf{id}, \{\mathsf{lb}_{i,b}^{(p+1)}\}, \boldsymbol{r}_p, r, \mathsf{id}', r', \mathsf{pad}](h'^{(p+1)}, h'^{(p+1)}, v'^{(p)})$$

$$= \begin{cases} \mathsf{HEnc}(\mathsf{pp}, h'^{(p+1)}, \{\mathsf{lb}_{i,b}^{(p+1)}\}; \boldsymbol{r}_p) & \text{if } \mathsf{id}[v_p'] = 0 \\ \mathsf{HEnc}(\mathsf{pp}, h'^{(p+1)}, \{\mathsf{lb}_{i,b}^{(p+1)}\}; \boldsymbol{r}_p) & \text{otherwise} \end{cases}$$

$$= \mathsf{HEnc}(\mathsf{pp}, h'^{(p+1)}, \{\mathsf{lb}_{i,b}^{(p+1)}\}; \boldsymbol{r}_p). \tag{12}$$

Equation 12 is identical to the RHS of Eq. 11 (first), up to the labels $\{\mathsf{lb}_i^{(p+1)}\}$ in Eq. 11 vs. $\{\mathsf{lb}_{i,b}^{(p+1)}\}$ in Eq. 12. By simulation security, the labels $\{\mathsf{lb}_i^{(p+1)}\}$ in Eq. 11 are computationally indistinguishable from labels $\{\mathsf{lb}_{i,z_{p+1}[i]}^{(p+1)}\}$. Thus $\{\mathsf{lb}_{i,z_{p+1}[i]}^{(p+1)}\}_{\mathbf{Hyb}_{1.p}} \overset{c}{\equiv} \{\mathsf{lb}_i^{(p+1)}\}_{\mathbf{Hyb}_{1.p+1}}$. By HE semantic security, $\mathsf{HEnc}(\mathsf{pp}, h'^{(p+1)}, \{\mathsf{lb}_{i,b}^{(p+1)}\}; \boldsymbol{r}_p) \overset{c}{\equiv} \mathsf{HEnc}(\mathsf{pp}, h'^{(p+1)}, \{\mathsf{lb}_i^{(p+1)}\}; \boldsymbol{r}_p)$, and hence $(\widetilde{C}_p, \{\mathsf{lb}_i^{(p)}\})_{\mathbf{Hyb}_{1.p}} \overset{c}{\equiv} (\widetilde{C}_p, \{\mathsf{lb}_i^{(p)}\})_{\mathbf{Hyb}_{1.p+1}}$ when $p > \ell$, which completes the proof of Lemma 7. □

7.2 Proof of Lemma 5

Lemma 5 states that $\mathbf{Hyb}_1 \overset{c}{\equiv} \mathbf{Hyb}_2$. So, we must show that $\mathsf{m}_2 := (\widetilde{C}_{\mathsf{d}_m}, \ldots, \widetilde{C}_0, \{\mathsf{cth}_{i,b}^{(0)}\}, r)$, as sampled in $\mathbf{Hyb}_1$, is computationally indistinguishable from random. We will argue that each element of m_2 is pseudorandom.

First consider the circuit $\widetilde{C}_{\mathsf{d}_m}$. It is formed as $(\widetilde{C}_{\mathsf{d}_m}, \{\mathsf{lb}_i^{(\mathsf{d}_m)}\}) \overset{\$}{\leftarrow} \mathsf{Sim}(\mathsf{F}, \{\mathsf{id}', r'\})$ where $\mathsf{id}', r' \overset{\$}{\leftarrow} \{0,1\}^\lambda$. Since the inputs id', r' are random, by anonymous security of garbled circuits the distribution $(\widetilde{C}_{\mathsf{d}_m}, \{\mathsf{lb}_i^{(\mathsf{d}_m)}\})$ is pseudorandom.

For w from $\mathsf{d}_m - 1$ to $\ell + 1$ the circuits are formed as $(\widetilde{C}_w, \{\mathsf{lb}_i^{(w)}\}) \overset{\$}{\leftarrow} \mathsf{Sim}(\mathsf{V}, \{\mathsf{cth}_{i,b}^{(w+1)}\})$ where $\{\mathsf{cth}_{i,b}^{(w+1)}\} \overset{\$}{\leftarrow} \mathsf{HEnc}(\mathsf{pp}, h'^{(w+1)}, \{\mathsf{lb}_i^{(w+1)}\})$. $\{\mathsf{cth}_{i,b}^{(w+1)}\}$ is pseudorandom by anonymous semantic security of HE, and so by anonymous security of GS, $(\widetilde{C}_w, \{\mathsf{lb}_i^{(w)}\})$ is also pseudorandom.

For $w = \ell$ we have $(\widetilde{C}_\ell, \{\mathsf{lb}_i^{(\ell)}\}) \overset{\$}{\leftarrow} \mathsf{Sim}(\mathsf{V}, \{\mathsf{id}', r', \mathsf{pad}\})$ where $\mathsf{id}', r' \overset{\$}{\leftarrow} \{0,1\}^\lambda$, $\mathsf{pad} \overset{\$}{\leftarrow} \{0,1\}^{2(n-1)}$, so again by anonymous security of garbled circuits, the distribution $(\widetilde{C}_\ell, \{\mathsf{lb}_i^{(\ell)}\})$ is pseudorandom.

For w from $\ell - 1$ to 0 we have $\{\mathsf{cth}_{i,b}^{(w+1)}\} \overset{\$}{\leftarrow} \mathsf{HEnc}(\mathsf{pp}, h_1^{(w+1)}, \{\mathsf{lb}_i^{(w+1)}\})$ and $(\widetilde{C}_w, \{\mathsf{lb}_i^{(w)}\}) \overset{\$}{\leftarrow} \mathsf{Sim}(\mathsf{V}, \{\mathsf{cth}_{i,b}^{(w+1)}\})$. Where, again, the use of $h_1^{(w+1)}$ in HEnc is from the assumption on pth. For all w from $\ell-1$ to 0, $\{\mathsf{cth}_{i,b}^{(w+1)}\}$ is pseudorandom by anonymous semantic security of HE, and thus by anonymous security of GS, $(\widetilde{C}_w, \{\mathsf{lb}_i^{(w)}\})$ is also pseudorandom.

Next in m_2 is the ciphertext, which in $\mathbf{Hyb}_1$ is formed as $\{\mathsf{cth}_{i,b}^{(0)}\} \overset{\$}{\leftarrow} \mathsf{HEnc}(\mathsf{pp}, h_{\mathsf{root}}, \{\mathsf{lb}_i^{(0)}\})$. $\{\mathsf{cth}_{i,b}^{(0)}\}$ is pseudorandom by anonymous semantic security of HE. The final element of m_2 is the signal string r, which is sampled uniformly at random. Hence m_2 is pseudorandom in the view of R, proving $\mathbf{Hyb}_1 \overset{c}{\equiv} \mathbf{Hyb}_2$ and completing the proof. □

Remark 1. In the proofs above, we assumed that the path induced by evaluating BP(id) always travelled to the left child. In the general case, the path in Eq. 6 ending in $v_1^{(\ell)}$ just needs to be changed to the path induced by BP(id) ending in the appropriate leaf $u \in T$. The proofs should then be updated accordingly.

Acknowledgements. S. Garg is supported in part by DARPA under Agreement No. HR00112020026, AFOSR Award FA9550-19-1-0200, NSF CNS Award 1936826, and research grants by Visa Inc, Supra, JP Morgan, BAIR Commons Meta Fund, Stellar Development Foundation, and a Bakar Fellows Spark Award. P. Miao is supported in part by the NSF CNS Award 2247352, a DPI Science Team Seed Grant, a Meta Award, and a Brown DSI Seed Grant. M. Hajiabadi is supported in part by an NSERC Discovery Grant 03270, and a Meta Research Award.

References

[ABD+21] Alamati, N., Branco, P., Döttling, N., Garg, S., Hajiabadi, M., Pu, S.: Laconic private set intersection and applications. In: Nissim, K., Waters, B. (eds.) TCC 2021, Part III. LNCS, vol. 13044, pp. 94–125. Springer, Cham (2021). https://doi.org/10.1007/978-3-030-90456-2_4

[ALOS22] Aranha, D.F., Lin, C., Orlandi, C., Simkin, M.: Laconic private set-intersection from pairings. In: Yin, H., Stavrou, A., Cremers, C., Shi, E. (eds.) ACM CCS 2022: 29th Conference on Computer and Communications Security, Los Angeles, CA, USA, 7–11 November 2022, pp. 111–124. ACM Press (2022)

[BFK+09] Barni, M., Failla, P., Kolesnikov, V., Lazzeretti, R., Sadeghi, A.-R., Schneider, T.: Secure evaluation of private linear branching programs with medical applications. In: Backes, M., Ning, P. (eds.) ESORICS 2009. LNCS, vol. 5789, pp. 424–439. Springer, Heidelberg (2009). https://doi.org/10.1007/978-3-642-04444-1_26

[BLSV18] Brakerski, Z., Lombardi, A., Segev, G., Vaikuntanathan, V.: Anonymous IBE, leakage resilience and circular security from new assumptions. In: Nielsen, J.B., Rijmen, V. (eds.) EUROCRYPT 2018, Part I. LNCS, vol. 10820, pp. 535–564. Springer, Cham (2018). https://doi.org/10.1007/978-3-319-78381-9_20

[BPSW07] Brickell, J., Porter, D.E., Shmatikov, V., Witchel, E.: Privacy-preserving remote diagnostics. In: Ning, P., De Capitani di Vimercati, S., Syverson, P.F. (eds.) ACM CCS 2007: 14th Conference on Computer and Communications Security, Alexandria, Virginia, USA, 28–31 October 2007, pp. 498–507. ACM Press (2007)

[CDG+17] Cho, C., Döttling, N., Garg, S., Gupta, D., Miao, P., Polychroniadou, A.: Laconic oblivious transfer and its applications. In: Katz, J., Shacham, H. (eds.) CRYPTO 2017, Part II. LNCS, vol. 10402, pp. 33–65. Springer, Cham (2017). https://doi.org/10.1007/978-3-319-63715-0_2

[CDPP22] Cong, K., Das, D., Park, J., Pereira, H.V.L.: SortingHat: efficient private decision tree evaluation via homomorphic encryption and transciphering. In: Yin, H., Stavrou, A., Cremers, C., Shi, E. (eds.) ACM CCS 2022: 29th Conference on Computer and Communications Security, Los Angeles, CA, USA, 7–11 November 2022, pp. 563–577. ACM Press (2022)

[CGH+21] Chase, M., Garg, S., Hajiabadi, M., Li, J., Miao, P.: Amortizing rate-1 OT and applications to PIR and PSI. In: Nissim, K., Waters, B. (eds.) TCC 2021, Part III. LNCS, vol. 13044, pp. 126–156. Springer, Cham (2021). https://doi.org/10.1007/978-3-030-90456-2_5

[DG17] Döttling, N., Garg, S.: Identity-based encryption from the Diffie-Hellman assumption. In: Katz, J., Shacham, H. (eds.) CRYPTO 2017, Part I. LNCS, vol. 10401, pp. 537–569. Springer, Cham (2017). https://doi.org/10.1007/978-3-319-63688-7_18

[DGGM19] Döttling, N., Garg, S., Goyal, V., Malavolta, G.: Laconic conditional disclosure of secrets and applications. In: Zuckerman, D. (ed.) 60th Annual Symposium on Foundations of Computer Science, Baltimore, MD, USA, 9–12 November 2019, pp. 661–685. IEEE Computer Society Press (2019)

[DGI+19] Döttling, N., Garg, S., Ishai, Y., Malavolta, G., Mour, T., Ostrovsky, R.: Trapdoor hash functions and their applications. In: Boldyreva, A., Micciancio, D. (eds.) CRYPTO 2019, Part III. LNCS, vol. 11694, pp. 3–32. Springer, Cham (2019). https://doi.org/10.1007/978-3-030-26954-8_1

[DKL+23] Döttling, N., Kolonelos, D., Lai, R.W.F., Lin, C., Malavolta, G., Rahimi, A.: Efficient laconic cryptography from learning with errors. In: Hazay, C., Stam, M. (eds.) EUROCRYPT 2023, Part III. LNCS, vol. 14006, pp. 417–446. Springer, Cham (2023). https://doi.org/10.1007/978-3-031-30620-4_14

[Gen09] Gentry, C.: Fully homomorphic encryption using ideal lattices. In: Mitzenmacher, M. (ed.) 41st Annual ACM Symposium on Theory of Computing, Bethesda, MD, USA, 31 May–2 June 2009, pp. 169–178. ACM Press (2009)

[GGH19] Garg, S., Gay, R., Hajiabadi, M.: New techniques for efficient trapdoor functions and applications. In: Ishai, Y., Rijmen, V. (eds.) EUROCRYPT 2019, Part III. LNCS, vol. 11478, pp. 33–63. Springer, Cham (2019). https://doi.org/10.1007/978-3-030-17659-4_2

[GHMR18] Garg, S., Hajiabadi, M., Mahmoody, M., Rahimi, A.: Registration-based encryption: removing private-key generator from IBE. In: Beimel, A., Dziembowski, S. (eds.) TCC 2018, Part I. LNCS, vol. 11239, pp. 689–718. Springer, Cham (2018). https://doi.org/10.1007/978-3-030-03807-6_25

[GHO20] Garg, S., Hajiabadi, M., Ostrovsky, R.: Efficient range-trapdoor functions and applications: rate-1 OT and more. In: Pass, R., Pietrzak, K. (eds.) TCC 2020, Part I. LNCS, vol. 12550, pp. 88–116. Springer, Cham (2020). https://doi.org/10.1007/978-3-030-64375-1_4

[GRS22] Garimella, G., Rosulek, M., Singh, J.: Structure-aware private set intersection, with applications to fuzzy matching. In: Dodis, Y., Shrimpton, T. (eds.) CRYPTO 2022, Part I. LNCS, vol. 13507, pp. 323–352. Springer, Cham (2022). https://doi.org/10.1007/978-3-031-15802-5_12

[GSW13] Gentry, C., Sahai, A., Waters, B.: Homomorphic encryption from learning with errors: conceptually-simpler, asymptotically-faster, attribute-based. In: Canetti, R., Garay, J.A. (eds.) CRYPTO 2013, Part I. LNCS, vol. 8042, pp. 75–92. Springer, Heidelberg (2013). https://doi.org/10.1007/978-3-642-40041-4_5

[IP07] Ishai, Y., Paskin, A.: Evaluating branching programs on encrypted data. In: Vadhan, S.P. (ed.) TCC 2007. LNCS, vol. 4392, pp. 575–594. Springer, Heidelberg (2007). https://doi.org/10.1007/978-3-540-70936-7_31

[KNL+19] Kiss, Á., Naderpour, M., Liu, J., Asokan, N., Schneider, T.: SoK: modular and efficient private decision tree evaluation. Proc. Priv. Enhancing Technol. **2019**(2), 187–208 (2019)

[QWW18] Quach, W., Wee, H., Wichs, D.: Laconic function evaluation and applications. In: Thorup, M. (ed.) 59th Annual Symposium on Foundations of Computer Science, Paris, France, 7–9 October 2018, pp. 859–870. IEEE Computer Society Press (2018)

[Rab81] Rabin, M.O.: How to exchange secrets with oblivious transfer. Technical report, TR-81, Aiken Computation Lab, Harvard University (1981)

[Rab05] Rabin, M.O.: How to exchange secrets with oblivious transfer. Cryptology ePrint Archive, Report 2005/187 (2005). https://eprint.iacr.org/2005/187

[Yao86] Yao, A.C.-C.: How to generate and exchange secrets (extended abstract). In: 27th Annual Symposium on Foundations of Computer Science, Toronto, Ontario, Canada, 27–29 October 1986, pp. 162–167. IEEE Computer Society Press (1986)

Rate-1 Fully Local Somewhere Extractable Hashing from DDH

Pedro Branco[1]($\boxtimes$), Nico Döttling[2], Akshayaram Srinivasan[3], and Riccardo Zanotto[2,4]

[1] Max-Planck Institute for Security and Privacy, Bochum, Germany
pedrodemelobranco@gmail.com
[2] CISPA Helmholtz Center for Information Security, Saarbrücken, Germany
[3] University of Toronto, Toronto, Canada
[4] Saarbrücken Graduate School of Computer Science, Saarbrücken, Germany

Abstract. Somewhere statistically binding (SSB) hashing allows us to sample a special hashing key such that the digest statistically binds the input at m secret locations. This hash function is said to be somewhere extractable (SE) if there is an additional trapdoor that allows the extraction of the input bits at the m locations from the digest.

Devadas, Goyal, Kalai, and Vaikuntanathan (FOCS 2022) introduced a variant of somewhere extractable hashing called rate-1 fully local SE hash functions. The rate-1 requirement states that the size of the digest is $m + \mathsf{poly}(\lambda)$ (where λ is the security parameter). The fully local property requires that for any index i, there is a "very short" opening showing that i-th bit of the hashed input is equal to b for some $b \in \{0,1\}$. The size of this opening is required to be independent of m and in particular, this means that its size is independent of the size of the digest. Devadas et al. gave such a construction from Learning with Errors (LWE).

In this work, we give a construction of a rate-1 fully local somewhere extractable hash function from Decisional Diffie-Hellman (DDH) and BARGs. Under the same assumptions, we give constructions of rate-1 BARG and RAM SNARG with partial input soundness whose proof sizes are only matched by prior constructions based on LWE.

1 Introduction

Keyed hash functions are fundamental building blocks in cryptography. They consist of two algorithms (Setup, Eval). Setup is a PPT algorithm that takes in the security parameter 1^λ and outputs a hashing key hk. Eval is a deterministic algorithm that takes in the hashing key hk and an input x and outputs a short digest h of the input. A key property that many applications require is collision resistance. This guarantees that no PPT adversary $\mathcal{A}$ on input the hashing key hk (sampled using the Setup algorithm) can find two different inputs x, x' such that $\mathsf{Eval}(\mathsf{hk}, x) = \mathsf{Eval}(\mathsf{hk}, x')$. However, for many applications collision-resistance is not sufficient and one requires more advanced properties from the hash function.

© International Association for Cryptologic Research 2024
Q. Tang and V. Teague (Eds.): PKC 2024, LNCS 14603, pp. 356–386, 2024.
https://doi.org/10.1007/978-3-031-57725-3_12

Somewhere Statistically Binding and Extractability. Somewhere statistically binding (SSB) hash functions [13,18] enhance collision resistance with stronger requirements. This family of hash function again consists of a pair of algorithms (Setup, Eval) where the Setup has a different syntax. Here, Setup takes in 1^λ and an index $i \in [n]$ (where n is the length of the input to the hash function) and outputs the hashing key hk. We require this hash function to satisfy two properties. The first property is hiding, which requires that the hashing key hk hides the location i from computationally bounded adversaries. The second property is statistical binding, which requires that the digest statistically binds to the location i. This means that any unbounded adversary should not be able to produce two inputs x and x' that differ at location i and hash to the same digest w.r.t. a hashing key hk that is sampled using Setup($1^\lambda, i$).

An SSB hash function is said to be somewhere extractable (SE) if Setup outputs a trapdoor td along with the hashing key hk. There exists an extraction algorithm Extract that takes the digest h and td and outputs x_i.

SE and SSB hash functions are usually augmented with two other algorithms (Open, Verify). The Open algorithm takes in the hk, input x and a location $j \in [n]$ and outputs an opening ρ. The Verify algorithm takes in the digest h, the index j, the bit x_j, and an opening ρ and either accepts or rejects the opening. For efficiency purposes, we require the size of the opening to be much smaller than the length of the input x. SSB and SE hash functions can be naturally extended to the setting where the hash key hk binds to a subset $I \subseteq [n]$. The hiding requirement is modified to guarantee that for any two subsets I and I' of the same size, the hash keys generated w.r.t. to I and I' are computationally indistinguishable.

SSB hash functions are used in constructing very low communication MPC protocols [13], iO for Turing machines and RAM programs [1,12,17], and laconic oblivious transfer [5,10]. Somewhere extractable hash functions are used in the recent constructions of Batch Arguments from NP and Succinct Non-Interactive Arguments for deterministic polynomial-time computation [7,8,14,16,21].

Rate-1 Fully Local Somewhere Extractability. In recent work, Devadas, Goyal, Kalai, and Vaikuntanathan [9] introduced another variant of somewhere extractability called rate-1 fully local somewhere extractable hash functions. The rate-1 property requires that the size of the digest is $m + \mathsf{poly}(\lambda)$ where m is the size of the binding set I used in generating the hash key hk. Since the digest has to bind to m locations, its size must be at least m. The above requirement states that the size of the digest incurs a fixed additive polynomial overhead in λ when compared to the lower bound. The fully local opening requirement states that the size of the opening ρ to any position is a fixed polynomial in λ and is independent of m. This, in particular, means that the size of the opening is independent of the size of the digest. In the same work, they gave a construction of rate-1 fully local SE hash functions from Learning with Errors [20].

1.1   Our Results

In this work, we give a construction of a rate-1 fully local SE hash function assuming the hardness of Decisional Diffie-Hellman (DDH) and the existence of somewhere extractable Batch Arguments (seBARGs) (see Definition 3). Formally,

Informal Theorem 1. *Assuming the hardness of DDH and a somewhere extractable BARG, there exists a rate-1 fully local SE hash function.*

The works of Waters and Wu [21] and Choudhuri et al. [6] gave constructions of somewhere extractable BARGs from k-Lin and sub-exponential DDH respectively. As a corollary, we get:

Corollary 1. *Assuming either sub-exponential hardness of DDH or polynomial hardness of DDH and k-Lin, there exists a rate-1 fully local SE hash function.*

Application-1: Rate-1 BARG. As a direct corollary of the work of Devadas et al. [9], we get a construction of rate-1 BARG.

Corollary 2. *Assuming the hardness of DDH and a somewhere extractable BARG, there exists a construction of a BARG for* NP *where the proof size is $m + \mathsf{poly}(\log k, \lambda)$. Here, m is the size of a single witness and k is the batch size.*

The prior construction of BARG for NP based on the same assumptions due to Paneth and Pass [19] has a proof size of $m + o(m) \cdot \mathsf{poly}(\log k, \lambda)$.[1] The only known construction of BARG that achieves the above proof size is due to Devadas et al. [9] but their work relies on the LWE assumption.

Application-2: RAM SNARG with Partial Input Soundness. A RAM SNARG [4,8] allows a verifier to verify the correctness of a RAM program with read-only access to a large database D that runs in time T and uses space S. The verifier is given a short digest h of the database and a proof π whose size is $\mathsf{poly}(\lambda, \log T, S)$. The traditional soundness for RAM SNARG requires the adversary to "commit" to the entire database. Recent work of Kalai et al. [15] considered a stronger soundness requirement called partial input soundness. This guarantees that if the memory is digested using a SE hash function that is extractable on a set of coordinates I, and if the RAM computation only reads coordinates in I, then soundness holds. In particular, this doesn't require the adversary to commit to (or, in other words, exhibit knowledge of) the entire database beforehand. Plugging in our rate-1 fully local SE hash function into the RAM SNARG construction given in Kalai et al. [15], we obtain the following corollary:

---

[1] We note that this work only requires a rate-1 SE hash function (without the fully local opening) property in addition to somewhere-extractable BARG. The work of Kalai et al. [15] gave a construction of such a SE hash function from rate-1 OT. Rate-1 OT can be instantiated from DDH/QR/LWE [11].

Corollary 3. *Assuming the hardness of DDH and a somewhere extractable BARG, there exists a construction of a RAM SNARG with partial input soundness where the size of the database digest is $m + \mathsf{poly}(\lambda)$ and size of the proof is $O(S) + \mathsf{poly}(\lambda, \log T)$. Here, m is the size of the index I in the partial input soundness.*

The above parameters were previously known only from LWE [9].

1.2 Technical Outline

We will now give an overview of our construction.

Rate-1 SEH from DDH. Our starting observation is that the DDH-based trapdoor hash construction of [11] in fact already gives us a rate-1 somewhere extractable hash function. We will very briefly outline this construction, since our construction uses specific properties of it. Specifically, let $\mathbb{G}$ be a cyclic group of prime order p generated by a generator g. The setup algorithm, on input a set $I = \{i_1, \ldots, i_m\} \subseteq [N]$ first chooses $a_1, \ldots, a_m$ uniformly random from $\mathbb{Z}_p$ and sets $h_0 = g$ and $h_k = g^{a_k}$ for $k = 1, \ldots, m$. Next, it chooses $r_1, \ldots, r_N \in \mathbb{Z}_p$ uniformly at random and sets $M_{k,j} = h_k^{r_j} \cdot g^{\delta_{j,i_k}}$, where $\delta_{i,j} = 1$ if $i = j$ and otherwise 0. The hashing key consists of the matrix $\mathbf{M} = (M_{k,j})_{k,j}$, whereas the trapdoors are given by $a_1, \ldots, a_m$.

Hashing proceeds as follows. Given a vector $\mathbf{x} = (x_1, \ldots, x_N)$, we compute $c_0, c_1, \ldots, c_m$ via $c_k = \prod_{j=1}^N M_{k,j}^{x_j}$. Note now that $c_1, \ldots, c_m$ is a batch ElGamal encryption of $x_{i_1}, \ldots, x_{i_m}$ with ciphertext header c_0, that is it holds that $g^{x_{i_k}} = c_k \cdot c_0^{-a_k}$ for $k = 1, \ldots, m$. This ciphertext is now *compressed* via the distributed discrete logarithm technique [2]. In a nutshell, there is an efficiently computable keyed function $f_K : \mathbb{G} \to \{0, 1\}$ such that we can efficiently find a key K such that it holds $f_K(c_k) = f_K(c_0^{a_k}) \oplus x_{i_k}$ for $k = 1, \ldots, m$. Importantly, to find such a key we do not need to know the a_k. Now, given such a key K, we compute $v_1, \ldots, v_m$ via $v_i = f_K(c_i)$. We set the hash value to be $v = (K, c_0, v_1, \ldots, v_m)$. Note that since the $v_1, \ldots, v_m$ are bits, such a hash value is of size $m + \mathsf{poly}(\lambda)$ bits.

Clearly, given a_k we can recover x_{i_k} from $K, c_0, v_1, \ldots, v_m$ via $x_{i_k} = f_K(c_0^{a_k}) \oplus v_k$ using the property of f_K detailed above.

The only security requirement we make for trapdoor hash functions is that they are *index hiding*, that is the hashing key, in this case the matrix $\mathbf{M}$, hides the index set $I = \{i_1, \ldots, i_m\}$. For this construction, this follows immediately from the IND-CPA security of batch ElGamal encryption, as for each $j = 1, \ldots, N$ it holds that $M_{1,j}, \ldots, M_{m,j}$ is a batch ElGamal ciphertext with header $M_{0,j}$.

There are two dilemmata with this construction however: first, the hashing key is non-compact, that is the size of the hashing key scales with the size of the database. Second, this construction does not support local opening.

While we do not know how to solve the first issue, we observe that this issue does not affect any of the applications of fully local somewhere extractable hash functions as long as there is a *succinct verification key* which can be used to check the validity of openings. We will therefore compute a verification key by computing a (non-rate 1) fully local somewhere extractable hash of the hashing key.

Full Locality. To address the second issue, we will take a similar avenue as [9]. Specifically, we will compute a second, non-rate 1 somewhere extractable hash h_x of the input x and prove consistency between the two hashes v and h_x. To facilitate this, we will use specific properties of how v is computed. Indeed, observe that each c_i is just a product of group elements $h_i^{x_1}, \ldots, h_i^{x_N}$. Recall that our goal is to make the size of the opening (essentially) independent of both N and m. Hence, the statement we are trying to prove cannot directly be proven with a BARG, as the product involves N terms. However, following an idea from [9], we can compute each c_i via a succinct sequence of local operations, each only involving two group elements. This is done via a binary multiplication tree. For the sake of simplicity, let N now be a power of two, i.e. $N = 2^T$. We define $z_{i,j}^{(0)} = M_{i,j}^{x_j}$ for $i \in [m]$ and $j \in [N]$. We can now recursively define the $z_{i,j}^{(t)}$ for $t = 1, \ldots, T$ via

$$z_{i,j}^{(t)} = z_{i,2j-1}^{(t-1)} \cdot z_{i,2j}^{(t)}. \tag{1}$$

Here, we just set $z_{i,j}^{(t)}$ to undefined if either $z_{i,2j-1}^{(t-1)}$ or $z_{i,2j}^{(t-1)}$ is undefined (i.e. $2j - 1$ or $2j$ is out of bounds). Now note that it holds routinely that $z_{i,1}^{(T)} = c_i$ via the recursive definition of the $z_{i,j}^{(t)}$.

The idea to prove consistency between v and h_x now comprises of 3 parts.

1. Prove for all i, j that $z_{i,j}^{(0)} = M_{i,j}^{x_j}$.
2. Prove for all i, j and all t that Eq. (1) holds.
3. Prove for all i that $v_i = f_K(z_{i,1}^{(T)})$.

Since all three items are local statements, we will enforce their validity using BARGs. To facilitate this, we will convert all statements into *index statements*. For item 1, the vector $\mathbf{x}$ is already implicitly given via the hash value h_x. As mentioned above, we will have an additional verification key which consists of an SEH hash h_M committing to the matrix $\mathbf{M}$. Moreover, for all $t = 1, \ldots, T$ let $z^{(t)} = (z_{i,j}^{(t)})_{i,j}$ and let $h^{(t)}$ be an SEH hash of $z^{(t)}$.

In our full construction of rate-1 fully local SEH, the hash value will consist of v, h_x, $h^{(1)}, \ldots, h^{(T)}$ as well as $T + 2$ BARGs (1 for item 1, T for item 2, and 1 for item 3). As the size of each BARG is independent of m and N, the total size of the hash value is still dominated by v and thus comes down to $m + T \cdot \mathsf{poly}(\lambda) = m + \mathsf{poly}(\lambda)$ (as $T = \log(N) = O(\lambda)$).

Finally, a local opening in this construction simply consists of a local opening of h_x.

Proving Security. We will now provide a high level discussion on how we establish the somewhere extractability property of our construction. Hence, assume we had a PPT adversary $\mathcal{A}$ who succeeds in providing a valid local opening for a position $i^* \in I$ such that the opened value differs from the value extracted using the trapdoor $a_1, \ldots, a_m$.

We will make use of the somewhere extractability properties of the hashes h_x, $h^{(1)}, \ldots, h^{(T)}$ and h_M. Specifically, it will suffice to make each of these hashes extractable at a constant number of locations. Hence the sizes of these hashes will still be $\mathsf{poly}(\lambda)$, and in particular independent of m and N.

As $|I| = m$, a security reduction can guess the index $j^* \in [m]$ such that $i^* = i_{j^*}$ with polynomial probability $1/m$, and produce a random output if the guess was wrong. The reduction will make h_x extractable at position i^*, and each $h^{(t)}$ extractable at locations $(0, j^{(t)})$ and $(j^*, j^{(t)})$, where the $j^{(t)}$ are on the root-to-leaf path to i^*. Due to the index hiding properties of the underlying SEH this modification is not noticed by the adversary.

Hence, the reduction will now be able to extract $z^{(t)}_{0,j^{(t)}}$ and $z^{(t)}_{j^*,j^{(t)}}$ for each $t = 1, \ldots, T$. Our critical observation is now the following: If $z^{(t)}_{0,j^{(t)}}$ and $z^{(t)}_{j^*,j^{(t)}}$ were correctly computed, then they form an ElGamal ciphertext of x_{i^*} under the secret key a_{j^*}, that is it would hold that

$$z^{(t)}_{j^*,j^{(t)}} = (z^{(t)}_{0,j^{(t)}})^{a_{j^*}} \cdot g^{x_{i^*}}.$$

This follows via the definition of $\mathbf{M}$ and the $z^{(0)}_{i,j}$. Namely, as $M_{0,j} = g^{r_j}$, $M_{j^*,j} = h_{j^*}^{r_j} \cdot g^{\delta_{j,i^*}}$ and $z^{(0)}_{0,j} = M^{x_j}_{0,j}$, $z^{(0)}_{j^*,j} = M^{x_j}_{j^*,j}$, it holds that $(z^{(0)}_{0,j}, z^{(0)}_{j^*,j})$ is an ElGamal encryption of x_{i^*} for $j = i^*$, and otherwise an encryption of 0.

Furthermore, the above property is efficiently testable given the trapdoor a_{j^*}, that is for $t = 1, \ldots, T$ the reduction can compute $X^{(t)} = z^{(t)}_{j^*,j^{(t)}} \cdot (z^{(t)}_{0,j^{(t)}})^{-a_{j^*}}$. Now, critically, if the opening provided by $\mathcal{A}$ opens to something different from x_{i^*}, then there must be an index $t^* \in [T]$ for which $X^{(t^*)}$ differs from $g^{x_{i^*}}$. The reduction can guess the smallest such index t^* with polynomial probability $1/T$.

If $t^* = 0$, we will routinely obtain a contradiction against the soundness of the BARG establishing item 1 above, whereas if $t^* = T$ we will obtain a contradiction against the soundness of the BARG establishing item 3. The challenging situation occurs if t^* lies in between 0 and T. To deal with this case, we make $h^{(t^*-1)}$ extractable at both children of $j^{(t^*)}$, which is not detectable as the underlying SEH is index hiding. Now, if the ElGamal ciphertext of one of the children is an encryption of 0 (which we can efficiently test), we immediately get a contradiction to the soundness of the BARG in item 2 for $t = t^*$ as we know by the minimality of t^* that the ElGamal ciphertext at the other child of $j^{(t^*)}$ is an encryption of x_{i^*}.

If the extracted ciphertext encrypts a non-zero value, we make $h^{(t^*-2)}$ extractable at both children of this node, which is again undetectable by the index hiding property. If both extracted ciphertexts encrypt 0, we again get a contradiction to the soundness of the corresponding BARG. Otherwise, we can guess with probability $1/2$ which one of the two children yields a non-zero ciphertext. We will maintain this invariant in the remaining hybrids: for one of the two children, the extracted ciphertext must decrypt to a non-zero value, unless the soundness of the corresponding BARG is violated. We can hence "push" this inconsistency all the way down to the leaf layer of the tree, and eventually get a contradiction to the soundness of the BARG in item 1.

To see that the reduction has polynomial advantage, note that the overall success probability against the BARG in item 2 comes down to

$$\epsilon' = \frac{1}{m \cdot T \cdot 2^T} \cdot \epsilon = \frac{1}{m \cdot T \cdot N} \cdot \epsilon,$$

where ϵ is the success probability of $\mathcal{A}$. Noting that ϵ' is also polynomial, we conclude this outline.

2   Preliminaries

In the following, let $\mathcal{G}$ be a (prime-order) *group generator*, that is, $\mathcal{G}$ is an algorithm that takes as an input a security parameter 1^λ and outputs $(\mathbb{G}, p, g)$, where $\mathbb{G}$ is the description of a multiplicative cyclic group, p is the order of the group which is always a prime number unless differently specified, and g is a generator of the group. In the following we state the decisional version of the Diffie-Hellman (DDH) assumption.

Definition 1 (Decisional Diffie-Hellman Assumption). *Let* $(\mathbb{G}, p, g) \leftarrow\!\!\$$ $\mathcal{G}(1^\lambda)$. *We say that the DDH assumption holds (with respect to* $\mathcal{G}$*) if for any PPT adversary* $\mathcal{A}$

$$\left| \Pr[1 \leftarrow \mathcal{A}((\mathbb{G}, p, g), (g^a, g^b, g^{ab}))] - \Pr[1 \leftarrow \mathcal{A}((\mathbb{G}, p, g), (g^a, g^b, g^c))] \right| \leq \mathsf{negl}(\lambda)$$

where $a, b, c \leftarrow\!\!\$ \mathbb{Z}_p$.

We additionally recall a shrinking procedure which compresses a DDH-based ciphertext into a rate-1 ciphertext.

Lemma 1 ([3,11]). *There exists a correct pair of algorithms* Shrink, ShrinkDec *such that given*

- $h_1 = g^{x_1}, \ldots, h_n = g^{x_n}$
- $c_0 = g^t$ *and* $c_i = h_i^t \cdot g^{m_i}$, *where* $m_1, \ldots, m_n$ *is a message and* $m_i \in \{0, 1\}$

it outputs

- $\mathsf{Shrink}(c_0, (c_1, \ldots, c_n)) = \mathsf{ct} = (K, d_0, (d_1, \ldots, d_n))$, *where the components are given by* $d_i = \mathsf{ShrinkComp}(K, c_i)$ *for* $i \in [n]$.
- $\mathsf{ShrinkDec}((x_1, \ldots, x_n), \mathsf{ct}) = (m_1, \ldots, m_n)$.

Moreover, $\mathsf{ShrinkDec}((x_1, \ldots, x_n), \mathsf{ct})$ *fails only with negligible probability in* λ, *and* $\mathsf{ShrinkComp}(K, c_i)$ *runs in expected polynomial time.*

In particular, the construction uses a pseudo-random function $\mathsf{PRF} : \{0, 1\}^\lambda \times \mathbb{G} \to \{0, 1\}^\tau$ *with output size* $\tau = \log(2n)$, *and* $\mathsf{ShrinkComp}(K, c_i)$ *computes the least* δ_i *such that* $\mathsf{PRF}(K, c_i \cdot g^{\delta_i}) = 0^\tau$ *and outputs* $\delta_i \mod 2$.

The compressing key K *is chosen such that* $\mathsf{PRF}(K, c_i/g) \neq 0$, *and that we have a bound* $\delta_i < D$, *where* $D = O(n\lambda)$.

2.1 Somewhere Extractable Hash Families

Definition 2 (Somewhere Extractable Hash). *A somewhere extractable hash family* SEH *consists of the following polynomial time algorithms:*

- Gen$(1^\lambda, N, i^*) \to$ (hk, td). *A probabilistic setup algorithm that takes as input the security parameter 1^λ, the message length N, and an index $i^* \in [N]$. It outputs a hashing key* hk *and a trapdoor* td.
- Hash(hk, x) $\to v$. *A deterministic algorithm that takes as input a hashing key* hk *and a message $x \in \{0,1\}^N$, and outputs a hash value $v \in \{0,1\}^{\ell_{hash}}$.*
- Open(hk, x, j) $\to (b, \rho)$. *A deterministic algorithm that takes as input a hashing key* hk, *a message x and an index $j \in [N]$. It outputs a bit $b \in \{0,1\}$ and an opening $\rho \in \{0,1\}^{\ell_{open}}$.*
- Verify(hk, v, j, b, ρ) $\to \{0,1\}$. *A deterministic algorithm that takes as input a hashing key* hk, *a hash value v, an index $i \in [N]$, a bit b and an opening ρ, and it outputs 1 (accept) or 0 (reject).*
- Extract(td, v) $\to u$. *A deterministic algorithm that takes as input the trapdoor* td *and a hash value v, and it outputs a bit $u \in \{0,1\}$.*

It is required to satisfy the following properties:

Efficiency. The size of the hashing key $|hk|$, the size of the hash ℓ_{hash}, the size of the opening ℓ_{open} and the running time of Verify are all bounded by $\mathrm{poly}(\lambda, \log N)$.

Opening Completeness. There exists a negligible function $\mathsf{negl}(\cdot)$ such that for any λ, any $N \le 2^\lambda$, any $i^* \in [N]$, any $j \in [N]$ and any $x \in \{0,1\}^N$,

$$
\Pr\left[
\begin{array}{l}
b = x_j \\
\land\ \mathsf{Verify}(\mathsf{hk}, v, j, b, \rho) = 1
\end{array}
:
\begin{array}{l}
(\mathsf{hk}, \mathsf{td}) \leftarrow \mathsf{Gen}(1^\lambda, N, i^*), \\
v = \mathsf{Hash}(\mathsf{hk}, x), \\
(b, \rho) = \mathsf{Open}(\mathsf{hk}, x, j)
\end{array}
\right] = 1 - \mathsf{negl}(\lambda)
$$

Index Hiding. For any poly-time adversary $\mathcal{A} = (\mathcal{A}_1, \mathcal{A}_2)$ there exists a negligible function $\mathsf{negl}(\cdot)$ such that $\Pr\left[\mathrm{HIDE}^{\mathcal{A}_1, \mathcal{A}_2}(1^\lambda) = 1\right] \le \frac{1}{2} + \mathsf{negl}(\lambda)$.

Experiment $\mathrm{HIDE}^{\mathcal{A}_1, \mathcal{A}_2}(1^\lambda)$
$(1^N, i_0^*, i_1^*) \leftarrow \mathcal{A}_1(1^\lambda)$
$b \leftarrow_\$ \{0,1\}$
$(\mathsf{hk}, \mathsf{td}) \leftarrow \mathsf{Gen}(1^\lambda, N, i_b^*)$
$b' \leftarrow \mathcal{A}_2(\mathsf{hk})$
return $b' = b$

Somewhere Statistically (Resp. Computational) Binding w.r.t. Opening. For any all-powerful (resp. poly-time) adversary $\mathcal{A} = (\mathcal{A}_1, \mathcal{A}_2)$ there exists a negligible function $\mathsf{negl}(\cdot)$ such that $\Pr\left[\mathrm{OPEN}^{\mathcal{A}_1, \mathcal{A}_2}(1^\lambda) = 1\right] \leq \mathsf{negl}(\lambda)$.

Experiment $\mathrm{OPEN}^{\mathcal{A}_1, \mathcal{A}_2}(1^\lambda)$
$(1^N, i^*) \leftarrow \mathcal{A}_1(1^\lambda)$
$(\mathsf{hk}, \mathsf{td}) \leftarrow \mathsf{Gen}(1^\lambda, N, i^*)$
$(v, j, b, \rho) \leftarrow \mathcal{A}_2(\mathsf{hk})$
$u = \mathsf{Extract}(\mathsf{td}, v)$
return $u \neq b \wedge \mathsf{Verify}(\mathsf{hk}, v, j, b, \rho)$

Remark 1 ([9,15]). Notice that we can easily convert any such SEH family into one that is extractable on m indices $i_1, \ldots, i_m$ by running each algorithm m times and concatenating the outputs.

Under this transformation, the sizes of ℓ_{hash}, ℓ_{open} and the efficiency of the Verify will be $|I| \cdot \mathsf{poly}(\lambda, \log N)$.

We will use the shorthand notation $\mathsf{Gen}(1^\lambda, N, I)$ to denote this construction, in which case $\mathsf{Extract}(\mathsf{td}, v)$ will output m bits $(u_i)_{i \in I}$.

Theorem 2 ([13]). *Assuming any FHE scheme, there exists a* SEH *family.*

Theorem 3 ([15]). *Assuming any rate-1 string OT with verifiable correctness, there exists a* SEH *family.*

Corollary 4. *There exists a* SEH *family from any of the* {DDH, $O(1)$-LIN, QR, DCR, LWE} *assumptions.*

2.2 Somewhere Extractable Batch Arguments

We recall the notion of batch arguments (BARGs), which is an argument system to succinctly prove that, given a language $\mathcal{L}$, multiple instances $x_1, \ldots, x_k$ all have witnesses $w_1, \ldots, w_k$, with a complexity less than $\sum |w_i|$.

In particular, let BatchCSAT be the following language:

$$\mathsf{BatchCSAT} = \{(C, x_1, \ldots, x_k) \ : \ \exists w_1, \ldots, w_k \text{ s.t. } \forall i \in [k], \ C(x_i, w_i) = 1\},$$

where $C : \{0,1\}^n \times \{0,1\}^m \to \{0,1\}$ is a boolean circuit that checks a relation with instance size n and witness size m.

Definition 3. *A somewhere extractable batch argument* seBARG *for* BatchCSAT *consists of the following polynomial time algorithms:*

- $\mathsf{Gen}(1^\lambda, k, 1^s, i^*) \to (\mathsf{crs}, \mathsf{td})$. *Given the number of instances k, an index i^* and a circuit size s, it outputs a* crs *and a trapdoor* td.

- $\mathsf{P}(\mathsf{crs}, C, \{x_i\}_{i \in [k]}, \{w_i\}_{i \in [k]}) \to \pi$. *Given a* crs, *a circuit* C, k *statements* $x_1, \ldots, x_k \in \{0,1\}^n$ *and* k *witnesses* $w_1, \ldots, w_k \in \{0,1\}^m$, *it generates a proof* π.
- $\mathsf{V}(\mathsf{crs}, C, \{x_i\}_{i \in [k]}, \pi) \to \{0,1\}$. *Given a* crs, *a circuit* C, k *statements* $\{x_i\}_{i \in [k]}$ *and a proof* π, *it outputs a bit* b.
- $\mathsf{Extract}(\mathsf{td}, C, \{x_i\}_{i \in [k]}, \pi) \to w^*$. *Given a trapdoor* td, *a circuit* C, k *statements* $\{x_i\}_{i \in [k]}$ *and a proof* π, *it outputs a witness* w^* *for instance* i^*.

L-succinctness. The crs and the proof π have length at most $L(k, \lambda) \cdot \mathsf{poly}(s)$, and the verifier runs in time $L(k, \lambda) \cdot \mathsf{poly}[s] + k \cdot \mathsf{poly}(n, \lambda)$.

Completeness. For all $\lambda \in \mathbb{N}$, all $k, n \in \mathsf{poly}(\lambda)$, all circuits $C : \{0,1\}^n \times \{0,1\}^m \to \{0,1\}$ at size most s and all $(x_1, \ldots, x_k)$ and $(w_1, \ldots, w_k)$ such that $C(x_i, w_i) = 1$ we have that

$$\Pr\left[1 \leftarrow \mathsf{V}(\mathsf{crs}, C, \{x_i\}_{i \in [k]}, \pi) : \begin{array}{l} (\mathsf{crs}, \mathsf{td}) \leftarrow \mathsf{Gen}(1^\lambda, k, 1^s, i^*) \\ \pi \leftarrow \mathsf{P}(\mathsf{crs}, C, \{x_i\}_{i \in [k]}, \{w_i\}_{i \in [k]}) \end{array}\right] = 1.$$

Index Hiding. For all $\lambda \in \mathbb{N}$, all $k, n \in \mathsf{poly}(\lambda)$, all PPT adversaries $\mathcal{A}$ and all indices $i_0, i_1 \in [k]$ we have that

$$\Pr\left[b \leftarrow \mathcal{A}(\mathsf{crs}) : \begin{array}{l} b \leftarrow_\$ \{0,1\} \\ (\mathsf{crs}, \mathsf{td}) \leftarrow \mathsf{Gen}(1^\lambda, k, 1^s, i_b) \end{array}\right] \leq \frac{1}{2} + \mathsf{negl}(\lambda).$$

Somewhere Argument of Knowledge. For all $\lambda \in \mathbb{N}$ there exists a PPT extractor Ext such that for any PPT adversary $\mathcal{A}$, there exists a negligible function $\mathsf{negl}(\cdot)$ such that for any polynomials $k, n = \mathsf{poly}(\lambda)$, and any index $i^* \in [k]$ we have that

$$\Pr\left[\begin{array}{c} 1 \leftarrow \mathsf{V}(\mathsf{crs}, C, \{x_i\}_{i \in [k]}, \pi) \\ \wedge \\ C(x_{i^*}, w^*) \neq 1 \end{array} : \begin{array}{l} (\mathsf{crs}, \mathsf{td}) \leftarrow \mathsf{Gen}(1^\lambda, k, 1^s, i^*) \\ (C, \{x_i\}_{i \in [k]}, \pi) \leftarrow \mathcal{A}(\mathsf{crs}) \\ w^* \leftarrow \mathsf{Ext}(\mathsf{td}, C, \{x_i\}_{i \in [k]}, \pi) \end{array}\right] \leq \mathsf{negl}(\lambda).$$

We remark that this notion is equivalent to the most common soundness notion of semi-adaptive soundness [15].

Index $\mathsf{seBARGs}$. We say that a seBARG scheme is an index seBARG if the instances $x_1, \ldots, x_k$ are all of the form $x_i = (x, i)$ with a common x; however, in the *L-succinctness* property we require that the verification algorithm runs in time $L(k, \lambda) \cdot \mathsf{poly}(s)$, since it doesn't have to read all the instances anymore.

Lemma 2 ([15]). *Assume the existence of*

- *An L-succinct index* BARG *proof system for* $\mathsf{BatchCSAT}$
- *A* SEH *family with statistical binding as in Definition 2*

Then there exists an L-succinct index seBARG *proof system.*

Lemma 3 ([6, 8, 21]). *There exists an index* seBARG *with proof size and verifier running time of* poly(λ, log k, $|C|$) *from* {DDH, k-LIN, LWE} *assumptions.*

Remark 2 ([9, 15]). As with the SEH hash families, we can easily make the seBARG extractable on a subset $I \subset [k]$ of indices by running all the algorithms in parallel, incurring in a multiplicative factor of $|I|$ increase of all running times and sizes.

In our construction of a flSEH we will then be using the following syntax and efficiency properties of an index seBARG.

Fix an index language $\mathcal{L}$ given by a relation $\mathcal{R}(x, i, w_i)$, where x represents the common part of the statement of the index seBARG. All the algorithms will then implicitly build the circuit C from the relation $\mathcal{R}$ and the value x for the common part of the instances.

- Gen(1^λ, k, I) $\rightarrow$ (crs, td). Given the number of instances k, and the extraction set $I \subset [k]$, it outputs a crs and a trapdoor td.
- P(crs, x, $\{w_i\}_{i \in [k]}$) $\rightarrow \pi$. Given a crs, a common statement x and k witnesses $w_1, \ldots, w_k \in \{0, 1\}^m$, it generates a proof π.
- V(crs, x, π) $\rightarrow \{0, 1\}$. Given a crs, a common statement x and a proof π, it outputs a bit b.
- Extract(td, x, π) $\rightarrow (w_i^*)_{i \in [k]}$. Given a trapdoor td, a common statement x and a proof π, it outputs witnesses w_i^* for all indices $i \in [k]$.

Efficiency. We require a (multi-extractable) index seBARG to have proofs of size $|\pi| = |I| \cdot$ poly(λ, log k, $|x|$, m).

Remark 3 (On large CRS). We remark that we do not impose any restrictions in the size of the crs, as it is done in previous works. The only restriction that we require is that the verifier runs in time logarithmically in k given RAM access to the crs. This is enough for most applications of seBARG as it is noted in [9].

3   Fully Local SEH from DDH

3.1   Definition

A Fully-Local Somewhere Extractable Hash family (flSEH) is a strengthening of the SEH hash family introduced by [9, 15], where the verification running time is required to be independent of the hash size (i.e. the number of binding positions).

In order to do so, we need to split the output of Hash into a *long value* and a *short digest*, and similarly split the key output by Gen into a *hashing key* and a (short) *verification key*.

The full syntax and properties are described below.

Definition 4 (Fully Local Somewhere Extractable Hash). *The syntax for a fully-local SEH hash family is the following:*

- Gen($1^\lambda, N, I$) → (hk, vk, td). *This is a probabilistic algorithm that takes as input the security parameter 1^λ, the message length N, and a set of indices $I \subset [N]$. It outputs a (long) hashing key* hk, *a (short) verification key* vk *and a trapdoor* td.
- Hash(hk, x) → (v, rt). *This is a deterministic algorithm that takes as input a hashing key* hk *and a message* $x \in \{0, 1\}^N$, *and outputs a (long) hash value v and a (short) digest* rt.
- Open(hk, x, i) → (b, ρ). *This is a deterministic algorithm that takes as input a hashing key* hk, *a message* x *and an index* i. *It outputs a bit $b \in \{0, 1\}$ and an opening* ρ.
- Verify(vk, rt, i, b, ρ) → $\{0, 1\}$. *This is a deterministic algorithm that takes as input the verification key* vk, *the short digest* rt, *an index* i, *a bit b and an opening* ρ. *It verifies the validity of the opening* (b, ρ) *against* rt.
- Validate(vk, v, rt) → $\{0, 1\}$. *This is a deterministic algorithm that takes as input the verification key* vk, *a hash value v and a digest* rt. *It checks the consistency of v and* rt.
- Extract(td, v) → u. *This is a deterministic algorithm that takes as input the trapdoor* td *and a hash value v, and it outputs an extracted message $u \in \{0, 1\}^{|I|}$.*

It is required to satisfy the following properties:

Efficiency. The running time of Verify is poly(λ, log N). Moreover, we say that a flSEH is *rate-1* if the length of the hash value v is $|I| + $ poly(λ).

Opening Completeness. There exists a negligible function negl($\cdot$) such that for any λ, any $N \leq 2^\lambda$, any $I \subset [N]$, any $j \in [N]$ and any $x \in \{0, 1\}^N$,

$$
\Pr\left[
\begin{array}{l}
b = x_j \\
\wedge\ \mathsf{Verify}(\mathsf{vk}, \mathsf{rt}, j, b, \rho) = 1
\end{array}
:
\begin{array}{l}
(\mathsf{hk}, \mathsf{vk}, \mathsf{td}) \leftarrow \mathsf{Gen}(1^\lambda, N, I), \\
(v, \mathsf{rt}) = \mathsf{Hash}(\mathsf{hk}, x), \\
(b, \rho) = \mathsf{Open}(\mathsf{hk}, x, j)
\end{array}
\right] = 1 - \mathsf{negl}(\lambda)
$$

Index Hiding. For any polynomial time adversary $\mathcal{A} = (\mathcal{A}_1, \mathcal{A}_2)$ there exists a negligible function negl($\cdot$) such that $\Pr\left[\mathsf{HIDE}^{\mathcal{A}_1, \mathcal{A}_2}(1^\lambda) = 1\right] \leq \frac{1}{2} + \mathsf{negl}(\lambda)$.

Experiment $\mathsf{HIDE}^{\mathcal{A}_1, \mathcal{A}_2}(1^\lambda)$
$(1^N, I_0, I_1) \leftarrow \mathcal{A}_1(1^\lambda)$
$b \leftarrow_\$ \{0, 1\}$
$(\mathsf{hk}, \mathsf{vk}, \mathsf{td}) \leftarrow \mathsf{Gen}(1^\lambda, N, I_b)$
$b' \leftarrow \mathcal{A}_2(\mathsf{hk}, \mathsf{vk})$
return $|I_0| = |I_1| \wedge b' = b$

Somewhere Extractability w.r.t Opening. For any polynomial time adversary $\mathcal{A} = (\mathcal{A}_1, \mathcal{A}_2)$ there exists a negligible function $\mathsf{negl}(\cdot)$ such that $\Pr\left[\mathrm{OPEN}^{\mathcal{A}_1, \mathcal{A}_2}(1^\lambda) = 1\right] \leq \mathsf{negl}(\lambda)$.

Experiment $\mathrm{OPEN}^{\mathcal{A}_1, \mathcal{A}_2}(1^\lambda)$

$(1^N, I) \leftarrow \mathcal{A}_1(1^\lambda)$

$(\mathsf{hk}, \mathsf{vk}, \mathsf{td}) \leftarrow \mathsf{Gen}(1^\lambda, N, I)$

$(v, \mathsf{rt}, (b_j)_{j \in I}, (\rho_j)_{j \in I}) \leftarrow \mathcal{A}_2(\mathsf{hk}, \mathsf{vk})$

$(x_j)_{j \in I} = \mathsf{Extract}(\mathsf{td}, v)$

return $\mathsf{Validate}(\mathsf{vk}, v, \mathsf{rt}) \wedge \left(\bigvee_{j \in I} x_j \neq b_j \wedge \mathsf{Verify}(\mathsf{vk}, \mathsf{rt}, j, b_j, \rho_j) \right)$

3.2 Construction

Our construction of a fully local SEH is, at its core, based on the DDH-based construction of trapdoor hash functions due to [11].

Fix a generator $g \in \mathbb{G}$ of a group $\mathbb{G}$ of prime order p; let $P = \lceil \log p \rceil$ be the bitlength of elements in $\mathbb{G}$.

For our purposes, we will need to open up the distributed discrete logarithm compression mechanism due to [3]; in particular, let PRF be a pseudo-random function and $\mathsf{Shrink} : \mathbb{G} \to \{0, 1\}$ the related compression function for the group $(\mathbb{G}, g)$, as described in Lemma 1.

Additional Ingredients. Our construction further requires as additional components a (non rate-1) somewhere extractable hash family SEH, and an index somewhere extractable batch argument system seBARG for NP. We will use seBARG with the following index languages.

– Let seBARG_0 be a BARG for the index language $\mathcal{L}_0$ defined by the relation

$$\mathcal{R}_0((\mathsf{hk_M}, \mathsf{hk}_x, \mathsf{hk}_z, h_\mathbf{M}, h_x, h_z), (i, j), (M_{i,j}, x_j, z_{i,j}, \rho_{i,j}^M, \rho_j^x, \rho_{i,j}^z))$$

that outputs 1 if and only if
- $\mathsf{SEH.Verify}(\mathsf{hk_M}, h_\mathbf{M}, (i, j), M_{i,j}, \rho_{i,j}^M) = 1$
- $\mathsf{SEH.Verify}(\mathsf{hk}_x, h_x, j, x_j, \rho_j^x) = 1$
- $\mathsf{SEH.Verify}(\mathsf{hk}_z, h_z, (i, j), z_{i,j}, \rho_{i,j}^z) = 1$
- $z_{i,j} = M_{i,j}^{x_j}$

In essence, this language ensures that group elements $z_{i,j}$ committed to in the hash value h_z are well-formed exponentiations of $M_{i,j}$ (committed to in $h_\mathbf{M}$) with x_j (committed to in h_x).

– Let seBARG_{mult} be a BARG for the language $\mathcal{L}_{mult}$ defined by the relation

$$\mathcal{R}_{mult}((\mathsf{hk}_1, \mathsf{hk}_2, h_1, h_2), (i, j), (z, z_l, z_r, \rho_z, \rho_{zl}, \rho_{zr}))$$

that checks the following statements

- SEH.Verify$(\mathsf{hk}_1, h_1, (i, j), z, \rho_z) = 1$
- SEH.Verify$(\mathsf{hk}_2, h_2, (i, 2j - 1), z_l, \rho_{zl}) = 1$
- SEH.Verify$(\mathsf{hk}_2, h_2, (i, 2j), z_r, \rho_{zr}) = 1$
- $z = z_l \cdot z_r$

This language ensures that the intermediate values $z^{(t)}$ are correctly computed in a binary tree structure.

- Let seBARG$_{fin}$ be a BARG for the language $\mathcal{L}_{fin}$ defined by the relation

$$\mathcal{R}_{fin}((K, \mathsf{hk}_\kappa, \mathsf{hk}_\mathbf{v}, \mathsf{hk}_z, h_\kappa, h_\mathbf{v}, h_z), (i, j), (v_i, z_i, \kappa_i, \rho_i^v, \rho_i^z, \rho_i^\kappa))$$

that checks all the following

- SEH.Verify$(\mathsf{hk}_\mathbf{v}, h_\mathbf{v}, i, v_i, \rho_i^v) = 1$
- SEH.Verify$(\mathsf{hk}_z, h_z, i, z_i, \rho_i^z) = 1$
- SEH.Verify$(\mathsf{hk}_\kappa, h_\kappa, i, \kappa_i, \rho_i^\kappa) = 1$
- $v_i = \kappa_i \mod 2$
- If $j < \kappa_i + 2$ check if $\mathsf{PRF}(K, z_i \cdot g^{j-2}) \neq 0$
- If $j = \kappa_i + 2$, check that $\mathsf{PRF}(K, z_i \cdot g^{\kappa_i}) = 0$.

This language checks that the final hash value $\mathbf{v}$ is correctly computed from compressing the last values $z^{(T)}$.

Construction. We now present the full construction.

Gen$(1^\lambda, N, I)$:

- Let $m = |I|$ and $I = \{i_1, \dots, i_m\}$.
- Let $T = \lceil \log N \rceil$; assume that actually $N = 2^T$, if need be by padding.
- Randomly sample $a_1, \dots, a_m$ from $\mathbb{Z}_p$, compute $h_k = g^{a_k}$, and set td $= (a_1, \dots, a_m)$.
- Randomly sample $r_1, \dots, r_N$ from $\mathbb{Z}_p$ and compute a matrix $\mathbf{M} \in \mathbb{G}^{(1+m) \times N}$ with $M_{0,j} = g^{r_j}$, and $M_{k,j} = h_k^{r_j} \cdot g^{\delta_{j, i_k}}$ for $k = 1, \dots, m$, i.e.

$$\mathbf{M} = \begin{pmatrix} g^{r_1} & g^{r_2} & \cdots & & \cdots & g^{r_N} \\ h_1^{r_1} & \cdots & h_1^{r_{i_1}} g & \cdots & & h_1^{r_N} \\ \vdots & \ddots & \ddots & & \ddots & \vdots \\ h_m^{r_1} & \cdots & & & h_m^{r_{i_m}} g & h_m^{r_N} \end{pmatrix}$$

- Compute $(\mathsf{hk}_x, *) = \mathsf{SEH}.\mathsf{Gen}(1^\lambda, N, \emptyset)$
- Compute $(\mathsf{hk}_\mathbf{M}, *) = \mathsf{SEH}.\mathsf{Gen}(1^\lambda, (m+1) \cdot N, \emptyset)$
- For all $t = 0, \dots, T$ compute $(\mathsf{hk}^{(t)}, *) = \mathsf{SEH}.\mathsf{Gen}(1^\lambda, (m+1) \cdot N/2^t, \emptyset)$
- Compute $(\mathsf{hk}_\mathbf{v}, *) = \mathsf{SEH}.\mathsf{Gen}(1^\lambda, m, \emptyset)$
- Compute $(\mathsf{hk}_\kappa, *) = \mathsf{SEH}.\mathsf{Gen}(1^\lambda, m, \emptyset)$
- Run $(\mathsf{crs}_0, *) = \mathsf{seBARG}_0.\mathsf{Gen}(1^\lambda, (m+1) \cdot N, \emptyset)$
- For all $t = 1, \dots, T$, run $(\mathsf{crs}_t, *) = \mathsf{seBARG}_{mult}.\mathsf{Gen}(1^\lambda, (m+1) \cdot N/2^t, \emptyset)$
- Run $(\mathsf{crs}_{fin}, *) = \mathsf{seBARG}_{fin}.\mathsf{Gen}(1^\lambda, m, \emptyset)$
- Compute $h_\mathbf{M} = \mathsf{SEH}.\mathsf{Hash}(\mathsf{hk}_\mathbf{M}, \mathbf{M})$.
- Set vk $= \left(\mathsf{hk}_x, \mathsf{hk}_\mathbf{M}, \{\mathsf{hk}^{(t)}\}_{t \in [T]}, \mathsf{hk}_\mathbf{v}, \mathsf{hk}_\kappa, \{\mathsf{crs}_t\}_{t \in [T]}, \mathsf{crs}_{fin}, h_\mathbf{M} \right)$.
- Set hk $= (\mathbf{M}, \mathsf{vk})$ and output hk, vk and td.

Hash(hk, x):

- Parse hk $= (\mathbf{M}, \mathsf{vk})$ and
  $$\mathsf{vk} = \left(\mathsf{hk}_x, \mathsf{hk}_\mathbf{M}, \{\mathsf{hk}^{(t)}\}_{t=0,\dots,T}, \mathsf{hk}_\mathbf{v}, \{\mathsf{crs}_t\}_{t=0,\dots,T}, \mathsf{crs}_{fin}, h_\mathbf{M}\right).$$
- Compute $c_k = \prod_{j=1}^N M_{k,j}^{x_j}$ for all $k = 0, \dots, m$.
- Compute $z_{i,j}^{(0)} = M_{i,j}^{x_j}$.
- Recursively compute $z_{i,j}^{(t+1)} = z_{i,2j-1}^{(t)} \cdot z_{i,2j}^{(t)}$, from $t = 0$ up until T. In particular, $z_i^{(T)}$ will only have one component, and $z_{i,1}^{(T)} = c_i$.
- Choose $K \leftarrow_\$ \{0,1\}^\lambda$ uniformly at random and for $k = 1, \dots, m$ proceed as follows
    • Compute the smallest $\kappa_k \in [0, D]$ such that $\mathsf{PRF}(K, c_i \cdot g^{\kappa_k}) = 0$, where D is the bound needed for the compression function.
    • If no such κ_k exists or if $\mathsf{PRF}(K, c_i/g) = 0$, resample $K \leftarrow_\$ \{0,1\}^\lambda$ and retry until both conditions are met.
    • Set $v_k = \kappa_k \mod 2$.
- Set $v = (K, c_0, \mathbf{v})$
- Compute $h_\kappa = \mathsf{SEH.Hash}(\mathsf{hk}_\kappa, \kappa)$.
- Compute $h_\mathbf{v} = \mathsf{SEH.Hash}(\mathsf{hk}_\mathbf{v}, \mathbf{v})$.
- Compute $h_x = \mathsf{SEH.Hash}(\mathsf{hk}_x, x)$.
- For all $t = 0, \dots, T$, compute $h^{(t)} = \mathsf{SEH.Hash}(\mathsf{hk}^{(t)}, z^{(t)})$.
- For all i, j compute the openings
    • $\rho_j^x = \mathsf{SEH.Open}(\mathsf{hk}_x, x, j)$
    • $\rho_{i,j}^z = \mathsf{SEH.Open}(\mathsf{hk}^{(0)}, z^{(0)}, (i,j))$
    • $\rho_{i,j}^M = \mathsf{SEH.Open}(\mathsf{hk}_\mathbf{M}, M, (i,j))$
- Given the witnesses $w_{i,j} = (M_{i,j}, x_j, z_{i,j}^{(0)}, \rho_{i,j}^M, \rho_j^x, \rho_{i,j}^z)$, compute
  $$\pi_0 = \mathsf{seBARG}_0.\mathsf{P}\left(\mathsf{crs}_0, (\mathsf{hk}_\mathbf{M}, \mathsf{hk}_x, \mathsf{hk}^{(0)}, h_\mathbf{M}, h_x, h^{(0)}), \{w_{i,j}\}_{i,j}\right).$$

- For all $t = 1, \dots, T$
    • For all i, j compute the openings
        * $\rho_{i,j}^z = \mathsf{SEH.Open}(\mathsf{hk}^{(t)}, z^{(t)}, (i,j))$
        * $\rho_{i,j}^{zl} = \mathsf{SEH.Open}(\mathsf{hk}^{(t-1)}, z^{(t-1)}, (i, 2j-1))$
        * $\rho_{i,j}^{zr} = \mathsf{SEH.Open}(\mathsf{hk}^{(t-1)}, z^{(t-1)}, (i, 2j))$
    • Using the witnesses $w_{i,j} = (z_{i,j}^{(t)}, z_{i,2j-1}^{(t-1)}, z_{i,2j}^{(t-1)}, \rho_{i,j}^z, \rho_{i,j}^{zl}, \rho_{i,j}^{zr})$, compute
  $$\pi_t = \mathsf{seBARG}_{mult}.\mathsf{P}\left(\mathsf{crs}_t, (\mathsf{hk}^{(t)}, \mathsf{hk}^{(t-1)}, h^{(t)}, h^{(t-1)}), \{w_{i,j}\}_{i,j}\right).$$

- For all $i = 1, \dots, m$ compute the openings
    • $\rho_i^z = \mathsf{SEH.Open}(\mathsf{hk}^{(T)}, z^{(T)}, i)$
    • $\rho_i^\kappa = \mathsf{SEH.Open}(\mathsf{hk}_\kappa, \kappa, i)$
    • $\rho_i^v = \mathsf{SEH.Open}(\mathsf{hk}_\mathbf{v}, \mathbf{v}, i)$

- From the witnesses $w_{i,j} = (v_i, z_{i,1}^{(T)}, \kappa_i, \rho_i^v, \rho_i^z, \rho_i^\kappa)$, compute

$$\pi_{fin} = \mathsf{seBARG}_{fin}.\mathsf{P}\left(\mathsf{crs}_{fin}, (K, \mathsf{hk}_\kappa, \mathsf{hk}_\mathbf{v}, \mathsf{hk}^{(T)}, h_\kappa, h_\mathbf{v}, h^{(T)}), \{w_{i,j}\}_{i,j}\right),$$

  where $i = 1, \ldots, m$ and $j = 1, \ldots, D$.
- Set $\mathsf{rt} = \left(h_x, \left(h^{(t)}, \pi_t\right)_{t=0,\ldots,T}, c_0, h_\mathbf{v}, K, h_\kappa, \pi_{fin}\right)$.
- Output (v, rt).

$\mathsf{Open}(\mathsf{hk}, x, i)$:

- Parse $\mathsf{hk} = (M, \mathsf{vk})$ and
  $\mathsf{vk} = \left(\mathsf{hk}_x, \mathsf{hk}_\mathbf{M}, \{\mathsf{hk}^{(t)}\}_{t=0,\ldots,T}, \mathsf{hk}_\mathbf{v}, \mathsf{hk}_\kappa, \{\mathsf{crs}_t\}_{t=0,\ldots,T}, \mathsf{crs}_{fin}, h_\mathbf{M}\right)$.
- Output $\mathsf{SEH.Open}(\mathsf{hk}_x, x, i)$

$\mathsf{Verify}(\mathsf{vk}, \mathsf{rt}, i, b, \rho)$:

- Parse $\mathsf{vk} = \left(\mathsf{hk}_x, \mathsf{hk}_\mathbf{M}, \{\mathsf{hk}^{(t)}\}_{t=0,\ldots,T}, \mathsf{hk}_\mathbf{v}, \mathsf{hk}_\kappa, \{\mathsf{crs}_t\}_{t=0,\ldots,T}, \mathsf{crs}_{fin}, h_\mathbf{M}\right)$.
- Parse $\mathsf{rt} = \left(h_x, \left(h^{(t)}, \pi_t\right)_{t=0,\ldots,T}, c_0, h_\mathbf{v}, K, h_\kappa, \pi_{fin}\right)$.
- Check that $\mathsf{seBARG}_0.\mathsf{V}\left(\mathsf{crs}_0, (\mathsf{hk}_\mathbf{M}, \mathsf{hk}_x, \mathsf{hk}^{(0)}, h_\mathbf{M}, h_x, h^{(0)}), \pi_0\right) = 1$.
- Check that $\mathsf{seBARG}_{mult}.\mathsf{V}\left(\mathsf{crs}_t, (\mathsf{hk}^{(t)}, \mathsf{hk}^{(t-1)}, h^{(t)}, h^{(t-1)}), \pi_t\right) = 1$ for all $t = 1, \ldots, T$.
- Check that $\mathsf{seBARG}_{fin}.\mathsf{V}\left(\mathsf{crs}_{fin}, (K, \mathsf{hk}_\kappa, \mathsf{hk}_\mathbf{v}, \mathsf{hk}^{(T)}, h_\kappa, h_\mathbf{v}, h^{(T)}), \pi_{fin}\right) = 1$.
- Check that $\mathsf{SEH.Verify}(\mathsf{hk}_x, h_x, i, b, \rho) = 1$.
- Output 1 if and only if all checks pass.

$\mathsf{Validate}(\mathsf{vk}, v, \mathsf{rt})$:

- Parse $\mathsf{vk} = \left(\mathsf{hk}_x, \mathsf{hk}_\mathbf{M}, \{\mathsf{hk}^{(t)}\}_{t=0,\ldots,T}, \mathsf{hk}_\mathbf{v}, \mathsf{hk}_\kappa, \{\mathsf{crs}_t\}_{t=0,\ldots,T}, \mathsf{crs}_{fin}, h_\mathbf{M}\right)$.
- Parse $\mathsf{rt} = \left(h_x, \left(h^{(t)}, \pi_t\right)_{t=0,\ldots,T}, c_{\mathsf{rt}}, h_\mathbf{v}, K_{\mathsf{rt}}, h_\kappa, \pi_{fin}\right)$.
- Parse $v = (K_v, c_v, \mathbf{v})$.
- Check that $c_v = c_{\mathsf{rt}}$ and $K_v = K_{\mathsf{rt}}$.
- Check that $\mathsf{SEH.Hash}(\mathsf{hk}_\mathbf{v}, \mathbf{v}) = h_\mathbf{v}$.

$\mathsf{Extract}(\mathsf{td}, v)$:

- Output $\mathsf{ShrinkDec}(\mathsf{td}, v)$.

3.3 Security Analysis

Lemma 4. *The construction in Sect. 3.2 is efficient and rate-1; in particular,* $|\mathsf{vk}|, |\mathsf{rt}|$ *and the running time of* Verify *are bounded by* $\mathsf{poly}(\lambda, \log N, \log |I|)$.

Proof. By the efficiency of the underlying SEH scheme, all the hashing keys $\mathsf{hk}_x, \mathsf{hk}_M, \mathsf{hk}^{(t)}, \mathsf{hk}_v, \mathsf{hk}_\kappa$ and all the openings that will be used as witnesses in the sebARGs for the languages $\mathcal{L}_0, \mathcal{L}_{mult}, \mathcal{L}_{fin}$ are of size $\mathsf{poly}(\lambda, \log(mNP))$, since our message is an $(m+1) \times N$ matrix of group elements.

This means that the circuit sizes for the sebARGs will be of size $\mathsf{poly}(\lambda, \log m, \log N)$, given also the efficiency of the algorithm SEH.Verify. Since we have $k = (m+1) \times N$ instances, by the succinctness of the index sebARG we get that the size of all the sebARG.crs and proofs sebARG.π, as well as the running time of sebARG.V, are bounded by $\mathsf{poly}(\lambda, \log m, \log N)$.

Thus, given that we only have $\log N$ many of $\mathsf{hk}^{(t)}, \pi_t$, we get that $|\mathsf{vk}|, |\mathsf{rt}|$ and the running time of Verify are bounded by $\mathsf{poly}(\lambda, \log N, \log |I|)$.

Finally, by construction we have that $|v| = |I| + \mathsf{poly}(\lambda)$, i.e. our construction is rate-1.

Lemma 5. *Assume that the DDH assumption holds in the group* $\mathbb{G}$. *Then the construction in Sect. 3.2 satisfies the index-hiding property.*

Proof. We can easily see that by repeated application of the DDH assumption the matrices outputted by the Gen algorithm are pseudorandom. For simplicity we can consider the 2-row matrices.

If (g^a, g^b, g^c) is a DDH challenge, where c is either ab or random, we see that

$$\begin{pmatrix} g^{r_1} & \cdots & g^a & \cdots & g^{r_N} \\ g^{br_1} & \cdots & g^{c+1} & \cdots & g^{br_N} \end{pmatrix}$$

follows the distribution of Gen in the case that $c = ab$, and is random at the i-th column if c is random.

Lemma 6. *Assume that* SEH *is a somewhere extractable hash function,* sebARG_0 *is a somewhere extractable BARG for the language* $\mathcal{L}_0$, sebARG_{mult} *is a somewhere extractable BARG for the language* $\mathcal{L}_{mult}$ *and* sebARG_{fin} *is a somewhere extractable BARG for the language* $\mathcal{L}_{fin}$, *where* $\mathcal{L}_0, \mathcal{L}_{mult}$ *and* $\mathcal{L}_{fin}$ *are defined in Sect. 3.2. Then the scheme constructed in Sect. 3.2 satisfies the opening completeness property.*

Proof. This follows directly from the completeness of the underlying SEH family and index sebARG system.

Theorem 4. *Assume that* SEH *is a somewhere extractable hash function,* sebARG_0 *is a somewhere extractable BARG for the language* $\mathcal{L}_0$, sebARG_{mult} *is a somewhere extractable BARG for the language* $\mathcal{L}_{mult}$ *and* sebARG_{fin} *is a somewhere extractable BARG for the language* $\mathcal{L}_{fin}$, *where* $\mathcal{L}_0, \mathcal{L}_{mult}$ *and* $\mathcal{L}_{fin}$ *are defined in Sect. 3.2. Then the scheme constructed in Sect. 3.2 is somewhere binding with respect to opening.*

Proof. Assume towards contradiction that there exists an a PPT adversary $\mathcal{A}$ with non-negligible success probability ϵ against the somewhere binding w.r.t. opening experiment. We will proceed in a sequence of hybrids to establish this contradiction.

Experiment Exp_0. Let Exp_0 be the real experiment, given as follows.

$\mathsf{Exp}_0(\mathcal{A})$
- $(\mathsf{hk}, \mathsf{vk}, \mathsf{td}) \leftarrow \mathsf{Gen}(1^\lambda, N, I)$
- $(v, \mathsf{rt}, (b_j), (\rho_j)) \leftarrow \mathcal{A}(\mathsf{hk}, \mathsf{vk})$
- $(\hat{b}_j) = \mathsf{Extract}(\mathsf{td}, v)$
- Output 1 if $\mathsf{Validate}(\mathsf{vk}, v, \mathsf{rt}) = 1$ and there exists a $j^* \in [m]$ such that $b_{j^*} \neq \hat{b}_{j^*}$ and $\mathsf{Verify}(\mathsf{vk}, \mathsf{rt}, j^*, b_{j^*}, \rho_{j^*}) = 1$, otherwise output 0.

By our assumption on $\mathcal{A}$ it holds that $\Pr[\mathsf{Exp}_0(\mathcal{A})] > \epsilon$.
Denote by E_{val} the event that in the experiment we have $\mathsf{Validate}(\mathsf{vk}, v, \mathsf{rt}) = 1$, and E_{cheat} the event that $\bigvee_{j \in I} \hat{b}_j \neq b_j \wedge \mathsf{Verify}(\mathsf{vk}, \mathsf{rt}, j, b_j, \rho_j) = 1$. Then

$$\Pr\left[\mathsf{Exp}_0(\mathcal{A})\right] = \Pr\left[E_{val} \cap E_{cheat}\right] = \Pr\left[E_{cheat} \mid E_{val}\right] \cdot \Pr\left[E_{val}\right] \leq$$
$$\leq \Pr\left[E_{cheat} \mid E_{val}\right]$$

In order to show that the hypothesis $\Pr\left[E_{cheat} \mid E_{val}\right] > \epsilon$ leads to a contradiction, we will then implicitly condition on E_{val} in all the next experiments; in particular, we assume that $\mathsf{SEH.Hash}(\mathsf{hk_v}, \mathbf{v}) = h_{\mathbf{v}}$ and that the decryption headers K, c_0 in v are the correct ones w.r.t. the digest rt.

Experiment Exp_1. In the second experiment Exp_1 we will change the success condition of the adversary. Specifically, the experiment guesses the index $j^* \leftarrow\$ [m]$ uniformly random in the very beginning, and outputs 0 if the mismatch between the extracted value and the opened value does not occur at index j^*. Exp_1 is given as follows.

$\mathsf{Exp}_1(\mathcal{A})$
- $j^* \leftarrow\$ [m]$
- $(\mathsf{hk}, \mathsf{vk}, \mathsf{td}) \leftarrow \mathsf{Gen}(1^\lambda, N, I)$
- $(v, \mathsf{rt}, (b_j), (\rho_j)) \leftarrow \mathcal{A}(\mathsf{hk}, \mathsf{vk})$
- $(\hat{b}_j) = \mathsf{Extract}(\mathsf{td}, v)$
- Output 1 if $b_{j^*} \neq \hat{b}_{j^*}$ and $\mathsf{Verify}(\mathsf{vk}, \mathsf{rt}, j^*, b_{j^*}, \rho_{j^*}) = 1$, otherwise output 0.

Define S be the set of indices i for which $b_i \neq \hat{b}_i$. Conditioned on $j^* \in S$, $\mathsf{Exp}_0(\mathcal{A})$ and $\mathsf{Exp}_1(\mathcal{A})$ are identically distributed. Hence it holds that

$$\Pr[\mathsf{Exp}_1(\mathcal{A}) = 1] = \underbrace{\Pr[\mathsf{Exp}_1(\mathcal{A}) = 1 \text{ and } j^* \in S]}_{=\Pr[\mathsf{Exp}_0(\mathcal{A})=1 \text{ and } j^* \in S]} + \underbrace{\Pr[\mathsf{Exp}_1(\mathcal{A}) = 1 \text{ and } j^* \notin S]}_{=0}$$
$$= \Pr[j^* \in S | \mathsf{Exp}_0(\mathcal{A}) = 1] \cdot \underbrace{\Pr[\mathsf{Exp}_0(\mathcal{A}) = 1]}_{>\epsilon}$$
$$> \Pr[j^* \in S | \mathsf{Exp}_0(\mathcal{A}) = 1] \cdot \epsilon$$
$$\geq \epsilon/m,$$

where the last inequality holds as S is non-empty conditioned on $\mathsf{Exp}_0(\mathcal{A}) = 1$ and j^* is independent of Exp_0.

Experiment Exp_2. In experiment Exp_2 we will modify the hashing keys hk_x, $\mathsf{hk}_{\mathbf{M}}$, $\mathsf{hk}^{(t)}$, $\mathsf{hk}_{\mathbf{v}}$ and hk_κ to be extractable on the root-to-leaf path corresponding to j^*, both for the "header" row and for the "payload" row.

Specifically, we modify the Gen algorithm such that hk_x, $\mathsf{hk}_{\mathbf{M}}$, $\mathsf{hk}^{(t)}$, hk_κ and $\mathsf{hk}_{\mathbf{v}}$ are generated as follows depending on j^*. Let $I = \{i_1, \ldots, i_m\}$ and define $i^* = i_{j^*}$ and $i_t^* = \lceil i^*/2^t \rceil$ for $t = 0, \ldots, T$.

- Compute $(\mathsf{hk}_x, \mathsf{td}_x) = \mathsf{SEH.Gen}(1^\lambda, N, \{i^*\})$
- Compute $(\mathsf{hk}_{\mathbf{M}}, \mathsf{td}_{\mathbf{M}}) = \mathsf{SEH.Gen}(1^\lambda, (m+1) \cdot N, \{(0, i^*), (j^*, i^*)\})$
- Compute $(\mathsf{hk}^{(t)}, \mathsf{td}^{(t)}) = \mathsf{SEH.Gen}(1^\lambda, (m+1) \cdot N/2^t, \{(0, i_t^*), (j^*, i_t^*)\})$ for all $t = 0, \ldots, T$
- Compute $(\mathsf{hk}_\kappa, \mathsf{td}_\kappa) = \mathsf{SEH.Gen}(1^\lambda, m, \{j^*\})$
- Compute $(\mathsf{hk}_{\mathbf{v}}, \mathsf{td}_{\mathbf{v}}) = \mathsf{SEH.Gen}(1^\lambda, m, \{j^*\})$

Computational indistinguishability between Exp_1 and Exp_2 follows routinely via a simple hybrid argument from the index-hiding property of SEH. Hence we have that

$$\Pr[\mathsf{Exp}_2(\mathcal{A}) = 1] \geq \Pr[\mathsf{Exp}_1(\mathcal{A}) = 1] - \mathsf{negl}(\lambda) \geq \epsilon/m - \mathsf{negl}(\lambda).$$

Experiment Exp_3. In this experiment we will extract M_{0,i^*} and M_{j^*,i^*} from $h_{\mathbf{M}}$, x_{i^*} from h_x, $z_{0,i_t^*}^{(t)}$ and $z_{j^*,i_t^*}^{(t)}$ from each $h^{(t)}$, κ_{j^*} from h_κ and v_{j^*} from $h_{\mathbf{v}}$, i.e.

- $M_{0,i^*} = \mathsf{SEH.Extract}(\mathsf{td}_{\mathbf{M}}, h_{\mathbf{M}}, (0, i^*))$
- $M_{j^*,i^*} = \mathsf{SEH.Extract}(\mathsf{td}_{\mathbf{M}}, h_{\mathbf{M}}, (j^*, i^*))$
- $x_{i^*} = \mathsf{SEH.Extract}(\mathsf{td}_x, h_x, i^*)$
- $z_{0,i_t^*}^{(t)} = \mathsf{SEH.Extract}(\mathsf{td}^{(t)}, h^{(t)}, (0, i_t^*))$
- $z_{j^*,i_t^*}^{(t)} = \mathsf{SEH.Extract}(\mathsf{td}^{(t)}, h^{(t)}, (j^*, i_t^*))$.
- $\kappa_{j^*} = \mathsf{SEH.Extract}(\mathsf{td}_\kappa, h_\kappa, j^*)$
- $v_{j^*} = \mathsf{SEH.Extract}(\mathsf{td}_{\mathbf{v}}, h_{\mathbf{v}}, j^*)$

Note that this modification does not affect the outcome of the experiment, hence it is merely syntactical, that is

$$\Pr[\mathsf{Exp}_3(\mathcal{A}) = 1] = \Pr[\mathsf{Exp}_2(\mathcal{A}) = 1] - \mathsf{negl}(\lambda) \geq \epsilon/m - \mathsf{negl}(\lambda).$$

We will now define events E_0, E_t for $t \in [T]$ and E_{fin} via

$$E_0 = 1 :\Leftrightarrow \left(z_{0,i^*}^{(0)} \neq M_{0,i^*}^{x_{i^*}} \text{ or } z_{j^*,i^*}^{(0)} \neq M_{j^*,i^*}^{x_{i^*}} \right)$$

$$E_t = 1 :\Leftrightarrow z_{j^*,i_t^*}^{(t)} \neq (z_{0,i_t^*}^{(t)})^{a_{j^*}} \cdot g^{x_{i^*}}$$

$$E_{fin} = 1 :\Leftrightarrow \left(v_{j^*} \neq \mathsf{ShrinkComp}(K, z_{j^*,1}^{(T)}) \text{ or } \mathsf{PRF}(K, z_{j^*,1}^{(T)}/g) = 0 \right)$$

where $\mathsf{td} = (a_1, \ldots a_m)$ is the trapdoor of the matrix $\mathbf{M}$. Now note that if none of the events E_0, E_t for some $t \in [T]$ or E_{fin} hold, then it *must hold* that $b_{j^*} = \hat{b}_{j^*}$.

Consequently, if Exp_3 outputs 1, then *at least one of these events must hold*, and therefore

$$
\begin{aligned}
\epsilon/m - \mathsf{negl}(\lambda) &\le \Pr[(E_0 \vee E_{fin} \vee \exists t \in [T] \text{ s.t. } E_t) \text{ and } \mathsf{Verify}(\mathsf{vk}, \mathsf{rt}, j^*, b_{j*}, \rho_{j*}) = 1] \\
&\le \Pr[E_0 \text{ and } \mathsf{Verify}(\mathsf{vk}, \mathsf{rt}, j^*, b_{j*}, \rho_{j*}) = 1] \\
&\quad + \Pr[E_{fin} \text{ and } \mathsf{Verify}(\mathsf{vk}, \mathsf{rt}, j^*, b_{j*}, \rho_{j*}) = 1] \\
&\quad + \Pr[\exists t \in [T] \text{ s.t. } E_t \text{ and } \mathsf{Verify}(\mathsf{vk}, \mathsf{rt}, j^*, b_{j*}, \rho_{j*}) = 1] \\
&\le \Pr[E_0 \text{ and } \mathsf{seBARG}_0.\mathsf{V}\left(\mathsf{crs}_0, (\mathsf{hk_M}, \mathsf{hk}_x, \mathsf{hk}^{(0)}, h_\mathbf{M}, h_x, h^{(0)}), \pi_0\right) = 1] \\
&\quad + \Pr[E_{fin} \text{ and } \mathsf{seBARG}_{fin}.\mathsf{V}\left(\mathsf{crs}_{fin}, (K, \mathsf{hk}_\kappa, \mathsf{hk}_\mathbf{v}, \mathsf{hk}^{(T)}, h_\kappa, h_\mathbf{v}, h^{(T)}), \pi_{fin}\right) = 1] \\
&\quad + \Pr[\exists t \in [T] \text{ s.t. } E_t \text{ and } \mathsf{seBARG}_{mult}.\mathsf{V}\left(\mathsf{crs}_t, (\mathsf{hk}^{(t)}, \mathsf{hk}^{(t-1)}, h^{(t)}, h^{(t-1)}), \pi_t\right) = 1]
\end{aligned}
$$

where the first inequality follows by the union bound,

That is, one of these three events must have non-negligible probability of occurrence. Hence we will now distinguish 3 cases.

1. Assume that

$$
\Pr[E_0 \text{ and } \mathsf{seBARG}_0.\mathsf{V}\left(\mathsf{crs}_0, (\mathsf{hk_M}, \mathsf{hk}_x, \mathsf{hk}^{(0)}, h_\mathbf{M}, h_x, h^{(0)}), \pi_0\right) = 1] > \epsilon_0
$$

for a non-negligible ϵ_0.
Define an experiment $\mathsf{Exp}_{3,0,1}$ which is identical to Exp_3, but outputs 1 if and only if E_0 and $\mathsf{seBARG}_0.\mathsf{V}\left(\mathsf{crs}_0, (\mathsf{hk_M}, \mathsf{hk}_x, \mathsf{hk}^{(0)}, h_\mathbf{M}, h_x, h^{(0)}), \pi_0\right) = 1$ holds. Clearly, by our assumption it holds that $\Pr[\mathsf{Exp}_{3,0,1} = 1] > \epsilon_0$. In the next experiment will make seBARG_0 extractable at positions $(0, i^*)$ and (j^*, i^*). Specifically, define an experiment $\mathsf{Exp}_{3,0,2}$ which is identical to $\mathsf{Exp}_{3,0,1}$ except that we compute crs_0 via

- $(\mathsf{crs}_0, \mathsf{td}_0^*) = \mathsf{seBARG}_0.\mathsf{Gen}(1^\lambda, (m+1) \cdot N, \{(0, i^*), (j^*, i^*)\})$

It follows routinely from the index-hiding property of seBARG_0 that $\mathsf{Exp}_{3,0,1}$ and $\mathsf{Exp}_{3,0,2}$ are computationally indistinguishable, that is it holds that

$$
\Pr[\mathsf{Exp}_{3,0,2} = 1] \ge \Pr[\mathsf{Exp}_{3,0,1} = 1] - \mathsf{negl}(\lambda) \ge \epsilon_0 - \mathsf{negl}(\lambda).
$$

Now we immediately get a contradiction against the somewhere argument of knowledge/somewhere soundness property of seBARG_0, as either the statement $z_{0,i^*}^{(0)} = M_{0,i^*}^{x_{i^*}}$ or the statement $z_{j^*,i^*}^{(0)} = M_{j^*,i^*}^{x_{i^*}}$ is false, and the keys hk_x, $\mathsf{hk_M}$ and $\mathsf{hk}^{(0)}$ are statistically binding to the corresponding positions.

2. Assume that

$$
\Pr[E_{fin} \text{ and } \mathsf{seBARG}_{fin}.\mathsf{V}\left(\mathsf{crs}_{fin}, (K, \mathsf{hk}_\kappa, \mathsf{hk}_\mathbf{v}, \mathsf{hk}^{(T)}, h_\kappa, h_\mathbf{v}, h^{(T)}), \pi_{fin}\right) = 1] > \epsilon_{fin}
$$

for a non-negligible ϵ_{fin}.
We modify Exp_3 into an experiment $\mathsf{Exp}_{3,fin,1}$ which outputs 1 if and only if E_{fin} and $\mathsf{seBARG}_{fin}.\mathsf{V}\left(\mathsf{crs}_{fin}, (K, \mathsf{hk}_\kappa, \mathsf{hk}_\mathbf{v}, \mathsf{hk}^{(T)}, h_\kappa, h_\mathbf{v}, h^{(T)}), \pi_{fin}\right) = 1$ hold. Again, by our assumption it holds immediately that $\Pr[\mathsf{Exp}_{3,fin,1} = 1] > \epsilon_{fin}$.
We also define events O_κ such that $O_\kappa = 1$ if and only if $\kappa < \kappa_{j*}$ such that

$$\mathsf{PRF}(K, z_{j^*,1}^{(T)} \cdot g^{\kappa}) = 0.$$

Notice that

$$\Pr[\mathsf{Exp}_{3,fin,1} = 1] = \Pr[\mathsf{Exp}_{3,fin,1} = 1 \text{ and } \exists \kappa, O_{\kappa} = 1] +$$
$$+ \Pr[\mathsf{Exp}_{3,fin,1} = 1 \text{ and } \forall \kappa, O_{\kappa} \neq 1]$$

We now define an experiment $\mathsf{Exp}_{3,fin,2}$ where we first make a guess $\kappa^* \in [0, \kappa_{j^*}]$ and then output 1 if also event $O_{\kappa^*} = 1$, i.e. if $\mathsf{PRF}(K, z_{j^*,1}^{(T)} \cdot g^{\kappa^*}) = 0$. Since our guess is independent from the experiment, we get that

$$\Pr[\mathsf{Exp}_{3,fin,2} = 1] \geq \Pr[\mathsf{Exp}_{3,fin,1} \text{ and } \exists \kappa, O_{\kappa} = 1]/D,$$

where $D = O(m\lambda)$.

We then define experiment $\mathsf{Exp}_{3,fin,3}$, where we make seBARG_{fin} extractable at index (j^*, κ^*). That is, experiment $\mathsf{Exp}_{3,fin,3}$ is identical to experiment $\mathsf{Exp}_{3,fin,2}$ except that we compute crs_{fin} via

- $(\mathsf{crs}_{fin}, \mathsf{td}_{fin}^*) = \mathsf{seBARG}_{fin}.\mathsf{Gen}(1^{\lambda}, m, \{(j^*, \kappa^*)\}).$

Indistinguishability of $\mathsf{Exp}_{3,fin,3}$ and $\mathsf{Exp}_{3,fin,2}$ follows from index-hiding of seBARG_{fin}. Moreover, since $\mathcal{L}_{fin}$ checks that $\mathsf{PRF}(K, z_{j^*,1}^{(T)} \cdot g^{\kappa^*}) \neq 0$, and we can extract a witness for the event O_{κ^*}, i.e. $\mathsf{PRF}(K, z_{j^*,1}^{(T)} \cdot g^{\kappa^*}) = 0$, we get that $\Pr[\mathsf{Exp}_{3,fin,3} = 1] \leq \mathsf{negl}(\lambda)$ by the soundness of seBARG_{fin}. This means that $\Pr[\mathsf{Exp}_{3,fin,1} \text{ and } \exists \kappa, O_{\kappa} = 1] \leq D \cdot \Pr[\mathsf{Exp}_{3,fin,2} = 1] \leq \mathsf{negl}(\lambda)$, and thus $\Pr[\mathsf{Exp}_{3,fin,1} = 1 \text{ and } \forall \kappa, O_{\kappa} \neq 1] \geq \epsilon_{fin} - \mathsf{negl}(\lambda)$.

Now we deal with the second part of the probability, $\Pr[\mathsf{Exp}_{3,fin,1} = 1 \text{ and } \forall \kappa, O_{\kappa} \neq 1]$. We define experiment $\mathsf{Exp}_{3,fin,4}$, which is identical to experiment $\mathsf{Exp}_{3,fin,1}$ except that we compute crs_{fin} via

- $(\mathsf{crs}_{fin}, \mathsf{td}_{fin}^*) = \mathsf{seBARG}_{fin}.\mathsf{Gen}(1^{\lambda}, m, \{(j^*, 0)\}).$

Computational indistinguishability of $\mathsf{Exp}_{3,fin,4}$ and $\mathsf{Exp}_{3,fin,1}$ follows again routinely from the index-hiding property of seBARG_{fin}. Consequently, it holds that

$$\Pr[\mathsf{Exp}_{3,fin,4} = 1 \text{ and } \forall \kappa, O_{\kappa} \neq 1] \geq \epsilon_{fin} - \mathsf{negl}(\lambda).$$

Notice now that given that all events O_{κ} are false, the computation $\mathsf{ShrinkComp}(K, z_{j^*,1}^{(T)})$ is correct. This means that the extracted witness, conditioned on the event E_{fin}, is not valid for the language $\mathcal{L}_{fin}$, thus breaking the somewhere argument of knowledge/somewhere soundness property of seBARG_{fin}, which is a contradiction.

3. Finally assume that

$$\Pr[\exists t \in [T] \text{ s.t. } E_t \text{ and } \mathsf{seBARG}_{mult}.\mathsf{V}\left(\mathsf{crs}_t, (\mathsf{hk}^{(t)}, \mathsf{hk}^{(t-1)}, h^{(t)}, h^{(t-1)}), \pi_t\right) = 1] > \epsilon'$$

for a non-negligible ϵ'. Now, let $\mathsf{Exp}'_{3,1}$ be identical to Exp_3, except that the experiment outputs 1 if and only if there exists a $t \in [T]$ s.t. E_t holds and $\mathsf{seBARG}_{mult}.\mathsf{V}\left(\mathsf{crs}_t, (\mathsf{hk}^{(t)}, \mathsf{hk}^{(t-1)}, h^{(t)}, h^{(t-1)}), \pi_t\right) = 1$. Clearly, by our assumption it holds that $\Pr[\mathsf{Exp}'_{3,1} = 1] > \epsilon'$.

In the next experiment $\mathsf{Exp}'_{3,2}$ we guess an index $t^* \leftarrow_\$ [T]$ such that t^* is the smallest t for which E_t holds. Specifically, $\mathsf{Exp}'_{3,2}$ outputs 0 if the guess t^* was wrong. Via the essentially same reasoning as in the step between Exp_0 and Exp_1 it holds that

$$\Pr[\mathsf{Exp}'_{3,2} = 1] \geq \Pr[\mathsf{Exp}'_{3,1} = 1]/T > \epsilon'/T.$$

In the next experiment, we make $\mathsf{hk}^{(t^*-1)}$ *also* extractable at the other child node of i_t^*, that is let

$$\bar{i}^*_{t^*-1} = \begin{cases} 2i_t^* - 1 & \text{if } i_{t^*-1}^* = 2i_t^* \\ 2i_t^* & \text{otherwise} \end{cases}.$$

Thus, in $\mathsf{Exp}'_{3,3}$ we will compute $\mathsf{hk}^{(t^*-1)}$ via

- $(\mathsf{hk}^{(t^*-1)}, \mathsf{td}^{(t^*-1)}) = \mathsf{SEH.Gen}(1^\lambda, (m+1) \cdot N/2^t, \{(0, i_{t^*-1}^*), (j^*, i_{t^*-1}^*), (0, \bar{i}^*_{t^*-1}), (j^*, \bar{i}^*_{t^*-1})\})$

Computational indistinguishability of $\mathsf{Exp}'_{3,2}$ and $\mathsf{Exp}'_{3,3}$ follows from the index-hiding property of SEH. Thus we have

$$\Pr[\mathsf{Exp}'_{3,3} = 1] \geq \Pr[\mathsf{Exp}'_{3,2} = 1] - \mathsf{negl}(\lambda) > \epsilon'/T - \mathsf{negl}(\lambda).$$

Note that by Remark 2, our notion of being able to extract at several points is essentially for notational convenience; we have a fresh key (and hash value) for each extraction slot, thus we can introduce a new extraction slots while maintaining the ability to extract at previously planted extraction slots. In the next hybrid $\mathsf{Exp}'_{3,4}$ we extract $h^{(t^*-1)}$ at $(0, \bar{i}^*_{t^*-1})$ and $(j^*, \bar{i}^*_{t^*-1})$, that is we compute

- $z_{0, \bar{i}^*_{t^*-1}}^{(t^*-1)} = \mathsf{SEH.Extract}(\mathsf{td}^{(t^*-1)}, h^{(t^*-1)}, (0, \bar{i}^*_{t^*-1}))$
- $z_{j^*, \bar{i}^*_{t^*-1}}^{(t^*-1)} = \mathsf{SEH.Extract}(\mathsf{td}^{(t^*-1)}, h^{(t^*-1)}, (j^*, \bar{i}^*_{t^*-1}))$

Notice that this modification has no effect on the output of the experiment. Moreover, in $\mathsf{Exp}'_{3,4}$ we also make seBARG_{mult} extractable at positions $(0, i_{t^*}^*)$ and $(j^*, i_{t^*}^*)$, that is, we will now generate $\mathsf{crs}^{(t^*)}$ via

- $(\mathsf{crs}^{(t^*)}, \hat{\mathsf{td}}^{(t^*)}) \leftarrow \mathsf{seBARG}_{mult}.\mathsf{Gen}(1^\lambda, (m+1) \cdot N/2^{t^*}, \{(0, i_{t^*}^*), (j^*, i_{t^*}^*)\})$.

By the index-hiding property of seBARG_{mult}, $\mathsf{Exp}'_{3,3}$ and $\mathsf{Exp}'_{3,4}$ are computationally indistinguishable, that is

$$\Pr[\mathsf{Exp}'_{3,4} = 1] \geq \Pr[\mathsf{Exp}'_{3,3} = 1] - \mathsf{negl}(\lambda) > \epsilon'/T - \mathsf{negl}(\lambda).$$

In $\mathsf{Exp}'_{3,5}$ we will introduce an additional condition which causes the experiment to output 0. Specifically, let F_{t^*} be the event that $(z_{0, \bar{i}^*_{t^*-1}}^{(t^*-1)}, z_{j^*, \bar{i}^*_{t^*-1}}^{(t^*-1)})$ is an encryption of 0, that is $F_{t^*} = 1$ if and only if

$$z_{j^*, \bar{i}^*_{t^*-1}}^{(t^*-1)} = (z_{0, \bar{i}^*_{t^*-1}}^{(t^*-1)})^{a_{j^*}}.$$

$\mathsf{Exp}'_{3,5}$ is identical to $\mathsf{Exp}'_{3,4}$, except that it outputs 0 if $F_{t^*} = 1$. Note that the event F_{t^*} can be efficiently tested for given a_{j^*}. We can appeal to the extractability property of seBARG_{mult} to argue that $\Pr[F_{t^*} = 1] \leq \mathsf{negl}(\lambda)$. Otherwise, we would get a violation of the somewhere extractability/somewhere soundness of seBARG_{mult}. Specifically, assume that F_{t^*} holds, i.e.

$$z_{j^*,\bar{i}_{t^*-1}}^{(t^*-1)} = (z_{0,\bar{i}_{t^*-1}}^{(t^*-1)})^{a_{j^*}}. \tag{2}$$

We will argue that this implies that either

$$z_{0,i_{t^*}^*}^{(t^*)} \neq z_{0,i_{t^*-1}^*}^{(t^*-1)} \cdot z_{0,\bar{i}_{t^*-1}^*}^{(t^*-1)}$$

or

$$z_{j^*,i_{t^*}^*}^{(t^*)} \neq z_{j^*,i_{t^*-1}^*}^{(t^*-1)} \cdot z_{j^*,\bar{i}_{t^*-1}^*}^{(t^*-1)},$$

which routinely implies a contradiction to the somewhere soundness of seBARG_{mult}. To see this, assume that both

$$z_{0,i_{t^*}^*}^{(t^*)} = z_{0,i_{t^*-1}^*}^{(t^*-1)} \cdot z_{0,\bar{i}_{t^*-1}^*}^{(t^*-1)}, \tag{3}$$

$$z_{j^*,i_{t^*}^*}^{(t^*)} = z_{j^*,i_{t^*-1}^*}^{(t^*-1)} \cdot z_{j^*,\bar{i}_{t^*-1}^*}^{(t^*-1)}. \tag{4}$$

Recall now that t^* is the smallest t for which $z_{j^*,i_t^*}^{(t)} \neq (z_{0,i_t^*}^{(t)})^{a_{j^*}} \cdot g^{x_{i^*}}$, hence it holds that

$$z_{j^*,i_{t^*-1}^*}^{(t^*-1)} = (z_{0,i_{t^*-1}^*}^{(t^*-1)})^{a_{j^*}} \cdot g^{x_{i^*}} \tag{5}$$

Thus, by exponentiating (3) and (4) by a_{j^*} and combining (2) and (5) we can conclude that

$$z_{j^*,i_{t^*}^*}^{(t^*)} = (z_{0,i_{t^*}^*}^{(t^*)})^{a_{j^*}} \cdot g^{x_{i^*}},$$

but this means that E_{t^*} *does not hold*, i.e. it is a contradiction to t^* be the smallest t for which E_t holds. Hence we conclude that

$$\Pr[\mathsf{Exp}'_{3,5} = 1] \geq \Pr[\mathsf{Exp}'_{3,4} = 1] - \mathsf{negl}(\lambda) > \epsilon'/T - \mathsf{negl}(\lambda).$$

Now, to simplify notation define $\tilde{i} = \bar{i}_{t^*-1}^*$. In experiment $\mathsf{Exp}'_{3,5}$ we have the guarantee that if the experiment outputs 1 (which happens with non-negligible probability $\epsilon'/T - \mathsf{negl}(\lambda)$), then we have the equation $z_{j^*,\tilde{i}}^{(t^*-1)} = (z_{0,\tilde{i}}^{(t^*-1)})^{a_{j^*}} \cdot g^\tau$ for a non-zero τ.

In the following hybrids, we will consider a path $\tilde{i}_{t^*-1}, \ldots, \tilde{i}_0$ from $\tilde{i}_{t^*-1} = \tilde{i}$ to a leaf node $\tilde{i}_0$ and establish the invariant that all ciphertexts $(z_{0,\tilde{i}_k}^{(k)}, z_{j^*,\tilde{i}_k}^{(k)})$ encrypt non-zero values, while maintaining non-negligible probabilities for the experiments to output 1. We will achieve this using the somewhere extractability of SEH and seBARG_{mult}. Eventually, once we reached a leaf-node we will arrive at a contradiction against the soundness of seBARG_0. We will thus consider a sequence of experiments $\mathsf{Exp}''_{k,0}, \mathsf{Exp}''_{k,1}, \mathsf{Exp}''_{k,2}, \mathsf{Exp}''_{k,3}, \mathsf{Exp}''_{k,4}$ for $k = t^* - 1, \ldots, 0$. We chain them by defining $\mathsf{Exp}''_{t^*,0} = \mathsf{Exp}'_{3,5}$ and $\mathsf{Exp}''_{k-1,0} = \mathsf{Exp}''_{k,4}$.

The experiment $\mathsf{Exp}''_{k,1}$ is identical to the experiment $\mathsf{Exp}''_{k,0}$, except that we make $\mathsf{hk}^{(k-1)}$ extractable at the children nodes of $(0, \tilde{i}_k)$ and $(j^*, \tilde{i}_k)$, i.e. at positions $(0, 2\tilde{i}_k - 1)$, $(0, 2\tilde{i}_k)$, $(j^*, 2\tilde{i}_k - 1)$, $(j^*, 2\tilde{i}_k)$. In particular, we generate $\mathsf{hk}^{(k-1)}$ via

- $(\mathsf{hk}^{(k-1)}, \mathsf{td}^{(k-1)}) = \mathsf{SEH.Gen}(1^\lambda, (m+1) \cdot N/2^{k-1}, \{(0, 2\tilde{i}_k - 1), (0, 2\tilde{i}_k),$
  $(j^*, 2\tilde{i}_k - 1), (j^*, 2\tilde{i}_k)\})$.

Computational indistinguishability of $\mathsf{Exp}''_{k,1}$ and its preceding experiment follows from the index-hiding property of SEH.

In experiment $\mathsf{Exp}''_{k,2}$, we make seBARG_{mult} extractable at positions $(0, \tilde{i}_k)$ and $(j^*, \tilde{i}_k)$.

- $(\mathsf{crs}^{(k-1)}, \hat{\mathsf{td}}^{(k-1)}) = \mathsf{seBARG}_{mult}.\mathsf{Gen}(1^\lambda, (m+1) \cdot N/2^t, \{(0, \tilde{i}_k), (j^*, \tilde{i}_k)\})$.

Computational indistinguishability follows from the index-hiding property of seBARG_{mult}.

In experiment $\mathsf{Exp}''_{k,3}$, we extract both ciphertexts at the children nodes of $\tilde{i}_k$, that is we compute

- $z^{(k-1)}_{0,2\tilde{i}_k-1} = \mathsf{SEH.Extract}(\mathsf{td}^{(k-1)}, h^{(k-1)}, (0, 2\tilde{i}_k - 1))$
- $z^{(k-1)}_{j^*,2\tilde{i}_k-1} = \mathsf{SEH.Extract}(\mathsf{td}^{(k-1)}, h^{(k-1)}, (j^*, 2\tilde{i}_k - 1))$
- $z^{(k-1)}_{0,2\tilde{i}_k} = \mathsf{SEH.Extract}(\mathsf{td}^{(k-1)}, h^{(k-1)}, (0, 2\tilde{i}_k))$
- $z^{(k-1)}_{j^*,2\tilde{i}_k} = \mathsf{SEH.Extract}(\mathsf{td}^{(k-1)}, h^{(k-1)}, (j^*, 2\tilde{i}_k))$

Furthermore, let F_k be the event that both $(z^{(k-1)}_{0,2\tilde{i}_k-1}, z^{(k-1)}_{j^*,2\tilde{i}_k-1})$ and $(z^{(k-1)}_{0,2\tilde{i}_k}, z^{(k-1)}_{j^*,2\tilde{i}_k})$ are encryptions of 0, that is it holds that both

$$z^{(k-1)}_{j^*,2\tilde{i}_k-1} = (z^{(k-1)}_{0,2\tilde{i}_k-1})^{a_{j^*}},$$
$$z^{(k-1)}_{j^*,2\tilde{i}_k} = (z^{(k-1)}_{0,2\tilde{i}_k})^{a_{j^*}}.$$

Note that we can efficiently test for this event given a_{j^*}.

In $\mathsf{Exp}''_{k,3}$ we add the additional condition that the experiment outputs 0 if the event F_k holds.

We will now argue that given that seBARG_{mult} is somewhere extractable/somewhere sound, the event F_k happens only with negligible probability. Given that F_k happens, we claim it must hold that either

$$z^{(k)}_{0,\tilde{i}_k} \neq z^{(k-1)}_{0,2\tilde{i}_k-1} \cdot z^{(k-1)}_{0,2\tilde{i}_k}$$

or

$$z^{(k)}_{j^*,\tilde{i}_k} \neq z^{(k-1)}_{j^*,2\tilde{i}_k-1} \cdot z^{(k-1)}_{j^*,2\tilde{i}_k}$$

which routinely leads to a contradiction to the somewhere extractability/somewhere soundness of seBARG_{mult}. Otherwise, if both equations

$$z^{(k)}_{0,\tilde{i}_k} = z^{(k-1)}_{0,2\tilde{i}_k-1} \cdot z^{(k-1)}_{0,2\tilde{i}_k},$$
$$z^{(k)}_{j^*,\tilde{i}_k} = z^{(k-1)}_{j^*,2\tilde{i}_k-1} \cdot z^{(k-1)}_{j^*,2\tilde{i}_k}$$

hold, then given the equations for the event F_k, this implies that

$$z^{(k)}_{j^*,\tilde{i}_k} = (z^{(k)}_{0,\tilde{i}_k})^{a_{j^*}},$$

i.e. $(z^{(k)}_{0,\tilde{i}_k}, z^{(k)}_{j^*,\tilde{i}_k})$ is an encryption of 0. But this violates our invariant that $(z^{(k)}_{0,\tilde{i}_k}, z^{(k)}_{j^*,\tilde{i}_k})$ is an encryption of a non-zero value. Hence the claim follows, and $\mathsf{Exp}''_{k,3}$ is computationally indistinguishable from $\mathsf{Exp}''_{k,2}$.

In $\mathsf{Exp}''_{k,4}$, we guess a random bit $\beta_{k-1} \leftarrow\!\!\$ \{0,1\}$ uniformly at random at the beginning of the experiment and set $\tilde{i}_{k-1} = 2\tilde{i}_k - 1$ if $\beta_{k-1} = 0$ and $\tilde{i}_{k-1} = 2\tilde{i}_k$ if $\beta_{k-1} = 1$. Let G_{k-1} be the event that $(z^{(k-1)}_{0,\tilde{i}_{k-1}}, z^{(k-1)}_{j^*,\tilde{i}_{k-1}})$ is an encryption of 0, i.e. $G_{k-1} = 1$ if and only if

$$z^{(k-1)}_{j^*,\tilde{i}_{k-1}} = (z^{(k-1)}_{0,\tilde{i}_{k-1}})^{a_{j^*}}.$$

Now, in $\mathsf{Exp}''_{k,4}$ we add the additional condition that the experiment outputs 0 if the event G_{k-1} holds. Since the bit β_{k-1} is chosen uniformly at random and we have the promise (from experiment $\mathsf{Exp}''_{k,3}$) that either $(z^{(k-1)}_{0,2\tilde{i}_k-1}, z^{(k-1)}_{j^*,2\tilde{i}_k-1})$ or $(z^{(k-1)}_{0,2\tilde{i}_k}, z^{(k-1)}_{j^*,2\tilde{i}_k})$ is an encryption of a non-zero value, we get that the event G_{k-1} has probability at least $1/2$, and therefore

$$\Pr[\mathsf{Exp}''_{k,4} = 1] \geq \Pr[\mathsf{Exp}''_{k,3} = 1]/2.$$

In particular, we have that

$$\Pr[\mathsf{Exp}''_{k,4} = 1] \geq \Pr[\mathsf{Exp}''_{k,0} = 1]/2 - \mathsf{negl}(\lambda),$$

and given that $\Pr[\mathsf{Exp}''_{k,0} = 1] = \Pr[\mathsf{Exp}''_{k+1,4} = 1]$, this implies that for the final experiment $\mathsf{Exp}''_{0,4}$ in this sequence it holds that

$$\Pr[\mathsf{Exp}''_{0,4} = 1] \geq \Pr[\mathsf{Exp}''_{t^*,1} = 1]/2^{t^*} \geq \Pr[\mathsf{Exp}''_{t^*,1} = 1]/2^T \geq \epsilon'/(2^T \cdot T) - \mathsf{negl}(\lambda),$$

which is non-negligible as ϵ' is non-negligible and $T = O(\log(\lambda))$.

In the final two experiments we will proceed analogously to the first case above, namely, we will make hk_x and hk_M extractable at positions corresponding to $\tilde{i}_0$ and establish a contradiction to the somewhere extractability/somewhere soundness of seBARG_0.

That is, in Exp'''_0 we switch hk_x to be extractable at position $\tilde{i}_0$ and hk_M to be extractable at positions $(0,\tilde{i}_0)$ and $(j^*,\tilde{i}_0)$, formally we compute

- $(\mathsf{hk}_x, \mathsf{td}_x) = \mathsf{SEH.Gen}(1^\lambda, N, \{i^*, \tilde{i}_0\})$
- $(\mathsf{hk}_M, \mathsf{td}_M) = \mathsf{SEH.Gen}(1^\lambda, (m+1) \cdot N, \{(0,i^*), (j^*,i^*), (0,\tilde{i}_0), (j^*,\tilde{i}_0)\})$

Computational indistinguishability of $\mathsf{Exp}''_{0,4}$ and Exp'''_0 follows routinely from the index-hiding property of SEH.

In experiment Exp'''_1, we switch crs_0 to be extractable at positions $(0,\tilde{i}_0)$ and $(j^*,\tilde{i}_0)$, that is we set

- $(\mathsf{crs}_0, \mathsf{td}_0) = \mathsf{seBARG}_0.\mathsf{Gen}(1^\lambda, (m+1) \cdot N, \{(0,\tilde{i}_0), (j^*,\tilde{i}_0)\})$.

Computational indistinguishability again follows routinely from the index-hiding property of seBARG_0.

We can now finally show a contradiction to the somewhere extractability/somewhere soundness property of seBARG_0.

Note that by our invariant $(z_{0,\tilde{i}_0}^{(0)}, z_{j^*,\tilde{i}_0}^{(0)})$ is an encryption of a non-zero value (conditioned on $\mathsf{Exp}_1''' = 1$). At the same time it holds that

$$M_{0,\tilde{i}_0}^{x_{\tilde{i}_0}} = g^{r_{\tilde{i}_0} \cdot x_{\tilde{i}_0}}$$
$$M_{j^*,\tilde{i}_0}^{x_{\tilde{i}_0}} = g^{a_j^* \cdot r_{\tilde{i}_0} \cdot x_{\tilde{i}_0}},$$

that is $(M_{0,\tilde{i}_0}^{x_{\tilde{i}_0}}, M_{j^*,\tilde{i}_0}^{x_{\tilde{i}_0}})$ is an encryption of 0. But this means that either

$$z_{0,\tilde{i}_0}^{(0)} \neq M_{0,\tilde{i}_0}^{x_{\tilde{i}_0}}$$

or

$$z_{j^*,\tilde{i}_0}^{(0)} \neq M_{j^*,\tilde{i}_0}^{x_{\tilde{i}_0}},$$

which routinely leads to a contradiction to the somewhere extractability of seBARG_0.

This concludes the proof.

4 Applications

4.1 Rate-1 seBARGs

Rate-1. Finally, we define the rate-1 property. A seBARG is said to be rate-1 if the proof is of size $|\pi| = m + o(m) \cdot \mathsf{poly}(\lambda, \log k)$.

The following lemma states that rate-1 BARGs exist given an index BARGs and a rate-1 fully-local SEH.

Lemma 7 ([9]). *Assuming the existence of an index seBARG and a rate-1 fully-local SEH, there exists a rate-1 seBARG.*

Instantiating the rate-1 flSEH with the construction from Sect. 3.2 and the BARG with one from Lemma 3, we obtain the following corollary.

Corollary 5. *There exists a rate-1 BARG from subexponential DDH or k-LIN where the proof has size $m + \mathsf{poly}(\lambda)$.*

Previously, this was known from the same assumptions by plugging the rate-1 SEH construction from [15] with the construction of [19] with proof size $m + \frac{3m}{\lambda} + \mathsf{poly}(\lambda)$.

4.2 Rate-1 BARGs with Short CRS

Our rate-1 BARG from Sect. 4.1 has a large CRS, that is, the size of the CRS grows with the number of instances. In this section, we show a generic transformation from rate-1 BARGs with large CRS to a rate-1 BARG with a compact CRS, that is, a CRS with size $\mathsf{poly}(\lambda)$ (independent of the number of instances).

In particular, we prove the following theorem.

Theorem 5. *Suppose* seBARG_0 *is a somewhere extractable BARG for language* $\mathcal{L}$ *with proof size* $m + \mathsf{poly}(\lambda, \log k)$ *and CRS size* $\mathsf{poly}(\lambda, k)$, *where* k *is the number of instances and* m *is the size of a witness for* $\mathcal{L}$. *Then there exists a somewhere extractable BARG* seBARG_1 *for* $\mathcal{L}$ *with proof size* $m + \mathsf{poly}(\lambda, \log k)$ *and CRS size* $\mathsf{poly}(\lambda, \log k)$.

Construction. We first sketch a construction of seBARG_1, which is based on a binary tree, where each node is a seBARG_0 proof that the two children are themselves valid seBARG_0 proofs, i.e. at each layer we use the BARG for just 2 statements.[2] Concretely, at the leaf level, let $\mathcal{L}_0 = \mathcal{L}$ be the base language for which we want a BARG. For each following layer $j \geq 1$, we define the language $\mathcal{L}_j$: a statement is a tuple $y_j = (x_1, \ldots, x_{2^j})$, a witness is a proof π, and the relation $\mathcal{R}_j$ is

$$\mathcal{R}_j(y_j, \pi) = \mathsf{seBARG}_0.\mathsf{V}(\mathsf{crs}_{j-1}, \mathcal{L}_{j-1}, \{(x_1, \ldots, x_{2^{j-1}}), (x_{1+2^{j-1}}, \ldots, x_{2^j})\}, \pi).$$

The algorithms $(\mathsf{Gen}, \mathsf{P}, \mathsf{Vf}, \mathsf{Extract})$ for seBARG_1 are then given by the following description.

- $\mathsf{seBARG}_1.\mathsf{Gen}(1^\lambda, k, 1^s, i^*) \to (\mathsf{crs}, \mathsf{td})$.
  Let $K = \lceil \log k \rceil$, and let $i_{K-1} i_{K-2} \ldots i_1 i_0$ be the binary representation of i^*; denote by $\bar{i}_j = \lfloor i^*/2^{j+1} \rfloor = i_{K-1} i_{K-2} \ldots i_{j+1}$.
  For each $j \in [K]$, run $(\mathsf{crs}_j, \mathsf{td}_j) = \mathsf{seBARG}_0.\mathsf{Gen}(1^\lambda, 2, 1^{s_j}, \bar{i}_j)$, where $s_0 = s$, and s_{j+1} is an upper bound to the size of the verification circuit $\mathcal{R}_j$ at layer j.
  Return $\mathsf{crs} = \{\mathsf{crs}_j\}$, $\mathsf{td} = \{\mathsf{td}_j\}$.
- $\mathsf{seBARG}_1.\mathsf{P}(\mathsf{crs}, C, \{x_i\}_{i\in[k]}, \{w_i\}_{i\in[k]}) \to \pi$.
  Recursively compute proofs in the following way: in the first step, compute

$$\pi_i^{(0)} = \mathsf{seBARG}_0.\mathsf{P}(\mathsf{crs}_0, \mathcal{L}, \{x_{2i}, x_{2i+1}\}, \{w_{2i}, w_{2i+1}\}).$$

Now, for any $1 \leq j \leq K - 1$ define $y_i^{(j)} = (x_{i \cdot 2^j}, \ldots, x_{(i+1) \cdot 2^j - 1})$. Then, recursively compute

$$\pi_i^{(j)} = \mathsf{seBARG}_0.\mathsf{P}\left(\mathsf{crs}_j, \mathcal{L}_j, \left\{y_{2i}^{(j)}, y_{2i+1}^{(j)}\right\}, \left\{\pi_{2i}^{(j-1)}, \pi_{2i+1}^{(j-1)}\right\}\right).$$

Output $\pi_0^{(K-1)}$ as the proof.

---

[2] This framework can also be trivially adapted to use a ℓ-ary tree, instead of a binary one. The resulting CRS has size $\log_\ell(k) \cdot \mathsf{poly}(\lambda, \ell)$.

- $\text{seBARG}_1.\text{V}(\text{crs}, C, \{x_i\}_{i\in[k]}, \pi) \to \{0,1\}$.
  Recursively recompute the $y_i^{(j)}$s and output the result of

  $$\text{seBARG}_0.\text{V}\left(\text{crs}_{K-1}, \mathcal{L}_{K-1}, \left\{y_0^{(K-1)}, y_1^{(K-1)}\right\}, \pi\right).$$

- $\text{seBARG}_1.\text{Extract}(\text{td}, C, \{x_i\}_{i\in[k]}, \pi) \to w^*$.
  Recursively extract the proofs until the last layer, and then extract the witness. In particular, recompute the $y_i^{(j)}$s, define $\pi^{(K-1)} = \pi$ and then recursively compute

  $$\pi^{(j-1)} = \text{seBARG}_0.\text{Extract}\left(\text{td}_j, \mathcal{L}_j, \left\{y_{2\tilde{i}_j}^{(j)}, y_{2\tilde{i}_j+1}^{(j)}\right\}, \pi^{(j)}\right).$$

  Finally, return

  $$w^* = \text{seBARG}_0.\text{Extract}\left(\text{td}_0, \mathcal{L}, \left\{x_{2\tilde{i}_0}, x_{2\tilde{i}_0+1}\right\}, \pi^{(0)}\right).$$

Properties. We sketch a proof for all the required properties of the resulting scheme seBARG_1.

CRS Succinctness. The CRS of seBARG_1 consists of $\log k$ many CRSs of seBARG_0 with a constant number of statements (in particular, 2). Thus, it is of size $\log k \cdot \text{poly}(\lambda)$.

Rate. Since seBARG_0 is rate-1, we have that $|\pi_i^{(j)}| = |\pi_i^{(j-1)}| + \text{poly}(\lambda)$. Thus, if m is the size of a witness for $\mathcal{L}$, the proof size of seBARG_1 is $m + \log k \cdot \text{poly}(\lambda)$.

Index Hiding. This property follows directly from index hiding of seBARG_0, since the crs of seBARG_1 is the union of many independent crs of seBARG_0.

Somewhere Argument of Knowledge. The following lemma establishes that seBARG_1 is a somewhere argument of knowledge, given that seBARG_0 is a somewhere argument of knowledge.

Lemma 8. *Let seBARG_0 be a somewhere extractable argument of knowledge, then seBARG_1 given above is also a somewhere argument of knowledge.*

Proof. Let $\mathcal{A}$ be an adversary against the somewhere argument-of-knowledge property of seBARG_1. In particular, let i^* the extractable index, and π the proof given by $\mathcal{A}$. We denote by $w^* = \text{seBARG}_1.\text{Extract}(\text{td}, C, \{x_i\}_{i\in[k]}, \pi)$ the extracted witness, and recall that the extraction algorithm also extracts witnesses $w_j = \pi^{(j)}$ for each layer. Consider then the following hybrids.

- Hybrid $\mathcal{H}_0$: This is the real experiment
- Hybrid $\mathcal{H}_k$ (for $k = 1, \ldots, K-1$): This is the same as hybrid $\mathcal{H}_{k-1}$, except that the experiment outputs 0 if the conditions $\mathcal{R}_j(y_{i_j}^{(j)}, w_j) \neq 1$ and
  $\text{seBARG}_0.V\left(\text{crs}_j, \left\{y_{2i_j}^{(j)}, y_{2i_j+1}^{(j)}\right\}, \pi^{(j)}\right) = 1$ hold, where $j = K - 1 - k$.

Note that the last experiment $\mathcal{H}_{K-1}$ aborts if $\mathcal{R}_0(x_{i^*}, w^*) \neq 1$. But since $x_{i^*} \notin \mathcal{L}_0 = \mathcal{L}$, this experiment always outputs 0, i.e. $\mathcal{A}$ has advantage 0 in this experiment.

It remains to show that experiments $\mathcal{H}_{k-1}$ and $\mathcal{H}_k$ are indistinguishable given that seBARG_0 is somewhere extractable. Concretely, if $|\Pr[\mathcal{H}_k = 1] - \Pr[\mathcal{H}_{k-1} = 1]| \geq \epsilon$ we can construct an adversary $\mathcal{A}'$ against the somewhere argument of knowledge property of seBARG_0 with advantage ϵ as follows. $\mathcal{A}'$ simulates $\mathcal{H}_{k-1}$ but only outputs the statements $y_{2i_j}^{(j)}$ and $y_{2i_j+1}^{(j)}$ as well as the proof $\pi^{(j)}$. If $y_{i_{j-1}}^{(j)} \in \mathcal{L}_j$ both experiments are identically distributed. Hence, it must holds that $y_{i_{j-1}}^{(j)} \notin \mathcal{L}_j$ but $\mathsf{seBARG}_0.V\left(\mathsf{crs}_j, \left\{y_{2i_j}^{(j)}, y_{2i_j+1}^{(j)}\right\}, \pi^{(j)}\right) = 1$ with probability at least ϵ. Hence $\mathcal{A}'$ breaks the somewhere argument of knowledge property of seBARG_0 with advantage ϵ, which concludes the proof.

4.3 RAM SNARGs with Partial Input Soundness

A RAM SNARG allows a verifier to verify that a RAM computation was well performed given just the hash of the input (or initial database) h and a proof π. Importantly, the verifier should run in time $\mathsf{poly}(\lambda, \log T)$ where T is the running time of the RAM computation.

Here, we are interested in RAM SNARGs that achieve a strong soundness property known as partial input soundness [15]. This guarantees that if the memory is digested using a SEH function that is extractable on a set of coordinates I, and if the RAM computation only reads coordinates in I, then soundness holds. We refer the reader to [9,15] for formal definitions.

It is known that a flexible RAM SNARG can be constructed from seBARGs and a fully-local SEH function.

Lemma 9 ([15]). *Assuming the existence of a* seBARG *and a fully-local* SEH, *there exists a RAM SNARG with partial input soundness.*

Let S be the size of a single intermediate state of the RAM computation. Then the RAM SNARG construction presented in [15] has proof size $S \cdot \mathsf{poly}(\lambda) + \mathsf{poly}(\lambda, \log T, S)$, where $S \cdot \mathsf{poly}(\lambda)$ corresponds to the output of the (fully-local) SEH and $\mathsf{poly}(\lambda, \log T, S)$ corresponds to the size of the seBARG proof. Additionally, assume that only V positions are read from the initial memory $\mathbf{X}$. Then the hash value of $\mathbf{X}$ has size $V \cdot \mathsf{poly}(\lambda)$.

If we instantiate the underlying seBARG with a rate-1 BARG (from Corollary 5) and the fully-local SEH with a rate-1 scheme (as the one from Sect. 3.2), we obtain the following corollary.

Corollary 6. *There exists a RAM SNARG with partial input soundness from subexponential DDH or k-LIN assumptions with proof size* $\mathcal{O}(S) + \mathsf{poly}(\lambda)$ *and an hash value (of the initial database) of size* $V + \mathsf{poly}(\lambda)$.

Acknowledgements. Pedro Branco was partially funded by the German Federal Ministry of Education and Research (BMBF) in the course of the 6GEM research hub under grant number 16KISK038.
Nico Döttling and Riccardo Zanotto: Funded by the European Union (ERC, LACONIC, 101041207). Views and opinions expressed are however those of the author(s) only and do not necessarily reflect those of the European Union or the European Research Council. Neither the European Union nor the granting authority can be held responsible for them.

References

1. Ananth, P., Lombardi, A.: Succinct garbling schemes from functional encryption through a local simulation paradigm. In: Beimel, A., Dziembowski, S. (eds.) TCC 2018, Part II. LNCS, vol. 11240, pp. 455–472. Springer, Heidelberg (2018). https://doi.org/10.1007/978-3-030-03810-6_17

2. Boyle, E., Gilboa, N., Ishai, Y.: Breaking the circuit size barrier for secure computation under DDH. In: Robshaw, M., Katz, J. (eds.) CRYPTO 2016, Part I. LNCS, vol. 9814, pp. 509–539. Springer, Heidelberg (2016). https://doi.org/10.1007/978-3-662-53018-4_19

3. Brakerski, Z., Branco, P., Döttling, N., Garg, S., Malavolta, G.: Constant ciphertext-rate non-committing encryption from standard assumptions. In: Pass, R., Pietrzak, K. (eds.) TCC 2020, Part I. LNCS, vol. 12550, pp. 58–87. Springer, Heidelberg (Nov (2020). https://doi.org/10.1007/978-3-030-64375-1_3

4. Brakerski, Z., Holmgren, J., Kalai, Y.T.: Non-interactive delegation and batch NP verification from standard computational assumptions. In: Hatami, H., McKenzie, P., King, V. (eds.) 49th ACM STOC, pp. 474–482. ACM Press (2017)

5. Cho, C., Döttling, N., Garg, S., Gupta, D., Miao, P., Polychroniadou, A.: Laconic oblivious transfer and its applications. In: Katz, J., Shacham, H. (eds.) CRYPTO 2017, Part II. LNCS, vol. 10402, pp. 33–65. Springer, Heidelberg (2017). https://doi.org/10.1007/978-3-319-63715-0_2

6. Choudhuri, A.R., Garg, S., Jain, A., Jin, Z., Zhang, J.: Correlation intractability and SNARGs from sub-exponential DDH. In: Handschuh, H., Lysyanskaya, A. (eds.) CRYPTO 2023. LNCS, pp. 635–668. Springer, Cham (2023). https://doi.org/10.1007/978-3-031-38551-3_20

7. Choudhuri, A.R., Jain, A., Jin, Z.: Non-interactive batch arguments for NP from standard assumptions. In: Malkin, T., Peikert, C. (eds.) CRYPTO 2021, Part IV. LNCS, vol. 12828, pp. 394–423. Springer, Heidelberg (2021). https://doi.org/10.1007/978-3-030-84259-8_14

8. Choudhuri, A.R., Jain, A., Jin, Z.: SNARGs for $\mathcal{P}$ from LWE. In: 62nd FOCS, pp. 68–79. IEEE Computer Society Press (2022)

9. Devadas, L., Goyal, R., Kalai, Y., Vaikuntanathan, V.: Rate-1 non-interactive arguments for batch-NP and applications. In: 63rd FOCS, pp. 1057–1068. IEEE Computer Society Press (2022)

10. Döttling, N., Garg, S.: Identity-based encryption from the Diffie-Hellman assumption. In: Katz, J., Shacham, H. (eds.) CRYPTO 2017, Part I. LNCS, vol. 10401, pp. 537–569. Springer, Heidelberg (2017). https://doi.org/10.1007/978-3-319-63688-7_18

11. Döttling, N., Garg, S., Ishai, Y., Malavolta, G., Mour, T., Ostrovsky, R.: Trapdoor hash functions and their applications. In: Boldyreva, A., Micciancio, D. (eds.) CRYPTO 2019, Part III. LNCS, vol. 11694, pp. 3–32. Springer, Heidelberg (2019). https://doi.org/10.1007/978-3-030-26954-8_1

12. Garg, S., Srinivasan, A.: A simple construction of iO for turing machines. In: Beimel, A., Dziembowski, S. (eds.) TCC 2018, Part II. LNCS, vol. 11240, pp. 425–454. Springer, Heidelberg (2018). https://doi.org/10.1007/978-3-030-03810-6_16

13. Hubacek, P., Wichs, D.: On the communication complexity of secure function evaluation with long output. In: Roughgarden, T. (ed.) ITCS 2015, pp. 163–172. ACM (2015)

14. Hulett, J., Jawale, R., Khurana, D., Srinivasan, A.: SNARGs for P from subexponential DDH and QR. In: Dunkelman, O., Dziembowski, S. (eds.) EUROCRYPT 2022, Part II. LNCS, vol. 13276, pp. 520–549. Springer, Heidelberg (2022). https://doi.org/10.1007/978-3-031-07085-3_18

15. Kalai, Y., Lombardi, A., Vaikuntanathan, V., Wichs, D.: Boosting batch arguments and ram delegation. In: Proceedings of the 55th Annual ACM Symposium on Theory of Computing, STOC 2023, pp. 1545–1552. Association for Computing Machinery, New York (2023). https://doi.org/10.1145/3564246.3585200

16. Kalai, Y.T., Vaikuntanathan, V., Zhang, R.Y.: Somewhere statistical soundness, post-quantum security, and SNARGs. In: Nissim, K., Waters, B. (eds.) TCC 2021, Part I. LNCS, vol. 13042, pp. 330–368. Springer, Heidelberg (2021). https://doi.org/10.1007/978-3-030-90459-3_12

17. Koppula, V., Lewko, A.B., Waters, B.: Indistinguishability obfuscation for turing machines with unbounded memory. In: Servedio, R.A., Rubinfeld, R. (eds.) 47th ACM STOC, pp. 419–428. ACM Press (2015)

18. Okamoto, T., Pietrzak, K., Waters, B., Wichs, D.: New realizations of somewhere statistically binding hashing and positional accumulators. In: Iwata, T., Cheon, J.H. (eds.) ASIACRYPT 2015, Part I. LNCS, vol. 9452, pp. 121–145. Springer, Heidelberg (2015). https://doi.org/10.1007/978-3-662-48797-6_6

19. Paneth, O., Pass, R.: Incrementally verifiable computation via rate-1 batch arguments. In: 63rd FOCS, pp. 1045–1056. IEEE Computer Society Press (2022)

20. Regev, O.: On lattices, learning with errors, random linear codes, and cryptography. In: Gabow, H.N., Fagin, R. (eds.) 37th ACM STOC, pp. 84–93. ACM Press (2005)

21. Waters, B., Wu, D.J.: Batch arguments for NP and more from standard bilinear group assumptions. In: Dodis, Y., Shrimpton, T. (eds.) CRYPTO 2022, Part II. LNCS, vol. 13508, pp. 433–463. Springer, Heidelberg (2022). https://doi.org/10.1007/978-3-031-15979-4_15

Private Set Operations from Multi-query Reverse Private Membership Test

Yu Chen[1,2,3](✉) ⓘ, Min Zhang[1,2,3] ⓘ, Cong Zhang[4] ⓘ, Minglang Dong[1,2,3] ⓘ,
and Weiran Liu[5] ⓘ

[1] School of Cyber Science and Technology, Shandong University, Qingdao 266237,
China
yuchen@sdu.edu.cn, {zm_min,minglang_dong}@mail.sdu.edu.cn
[2] State Key Laboratory of Cryptology, P.O. Box 5159, Beijing 100878, China
[3] Key Laboratory of Cryptologic Technology and Information Security,
Ministry of Education, Shandong University, Qingdao 266237, China
[4] Institute for Advanced Study, BNRist, Tsinghua University, Beijing, China
zhangcong@mail.tsinghua.edu.cn
[5] Alibaba Group, Hangzhou, China
weiran.lwr@alibaba-inc.com

Abstract. Private set operations allow two parties to perform secure computation on their private sets, including intersection, union and functions of intersection/union. In this paper, we put forth a framework to perform private set operations. The technical core of our framework is the multi-query reverse private membership test (mqRPMT) protocol (Zhang et al., USENIX Security 2023). We present two constructions of mqRPMT from newly introduced cryptographic notions, one is based on commutative weak pseudorandom function (cwPRF), and the other is based on permuted oblivious pseudorandom function (pOPRF). Both cwPRF and pOPRF can be realized from the decisional Diffie-Hellman (DDH)-like assumptions in the random oracle model.

We demonstrate the practicality of our framework with implementations. By plugging our cwPRF-based mqRPMT into the framework, we obtain various PSO protocols that are superior or competitive to the state-of-the-art protocols. For intersection functionality, our protocol is faster than the most efficient one for small sets. For cardinality functionality, our protocol achieves a $2.4 - 10.5\times$ speedup and a $10.9 - 14.8\times$ reduction in communication cost. For cardinality-with-sum functionality, our protocol achieves a $28.5 - 76.3\times$ speedup and $7.4\times$ reduction in communication cost. For union functionality, our protocol is the first one that achieves strictly linear complexity, and requires the lowest concrete computation and communication costs in all settings, achieving a $2.7 - 17\times$ speedup and about $2\times$ reduction in communication cost. Furthermore, our improvement on PSU also translates to related functionality, yielding the most efficient private-ID protocol to date.

Keywords: PSO · PSU · multi-query RPMT · commutative weak PRF · permuted OPRF

ⓒ International Association for Cryptologic Research 2024
Q. Tang and V. Teague (Eds.): PKC 2024, LNCS 14603, pp. 387–416, 2024.
https://doi.org/10.1007/978-3-031-57725-3_13

1   Introduction

Consider several parties, each with a private set of items, want to perform computation on their private sets without revealing any other information to each other. Private set operation (PSO) refers to such family of interactive cryptographic protocols that fulfill this task, which take private sets as inputs and compute the desired function, delivering the result to the participants. In this work, we focus on two-party PSO protocols with semi-honest security. In what follows, we briefly review related works in terms of typical functionalities.

Private Set Intersection (PSI). PSI allows two parties, the sender and the receiver, to compute the intersection of their private sets X and Y, such that the receiver only learns $X \cap Y$ and the sender learns nothing. PSI has found numerous applications including privacy-preserving location sharing [NTL+11], private contact discovery [DRRT18], DNA testing and pattern matching [TKC07]. Due to its importance and wide applications, in the past two decades PSI has been extensively studied in a long sequence of works and has become truly practical with extremely fast implementations. The most efficient PSI protocols [KKRT16, PRTY19, CM20, GPR+21, RS21] mainly rely on symmetric-key operations, except $O(\kappa)$ public-key operations (where κ is a computational security parameter) in base OT used in the OT extension protocol. We refer to [PSZ18] for a good survey of different PSI paradigms.

Private Computing on Set Intersection (PCSI). Certain real-world application scenarios only require partial/aggregated information about the intersection. In this setting fine-grained private computation on set intersection (PCSI) is needed, such as PSI-card for intersection cardinality [HFH99, AES03, CGT12], PSI-card-sum for intersection cardinality and sum [IKN+20, GMR+21]. For general-purpose PCSI (also known as circuit-PSI) [HEK12, PSTY19], the parties learn secret shares of elements in the set intersection, which can be further fed into generic 2PC to compute $g(X \cap Y)$ for arbitrary function g.

Private Set Union (PSU). PSU allows two parties, the sender and the receiver, to compute the union of their private sets X and Y, such that the receiver only learns $X \cup Y$ and the sender learns nothing. Like PSI, PSU also has many applications in practice, such as cyber risk assessment and management [LV04], IP blacklist and vulnerability data aggregation [HLS+16], private DB supporting full join [KRTW19] and private ID [GMR+21]. Existing PSU protocols can be broadly divided into two categories based on the underlying cryptographic techniques used. The first category mainly relies on public-key techniques [KS05, Fri07, HN10, DC17], while the second category mainly relies on symmetric-key techniques [KRTW19, GMR+21, JSZ+22]. We refer to [ZCL+23] for a comprehensive survey of existing PSU protocols.

Among PSO protocols, PSI has been extensively studied. Numerous PSI protocols achieve linear complexity, and the current state-of-the-art PSI [RR22] is almost as efficient as the naive insecure hash-based protocol. In contrast, the study of PCSI and PSU is less satisfactory. In the case of PCSI, while a few protocols [PSTY19, IKN+20] achieve linear complexity, their practical performance is poor. As shown in [GMR+21], even in the simplest case of semi-honest PCSI - like PSI-card - is concretely about 20× slower and requires over 30× more communication than PSI. In the case of PSU, no protocol with linear complexity in either balanced or unbalanced setting is known for a long time being. It is until very recently, Zhang et al. [ZCL+23] make a breakthrough by proposing the first PSU with linear complexity. However, their work does not close this issue. Their concrete PSU protocols have a large constant term in computation complexity, incurring a significant efficiency gap compared with PSI: roughly 25× slower and requires at least 3× more communication than PSI.

It is somewhat surprising that different PSO protocols have significantly different efficiency. One may wonder: what is the reason for this discrepancy? Observe that PSI can be essentially viewed as multi-query private membership test (mqPMT), which has efficient realizations in both balanced and unbalanced settings. However, mqPMT generally does not imply PCSI or PSU. The reason is that mqPMT reveals information about the intersection, which should be hidden from the receiver in PCSI and PSU.

1.1 Motivation

Our motivation of this work is threefold. First, the above discussion indicates that the most efficient PSI protocols may not be easily adapted to PCSI and PSU protocols. Consequently, constructions of different PSO protocols differ vastly in the types of techniques they employ, requiring significant engineering effort and making it difficult to deploy PSO systematically. This calls for a modular approach that allows for an easier navigation in the huge design space. We are thus motivated to seek for a common principal that enables all private set operations through a unified framework. Second, given the large efficiency gap between PSI and other related protocols, we are also motivated to give efficient instantiations of the framework to narrow the gap. Last but not least, it is worth noting that the seminal PSI protocol, DH-PSI [Mea86] (related ideas were appeared in [Sha80, HFH99]), which was derived from the Diffie-Hellman key-exchange protocol, based on the decisional Diffie-Hellman (DDH) assumption, is still the most easily understood and implemented one among many PSI protocols for over four decades. Somewhat surprisingly, no PSU counterpart of DH-PSI has been discovered yet. It is curious to know whether the DDH assumption is also useful in the PSU setting. In sum, our work focus on the following questions:

Is there a central building block that enables a unified framework for all private set operations? If so, can we give efficient instantiations with optimal asymptotic complexity and good concrete efficiency? And finally, can the DDH assumption be used to construct efficient PSU protocols?

1.2 Our Contribution

We provide affirmative answers to the aforementioned questions. Our main results are summarized as below.

A Framework of PSO. We identify that multi-query reverse private membership test (mqRPMT) [ZCL+23] is actually a "Swiss Army Knife" for various private set operations. mqRPMT already implies PSI-card by itself; by coupling with OT, mqRPMT implies PSI and PSU; by additionally coupling with simple secret sharing, mqRPMT implies PSI-card-sum and PSI-card-secret-sharing, where the latter further admits general-purpose PCSI with cardinality. Therefore, mqRPMT enables a unified PSO framework, which can perform a variety of private set operations in a flexible manner.

Efficient Construction of mqRPMT. We present two generic constructions of mqRPMT. The first is based on a newly formalized cryptographic primitive called commutative weak PRF (cwPRF), while the second is based on a newly introduced secure protocol called permuted oblivious PRF (pOPRF). Both of them can be realized from DDH-like assumptions in the random oracle model, yielding incredibly simple mqRPMT constructions with linear communication and computation complexity. Note that the complexity of our PSO framework is dominated by the underlying mqRPMT. Therefore, all resulting PSO protocols inherit optimal linear complexity. Notably, the obtained PSU protocol is arguably the most simple and efficient one among existing PSU protocols.

Evaluations. We give efficient implementation of our generic framework from the cwPRF-based mqRPMT protocol. The experimental results demonstrate that all PSO protocols derived from our generic framework are superior or competitive to the state-of-the-art corresponding protocols.

1.3 Technical Overview

PSO from mqRPMT. As discussed above, mqPMT (equivalent to PSI) is generally not applicable for computing PCSI and PSU. We examine the reverse direction, i.e., whether the core protocol underlying PSU can be used for computing PSI and PCSI. We identify that the recently emerged mqRPMT protocol [ZCL+23], which is a generalization of RPMT formalized in [KRTW19], is actually a central protocol underlying all the existing PSU protocols. Roughly speaking, mqRPMT is a two-party protocol between a server holding a set Y and a client holding a vector $X = (x_1, \ldots, x_n)$. After the execution, the server learns an indication bit vector $(e_1, \ldots, e_n)$ such that $e_i = 1$ if and only if $x_i \in Y$ but without knowing x_i, while the client learns nothing. Superficially, mqRPMT is similar to mqPMT, except that it is the server but not the client learns the test results. This subtle difference turns out to be crucial. To see this, note that in mqRPMT the intersection information (i.e. x_i and e_i) is shared between two parties, while in mqPMT the intersection information is entirely known by the client. In light of this difference, mqRPMT is not only particularly suitable for functionalities that have to keep intersection private, but also retains the necessary information to compute the intersection.

More precisely, we can build a family of PSO protocols from mqRPMT in a modular fashion. PSI-card protocol is immediate since the cardinality of intersection is exactly the Hamming weight of indication vector. PSI (resp. PSU) protocol can be created by having the receiver (playing the role of server) and the sender (playing the role of client) invoke a mqRPMT protocol in the first place, then carry out n one-sided OTs with $1 - e_i$ (resp. e_i) and x_i. PSI-card-sum and PSI-card-secret-sharing protocols can be constructed by additionally coupling with OT and simple secret-sharing trick. We defer the construction details to Sect. 6.

Next, we give two generic constructions of mqRPMT. For clarity, we explicitly parameterize RPMT and PMT with two parameters n_1 and n_2, namely (n_1, n_2)-(R)PMT, where n_1 is the size of server's set Y, n_2 is the length of client's vector X, a.k.a. the number of membership test queries.

mqRPMT from cwPRF. Observe that private equality test (PEQT) protocol [PSZ14] not only can be viewed as an extreme case of mqPMT, but also can be viewed as an extreme case of mqRPMT. Under the parameterized notions, PEQT is essentially $(1, 1)$-PMT and $(1, 1)$-RPMT. We choose PEQT as the starting point of our first mqRPMT construction.

The basic idea of building $(1, 1)$-RPMT protocol amenable to extension is using *oblivious joint encoding*, by which an element can only be encoded to a codeword by two parties in a joint manner, while the process reveals nothing to the party without the element. To implement this idea, we formalize a new cryptographic primitive called commutative weak PRF (cwPRF). Let $F : K \times D \to R$ be a family of weak PRF, where $R \subseteq D$. F is commutative if $F_{k_1}(F_{k_2}(x)) = F_{k_2}(F_{k_1}(x))$ for any $k_1, k_2 \in K$ and any $x \in D$. In other words, the two composite functions $F_{k_1} \circ F_{k_2}$ and $F_{k_2} \circ F_{k_1}$ are essentially the same function, denoted by $\hat{F}$.

Now we are ready to describe the construction of $(1, 1)$-RPMT from cwPRF. The server P_1 holding y and the client P_2 holding x can conduct PEQT functionality via the following steps: (1) P_1 and P_2 generate cwPRF key k_1 and k_2 respectively, and map their items to domain D of F using a common cryptographic hash function H, which will be modeled as a random oracle; (2) P_1 computes and sends $F_{k_1}(\mathsf{H}(y))$ to P_2; (3) P_2 computes and sends $F_{k_2}(\mathsf{H}(x))$ and $F_{k_2}(F_{k_1}(\mathsf{H}(y)))$ to P_1; (4) P_1 then learns the test result by comparing $F_{k_1}(F_{k_2}(\mathsf{H}(x))) =? F_{k_2}(F_{k_1}(\mathsf{H}(y)))$. The commutative property of F ensures the correctness. The weak pseudorandomness of F guarantees that P_2 learns nothing and P_1 learns nothing more than the test result. In the above construction, $F_{k_2}(F_{k_1}(\mathsf{H}(\cdot))) = F_{k_1}(F_{k_2}(\mathsf{H}(\cdot))) = \hat{F}_k(\mathsf{H}(\cdot))$ serves as a pseudorandom encoding function in the joint view, while $F_{k_1}(\mathsf{H}(\cdot))$ and $F_{k_2}(\mathsf{H}(\cdot))$ serve as a partial encoding function in the individual views of the server and client respectively.

We then extend the above $(1, 1)$-RPMT protocol to $(n_1, 1)$-RPMT. Note that naive repetition by sending back $F_{k_2}(F_{k_1}(\mathsf{H}(y_i)))$ for each $y_i \in Y$ in the same order of the server's first move message $F_{k_1}(\mathsf{H}(y_i))$ does not lead to a secure $(n_1, 1)$-RPMT. This is because $\{\hat{F}_k(\mathsf{H}(y_i))\}_{i \in [n_1]}$ constitutes an order-preserving pseudorandom encoding of $(y_1, \ldots, y_{n_1})$, and as a consequence, the server will learn the exact value of x if $x \in Y$. The idea to perform the membership test in an oblivious manner is making the pseudorandom encoding of $(y_1, \ldots, y_{n_1})$ independent of the order known by the server. A straightforward approach is to shuffle $\{\hat{F}_k(\mathsf{H}(y_i))\}$. This yields a $(n_1, 1)$-RPMT protocol from cwPRF, which can be batched to a full-fledged (n_1, n_2)-RPMT protocol by reusing the encoding key k_2. A simple calculation shows that for a (n_1, n_2)-RPMT protocol, the computation cost is $(n_1 + n_2)$ mappings, $(2n_1 + n_2)$ evaluations of F, n_2 lookups and one shuffling, and the communication cost is $(2n_1 + n_2)$ elements in the range of F. The resulting mqRPMT protocol is optimal in the sense that both computation and communication complexity are linear to the set size. To further reduce the communication cost, we can insert $\{\hat{F}(\mathsf{H}(y_i))\}$ into an order-hiding data structure such as a Bloom filter [Blo70] instead of shuffling them.

In Sect. 4.2, we show that cwPRF can be realized from DDH-like assumptions. Combining this with the above results, DDH implies all PSO protocols. Remarkably, it strikes back with an incredibly simple PSU protocol, once again demonstrating that the DDH assumption is truly a golden mine in cryptography.

mqRPMT from permuted OPRF. We choose $(n, 1)$-RPMT as the starting point of our second mqRPMT construction. The idea is *oblivious permuted encoding*, in which only one party say P_2 is able to encode, and the other party say P_1 learns the codewords of its elements $(y_1, \ldots, y_n)$ in a permuted order, while both parties learn nothing more. A tempting approach to implement this idea is using multi-point OPRF that underlies many PSI protocols [PRTY19, CM20]. More precisely, having P_1 (acts as the OPRF's client) and P_2 (acts as the OPRF's server) engage in an OPRF protocol. Eventually, P_1 obtains PRF values of $(y_1, \ldots, y_n)$ as encodings, and P_2 obtains a PRF key k. However, OPRF does not readily enable oblivious permuted encoding, because the standard OPRF functionality always gives the PRF values with the same order of inputs. To remedy this issue, we introduce a new cryptographic protocol called permuted OPRF (pOPRF). pOPRF can be viewed as a generalization of OPRF. The difference is that the server additionally obtains a random permutation π over $[n]$ besides PRF key k, while the client obtains PRF values in a permuted order as per π. pOPRF immediately implies a $(n, 1)$-RPMT protocol: The server P_1 with $Y = (y_1, \ldots, y_n)$ (acts as the pOPRF's client) and the client P_2 with $X = \{x\}$ (acts as the pOPRF's server) first engage in a pOPRF protocol. As a result, P_1 obtains $\{F_k(y_{\pi(i)})\}_{i \in [n]}$, and P_2 obtains a PRF key k and a permutation π over $[n]$. P_2 then computes and sends $F_k(x)$ to the server as an RPMT query for x. Finally, P_1 learns if $x \in Y$ by testing whether $F_k(x) \in \{F_k(y_{\pi(i)})\}_{i \in [n]}$, but learns nothing more since its received PRF values are of permuted order. At a high level, $F_k(\cdot)$ serves as an encoding function in mqRPMT-client's view, while $F_k(\pi(\cdot))$ serves as a permuted pseudorandom encoding function in mqRPMT-server's view. Extending the above $(n, 1)$-RPMT to full-fledged (n_1, n_2)-RPMT is straightforward by having the client reuse k and send $\{F_k(x_i)\}_{i \in [n_2]}$ as RPMT queries.

Given the above, it remains to investigate how to build pOPRF. Recall that a common approach to build OPRF is "mask-then-unmask", we choose OPRF along this line as the starting point. The rough idea is exploiting the input homomorphism to mask inputs[1], then unmask the outputs. If the mask procedure is

---

[1] Standard pseudorandomness denies input homomorphism. Rigorously speaking, we utilize the homomorphism over intermediate input.

different per input, then different unmask procedure must be carried out accordingly. For this reason, OPRF protocols of this case cannot be easily adapted to pOPRF, since the receiver is unable to perform the unmask procedure over permuted masked outputs correctly, namely, to recover outputs in permuted order. The above analysis indicates us that if the masking procedure can be done via a universal manner, then the client might be able to unmask the permuted masked outputs correctly. Observe that the simplest way to perform unified masking is to apply a weak pseudorandom function F_s to the intermediate input $H(x)$, where H is a cryptographic hash function that maps input x to the domain of F_s. To enable efficient unmasking, we further require that F_s is a permutation and commutative with respect to F_k. This yields a simple pOPRF construction from commutative weak pseudorandom permutation. More precisely, to build pOPRF, the server picks a random PRP key k for F, while the client with input $X = (x_1, \ldots, x_n)$ picks a random PRP key s for F. The client then sends $\{F_s(H(x_i))\}_{i \in [n]}$ to the server. Upon receiving the masked intermediate inputs, the server applies F_k to them, then sends the results in permuted order, a.k.a. $\{F_k(F_s(H(x_{\pi(i)})))\}_{i \in [n]}$. Finally, the client applies F_s^{-1} to the permuted masked outputs, and will obtain $\{F_k(H(x_{\pi(i)}))\}_{i \in [n]}$ by the commutative property.

Note that many efficient OPRF constructions [PRTY19, CM20, RS21] seem not amenable to pOPRF due to the lack of nice algebra structures. This somehow explains the efficiency gap between the state-of-the-art PSI and PCSI/PSU.

1.4   Related Works

We review previous PSI-card, PSI-card-sum and PSU protocols that are relevant to our work. Ion et al. [IKN+20] showed how to transform single-point OPRF-based [PSZ14, KKRT16], garbled Bloom filter-based [DCW13, RR17], and DDH-based [HFH99] PSI protocols into ones for computing PSI-card-sum by leveraging additively homomorphic encryption (AHE). However, their conversions are inefficient due to the usage of AHE, and as noted by the authors, detailed conversions to each category of protocols differ significantly, especially in the way of making use of the underlying AHE. In contrast, we distill Sigma-mqPMT from a broad class of PSI protocols, then show how to tweak it to mqRPMT* in a generic and black-box manner, without relying on any additional cryptographic tools. Our abstraction of Sigma-mqPMT is more broadly applicable, and our conversion works at a higher level. Miao et al. [MPR+20] put forward shuffled distributed oblivious PRF as a central tool to build PSI-card-sum with malicious security. Compared to shuffled distributed OPRF, our notion of permuted OPRF is much simpler and should be best viewed as a useful extension of standard OPRF. The conceptual simplicity lends it to be easily built from commutative weak pseudorandom permutation and find more potential applications. For example, permuted OPRF immediately implies permuted matrix private equality test, which is a key tool in building FHE-based PSU [TCLZ23]. Davidson and Cid [DC17] proposed a framework for constructing PSI, PSU, and PSI-card. Their protocols have linear complexity, but both the computation and communication complexity additionally rely on the statistical security parameter λ (a typical concrete choice is 40), resulting in low performance in practice. Kolesnikov et al. [KRTW19] proposed the notion of reverse private membership test (RPMT), then used it to build a PSU protocol whose performance is much better than [DC17]. Garimella et al. [GMR+21] proposed a framework for all private set operations from permuted characteristic, which could be viewed as a variant of RPMT. Nevertheless, the oblivious shuffle in permuted characteristic functionality is not necessary for PSO, but seems unavoidable due to the use of oblivious switching networks, which in turn incurs superlinear complexity to permuted characteristic protocol and all the enabling PSO protocols. Besides, we note that the PSI-card-sum functionality defined in [GMR+21] differs from the original functionality defined in [IKN+20]. The distinction is that in the original functionality of PSI-card-sum, both parties are given the cardinality of intersection, and the party initially holding values is also given the intersection sum, while in the functionality described in [GMR+21], the party without holding values is given the cardinality and sum of the intersection. To distinguish this subtle difference, we refer to the functionality presented in [GMR+21] as reverse PSI-card-sum.

Very recently, Zhang et al. [ZCL+23] extended the notion of RPMT [KRTW19] to multi-query RPMT (mqRPMT), and proposed a generic construction from oblivious key-value store (OKVS) [GPR+21], set-membership encryption and oblivious vector decryption-then-test protocol. By instantiating their generic construction from symmetric-key and public-key encryption respectively, they obtained two concrete mqRPMT protocols with linear complexity. However, their two mqRPMT protocols have a large multiplicative constant (the statistical security parameter) in computation complexity, and so is the resulting PSU protocol. Besides, as noted by the authors, their more efficient PKE-based mqRPMT protocol is leaky, failing to meet the standard security. Compared with their work, our generic construction of mqRPMT is much simpler, and our two concrete instantiations meet the standard definition yet achieve strict linear complexity.[2] Moreover, we identify mqRPMT as a central building block for a family of private set operations, while their focus is limited to PSU.

Other Related Works. PSO are primarily designed for the balanced scenario, where the sizes of two sets are approximately the same. Recently, a line of research has started considering the unbalanced scenario, where one set is much larger than the other. Hereafter, let the sizes of small and large sets be m and n, respectively. [CLR17,CHLR18,CMdG+21] showed how to leverage FHE to build PSI protocols suitable for unbalanced scenario with communication complexity $O(m \log n)$, which is linear to the size of small set but logarithmic to the size of large set. A body of follow-up works achieved the same complexity for other functionalities. [CHLR18] proposed circuit-PSI, PSI-card and PSI-card-sum protocols based on generic 2PC technique, and then [SJ23,WY23] provided the associated implementations. [TCLZ23] created the first unbalanced PSU

---

[2] In the context of PSO, strict linear complexity means that the complexity grows linearly only to the sets sizes.

protocol by tweaking the technique due to [CLR17]. Another line of research extended PSO to multi-party settings: [KMP+17,NTY21] for PSI, [CDGB22] for PSI-card(-sum), and [LG23] for PSU.

1.5 Roadmap

In Sect. 2 we recall the standard definitions of MPC and PSO. In Sect. 3 we introduce the ingredients we use to build the PSO framework. In Sect. 4 and Sect. 5 we give two generic constructions of mqRPMT from newly formalized cwPRF and newly introduced permuted OPRF, respectively. In Sect. 6 we show how to build the PSO framework from mqRPMT, and also present a modular construction of private-ID from distributed OPRF and PSU. In Sect. 7 we provide a performance analysis of our implementation, and compare our experimental results to the related state-of-the-art protocols. Due to space limit, we defer all the security proofs and additional results to the full version of this paper https://eprint.iacr.org/2022/652.

2 Preliminaries

Notation. We use κ and λ to denote the computational and statistical parameter respectively. Let $\mathbb{Z}_n$ be the set $\{0, 1, \ldots, n-1\}$, $\mathbb{Z}_n^* = \{x \in \mathbb{Z}_n \mid \gcd(x, n) = 1\}$. We use $[n]$ to denote the set $\{1, \ldots, n\}$, and use $\mathsf{Perm}[n]$ to denote all the permutations over the set $\{1, \ldots, n\}$. We assume that every set X has a default order (e.g. lexicographical order), and write it as $X = \{x_1, \ldots, x_n\}$. For a set X, we use $|X|$ to denote its size and use $x \xleftarrow{\text{R}} X$ to denote sampling x uniformly at random from X. We use $(x_1, \ldots, x_n)$ to denote a vector, and its i-th element is x_i. A function is negligible in κ, written $\mathsf{negl}(\kappa)$, if it vanishes faster than the inverse of any polynomial in κ. A probabilistic polynomial time (PPT) algorithm is a randomized algorithm that runs in polynomial time.

2.1 MPC in the Semi-honest Model

We use the standard notion of security in the presence of semi-honest adversaries. Let Π be a two-party protocol for computing the function $f(x_1, x_2)$, where party P_i has input x_i, and $\mathsf{output}(x_1, x_2)$ be the output of both parties in the protocol. For each party P_i where $i \in \{1, 2\}$, let $\mathsf{View}_{P_i}(x_1, x_2)$ denote the view of party P_i during an honest execution of Π on inputs x_1 and x_2, which consists of P_i's input, random tape, and all messages P_i received in the protocol.

Definition 1. *Two-party protocol Π securely realizes f in the presence of semi-honest adversaries if there exists a simulator Sim such that for all inputs x_1, x_2 and all $i \in \{1, 2\}$:*

$$\{\, \mathit{View}_{P_i}(x_1, x_2), \mathsf{output}(x_1, x_2)\} \approx_c \{\mathsf{Sim}(i, x_i, f(x_1, x_2)), f(x_1, x_2)\}$$

Roughly speaking, a protocol is secure if P_i with x_i learns no more information other than $f(x_1, x_2)$ and x_i.

2.2 Private Set Operation

PSO is a special case of secure two-party computation. We call the two parties engaging in PSO the *sender* and the *receiver*. The sender holds a set X of size n_1, and the receiver holds a set Y of size n_2 (we set $n_1 = n_2 = n$ in the balanced setting). Figure 1 formally defines the ideal functionality for PSO that computes the intersection, union, cardinality, intersection sum with cardinality and intersection secret-sharing with cardinality.

Parameters: The receiver P_1's input size n_1 and the sender P_2's input size n_2.
Inputs: The receiver P_1 inputs a set of elements $Y = \{y_1, \ldots, y_{n_1}\}$ where $y_i \in \{0,1\}^\ell$. The sender P_2 inputs a set of elements $X = \{x_1, \ldots, x_{n_2}\}$ where $x_i \in \{0,1\}^\ell$ and possibly a set of values $V = \{v_1, \ldots, v_{n_2}\}$ where $v_i \in \mathbb{Z}_p$ for some integer modular p.
Output:

- **intersection:** The receiver P_1 gets $X \cap Y$.
- **union:** The receiver P_1 gets $X \cup Y$.
- **union*:** The receiver P_1 gets $X \cup Y$. The sender P_2 gets $|X \cap Y|$.
- **card:** The receiver P_1 gets $|X \cap Y|$.
- **card-sum:** The receiver P_1 gets $|X \cap Y|$. The sender P_2 gets $|X \cap Y|$ and $S = \sum_{i: x_i \in Y} v_i$.
- **card-secret-sharing:** The receiver P_1 gets $|X \cap Y|$ and $\{z_i^1\}_{i \in [n_2]}$. The sender P_2 gets $\{z_i^2\}_{i \in [n_2]}$. For each (z_i^1, z_i^2), $z_i^1 \oplus z_i^2 = x_i$ if $x_i \in Y$ and $z_i^1 \oplus z_i^2 = 0$ otherwise.

Fig. 1. Ideal functionality $\mathcal{F}_{\mathsf{PSO}}$ for PSO

In this work, we restrict ourselves to two-party PSO with semi-honest security in the balanced setting.

3 Protocol Building Blocks

3.1 Oblivious Transfer

Oblivious Transfer (OT) [Rab05] is a central cryptographic primitive in the area of secure computation. In the most common 1-out-of-2 OT, a sender with two input strings (m_0, m_1) interacts with a receiver with an input choice bit $b \in \{0, 1\}$, and finally the receiver only learns m_b while the sender learns nothing. In some cases, it suffices to use a "one-sided" version of OT, which conditionally transfers the only item of the sender or nothing to the receiver depending on the choice bit. Though expensive public-key operations are unavoidable for a single OT, a powerful technique called OT extension [IKNP03,KK13,ALSZ15] allows one to carry out n OTs by only performing $O(\kappa)$ public-key operations and $O(n)$ fast symmetric-key operations.

3.2 Multi-query Reverse Private Membership Test

Multi-query reverse private membership test (mqRPMT) [ZCL+23] is a protocol where the client with input vector $(x_1, \ldots, x_n)$ interacts with a server holding a set Y. As a result, the server learns only a bit vector $(e_1, \ldots, e_n)$ in which e_i indicates that whether $x_i \in Y$. Figure 2 formally defines the ideal functionality for mqRPMT. We also consider a relaxed version of mqRPMT called mqRPMT*, in which the client is also given $|X \cap Y|$.

Parameters: The server P_1's set size n_1 and number of RPMT queries n_2 by the client P_2.

Inputs: The server P_1 inputs a set $Y = (y_1, \ldots, y_{n_1})$, where $y_i \in \{0,1\}^\ell$. The client P_2 inputs a set $X = (x_1, \ldots, x_{n_2})$ (should be interpreted as a vector), where $x_i \in \{0,1\}^\ell$.

Output: The server P_1 gets a vector $\vec{e} = (e_1, \ldots, e_{n_2}) \in \{0,1\}^{n_2}$, where $e_i = 1$ if $x_i \in Y$ and $e_i = 0$ otherwise. The client P_2 gets nothing.

Fig. 2. Ideal functionality $\mathcal{F}_{\mathsf{mqRPMT}}$ for multi-query RPMT

4 The First Generic Construction of mqRPMT

4.1 Definition of Commutative Weak PRF

We first formally define two standard properties for keyed functions.

Composable. For a family of keyed functions $F : K \times D \to R$, F is 2-composable if $R \subseteq D$, namely, for any $k_1, k_2 \in K$, the function $F_{k_1}(F_{k_2}(\cdot))$ is well-defined. In this work, we are interested in a special case namely $R = D$.

Commutative. For a family of composable keyed functions, we say it is commutative if: $\forall k_1, k_2 \in K, \forall x \in D : F_{k_1}(F_{k_2}(x)) = F_{k_2}(F_{k_1}(x))$.

It is easy to see that the standard pseudorandomness denies commutative property. Consider the following attack against the standard pseudorandomness of F_k as below: the adversary $\mathcal{A}$ picks $k' \xleftarrow{\text{R}} K$, $x \xleftarrow{\text{R}} D$, and then queries the real-or-random oracle at point $F_{k'}(x)$ and point x respectively, receiving back responses y' and y. $\mathcal{A}$ then outputs '1' iff $F_{k'}(y) = y'$. Clearly, $\mathcal{A}$ breaks the pseudorandomness with advantage $1/2$. Provided commutative property exists, the best security we can expect is weak pseudorandomness. Looking ahead, weak pseudorandomness and commutative property may co-exist based on some well-studied assumptions.

Definition 2 (Commutative Weak PRF). *Let F be a family of keyed functions $K \times D \to D$. F is called commutative weak PRF if it satisfies weak pseudorandomness and commutative property simultaneously. If F is a permutation, we say F is a commutative weak pseudorandom permutation (cwPRP).*

Remark 1 (cwPRF vs. Commutative Encryption). We note that our notion of cwPRF is similar to but strictly weaker than a previous notion called commutative encryption [AES03]. The difference is that cwPRF neither requires F_k be a permutation nor F_k^{-1} be efficiently computable.

4.2 Construction of Commutative Weak PRF

We observe that the classic weak PRF based on the DDH assumption already satisfies commutative property. This gives us a simple cwPRF construction from the DDH-like assumption. It is still interesting to know if cwPRF can be built from other assumptions. Note that cwPRF naturally yields a non-interactive key exchange (NIKE) protocol, while the recent result of Guo et al. [GKRS22] indicated that it would be difficult to construct NIKE from lattice-based assumptions. Therefore, giving lattice-based cwPRF or proving impossibility will lead to progress on some other well-studied questions in cryptography.

4.3 mqRPMT from Commutative Weak PRF

In Fig. 3, we show how to build mqRPMT from cwPRF $F : K \times D \to D$ and cryptographic hash function $H : \{0,1\}^\ell \to D$.

Parameters: The server P_1's set size n_1 and the client P_2's set size n_2, cwPRF $F : K \times D \to D$, and hash function $H : \{0,1\}^\ell \to D$.

Inputs: The server P_1 inputs a set $Y = \{y_1, \ldots, y_{n_1}\}$, where $y_i \in \{0,1\}^\ell$. The client P_2 inputs a set $X = \{x_1, \ldots, x_{n_2}\}$ (should be interpreted as a vector), where $x_i \in \{0,1\}^\ell$.

Protocol:

1. P_1 picks $k_1 \xleftarrow{R} K$, then computes and sends $\{F_{k_1}(H(y_i))\}_{i \in [n_1]}$ to P_2.

2. P_2 picks $k_2 \xleftarrow{R} K$, then:
   (a) computes and sends $\{F_{k_2}(H(x_i)))\}_{i \in [n_2]}$ to P_1.
   (b) computes $\{F_{k_2}(F_{k_1}(H(y_i)))\}_{i \in [n_1]}$, picks a random permutation π over $[n_1]$, then sends $\{F_{k_2}(F_{k_1}(H(y_{\pi(i)})))\}_{i \in [n_1]}$ to P_1. Instead of explicit shuffling, an alternative choice is inserting $\{F_{k_2}(F_{k_1}(H(y_i)))\}_{i \in [n_1]}$ to a Bloom filter and then sending the filter to P_1. We slightly abuse the notation, and still use Ω to denote the Bloom filter.

3. P_1 computes $\{F_{k_1}(F_{k_2}(H(x_i)))\}_{i \in [n_2]}$, sets $e_i = 1$ iff $F_{k_1}(F_{k_2}(H(x_i))) \in \Omega$.

Fig. 3. Multi-query RPMT from commutative weak PRF

Correctness. The protocol is correct except the event E that $F_{k_1}(F_{k_2}(H(x))) = F_{k_1}(F_{k_2}(H(y)))$ for some $x \neq y$ occurs. In what follows, we fix a tuple (x, y) such that $x \neq y$. Let E_0 be the event $H(x) = H(y)$. By the collision resistance of H, we have $\Pr[E_0] = 2^{-\kappa}$. Let E_1 be the event that $H(x) \neq H(y)$ but $F_{k_1}(F_{k_2}(H(x))) = $

$F_{k_1}(F_{k_2}(\mathsf{H}(y)))$, which can further be divided into sub-cases E_{10}-$F_{k_2}(\mathsf{H}(x)) = F_{k_2}(\mathsf{H}(y))$ and E_{11}-$F_{k_2}(\mathsf{H}(x)) \neq F_{k_2}(\mathsf{H}(y)) \wedge F_{k_1}(F_{k_2}(\mathsf{H}(x))) = F_{k_1}(F_{k_2}(\mathsf{H}(y)))$. By the weak pseudorandomness of F, we have $\Pr[E_{10}] = (1 - \Pr[E_0]) \cdot 1/|D|$, and $\Pr[E_{11}] = (1 - \Pr[E_0]) \cdot (1 - 1/|D|) \cdot 1/|D|$. If $|D| = \omega(\kappa)$, then both $\Pr[E_0]$, $\Pr[E_{10}]$ and $\Pr[E_{11}]$ are negligible in κ. Therefore, by union bound we have $\Pr[E] \leq n_1 n_2 \cdot (\Pr[E_0] + \Pr[E_{10}] + \Pr[E_{11}]) = \mathsf{negl}(\kappa)$.

Theorem 1. *The mqRPMT protocol described in Fig. 3 is secure in the semi-honest model assuming* H *is a random oracle and* F *is a family of cwPRFs.*

Complexity Analysis. We now analyze the complexity of the above (n_1, n_2)-mqRPMT protocol. Simple calculation shows that the total computation cost is $(n_1 + n_2)$ hashings, $(2n_1 + 2n_2)$ evaluations of cwPRF F, n_2 lookups whose complexity is $O(1)$, and one shuffling whose complexity is $O(n_1)$, while the total communication cost is $(2n_1 + n_2)$ elements in range D. In summary, both the computation and communication complexity are strictly linear in set sizes.

Optimization. The protocol can be further improved by inserting the elements $\{F_{k_2}(F_{k_1}(\mathsf{H}(y_i)))\}_{i \in [n_1]}$ to a Bloom filter instead of explicitly shuffling them in the last move. In this way, the length of last message can be reduced from to n_1 group elements to $1.44\lambda \cdot n_1$ bits (with false positive probability $2^{-\lambda}$), where λ is the statistical security parameter and the typical choice is 40.

It is worth to highlight that our usage of Bloom filter is novel here since we additionally exploit its order-hiding property to ensure security[3]. To the best of knowledge, Bloom filter merely serves as a space-efficient data structure in previous works [KLS+17, RA18] to reduce communication cost.

5 The Second Generic Construction of mqRPMT

5.1 Definition of Permuted OPRF

An oblivious pseudorandom function (OPRF) [FIPR05] is a two-party protocol in which the server learns (or chooses) a PRF key k and the client learns $F_k(x_1), \ldots, F_k(x_n)$, where F is a pseudorandom function (PRF) and $(x_1, \ldots, x_n)$ are the client's inputs. Nothing about the client's inputs is revealed to the server and nothing more about the key k is revealed to the client.

We consider an extension of OPRF called permuted OPRF (pOPRF). Roughly speaking, the server additionally picks a random permutation π over $[n]$, and the client learns its PRF values in permuted order, namely, $y_i = F_k(x_{\pi(i)})$. Figure 4 formally defines the ideal functionality for pOPRF.

---

[3] Formally, order-hiding property means that the data structure does not reveal the adding order of elements. Recall that an empty Bloom filter is a bit array of m bits (all set to 0), and adding an element x is done by setting the bits at positions $\{h_1(x), \ldots, h_k(x)\}$. to be 1, where $\{h_i\}_{i=1}^k$ are k distinct hash functions. Clearly, Bloom filter satisfies order-hiding property since the resulting Bloom filter is independent of the adding order. We also stress that the choice of Bloom filter is not arbitrary here, cause other filters such as Cuckoo filter and Vacuum filter do not satisfy order-hiding property.

Parameters: Number of OPRF queries n.
Inputs: The server P_1 inputs nothing. The client P_2 inputs a set $X = (x_1, \ldots, x_n)$, where $x_i \in \{0,1\}^\ell$.
Output: The server P_1 gets a random PRF key k and a random permutation π over $[n]$. The client P_2 gets $y_i = F_k(x_{\pi(i)})$.

Fig. 4. Ideal functionality $\mathcal{F}_{\mathsf{pOPRF}}$ for permuted OPRF

5.2   Construction of Permuted OPRF

As we sketched in the introduction part, we can create a permuted OPRF from cwPRP F with the help of random oracle. At a high level, the universal masking procedure is done by applying a weak PRF $F_s(\cdot)$ to $\mathsf{H}(x)$, and the unmasking process is enabled by the commutative property of F and the fact that $F_s(\cdot)$ is an efficiently invertible permutation. We depict the construction in Fig. 5.

$$F : K \times D \to D, \mathsf{H} : \{0,1\}^\ell \to D$$

P_1 (server)
$$$P_2$ (client)
$$$X = (x_1, \ldots, x_n)$

$$\xleftarrow{\{F_s(\mathsf{H}(x_i))\}_{i\in[n]}}$$
$$$s \xleftarrow{\mathrm{R}} K$

$k \xleftarrow{\mathrm{R}} K, \pi \xleftarrow{\mathrm{R}} [n]$ $\quad\xrightarrow{\{F_k(F_s(\mathsf{H}(x_{\pi(i)})))\}_{i\in[n]}}\quad$ $F_k(\mathsf{H}(x_{\pi(i)})) \leftarrow F_s^{-1}(F_k(F_s(\mathsf{H}(x_{\pi(i)}))))$

Fig. 5. Permuted OPRF from cwPRP

Theorem 2. *The above permuted OPRF protocol is secure in the semi-honest model assuming* H *is a random oracle and* F *is a family of cwPRPs.*

5.3   mqRPMT from Permuted OPRF

In Fig. 6, we show how to build mqRPMT from permuted OPRF for $F : K \times D \to R$. For simplicity, we assume that $\{0,1\}^\ell \subseteq D$. Otherwise, we can always map $\{0,1\}^\ell$ to D using a collision resistant hash function.

Parameters: The server P_1's set size n_1 and the client P_2's set size n_2, a permuted OPRF for $F : K \times D \to R$.
Inputs: The server P_1 inputs a set $Y = \{y_1, \ldots, y_{n_1}\}$, where $y_i \in \{0,1\}^\ell$. The client P_2 inputs a set $X = \{x_1, \ldots, x_{n_2}\}$, where $x_i \in \{0,1\}^\ell$.
Protocol:

1. P_1 with inputs $Y = \{y_1, \ldots, y_{n_1}\}$ and P_2 engage in a permuted OPRF protocol. P_1 acts as the pOPRF's client, while P_2 acts as the pOPRF's server. At the end of the protocol, P_1 obtains $\{F_k(y_{\pi(i)})\}_{i \in [n_1]}$, P_2 obtains a PRF key k and a random permutation π over $[n_1]$.
2. P_2 computes and sends $(F_k(x_1), \ldots, F_k(x_{n_2}))$ to P_1.
3. P_1 sets $e_i = 1$ iff $F_k(x_i) \in \{F_k(y_{\pi(i)})\}_{i \in [n_1]}$.

Fig. 6. mqRPMT from permuted OPRF

Correctness. The above protocol is correct except the event $E = \vee_{i,j} E_{ij}$ occurs, where E_{ij} denotes $F_k(x_i) = F_k(y_j)$ but $x_i \neq y_j$. By pseudorandomness of F, we have $\Pr[E_{ij}] = 2^{-\ell}$. Apply the union bound, we have $\Pr[E] \leq n_1 n_2 \cdot \Pr[E_{ij}] = n_1 n_2 / 2^\ell = \mathsf{negl}(\lambda)$.

Theorem 3. *The above mqRPMT protocol described in Fig. 6 is secure in the semi-honest model assuming the security of permuted OPRF.*

Performance Analysis. We now analyze the performance the above (n_1, n_2)-mqRPMT protocol based on the cwPRP-based permuted OPRF. Simple calculation shows that the total computation cost is $(n_1 + n_2)$ hashings, $2n_1 + n_2$ evaluations, n_2 inversions, n_2 lookups whose complexity is $O(1)$, and one shuffling whose complexity is $O(n_1)$, while the total communication cost is $(2n_1 + n_2)$ group elements in range D. In summary, both the computation and communication complexities are strictly linear in set sizes.

Comparison of the Two Constructions of mqRPMT. We have presented two generic constructions of mqRPMT, the first is from cwPRF, while the second is from pOPRF. We summarize their differences as below.

- cwPRF-based construction admits fast implementation from the NIKE protocol called X25519 based on Curve25519 (since X25519 implies a cwPRF), and can further utilize the Bloom filter to reduce communication cost as well as improve efficiency.
- Compared with the cwPRF-based construction, the pOPRF-based construction does not admit fast implementation from X25519 anymore (since X25519 does not imply a cwPRP and thus further a pOPRF), and the Bloom filter optimization is not applicable (since the set is already fixed in pOPRF phase). Nevertheless, the pOPRF-based mqRPMT construction can be viewed as a counterpart of OPRF-based mqPMT construction, and thus is more of theoretical interest. So far, we only know how to build pOPRF based on

assumptions with nice algebra structure, but not from efficient symmetric-key primitives. This somehow explains the efficiency gap between mqPMT and mqRPMT.

6 Applications of mqRPMT

6.1 PSO Framework from mqRPMT

In Fig. 7, we show how to build a PSO framework centering around mqRPMT.

Parameters: The receiver P_1's set size n_1 and the client P_2's set size n_2.
Inputs: The receiver P_1 inputs a set $Y = \{y_1, \ldots, y_{n_1}\}$, where $y_i \in \{0,1\}^\ell$. The sender P_2 inputs a set $X = \{x_1, \ldots, x_{n_2}\}$ and $V = \{v_1, \ldots, v_{n_2}\}$, where $x_i \in \{0,1\}^\ell$ and $v_i \in \mathbb{Z}_p$. Let q be a big integer greater than $n_2 \cdot p$.
Protocol:

0. P_2 shuffles the set $\{x_1, \ldots, x_{n_2}\}$ and $\{v_1, \ldots, v_{n_2}\}$ using the same random permutation over $[n_2]$. For simplicity, we still use the original notation to denote the resulting vectors after permutation.

1. P_1 (playing the role of server) with Y and P_2 (playing the role of client) with $X = \{x_1, \ldots, x_{n_2}\}$ invoke $\mathcal{F}_{\mathsf{mqRPMT}}$. P_1 obtains an indication bit vector $\vec{e} = (e_1, \ldots, e_{n_2})$. P_2 obtains nothing.
   - **cardinality:** P_1 learns the cardinality by calculating the Hamming weight of $\vec{e}$.

2. P_1 and P_2 invoke n_2 instances of OT via $\mathcal{F}_{\mathsf{OT}}$. P_1 uses $\vec{e}$ as the choice bits.
   - **intersection:** P_1 holding e_i and P_2 holding $(\bot, x_i)$ invoke one-sided OT n_2 times. P_1 learns $\{x_i \mid e_i = 1\}_{i \in [n_2]} = X \cap Y$.
   - **union:** P_1 holding e_i and P_2 holding $(x_i, \bot)$ invoke one-sided OT n_2 times. P_1 learns $\{x_i \mid e_i = 0\}_{i \in [n_2]} = X \backslash Y$, and outputs $\{X \backslash Y\} \cup Y = X \cup Y$.
   - **card-sum:** P_2 randomly picks $r_i \in \mathbb{Z}_q$ and computes $r' = \sum_{i=1}^{n_2} r_i \bmod q$. Subsequently, P_1 holding e_i and P_2 holding $(r_i, r_i + v_i)$ invoke 1-out-of-2 OT n_2 times. P_1 learns $S' = \sum_{i=1}^{n_2} r_i + e_i \cdot v_i \bmod q$, then sends S' and the Hamming weight of $\vec{e}$ to P_2. P_2 computes $S = (S' - r') \bmod q$.
   - **card-secret-sharing:** P_2 randomly picks $r_i \in \{0,1\}^\ell$. Subsequently, P_1 holding e_i and P_2 holding $(r_i, r_i \oplus x_i)$ invoke 1-out-of-2 OT n_2 times. P_1 learns $\{z_i\}_{i \in [n_2]}$, and thus $\{(z_i, r_i \oplus x_i)\}_{e_i=1}$ constitutes the shares of intersection values.

Fig. 7. PSO from mqRPMT

We prove the security of the above PSO framework by the case of PSU. The security proof of other functionality is similar.

Theorem 4. *The PSU derived from the above framework is semi-honest secure by assuming the semi-honest security of mqRPMT and OT.*

In what follows, we compare the protocols derived from our framework to existing protocols with focus on conceptual differences, and defer the performance comparisons to Sect. 7.

We first compare our PSU protocol to prior PSU protocols. [KS05, Fri07, DC17] proposed the first three PSU protocols from public-key techniques, with the complexity gradually dropping from quadratic to linear. Later, [KRTW19, GMR+21, JSZ+22] proposed three PSU protocols from symmetric-key techniques. Despite their protocols achieve much better performance than previous ones based on public-key techniques, all of them require superlinear complexity. Recently, Zhang et al. [ZCL+23] created a more efficient PSU protocol with linear complexity. Both our protocol and their protocol are derived from the same core protocol—mqRPMT, but with different instantiations. Our concrete mqRPMT protocols are much simpler and efficient, yielding the first PSU protocols with strict linear complexity.

We then discuss the relationship between our PSI-card protocol and prior related protocols. Huberman et al. [HFH99] proposed the first PSI-card protocol but did not provided security proof. Agrawal et al. [AES03] explained and proved the classic protocol via the notion of "commutative encryption". Later, De Cristofaro et al. [CGT12] gave a close variant of the classic protocol. Our PSI-card protocol is generically derived from the more abstract mqRPMT, which in turn can be built from cwPRF or pOPRF. By instantiating the underlying cwPRF and pOPRF from the DDH assumption, we recover the PSI-card protocols in [HFH99, CGT12] respectively. In a nutshell, our generic mqRPMT-based PSI-card construction not only encompasses existing concrete protocols at a high level, but also readily profits from the possible improvements on the underlying mqRPMT (e.g., Bloom filter optimization and post-quantum secure realization based on the EGA assumption).

We continue to compare our PSI-card-sum protocol with closely related protocols [IKN+20, GMR+21]. As mentioned in the introduction part, the PSI-card-sum protocols presented in [IKN+20] are built from concrete primitives (e.g. DH-protocol, ROT-protocol, Phasing+OPPRF etc.) with generic 2PC techniques or AHE schemes. Compared to [IKN+20], our protocol is built from mqRPMT and lightweight OT, which is more general and efficient. The protocol presented in [GMR+21] is built from permuted characteristic (permuted mqRPMT under our terminology) and secret sharing. Compared to [GMR+21], our protocol has the following differences: (i) mqRPMT underlying our protocol is conceptually simpler than permuted characteristic. More importantly, mqRPMT admits instantiations with optimal linear complexity, while the current best instantiation of permuted characteristic requires superlinear complexity. (ii) The protocol in [GMR+21] deviates from the standard functionality (as mentioned earlier in the introduction part), while our protocol meets the standard functionality of PSI-card-sum as defined in [IKN+20]. We do so by removing the constraint $\sum_{i=1}^{n} r_i = 0$ on the receiver side (as did in [GMR+21]), and having the sender send back the masked sum value to the receiver, and the receiver finally recovers the intersection sum by unmasking.

Finally, we compare our PSI card-secret-sharing protocol to the closely related circuit-PSI [HEK12, PSTY19, RS21]. The only difference on functionality is that our protocol additionally leaks the cardinality to the receiver. Nevertheless, as pointed out in [GMR+21], in many applications of interest the functions that need to be computed already contain such leakage. Garimella et al. [GMR+21] proposed a similar functionality called secret-shared intersection, in which the parties get the shares of intersection elements. As a result, their functionality leaks the cardinality to both the sender and the receiver.

6.2   Private-ID

Recently, Buddhavarapu et al. [BKM+20] proposed a two-party functionality called private-ID, which assigns two parties, each holding a set of items, a truly random identifier per item (where identical items receive the same identifier). As a result, each party obtains identifiers to his own set, as well as identifiers associated with the union of their input sets. With private-ID, two parties can sort their private set with respect to a global set of identifiers, and then can proceed any desired private computation item by item, being assured that identical items are aligned. Buddhavarapu et al. [BKM+20] also gave a concrete DDH-based private-ID protocol. Garimella et al. [GMR+21] showed how to build private-ID from OPRF and PSU. Roughly speaking, their approach proceeds in two phases. In phase 1, P_1 holding X and P_2 holding Y run an OPRF twice by switching the roles, so that first P_1 learns k_1 and P_2 learns $F_{k_1}(y_i)$, and second P_2 learns k_2 and P_1 learns $F_{k_2}(x_i)$. The random identifier of an item z is thus defined as $id_z = F_{k_1}(z) \oplus F_{k_2}(z)$. After phase 1, both parties can compute identifiers for their own items. In phase 2, they simply engage a PSU protocol on their sets $id(X)$ and $id(Y)$ to finish private-ID.

Our method is largely inspired by the approach presented in [GMR+21]. We first observe that in phase 1, two parties essentially need to engage a *distributed* OPRF protocol, as we formally depict in Fig. 8. The random identifier of an item z is defined as $G_{k_1,k_2}(z)$, where G is a PRF determined by key (k_1, k_2). Furthermore, note that $id(X)$ and $id(Y)$ are pseudorandom, which means in phase 2 a *distributional* PSU protocol suffices, whose semi-honest security is additionally defined over the input distribution. Such relaxation may lead to remarkable efficiency improvement.

In this work, we instantiate the generic private-ID construction as below: (1) realize the distributed OPRF protocol by running currently the most efficient multi-point OPRF of [RR22] built from VOLE and improved OKVS twice in reverse order; (2) run the PSU protocol from cwPRF-based mqRPMT with the obtained two sets of pseudorandom identifiers as inputs to fulfill the private-ID functionality.

Distributional PSU. Standard security notions for MPC are defined w.r.t. any private inputs. This treatment facilitates secure composition of different protocols. We find that in certain settings it is meaningful to consider a weaker security notion by allowing the real-ideal indistinguishability to also base on the

---

Parameters: PRF $G : K \times D \to R$, where $K = K_1 \times K_2$.
Inputs: P_1 inputs a set $X = \{x_1, \ldots, x_{n_1}\}$, where $x_i \in D$. P_2 inputs a set $Y = \{y_1, \ldots, y_{n_2}\}$, where $y_i \in D$.
Output: P_1 gets $\{G_{k_1,k_2}(x_i)\}_{i \in [n_1]}$ and k_1. P_2 gets $\{G_{k_1,k_2}(y_i)\}_{i \in [n_2]}$ and k_2.

Fig. 8. Ideal functionality for distributed OPRF

distribution of private inputs. This is because such relaxed security suffices if the protocol's input is another protocol's output which obeys some distribution, and the relaxation may admit efficiency improvement. Suppose choosing the DDH-based distributed OPRF and DDH-based PSU in the same elliptic curve (EC) group as ingredients, faithful implementation according to the above recipe requires $4n$ hash-to-point operations. Observe that the output of distributed DDH-based OPRF are already pseudorandom EC points. In this case, it suffices to use distributional DDH-based PSU instead, and thus can save $2n$ hash-to-point operations, which are costly in the real-world implementation.

7   Performance

We describe details of our implementation and report the performance of the following set operations: (1) **psi:** intersection of the sets; (2) **psi-card:** cardinality of the intersection; (3) **psi-card-sum:** sum of the associated values for every item in the intersection with cardinality; (4) **psu:** union of the sets; (5) **private-ID:** a universal identifier for every item in the union. We compare our work with the current fastest known protocol implementation for each functionality.

7.1   Implementation Details

Our protocols are written in C++, which can be found at https://github.com/yuchen1024/Kunlun/mpc. The code is organized in a modular and unified fashion in consistent with our paper: first implement the core mqRPMT protocol, then build various PSO protocols upon it. Besides, it only requires OpenSSL [Opea] as the main 3rd party library, and can smoothly run on both Linux and x86_64 MacOS platforms.

7.2   Experimental Setup

We run all our protocols and related protocols on Ubuntu 20.04 with a single Intel i7-11700 2.50 GHz CPU (8 physical cores) and 16 GB RAM. We simulate the network connection using Linux `tc` command. In the LAN setting, the bandwidth is set to be 10 Gbps with 0.1 ms RTT latency. In the WAN setting, the bandwidth is set to be 50 Mbps with 80 ms RTT latency. We use `iptables` command to calculate the communication cost, and use running time (the maximal time from protocol begin to end in the sender and the receiver side, including messages transmission time) to measure the computation cost. For a fair comparison, we stick to the following setting for all protocols being evaluated:

– We set the computational security parameter $\kappa = 128$ and the statistical security parameter $\lambda = 40$.
– We test the balanced scenario by setting the input set size $n_1 = n_2$ (our implementation supports unbalanced scenario as well), and randomly generate two input sets with 128 bits item length conditioned on the intersection size being roughly $0.5n$. The exception is the implementation of protocol in [GMR+21], whose item length is set as 61 bits in default and cannot exceed 64 bits since each element is represented as a uint64_t integer.
– The PSI-card-sum protocol [IKN+20] and the private-id protocol [BKM+20] are two of the related works we are going to compare. The former implementation is built upon NIST P-256 (also known as secp256r1 and prime256v1), while the latter implementation is built upon Curve25519. For a comprehensive comparison, our implementation supports flexible switching between standard elliptic curve NIST P-256 and special elliptic curve Curve25519. For protocols based on NIST P-256, we denote the ones not using or using point compression technique with ♦ and ▼ respectively. For protocols based on Curve25519, we denote them with ★.

7.3   Evaluation of mqRPMT

We first report the performance of our cwPRF-based mqRPMT protocol (optimized with Bloom filter) described in Sect. 4.3, which dominates the communication and computation overheads of its enabling PSO protocols. We test our protocol up to 4 threads, since both the server and the client run on a single CPU with 8 physical cores. Our cwPRF-based mqRPMT achieves optimal linear complexity, and thus is scalable, which is demonstrated by the experimental results in Table 1. Moreover, the computation tasks on both sides in our cwPRF-based mqRPMT are highly parallelable, thus we can effortlessly using OpenMP [Opeb] to make the program multi-threaded.

7.4   Benchmark Comparison of PSO Protocols

We derive all kinds of PSO protocols from cwPRF-based mqRPMT protocol, and compare them with the state-of-the-art related protocols. We report the performances for three input sizes $n = \{2^{12}, 2^{16}, 2^{20}\}$ all executed over a single thread in LAN and WAN settings. When testing the PSI-card, PSI-cardsum and PSU protocols in [GMR+21], we set the number of mega-bins as $\{1305, 16130, 210255\}$ and the number of items in each mega-bin as $\{51, 62, 72\}$ for set sizes $n = \{2^{12}, 2^{16}, 2^{20}\}$ respectively. These parameter choices have been tested to be much more optimal than their default ones.

PSI. We first compare our mqRPMT-based PSI protocol to the classical DH-PSI protocol reported in [PRTY19] and the one re-implemented by ourselves.

Table 1. Communication cost and running time of mqRPMT.

| Protocol | T | Running time (s) | | | | | | Comm. (MB) | | |
| | | LAN | | | WAN | | | total | | |
		2^{12}	2^{16}	2^{20}	2^{12}	2^{16}	2^{20}	2^{12}	2^{16}	2^{20}
mqRPMT♦	1	0.50	7.20	114.16	1.39	9.68	136.27	0.52	8.35	133.6
	2	0.31	3.89	62.09	1.14	6.54	86.60			
	4	0.22	2.37	40.41	1.11	5.08	62.77			
Speedup		1.6–2.3 ×	1.9–3.0 ×	1.8–2.8 ×	1.2–1.3 ×	1.5–1.9 ×	1.6-2.2 ×	–	–	–
mqRPMT▼	1	0.50	8.00	128.00	1.35	10.15	141.52	0.27	4.35	69.6
	2	0.32	5.05	80.69	1.18	7.11	94.19			
	4	0.23	3.54	58.40	1.08	5.54	71.26			
Speedup		1.6-2.2 ×	1.6-2.3 ×	1.6-2.2 ×	1.1-1.3×	1.4-1.8 ×	1.5-2 ×	–	–	–
mqRPMT★	1	0.26	3.51	54.85	0.81	5.41	68.68	0.26	4.23	67.66
	2	0.15	1.79	28.24	0.75	3.83	41.38			
	4	0.10	1.07	15.32	0.72	3.09	28.31			
Speedup		1.7-2.6 ×	2.0-3.3 ×	1.9-3.6 ×	1.1-1.1 ×	1.4-1.8 ×	1.7-2.4 ×	–	–	–

We remark that the PSI protocols in comparison are not competitive to the state-of-the-art PSI protocol. We include them merely for illustrative purpose and completeness. PSI protocols build upon public-key techniques are used to be thought inefficient, but our experiment results demonstrate that they could be practical by leveraging modern crypto library and carefully choosing optimized parameters. By using fast elliptic curve operations provided by OpenSSL, our mqRPMT-based PSI protocol is $3.4 - 10.5\times$ faster than the DH-PSI protocol[4] implemented in [PRTY19]. By further exploiting the features of Curve25519 in important ways (see Sect. 7.5 in details), our re-implemented DH-PSI protocol (denoted by DH-PSI★) achieves a $6.3 - 26.1\times$ speedup, which is arguably the most efficient DH-PSI implementation known to date (Table 2).

Recently, Rosulek and Trieu [RT21] proposed a PSI protocol based on Diffie-Hellman key agreement, which requires the least time and communication of any known PSI protocols for small sets. Somewhat surprisingly, Table 3 shows that for small sets our mqRPMT-based PSI protocol is faster than their protocol in the LAN setting, and our re-implemented DH-PSI protocol is much faster than their protocol in all settings with marginally larger communication cost.

PSI-card. We compare our mqRPMT-based PSI-card protocol to the PSI-card protocol in [GMR+21]. Table 4 shows that our protocol achieves a $2.4 - 10.5\times$ speedup, and reduces the communication cost by a factor of $10.9 - 14.8\times$.

---

[4] We remark that except inefficiency, their implementation also has a severe security issue. More precisely, they realize the hash-to-point function $\{0,1\}^* \to \mathbb{G}$ as $x \mapsto g^{H(x)}$, where H is some cryptographic hash function. However, such hash-to-point function cannot be modeled as random oracle anymore since it exposes the algebra structure of output in the clear, and hence totally compromise security. Similar issue also appears in libPSI.

Table 2. Communication cost and running time of PSI protocol.

PSI	Running time (s)						Comm. (MB)		
	LAN			WAN			total		
	2^{12}	2^{16}	2^{20}	2^{12}	2^{16}	2^{20}	2^{12}	2^{16}	2^{20}
[PRTY19]★	5.51	88.64	1418.20	5.82	90.79	1498.67	0.30	4.74	76.60
Our PSI♦	0.50	7.24	114.66	1.71	10.50	142.45	0.67	10.38	165.77
Our PSI▼	0.55	8.04	128.18	1.73	11.02	148.18	0.41	6.38	101.63
Our PSI★	0.29	3.56	55.11	1.19	6.38	75.56	0.40	6.25	99.71
DH-PSI★	0.22	3.39	54.79	0.92	5.57	69.31	0.28	4.57	74.1

Table 3. Communication cost and running time of PSI protocol on small sets.

PSI	Running time (ms)						Comm. (KB)		
	LAN			WAN			total		
	2^8	2^9	2^{10}	2^8	2^9	2^{10}	2^8	2^9	2^{10}
[RT21]★	50.0	71.0	147.3	224.1	260.2	457.9	17.9	34.1	66.3
Our PSI★	41.9	69.5	99.3	577.0	582.9	646.1	38.6	63.5	113.3
DH-PSI★	16.49	31.80	56.91	210.42	227.33	252.32	18.48	36.68	72.8

Table 4. Communication cost and running time of PSI-card protocol.

PSI-card	Running time (s)						Comm. (MB)		
	LAN			WAN			total		
	2^{12}	2^{16}	2^{20}	2^{12}	2^{16}	2^{20}	2^{12}	2^{16}	2^{20}
[GMR+21]	1.00	8.41	126.01	8.60	27.46	323.52	2.93	55.49	1030
Our PSI-card♦	0.49	7.20	114.31	1.30	9.68	136.06	0.53	8.59	137.31
Our PSI-card▼	0.53	8.00	128.00	1.35	10.16	141.31	0.28	4.58	73.20
Our PSI-card★	0.27	3.51	54.89	0.82	5.42	68.31	0.27	4.46	71.30

PSI-card-sum. We compare our mqRPMT-based PSI-card-sum protocol to the PSI-card-sum protocol (the most efficient and also the deployed one based on DH-protocol+Paillier) in [IKN+20].[5] As shown in Table 5, compared with the

---

[5] We do not compare the protocol described in [GMR+21] since its functionality is not the standard one, as we elaborated in the introduction. Putting aside the functionality difference, our protocol is still more advantageous than the protocol of [GMR+21] since our random masking trick is much simpler and efficient than the AHE-based technique adopted by the latter. In more detail, the upper bound of intersection sum in [GMR+21] is closely tied to the AHE scheme in use, which requires sophisticated parameter tuning and ciphertext packing techniques. Whereas in our protocol, the upper bound of intersection sum can be flexibly adjusted according to applications.

protocol presented in [IKN+20], our protocol achieves a 28.5 − 76.3× improvement in running time and a 7.4× reduction in communication cost.

Table 5. Communication cost and running time of PSI-card-sum protocol.

PSI-card-sum	Running time (s)						Comm. (MB)		
	LAN			WAN			total		
	2^{12}	2^{16}	2^{20}	2^{12}	2^{16}	2^{20}	2^{12}	2^{16}	2^{20}
[IKN+20]▼ (deployed)	23.64	176.34	−	30.10	186.29	−	2.72	43.24	−
Our PSI-card-sum◆	0.51	7.22	113.66	1.46	9.68	136.27	0.65	10.12	161.40
Our PSI-card-sum▼	0.57	8.12	129.66	1.94	11.83	157.66	0.39	6.10	97.34
Our PSI-card-sum★	0.31	3.73	57.44	1.36	6.53	76.16	0.37	5.75	95.30

We assume each associated value is a non-negative integer in $[0, 2^{32})$ conditioned on the upper bound of intersection sum being 2^{32}. We note that the implementation of [IKN+20] only works in our environment at set sizes 2^{12} and 2^{16}. For set size 2^{20}, we encounter a run time error reported in [Pri] that has not been fixed yet. The corresponding cells are marked with "−".

PSU. We compare our mqRPMT-based PSU protocol to the state-of-the-art PSU protocols in [GMR+21, ZCL+23, JSZ+22]. [ZCL+23] provides two PSU protocols from public-key and symmetric-key respectively. [JSZ+22] also provides two PSU protocols called PSU-S and PSU-R. We choose the most efficient PKE-PSU [ZCL+23] and PSU-R [JSZ+22] for comparison. Among all the mentioned PSU protocols, only our PSU protocol achieves strict linear communication and computation complexity. The experimental results in Table 6 indicate that our PSU protocol is the most superior one. Comparing to the state-of-the-art PSU protocol of [ZCL+23][6], our protocol achieves a 2.7 − 17× improvement in running time and a 2× reduction in communication cost.

Private-ID. We compare our private-ID protocol described in Sect. 6.2 to the state-of-the-art protocols in [BKM+20, GMR+21]. As shown in Table 7, our private-ID protocol achieves a 2.7 − 4.8× speedup comparing to the current most computation efficient private-ID protocol [GMR+21], while requires 1.3× less communication for sufficiently large sets[7] than the current most communication efficient private-ID protocol [BKM+20]. Hence, our private-ID protocol is arguably the most computation and communication efficient one to date.

---

[6] A recent work [BPSY23] proposed a new construction of OKVS and used it to improve the performance of the PSU protocol in [ZCL+23] by approximately 30%. However, if suitable parameters of the new OKVS construction exist when set sizes are less than 2^{10} is unclear. Our PSU protocol still performs the best even comparing with their optimized protocol.

[7] We note that our protocol requires more communication for sets of size 2^{12}. This is because the underlying multi-point OPRF [RR22] is built using VOLE, which has noticeable startup cost, arising relatively large constant terms in the computation and communication complexities of multi-point OPRF.

Table 6. Communication cost and running time of PSU protocol.

PSU	Running time (s)						Comm. (MB)		
	LAN			WAN			total		
	2^{12}	2^{16}	2^{20}	2^{12}	2^{16}	2^{20}	2^{12}	2^{16}	2^{20}
[GMR+21]	1.16	10.06	151.34	10.34	38.52	349.43	3.85	67.38	1155
[ZCL+23]♦	4.87	12.19	141.38	5.78	15.75	182.88	1.35	21.41	342.38
[ZCL+23]▾	5.10	15.13	187.29	5.82	17.37	210.06	0.77	12.20	195.17
[JSZ+22]	2.29	8.50	516.04	5.33	27.00	736.30	3.59	70.37	1341.55
Our PSU♦	0.52	7.27	114.44	1.70	10.56	143.29	0.69	10.61	169.37
Our PSU▾	0.57	8.04	128.20	1.76	10.92	148.15	0.42	6.61	105.23
Our PSU★	0.30	3.55	55.48	1.19	6.38	74.96	0.41	6.48	103.31

Table 7. Communication cost and running time of private-ID protocol.

Private-ID	Running time (ms)						Comm. (MB)		
	LAN			WAN			total		
	2^{12}	2^{16}	2^{20}	2^{12}	2^{16}	2^{20}	2^{12}	2^{16}	2^{20}
[GMR+21]	1.65	11.023	158.76	13.82	43.00	385.12	4.43	76.57	1293
[BKM+20]★	2.21	37.56	671.75	7.98	46.97	710.94	1.00	15.97	226.70
Our Private-ID♦	0.55	7.28	115.63	5.34	14.83	163.43	3.12	16.91	237.55
Our Private-ID▾	0.65	8.43	134.16	5.69	15.68	169.05	2.85	12.91	173.50
Our Private-ID★	0.34	3.78	59.76	5.04	10.87	94.89	2.82	12.74	171.54

7.5   Tips for ECC-Based Implementations

In what follows, we summarize the lessons we learned during the implementation of ECC-based protocols, with the hope to uncover some dark details and correct imprecise impressions.

We first highlight the following two caveats when implementing with standard elliptic curves:

Pros and cons of point compression technique. Point compression is a standard trick in elliptic-curve cryptography (ECC), which can roughly reduce the storage cost of EC point by half, at the cost of performing decompression when needed. Point decompression was empirically thought to be cheap, but experiment indicates that it could be as expensive as scalar multiplication. Our perspective is that point compression offers a natural trade-offs between communication and computation. The above experimental results demonstrate that the total running time gives a large weight to communication cost in bandwidth constrained scenarios. Therefore, in the WAN setting (involving parties cannot be co-located) we recommend not to apply point compression trick, while in the LAN setting (involving parties are co-located) we recommend to apply point compression trick. A quick take-away is that point compression trick pays off in the setting where communication is much more expensive than computation.

Tricky hash-to-point operation. The hash to point operation is very tricky in ECC. So far, there is no universal method to securely map arbitrary bit strings to points on elliptic curves. Here, the vague term "securely" indicates the hash function could be modeled as a random oracle. A folklore method is the "try-and-increment" algorithm [BLS01], which is also the method adopted in this work. Nevertheless, even such simple hash-to-point operation could be as expensive as scalar multiplication, which should be avoided if possible.

Regarding the two caveats discussed above, the following questions arise: (1) is it possible to get the best of two worlds of point compression; (2) could the hash-to-point operation be cheaper. Luckily, the answers are affirmative under some circumstances.

With the aim to avoid ASIACRYPT potential implementation pitfalls, Bernstein [Ber06] built a Montgomery curve called Curve25519 in 2006, in which 25519 indicates that the characteristic of the base field is $2^{255} - 19$. Due to many efficiency/security advantages, Curve25519 has been widely deployed in numerous applications and has become the *de facto* alternative to NIST P-256. Here, we highlight two notable features of Curve25519: (i) one can perform *somewhat* scalar multiplication using only X coordinate; (ii) by design, any 32-byte bit array corresponds the X coordinate of a valid EC point. Please refer to [Kle21] for more technique details. Exactly by leveraging these two features, Bernstein constructed a non-interactive key exchange (NIKE) protocol called X25519 based on Curve25519, which outperforms other EC NIKE protocols since it only depends on the X coordinate of the EC point.

Recall that our cwPRF-based mqRPMT protocol can be realized from any EC NIKE protocol and associated hash-to-point function. Compared with standard EC curves like NIST P-256, Curve25519 is particularly beneficial for the implementation of our protocol. More precisely, feature (i) brings us the best of two worlds of point compression (without making trade-off anymore), while feature (ii) makes the hash-to-point function almost free, simply hashing the input to a 32-byte bit array via standard cryptographic hash function. To the best of our knowledge, this is the first time that Curve25519 fully unleashes its power in the area of private set operations. In general, Curve25519 is a perfect match for schemes/protocols enabled by cwPRF.

Public-key operations are always rashly thought to be much expensive than symmetric-key operations, and thus the design discipline of many practical protocols opts to avoid public-key operations as much as possible. Our experimental results indicate that this impression is not precise anymore after rapid advances on ECC-based cryptography in recent years. By leveraging optimized implementation, public-key operations could be as efficient as symmetric-key operations. As a concrete example, in EC group with 128 bit security level one EC point scalar operation takes 0.026 ms and one EC point addition takes 0.00028 ms on a laptop.

8 Summary and Perspective

This work demonstrates that mqRPMT protocol is complete for most private set operations. In particular, we created a unified PSO framework from mqRPMT, which is rather attractive given its conceptual simplicity and modular nature. The high level abstraction is useful for allowing us to interpret various PSO protocols through the lens of mqRPMT, and helps to greatly reduces the deployment and maintenance costs of PSO in the real world. We also presented two generic constructions of mqRPMT and instantiated them from the DDH assumption, yielding a family of PSO protocols with optimal asymptotic complexity and good concrete efficiency that are superior or competitive to existing ones. In summary, we regard the PSO framework from mqRPMT together with its efficient implementations as the main contribution of this work. We emphasize that our framework does not intend to fully cover the current state of the art, which is a rapidly moving target. Instead, it mainly aims to distill common principles and clean abstractions that can apply broadly and systematically.

Along the way of constructing mqRPMT, we introduced cwPRF and pOPRF. The notion of cwPRF can be viewed as the right cryptographic abstraction of the celebrated DH functions, demonstrating the versatility of the DDH assumption. The notion of pOPRF is of independent interest. It enriches the OPRF family, and helps us to understand which OPRF-based PSI protocols can (or cannot) be adapted to PCSI/PSU protocols. We left more applications and efficient constructions of pOPRF as an interesting problem.

Acknowledgement. We thank the anonymous reviewers for their valuable comments on this paper. We thank Yilei Chen for helpful discussions on the post-quantum constructions of cwPRF. This work was supported by the National Key Research and Development Program of China (Grant No. 2021YFA1000600), the National Natural Science Foundation of China (Grant No. 62272269 and No. 61932019), Taishan Scholar Program of Shandong Province, and Major Programs of the National Social Science Foundation of China (Grant No. 22&ZD147).

References

[AES03] Agrawal, R., Evfimievski, A.V., Srikant, R.: Information sharing across private databases. In: ACM SIGMOD 2003, pp. 86–97 (2003)

[ALSZ15] Asharov, G., Lindell, Y., Schneider, T., Zohner, M.: More efficient oblivious transfer extensions with security for malicious adversaries. In: Oswald, E., Fischlin, M. (eds.) EUROCRYPT 2015. LNCS, vol. 9056, pp. 673–701. Springer, Heidelberg (2015). https://doi.org/10.1007/978-3-662-46800-5_26

[Ber06] Bernstein, D.J.: Curve25519: new Diffie-Hellman speed records. In: Yung, M., Dodis, Y., Kiayias, A., Malkin, T. (eds.) PKC 2006. LNCS, vol. 3958, pp. 207–228. Springer, Heidelberg (2006). https://doi.org/10.1007/11745853_14

[BKM+20] Buddhavarapu, P., Knox, A., Mohassel, P., Sengupta, S., Taubeneck, E., Vlaskin, V.: Private matching for computer (2020). https://eprint.iacr.org/2020/599

[Blo70] Burton, H.: Bloom. Commun. ACM **13**(7), 422–426 (1970)

[BLS01] Boneh, D., Lynn, B., Shacham, H.: Short signatures from the Weil pairing. In: Boyd, C. (ed.) Short signatures from the weil pairing. LNCS, vol. 2248, pp. 514–532. Springer, Heidelberg (2001). https://doi.org/10.1007/3-540-45682-1_30

[BPSY23] Bienstock, A., Patel, S., Seo, J.Y., Yeo, K.: Near-optimal oblivious key-value stores for efficient PSI, PSU and volume-hiding multi-maps. In: USENIX Security 2023, pp. 301–318 (2023)

[CDGB22] Chen, Y., Ding, N., Dawu, G., Bian, Y.: Practical multi-party private set intersection cardinality and intersection-sum under arbitrary collusion. In: Deng, Y., Yung, M. (eds.) Information Security and Cryptology. Inscrypt 2022. LNCS, vol. 13837, pp. 169–191. Springer, Cham (2022). https://doi.org/10.1007/978-3-031-26553-2_9

[CGT12] De Cristofaro, E., Gasti, P., Tsudik, G.: Fast and private computation of cardinality of set intersection and union. In: Pieprzyk, J., Sadeghi, A.-R., Manulis, M. (eds.) CANS 2012. LNCS, vol. 7712, pp. 218–231. Springer, Heidelberg (2012). https://doi.org/10.1007/978-3-642-35404-5_17

[CHLR18] Chen, H., Huang, Z., Laine, K., Rindal, P.: Labeled PSI from fully homomorphic encryption with malicious security. In: ACM CCS 2018, pp. 1223–1237 (2018)

[CLR17] Chen, H., Laine, K., Rindal, P.: Fast private set intersection from homomorphic encryption. In: ACM CCS 2017, pp. 1243–1255 (2017)

[CM20] Chase, M., Miao, P.: Private set intersection in the internet setting from lightweight oblivious PRF. In: Micciancio, D., Ristenpart, T. (eds.) CRYPTO 2020. LNCS, vol. 12172, pp. 34–63. Springer, Cham (2020). https://doi.org/10.1007/978-3-030-56877-1_2

[CMdG+21] Cong, K., et al.: Labeled PSI from Homomorphic Encryption with Reduced Computation and Communication. In: ACM CCS 2021, pp. 1135–1150. ACM (2021)

[DC17] Davidson, A., Cid, C.: An efficient toolkit for computing private set operations. In: ACISP 2017 (2017)

[DCW13] Dong, C., Chen, L., Wen, Z.: When private set intersection meets big data: an efficient and scalable protocol. In: ACM CCS 2013, pp. 789–800 (2013)

[DRRT18] Demmler, D., Rindal, P., Rosulek, M., Trieu, N.: PIR-PSI: scaling private contact discovery. Proc. Priv. Enhanc. Technol. **2018**(4), 159–178 (2018)

[FIPR05] Freedman, M.J., Ishai, Y., Pinkas, B., Reingold, O.: Keyword search and oblivious pseudorandom functions. In: TCC 2005, pp. 303–324 (2005)

[Fri07] Frikken, K.: Privacy-preserving set union. In: Katz, J., Yung, M. (eds.) ACNS 2007. LNCS, vol. 4521, pp. 237–252. Springer, Heidelberg (2007). https://doi.org/10.1007/978-3-540-72738-5_16

[GKRS22] Guo, S., Kamath, P., Rosen, A., Sotiraki, K.: Limits on the efficiency of (ring) LWE-based non-interactive key exchange. J. Cryptol. **35**, 1 (2022)

[GMR+21] Garimella, G., Mohassel, P., Rosulek, M., Sadeghian, S., Singh, J.: Private set operations from oblivious switching. In: Garay, J.A. (ed.) PKC 2021. LNCS, vol. 12711, pp. 591–617. Springer, Cham (2021). https://doi.org/10.1007/978-3-030-75248-4_21

[GPR+21] Garimella, G., Pinkas, B., Rosulek, M., Trieu, N., Yanai, A.: Oblivious key-value stores and amplification for private set intersection. In: Malkin, T., Peikert, C. (eds.) CRYPTO 2021. LNCS, vol. 12826, pp. 395–425. Springer, Cham (2021). https://doi.org/10.1007/978-3-030-84245-1_14

[HEK12] Huang, Y., Evans, D., Katz, J.: Private set intersection: are garbled circuits better than custom protocols? In: NDSS 2012 (2012)

[HFH99] Huberman, B.A., Franklin, M.K., Hogg, T.: Enhancing privacy and trust in electronic communities. In: ACM Conference on Electronic Commerce, pp. 78–86 (1999)

[HLS+16] Hogan, K., et al.: Secure multiparty computation for cooperative cyber risk assessment. In: IEEE Cybersecurity Development, SecDev 2016, pp. 75–76 (2016)

[HN10] Hazay, C., Nissim, K.: Efficient set operations in the presence of malicious adversaries. In: Nguyen, P.Q., Pointcheval, D. (eds.) PKC 2010. LNCS, vol. 6056, pp. 312–331. Springer, Heidelberg (2010). https://doi.org/10.1007/978-3-642-13013-7_19

[IKN+20] Ion, M., et al.: On deploying secure computing: private intersection-sum-with-cardinality. In: IEEE EuroS&P 2020, pp. 370–389 (2020)

[IKNP03] Ishai, Y., Kilian, J., Nissim, K., Petrank, E.: Extending oblivious transfers efficiently. In: Boneh, D. (ed.) CRYPTO 2003. LNCS, vol. 2729, pp. 145–161. Springer, Heidelberg (2003). https://doi.org/10.1007/978-3-540-45146-4_9

[JSZ+22] Jia, Y., Sun, S.-F., Zhou, H.-S., Du, J., Gu, D.: Shuffle-based private set union: faster and more secure. In: USENIX 2022 (2022)

[KK13] Kolesnikov, V., Kumaresan, R.: Improved OT extension for transferring short secrets. In: Canetti, R., Garay, J.A. (eds.) CRYPTO 2013. LNCS, vol. 8043, pp. 54–70. Springer, Heidelberg (2013). https://doi.org/10.1007/978-3-642-40084-1_4

[KKRT16] Kolesnikov, V., Kumaresan, R., Rosulek, M., Trieu, N.: Efficient batched oblivious PRF with applications to private set intersection. In: ACM CCS 2016, pp. 818–829 (2016)

[Kle21] Kleppmann, M.: Implementing curve25519/x25519: a tutorial on elliptic curve cryptography (2021). https://www.cl.cam.ac.uk/teaching/2122/Crypto/curve25519.pdf

[KLS+17] Kiss, Á., Liu, J., Schneider, T., Asokan, N., Pinkas, B.: Private set intersection for unequal set sizes with mobile applications. Proc. Priv. Enhanc. Technol. 4, 177–197 (2017)

[KMP+17] Kolesnikov, V., Matania, N., Pinkas, B., Rosulek, M., Trieu, N.: Practical multi-party private set intersection from symmetric-key techniques. In: ACM CCS 2017, pp. 1257–1272 (2017)

[KRTW19] Kolesnikov, V., Rosulek, M., Trieu, N., Wang, X.: Scalable private set union from symmetric-key techniques. In: Galbraith, S.D., Moriai, S. (eds.) ASIACRYPT 2019. LNCS, vol. 11922, pp. 636–666. Springer, Cham (2019). https://doi.org/10.1007/978-3-030-34621-8_23

[KS05] Kissner, L., Song, D.: Privacy-preserving set operations. In: Shoup, V. (ed.) CRYPTO 2005. LNCS, vol. 3621, pp. 241–257. Springer, Heidelberg (2005). https://doi.org/10.1007/11535218_15

[LG23] Liu, X., Gao, Y.: Scalable multi-party private set union from multi-query secret-shared private membership test. In: Guo, J., Steinfeld, R. (eds.) Advances in Cryptology. ASIACRYPT 2023. LNCS, vol. 14438, pp. 237–271. Springer, Singapore (2023). https://doi.org/10.1007/978-981-99-8721-4_8

[LV04] Lenstra, A., Voss, T.: Information security risk assessment, aggregation, and mitigation. In: Wang, H., Pieprzyk, J., Varadharajan, V. (eds.) ACISP 2004. LNCS, vol. 3108, pp. 391–401. Springer, Heidelberg (2004). https://doi.org/10.1007/978-3-540-27800-9_34

[Mea86] Meadows, C.A.: A more efficient cryptographic matchmaking protocol for use in the absence of a continuously available third party. In: IEEE Symposium on Security and Privacy, pp. 134–137 (1986)

[MPR+20] Miao, P., Patel, S., Raykova, M., Seth, K., Yung, M.: Two-sided malicious security for private intersection-sum with cardinality. In: Micciancio, D., Ristenpart, T. (eds.) CRYPTO 2020. LNCS, vol. 12172, pp. 3–33. Springer, Cham (2020). https://doi.org/10.1007/978-3-030-56877-1_1

[NTL+11] Narayanan, A., Thiagarajan, N., Lakhani, M., Hamburg, M., Boneh, D.: Location privacy via private proximity testing. In: NDSS 2011 (2011)

[NTY21] Nevo, O., Trieu, N., Yanai, A.: Simple, fast malicious multiparty private set intersection. In: ACM CCS 2021, pp. 1151–1165 (2021)

[Opea] https://github.com/openssl

[Opeb] https://www.openmp.org/resources/openmp-compilers-tools/

[Pri] https://github.com/google/private-join-and-compute/issues/16

[PRTY19] Pinkas, B., Rosulek, M., Trieu, N., Yanai, A.: SpOT-light: lightweight private set intersection from sparse OT extension. In: Boldyreva, A., Micciancio, D. (eds.) CRYPTO 2019. LNCS, vol. 11694, pp. 401–431. Springer, Cham (2019). https://doi.org/10.1007/978-3-030-26954-8_13

[PSTY19] Pinkas, B., Schneider, T., Tkachenko, O., Yanai, A.: Efficient circuit-based PSI with linear communication. In: Ishai, Y., Rijmen, V. (eds.) EUROCRYPT 2019. LNCS, vol. 11478, pp. 122–153. Springer, Cham (2019). https://doi.org/10.1007/978-3-030-17659-4_5

[PSZ14] Pinkas, B., Schneider, T., Zohner, M.: Faster private set intersection based on OT extension. In: USENIX 2014, pp. 797–812 (2014)

[PSZ18] Pinkas, B., Schneider, T., Zohner, M.: Scalable private set intersection based on OT extension. ACM Trans. Priv. Secur. $21(2)$, 7:1-7:35 (2018)

[RA18] Resende, A.C.D., Aranha, D.F.: Faster unbalanced private set intersection. In: Meiklejohn, S., Sako, K. (eds.) FC 2018. LNCS, vol. 10957, pp. 203–221. Springer, Heidelberg (2018). https://doi.org/10.1007/978-3-662-58387-6_11

[Rab05] Rabin, M.O.: How to exchange secrets with oblivious transfer (2005). https://eprint.iacr.org/2005/187

[RR17] Rindal, P., Rosulek, M.: Improved private set intersection against malicious adversaries. In: Coron, J.-S., Nielsen, J.B. (eds.) EUROCRYPT 2017. LNCS, vol. 10210, pp. 235–259. Springer, Cham (2017). https://doi.org/10.1007/978-3-319-56620-7_9

[RR22] Raghuraman, S., Rindal, P.: Blazing fast PSI from improved OKVS and subfield VOLE. In: ACM CCS 2022 (2022)

[RS21] Rindal, P., Schoppmann, P.: VOLE-PSI: fast OPRF and circuit-PSI from vector-OLE. In: Canteaut, A., Standaert, F.-X. (eds.) EUROCRYPT 2021. LNCS, vol. 12697, pp. 901–930. Springer, Cham (2021). https://doi.org/10.1007/978-3-030-77886-6_31

[RT21] Rosulek, M., Trieu, N.: Compact and malicious private set intersection for small sets. In: ACM CCS 2021, pp. 1166–1181 (2021)

[Sha80] Shamir, A.: On the power of commutativity in cryptography. In: de Bakker, J., van Leeuwen, J. (eds.) ICALP 1980. LNCS, vol. 85, pp. 582–595. Springer, Heidelberg (1980). https://doi.org/10.1007/3-540-10003-2_100

[SJ23] Son, Y., Jeong, J.: PSI with computation or circuit-psi for unbalanced sets from homomorphic encryption. In: ASIA CCS 2023, pp. 342–356. ACM (2023)

[TCLZ23] Tu, B., Chen, Y., Liu, Q., Zhang, C.: Fast unbalanced private set union from fully homomorphic encryption (2023)

[TKC07] Troncoso-Pastoriza, J.R., Katzenbeisser, S., Celik, M.U.: Privacy preserving error resilient DNA searching through oblivious automata. In: ACM CCS 2007, pp. 519–528 (2007)

[WY23] Wu, M., Yuen, T.H.: Efficient unbalanced private set intersection cardinality and user-friendly privacy-preserving contact tracing. In: USENIX Security 2023 (2023)

[ZCL+23] Zhang, C., Chen, Y., Liu,W., Zhang, M., Lin, D.: Optimal private set union from multi-query reverse private membership test. In: USENIX 2023 (2023). https://eprint.iacr.org/2022/358

Author Index

© International Association for Cryptologic Research 2024
Q. Tang and V. Teague (Eds.): PKC 2024, LNCS 14603, p. 417, 2024.
https://doi.org/10.1007/978-3-031-57725-3

Printed in the United States
by Baker & Taylor Publisher Services